THE GUINNESS
WHO'S WHO OF

film
MUSICALS
& MUSICAL FILMS

General Editor: Colin Larkin

GUINNESS PUBLISHING

Dedicated to Gene Kelly
for the best three and a half minutes on film in the rain

FIRST PUBLISHED IN 1994 BY
GUINNESS PUBLISHING LTD
33 LONDON ROAD, ENFIELD, MIDDLESEX EN2 6DJ, ENGLAND
ALL EDITORIAL CORRESPONDENCE TO SQUARE ONE BOOKS

GUINNESS IS A REGISTERED TRADEMARK OF GUINNESS PUBLISHING LTD

´ BRITISH LIBRARY CATALOGUING-IN-PUBLICATION DATA
A CATALOGUE RECORD FOR THIS BOOK IS AVAILABLE FROM THE BRITISH LIBRARY

ISBN 0-85112-787-8

CONCEIVED, DESIGNED, EDITED AND PRODUCED BY
SQUARE ONE BOOKS LTD
IRON BRIDGE HOUSE, 3 BRIDGE APPROACH, CHALK FARM, LONDON NW1 8BD

EDITOR AND DESIGNER: COLIN LARKIN
ASSISTANT EDITOR: ALEX OGG
PRODUCTION EDITORS: SUSAN PIPE AND JOHN MARTLAND
SPECIAL THANKS: BRIAN HOGG, DIANA NECHANICKY, TONY GALE, MARK COHEN,
SIMON DUNCAN, DAVID ROBERTS AND SARAH SILVÉ

IMAGE SET BY L & S COMMUNICATIONS LTD

PRINTED AND BOUND IN GREAT BRITAIN BY THE BATH PRESS

EDITORS NOTE

The Guinness Who's Who Of Film Musicals & Musical Films forms a part of the multi-volume Guinness Encyclopedia Of Popular Music. There are now 14 titles available in the series, with further volumes planned.

Already available:
The Guinness Who's Who Of Indie And New Wave Music.
The Guinness Who's Who Of Heavy Metal.
The Guinness Who's Who Of Fifties Music.
The Guinness Who's Who Of Sixties Music.
The Guinness Who's Who Of Seventies Music.
The Guinness Who's Who Of Jazz.
The Guinness Who's Who Of Country Music.
The Guinness Who's Who Of Blues.
The Guinness Who's Who Of Soul.
The Guinness Who's Who Of Folk Music.
The Guinness Who's Who Of Stage Musicals.
The Guinness Who's Who Of Dance, Rap & Techno
The Guinness Who's Who Of Reggae

Tony Gale and Pictorial Press supplied all the photographs used in this volume.

This book documents the rise of the musical film format from its origins in the 30s through to the present day. Its intention is to cover the fascinating variety of work produced over the ensuing years and put these achievements into context.

Arguably the first film musical proper arrived in 1927 with Al Jolson's The Jazz Singer, before springing into life with the advent of a new decade. The titles of some of the shows from this period offer a resonance beyond their immediate audiences, and they have passed into the fabric of our culture. Busby Berkeley's 42nd Street and Dames and Fred Astaire and Ginger Rogers' standards such as Top Hat and Swing Time share an appeal which is timeless. Judy Garland's The Wizard Of Oz, meanwhile, requires less introduction still.

A second golden era for the film musical flourished during the 40s and 50s, when a host of stars made their names in this field, including Gene Kelly, Frank Sinatra, Danny Kaye, Rita Hayworth, Mario Lanza and Marilyn Monroe, plus Bob Hope, Bing Crosby and Dorothy Lamour in their distinctive road movies. The lyrics and music which accompanied the dialogue in films such as Singin' In The Rain, Meet Me In St Louis, Gentlemen Prefer Blondes, Oklahoma and South Pacific has given these productions a continually replenished audience down the generations.

The intervening years have continued the format's tradition for strong entertainment values whilst updating the setting. Favourites include The Sound Of Music, Mary Poppins, The Jungle Book, in addition to the personality-based efforts from Elvis Presley, Cliff Richard and the Beatles. Also explored are the modern standbys of Grease, Saturday Night Fever and The Rocky Horror Show.

The following publications have been used to check facts: Halliwell's Film Guide. Halliwell's Filmgoer's Companion. The Hollywood Musical, Clive Hirschhorn. Leonard Maltin's Movie And Video Guide. Quinlan's Illustrated Guide To Film Directors. The British Film Catalogue 1895-1985, Denis Gifford. British Film Music, John Huntley. 60 Years Of The Oscar, Robert Osborne. Hollywood Musicals Year By Year, Stanley Green. The International Film

Encyclopedia, Ephraim Katz. *The Movies' Greatest Musicals-Produced In Hollywood USA By The Freed Unit*, Hugh Fordin.

The majority of the box-office returns quoted in this book have been taken from *Variety*'s lists of 'All-Time Film Rental Champs'. It has also been an invaluable source of news and other information.

Thanks to the Performing Right Society and the British Film Institute's library and film information services.

Brian Hogg assisted with a few last minute entries at very short notice, Alex Ogg and Susan Pipe were as always, key figures in going to press (a bit late this time).

Finally to John Martland who was responsible for the vast majority of the text, the biggest credit must be given. Martland is so modest it hurts. Maybe it should be left to me to say that he is one of the most knowledgeable and enthusiastic people on Stage and Film I have ever known. To have him as a full time member of the editorial team is one of our greatest strengths.

Colin Larkin, August 1994

A

Adamson, Harold

b. 10 December 1906, Greenville, New Jersey, USA, d. 17 August 1980. Adamson began writing poetry for his school newspaper and sketches for school shows; at the University of Kansas he wrote songs and worked with a professional company during vacations before going on to Harvard. Here he wrote for the famous 'Hasty Pudding' shows, cradle of much Broadway talent. In 1931 Adamson was on Broadway writing for Earl Carroll's *Vanities* and Florenz Ziegfeld's *Smiles*, in which he had his first hit with the lyric (co-written with Mack Gordon) for Vincent Youmans' 'Time On My Hands'. This was the first of many collaborations with the greatest composers. Adamson also wrote for Hoagy Carmichael ('My Resistance Is Low', 'Aint There Anyone Here For Love' and 'When Love Goes Wrong'), Walter Donaldson ('It's Been So Long'), Vincent Youmans and Mack Gordon ('Time On My Hands'), Burton Lane ('Everything I Have Is Yours'), Victor Young ('Around The World'), Harry Warren and Leo McCarey ('An Affair To Remember'), Ferde Grofe ('Daybreak'), Eldo Di Lazzaro ('Ferryboat Serenade' and 'The Woodpecker Song'), Jan Savitt ('720 In The Books') and Jan Savitt and Johnny Watson ('It's A Wonderful World'). He also collaborated with Vernon Duke and Duke Ellington. From 1932 he worked mainly in Hollywood on films such as *Dancing Lady* ('Everything I Have Is Yours'), *Reckless* ('Everything's Been Done Before'), *Great Ziegfeld* ('You'), *Suzy* ('Did I Remember?'), *Banjo On My Knee* ('There's Something In The Air'), *Top Of The Town* ('Where Are You?'), *That Certain Age* ('My Own'), *Mad About Music* ('I Love To Whistle'), *Thousands Cheer* ('Daybreak'), *Higher & Higher* ('I Couldn't Sleep A Wink Last Night', 'A Lovely Way To Spend An Evening'), *Four Jills In A Jeep* ('How Blue The Night'), *Date With Judy* ('It's A Most Unusual Day'), *Gentlemen Prefer Blondes* ('When Love Goes Wrong'), also writing title tunes for *You're A Sweetheart*, *Around The World In 80 Days* and *Affair To Remember*.

Addinsell, Richard

b. Richard Stewart Addinsell, 13 January 1904, Oxford, England, d. 14 November 1977, London, England. A composer, for the theatre and for feature films. Addinsell read law at Hertford College, Oxford, but was more interested in music and the theatre. He studied briefly at the Royal College of Music, and then in Berlin and Vienna. During the late 20s he began to contribute music to revues and shows such as

Little Miss Danger, *R.S.V.P.*, *The Charlot Show* and *Adam's Opera*. In 1931 he supplied the music for the incidental songs in *The Good Companions* (from J.B. Priestley's novel), and, for some 30 years, continued to write for the theatre, often in collaboration with the entertainer Joyce Grenfell. He provided material for several shows in which she also appeared, such as *Tuppence Coloured* (1947), *Penny Plain* (1951), *Joyce Grenfell Requests The Pleasure* (1954), *Joyce Grenfell - A Miscellany* (1957), and some 60s productions. It was for his firm work, however, that Addinsell is probably best remembered. From 1936, through to the early 60s, he wrote the music for some of the best British films, particularly those of the 'stiff upper lip' variety, so prevalent around the time of World War II. His scores included *The Amateur Gentleman* (1936), *Dark Journey*, *Farewell Again*, *South Riding*, *Fire Over England*, *Vessel Of Wrath*, *Goodbye, Mr. Chips*, *The Lion Has Wings*, *Contraband*, *Men Of The Lightships*, *Gaslight*, *Dangerous Moonlight*, *Love On The Dole*, *The Siege Of Tobruk*, *Blithe Spirit*, *Diary For Timothy*, *The Passionate Friends*, *The Black Rose*, *Scrooge*, *Encore*, *Tom Brown's Schooldays*, *Sea Devils*, *Beau Brummell*, *The Prince And The Showgirl*, *The Admirable Crichton*, *A Tale Of Two Cities*, *Loss Of Innocence*, *The Greengage Summer*, *The Waltz Of The Toreadors*, and *The Roman Spring Of Mrs. Stone* (1962). The score of *Dangerous Moonlight* (1941), contained Addinsell's most well-known composition, 'The Warsaw Concerto', played on the soundtrack by pianist Louis Kentner, with the London Symphony Orchestra. The piece became enormously popular, and was a hit for saxophonist Freddy Martin and his orchestra in the USA. Addinsell died 1977, but just over 10 years later, his music was heard again in London Theatres when the revue *Re: Joyce*, 'A celebration of the work of Joyce Grenfell', starring Maureen Lipman, opened in the West End in 1988, and returned twice more, with a televised version being shown at Christmas 1991.

Addison, John

b. John Mervin Addison, 16 March 1920, Cobham, Surrey, England. A composer, for the theatre, but worked mainly in film music. Addison studied composition, and several instruments including the piano, oboe and clarinet, at the Royal College of Music, just before, and after, World War II. He was appointed Professor of Composition at the college, 1950-57; his own classical compositions included music for the ballet, chamber orchestra and a trumpet concerto. For the theatre, in the 50s he collaborated with *avant garde* choreographer John Cranko on shows such as *Cranks* and *Keep Your Hair On*, and much later, in the early 70s, wrote the music to lyrics by David Heneker, for *The Amazons* and *Popkiss*. He also contributed music for several plays, including *Luther*, *A Patriot For Me*, *Bloomsbury*, *The Entertainer*, and *Antony And Cleopatra*. In the film world, he wrote the best of British, particularly during the 60s. His scores included *Seven Days To Noon*, *The Man Between*, *Private's Progress*, *Reach For The Sky* (the popular bio-pic of flying ace Douglas Bader, starring Kenneth More), *Lucky Jim*, *I Was Monty's Double*, *Look Back In Anger*, *A French Mistress*, *The Entertainer*, *School For Scoundrels*, *A Taste Of Honey*, *The Girl In The Headlines*, *Girl With Green Eyes*, *Tom Jones* (1963), (starring Albert Finney, and for which Addison won an Academy Award), *Guns At Batasi*, *The Amorous Adventures of Moll Flanders*, *The Loved Ones*, *Torn Curtain*, *A Fine Madness*, *The Honey Pot*, *Smashing Time*, *The Charge Of The Light Brigade*, *Start The Revolution Without Me*, *Country Dance*, *Mr. Forbush And The Penguins*, *Sleuth* (nominated for an Oscar), *Dead Cert*, *A Bridge Too Far*, *The Seven Per Cent Solution*, *The Pilot*, *Strange Invaders*, *The Ultimate Solution of Grace Quigley*, and *Code Name: Emerald* (1985). Addison also composed extensively for UK television, for programmes such as *Sambo And The Snow Mountain*, *The Search For Ulysses*, US shows such as *Grady* series (NBC), *Black Beauty*, *The Bastard*, *Centennial*, *Like Normal People*, *Love's Savage Fury* and *The French Atlantic Affair*, *Charles And Diana*, *A Royal Love Story*, *Eleanor-First Lady Of The World*, *Mistress Of Paradise*, *Mail Order Bride*, *Ellis Island* and *Murder She Wrote* (series). In the 80s, with programmes such as *Something In Common*, *Thirteen At Dinner*, *Deadman's Folly*, *Bigger Than A Breadbox*, *The Pumpkin Competition*, *Mr. Boogedy*, *Something In Common*, *Bridge Of Boogedy*, *Strange Voices*, *Beryl Markham*, *A Shadow Of The Sun* and *The Phantom Of The Opera*.

After Hours

Superb pilot made in 1961 for a US television series that never was. A simple nightclub setting has a band led by Coleman Hawkins and Roy Eldridge with Johnny Guarnieri, Barry Galbraith, Milt Hinton and William 'Cozy' Cole. Amongst the songs are 'Lover Man' and a red-hot 'Sunday' during which Eldridge is so carried away he overruns his solo to the obvious delight of a momentarily upstaged Hawkins.

Aladdin

The third and most successful of Walt Disney Pictures' trio of high-tech, computer enhanced animated box-office sensations of the late 80s/early 90s. *Aladdin* was released late in 1992, and in hardly any time at all had generated US rentals in excess of over $50 million. Unlike its two predecessors, *The Little Mermaid* and *Beauty And The Beast*, the film was not welcomed with open arms worldwide. The seemingly harmless traditional story involved Jasmine, the Sultan's daughter, who escapes from the royal castle and an arranged marriage, and falls for the pauper Aladdin. However, there were accusations of racism, and the Arab-American Anti-Discrimination Committee was unhappy about *Aladdin*'s depiction of their people 'as sleazy, nasty and mean'. They also objected to a section of the opening song in which an Arab trader sings: 'Oh, I come from a land/From a faraway place/Where the caravan camels roam/Where they cut off your ear/If they don't like your face/It's barbaric, but hey, it's home.' On foreign prints and the video release, the last three lines were amended to: 'Where it's flat and immense/And the heat is intense/It's barbaric, but hey, it's home', but, despite further protests, Disney refused to remove the word 'barbaric'. That song, 'Arabian Nights', and others such as 'Friend Like Me' and 'Prince Ali', had been written by Alan Menken and Howard Ashman before the latter died in 1991. Together with his new lyricist, Tim Rice, Menken completed a hat-trick of Academy Awards with the song 'A Whole New World', and won another Oscar for the film's original score. 'A Whole New World' went to the top of the US chart in a version by Peabo Bryson and Regina Belle. The voices for the main characters were provided by Aladdin (Scott Weinger, Brad Kane singing), Jasmine (Linda Larkin, Lea Salonga singing), and Robin Williams as the Genie. Williams was sensational, metamorphosing into a variety of hilarious impersonations which included actors such as Jack Nicholson, and various political and television personalities. *Aladdin* was directed by John Musker and Ron Clement and, early in 1993, was being hailed by Disney as the highest-grossing release in the Studio's 69-year history. A year later the soundtrack recording attracted five Grammy Awards.

Alexander's Ragtime Band

Released in 1938, one of the most entertaining musicals of the decade celebrated the work of one of America's all-time great songwriters - Irving Berlin. The slight plot concerning the erratic domestic and professional arrangements of bandleader Alexander (Tyrone Power) and singer Stella Kirby (Alice Faye), was merely an occasional diversion compared to the continual flow of wonderful songs which effectively traced the evolution of popular song through a period of nearly 30 years. They included 'Alexander's Ragtime Band', 'Ragtime Violin', 'Everybody's Doing It', 'When The Midnight Choo-Choo Leaves For Alabam', 'That International Rag', 'For Your Country And My Country', 'Oh, How I Hate To Get Up In The Morning', 'I Can Always Find A Little Sunshine In The YMCA', 'A Pretty Girl Is Like A Melody', 'Say It With Music', 'Everybody Step', 'Pack Up Your Sins And Go To The Devil', 'All Alone', 'What'll I Do?', 'Remember', 'Easter Parade', 'Heat Wave', and 'Now It Can Be Told' which Berlin wrote especially for the film. Also involved in the screenplay, which was written by Kathryn Scola and Lamar Trotti, were Ethel Merman, Don Ameche, Jack Haley, Jean Hersholt, Dixie Dunbar, Chick Chandler, John Carradine, and a host of others.

Alexander's Ragtime Band

Photographed in black and white, and directed by Darryl F. Zanuck and Harry Joe Brown, *Alexander's Ragtime Band* was the first in a long and enjoyable series of lavish, all-star musicals produced by 20th Century-Fox.

All Night Long

Even in 1961, adapting William Shakespeare to outwardly incongruous settings was not a new departure for film-makers. Setting the Bard to a jazz background was. This is *Othello* with quite a few differences. With a good cast, including Richard Attenborough, Betsy Blair and Keith Michell supporting 'drummer' Patrick McGoohan, good direction, Basil Dearden, and an adequate script, Nel King and Peter Achilles, *All Night Long* has the makings but the end result is curiously dull. In retrospect, the soundtrack is the best thing about the film. Not surprising when the musicians heard (and occasionally seen) include Harry Beckett, Dave Brubeck, Keith Christie, Bert Courtley, John Dankworth, Allan Ganley (ghosting for McGoohan), Tubby Hayes, Cleo Laine, Charles Mingus, and Kenny Napper. The film's musical director, Phillip Green, co-ordinated into the score works by Hayes, Mingus, Napper and Duke Ellington.

All That Jazz

A kind of musical *This Is Your Life - Bob Fosse* was how the critics summed up this sometimes grim but always brilliant exposé of the agony and ecstasy (not much of that in this case) entailed in the creation of a Broadway musical. Bob Fosse's character, Joe Gideon - the obsessive, hard-drinking, womanising, perfectionist choreographer-director- is played by Roy Schneider, with Leland Palmer as Fosse's one time wife, Gwen Verdon, Ann Reinking as his mistress, and Erzsebet Foldi in the role of daughter Nicole. The spectre of Death (in the form of Jessica Lange) is never far away throughout the string of spectacular production numbers which culminate in a recreation - right there on stage - of Fosse's open-heart operation during which Schneider lies, connected to all the drips and monitors, surrounded by lightly clad showgirls waving feather boas: bizarre, to say the least. The main difference from the reality is that while Gideon dies, Fosse happily survived following his surgery, to work on for a number of years. Also taking part in this unpleasant (some said distasteful) look at the normally glamorous world of show business were Ben Vereen, Cliff Gorman, John Lithgow, and Keith Gordon. A marvellous opening sequence based around 'On Broadway' (Barry Mann-

Cynthia Weill-Jerry Leiber-Mike Stoller) kicks off the proceedings in great style, and the remainder of a varied selection of musical numbers included 'Everything Old Is New Again' (Peter Allen-Carole Bayer Sager), 'There'll Be Some Changes Made' (W. Benton Overstreet-Billy Higgins), 'Bye Bye Love' (Felice and Boudleux Bryant), 'Some Of These Days' (Shelton Brooks), 'After You've Gone' (Henry Creamer-Turner Layton), 'Who's Sorry Now?', (Bert Kalmar-Harry Ruby-Ted Snyder), and 'Going Home Now' (Ralph Burns). Bob Fosse's choreography was magnificent throughout, and he also directed and co-wrote the screenplay with Robert Alan Arthur who produced the film for 20th Century-Fox and Columbia in 1979. It was photographed in Technicolor and Panavision by Giuseppe Rotunno. *All That Jazz* grossed over $20 million in the USA, ensuring it a place in the Top 10 musicals of the decade.

Allyson, June

b. Ella Geisman, 7 October 1917, Bronx, New York, USA. An attractive actress and singer with a distinctive husky voice, often cast as the archetypal cute girl-next-door, and probably best remembered for her portrayal of the bandleader's wife (opposite James Stewart) in *The Glenn Miller Story* (1954). Allyson was raised by her mother who worked as a waitress to make-ends-meet. At the age of nine she was confined to a wheelchair for a time after being injured by a falling tree, and took up dancing to strengthen her back. In the late 30s and early 40s she had small roles in the Broadway musicals *Sing Out The News*, *Very Warm For May*, *Higher And Higher* and *Panama Hattie*, and had a leading part in *Best Foot Forward* (1941). She recreated her role in the latter show for the 1943 film version, and in the same year appeared in *Girl Crazy* and the multi-star extravaganza *Thousands Cheer*. From then on she starred in a string of mostly MGM musicals which included *Meet The People*, *Two Girls And A Sailor*, *Music For Millions*, *Two Sisters From Boston*, *Till The Clouds Roll By*, *Good News*, *Words And Music*, *The Glenn Miller Story*, *You Can't Run Away From It*, and *The Opposite Sex* (1956). In addition she appeared in an equal number of straight sugary films such as the 1949 remake of *Little Women* and the dramatic and highly emotional *The Shrike* (1955) with Jose Ferrer. She and her husband, actor Dick Powell, were active on US television throughout the 50s and early 60s - they both had their own shows - but after his death in 1963 Allyson withdrew for a time. Later, she continued to work in films, nightclubs, and on stage and television. In 1989 she was re-united in London with some of the other stars of classic movie musicals, such as Ann Miller, Dorothy Lamour and Alice Faye, for the lavish one-night-only production of *The MGM Ladies And The Hollywood Great Stars*.

Ameche, Don

b. Dominic Felix Amici, 31 May 1908, Kenosha, Wisconsin, USA, d. 6 December 1993, Scottsdale, Arizona, USA. A suave, romantic leading man with an appealing style and mellifluous voice, who was one of the most popular movie actors in Hollywood movies from the mid-30s through to the late 40s. Ameche worked in radio before signing for 20th Century-Fox in 1936. He appeared in several straight roles, before making a big impact in the musicals *One In A Million* (with Sonja Henie) and *Old Chicago* (1938) with Alice Faye and Tyrone Power. The trio came together again for *Alexander's Ragtime Band* which was released in the same year. He proved a suitably dashing D'Artagnan in another musical, *The Three Musketeers*, and then came what is probably his best-remembered part in *The Story Of Alexander Graham Bell* (1939), which was so effective that it sparked off a popular joke that Ameche himself had invented the telephone. From then on, and throughout the 40s, he was smooth and splendid in numerous films, including musicals such as *Hollywood Cavalcade*, *Swanee River* (as composer Stephen Foster), *Lillian Russell*, *Down Argentine Way* and *Moon Over Miami*, (both with Betty Grable), *Kiss The Boys Goodbye* (with Mary Martin), *Something To Shout About*, *Greenwich Village*, and *Slightly French* (1949). After that the film roles dried up and he moved to New York and began working in the relatively new medium of television, becoming involved in a long-running circus series in which he played a ringmaster. He also starred in three Broadway musicals, Cole Porter's *Silk Stockings* (1955) with Hildegarde Neff, *Goldilocks* (1958) with Elaine Stritch, and the short-lived *Thirteen Daughters* (1961). After playing a few minor movie roles in the 60s and 70s, he made his big comeback in the Eddie Murphy comedy *Trading Places* (1983), and then won the Oscar for best supporting actor in *Cocoon* (1984). This was followed by the inevitable sequel, *Cocoon: The Return* (1988), and one or two other good parts. His last film was *Folks!* in 1992. He completed his role in *Corrina, Corrina* with Whoopi Goldberg a month before he died of prostate cancer at the age of 85.

American Graffiti

Written By George Lucas and produced by Francis Ford Coppola, *American Graffiti* was a haunting, affectionate paean to small-town America during the early 60s. The sense of innocence and loss it evoked was enhanced by an extensive soundtrack, the bulk of which featured songs drawn from the previous decade. The cast is thus already imbued with a sense of nostalgia, capturing to perfection the uncertainty of the post-Elvis Presley, pre-Beatles era. The accompanying album is a joy from beginning to end, collecting classic songs by Buddy Holly, Chuck Berry, the Beach Boys, Del Shannon and many more. It is highly satisfying in its own right, but takes on an extra resonance when combined with one of the finest 'rock' films of any era.

American In Paris, An

One of the most enchanting of all film musicals, *An American In Paris* was released in 1951 and became one of the top money-makers of the decade. It has endured simply because of the all-round high-class talent involved. Alan Jay Lerner's screenplay is set in Paris, where Jerry Mulligan (Gene Kelly) is gaining far more personal fulfilment as a painter than he did in his former occupation as a GI. Other areas of his life are not so satisfying: a wealthy American, the rather more mature Milo Richards (Nina Foch), seems more interested in him than in his canvases; and the girl he falls in love with, Lise Bourvier (the delightful dancer Leslie Caron in her screen debut), is promised to another, Henri Baurel (Georges Guetary), who happens to be Jerry's best friend. Naturally, it all ends happily, with Jerry keeping his friend and getting the girl. The story, anyway, was subservient to the songs - a great collection from George and Ira Gershwin which included 'By Strauss', 'I'll Build A Stairway To Paradise', 'Embraceable You', 'Love Is Here To Stay', 'Tra-La-La', and "S Wonderful'. The film's climax was a spectacular 18 minutes-long ballet during which Kelly (who choreographed the complete film) found himself in various Parisian locations, each which was presented in the style of a famous painter. Among the other highlights were Kelly's French lesson for an eager and engaging bunch of kids via 'I Got Rhythm', and a dream sequence during which Oscar Levant conducts part of the 'Piano Concerto In F' and every member of the orchestra seems to be him! A Technicolor production from Arthur Freed's MGM unit, *An American In Paris* was directed with supreme style and flair by Vincente Minnelli. It won Academy Awards for best picture, screenplay, musical arrangements (Saul Chaplin and Johnny Green), cinematography and art/set direction. At the same Awards ceremony - in 1952 - Gene Kelly received a special Oscar for his versatility as an actor, singer, director, dancer - and especially - choreographer.

Anchors Aweigh

Considering Frank Sinatra's life-long attraction to females the world over, it seems somewhat incongruous that in this, his first major film in 1945, he played a bashful sailor named Clarence Doolittle who has to seek advice on 'how to handle a woman' from his shipmate, Joseph Brady (Gene Kelly) - 'the best wolf in the whole US Navy'. On leave in Hollywood, the pair become involved with a very small boy (Dean Stockwell) who is just leaving home to join the navy, and his singing guardian aunt (Kathryn Grayson) who yearns to audition for the Spanish pianist and conductor José Iturbi. After the usual complications, Kelly gets Grayson, Grayson passes the audition, and Sinatra finally conquers his shyness with a girl (Pamela Britton) from his own hometown of Brooklyn. The principal songs were by Sammy Cahn and Jule Styne and included three lovely ballads for Sinatra, 'What Makes The Sunset?', 'The Charm Of You', and 'I Fall In Love Too Easily', along with two amusing duets with Kelly, 'I Begged Her' and 'We Hate To Leave'. Among the songs by other composers were 'Cradle Song' (Sinatra), 'If You Knew Susie' (Kelly and Sinatra), and 'Jealousy' and 'My Heart Sings', which were sung by Grayson. She and Iturbi also performed several classical pieces. All that music stretched the film's running time to a marathon 140 minutes. It was photographed in Techicolor, directed by George Sidney, with a screenplay by Isobel Lennart. Gene Kelly choreographed, and also provided one of the film's highlights when he 'danced' with the Jerry, an animated mouse, while singing 'The Worry Song' by Ralph Freed and Sammy Fain. Four full-length Disney animated features were the most popular films of any kind in the 40s, each taking over $40 million in the US alone. *Anchors Aweigh* earned about a tenth of that.

Andrews Sisters

Laverne (b. 6 July 1915, Minnesota, Louisiana, USA, d. 8 May 1967), Maxene (b. 3 January 1918, Minnesota, Louisiana, USA) and Patti, lead singer and soloist (b. 16 February 1920, Minnesota, Louisiana, USA). In the early-30s the Sisters appeared in vaudeville and toured with the Larry Rich band before joining Leon Belasco at New York's Hotel Edison in 1937. With their new manager Lou Levy, later to marry Maxene, they signed for Decca Records and almost immediately had a massive hit in 1938 with 'Bei Mir Bist Du Schon', a Yiddish song from 1933, with a new lyric by Saul Chaplin and Sammy Cahn. This was followed by the novelty 'Hold Tight, Hold Tight', and 'Roll Out The Barrel', an Americanized version of the old Czechoslovakian melody, 'The Beer Barrel Polka', which became one of World War II's smash hits and helped them become the most popular girl vocal group of the war years. They went to Hollywood in 1940 to appear in the film *Argentine Nights* with the Ritz Brothers, and featured in several movies starring comedians Abbott and Costello, including *Buck Privates* in which they sang 'Boogie Woogie Bugle Boy'. In *Hollywood Canteen*, Warner's 1944 star-studded morale booster, the Sisters sang 'Don't Fence Me In', later a chart-topper with Bing Crosby. Their fruitful career-long collaboration with Crosby also included 'Pistol Packin' Mama', 'Is You Is, Or Is You Ain't My Baby?', 'Ac-Cent-Tchu-Ate The Positive', 'The Three Caballeros', 'Along The Navajo Trail', 'Jingle Bells' and 'Sparrow In The Tree Top'. They also recorded with several other artists such as Les Paul ('Rumours Are Flying'), Burl Ives ('Blue Tail Fly'), Danny Kaye ('Civilisation' and 'Woody Woodpecker'), Carmen Miranda ('Cuanto La Gusta'), Guy Lombardo ('Christmas Island'), and country singer Ernest Tubbs ('I'm Bitin' My Fingernails And Thinking Of You'). Their own un-aided hits, accompanied mainly by the Vic Schoen Orchestra, were a mixture of novelty, commercial boogie-woogie, calypso, jazzy numbers and heart-felt ballads. Following that first Yiddish hit in 1938 they were consistently in the charts with records such as 'Says My Heart', 'Say Si Si', 'Beat Me, Daddy, Eight To The Bar', 'I, Yi, Yi, Yi, Yi, (I Like You Very Much)', 'I'll Be With You In Apple Blossom Time', 'Three Little Sisters', 'Strip Polka', 'Straighten Up And Fly Right', and 'Underneath The Arches'/'You Call Everybody Darling' which was recorded in the UK, and accompanied by the Billy Ternent Orchestra. In 1949 Patti Andrews topped the US chart with her solo record, 'I Can Dream, Can't I?'/'I Wanna Be Loved', and in 1953 left the group to go solo. The Sisters still worked together occasionally right up to Laverne's death in 1967. At their peak for just over a decade, their immediately identifiable close harmony sound, coupled with a swinging, vigorous delivery eventually gained them world record sales in excess of 60 million, making them, perhaps, the most successful and popular female group ever. Bette Midler's frenetic revival of 'Boogie Woogie Bugle Boy' in 1973 revived some interest in their records, and in 1974 Patti and Maxene were reunited for *Over Here*, a Broadway musical with a World War II setting which ran for over a year. In the early-80s Maxene underwent heart surgery but in 1985 was still able to record her first solo album, *Maxene*, a mixture of new material and some of the group's old hits. Patti continues to work, touring the UK in 1990 on a wave of wartime nostalgia with the current Glenn Miller Orchestra.

Albums: *Curtain Call* (1956), *Jingle Bells* (1956), *By Popular Demand* (1957), *The Andrew Sisters In Hi-Fi* (1957), *Fresh And Fancy Free* (1957), *Dancing Twenties* (1958), *The Andrews Sisters Present* (1963), *Great Country Hits* (1964), *The Andrews Sisters Go Hawaiian* (1965). Compilations: *The Best Of The Andrews Sisters* (1973), *Boogie Woogie Bugle Girls* (1973), *In The Mood* (1974), *Beat Me Daddy Eight To The Bar* (1982), *Jumpin' Jive* (1986), *16 Golden Classics* (1987), *Hold Tight - It's The Andrews Sisters* (1987), *Rarities* (1988), *Christmas With The Andrews Sisters* (1988), *Sing Sing Sing* (1988), *Says My Heart* (1989). Solo albums: Patti And Maxene Andrews *Over Here* (1974, stage cast), Maxene Andrews *Maxene* (1985).

Andrews, Julie

b. Julia Wells, 1 October 1935, Walton-On-Thames, Surrey, England. After singing lessons with Madam Lillian Stiles-Allan, which formed her precise vocal style and typically English delivery, she made her professional debut in her parent's variety act at the age of 10. Two years later she performed at the London Hippodrome in the Pat Kirkwood musical, *Starlight Roof*, and the following year appeared in the Royal Command Performance. On BBC radio, she was Archie Andrew's playmate in *Educating Archie*, while appearing on stage in the title role of *Humpty Dumpty* at the London Casino at the age of 13. Her big break came in 1954 when she played Polly Brown in the Broadway production of Sandy Wilson's *The Boy Friend*. Having insisted on only a one-year contract for the latter, she was available to star with Rex Harrison in one of Broadway's major musicals, Lerner & Loewe's *My Fair Lady*, later repeating her performance in London before returning to Broadway as Queen Guinevere, with Richard Burton as King Arthur, in *Camelot*. To her chagrin, she was not required for the movie versions of the last two shows but, instead, gained an Oscar for her performance as the 'flying nanny' in the title role of Disney's *Mary Poppins* in 1964. Since then, her career in film musicals has taken her from the blockbuster heights of *The Sound Of Music* to the critical depths of the Gertrude Lawrence bio-pic *Star*, with *Thoroughly Modern Millie*, and a transvestite role in *Victor/Victoria*, in-between. The latter film, and her straight roles in movies such as *10* and *S.O.B.*which were directed by her second husband Blake Edwards, have sometimes seemed a direct effort to counter her life-long cosy, old fashioned image. Nevertheless, she has been a major film star for over 25 years, and in 1989 was awarded BAFTA's Silver Mask in recognition of her outstanding contribution to the medium. She was not so successful on the small screen, and her 1992 ABC comedy series *Julie* received poor reviews. In the same year, she sang the role of Anna in a CD recording of *The King And I*, amid general amazement that she had never played the part on the stage; British actor Ben Kinsgsley was her regal partner in the studio. In 1993 Andrews returned to the New York stage for the first time since *Camelot* (1960), and attracted ecstatic reviews for her performance in the Off-Broadway Sondheim revue *Putting It Together*.

Albums: *My Fair Lady* (1956, Broadway Cast) *Camelot* (1961, Broadway Cast), with Carol Burnett *Julie And Carol At Carnegie Hall* (1962), *Mary Poppins* (1964, film soundtrack), *The Sound Of Music* (1965, film soundtrack), *A Christmas Treasure* (1968), *Love Me Tender* (1983), *The Secret Of Christmas* (1977), *Broadway's Fair* (1984), *The Sound Of Christmas* (1987), *Julie Andrews And Carol Burnett At The Lincoln Center* (1989), *Love Julie* (1989), *The King And I* (1992, studio cast).

Further reading: *Life Story Of A Superstar*, John Cottrell. *Julie Andrews*, Robert Windeler.

Annette

b. Annette Funicello, 22 October 1942, Utica, New York, USA. Initially billed as 'Annette', this singer/actress rose to fame under the aegis of the Walt Disney organization. A one-time Mouseketeer, she enjoyed several hit singles between 1959 and 1961 which included two US Top 10 entries, 'Tall Paul' and 'O Dio Mio', as well as the enduring 'Pineapple Princess'. During the 60s Annette starred alongside Frankie Avalon in a series of 'quickie' beach films, including *Beach Party*, *Bikini Beach* (both 1964) and *How To Stuff A Wild Bikini* (1965), which combined slim plots, teenage themes and cameos from often-transitory pop stars. *The Monkey's Uncle* (1964) drew its appeal from an appearance by the Beach Boys and musical contributions from their leader, Brian Wilson. The latter assisted songwriter/producer Gary Usher in creating material for *Muscle Beach Party*, Annette's strongest album, which also featured back-up from the all-female group, the Honeys. Funicello later appeared in the Monkees' cult film *Head* (1968), but was unable to sustain thespian and recording successes into the next decade.

Albums: *Annette Sings Anka* (1960), *Hawaiiannette* (1960), *Songs From Annette And Other Walt Disney Serials* (early 60s), *Tubby The Tuba And Other Songs About Music* (early 60s), *Annette, Italiannette* (early 60s), *Dance Annette* (early 60s), *The Story Of My Teens* (early 60s), *Teen Street* (early 60s), *Annette On Campus* (early 60s), *Annette At Bikini Beach* (early 60s), *Pajama Party* (early 60s), *Annette Sings Golden Surfin' Hits*, (early 60s) *Something Borrowed, Something Blue* (early 60s), *Annette Funicello* (early 60s), *Annette's Beach Party* (1963), *Muscle Beach Party* (1964).

Annie

Adapted from the Broadway musical which opened in 1977 and ran for over 2,000 performances, this screen version, which cost over $50 million to produce, was generally regarded as an all-round disaster. Carol Sobieski's screenplay differed in several respects from Thomas Meehan's Broadway libretto and its original source, Harold Gray's comic strip, *Little Orphan Annie*. However, the story still takes place in 1933 in New York, when, after visiting his house, Annie (Aileen Quinn) is adopted by the millionaire industrialist Oliver 'Daddy' Warbucks (Albert Finney). Annie, with her dog Sandy, is trying to escape the clutches of the cruel and callous orphanage manager, Miss Hannigan (Carol Burnett), and hoping to find her real parents. Several of the Charles Strouse and Martin Charnin songs from their original score were dropped, and new ones written. Among those retained were the show's big hit, 'Tomorrow', along with 'It's The

Annie Get Your Gun

Hard-Knock Life', 'Maybe', 'I Think I'm Gonna Like It Here', 'You're Never Fully Dressed Without A Smile', and 'I Don't Need Anything But You'. Neither Finney nor director John Huston had had much previous experience with musicals, and they both came in for adverse criticism, along with choreographer Arlene Phillips. The main problem though was that it was all too extravagant: once again Hollywood had taken a small and charming concept and blown it up out of proportion.

Annie Get Your Gun

Like many other films boasting Irving Berlin scores, *Annie Get Your Gun* is rarely seen nowadays, and is not listed as having been released on video - at least in the UK. While he was alive it was said that the composer's financial demands prevented his work being continually enjoyed in the cinema and on television, and perhaps, now that he has gone, his estate is continuing with that policy. This film was released in 1950, five years after Ethel Merman's triumphant opening night in the original Broadway show. Unlike many other Broadway to Hollywood transfers, *Annie*'s screen debut for MGM was generally regarded as being highly satisfactory. Judy Garland was the first choice to play the lead, but a recurrence of the usual problems gave Betty Hutton the best role of her career. She played sharpshooter Annie Oakley who deliberately loses a shooting match with her rival, Frank Butler (Howard Keel), so that he will not consider her a threat to his masculinity, and they can be married. Of course this scenario took place long before the rise of feminism - in the days when men were men, and women were expected to be grateful. Although he had made a previous screen appearance in the UK while appearing in the West End in *Oklahoma!*, this was Keel's first Hollywood musical and he was in fine voice and gave an impressive performance. Among the rest of the cast were Louis Calhern (Buffalo Bill), J. Carrol Naish (Sitting Bull), Keenan Wynn, Edward Arnold, and Benay Venuta. Berlin's superb stage score survived practically intact in its screen reincarnation; the main casualty being the lovely ballad, 'Moonshine Lullaby'. All the big hits were there, including 'Doin' What Comes Natur'lly', 'I Got The Sun In The Morning', 'You Can't Get A Man With A Gun', 'The Girl That I Marry', 'They Say It's Wonderful', 'My Defenses Are Down', 'Anything You Can Do', along with Hutton's highly amusing 'I'm An Indian, Too', and the rousing 'There's No Business Like Show Business'. *Annie Get Your Gun* was photographed in Technicolor and directed by George Sidney, with choreography by Robert Alton. It was the top musical money-spinner

Anything Goes

of 1950, and won Academy Awards for 'scoring of a musical picture' for Adolph Deutsch and Roger Edens.

Anything Goes

In 1936, two years after the original show opened on Broadway, Paramount released this reasonably faithful screen version. Ethel Merman recreated her stage role as nightclub singer Reno Sweeney, whose friend, Billy Crocker (Bing Crosby), stows away on an ocean liner so that he can be close to his beloved Hope Harcourt (Ida Lupino). After the inevitable complications which involve a Reverend gentleman (Charlie Ruggles) - who is really America's Public Enemy No. 13 - everyone is paired off satisfactorily, including Reno herself who bags a member of the English aristocracy. The majority of Cole Porter's songs from the stage production were axed, but fortunately three of the survivors, 'Anything Goes', 'I Get A Kick Out Of You', and 'You're The Top', were Merman specialities. The numbers that were added included 'Shanghai-Di-Ho', 'My Heart And I', 'Hopelessly In Love' (all written by Frederick Hollander and Leo Robin), and 'Sailor Beware' (Richard Whiting-Leo Robin), and the engaging 'Moonburn' by Hoagy Carmichael and Edward Heyman, which was smoothly delivered by Crosby. Howard Lindsay, Russel Crouse and Guy Bolton adapted the screenplay from their original libretto which was written in collaboration with P.G. Wodehouse, and the film was directed by Lewis Milestone. When Anything Goes was remade in Technicolor by Paramount 20 years later, Crosby was retained, and in Sidney Sheldon's new story, he and Donald O'Connor went on a talent-spotting cruise and came up with Mitzi Gaynor and Jeanmaire - which was not a bad result. The musical aspect was pretty satisfying too, with Sammy Cahn and Jimmy Van Heusen supplementing Porter's score with three numbers, 'You Can Bounce Right Back', 'You Gotta Give The People Hoke', and 'A Second-Hand Turban And A Crystal Ball'. Phil Harris, who is always worth seeing, was also in the cast, and the film was choreographed by Nick Castle and Roland Petit, and directed by Robert Lewis.

Arlen, Harold

b. Hyman Arluck, 15 February 1905, Buffalo, New York, USA, d. 23 April 1986. The son of a cantor, Arlen sang in his father's synagogue, but was soon playing ragtime piano in local bands and accompanying silent pictures. In the early 20s he played and arranged for the Buffalodians band, - then in 1925 shook off small-town connections when he took a job in New York City, arranging for Fletcher Henderson and working in radio and theatre, as a rehearsal pianist. Indeed, his first composition began as a rehearsal vamp and was developed into 'Get Happy', with lyrics by Ted Koehler. Arlen was soon composing songs regularly and in collaboration with Koehler wrote eight Cotton Club revues, one of which included a song, 'Stormy Weather', which Ethel Waters made into an American classic. In 1934 Arlen went to Hollywood to write songs, but continued composing for Broadway musicals. Apart from Koehler, his lyricists have included Dorothy Fields, Les Robin, Johnny Mercer, Yip Harburg and Ira Gershwin. Among the stage shows for which Arlen wrote were Earl Carroll Vanities (which included 'I've Got The World On A String' and 'I Gotta Right To Sing The Blues'), Rhythm Mania ('The Devil And The Deep Blue Sea') and St. Louis Woman ('Come Rain Or Come Shine'). In Hollywood he worked on Take A Chance (1937), which included 'It's Only A Paper Moon', Star-Spangled Rhythm (1941, 'Hit The Road To Dreamland'), The Sky's The Limit (1943, 'One For My Baby' and 'My Shining Hour'). Among other great successes, mostly written for films but which have become an integral part of American music, are 'The Man That Got Away', 'Let's Fall In Love', 'Blues In The Night', 'That Old Black Magic', and a song written for (but almost cut from) the 1939 film The Wizard Of Oz, 'Over The Rainbow'. Arlen's songs have been recorded by countless singers and used frequently by jazz artists. He also made occasional records himself, singing with Duke Ellington and with Barbra Streisand. In 1993 a revue entitled Sweet And Hot: The Songs Of Harold Arlen, was circulating in the USA.

Selected albums: Harold Sings Arlen (With Friend) (1966), Harold Arlen In Hollywood (1979), Harold Sings Arlen (1983), I Love To Sing (1988).

Arnold, Malcolm

b. 21 October 1921, Northampton, England. A composer, conductor, arranger and trumpet player. Arnold became aware of music at the age of four, and taught himself to play trumpet - his inspiration was Louis Armstrong. He began his career in 1941 as an instrumentalist with the London Philharmonic Orchestra, and returned to the orchestra in 1946 after brief service in World War II, and a spell with the BBC Symphony Orchestra. During these times he was also composing; one of his best known pieces, 'Sea Shanties', was written in 1943. He became a full time composer in the early 50s, and soon won much critical acclaim as 'one of the great hopes of British music'. His work schedule was exhausting; from 1951-56 he is said to have written the music for over 70 films; as well as three operas, ballet music, concertos and other classical and light works. One of his more unusual compositions was the 'Grand Overture' for a Gerald Hoffnung concert, in which the more conventional instruments of the orchestra were augmented by three vacuum cleaners and an electric polisher. His film scores, many of which complemented classic British productions, including *The Sound Barrier* (1952), *The Holly And The Ivy*, *The Captain's Paradise*, *Hobson's Choice*, *Prize Of Gold*, *I Am A Camera*, *Trapeze*, *Tiger In The Smoke*, *The Deep Blue Sea*, *Island In The Sun*, *The Bridge On The River Kwai* (one of the film's six Oscars went to Arnold), *Blue Murder At St. Trinians*, *The Inn Of The Sixth Happiness* (the film theme won an Ivor Novello Award in 1959), *The Key*, *The Root Of Heaven*, *Dunkirk*, *Tunes Of Glory*, *The Angry Silence*, *No Love For Johnnie*, *The Inspector*, *Whistle Down The Wind*, *The Lion*, *Nine Hours To Rama*, *The Chalk Garden*, *The Heroes Of Telemark*, *The Thin Red Line*, *Sky West And Crooked*, and *The Reckoning* (1969). During the 60s the whole thing went sour. Arnold was ignored, even reviled, by the critics and sections of the concert and broadcasting establishment. He was called 'a clown', and his work was regarded as 'out of phase' with the current trends in music. There were alcohol problems, he suffered several nervous breakdowns, and attempted suicide more than once. He continued to write, when he was able, and was particularly interested in brass band music, but his work generally went unappreciated. His ninth and final symphony, written in 1986, still had not received a proper premiere by 1991, when low-key celebrations for his 70th birthday involved a concert at London's Queen Elizabeth Hall, which included his double violin concerto, commissioned by Yehudi Menuhin in 1962. In 1993, Malcolm Arnold received a knighthood in the Queen's New Year honours list.

Further reading: *Malcolm Arnold: A Catalogue Of His Music*, A. Poulton.

Ashman, Howard

b. 1951, Baltimore, Maryland, USA, d. 14 March 1991. A lyricist, librettist, playwright and director. After studying at Boston University and Indiana University, where he gained a master's degree in 1974, Ashman moved to New York and worked for publishers Grosset & Dunlap, while starting to write plays. One of his earliest works, *Dreamstuff*, a musical version of *The Tempest*, was staged at the WPA Theatre, New York, where Ashman served as artistic director from 1977-82. In 1979, the WPA presented a musical version of Kurt Vonnegut's *God Bless You, Mr Rosewater*, written by Ashman in collaboration with composer Alan Menken, which became a cult hit. In 1982, again at the WPA, they had even bigger success with *Little Shop Of Horrors*, the story of Audrey II, a man-eating plant. The show became the highest grossing and third-longest-running musical in off-Broadway history. It won the New York Drama Critics Award 1982-83, and the London Evening Standard Award for 'Best Musical'. As well as writing the book and lyrics, Ashman directed the stage show, and the 1961 film version, from which the song, 'Mean Green Mother From Outer Space', was

nominated for an Academy Award. Disenchanted with Broadway following his flop show, *Smile*, with music by Marvin Hamlisch (1988), Ashman moved to Hollywood, and the animated features of Walt Disney. One of Ashman's own songs, with the ironic title: 'Once Upon A Time In New York', was sung by Huey Lewis in *Oliver & Company* (1988), and the following year he was back with Menken for *The Little Mermaid*. Two of their songs for the film, 'Kiss The Girl' and 'Under The Sea' were nominated for Academy Awards. The latter won, and Menken also received the Oscar for 'Best Score'. Two years later they did it again, with their music and lyrics for *Beauty And The Beast* (1991); 'Disney's latest animated triumph, boasts the most appealing musical comedy score in years, dammit'. Three songs from the film were nominated by the Academy, this time with the title number emerging as the winner, along with the score. Menken received an unprecedented five BMI awards for this work on the film. In Ashman's case his Academy Award was posthumous - he died of AIDS on 14 March 1991, in New York, USA. Menken signed a long-term contract with Disney, the first result of which was *Newsies*, a turn-of-the-century story, using real actors, with lyrics by Jack Feldman. Before Ashman died, he had been working with Menken on the songs for *Aladdin*, and one of them, 'Friend Like Me', was eventually nominated for an Academy Award. Menken completed work on the film with British lyricist, Tim Rice, and their 'Whole New World' won the Oscar, as did Menken's score. 'Whole New World' also won a Golden Globe award, and the version by Peabo Bryson and Regina Belle topped the US chart in 1993.

Astaire, Fred

b. Frederick Austerlitz, 10 May 1899, Omaha, Nebraska, USA, d. 22 June 1987. By the age of seven Astaire was dancing in vaudeville with his sister, Adele (b. 18 September 1896, d. 25 January 1981). The duo made their Broadway debut in 1917 and the following year were a huge success in *The Passing Show Of 1918*. During the 20s they continued to dance to great acclaim in New York and London, their shows including *Lady, Be Good!* (1924) and *Funny Face* (1927). They danced on into the 30s in *The Band Wagon* (1931). but with *The Gay Divorce*, (1932) their partnership came to an end. Adele married Charles Cavendish, the younger son of the Duke of Devonshire. The Astaires had dabbled with motion pictures, perhaps as early as 1915 (although their role in a Mary Pickford feature from this year is barely supported by the flickering remains), but a screen test for a film version of *Funny Face* had resulted in an offhand summary of Adele as 'lively' and the now infamous dismissal of Astaire: 'Can't act. Can't sing. Balding. Can dance a little.' Despite this negative view of his screen potential, Astaire, now in need of a new direction for his career, again tried Hollywood. He had a small part in *Dancing Lady* (1933) and was then teamed with Ginger Rogers for a small spot in *Flying Down To Rio* (1933). Their dance duet was a sensation and soon thereafter they were back on the screen, this time as headliners in *The Gay Divorcee* (1934). A string of highly successful films followed, among them *Roberta* and *Top Hat* (both 1935), *Follow The Fleet* and *Swing Time* (both 1936), *Shall We Dance?* (1937) and *The Story Of Vernon And Irene Castle* (1939). Astaire then made a succession of films with different dancing partners, including Paulette Goddard in *Second Chorus* (1940), Rita Hayworth in *You'll Never Get Rich* (1941) and *You Were Never Lovelier* (1942), and Lucille Bremer in *Yolanda And The Thief* (1945) and *Ziegfeld Follies* (1946). His singing co-leads included Bing Crosby in *Holiday Inn* (1942) and *Blue Skies* (1946) and Judy Garland in *Ziegfeld Follies* and *Easter Parade* (1948). He was reunited with Rogers in *The Barkleys Of Broadway* (1949) and danced with Vera Ellen, Betty Hutton, Jane Powell, Cyd Charisse, Leslie Caron, Audrey Hepburn and others throughout the rest of the 40s and on through the 50s. By the late 50s he was more interested in acting than dancing and singing and began a new stage in his film career with a straight role in *On The Beach* (1959). A brief return to a musical came with *Finian's Rainbow* (1968), but apart from hosting, with Gene Kelly, three compilation-films of musical clips, he had abandoned this side of his work. During the 50s, 60s and 70s he also appeared on US television, mostly in acting roles but occasionally, as with *An Evening With Fred Astaire* (1958), *Another Evening With Fred Astaire* (1959) and *The Fred Astaire Show* (1968), to sing and dance (in the three cases cited, with Barrie Chase). By the early 80s, for all practical purposes he had retired. Off-screen Astaire led a happy and usually quiet life. His first marriage lasted from 1933 to 1954, when his wife died in her mid-40s; they had two children, Fred Jnr. and Phyllis Ava. He remarried in 1980, his second wife surviving his death on 22 June 1987. Astaire made his recording debut in 1923, singing with Adele, and in 1926 the couple recorded a selection of tunes by George Gershwin with the composer at the piano. He recorded steadily but infrequently during the 30s and 40s, and in 1952 made his first long playing record for Norman Granz, *The Astaire Story*, on which he was accompanied by jazz pianist Oscar Peterson. He continued to make records into the mid-70s, usually of songs from his films or television shows, while soundtrack albums and compilations from many of his earlier film appearances continued to be issued. As a singer, Astaire presented songs with no artifice and never did anything to dispel the impression that he was merely an amateur with few natural gifts. Yet for all this his interpretations of popular songs were frequently just what their composers and lyricists wanted, and many such writers commended him for the engaging manner in which he delivered their material. A key factor in their approval may well have lain in his decision, perhaps forced upon him by the limitations of his vocal range, to sing simply, directly and as written. Among the composers who rated him highly were masters of the Great American Popular Songbook such as Irving Berlin, Jerome Kern, Cole Porter, Gershwin, Harold Arlen, Johnny Mercer and Harry Warren.

As an actor, he was usually adequate and sometimes a little more so, but rarely immersed himself so completely in a role that he ceased to be himself and, indeed, did little to disprove the first part of his screen test summation. As a dancer, however, it is impossible to assess his contribution to stage, television and especially to musical films without superlatives. Like so many great artists, the ease with which Astaire danced made it seem as though anyone could do what he did. Indeed, this quality might well have been part of his popularity. He looked so ordinary that any male members of the audience, even those with two left feet, were convinced that given the opportunity they could do as well. In fact, the consummate ease of his screen dancing was the end result of countless hours of hard work, usually alone or with his longtime friend, colleague, co-choreographer and occasional stand-in, Hermes Pan. (Ginger Rogers, with whom Astaire had an uneasy off-screen relationship, recalled rehearsing one number until her feet bled.) For slow numbers he floated with an elegant grace and, when the tempo quickened, the elegance remained, as did the impression that he was forever dancing just a fraction above the ground. The sweatily energetic movements of many other screen dancers was, perhaps, more cinematic, but it was always something that Astaire would not have considered even for a moment. Alone, he created an entirely original form of screen dance and after his first films, all previous perceptions of dance were irrevocably altered. In the world of showbiz, where every artist is labelled 'great' and words like 'genius' have long ago ceased to have realistic currency, Fred Astaire truly was a great artist and a dancer of genius.

Selected albums: *The Astaire Story* (1952), *Three Evenings With Fred Astaire* (1958-60), *Another Evening With Fred Astaire* (1959), with Bing Crosby *A Couple Of Song And Dance Men* (1975), with Bing Crosby *How Lucky Can You Get!* (1993). Compilations: *Lady, Be Good!* (1924-33), *Starring Fred Astaire And Ginger Rogers* (1936-37), *Dancing, Swinging, Singing And Romancing* (1941-46), *Crazy Feet* (1983), *Fred Astaire Collection* (1985), *An Evening With* (1987), *Easy To Dance With* (1987), *Starring Fred Astaire* (1987), *Top Hat, White Tie And Tails* (1987), *Astairable Fred* (1988), *Cheek To Cheek* (1988), *Puttin' On The Ritz* (1988), *The Fred Astaire And Ginger Rogers Story* (1989), *The Cream Of* (1993).

At Long Last Love

Released by 20th Century-Fox in 1975, this film was regarded as an attempt by writer-director Peter Bogdanovich to recapture the magic of the classic Fred Astaire-Ginger Rogers RKO musicals of the 30s. However, while the picture was lovely to look at, courtesy of the brilliant art deco sets and Laszlo Kovac's dazzling Technicolor photography, Burt Reynolds and Cybill Shepherd's song-and-dance talents were minimal, and the whole affair was a dreadful $6 million flop. It was a shame, because Bogdanovich's screenplay was endearingly scatty - just like the 30s originals - and the score contained some wonderful Cole Porter songs. Most of them, such as 'You're The Top', 'It's De-Lovely', 'Well, Did You Evah?', 'I Get A Kick Out Of You', 'Most Gentlemen Don't Like Love', 'Just One Of Those Things', and 'Friendship', were much-loved favourites, but other, less-familiar delights included 'But In The Morning, No', 'From Alpha To Omega', and 'Which'. Even with some valiant support from Eileen Brennan, Madeline Kahn, Duilio del Prete, Mildred Natwick, and John Hillerman, nothing worthwhile could be salvaged from the wreck. Footnote: Cybill Shepherd says that they sang 'live' - the first time it had been done in films since the 30s.

Auric, Georges

b. 15 February 1899, Lodève, Hérault, France, d. 23 July 1983, Paris, France. A composer of many classical pieces including an opera, and ballet, choral and instrumental music. From 1930 until the early 60s he contributed the scores to French films such as *Quand J'étais*, *A Nous La Liberté*, *Orphée*, and *Belles De Nuit*. He also wrote the music for numerous English speaking movies, including several classic Ealing comedies. His scores included *Dead Of Night* (1945), *Caesar And Cleopatra*, *Hue And Cry*, *It Always Rains On Sunday*, *Another Shore*, *Corridors Of Mirrors*, *Silent Dust*, *Passport To Pimlico*, *The Queen Of Spades*, *The Spider And The Fly*, *Cage Of Gold*, *The Galloping Major*, *The Lavender Hill Mob*, *Moulin Rouge*, *Roman Holiday*, *The Wages Of Fear*, *Father Brown*, *Rififi*, *The Witches Of Salem*, *Gervaise*, *The Picasso Mystery*, *Bonjour Tristesse*, *Heaven Knows Mr Allison*, *Heaven Fell That Night*, *The Innocents*, *The Mind Benders*, *Thomas The Impostor*, *Therese And Isabelle*, and *The Christmas Tree* (1969). The haunting theme from *Moulin Rouge* (1952), with a lyric by Bill Engvick, ('Whenever we kiss, I worry and wonder/Your lips may be here, but where is your heart?'), became a hit in the USA for Percy Faith and his Orchestra, with the vocal by Felicia Sanders; and a record of the title music from *Bonjour Tristesse* (1957), with words added by the film's screenwriter, Arthur Laurents, was popular for Gogi Grant. Auric published his autobiography in 1974, and died in 1983.

Avalon, Frankie

b. Francis Avallone, 18 September 1939, Philadelphia, USA. The photogenic 50s teen idol started as a trumpet-playing child prodigy. His first recordings in 1954 were the instrumentals 'Trumpet Sorrento' and 'Trumpet Tarantella' on X-Vik Records (an RCA Records subsidiary). In the mid-50s, he appeared on many television and radio shows including those of Paul Whiteman, Jackie Gleason and Ray Anthony. He joined Rocco & The Saints and was seen singing with them in the 1957 film *Jamboree* (*Disc Jockey Jamboree* in the UK). Avalon signed to Chancellor Records and in 1958 his third single for them 'Dede Dinah' reached the US Top 10. It was the first of his 25 US chart entries, many of which were written by his hard-working manager, Bob Marucci.

Despite the fact that he had a weak voice, he quickly became one of the top stars in the US and managed two chart toppers in 1959 'Venus' and 'Why', which were his only UK Top 20 entries. He had to wait until his 21st birthday in 1961 to receive the $100,000 he had earned to date and by that time he had passed his peak as a singer and turned his attention to acting. His acting career was also successful, with appearances in many films including a string of beach movies, alongside fellow 50s pop star Annette. He also appeared in the very successful 1978 film, *Grease*. He later recorded with little success on United Artists, Reprise, Metromedia, Regalia, Delite, Amos and Bobcat. Apart from his film and occasional television appearances, Avalon still performs on the supper-club circuit. Alongside his fellow Chancellor Records artist Fabian, he is often put down by rock critics, yet remains one of the American public's best loved 50s teen idols.

Selected albums: *Frankie Avalon* (1958), *The Young Frankie Avalon* (1959), *Swingin' On A Rainbow* (1959), *Young And In Love* (1960), *Summer Scene* (1960), *And Now About Mr. Avalon* (1961), *Italiano* (1962), *You Are Mine* (1962), *Frankie Avalon Christmas Album* (1962), *Muscle Beach Party* (1964, film soundtrack), *I'll Take Sweden* (1965, film soundtrack), *I Want You Near Me* (1970), *Bobby Sox To Stockings* (1984), *Frankie Avalon* (1987). Selected compilations: *A Whole Lotta Frankie* (1961), *15 Greatest Hits* (1964), *Best Of Frankie Avalon* (1984), *Frankie Avalon: Collection* (1990), *Venus And Other Hits* (1993).

B

Babes In Arms

Adapted for the screen by Jack McGowan and Kay Van Riper from the 1937 Broadway musical of the same name, *Babes In Arms*, which was released by MGM two years later, retained only two of the songs - 'Babes In Arms' and 'Where Or When' - by Richard Rodgers and Lorenz Hart which had made the show so appealing. The story was much the same though: a bunch of kids, whose vaudevillian parents are in a more or less permanent 'resting' situation, mount their own successful show and make the old folks proud. This theme of 'my uncle's got a barn, so we can do the show there', was used in many a future movie, and the idea was even worked into the title of a BBC radio quiz programme - *Let's Do The Show Right Here!* - more than 50 years later. Two of the best-loved stars in movie history, Judy Garland and Mickey Rooney, were teamed for the first time in *Babes In Arms*, and the magic was immediate: even at the age of 17, Garland's way with a song was awesome. There were some good numbers for her and the rest of the cast to work on too, including four with lyrics by the film's producer Arthur Freed, 'You Are My Lucky Star', 'Broadway Rhythm' and 'Good Morning' (all with Nacio Herb Brown), and 'I Cried For You' (with Abe Lyman and Gus Arnheim). The rest of the score included 'God's Country' (Harold Arlen-E.Y. 'Yip' Harburg), 'I'm Just Wild About Harry' (Eubie Blake-Noble Sissle), and 'Ja-Da' (Bob Carleton). *Babes In Arms* gave a boost to the already burgeoning career of director-choreographer Busby Berkeley who collaborated with Garland, Rooney, and Freed on three more movie milestones.

The first of these, *Strike Up The Band* (1940), borrowed George and Ira Gershwin's title song from the 1930 Broadway musical of that name, but nothing else. In the screenplay, by John Monks Jnr. and Fred Finklehoffe, Mickey Rooney assembles a school orchestra - with Judy Garland as the star vocalist - and, from his position on drums, drives them to the winning position in a nationwide radio competition fronted by Paul Whiteman. The legendary bandleader and his orchestra were joined in the cast by June Preisser, William Tracy, Larry Nunn, Margaret Early, and Ann Shoemaker. Several of the songs were written by Freed's close musical associate, Roger Eden, including 'Do The La Conga', 'Nobody', 'Drummer Boy', 'Nell Of New Rochelle', and 'Our Love Affair' (lyric-Freed).

MGM's third vehicle for Garland and Rooney was *Babes On Broadway* (1941), and the formula worked yet again. This time the show that just had to be put on was in aid of under-privileged children. The musical highlight was a delightful duet by Garland and Rooney on Ralph Freed and Burton Lane's 'How About You?', but there were lots of other good numbers, including 'Babes On Broadway' and 'Blackout Over Broadway' (both Ralph Freed-Lane), 'Hoe Down' (Ralph Freed-Roger Edens), 'Chin Up! Cheerio! Carry On! (Ralph Freed), and 'Anything Can Happen In New York (Lane-Harburg). Several older songs such as 'Mary Is A Grand Old Name', 'Yankee Doodle Boy', 'By The Light Of The Silvery Moon', 'Alabamy Bound', and 'Waiting For The Robert E. Lee' are used in a scene in which both of the young stars impersonate some legendary entertainers of the past and present: Rooney's uncanny (and hilarious) impression of Carmen Miranda (complete with tutti-frutti hat) still lingers in the memory.

The final film in which Garland, Rooney, Arthur Freed and Busby Berkeley pooled their remarkable talents was *Girl Crazy* (1943). There had been an earlier film version - in 1932 - of the classic Broadway show with its outstanding score by George and Ira Gershwin, and for this remake most of the original storyline was retained, although a few locations were shifted around. Young philanderer Danny Churchill (Rooney), is chased out of town by his father and ends up in a males-only college out West. Not to be outdone, he falls for one of the dean's granddaughters (Judy Garland), who joins with Danny to get the college out of debt by . . . putting on a show. The film contained the entire Broadway score, plus another famous Gershwin song, 'Fascinating Rhythm'. 'Bidin' My Time', which had been sung in the original show by a cowboy quartet, now took on a new dimension when given the Garland treatment. The other numbers included 'Sam And Delilah', 'Treat Me Rough', 'Bronco Busters', 'Embraceable You', 'Barbary Coast', 'Cactus Time In Arizona', 'Could You Use Me?', and 'But Not For Me'. Tommy Dorsey And His Orchestra were featured in several numbers including the rousing finale 'I Got Rhythm'. Roger Edens contributed one new song, 'Happy Birthday, Ginger' - perhaps an allusion to Ginger Rogers who played the ingénue in the Broadway production. After *Girl Crazy*, Rooney went back to his Andy Hardy pictures, among other projects, and Judy Garland joined Gene Kelly in his first feature film, *For Me And My Gal*.

Bacharach, Burt

b. 12 May 1928, Kansas City, Missouri, USA. As a composer and arranger, Bacharach is rightly regarded as one of the most important figures in contemporary music. Although his father was a journalist, it was music rather than lyrics which were to prove Bacharach's forte. Bred in New York, Burt was a jazz aficionado and played in various ensembles during the 40s. He studied musical theory and composition at university and served in the US Army between 1950 and 1952. Following his discharge, he worked as a pianist, arranger and conductor for a number of artists including Vic Damone, Steve Lawrence, Polly Bergen and the Ames Brothers. From 1956-58, Bacharach worked as musical director for Marlene Dietrich, a period in which he also registered his first hit as a composer. The song in question was the Five Blobs' 'The Blob', a tune written for a horror b-movie. Bacharach's co-composer on that hit was Mack David, but a more fruitful partnership followed when Burt was introduced to his collaborator's brother, Hal David. In 1958, Bacharach/David enjoyed their first hit with 'The Story Of My Life', a US Top 20 for Marty Robbins. In the UK, the song became an instant standard, courtesy of the chart-topping Michael Holliday and three other hit versions by Gary Miller, Alma Cogan and Dave King. Even greater success followed with Perry Como's reading of the engagingly melodic 'Magic Moments' which topped the UK charts for an astonishing eight weeks (number 4 in the US). Despite their chart-topping songwriting success, the Bacharach/David team did not work together exclusively until as late as 1962. In the meantime, Bacharach found a new songwriting partner, Bob Hilliard, with whom he composed several recordings for the Drifters. They also enjoyed minor success with Chuck Jackson's 'Any Day Now' (later recorded by Elvis Presley). It was during the early 60s that the Bacharach/David team recommenced their collaboration in earnest and many of their recordings brought success to both USA and UK artists. Frankie Vaughan's 'Tower Of Strength' gave them their third UK number 1, as well as another US Top 10 hit in a version by Gene McDaniels. The highly talented Gene Pitney, himself a songwriter, achieved two of his early hits with the duo's 'The Man Who Shot Liberty Valence' and 'Twenty Four Hours From Tulsa'. Other well-known Bacharach/David standards from the early/mid-60s included 'Wives And Lovers' and 'What The World Needs Now Is Love' (successfully covered by Jack Jones and Jackie DeShannon, respectively). From 1962 onwards the formidable Bacharach/David writing team steered the career of songstress Dionne Warwick with a breathtaking array of quality hit songs including 'Don't Make Me Over', 'Anyone Who Had A Heart', 'Walk On By', 'You'll Never Get To Heaven', 'Reach Out For Me', 'Are You There (With Another Girl)', 'Message To Michael', 'Trains And Boats And Planes', 'I Just Don't Know What To Do With Myself', Alfie', 'The Windows Of The World', 'I Say A Little Prayer', Valley Of The Dolls' and 'Do You Know The Way To San Jose?'. Interestingly, the songwriting duo maintained a quotient of number 1 singles in the UK, thanks to

class covers by Cilla Black ('Anyone Who Had A Heart'), Sandie Shaw ('There's Always Something There To Remind Me'), the Walker Brothers ('Make It Easy On Yourself') and Herb Alpert ('This Guy's In Love With You'). Looking back at this remarkable series of hits, one notices the strength of Bacharach's melodies and the deftness of touch that so neatly complemented David's soul-tortured, romantic lyrics. Since writing the theme song to *The Man Who Shot Liberty Valence*, Bacharach/David were popular choices as composers of film scores. The comedy *What's New Pussycat?* brought them an Oscar nomination and another hit when the theme was recorded by Tom Jones. Dusty Springfield recorded numerous Bacharach songs on her albums throughout the 60s and together with Warwick, they were arguably the best interpreters of his material. Further hits and Academy Award nominations followed between 1967 and 1968 with *Alfie* and *Casino Royale* (which featured 'The Look Of Love'). Finally, in 1969, a double Oscar celebration was achieved with the score from *Butch Cassidy And The Sundance Kid* and its award-winning standard 'Raindrops Keep Falling On My Head'.

Although there were opportunities to write further movie material during the late 60s, the duo were determined to complete their own musical, *Promises Promises*. The show proved enormously successful and enjoyed a lengthy Broadway run. Although Bacharach's reputation rests mainly on his songwriting, he has had a sporadic career as a recording artist. After a minor US hit with 'Saturday Sunshine' in 1963, he outmanoeuvred Billy J. Kramer And The Dakotas in the 1965 chart race involving 'Trains And Boats And Planes'. Personal appearances at such prestigious venues as the Greek Theatre in Los Angeles and the Riviera Hotel in Las Vegas have produced 'standing room only' notices, while television specials based on his songs proved very popular.

By 1970, Bacharach seemed blessed with the hit Midas touch and the Carpenters' beautiful reading of 'Close To You' suggested that a further wealth of standards would follow. Remarkably, however, this inveterate hitmaker would not enjoy another chart success for over 10 years. An acrimonious split with partner Hal David broke the classic songwriting spell. A barren period was possibly exacerbated by the concurrent break up of Burt's marriage to actress Angie Dickinson and the loss of his most consistent hitmaker Dionne Warwick. Bacharach's desultory decade was alleviated by a series of albums for A&M Records, which featured his own readings of his compositions. Although the late 60s recording *Make It Easy On Yourself* and the 1971 *Burt Bacharach* were chart successes, the curse of the 70s was once more evident when *Living Together* sold poorly. Worse followed when his musical *Lost Horizon* emerged as a commercial disaster. His succeeding albums *Futures* and *Woman* also fared badly and none of his new compositions proved chartworthy.

It was not until 1981 that Bacharach's dry run ended. At last he found a lyricist of genuine commercial fire in Carole Bayer Sager. Their Oscar-winning 'Arthur's Theme' (co-written with Peter Allen and singer Christopher Cross) returned Bacharach to the charts and in 1982 he married Sager. Together, they provided hits for Roberta Flack ('Making Love') and Neil Diamond ('Heartlight'). 1986 saw Bacharach re-enacting the success level so familiar during the late 60s, with two US number 1 hits 'That's What Friends Are For' (an AIDS charity record by Warwick and 'Friends' - Elton John, Gladys Knight and Stevie Wonder) and 'On My Own' (a duet between Patti Labelle and Michael McDonald).

In the late 80s Bacharach collaborated with Sager on film songs such as 'They Don't Make Them Like They Use To' (for *Tough Guys*), 'Everchanging Time' (with Bill Conti for *Baby Boom*), and 'Love Is My Decision' (with Christopher Cross and Peter Allen for *Arthur 2: On The Rocks*). He also wrote the score for the latter film. In 1989 the American vocalist Sybil revived 'Don't Make Me Over', Warwick's first hit with a Bacharach and David song, and a year later the UK group Deacon Blue went to number 2 with their *Four Bacharach And David Songs* EP. In 1992, some months after Bacharach had announced that his nine-year-old marriage to Sager was over, he and David finally got together again to write some songs, including 'Sunny Weather Lover' for Dionne Warwick's new album. Two years after that, a musical revue entitled *Back To Bacharach And David* opened in New York.

Albums: *Hit Maker - Burt Bacharach* (1965), *Reach Out* (1967), *Make It Easy On Yourself* (1969), *Burt Bacharach* (1971), *Living Together* (1973), *Futures* (1977), *Woman* (1979). Compilations: *Portrait In Music* (1971), *Burt Bacharach's Greatest Hits* (1974).

Bailey, Pearl

b. 29 March 1918, Newport News, Virginia, USA, d. 17 August 1990, Philadephia, Pennsylvania, USA. Pearlie Mae, as she was known, was an uninhibited performer, who mumbled her way through some songs and filled others with outrageous asides and sly innuendoes. She entered the world of entertainment as a dancer but later sang in vaudeville, graduating to the New York nightclub circuit in the early 40s. After working with the Noble Sissle Orchestra, she became band-vocalist with Cootie Williams with whom she recorded 'Tessa's Torch Song' previously sung by Dinah Shore in the movie *Up In Arms*. Bailey received strong critical acclaim after substituting for Rosetta Tharpe in a show, and was subsequently signed to star in the 1946 Harold Arlen/Johnny Mercer Broadway musical *St. Louis Woman*. A year

later her slurred version of 'Tired' was the highlight of the movie *Variety Girl*. Subsequently her best films were *Carmen Jones* (1954), *St. Louis Blues* (1958) and *Porgy And Bess* (1959). During her stay with Columbia Records (1945-50) Bailey recorded a series of duets with Frank Sinatra, trumpeter Oran 'Hot Lips' Page and comedienne Moms Mabley. She also recorded some solo tracks with outstanding arrangers/conductors, Gil Evans and Tadd Dameron. Upon joining the Coral label in 1951, she employed Don Redman as her regular musical director, the association lasting for 10 years. In 1952, she had her biggest hit record 'Takes Two To Tango'. In that same year she married drummer Louie Bellson and he took over from Redman as her musical director in 1961. Although few of her records have sold in vast quantities, Bailey had always been a crowd-pulling, on-stage performer and, following her early stage triumph in *St. Louis Woman*, was later cast in other shows including *The House Of Flowers*, *Bless You All*, *Arms And The Girl* and an all-black cast version of *Hello, Dolly!*. She has also starred in several US television specials, playing down the double-entendre that caused one of her albums, *For Adults Only*, to be 'restricted from air-play'.

Selected albums: *Pearl Bailey A-Broad* (1957), *Gems* (1958), *For Adults Only* (1958), *Sings!* (1959), *St. Louis Blues* (1959), *Porgy & Bess & Others* (1959), *More Songs For Adults* (1960), *Songs Of Bad Old Days* (1960), *Naughty But Nice* (1961), *Songs She Loves By Arlen* (1962), *Come On Let's Play With Pearlie Mae* (1962), *Intoxicating* (1964), *Songs By Jimmy Van Heusen* (1964), *For Women Only* (1965), *Birth Of The Blues* (c.60s), *Cultered Pearl* (c.60s), *The Definitive* (c.60s), *For Adult Listening* (c.60s), *C'est La Vie* (c.60s), *Risque World* (c.60s), *The Best Of - The Roulette Years* (1991).

Further reading: *The Raw Pearl*, Pearl Bailey.

Ball Of Fire

Hollywood has never been averse to squeezing the last drop of loot out of a good idea. This 1941 film broadly re-jigged *Snow White And The Seven Dwarfs* (1937) and obviously appealed to director Howard Hawks so much that seven years later he remade it as *A Song Is Born*. A group of professors have been cooped up writing an encyclopedia when a chance visitor from the outside makes them realize that, musically speaking, they are out of touch. One of their number, Gary Cooper, is sent forth to discover what is happening in the contemporary popular music business and meets band singer Barbara Stanwyck with whom he becomes romantically involved. The Gene Krupa band, featuring the leader and Roy Eldridge, performs 'Drum Boogie' with Stanwyck, apparently ghosted by Martha Tilton (presumably because Irene Daye was in the process of leaving the band around this time). Good fun and all very professional, but not to be taken seriously by jazz fans.

Bambi (see **Disney, Walt**)

Band Wagon, The

Taking the title from a highly successful 1931 Broadway revue which had a score by Arthur Schwartz and Howard Dietz, but no plot, Betty Comden and Adolph Green provided the screenplay for arguably the best and wittiest backstage film musical of them all. It dealt with an ageing, has-been hoofer, Tony Hunter (Fred Astaire), whose New York comeback is being masterminded and written by Lily and Lester Marton (Oscar Levant and Nanette Fabray), two characters reputedly based on Comden and Green themselves. Ballerina Gabrielle Gerard (Cyd Charisse) reluctantly agrees to become Hunter's co-star, and Jerry Cordova (Jack Buchanan), the reigning theatrical virtuoso and super-egotist, is called in to direct, but his extravagant efforts result in something nearer *Faust* than *Funny Face*. However, all is not lost: after the cast have revamped the show (with the help of Cordova who turns out to be a nice modest - even insecure - guy underneath), it looks like it will run for years. Schwartz and Dietz's score was full of marvellous songs, including 'A Shine On Your Shoes', 'By Myself' (Astaire), 'I Guess I'll Have To Change My Plan' (Astaire-Buchanan), the ingenious 'Triplets' (Astaire-Buchanan-Fabray), 'New

Sun In The Sky' (Charisse, dubbed by India Adams), and several others involving the principals and chorus, such as 'I Love Louisa', 'Louisiana Hayride', 'You And The Night And The Music', 'Dancing In The Dark', and 'Something To Remember Me By'. The one new number was 'That's Entertainment', which, along with Irving Berlin's 'There's No Business Like Show Business', attempts to explain why, despite Noël Coward's reservations, the show must always go on. Cyd Charisse and Fred Astaire's dancing was a dream, especially in the ethereal 'Dancing In The Dark' sequence and the 'Girl Hunt' ballet. Much of the credit for the film's oustanding success was due to director Vincente Minnelli, choreographer Michael Kidd, and producer Arthur Freed whose special musicals unit at MGM had created yet another winner.

Barkleys Of Broadway, The

After Judy Garland, his original co-star, withdrew through illness, Fred Astaire was reunited for the last time with his most famous dance partner, Ginger Rogers, for this 1949 production from Arthur Freed's MGM unit. Betty Comden and Adolph Green's screenplay cast the pair as husband and wife, Josh and Dinah Barkley, an enduring musical comedy couple whose comfortable and lucrative life is temporarily

The Band Wagon

disturbed when Dinah gets an urge to become 'a great tragic actress'. Fortunately, she eventually comes to her senses, and the old Rogers/Astaire magic - not seen on the screen since they portrayed another famous dance team in *The Story Of Vernon And Irene Castle* in 1939 - was shining as bright as ever in Harry Warren and Ira Gershwin's numbers such as 'Swing Trot', 'Bouncin' The Blues', 'You'd Be Hard To Replace', 'Weekend In The Country', and 'Manhattan Downbeat'. Two of the many highlights included Fred and Ginger kitted out with kilts and excruciating Scottish accents in 'My One And Only Highland Fling', and 'Shoes With Wings On', in which Fred dances while being 'bombarded' from all directions by flying pairs of shoes. This, and the other memorable and innovative routines, were choreographed by Robert Alton and Hermes Pan. There was a lovely and poignant moment towards the end of the film when Fred and Ginger are reunited to the strains of George and Ira Gershwin's 'They Can't Take That Away From Me', a number that Fred introduced in the 1937 film *Shall We Dance*. *The Barkleys Of Broadway* was photographed in Techicolor, and directed by Charles Walters. The cast also included Oscar Levant, Billie Burke, Gale Robbins, Jacques Francois, George Zucco, and Clinton Sundberg. It was released in the UK under the title of *The Gay Barkleys*.

Barry, John

b. Jonathan Barry Prendergast, 3 November 1933, York, Yorkshire, England. Renowned as one of the leading composers of film soundtrack music, Barry began his career leading the John Barry Seven. This rousing instrumental unit scored several notable UK hits between 1960-62, the best-known of which were 'Hit And Miss' and a version of the Ventures' 'Walk Don't Run' (both 1960). The former, which reached number 11 in the UK charts, was the theme to *Juke Box Jury*, BBC television's long-running record release show. Barry made regular appearances on several early pop programmes, including *Oh Boy* and *Drumbeat* and also enjoyed concurrent fame as a writer and arranger, scoring the distinctive pizzicato strings on numerous Adam Faith hits including the number 1 'What Do You Want' (1959). He also composed the soundtrack to *Beat Girl*, the singer's film debut, and later took up a senior A&R post with the independent Ember label. In 1962 Barry had a UK Top 20 hit with the 'James Bond Theme' which was part of Monty Norman's score for the film *Dr. No*, the first in a highly successful series. He produced music for several subsequent Bond films, including *From Russia With Love*, *Goldfinger* and *You Only Live Twice*, the title songs from which provided hit singles for Matt Monro (1963), Shirley Bassey (1964) and Nancy Sinatra (1967). Such success led to a series of stylish soundtracks which encompassed contrasting moods

and music, including *The Ipcress File*, *The Knack* (both 1965); *Born Free* (which won an Oscar in 1966); *Midnight Cowboy* (1969) and *Mary, Queen Of Scots* (1971). Although his theme songs have enjoyed a high commercial profile, it is Barry's imaginative incidental music which has assured his peerless reputation. By contrast he pursued another lucrative direction composing television commercials for disparate household items.

His consistency remained intact throughout the 70s and 80s, although several attendant films, including *King Kong* (1976) and *Howard The Duck* (1986), were highly criticized. 'Down Deep Inside', the theme from *The Deep* (1977), was a UK Top 5 hit for Donna Summer and this disco-influenced composition emphasized the writer's versatility. *Out Of Africa* (1985), *The Living Daylights* and *Hearts Of Fire* (both 1987) demonstrated his accustomed flair while *Dances With Wolves* (1990) earned him an Oscar. In the early 90s, his scores included *Ruby Cairo*, *Indecent Proposal*, and Richard Attenborough's *Chaplin*, for which Barry received an Oscar nomination, and *My Life* (1993). His orchestrations combine elements of classical, jazz and popular themes and command the respect of enthusiastic aficionados.

Albums: as performer, composer, arranger or conductor *Six-Five Special* (1957), *Oh Boy* (1958), *Drumbeat* (1959), *Beat Girl* (1959), *Stringbeat* (1961), *Man In The Middle* (1962), *Dr. No* (1962), *It's All Happening* (1963), *Zulu* (1963), *Elizabeth Taylor In London* (1963), *From Russia With Love* (1963), *The Man In The Middle* (1964), *Goldfinger* (1964), *The Ipcress File* (1965), *Sophia Loren In Rome* (1965), *King Rat* (1965), *The Knack...& How To Get It* (1965), *Four In The Morning* (1965), *Thunderball* (1965), *Passion Flower Hotel* (1965), *The Wrong Box* (1966), *The Chase* (1966), *Born Free* (1966), *The Quiller Memorandum* (1966), *You Only Live Twice* (1967), *Dutchman* (1967), *The Whisperers* (1967), *Deadfall* (1968), *Petulia* (1968), *Boom* (1968), *The Lion In Winter* (1968), *On Her Majesty's Secret Service* (1969), *Midnight Cowboy* (1969), *The Last Valley* (1970), *Diamonds Are Forever* (1971), *Follow Me* (1971), *Lolita My Love* (1971), *The Persuaders* (1971), *Mary Queen Of Scots* (1971), *Alice's Adventures In Wonderland* (1972), *The John Barry Concert* (1972), *A Doll's House* (1973), *Billy* (1974), *The Dove* (1974), *The Man With The Golden Gun* (1974), *The Day Of The Locust* (1974), *Americans* (1975), *Robin And Marian* (1976), *King Kong* (1976), *The Deep* (1977), *The Game Of Death* (1978), *Starcrash* (1978), *The Black Hole* (1979), *Moonraker* (1979), *Inside Moves* (1980), *The Legend Of The Lone Ranger* (1981), *Frances* (1982), *High Road To China* (1983), *The Golden Seal* (1983), *Body Heat* (1983), *Until September* (1984), *Jagged Edge* (1985), *Out Of Africa* (1985), *A View To A Kill* (1985), *Peggy Sue Got Married* (1986), *Howard The Duck* (1986), *Golden Child* (1986), *Somewhere In Time* (1986), *Living Daylights* (1987),

Dances With Wolves (1990). Compilations: *The Great Movie Sounds Of John Barry* (1966), *John Barry Conducts His Great Movie Hits* (1967), *Ready When You Are, John Barry* (1970), *John Barry Revisited* (1971), *Play It Again* (1974), *The Music Of John Barry* (1976), *The Very Best Of John Barry* (1977), *The John Barry Seven And Orchestra* (1979), *The Best Of John Barry* (1981), *The Big Screen Hits Of John Barry* (1981), *James Bond's Greatest Hits* (1982), *Music From The Big Screen* (1986), *Hit Or Miss* (1988), *The Film Music Of John Barry* (1989), *John Barry Themes* (1989), *The Ember Years Vol. 1* (1992), *The Ember Years Vol. 2* (1992), *Moviola* (1992), *The Best Of EMI Years Vol. 2* (1993).

Beauty And The Beast

After Walt Disney's tremendous success with *The Little Mermaid* in 1989, this blockbuster came along two years later and was immediately considered to be equal to the Studio's animated gems of the distant past including *Cinderella*, *Snow White And The Seven Dwarfs*, and *Peter Pan*. The memory of earlier movie treatments of the classic French fairytale, such as Jean Cocteau's highly regarded 1946 version, were overwhelmed by the all-round brilliance of this triumph of animated storytelling, which was enhanced by spectacular extra computer graphics images by Jim Hillin. In Linda Woolverton's screenplay Belle is portrayed as a modern, emancipated, well-read young lady who is kidnapped by the Beast and incarcerated in his castle, which by a stroke of good fortune houses a fine library. After overcoming her initial fear and revulsion, Belle forges a caring relationship with her captor when she becomes aware of his inner beauty and sensitivity. Belle's voice is provided by Paige O'Hara, and Robby Benson gives the Beast just the right mixture of terror and tenderness. There are also several well-known voices behind the supporting cast which is mostly made up of objects from around the castle, such as Lumiere the candelabra (Jerry Orbach), Mrs. Potts the teapot (Angela Lansbury), her teacup son Chip (Bradley Michael Pierce), Cogsworth the mantel clock (David Ogden Stiers), Featherduster (Kimmy Robertson), Wardrobe (Jo Anne Worley), Gaston (Richard White), Belle's determined but unrequited suitor. Composer Alan Menken and lyricist Howard Ashman excelled themselves with a bunch of witty and tuneful songs; even the *Variety* theatre critic wryly acknowledged that *Beauty And The Beast* 'boasted the most appealing musical comedy score in years, dammit'. For the second year in succession, Menken took the Academy Award for original score, and he and Ashman won another Oscar for the film's enchanting title song which was introduced by Mrs. Potts, and sung over the end titles by Celine Dion and Peabo Bryson; their version entered the US Top 10. Two other numbers, 'Belle' and 'Be Our Guest', were also nominated for Oscars. *Beauty And The Beast* won five Grammys, three

Golden Globe Awards including best picture (musical or comedy), and was the first animated feature to be nominated for an Academy Award for best picture. No doubt real-live actors all over the world breathed a collective sigh of relief when the Academy's voting panel preferred the grim and grisly *The Silence Of The Lambs*. Directed by Gary Trousdale and Kirk Wise, the picture was dedicated to lyricist and executive producer Howard Ashman who died a few months before it was released.

Belafonte, Harry

b. Harold George Belafonte, 1 March 1927, New York, USA. In recent years, the former 'King Of Calypso' has become better known for his work with UNICEF and his enterprise with USA For Africa. Prior to that, Belafonte had an extraordinarily varied life. His early career was spent as an actor, until he had time to demonstrate his silky smooth and gently relaxing singing voice. He appeared as Joe in Oscar Hammerstein's *Carmen Jones*; an adaptation of *Carmen* by Bizet, and in 1956 he was snapped up by RCA Victor. Belafonte was then at the forefront of the calypso craze which was a perfect vehicle for his happy-go-lucky folk songs. Early hits included 'Jamaica Farewell', 'Mary's Boy Child' and the classic transatlantic hit 'Banana Boat Song' with its unforgettable refrain; 'Day-oh, dayyy-oh, daylight come and me wanna go home'. *Calypso* became the first ever album to sell a million copies, and spent 31 weeks at the top of the US charts. Belafonte continued throughout the 50s with incredible success. He was able to cross over into many markets appealing to pop, folk, jazz as well as the with ethnic population with whom he became closely associated, particularly during the civil rights movement. He appeared in many films including *Island In The Sun*, singing the title song and *Odds Against Tomorrow*. His success as an album artist was considerable; between 1956 and 1962 he was hardly ever absent from the album chart. *Belafonte At Carnegie Hall* spent over three years in the charts, and similar success befell *Belafonte Returns To Carnegie Hall*, featuring Miriam Makeba, the Chad Mitchell Trio and Odetta with the memorable recording of 'There's A Hole In My Bucket'. Throughout the 60s Belafonte was an ambassador of human rights and a most articulate speaker at rallies and on television. His appeal as a concert hall attraction was immense, no less than seven of his albums were recorded in concert. Although his appearances in the best-sellers had stopped by the 70s he remained an active performer, recording artist and continued to appear on film, although in lightweight movies like *Buck And The Preacher* and *Uptown Saturday Night*. In the mid-80s he was a leading light in the USA For Africa appeal and sang on 'We Are The World'. His sterling work continued into the 90s with UNICEF. Belafonte was

Bells Are Ringing

one of the few black artists who broke down barriers of class and race and should be counted with Martin Luther King as a major figure in achieving equal rights for blacks in America, although he did it through popular music in a less obvious way.

Albums: *Mark Twain And Other Folk Favorites* (1955), *Belafonte* (1956), *Calypso* (1956), *An Evening With Belafonte* (1957), *Belafonte Sings Of The Caribbean* (1957), *Belafonte Sings The Blues* (1958), *Love Is A Gentle Thing* (1959), *Porgy And Bess* (1959), *Belafonte At Carnegie Hall* (1959), *My Lord What A Mornin'* (1960), *Belafonte Returns To Carnegie Hall* (1960), *Jump Up Calypso* (1961), *The Midnight Special* (1962), *The Many Moods Of Belafonte* (1962), *To Wish You A Merry Christmas* (1962), *Streets I Have Walked* (1963), *Belafonte At The Greek Theatre* (1964), *Ballads Blues And Boasters* (1964), *An Evening With Belafonte/Makeba* (1965), *An Evening With Belafonte/Mouskouri* (1966), *In My Quiet Room* (1966), *Calypso In Brass* (1967), *Belafonte On Campus* (1967), *Homeward Bound* (1970), *Turn The World Around* (1977), *Loving You Is Where I Belong* (1981), *Paradise In Gazankulu* (1988). Compilations: *Collection - Castle Collector Series* (1987), *Banana Boat Song* (1988), *All Time Greatest Hits* (1989), *The Very Best Of* (1992).

Bells Are Ringing

As Broadway-to-Hollywood transplants go, *Bells Are Ringing* was pretty satisfactory mainly due to the presence of Judy Holliday. She recreated her stage role as Ella Peterson, the somewhat scatty telephone operator at Susanswerphone, who considers her clients 'family', and their problems her own. After sympathising with her dentist who is more interested in music than molars, she turns her attention to Jeff Moss (Dean Martin), a playwright whose output is, as the Americans say, 'batting zero'. As they fall in love, he takes her to a smart party where, after she gets her 'Ethels' (Waters, Barrymore, and Merman) mixed up with her 'Marys' (Pickford, Martin, and Astor), the sophisticated theatre crowd explain that it's simply a question of being able to 'Drop That Name'. That neat number, and the rest of the score, were written by Jule Styne (music) and Betty Comden and Adolph Green (lyrics and screenplay). Most of the songs from the Broadway production survived, although the absence of 'Long Before I Knew You' was a pity. It was replaced by 'Better Than A Dream', and another newcomer, 'Do It Yourself', was slipped in alongside originals such as 'It's A Simple Life', 'It's A Perfect Relationship', 'I Met A Girl', 'It's A Simple Little System', 'The Midas Touch', and the popular duo, 'Just In Time' and 'The Party's Over'. Just before the film reaches its inevitable happy ending, Ella becomes tired of her complicated telephonic involvement in other people's lives, and yearns to return to her more simple existence in the delightful 'I'm Going Back (where I can be me/At the Bonjour Tristesse Brassiere Company)'. The rest of the fine cast, a few of whom were also in the Broadway show, included Fred Clark, Eddie Foy Jnr., Dort Clark, Jean Stapleton, Frank Gorshin, Bernie West, and Gerry Mulligan. The film, which was photographed in Metrocolor and released by MGM in 1960, was directed by Vincente Minnelli, choreographed by Charles O'Curran, and produced by Arthur Freed.

Benny Goodman Story, The

Hollywood bio-pics almost always present the same paradox: If the subject is interesting enough to make a film of his/her life, why mess with the facts? Goodman, portrayed by Steve Allen but providing his own playing for the soundtrack, had a rags-to-riches life story that simultaneously fulfils the American Dream and every screenwriter's wildest fantasy. Unfortunately, Goodman in real life was a single-minded perfectionist who became a household name and a millionaire before he had reached 30. Put another way, what he did was practice, practice, practice and when he was not doing that he performed. Not much visual drama there, except in the performing part, so the reality of his dedication was jettisoned in favour of a sloppy story about a home-loving boy who made good. Along the way, Goodman whines periodically to his Ma, 'Don't be that way'. This allows the scriptwriter to introduce the tune of that name as a dutiful son's grateful acknowledgement to his mother, thus overlooking the fact that Edgar Sampson wrote the song for another bandleader, Chick Webb. Goodman's mile-wide streak of ruthlessness was also overlooked. No matter, the film has some nice musical moments from Allen/Goodman, Teddy Wilson, Lionel Hampton and Gene Krupa in the small group numbers. The specially assembled big band includes Buck Clayton, Stan Getz, Conrad Gozzo, Urbie Green, Manny Klein and Murray McEachern and plays very well even if it does not sound too much like the real Goodman band of the late 30s. Ben Pollack and Kid Ory also appear, as does Harry James (in a close-up solo feature but not in long-shot - contractual reasons were suggested, amongst which was too little money). For all this 1955 film's flaws, amongst which is the famous 1938 Carnegie Hall concert attended by 'longhairs' - in real life the seats were packed with swing-era fans and jitterbugs - it remains one of the least embarrassing of the earlier jazz-bio-pics.

Bergman, Alan And Marilyn

For over two decades, the Bergmans have been among the leading lyricists of songs for Hollywood films. Among the husband and wife partnership's earliest work for the screen was the theme for 'In The Heat Of The Night' (1967), co-written with Quincy Jones and sung by Ray Charles. The following year the Bergmans began one of their most important collaborations with a soundtrack composer when they wrote 'Windmills Of Your Mind' with Michel Legrand for *The Thomas Crown Affair*. Sung by Noel Harrison it was an international hit in 1969. The Bergman-Legrand team were also responsible for 'What Are You Doing The Rest Of Your Life' which appeared in the 1969 movie *The Happy Ending*, 'How Do You Keep The Music Playing' for *Best Friends* (1982) and 'The Way He Makes Me Feel' for the Barbra Streisand film *Yentl* (1983).

Streisand was the first to feature perhaps the Bergmans' most famous song, 'The Way We Were' in the 1973 film of the same name. The music for this yearning ballad was composed by Marvin Hamlisch and the Oscar-winning song was given an epic soul-tinged treatment by Gladys Knight. The same team wrote 'The Last Time I Felt Like This', for *Same Time, Next Year* (1978). Among Alan and Marilyn Bergman's other collaborators have been Dave Grusin ('It Might Be You' for *Tootsie* in 1982), Henry Mancini ('Little Boys' for *The Man Who Loved Women* in 1983) and James Newton Howard, who provided the melody in 1991 for 'Places That Belong To You', performed by Barbra Streisand in *Prince Of Tides*. Streisand herself co-wrote 'Two People', the theme from *Nuts*, with the Bergmans. The couple have also provided themes for US television series, including *Alice* (1976) and *Powers That Be* (1990), where they again worked with Hamlisch. With a talent precisely tailored to providing cinema theme songs, among the few lyrics written by Alan and Marilyn Bergman for the recording studio was 'I Believe In Love', which became a minor hit for Kenny Loggins in 1977.

Berkeley, Busby

b. William Berkeley Enos, 29 November 1895, Los Angeles, California, USA, d. 1976. A legendary choreographer and director, renowned for his innovative work on the 'Depression Era' musical films of the 30s. Stories abound about him building a monorail along which the camera travelled at the most unusual angles, and his habit of cutting a hole in the studio roof just so that he could get that one special shot. Although Berkeley's mother was an actress and he appeared in a number of small stage productions as a youngster, he had no formal theatrical training and attended the Mohegan Lake Military Academy near New York before working in a shoe factory for three years. After a brief spell in the US Army in 1917, Berkeley played small roles in a number of plays and musicals before taking up directing in the early 20s. For most of the decade he served primarily as a dance director on Broadway shows such as *Holka Polka, A*

Connecticut Yankee, *Present Arms*, *Good Boy*, *Street Singer*, and *The International Review* (1930). Samuel Goldwyn is credited with taking Berkeley to Hollywood in 1930 to stage the production numbers for the Eddie Cantor vehicle *Whoopee!*. His work on that film, which introduced his trademark 'top shots' and close-ups of the chorus girls, was further developed in the other United Artists films for which he staged the dances, *Palmy Days*, *The Kid From Spain*, and *Roman Scandals*. However, it was not until 1933 and *42nd Street*, the first of Berkeley's films for Warner Brothers, that the dance director's elaborate musical numbers, with the girls arranged in a series of complicated kaleidoscopic patterns which were continually moving in different directions, began to be fully appreciated. Dick Powell and Ruby Keeler were the stars of this slight backstage story, and they were in some of the other films to which he brought his highly individual flair and imagination. These included *Gold Diggers Of 1933*, *Footlight Parade*, *Wonder Bar*, *Fashions Of 1934*, *Twenty Million Sweethearts*, *Dames*, *Go Into Your Dance*, *In Caliente*, *Stars Over Broadway*, *Gold Diggers Of 1937*, *The Singing Marine*, *Varsity Show*, and *Gold Diggers In Paris* (1938). Berkeley left Warner Brothers in 1939 to continue to 'create and stage the dances and ensembles' for MGM and other studios for musicals such as *Broadway Serenade*, *Ziegfeld Girl*, *Lady Be Good*, *Born To Sing*, *Girl Crazy*, *Two Weeks With Love*, *Call Me Mister*, *Two Tickets To Broadway*, *Million Dollar Mermaid*, *Small Town Girl*, *Easy To Love*, and *Rose Marie* (1954). By then he and his kind of elaborate production numbers were out of fashion, but he returned in 1962 to stage the dance numbers for his last screen project, *Billy Rose's Jumbo*. From *Gold Diggers Of 1935* onwards, Berkeley was overall director of a number of films. The musicals among them included *Bright Lights* (1935), *I Live For Love*, *Stage Struck*, *Hollywood Hotel*, *Babes In Arms*, *Strike Up The Band*, *Babes On Broadway*, *For Me And My Gal*, *The Gang's All Here*, *Cinderella Jones*, and *Take Me Out To The Ball Game* (1949). In the mid-60s Berkeley benefited from a general upsurge of interest in the films of the 30s, and there were several retrospective seasons of his work in the US and other countries around the world. In 1971 he was the production supervisor for a Broadway revival of the musical *No, No, Nanette*, which starred Ruby Keeler and ran for 861 performances. Looking back on his career, he said: 'What I mostly remember is stress and strain and exhaustion.' His brilliant achievements were contrasted by a shambolic private live - he was married at least five times - and in 1946 he attempted suicide after his mother died It is also reported that in 1935 he was charged with second-degree murder after driving into another car, killing the three occupants. After two trials ended with hung juries, he was finally acquitted.

Berlin, Irving

b. Israel Baline, 11 May 1888, Temun, Siberia, Russia, d. 22 September 1989. Despite his foreign birth, Berlin became one of the most American of all songwriters. When he was four-years-old his family escaped a pogrom and travelled to the USA. His father was a cantor in his homeland, but in their new country had to earn his living as a meat inspector in New York City, singing in the synagogue only when the regular cantor was unavailable. An indifferent student, Berlin was happier singing, but in 1896, following the death of his father, he was obliged to work. At the age of 14 he began singing in saloons and on street corners. It was while engaged in this latter activity that he was 'discovered' and recommended to songwriter and publisher Harry Von Tilzer, who hired him to sing songs from the balcony of a 14th Street theatre. By 1906 Berlin had not advanced far, working as a singing waiter in Pelham's, a Chinatown restaurant frequented by New York's upper set, but he had taught himself to play piano and had started to write his own material. His first published song (lyrics only, music by Michael Nicholson) was 'Marie From Sunny Italy', from which he earned 37 cents and, apparently through a misprint on the sheet music, acquired the name by which he was thereafter known.

During the next few years he continued to write words and music, but also hung onto his work as a singing waiter. Several of the songs he wrote in these years were in Yiddish and were popular successes for artists such as Eddie Cantor and Fanny Brice. His first real songwriting success was 'My Wife's Gone To The Country' (1909, music by George Whiting), which was featured by Cantor. Like many other songwriters of the day, Berlin was fascinated by ragtime and tried his hand at several numbers, many of which had little to do with the reality of this musical form except in their titling. In 1910, however, he had his first massive hit with such a song. 'Alexander's Ragtime Band', for which he wrote both words and music, made him a household name. Berlin capitalized upon the success of this song with 'Everybody's Doin' It' (1911), 'The International Rag' (1913) and others. In 1914, he scored a Broadway show, *Watch Your Step*, for dancers Vernon And Irene Castle, which included 'Play A Simple Melody', and followed it in 1915 with *Stop! Look! Listen!* which included 'I Love A Piano'. In addition to shows he wrote lasting popular pieces such as 'Woodman Spare That Tree' (1911), 'When The Midnight Choo Choo Leaves For Alabam' (1912), 'When I Lost You' (1913), his first major ballad, and the sentimental 'When I Leave The World Behind' (1915). During World War I Berlin was active in the theatre, writing an outstanding ballad in 'Kiss Me Again' and a handful of patriotic songs with only limited appeal. In 1918 he was drafted into the army and encouraged to write a show for the troops. For this hastily conceived and executed work he produced two memorable songs, 'Mandy' and 'Oh, How I Hate To Get Up In The Morning'. After the war came a steady stream of successful shows and popular songs, among the latter were 'A Pretty Girl Is Like A Melody' (1919), 'Say It With Music', 'All By Myself' (both 1921), 'All Alone' and 'What'll I Do' (both 1923). In 1925 he met, fell in love with, and a year later married Ellin Mackay, a member of New York's elite. One result of his meeting Mackay was a succession of fine ballads, including 'Remember' and 'Always' (both 1925). Although he was by now the biggest name in American songwriting, Berlin was always happy to contribute songs to the shows of others and in 1926 wrote 'Blue Skies' for *Betsy*, a show co-written by Richard Rodgers and Lorenz Hart. Among his songs of the late 20s were 'Shaking The Blues Away', 'The Song Is Ended' (1927), 'Marie' (1928), 'Let Me Sing - And I'm Happy' and 'Puttin' On The Ritz' (both 1930). In 1932, following a period of almost two years during which he appeared to have dried up, he recovered his confidence with 'Say It Isn't So' and 'Soft Lights And Sweet Music'. The following year he had a major Broadway success with *As Thousands Cheer*, a show which included 'Heat Wave' and the timeless 'Easter Parade'. During the 30s Hollywood was churning out numerous film musicals and, inevitably, Berlin was lured there to write scores for a succession of productions, some of which owe any subsequent fame to his contribution. Among the best of his films were *Top Hat* (1935), *Follow The Fleet* (1936) and *Carefree* (1938), all vehicles for newly-discovered hot properties, Fred Astaire and Ginger Rogers. Songs from these films included 'Cheek To Cheek', 'Isn't It A Lovely Day', 'Top Hat, White Tie And Tails', 'Let's Face The Music And Dance' and 'Change Partners'. *Alexander's Ragtime Band* (1938) was a feast for Berlin fans, with more than two dozen of his hit songs plus a new song, 'Now It Can Be Told'. Towards the end of the 30s, with rumblings of war coming from Europe, Berlin wrote a song especially for Kate Smith. This was 'God Bless America', a song which for a while was a serious contender as a national anthem.

As successful in films as he had been with stage musicals, Berlin again conquered Broadway, this time with *Louisiana Purchase* (1940), from which the hit song was 'Tomorrow Is A Lovely Day'. America's entry into the war roused Berlin's patriotism to new heights with a show, *This Is The Army* (1942), for which he wrote 'This Is The Army Mr. Jones' and 'I Left My Heart At The Stage Door Canteen'. A concurrent film project was *Holiday Inn*, which included two new classics, 'White Christmas' and 'Be Careful It's My Heart'. After the war Berlin, belying the fact that he had been writing hit songs for more

than 30 years, struck a new lode of inspiration with *Annie Get Your Gun* (1946), brimming with hits, and after the less successful *Miss Liberty* (1949), found gold again with *Call Me Madam* (1950), which was followed by another downturn with *Mr President* (1962), his last Broadway musical. His post-war films included *Blue Skies* (1946), *Easter Parade* (1948) and *White Christmas* (1954), which mostly reprised old songs but included such new material as 'You Keep Coming Back Like A Song', 'A Couple Of Swells', 'It Only Happens When I Dance With You' and 'Count Your Blessing Instead Of Sheep'. By the 50s Berlin's musical inspiration had subsided and he wrote little more, although a 1966 song, 'An Old Fashioned Girl', was briefly popular. Despite, or perhaps because of, his foreign birth, Berlin was intensely American both in his personal patriotism and acute sense of what made American popular music distinctive. For the last 30 years of his long life, Berlin lived in semi-seclusion, ignoring media attempts to laud his achievements even at such significant milestones as his 100th birthday. He died in September 1989.

Further reading: *The Story Of Irving Berlin*, David Ewen. *Irving Berlin*, Michael Freedland. *Irving Berlin And Ragtime America*, I. Whitcomb, *As Thousands Cheer: The Life Of Irving Berlin*, L. Bergreen.

Bernstein, Elmer

b. 4 April 1922, New York, USA. An important and prolific arranger-conductor, and composer of over 100 films scores, including biblical epics, westerns, comedies, thrillers and social dramas. Bernstein was hailed as a 'musical genius' in the classical field at the age of 12. Despite being a talented actor, dancer and painter, he devoted himself to becoming a concert pianist and toured nationally while still in his teens. His education at New York University was interrupted when he joined the United States Air Force during World War II. Throughout his four years service he composed and conducted music for propaganda programmes, and produced musical therapy projects for operationally fatigued personnel. After the war he attended the Juilliard School of Music and studied composition with the distinguished composer, Roger Sessions. Bernstein moved to Hollywood and started writing film scores in 1950 and, two years later, wrote the background music for *Sudden Fear*, a suspense thriller starring Joan Crawford and Jack Palance. Agent and producer Ingo Preminger, impressed by the Bernstein music, recommended him to his brother Otto, for the latter's 1955 film project, *The Man With The Golden Arm*. A tense, controversial movie, its theme of drug addiction, accompanied by the Berstein modern jazz score, played by top instrumentalists such as Shelly Manne, Shorty Rogers, Pete Candoli and Milt Bernhart, caused distribution problems in some American states. The film won Oscar nominations for

Frank Sinatra in the role of Frankie Machin, the junkie and would-be drummer, and for Bernstein's powerful, exciting music score. Bernstein made the US Top 20 with his record of the film's 'Main Title', and Billy May entered the UK Top 10 with his version. In 1956, Bernstein wrote the score for Cecil B. De Mille's epic *The Ten Commandments*, starring Charlton Heston. Thereafter, he provided the background music for an impressive array of movies with varied styles and subjects, including *Fear Strikes Out* (1957), *Sweet Smell Of Success* (1957), *God's Little Acre* (1958), *Some Came Running* (1958), *The Rat Race* (1960), *The Birdman Of Alcatraz* (1962), *The Great Escape* (1963), *A Walk In The Spring Rain* (1970), *The Shootist* (1976), *National Lampoon's Animal House* (1978), *An American Werewolf In London* (1981), *Ghostbusters* (1984), *!Three Amigos!* (1986), *Amazing Grace And Chuck* (1987), *Slipstream* (1988), *DA* (1988), (*My Left Foot* (1989), *The Grifters* (1990), *The Field* (1990), *Rambling Rose* (1991), *Oscar* (1991) *A Rage In Harlem* (1991), *The Babe* (1992), *The Cemetery Club* (1993), *Mad Dog And Glory* (1993), and *The Good Son* (1993). In 1991, Bernstein was the musical director, and arranger (or re-arranger) of Bernard Herrman's original score for the 1962 classic, *Cape Fear*. He received Academy Award nominations for his work on the highly-acclaimed western, *The Magnificent Seven* (1960), *Summer And Smoke* (1961), the title song for *Walk On The Wild Side* (1961), with a lyric by Mack David; *To Kill A Mockingbird* (1962), said to be Bernstein's favourite of his own scores; the scores for *Return Of The Seven* (1966), and *Hawaii* (1966) (and a song from *Hawaii*, 'Wishing Doll', lyric by Mack David); the title song from *True Grit* (1969), lyric by Don Black; a song from *Gold* (1974), 'Wherever Love Takes Me', lyric by Don Black; and *Trading Places* (1983). Bernstein won an Oscar for his original music score for the 20's spoof, *Thoroughly Modern Millie* (1967), in which Beatrice Lillie contrived to steal the picture from Julie Andrews. Coincidentally, Bernstein was the musical arranger and conductor at the Academy Awards ceremony when his award was announced, so he had to relinquish the baton before going on stage to receive his Oscar. Apart from films, Bernstein worked extensively in television. In 1958 he signed for US Revue Productions to provide background music for television dramas. One of his most notable scores was for *Staccato* (1959) (later re-titled *Johnny Staccato*), a series about a jazz musician turned private eye, starring John Cassavetes. The shows were a big hit in the UK, where Bernstein's recording of 'Staccato's Theme' rose to Number 4 in the singles chart in 1959, and re-entered the following year. On a somewhat larger scale, instrumentally, an 81-piece symphony orchestra was contracted to record Berstein's score for Martin Scorsese's 1993 film, *Age Of Innocence*, which was nominated for an Oscar.

Selected albums: *What Is Jazz?* (1958), *Desire Under The Elms* (1959), *God's Little Acre* (1959), *King Go Forth* (1959), *Some Came Running (*1960), *Walk On the Wild Side* (1962), *To Kill A Mocking Bird* (1962), *Movie And TV Themes* (1963), *The Great Escape* (1963), *The Carpetbaggers* (1964), *Hallelujah Trail* (1965), *The Sons Of Katie Elder* (1965), *The Ten Commandements* (1966).

Bernstein, Leonard

b. Louis Bernstein, 25 August 1918, Lawrence, Massachusetts, USA, d. 14 October 1990, New York, USA. Bernstein was a major and charismatic figure in modern classical music, and the Broadway musical theatre. He was also a conductor, composer, pianist, author and lecturer. A son of immigrant Russian Jews, Bernstein started to play the piano at the age of 10. In his teens he showed an early interest in the theatre by organizing productions such as *The Mikado*, and an unconventional adaptation of *Carmen*, in which he played the title role. Determined to make a career in music, despite his father's insistence that 'music just keeps people awake at night', Bernstein eschewed the family beauty parlour business. He went on to study firstly with Walter Piston and Edward Burlingaunt Hill at Harvard, then with Fritz Reiner, Isabella Vengerova and Randall Thompson at the Curtis Institute in Philadephia, and finally with Serge Koussevitzky at the Berkshire Music Institute at Tanglewood. Bernstein had gone to Harvard regarding himself as a pianist but became influenced by Dimitri Mitropoulos and Aaron Copland. They inspired him to write his first symphony, *Jeremiah*. By 1943 he was chosen by Artur Rodzinski to work as his assistant at the New York Philharmonic. On 14 November 1943, Bernstein deputized at the last minute for the ailing Bruno Walter, and conducted the New York Philharmonic in a concert which was broadcast live on network radio. The next day, for what would not be the last time, he made the front pages and became a celebrity over-night. In the same year he wrote the music for *Fancy Free*, a ballet, choreographed by Jerome Robbins, about three young sailors on 24 hours shore leave in New York City. It was so successful that they expanded it into a Broadway musical, with libretto and lyrics by Betty Comden and Adolph Green. Retitled *On The Town* and directed by George Abbott, it opened in 1944, with a youthful, vibrant score which included the anthem 'New York, New York', 'Lonely Town', 'I Get Carried Away' and 'Lucky To Be Me'. The 1949 film version, starring Frank Sinatra and Gene Kelly, and directed by Kelly and Stanley Donen, is often regarded as innovatory in its use of real New York locations, although Bernstein's score was somewhat truncated in the transfer. In 1950 Bernstein wrote both music and lyrics for a musical version of J. M. Barrie's *Peter Pan*, starring Jean Arthur and Boris Karloff. His next Broadway project, *Wonderful Town*

(1953), adapted from the play, *My Sister Eileen*, by Joseph Fields and Jerome Chodorov, again had lyrics by Comden and Green, and starred Rosalind Russell, returning to Broadway after a distinguished career in Hollywood. Bernstein's spirited, contemporary score for which he won a Tony Award, included 'Conversation Piece', 'Conga', 'Swing', 'What A Waste', 'Ohio', 'A Quiet Girl' and 'A Little Bit Of Love'. The show had a successful revival in London in 1986, with Maureen Lipman in the starring role. *Candide* (1956) was one of Bernstein's most controversial works. Lillian Hellman's adaptation of the Voltaire classic, sometimes termed a 'comic operetta', ran for only 73 performances on Broadway. Bernstein's score was much admired though, and one of the most attractive numbers, 'Glitter And Be Gay', was sung with great effect by Barbara Cook, one year before her Broadway triumph in Meredith Willson's *The Music Man*. *Candide* has been revived continually since 1956, at least twice by producer Hal Prince. It was his greatly revised production, including additional lyrics by Stephen Sondheim and John Latouche, to the originals by Richard Wilbur, which ran for 740 performances on Broadway in 1974. The Scottish Opera's production, directed by Jonathan Miller in 1988, is said to have met with the composer's approval, and Bernstein conducted a concert version of the score at London's Barbican Theatre in 1989, which proved his last appearance in the UK.

Bernstein's greatest triumph in the popular field came with *West Side Story* in 1957. This brilliant musical adaptation of Shakespeare's *Romeo And Juliet* was set in the New York streets and highlighted the violence of the rival gangs, the Jets and the Sharks. With a book by Arthur Laurents, lyrics by Sondheim in his first Broadway production, and directed by Jerome Robbins, Bernstein created one of the most dynamic and exciting shows in the history of the musical theatre. The songs included 'Jet Song', 'Something's Coming', 'Maria', 'Tonight', 'America', 'Cool', 'I Feel Pretty', 'Somewhere' and 'Gee, Officer Krupke!'. In 1961, the film version gained 10 Oscars, including 'Best Picture'. Bernstein's music was not eligible because it had not been written for the screen. In 1984, he conducted the complete score of *West Side Story* for the first time, in a recording for Deutsche Grammophon, with a cast of opera singers including Kiri Te Kanawa, José Carreras, Tatania Troyanos and Kurt Allman. Bernstein's last Broadway show, *1600 Pennsylvania Avenue* (1976) was an anti-climax. A story about American presidents, with book and lyrics by Alan Jay Lerner, it closed after only seven performances. Among Bernstein's many other works was the score for the Marlon Brando film, *On The Waterfront* (1954), for which he was nominated for an Oscar; a jazz piece, 'Prelude, Fugue and Riffs', premiered on US television by Benny Goodman in

1955; and 'My Twelve Tone Melody' written for Irving Berlin's 100th birthday in 1988. In his classical career, which ran parallel to his work in the popular field, he was highly accomplished, composing three symphonies, a full length opera, and several choral works. He was music director of the New York Philharmonic from 1958-69, conducted most of the world's premier orchestras, and recorded many of the major classical works. In the first week of October 1990, he announced his retirement from conducting because of ill health, and expressed an intention to concentrate on composing. He died one week later on 14 October 1990. In 1993, BBC Radio marked the 75th anniversary of his birth by devoting a complete day to programmes about his varied and distinguished career. A year later, *The Leonard Bernstein Revue: A Helluva Town*, played the Rainbow & Stars in New York.

Selected albums: *Bernstein Conducts Bernstein* (1984), *West Side Story* (1985), *Bernstein's America* (1988).

Further reading: *The Joy Of Music*, Leonard Bernstein. *Leonard Bernstein*, John Briggs. *Leonard Bernstein*, Peter Gadenwitz. *Leonard Bernstein*, Joan Peyser.

Best Foot Forward

The story of an ordinary guy inviting a famous movie star to be his date at the school dance has a familiar ring to it. This particular example was adapted from the 1941 Broadway musical of the same name which had been based on a book by John Cecil Holmes. Lucille Ball was the glamour girl who, in the cause of public relations and personal publicity, answers the call from young Tommy Dix and hastens to the Winsocki Military Academy to join several veterans of the original stage production who included June Allyson, Nancy Walker, Kenny Bowers, Jack Jordan Jnr., and Dix himself. Also in the cast were William Gaxton, Virginia Weidler, Gloria De Haven, Beverley Tyler, Chill Wills, and Henry O'Neill. Songwriters Hugh Martin and Ralph Blane made their Hollywood debut with a mixture of lively and romantic numbers which included 'Three Men On A Date', 'You're Lucky', 'My First Promise', 'Shady Lady Bird', 'Alive And Kicking', 'The Three 'B's'', 'Wish I May Wish I Might', 'Ev'ry Time', and 'Buckle Down, Winsocki'. Two instrumentals, 'Two O'Clock Jump' (Harry James-Count Basie-Benny Goodman) and 'The Flight Of The Bumble Bee' (Rimsky-Korsakov) were used as showcases for guest artist Harry James And His Orchestra. Irving Brecher and Fred Finklehoffe wrote the screenplay and the imaginative and spirited choreography was designed by Charles Walters. Edward Buzzell was the director, and *Best Foot Forward* was shot in Technicolor by producer Arthur Freed's MGM unit which did this kind of film so well.

Best Things In Life Are Free, The

This highly entertaining film biography of De Sylva, Brown And Henderson, one of the top songwriting teams of the 20s and 30s, was released in 1956. The sheer pleasure of listening to the constant stream of singable happy songs, diverted the attention from a screenplay by William Bowers and Phoebe Ephron which, as usual with bio-pics, made the subjects' interesting lives seem ordinary. In this case, the composer Ray Henderson (Dan Dailey), gives up teaching children to work with two men who behave like children, Buddy De Sylva (Gordon MacRae) and Ray Brown (Ernest Borgnine). Their tempestuous working relationship results in hit after hit for Broadway shows before De Sylva gets a taste for the Hollywood 'big time' and goes off to produce early films. In no time at all he realises the error of his ways and is reunited with his two buddies, and with Kitty Kane (Sheree North), the girl he left behind. She has reflected on his absence with the lovely ballad, 'Without Love' (dubbed by Eileen Wilson), a rare quiet moment in an otherwise jolly collection of the composers' numbers which included 'Birth Of The Blues', 'You Try Somebody Else', 'Button Up Your Overcoat', 'Sunny Side Up', 'If I Had A Talking Picture Of You', 'This Is My Lucky Day', 'Black Bottom', and 'The Best Things In Life Are Free'. One of the film's most amusing scenes comes when the songwriters, forced against their will to write a number for Al Jolson (played by Norman Brooks), try to come up with a 'stinker' but it turns out to be 'Sonny Boy'! The film was produced by 20th Century-Fox in CinemaScope and Technicolor and directed by Michael Curtiz.

Big Ben

No, not the bell in the clock tower of the Mother of Parliaments. This is that other giant named Ben, tenor saxophonist Ben Webster. An enjoyable and thoughtful short documentary made in 1967 from Dutch film-maker Johann van der Kenben. Interviews and music are all good, the subject's solos sublime.

Big Broadcast, The

By 1932, when this film was released by Paramount, Bing Crosby was the radio sensation of America. His relaxed singing style and self-deprecating humour transferred easily to film, and, later, the more intimate medium of television. In George Marion Jnr.'s screenplay for *The Big Broadcast*, Bing plays a radio crooner who serenades the lovely Leila Hyams, but she prefers well-heeled Texan Stuart Erwin. Crosby loses the girl, but gets a job when the radio station is saved from extinction by Erwin's dollars. There were songs and stars galore in a picture in which several of the performers sang numbers that were to become indelibly identified with them, such as 'Please' and 'Where The Blue Of The Night Meets The Gold Of

The Day' (Crosby), 'Trees' (Donald Novis), and 'When The Moon Comes Over The Mountain' (Kate Smith). Among the other musical items played and sung were 'Tiger Rag' (Mills Brothers), 'Kickin' The Gong Around' (Cab Calloway And His Orchestra), 'It Was So Beautiful' (Smith), 'Shout, Sister, Shout' (Boswell Sisters), 'Minnie The Moocher' (Calloway), 'Marta' (Arthur Tracy), 'Goodbye Blues' (Mills Brothers), 'Dinah' (Crosby), and 'Here Lies Love' (Tracy, Crosby and the Vincent Lopez Orchestra). Also in the cast were George Burns, Gracie Allen, and Eddie Lang. The film, which was directed by Paramount veteran Frank Tuttle, became so successful that it spawned three sequels.

Although Bing Crosby turned up again in *The Big Broadcast Of 1936* (released 1935), Jack Oakie was the romantic radio crooner this time - except that he actually wasn't - because, unknown to his nation-wide listening audience, someone else is paid to do the singing for him. Complications arise when a wealthy countess played by Lyda Roberti falls in love with the voice - and whisks him off to her own private Shangri-la. Burns and Allen were in attendance again, and also in the cast were Akim Tamiroff, Wendy Barrie, Henry Wadsworth, and Benny Baker. Brief, but effective contributions came from Amos 'N Andy, Bill 'Bojangles' Robinson, the Nicholas Brothers, the Vienna Boys' Choir, and Ray Noble And His Orchestra. Highlights included Ethel Merman's 'man-hungry' 'It's The Animal In Me', and Crosby's smooth and soulful 'I Wished On The Moon' which became a big US hit for him, and for Little Jack Little And His Orchestra. The rest of the songs, such as 'Miss Brown To You', 'Double Trouble', 'Why Dream?', and 'Through The Doorway Of Dreams I Saw You', were not particularly memorable, but the whole package, which had a screenplay by Walter DeLeon, Francis Martin and Ralph Spence, and was directed by Norman Taurog, proved to be fast and furious fun, and led to more of the same or similar a year later.

Songwriters Ralph Rainger and Leo Robin, who, in association with Richard Whiting and Dorothy Parker, had written most of the songs for the 1936 edition, provided the complete score for *The Big Broadcast Of 1937* (made in 1936). Numbers such as 'You Came To My Rescue', 'Hi-Ho The Radio', 'La Bomba', 'I'm Talking Through My Heart', and 'Here's Love In Your Eye', punctuated Walter DeLeon and Francis Martin's token story which involved Jack Benny, a great radio favourite at the time, along with a fascinating mixture of comedic and musical talent such as Burns And Allen, Bob Burns, Martha Raye, Benny Fields, Benny Goodman And His Orchestra, Leopold Stokowski and the Philadelphia Orchestra, Eleanore Whitney, Frank Forrest, and mouth organist Larry Adler. The engaging 'Here's Love In Your Eye' became a hit on

The Big Broadcast Of 1938

record for Benny Goodman, and for trumpeter Henry Allen And His Orchestra.

In *The Big Broadcast Of 1938*, Shirley Ross, who, with Ray Milland, had provided the love interest in the 1937 film, joined with screen newcomer, Bob Hope, to introduce one of the most enduring of all popular songs, 'Thanks For The Memory'. That number was the highlight of another Robin and Rainger score which included several other memorable moments such as 'Mama, That Moon Is Here Again' (sung by Martha Raye), 'This Little Ripple Had Rhythm' (Shep Fields And His Orchestra), and 'You Took The Words Right Out Of My Heart' (Dorothy Lamour). Comedian W.C. Fields headlined the cast which also featured South American singer Tito Guizar and opera diva Kirsten Flagstad. Fields strutted his usual stuff in a story by Walter DeLeon, Francis Martin and Ken Englund which was directed by Mitchell Leisen and set around a trans-oceanic race. Of course, one of the two large liners had to organize a celebrity radio show during the voyage, thereby justifying the film's title.

All four of Paramount's *Big Broadcast* films were highly entertaining and big money-spinners. Shirley Ross and Bob Hope's big hit from the last of them, 'Thanks For The Memory', won an Academy Award and became the title of another 1938 picture in which they appeared together. In that one, the duo introduced yet another all-time standard, Frank Loesser and Hoagy Carmichael's 'Two Sleepy People' ('Here we are, out of cigarettes . . .').

Billy Rose's Diamond Horseshoe

There really was an establishment with this name in New York which was owned and operated by the master-showman and songwriter himself, along with the New York Supper Club and two theatres. Much of the action in writer-director George Seaton's screenplay consisted of lavish set-piece musical numbers, but he provided ample opportunity for the more intimate love scenes between two of 20th Century-Fox's brightest stars, Betty Grable and Dick Haymes. Grable plays one of the showgirls who prefers dollar signs to doctors, which is unfortunate for Haymes who is a typically improverished medical student. Things improve after Haymes gives her the treatment via two lovely ballads by Harry Warren and Mack Gordon, 'The More I See You' and 'I Wish I Knew'. Warren and Gordon contributed several other numbers, including the rousing 'Welcome To The Diamond Horseshoe', 'Play Me An Old Fashioned Melody', 'A Nickel's Worth Of Jive', 'Cooking Up A Show', and 'In Acapulco'. William Gaxton, a trouper in the old tradition, played Haymes' father, and Phil Silvers was always funny, floating around backstage just as he did in *Cover Girl*. The rest of the cast, which included Margaret Dumont (always good comic value), Carmen Cavallero, and Beatrice Kay, were admirable, but it was the superb baritone voice of

Dick Haymes, in only his second leading role, which took the honours. The film was photographed in Technicolor and released in 1945.

Billy Rose's Jumbo

Twenty seven years after he starred on Broadway in master showman Billy's Rose's mixture of circus and musical comedy, Jimmy Durante was present again in this 1962 screen version. Screenwriter Sidney Sheldon's somewhat liberal adaptation of the original stage libretto cast Durante as the owner of a circus with financial problems and ripe for a takeover. First in line as the potential new owner is Dean Jagger, the boss of a rival outfit. Jagger's son, played by Stephen Boyd, gains control of the crippled carnival by devious means, but is eventually won over by the decency of Durante and the delicious charms of his daughter, Doris Day. The film ends on an optimistic note with Durante and his wife (Martha Raye), Day, and Boyd looking to the future and singing 'Sawdust, Spangles And Dreams'. That number was written by Roger Edens, but the rest of the songs - some of which survived from the original stage show - were the work of Richard Rodgers and Lorenz Hart. They included Durante's endearing and individual rendering of 'The Most Beautiful Girl In The World' and a tender version of 'This Can't Be Love' by Doris Day, along with several other memorable songs such as 'Little Girl Blue', 'Over And Over Again', 'My Romance', 'The Circus Is On Parade', and 'Why Can't I?'. Fine performances all round, especially from Durante and Raye, and Jumbo the elephant played a big part, too. William Daniels was responsible for the impressive photography in Metrocolor and Panavision, and the director was Charles Walters. The film was the last to be choreographed by the legendary Busby Berkeley.

Bird

In defence of any bio-pic about a seminal figure in the arts, it has to be said that depicting on film the creative process and the manner in which an individual can inspire a generation is pretty nearly impossible. So it proves in this account of the life of Charlie Parker. This 1988 film also misses Parker's articulateness and his sharp and ready wit. For all these shortcomings, however, *Bird* is an honestly-conceived and well-made attempt at portraying this erratic genius of jazz. Drawing heavily upon Chan Parker's account of her common-law husband's life, rather than upon reminiscences of his musical peers, the film frequently but perhaps misleadingly stresses the turbulent life of one of the half-dozen greatest figures in all jazz history while allowing his importance to jazz slip by as if it were almost incidental to his private life. Nevertheless, director Client Eastwood's admiration and affection for his subject makes up for most of the film's historical uncertainty and is infinitely superior to the rag-tag 50s bio-pics of swing era favourites such as Benny Goodman, Gene Krupa and Glenn Miller. Clearly, Eastwood worked on the project for love not money, and with a solid if uncharasmatic central performance from Forest Whitaker, *Bird* surprisingly proved to have box-office appeal that far transcended the hard-core jazz audience. The soundtrack is a brilliant display of latter-day technology allied to astute and perceptive musical understanding. Overseen by Lennie Niehaus, Parker's solos from some of his original recordings were detached from their sometimes scrappy surroundings, then provided with newly-recorded accompaniment by leading latter-day bop musicians. The end result is musical excellence even if, predictably perhaps, the film and its re-jigged music was received in some quarters with a marked lack of enthusiasm. Amongst the musicians appearing on the soundtrack are Monty Alexander, Chuck Berghofer, Ray Brown, Conte Candoli, Ron Carter, Pete Christlieb, Bob Cooper, Walter Davis Jnr., Jon Faddis, John Guerin, Barry Harris, Pete Jolly, Bill Watrous, Red Rodney (portrayed in the film by Michael Zelniker and Charles McPherson, who provided all of the non-original Parker performances.

Birth Of The Blues

Released by Paramount in 1941, this film is remembered mainly for one song, Johnny Mercer's 'The Waiter And The Porter And The Upstairs Maid', which was performed in exuberant fashion by Bing Crosby, Jack Teagarden, and Mary Martin. Harry Tugend and Walter DeLeon's screenplay was set in New Orleans at a time when the 'devil' jazz music was threatening the cosy world of opulent operettas. Throughout his life Crosby was associated with jazz and many of its exalted exponents including Louis Armstrong with whom he collaborated so memorably in *High Society*. In *Birth Of The Blues*, as well as crooning, Crosby is the clarinet-playing leader of the Hot Shots, a swinging group supposedly based on the Original Dixieland Jazz Band. Brian Donlevy, an actor who later made a career out of playing the tough-guy-with-the-soft heart, was the hot trumpeter for the Hot Shots, and Mary Martin obliged with the cool vocals. The rest of the numbers included 'Wait 'Til The Sun Shines, Nellie' (Harry Von Tilzer, Andrew Stirling), 'My Melancholy Baby' (George A. Norton, Ernie Burnett), 'Cuddle Up A Litle Closer' (Karl Hoschna, Otto Harbach), 'By The Light Of The Silvery Moon' (Gus Edwards, Edward Madden), 'The Birth Of The Blues' (De Sylva, Brown And Henderson), 'St. Louis Blues' (W.C. Handy), and several other jazzy oldies. Jack Benny's long-time comic companion, Eddie 'Rochester' Anderson, was also in the cast, and the film was directed by Victor Schertzinger.

Bix 'Ain't None Of Them Play Like That'

An exceptionally well-researched and presented documentary released in 1981. Canadian film-maker Brigitte Berman traces the life of the legendary Bix Beiderbecke through some film, many stills and numerous interviews all backed by a sublime soundtrack. The subject's catastrophic decline through alcohol and his habitual disregard of things like sleep and food in favour of playing and drinking is sympathetically but unglamorously explored. A deeply moving moment emerges with the revelation that on a visit to his disapproving parents' house Bix found in a closet all his records, which he had proudly sent home, still enclosed in their wrappings. The standards of jazz documentaries were raised by this film and it can be wholeheartedly recommended to anyone, regardless of personal taste in jazz, for its immediacy and understanding.

Black, Don

b. 21 June 1938, Hackney, London, England. A prolific lyricist for film songs, stage musicals and Tin Pan Alley. One of five children, three boys and two girls, he worked part-time as an usher at the London Palladium before getting a job as an office boy and sometimes journalist with the *New Musical Express* in the early 50s. Then, after a brief sojourn as a stand-up comic in the dying days of the music halls, he gravitated towards London's Denmark Street, the centre of UK music publishing, where he worked as a song plugger for firms owned by Dave Toff and Joe 'Mr. Piano' Henderson. He met Matt Monro in 1960, when the singer was about to make his breakthrough with Cyril Ornadel and Norman Newell's 'Portrait Of My Love'. Encouraged by Monro, Black began to develop his talent for lyric writing. Together with another popular vocalist, Al Saxon, Black wrote 'April Fool', which Monro included on his *Love Is The Same Anywhere*. In 1964 Black collaborated with the German composer, Udo Jurgens, and together they turned Jurgens' Eurovision Song Contest entry, 'Warum Nur Warum', into 'Walk Away', which became a UK Top 5 hit for Monro. The singer also charted with 'For Mama', which Black wrote with Charles Aznavour. It was also popular for Connie Francis and Jerry Vale in the USA. In 1965 Black made his breakthrough into films with the lyric of the title number for *Thunderball*, the third James Bond movie. The song was popularized by Tom Jones, and it marked the beginning of a fruitful collaboration with composer John Barry. As well as providing Bond with two more themes, 'Diamonds Are Forever' (1971, Shirley Bassey), for which they received an Ivor Novello Award; and 'The Man With The Golden Gun' (1974, Lulu), the songwriters received a second 'Ivor', and an Academy Award, for their title song to *Born Free* in 1966. Black has been nominated on four other occasions: for 'True Grit' (with Elmer

Bernstein, 1969), 'Ben' (Walter Scharf, a US number 1 for Michael Jackson in 1972, and a UK hit for Marti Webb in 1985), 'Wherever Love Takes Me', from Gold (Bernstein, 1972), and 'Come To Me', from *The Pink Panther Strikes Again* (Henry Mancini, 1976). It has been estimated that Black's lyrics have been heard in well over 100 movies, including *To Sir With Love* (title song, with Mark London, 1972, a US number 1 for Lulu), *Pretty Polly* (title song, Michel Legrand, 1967), *I'll Never Forget What's 'Is Name* ('One Day Soon', Francis Lai, 1968), *The Italian Job* ('On Days Like These', Quincy Jones, 1969), *Satan's Harvest* ('Two People', Denis King, 1969), *Hoffman* ('If There Ever Is A Next Time', Ron Grainer, 1970), *Mary Queen Of Scots* ('Wish Was Then', John Barry, 1971), *Alice's Adventures In Wonderland* (several songs with Barry, 1972), *The Tamarind Seed* ('Play It Again', Barry, 1974), *The Dove* ('Sail The Summer Winds', Barry, 1974), and *The Wilby Conspiracy* ('All The Wishing In The World', Stanley Myers, 1975). In 1970, Matt Monro invited Don Black to become his manager, and he remained in that role until the singer died in 1985. Black considered Monro to be one of the finest interpreters of his lyrics, particularly with regard to 'If I Never Sing Another Song', which Black wrote with Udo Jurgens in 1977. The song became a favourite closing number for many artists, including Johnnie Ray and Eddie Fisher. In 1971, Black augmented his already heavy work load by becoming involved with stage musicals. His first score, written with composer Walter Scharf, was for *Maybe That's Your Problem*, which had a limited run (18 performances) at London's Roundhouse Theatre. The subject of the piece was premature ejaculation (Black says that his friend, Alan Jay Lerner, suggested that it should be called Shortcomings), but the critics called it 'a dismal piece'. However, one of the performers was Elaine Paige, just seven years before *Evita*. Paige was also in *Billy*, London's hit musical of 1974. Adapted from the straight play, *Billy Liar*, which was set in the north of England, Black and John Barry's score captured the 'feel' and the dialect of the original. The songs included 'Some Of Us Belong To The Stars', 'I Missed The Last Rainbow', 'Any Minute Now', and 'It Were All Green Fields When I Were A Lad', which was subsequently recorded by Stanley Holloway. The show, which ran for over 900 performances, made a star of Michael Crawford in his musical comedy debut. Black's collaborator on the score for his next show, *Barmitzvah Boy* (1978), was Jule Styne, the legendary composer of shows such as *Funny Girl* and *Gypsy*, amongst others. Although *Barmitzvah Boy* had a disappointingly short run, it did impress Andrew Lloyd Webber, who engaged Black to write the lyrics for his song cycle, *Tell Me On Sunday*, a television programme and album, which featured Marti Webb. Considered too short for theatrical presentation, on the recommendation of

Cameron Mackintosh it was combined with Lloyd Webber's *Variations* to form *Song And Dance*, a two part 'theatrical concert'. In the first half, Webb, playing an English girl domiciled in the USA, 'wended her way through a succession of unsatisfactory love affairs' via songs such as 'Take That Look Off Your Face', which gave her a UK Top 5 hit and gained Black another Ivor Novello Award; 'Nothing Like You've Ever Known', 'Capped Teeth And Caesar Salad', and 'Tell Me On Sunday'. Wayne Sleep and his company of eight dancers performed the second half, to the music of *Variations*. The show ran in the West End for 781 performances before being re-modelled and expanded for Broadway, where it starred Bernadette Peters, who received a Tony Award for her performance. Black teamed with Benny Andersson and Bjorn Ulvaeus, two former members of Abba, for the aptly title, *Abbacadabra*, a Christmas show which played to packed houses in 1983. Earlier that year, he had written the score for *Dear Anyone* with Geoff Stephens, a successful composer of pop hits such as 'Winchester Cathedral', 'You Won't Find Another Fool Like Me' and 'There's A Kind Of Hush'. The show first surfaced as a concept album in 1978, and one of its numbers, 'I'll Put You Together Again', became a Top 20 hit for the group, Hot Chocolate. The 1983 stage presentation did not last too long, and neither did *Budgie* (1988). Against a background of 'the sleezy subculture of London's Soho', the show starred Adam Faith and Anita Dobson. Black's lyrics combined with Mort Shuman's music for songs such as 'Why Not Me?', 'There Is Love And There Is Love', 'In One Of My Weaker Moments', and 'They're Naked And They Move', but to no avail - Don Black, as co-producer, presided over a £1,000,000 flop. Two years earlier, Anita Dobson had had a big UK hit with 'Anyone Can Fall In Love', when Black added a lyric to Simon May and Leslie Osborn's theme for *Eastenders*, one of Britain's top television soaps, and he collaborated with the composers again for 'Always There', a vocal version of their music for *Howard's Way*, which gave Marti Webb a UK hit. In 1989, Black resumed his partnership with Andrew Lloyd Webber for *Aspects Of Love*. Together with *Phantom Of The Opera* lyricist, Charles Hart, they fashioned a musical treatment of David Garnett's 1955 novel, which turned out to be more intimate than some of Lloyd Webber's other works, but still retained the operatic form. The show starred Michael Ball and Ann Crumb, and it nearly had a 'James Bond', when Roger Moore was originally cast as George Dillingham, but he withdrew before the show opened. Ball took the big ballad, 'Love Changes Everything', to number 2 in the UK, and the score also featured the 'subtle, aching melancholy' of 'The First Man You Remember'. *Aspects Of Love* was not considered a hit by Lloyd Webber's standards - it ran

for three years in the West End, and for one year on Broadway - and the London Cast recording topped the UK album chart. In the 90s, Don Black's activities remain numerous and diverse. In 1992, together with Chris Walker, he provided extra lyrics for the London stage production of *Radio Times*; wrote additional songs for a revival of *Billy* by the National Youth Music Theatre at the Edinburgh Festival; renewed his partnership with Geoff Stephens for a concept album of a 'revuesical' entitled *Off The Wall*, the story of 'six characters determined to end it all by throwing themselves off a ledge on the 34th storey of a London highrise building'; wrote, with Lloyd Webber, the Barcelona Olympics anthem, 'Friends For Life' ('Amigos Para Siempre'), which was recorded by Sarah Brightman and Jose Carreras; and collaborated with David Dundas on 'Keep Your Dreams Alive', for the animated feature, *Freddie As F.R.O.7*. He spent a good deal of the year with Andrew Lloyd Webber and Christopher Hampton, writing a musical treatment of the Hollywood classic, *Sunset Boulevard*, which was set to open in London in June 1993. Black has held the positions of chairman and vice-president of the British Academy of Songwriters, Composers and Authors, and has, for the past few years, been the genial chairman of the voting panel for the Vivian Ellis Prize, a national competition to encourage new writers for the musical stage.
Selected album: *Matt Monro Sings Don Black* (1990).

Black And Tan

Directed by Dudley Murphy in 1929, who, in the same year, made *St. Louis Blues* with Bessie Smith, this early talkie short remains one of the few films to use jazz as its *raison d'etre*. A slight but melodramatic storyline has showgirl Fredi Washington literally dancing her life away to ensure her musical colleagues get the big break they have been waiting for. The musicians involved are Duke Ellington And His Orchestra (their screen debut) including Barney Bigard, Harry Carney, Johnny Hodges, Joe Nanton, Artie Whetsol and Cootie Williams. Amongst the musical numbers are 'The Duke Steps Out', 'Black Beauty' and, of course, an eloquent version of 'Black And Tan Fantasy'.

Blaine, Vivian

b. Vivian Stapleton, 21 November 1921, Newark, New Jersey, USA. A vivacious actress and singer who created one of the American musical theatre's best-loved characters, Miss Adelaide, in Frank Loesser's *Guys And Dolls*. Vivian Blaine appeared on the stage of her local theatre, and later attended the American Academy of Dramatic Art. She subsequently toured in various musicals and in vaudeville before making her Broadway debut in *Guys And Dolls* in 1950. She gave a delightful performance as the dancegirl who has been waiting for 14 years in the hope that her fiancé,

Nathan Detroit, will finally abandon his floating crap game and marry her. Her frustration boils over in 'Sue Me', and she is splendid in the ensemble numbers with the girls at the 'Hot Box', 'Take Back Your Mink' and 'A Bushel And A Peck', but the stand-out song is 'Adelaide's Lament' in which she shares the knowledge, just gleaned from a book - of all things - that there is a direct relationship between long engagements and ill health: 'The average unmarried female, basically insecure/Due to some long frustration may react/With psychosomatic symptoms, difficult to endure/Affecting the upper respiratory tract . . . In other words just from waiting around for that plain little band of gold/A person - can develop a cold.' In 1953 she repeated her success at the London Coliseum, and was back on Broadway five years later with *Say, Darling* in which she starred with Robert Morse, David Wayne, and Johnny Desmond. She subsequently toured extensively in a wide range of straight plays and musical revivals including *Zorba*, *Follies*, *Hello, Dolly!*, *Gypsy*, and *I Do! I Do!*. She succeeded Jane Russell in the role of Jo Anne in the Broadway production of *Company*, and has also performed in cabaret. In addition to her stage work, Vivian Blaine has appeared in several film musicals including *Jitterbugs*, *Something For The Boys*, *Nob Hill*, *State Fair* (1945 version), *Doll Face*, *If I'm Lucky*, *Three Little Girls In Blue*, *Skirts Ahoy*, and *Guys And Dolls* (1955). Since then - through to the 80s - her film work has consisted of mainly straight roles in features and on US television.
Selected albums: *Singing Selections From Pal Joey & Annie Get Your Gun* (c.50s), *Broadway's All Time Hits* (c.50s).

Blossom Time

This lavish, but idealized film biography of composer Franz Schubert, which was released in 1934, gave the celebrated tenor Richard Tauber his most famous screen role. Set in Vienna in the 1820's, Franz Schulz's romantic screenplay, which was adapted from a story by John Drinkwater, Roger Burford, Paul Perez, and G.H. Clutsam, concerns the struggle for recognition by a middle-aged (Tauber was 42), unknown genius who sacrifices his love for the sweet young Vicki Wimpassinger (Jane Baxter) because he realises that she is passionately in love with a dashing young officer, Rudi (Carl Esmond). Paul Graetz, as Vicki's father, Alois, provided the comic relief, and also cast were Athene Seyler, Charles Carson, Marguerite Allen, Edward Chapman, Lester Matthews, Gibb McLaughlin, and Frederick Lloyd. Schubert's magnificent music was heard throughout, with Tauber providing a thrilling finalé with 'Impatience (Thine Is My Heart)' which had a lyric by John Drinkwater. *Blossom Time* was produced in the UK by Walter C. Mycroft for British International Pictures (BIP). The director was Paul Stein who

Blue Skies

continued to direct film musicals until after World War II.

Blue Skies

Released by Paramount in 1946, *Blue Skies* was similar in style and content to *Holiday Inn* (1942) in that it starred Bing Crosby and Fred Astaire as a former song-and-dance duo weaving their way through a great bunch of Irving Berlin songs. Arthur Sheekman's screenplay told of Johnny Adams (Crosby), a singer who buys and sells nightclubs on the side, while good old reliable Jed Potter (Astaire) looks on and disapproves. They are both chasing the same girl, Mary O'Hara (Joan Caufield), who marries Johnny, but his instability eventually leads to their divorce and her disappearance. Many years later the trio are reunited in a radio studio to the strains of 'You Keep Coming Back Like A Song'. The film's many highlights included 'A Couple Of Song And Dance Men' (Crosby and Astaire), 'I've Got My Captain Working For Me Now' (Crosby and Billy De Wolfe), '(I'll See You In) C-U-B-A' (Crosby and Olga San Juan), and 'Puttin' On The Ritz', which was brilliantly danced by Astaire accompanied by eight other images of himself. The rest of the score featured some of the best of Berlin, and included 'Always', 'You'd Be Surprised', 'A Pretty Girl Is Like A Melody', 'Not For All The Rice In China', 'How Deep Is The Ocean?', 'This Is The Army Mr Jones', '(Running Around In Circles) Getting Nowhere', 'Russian Lullaby', 'White Christmas', and 'Heatwave'. Most of the choreography for the musical numbers was by Hermes Pan. *Blue Skies* was photographed in Technicolor and directed by Stuart Heisler. It proved to be a box-office smash, and became one of the Top 10 musicals of the 40s.

Blues In The Night

The Big Band Era was still in full swing when this unassuming little film was released by Warner Brothers in 1941. The story reflected what had been going on for many years all over the USA - a group of dedicated jazz musicians enduring the grind of one-night stands, with all their attendant problems and temptations. Robert Rossen's screenplay was adapted from the play, *Hot Nocturne*, by Edwin Gilbert, and cast Richard Whorf as the band's leader whose affair with Betty Field - an actress who specialised in neurotic roles - ends in tragedy. Priscilla Lane, Jack Carson, Elia Kazan, Lloyd Nolan, Peter Whitney, Wallace Ford, Bill Halop were in it as well, and there were guest appearances by the real-life orchestras of Jimmy Lunceford and Will Osborne. The top-class score by Harold Arlen and Johnny Mercer contained two of their all-time standards, the beautiful 'Blues In The Night' ('My Momma Done Tol' Me/When I was in knee pants . . .') which was introduced by William Gillespie, and the pretty 'This Time The

Dream's On Me'. The other numbers were 'Says Who, Says You, Says Me' and 'Hang On To Your Lids, Kids'. With that kind of music and the snappy dialogue long associated with jazz music fraternity, *Blues In The Night*, which was directed by Anatole Litvak, provided an engaging, if not absorbing, 90 minutes or so of entertainment for the fans.

Boles, John

b. 28 August 1895 or 1898, Greenville, Texas, USA, d. 27 February 1969, San Angelo, Texas, USA. An archetypal handsome leading man with a fine baritone voice who was in several popular movie musicals of the 30s. After graduating from the University of Texas, Boles completed military service during World War I before studying singing in Paris and New York. In the early 20s he had minor roles in several Broadway shows including *Little Jessie James* and *Mercenary Mary*, which was followed by a good part in *Kitty's Kisses* (1926). During the late 20s he was suitably strong and manly in silent films, and, at the same time, also came into his own in a string of movie musicals which included *The Desert Song*, *Rio Rita*, *The King Of Jazz*, *One Heavenly Night*, *My Lips Betray*, *Music In The Air*, *Bottoms Up*, *Stand Up And Cheer*, *Curly Top*, *Redheads On Parade*, *Rose Of The Rancho*, *Romance In The Dark* (1938) and *Thousands Cheer* (1943). These films represented only a small fraction of his output which mainly consisted of dramatic, non-musical roles. In the 40s and early 50s he appeared in revivals of stage musicals such as *Show Boat*, and in 1946 co-starred with Mary Martin and Kenny Baker in the Broadway hit musical, *One Touch Of Venus*. After joining other veteran stars such as Paulette Goddard and Gypsy Rose Lee in the poorly-received satirical picture *Babes In Bagdhad* in 1952, he retired from show business shortly afterwards.

Bolger, Ray

b. Raymond Wallace Bolger, 10 January 1904, Boston, Massachusetts, USA, d. 15 January 1987, Los Angeles, California, USA. An eccentric, rubber-legged dancer with a style and image that had to be seen to be believed. He started out as a comedian in 1922 with the Bob Ott Musical Repertory Company and four years later gained a small part in a Broadway show called *The Merry Whirl*. After a spell in vaudeville, he returned to Broadway in the late 20s and 30s in shows such as *Heads Up*, *George White's Scandals*, *Life Begins At 8:40*, and *On Your Toes* (1936). Bolger shot to stardom in the latter show in which he introduced the lovely 'There's A Small Hotel', and performed an hilarious eccentric dance in Richard Rodgers' famous 'Slaughter On Tenth Avenue' ballet. After leaving the show he moved to Hollywood and appeared in *The Great Ziegfeld*, *Rosalie*, *Sweethearts*, and one of the most memorable films of all-time, *The Wizard Of Oz* (1939), in which he played the

Born To Dance

Scarecrow in search of a brain. After returning to New York for the short-lived musical *Keep Off The Grass* (1940), he made one more film, *Sunny* (1941), before leaving for the South Pacific where he entertained troops with the USO during World War II. He was back on Broadway in 1942 for *By Jupiter*, and then the revue *Three To Make Ready* in which he stopped the show regularly with the charming 'That Old Soft Shoe', complete with straw hat and cane. Frank Loesser's *Where's Charley?* came along in 1948 and gave Bolger his greatest role; he introduced the gentle 'Once In Love With Amy', and it subsequently became his signature tune. During the 40s and 50s he made several more films including *Stage Door Canteen*, *Four Jacks And A Jill*, *The Harvey Girls*, *Look For The Silver Lining*, *Where's Charley?*, and *April In Paris*. In 1962 and 1969 he appeared in two more stage musicals, *All American* and *Come Summer*, but mostly during the 60s and 70s he mixed feature films such as *Babes In Toyland*, *The Daydreamer*, *The Runner Stumbles*, and *Just You And Me Kid*, with television movies which included *The Entertainer*, *The Captains And The Kings*, and *Only Heaven Knows*. In 1984, in the MGM extravaganza *That's Entertainment*, he looked back affectionately on a career that had spanned well over half a century. Three years later he died of cancer at the age of 83.

Born To Dance

Eleanor Powell, one of the big screen's most accomplished tap dancers, was the star of this 1937 MGM release in which two of Cole Porter's all-time standards, 'I've Got You Under My Skin' and 'Easy To Love', were introduced. James Stewart's charming version of the latter song came during one of the film's quieter moments in Jack McGowan and Sid Silvers' screenplay during which a group of sailors on shore leave get mixed up in the world of show-business. After the usual complications, Stewart ends up with Powell, of course, who gets her big chance on Broadway when replacing Virginia Bruce, the indisposed (and extremely temperamental) star of the show. For maximum enjoyment of this film, the fact that Powell is a dancer and Bruce a singer is an issue that is better ignored. Virginia Bruce is the lucky lady who is given first chance at 'I've Got You Under My Skin', and Powell is particularly scintillating on 'Rap Tap On Wood' and the spectacular finale, 'Swingin' The Jinx Away', which takes place on the foredeck of a battleship populated by an enormous cast and a band that looks as if it should be in *The Music Man*. The rest of the classy Porter numbers included 'Hey, Babe, Hey', 'Rolling Home', 'Entrance Of Lucy James', and 'Love Me, Love My Pekinese', an amusing item given the full treatment by Virginia Bruce. Two of James

Stewart's shipmates, Buddy Ebsen and Sid Silvers, were prominent in a lively cast which also included Frances Langford and Una Merkel. The spirited choreography was by Dave Gould, and the picture was directed by Roy Del Routh.

Born To Swing

An outstanding documentary made in 1973 by John Jeremy, which draws on interviews (with Buck Clayton, John Hammond, Andy Kirk, Gene Krupa and others), still photographs (by Valerie Wilmer), archive film of the Count Basie band of the early 40s, and, most tellingly, ex-Basie sidemen in musical action. Amongst those still playing (in 1972) and swinging magnificently, are Eddie Durham, Jo Jones, Joe Newman, Gene Ramey, Buddy Tate, Earle Warren and Dicky Wells. Made in the UK and first screened on BBC TV, the film has a linking commentary spoken by Humphrey Lyttelton.

Brewster's Millions

This 1935 musical is often regarded as British song-and-dance-man Jack Buchanan's best home-grown film - the qualification is necessary because of his appearance with Fred Astaire in the wonderful Hollywood movie of The Band Wagon (1953). As Jack Brewster, Buchanan is faced with the farcical task of losing £500,000 in a couple of months in order to inherit the sum of £6 million. Inevitably, everything he invests in - including a musical show which is supposed to be a guaranteed flop - yields a handsome profit. After buying a lavish yacht and taking a large party to Monte Carlo and Italy, he finances a local carnival and evades potential kidnappers by functioning as the rear end of a papier-maché dragon. All this provides a great excuse for some extremely elaborate production numbers, one of which, 'The Caranga', bore an uncanny resemblance to 'The Carioca', a dance that became all the rage after it was featured in the Fred Astaire-Ginger Rogers movie Flying Down To Rio. Thornton Freeland, the director of that film, also directed Brewster's Millions. Composer Ray Noble and lyricist Douglas Furber contributed a further three songs, 'I Think I Can', 'One Good Tune Deserves Another', and 'Pull Down The Blind'. Surrounded by a host of lovely girls and some lovely scenery, Buchanan is in his element, both comically and musically. He receives strong support from Lili Damita and the rest of the cast which included Nancy O'Neil, Sydney Fairbrother, Ian McLean, Allan Aynesworth, Lawrence Hanray, Dennis Hoey, Henry Wenman, Amy Venesa, Sebastian Shaw, and Antony Holles. Herbert Wilcox was the producer for the British and Dominion Films Corporation. The screenplay, by Arthur Wimperis, Paul Gangelin, Douglas Furber, Clifford Grey, Donovan Pedelty and Wolfgan Wilhem, was based on the 1906 play by George Barr McCutcheon and Winchell Smith,

which itself was adapted from McCutcheon's original novel. Brewster's Millions was remade in America in 1945 (with Dennis O'Keefe) and 1985 (with Richard Pryor), and another version, entitled Three On A Spree, was produced in the UK in 1961 starring Jack Watling. Due no doubt to inflation, Brewster now had to get rid of £1 million in order to inherit £8 million. The 1951 West End musical Zip Goes A Million, starring George Formby, was yet another production based on the same format.

Brice, Fanny

b. 29 October 1891, New York City, New York, USA, d. 29 May 1951. In her early teens Brice appeared on the stage in both legitimate musical shows and in vaudeville. In 1910 she was booked into Florenz Ziegfeld's Follies and appeared in his shows regularly for the next dozen years, gradually rising to become one of Broadway's biggest stars. She also appeared in other Broadway shows including Music Box Revue (1928), in which she co-starred with Bobby Clark, and one, Fanny, written especially for her after she became a star. For the most part her act consisted of comic patter and novelty songs, many of which she sang in a Brooklyn dialect. Among her hits in this area of music was 'Second-Hand Rose'. Despite her plain features and gawky stage presence, or perhaps because of the affinity audiences felt with her for these characteristics, she later sang torch songs with great success. Among the songs in this style were 'When A Woman Loves A Man' and 'My Man', the number with which she was most closely linked. She made her first film appearance in 1928 in My Man, but her real forte was the stage and she made only spasmodic journeys to Hollywood for Night Club (1929), Be Yourself (1930), The Great Zeigfeld (1936), Everybody Sing (1938), and Ziegfeld Follies (1945). Brice was also successful on radio, appearing in the title role of the popular series, Baby Snooks, which ran for six years from 1939. She died in 1951, but in 1964 her career and chequered private life (she was married to gambler Nicky Arnstein and showman Billy Rose) became the subject of a hit Broadway show. Funny Girl, written by Jule Styne and Bob Merrill and starring Barbra Streisand as Brice, ran for 1,348 performances and four years later provided the basis for a successful film and a 1978 sequel, Funny Lady. Two other films were (allegedly) based on her life: Broadway Thru A Keyhole (1933) and Rose Of Washington Square (1938).
Further reading: The Fabulous Fanny-The Story Of Fanny Brice, N. Katkov. Fanny Brice-The Original Funny Girl, Herbert G. Goldman.

Bricusse, Leslie

b. 29 January 1931, London, England. A composer, lyricist, librettist and screenwriter, Bricusse was influenced by the MGM musicals of the 40s, pariicularly *Words And Music*, the Richard Rodgers and Lorenz Hart bio-pic. He originally intended to be a journalist, but, while studying at Cambridge University, started to write, direct and appear in the Cambridge footlights revues. In 1953, he wrote the music and lyrics (with Robin Beaumont) for *Lady At the Wheel*, a musical with the Monte Carlo rally as its setting, which included songs such as 'The Early Birdie', 'Pete Y'Know', 'Love Is' and a comedy tango, 'Siesta'. It was presented at the local Arts Theatre, and, five years later, had a limited run in the West End. Well before that, in 1954-5, Bricusse had appeared on the London stage himself, and with a theatrical legend, in *An Evening With Beatrice Lillie*. For a while during the 50s, he was under contract as a writer at Pinewood Film Studios, and, in 1954, wrote the screenplay, and the songs (with Beaumont), for *Charley Moon,* which starred Max Bygraves. The popular singer/comedian took one of the numbers, 'Out Of Town', into the UK Top 20, and it gained Bricusse his first Ivor Novello Award: he won several others, including one for 'My Kind Of Girl' (words and music by Bricusse), which was a UK Top 5 hit for Matt Monro in 1961. Bricusse also wrote a good deal of special material for Bygraves, including one of his 'catch-phrase' songs, 'A Good Idea - Son!'. Early in 1961, Bricusse went to New York to write for another Beatrice Lillie revue, taking Anthony Newley with him to develop ideas for a show of their own. The result, *Stop The World - I Want To Get Off*, written in around three weeks, opened in London's West End in July of that year, and stayed there until November 1962. It later ran for over 500 performances on Broadway, and was filmed in 1966. Book, music and lyrics were jointly credited to Bricusse and Newley - the latter starred as the central character, Littlechap, in London and New York. The score included several hit songs, including 'What Kind Of Fool Am I?', 'Once In A Lifetime' and 'Gonna Build A Mountain', as well as other, more specialized numbers, such as 'Lumbered', 'Typically English' and 'Someone Nice Like You'. While Newley went off to appear in the off-beat, parochial movie, *The World Of Sammy Lee*, Bricusse collaborated with Cyril Ornadel on the score for the musical, *Pickwick* (1963), which starred the 'Goon with the golden voice', Harry Secombe, in the title role. His recording of the show's big ballad, 'If I Ruled The World', was a Top 20 hit in the UK, and, later, after the Broadway production had flopped, it became part of Tony Bennett's repertoire. Reunited in 1964, Bricusse and Newley's next major stage project, *The Roar Of The Greasepaint - The Smell Of The Crowd* (1965), was regarded as similar to their previous effort, a moral tale of a downtrodden little man, bucking the system. It toured (Bricusse: 'We managed to empty every provincial theatre in England'), but did not play the West End. Bricusse, and others, felt that comedian, Norman

Wisdom, was miscast in the central role, and Newley took over for the Broadway run of 232 performances. Once again, though, the hit songs were there - in this case, 'Who Can I Turn To?' and 'A Wonderful Day Like Today', plus other items such as 'This Dream', 'The Beautiful Land', 'The Joker', 'Where Would You Be Without Me?', 'Nothing Can Stop Me Now' and 'Feeling Good'. The latter number was popularized in the USA by Joe Sherman, and received an impressive, extended treatment from Steve Winwood's UK rock group, Traffic, on their live *Last Exit* (1969). In 1964, Bricusse and Newley turned their attention to the big screen, providing the lyric to John Barry's music for the title song to the James Bond movie, *Goldfinger* (1964), which Shirley Bassey sang over the titles. Bricusse and Barry later wrote another Bond theme for *You Only Live Twice* (1968), popularized by Nancy Sinatra. In 1967, Bricusse wrote the screenplay and the complete song score for *Doctor Dolittle*, which starred Newley, along with Rex Harrison, who sang the Oscar-winning 'Talk To The Animals'. Considered an 'expensive dud', there was no mention of a *Doctor Dolittle II*. Far more to the public's taste was Roald Dahl's *Willy Wonka And The Chocolate Factory* (1971). Bricusse and Newley's score contained 'The Candy Man', a song which gave Sammy Davis Jnr. a US number 1 in the following year. Davis was one of the songwriting team's favourite people - Bricusse estimates that he recorded at least 60 of his songs, including a complete album of *Doctor Dolittle*. Davis also starred in a revival of *Stop The World - I Want To Get Off* during the 1978-79 Broadway season.

After writing several numbers for a 1971 US television adaptation of *Peter Pan*, which starred Danny Kaye and Mia Farrow, Bricusse and Newley returned to the stage with *The Good Old Bad Old Days*. Newley directed and starred in the show, which ran for 10 months in London, and included the jolly title song and several other appealing numbers, such as 'I Do Not Love You', 'It's A Musical World', 'The People Tree' and 'The Good Things In Life'. Since then, their back catalogue has been re-packaged in productions such as *The Travelling Music Show* (1978), with Bruce Forsyth; and *Once Upon A Song*, in which Newley occasionally appears when he is not singing for big dollars in Las Vegas. Also in 1978, Bricusse collaborated with composer Armando Trovajoli on *Beyond the Rainbow*, an English language version of the Italian musical *Aggiungi Una Posta Alla Tavola*, which ran for six months in London - a good deal longer than his own *Kings And Clowns*. He also wrote some new songs for a Chichester Festival Theatre production of his film score for *Goodbye, Mr Chips* (1982). By then, he was generally wearing his Hollywood hat, and had received Oscar nominations for his work on *Goodbye, Mr Chips* (1969, original song score, with John Willams), *Scrooge* (1970, original song score with Ian Fraser and Herbert W. Spencer, and his own song, 'Thank You Very Much'), *That's Life* (1986, 'Life In a Looking Glass', with Henry Mancin), *Home Alone* (1990, 'Somewhere In My Memory', with John Williams), and *Hook* (1991, 'When You're Alone', with John Williams). He won his second Academy Award in 1982, in collaboration with Henry Mancini, for the original song score for *Victor/Victoria*. Bricusse and Newley were inducted into the Songwriters' Hall Of Fame in 1989, a year that otherwise proved something of a disappointment for partners: an updated version of *Stop The World*, directed by, and starring Newley, staggered along for five weeks in London, and Bricusse's *Sherlock Holmes*, with Ron Moody and Liz Robertson, opened there as well, to disappointing reviews. The latter show resurfaced in 1993, and toured the UK with Robert Powell in the title role, shortly after *Scrooge,* Bricusse's stage adaptation of his film score, had enjoyed a limited run at the Alexandra Theatre in Birmingham, England, with Newley in the title role. Also in 1993, Harry Secombe recreated his orginal role in *Pickwick* at Chichester and in the West End, and Broadway was buzzing with talk of possible stage productions of *Victor/Victoria*, and *Jekyll & Hyde*, a show that Bricusse wrote with Frank Wildhorn which was released on CD in 1990.

Brigadoon

Despite the acknowledged brilliance of the MGM team that transferred the 1947 Broadway musical *Brigadoon* to the big screen (notably producer Arthur Freed and director Vincente Minnelli), for many the magic touch so evident in their other creations was missing on this occasion. Alan Jay Lerner's mystical tale is set in a Scottish Highlands village which only comes to life once every hundred years, and where two Americans, Tommy Albright (Gene Kelly) and Jeff Douglas (Van Johnson), happen to stray during a hunting holiday. Albright falls in love with Fiona (Cyd Charisse), one of the townspeople, and yet initially the thoughts of his life and girl back home in the USA pull him away and he is unable to make the sacrifice and remain part of the sleeping village. It is only a minor miracle brought on by the strength of Kelly's love that re-awakens the village temporarily so he can once again, and forever, be with his true love. Many reasons have been cited for the rather staged *Brigadoon* not working quite as well as other Freed creations. These include the decisions to photograph the film in Ansco Color and CinemaScope and on location due to financial restraints which resulted in the use of artificial-looking studio backdrops; and the exclusion of some of the show's most endearing numbers such as 'There But For You Go I' and

Brigadoon

'Come To Me, Bend To Me'. And yet despite these factors, the film, released in September 1954, certainly has its enchanting moments. Some sequences are widely considered to be misjudged, but it is hard to fault Charisse and Kelly (also the film's choreographer) when they are dancing to 'Heather On The Hill' (Charisse dubbed by Carole Richards), or Kelly's expression of joy in 'Almost Like Being In Love'. Other songs in what is a lovely score, written by Frederick Loewe, with charming lyrics from Alan Jay Lerner, included 'Brigadoon', 'Waitin' For My Dearie', 'Once In The Highlands', and the rousing ensemble piece, 'I'll Go Home With Bonnie Jean'. Most of the comic moments are left to Van Johnson, who, as Kelly's cynical companion, prefers to dream with the help of alcohol rather than women. Despite its flaws, *Brigadoon*, with its romantic and fairy tale atmosphere, is still fondly regarded by many a musicals admirer.

Broadway Melody, The

Al Jolson had already dispensed a few musical morsels in the otherwise silent *The Jazz Singer*, the first feature length 'talking' picture in 1927, but this film, which was released by MGM two years later, launched the movie musical proper, and more than lived up to its billing as the first 'All Talking! All Singing! All Dancing!' motion picture. The witty and realistic screenplay by James Gleason, Norman Houston, and Edmund Goulding, tells of a vaudeville sister act, played by Bessie Love and Anita Page, who split up when handsome song-and-dance-man (Charles King) jilts Love and marries Page. Bessie Love, one of the biggest stars of the silent era, proved more than equal to the talkie challenge and turned in a fine emotional performance. The strong supporting cast included Jed Prouty, Kenneth Thompson, Eddie Kane, Mary Doran, and James Gleason. Nacio Herb Brown and Arthur Freed came up with a first-rate score which included two future standards, 'The Broadway Melody' and the tender 'You Were Meant For Me', both superbly delivered by Charles King, and the remainder of the score included 'The Boy Friend', 'Harmony Babies From Melody Lane', 'Love Boat', and 'The Wedding Of The Painted Doll'. The latter accompanied a sequence shot in two-colour Technicolor. Another song, 'Truthful Parson Brown', written by Willard Robison (he later composed the classic 'Cottage For Sale'), was performed by the Biltmore Trio and Orchestra. George Cunningham staged the dances, and Harry Beaumont was the director. Irving Thalberg produced this historic picture, which, although primitive in many respects, was dramatically and musically wonderful, and inspired a host of similar backstage movie musicals during the 30s, including MGM's own occasional series which began with:
Broadway Melody Of 1936. Apart from a chorus of

'The Broadway Melody' in the first scene and the presence of songwriters Nacio Herb Brown and Arthur Freed, this 1936 edition bore little resemblance to its predecessor. Jack McGowan and Sid Silvers' screenplay, which was based on a story by Moss Hart, concerns newspaper (and radio) gossip columnist Bert Keeler (Jack Benny). His editor, fed up with Benny's 'baby arrival' stories, demands 'the sort of stuff you get peeking through keyholes'. Keeler obliges, and becomes involved in a feud with Broadway producer Robert Gordon (Robert Taylor). After booking Mademoiselle Belle Arlette (a figment of Keeler's imagination) as his new leading lady, Gordon's show is saved from disaster by starstruck novice Irene Foster (Eleanor Powell), who, after dancing up a storm in the spectacular 'Broadway Rhythm' finalé, dances straight into Gordon's arms. Frances Langford, playing herself, introduced the lovely 'You Are My Lucky Star', and the rest of Brown and Freed's appealing score included 'I've Got A Feeling You're Foolin', 'Sing Before Breakfast', and 'On A Sunday Afternoon'. The latter number was sung and danced by the engaging duo of Buddy and Vilma Ebsen. Among the rest of the supporting cast were Una Merkel, Sid Silvers, June Knight, Harry Stockwell, and Nick Long Jnr. The dances were created and staged by Dave Gould, and the 'Lucky Star Ballet' was staged by Albertina Rasch. Roy Del Ruth directed, and the producer was John Considine Jnr.
Broadway Melody Of 1938. Very much a follow-up to the previous edition, with Robert Taylor, Eleanor Powell, and Buddy Ebsen on hand again, along with songwriters Nacio Herb Brown and Arthur Freed, choreographer Dave Gould, director Roy Del Routh, and screenwriters Jack McGowan and Sid Silvers. In the latter's slight and samey story, Powell is still trying to make it big in Taylor's Broadway show. However, this time she provides the finance, as well as the talent, when the racehorse that she co-owns (who is partial to opera as well as oats), wins $25,000 after being urged on by a passionate rendering of Rossini's 'Largo Al Factotum' over the racecourse PA system. Also involved were George Murphy, Binnie Barnes, Raymond Walburn, Charles Igor Gorin, Willie Howard, Robert Benchley, Charley Grapewin, and Robert Wildhack, but it was 15-years-old Judy Garland who stole the picture with one number - 'Dear Mr. Gable'. Roger Edens added a new verse and some patter to the old Jimmy Monaco-Joseph McCarthy number 'You Made Me Love You', and when Judy sang it while 'writing' a note to a picture of 'The King' which she kept on her dressing table, there was not a dry eye in movie houses worldwide. Sophie Tucker played Garland's mother, so naturally one of her specialities - 'Some Of These Days' - was in the film, and Tucker also sang Brown and Freed's latest 'Broadway' song, 'Your Broadway And My Broadway'. The rest of the numbers included 'Yours

The Broadway Melody Of 1940

And Mine', 'Everybody Sing', 'I'm Feelin' Like A Million', and 'Sun Showers' (all Brown-Freed). Jack Cummings was the producer.

Broadway Melody Of 1940. To movie buffs (and others) that title conjures of the complicated 'Begin The Beguine' number which was danced exquisitely by Eleanor Powell and Fred Astaire on a vast mirrored surface - especially the tap-dancing section when the couple, dressed in white, are accompanied by Roger Edens' 'swing' arrangement with clarinet lead. However, the rest of the picture was fine, too, with a top-notch Cole Porter score which included the amusing 'Please Don't Monkey With Broadway', 'Between You And Me', 'I've Got My Eyes On You', and the enduring standard, 'I Concentrate On You'. In Leon Gordon and George Oppenheimer's screenplay, which was based on an original story by Jack McGowan and Dore Schary, Astaire and George Murphy are a couple of song and dance men who break up after being involved in a mix-up during which Murphy is chosen for the Broadway role intended for Astaire. The dances were staged by Bobby Connolly, and also taking part in the fun and games were Frank Morgan, Ian Hunter, Florence Rice, Lynne Carver, and Ann Morriss. Jack Cummings was the producer and Norman Taurog directed an immensely entertaining climax to this MGM Broadway Melody series, which ended on the highest possible note with that 'Begin The Beguine' finalé.

Brodszky, Nicholas

b. 1905, Odessa, Russia, d. 24 December 1958, Hollywood, California, USA. After some musical training in Russia as a child, Brodszky continued his studies in Rome, Vienna and Budapest. From 1930 onwards he wrote music for European films and operetta, and in 1937 travelled to England and collaborated with lyricist A.P. Herbert on the score for the West End revue, *Home And Beauty*, which starred Gitta Alpar and Binnie Hale. During the next 10 years he composed the scores for several British movies, including *French Without Tears, Freedom Radio, Quiet Wedding, Unpublished Story, Tomorrow We Live, The Way To The Stars, English Without Tears, Carnival,* and *A Man About The House* (1947). In this phase of his career it is often said that he relied heavily on collaborators such as Clive Richardson, Charles Williams, Sidney Torch, Philip Green, and Roy Douglas. Brodszky really hit the big time when he moved to the USA and teamed with popular lyricist Sammy Cahn on 'Be My Love' for the Mario Lanza picture *The Toast Of New Orleans* (1950). It was the first of five songs of his to be nominated for an Oscar. Three of the others were with Cahn: 'Wonder Why' (from *Rich, Young And Pretty*), the title song for another Lanza vehicle, *Because You're Mine,* and 'I'll Never Stop Loving You' which was introduced in the

Ruth Etting bio-pic *Love Me Or Leave Me* by Doris Day. The other nominee was 'My Flaming Heart' from *Small Town Girl* which had a lyric by Leo Robin. There were several other appealing songs in *Rich, Young And Pretty,* including 'How Do You Like Your Eggs In The Morning?', which was sung by Jane Powell, Vic Damone and the Four Freshmen; and 'We Never Talk Much', a delightful number performed in the movie by Danielle Darrieux and Fernando Lamas and later recorded with some success by Dean Martin and Line Renaud. Brodszky's other work for pictures included 'Beloved', 'Summertime In Heidelberg' and 'I'll Walk With God', all with Paul Francis Webster for *The Student Prince*; and 'Hell Hath No Fury' (*Meet Me In Las Vegas*), 'Now, Baby, Now' and others (*The Opposite Sex*); and 'You I Love', 'Money Is A Problem', 'Only Trust Your Heart' and the title song for *Ten Thousand Bedrooms* (all with Cahn). Brodszky died in 1958, shortly after that score was completed.

Brown, Nacio Herb

b. 22 February 1896, Deming, New Mexico, USA, d. 28 September 1964, San Francisco, California, USA. After studying piano with his mother (his father was the local sherrif), Brown graduated from Musical Art High School, Los Angeles, but then took a course in business administration. Before long, however, he was playing piano as accompanist to vaudeville singer Alice Doll. A year later he became a tailor in Hollywood, dabbling in real estate on the side, and by 1920 was wealthy enough to hang up his tailors' scissors and start writing songs. His first was 'Coral Sea', written in 1920 with Alice Doll's husband, Jack (who used the pseudonym Zany King). Later in the decade he collaborated with Richard Whiting (father of singer Margaret Whiting) and Arthur Freed, with whom he wrote songs for the movie *The Broadway Melody* (1929). This collaboration produced the songs 'Broadway Melody', 'You Were Meant For Me' and 'The Wedding Of The Painted Doll'. Another film of the same year, *The Hollywood Revue,* featured 'Singin' In The Rain'. Brown also collaborated with Whiting and Buddy De Sylva on 'Eadie Was A Lady' for the 1932 Broadway show *Take A Chance.* Brown continued to collaborate with Freed on film songs, one of which was 'All I Do Is Dream Of You', written for *Sadie McKay* (1934) and reprised in 1953 in *Singin' In The Rain.* Also heard again in that film were the Freed-Brown songs, 'You Are My Lucky Star' and 'I've Got A Feelin' You're Foolin'', written for *The Broadway Melody Of 1936.* The team also wrote 'Alone' for the Marx Brothers film *A Night At The Opera* (1935). The 1939 film *Babes In Arms,* which starred Mickey Rooney and Judy Garland, included 'Good Morning', yet another song to delight a later generation of filmgoers in *Singin' In The Rain.* In the early 40s Brown had other collaborators for songs such as 'You Stepped Out Of A Dream' (with Gus Kahn) and 'Love Is Where You Find It' (with Earl K. Brent). Brown retired at the end of the 40s, but saw his music revived thanks largely to *Singin' In The Rain*, a film produced by Freed and said to trace aspects of the life of the duo. In celebration of their return to acclaim, they wrote one original song for the film, 'Make 'Em Laugh'. In February 1960 the authorities in Deming celebrated the 64th birthday of their most famous citizen by naming a city park after him. Brown died in September 1964.

Buchanan, Jack

b. 2 April 1890, Helensburgh, Strathclyde, Scotland, d. 20 October 1957, London, England. A major UK musical comedy, revue and film star, choreographer, director, producer and manager with a disarming, casual style, Buchanan's career spanned 40 years. He played in amateur dramatics and local music halls before moving to London to work as an understudy and chorus boy. Rejected for military service at the start of World War I because of poor health, he taught himself to dance, and played a leading role in the touring version of the West End hit musical comedy *Tonight's The Night* in 1915. His big break came two years later when he took over from Jack Hulbert in producer Andre Charlot's revue *Bubbly*, followed by another Charlot show, *A To Z*, in 1921. In the latter Buchanan sang one of his all-time hits 'And Her Mother Came Too', with Ivor Novello's music and a lyric by Dion Titheradge. Also in the cast were Beatrice Lillie and a young Gertrude Lawrence. After branching out into management with the musical farce *Battling Butler* at the New Oxford Theatre, Buchanan went to New York with Lillie and Lawrence to appear in *Andre Charlot's Revue Of 1924* at the Times Square Theater. Buchanan was a substantial success on Broadway, and returned in 1926 with another Charlot revue in which he duetted with Lawrence on 'A Cup Of Coffee, A Sandwich, And You'. The recording reached number 5 in the chart and was his only US hit. Back in London in 1926 he was at his peak in Jerome Kern's *Sunny*. With Elsie Randolph as his regular leading lady, he appeared in dancing musicals such as *That's A Good Girl*, *Mr Whittington*, *This'll Make You Whistle*, and their last show together in 1943, *It's Time To Dance*. He also went back to New York for *Wake Up And Dream!* with Jessie Matthews, and *Between The Devil* with Evelyn Laye. Songs such as, 'Who', 'Goodnight Vienna', 'I Think I Can', 'There's Always Tomorrow', 'Fancy Our Meeting', 'Sweet So And So', 'Weep No More My Baby', 'By Myself' and 'I'm In A Dancing Mood', were delivered in a seemingly fragile, 'typically English' style. In his show *Stand Up And Sing* at the London Hippodrome in 1931, a very young Anna Neagle was discovered by film producer Herbert Wilcox who started her on the road to a long

and distinguished film career by putting her into the Buchanan film *Goodnight Vienna*. Buchanan's own film career had started in 1925 with the silent, *Bulldog Drummond's Third Round*, and included a series of comedies, light dramas and farces such as *Yes, Mr Brown*, *Brewster's Millions* and *The Gang's All Here*. His first movie musical was *Paris*, with Corsican actress/singer Irene Bordoni, and he made several more including *Monte Carlo*, directed by Ernest Lubitsch, and co-starring Jeanette MacDonald, plus a few celluloid transfers of his hit stage productions. In 1953, the top UK and US song-and-dance men met in *The Band Wagon*. Buchanan and Fred Astaire's duet 'I Guess I'll Have To Change My Plan', and their clever version, with Nanette Fabray, of 'Triplets' fame, made this one of MGM's most acclaimed musical films, and the pinnacle of Buchanan's career. Compilations: *That's A Good Girl* (1979), *The Golden Age Of Jack Buchanan* (1984), *Elegance* (1985), *This'll Make You Whistle* (1990).
Further reading: *Top Hat And Tails*, Michael Marshall.

Bugsy Malone

Alan Parker properly put the old adage 'never work with children' to shame with his 1976 musical gangster spoof *Bugsy Malone*. With every role played by young people of varying ages, writer/director Parker tells the tongue-in-cheek tale of gang warfare in 20s New York - where no one is safe from the 'fatal' effects of the dreaded splurge gun. However, in the bitter battle between Fat Sam (goodie) and Dandy Dan (baddie), the guns do not shoot bullets; instead the ammunition is whipped cream. Paul Williams' score was skilfully integrated into the plot which sees Bugsy (a very young Scott Baio) emerging from an advanced state of apathy to help Fat Sam (John Cassisi), and fall in love with Blousey Brown (a name, he says, that sounds like a stale loaf of bread). 'With an Irish father and an Italian mother,' remarks Fat Sam, 'naturally Bugsy has grown up a little confused.' Made in Britain and released at a time when the Hollywood musical was a thing of the past, young audiences were given a taste of what they had missed with well-choreographed production numbers (the custard pie-throwing finale 'You Give A Little Love' is sentimental but enchanting), comic sequences such as 'So You Wanna Be A Boxer', and melancholy lost-love songs for Blousey - 'I'm Feeling Fine' and 'Ordinary Fool'. The film received mixed reviews from the critics but was popular with audiences, as was the album which included songs sung by the composer himself. Made by Rank/Bugsy Malone Productions (producers Allan Marshall and David Puttnam), Parker claims that the inspiration for the musical came in a 'drugstore-come-restaurant' in Las Vegas called Fox's Deli. Considered a novelty film by many, it neverthelesss helped to propel a few youngsters to future stardom, notably double Oscar winner Jodie Foster, whose portrayal of Sam's girlfried Tallulah, is one of the film's highlights.

Burke, Johnny

b. 3 October 1908, Antioch, California, USA, d. 25 February 1964, New York, USA. Brought up in Chicago, Burke studied piano and drama and in 1926 began work as a piano salesman with Irving Berlin Inc. In New York, doing this same job with the same company, he began writing lyrics and in 1933 had a hit with 'Annie Doesn't Live Here Anymore' (music by Harold Spina and a hit for Guy Lombardo). After a string of minor songs, with Spina, which were recorded by various popular artists of the day, among them Paul Whiteman, Ozzie Nelson and Ben Pollack, he had another hit with 'My Very Good Friend The Milkman' which was recorded by Fats Waller. In 1936 he went to Hollywood and there began a sustained period of creative activity and success. Burke made his name as a lyricist to Bing Crosby, working with many co-composers such as Arthur Johnston: 'Pennies From Heaven', 'One, Two, Button Your Shoe' from *Pennies From Heaven* (1936) and 'The Moon Got In My Eyes', 'All You Want To Do Is Dance' from *Double Or Nothing* (1937), and with Jimmy Monaco: 'I've Got A Pocketful Of Dreams', 'Don't Let That Moon Get Away' from *Sing, You Sinners* (1938), 'An Apple For The Teacher' from *The Star Maker*, 'East Side Of Heaven', 'Sing A Song Of Moonbeams' from *East Side Of Heaven* (1939) and 'Too Romantic', 'Sweet Potato Piper' from the first Bob Hope and Bing Crosby 'Road' film, *Road To Singapore* (1940). Burke's most famous collaboration was with Jimmy Van Heusen which began in 1940. The team supplied songs for 16 Crosby films, including *Road To Zanzibar* (1941), *Road To Morocco* (1942), *Dixie* (1943), *Going My Way* (1944) (which featured the Academy Award winning 'Swinging On A Star'), *The Bells Of St Mary's* (1945), *Road To Utopia* (1945), *Road To Rio* (1947), *A Connecticut Yankee In King Arthur's Court* (1949) and *Riding High* (1950). Besides working on other films, Van Heusen and Burke also wrote the score for the 1953 Broadway musical *Carnival In Flanders*, which contained the songs, 'Here's That Rainy Day' and 'It's An Old Spanish Custom'. Other Van Heusen-Burke songs during this period included 'Oh, You Crazy Moon', 'Suddenly It's Spring' and 'Like Someone In Love'. Burke wrote many more very popular songs, including 'Scatterbrain', with Frankie Masters and Keene-Bean; 'What's New', with Bob Haggart; and 'Misty', with jazz pianist Erroll Garner. He continued working until shortly before his death in February 1964.

Burns, Ralph

b. 29 June 1922, Newton, Massachusetts, USA. After studying music at the New England Conservatory in Boston, Burns worked with several late swing era bands, including Charlie Barnet's, as both pianist and arranger. His best-known period was as a member of Woody Herman's First Herd, during which time he was not only one-fourth of a great rhythm section (the others being Billy Bauer, Chubby Jackson and Dave Tough), but also arranged some of the band's most successful numbers (in some cases formalizing classic head arrangements, like that of 'Apple Honey'). In 1945 Burns decided to concentrate on writing and arranging, and contributed some exciting charts for Herman's Four Brothers band. He also composed some longer works, amongst which are 'Lady McGowan's Dream' and 'Summer Sequence', both recorded by Herman. When the record company decided to reissue 'Summer Sequence', they requested that a further section be added to the original three-part suite to fill the fourth side of a pair of 78 rpm releases. Burns obliged, and although some years had elapsed since the recording of the first three parts and the Herman band's personnel and style had substantially altered, he was able to recapture the mood successfully. The new piece, entitled 'Early Autumn', became a favourite of many jazz players, including Stan Getz. Freelancing in the 50s and 60s, Burns gradually moved away from jazz and into the film studios, although even here, as in *New York, New York* (1977), he was sometimes able to make use of his extensive knowledge of the jazz world. He won Academy Awards for his work on *Cabaret* (1972) and *All That Jazz* (1979), and continued to score for a mixture of feature and television movies such as *Lenny, Piaf, Lucky Lady, Movie Movie, Make Me An Offer, Urban Cowboy, Golden Gate, Pennies From Heaven*, (with Marvin Hamlisch), *Annie, Kiss Me Goodbye, My Favourite Year, Star 80, Ernie Kovacs-Between The Laughter, A Chorus Line; Moving Violations, The Christmas Star, In The Mood, Bert Rigby, You're A Fool, Sweet Bird Of Youth, All Dogs Go To Heaven*, and *The Josephine Baker Story* (1991).
Selected albums: with Woody Herman *Summer Sequence* (1945-47), *Piaf* (1974, film soundtrack), *Ralph Burns Conducts* (1988, rec. 1951-54), *Bijou* (1988, rec. 1955).

Bye Bye Birdie

Dick Van Dyke, one of the most popular comic actors on US and UK television, made his big screen debut in this 1963 Columbia adaptation of the hit Broadway show. Van Dyke reprised his stage role as the flamboyant manager and promoter of Conrad Birdie (Jesse Pearson), the rock 'n' roll singing sensation, who, in one final extravagant publicity stunt before he enters the US Army (à la Elvis Presley), sings Albert's latest song, 'One Last Kiss', on the *Ed Sullivan Show* while bestowing same on his biggest fan, Kim McAfee (Ann-Margret). The other members of a particularly strong cast included Janet Leigh (as Albert's secretary).

Bobby Rydell, Maureen Stapleton, Paul Lynde, Frank Albertson, and Ed Sullivan himself. As usual, several of the original songs from the stage show were lost in the transfer to film, but the survivors included some of Charles Strouse and Lee Adams' most amusing and entertaining numbers such as 'Put On A Happy Face', 'A Lot Of Livin' To Do', 'Kids', 'Honestly Sincere', 'How Lovely To Be A Woman', 'One Last Kiss', and 'The Telephone Hour', which was performed by Rydell and the 'kids', and is generally held to be the film's musical highspot. Screenplay writer Irving Brecher made only a few changes to Michael Stewart's original libretto, and Onna White, whose work had enhanced *The Music Man* the year before, choreographed the proceedings with style. The film, which was photographed in Eastman Color and Panavision, was directed by Fred Kohlmar.

C

Cabaret

One of the relatively few film musicals to be considered a vast improvement on the original Broadway show, *Cabaret* underwent substantial revisions before it came to the big screen courtesy of Allied Artists and ABC Picture Corporation in 1972. Screenwriter Jay Presson Allen and his 'research consultant', Hugh Wheeler, reportedly supplemented their adaptation of Joe Masteroff's 1966 stage libretto with further information from its source, Christopher Isherwood's collection of *Berlin Stories* and John Van Druten's play *I Am A Camera*. Although there were several changes in characterization, the basic story of the decadence and corruption prevalent in Berlin during the emergence of Nazism immediately prior to World War II, still came through loud and clear. Liza Minnelli, in her first leading role in a film musical, gave a sensational performance as Sally Bowles, the tawdry American singer who shares her lover, the English writer Brian Roberts (Michael York), with a bisexual aristocrat. Joel Grey recreated the menacing 'Emcee' at the Kit Kat Club, a part which had brought him much acclaim on Broadway, and he joined Minnelli in two of the film's musical highspots, 'Mein Herr' and 'Money, Money', both written especially for the film. The surviving songs from John Kander and Fred Ebb's original Broadway score included Grey's extravagant but sinister 'Willkommen', 'Two Ladies', 'If You Could See Her', 'Tomorrow Belongs To Me', 'Heiraten (Married)', and the titles song which Minnelli made forever her own. She also gave a highly emotional reading of 'Maybe This Time', which Kander and Ebb - who could almost be regarded as her 'personal' songwriters - had composed for her some years previously. Bob Fosse, who was probably still nursing the bruises from the adverse critical reaction to his work on the film of *Sweet Charity*, staged the dances and musical numbers, and won an Academy Award for his inspired direction. Other Oscars went to Minnelli, Grey, Geoffrey Unsworth (for his brilliant Technicolor photography), Ralph Burns (musical director). *Cabaret* also scooped the technical awards for best sound, film editing, art/set direction, music scoring, and cinematography. Presumably the Awards Committee was faced with an offer they could not refuse, because *Cabaret* was beaten for best film by *The Godfather*. The musical also trailed some $66 million dollars behind the Marlon Brando film at the box-office.

Cabin In The Sky

Adapted from the 1940 Broadway musical, this film version was released by MGM three years later. Joseph Schrank's screenplay is set in the Negro south, with Ethel Waters recreating her stage role as Petunia, the wife of Little Joe (Eddie 'Rochester' Anderson), a no-good gambling man. Little Joe is fatally injured in a fight and is destined for the fiery furnace until Petunia's fervent prayers result in a six months earthbound extension so that he can mend his ways. After being lobbied by representatives from the various ultimate destinations, the Lord's General (Kenneth Spencer) and Lucifer Jnr. (Rex Ingram) - with additional interference from one of the Devil's delicious disciples, Georgia Brown (Lena Horne) - Little Joe eventually is allowed through the Pearly Gates, along with Petunia who, by then, has qualified for entry herself. Also in the cast were the jazz greats Louis Armstrong and the Duke Ellington Orchestra. The original stage production's score was by composer Vernon Duke and lyricist John Latouche, but most of their work was lost in the show's transfer to the screen. Fortunately one of the songs to survive was 'Taking A Chance On Love' (lyric with Ted Fetter), which was given a memorable reading by Ethel Waters. Other songs by various composers included 'Honey In The Honeycomb', 'Cabin In The Sky', 'Shine', 'Life's Full Of Consequences', 'In My Old Virginia Home', and the lovely 'Happiness Is Just A Thing Called Joe', written by Harold Arlen and E.Y. 'Yip' Harburg. That song became an enduring standard and was immortalised by Judy Garland. *Cabin In The Sky* was an Arthur Freed production, and is remembered as the first Hollywood directorial assignment in Vincente Minnelli's distinguished career.

Cabin In The Sky

Caesar, Irving

b. Isodore Caesar, 4 July 1895, New York City, New York, USA. After studying music while at school, Caesar worked in commerce for several years, mostly for the Ford Motor Company. Highly literate, and a graduate of several educational establishments for advanced students, he began writing lyrics for his own amusement. George Gershwin, a childhood friend, collaborated with him on some mildly successful songs written between 1916 and 1919. The pair then had a huge success with 'Swanee', a song that was taken up by Al Jolson. Caesar wrote many songs with a succession of collaborators during the 20s, among them 'Tea For Two' and 'I Want To Be Happy', both from *No, No Nanette* (1925, music by Vincent Youmans), 'Sometimes I'm Happy' from *Hit The Deck* (1927, Youmans again) and 'Crazy Rhythm' (1928, music by Joseph Meyer and Roger Wolfe Kahn). He also worked in Hollywood, writing lyrics for 'Count Your Blessings' (music by Gerald Marks), which was used in *Palooka* (1934), and 'Animal Crackers In My Soup' (music by Ray Henderson), which was sung by Shirley Temple in *Curly Top* (1935). In 1936 he co-wrote lyrics for 'Is It True What They Say About Dixie' with Sammy Lerner (music by Marks). Although he continued to write lyrics throughout most of his life, his best work was done before the outbreak of World War II. In his later years he often wrote to commissions from government departments on such subjects as safety and health.

Caesar's best-known number, 'Tea For Two', has been recorded by numerous artists in a wide variety of styles over the years, and became the title of a film starring Doris Day and Gordon MacRea in 1950. Over 40 years later, in July 1992, the song was the subject of a BBC radio programme in which Caesar related how it came to be written. The show also confirmed that he was still very much alive - and working - at the age of 97.

Cagney, James

b. James Francis Cagney, 17 July 1899, New York, New York, USA, d. 30 March 1986, Stanfordville, New York USA. One of Hollywood's all-time great stars: a versatile actor with a tough guy image, renowned for his gangster movies, who appeared in several highly entertaining screen musicals. One of five children of an Irish-American father and an Irish-Norwegian mother, Cagney attended Columbia University but left to find full-time work after his father died at the age of 41 in the influenza epidemic of 1918. He had a variety of jobs before finding a place in the chorus of the Broadway musical comedy *Pitter Patter* in 1920. Also in the chorus was Frances

Willard Vernon, and the couple were married in 1922 and worked together in vaudeville for a few years before Cagney began to appear in stage melodramas, and musicals such as *The Grand Street Follies* of 1928 and 1929. In 1930 Cagney joined the Warner Brothers Studio in Hollywood and proceeded to make the classic gangster movies for which he is so famous, including *Public Enemy*, *Angels With Dirty Faces*, and *The Roaring Twenties*. In 1933 he played the lead in one of the best musicals of the decade, *Footlight Parade*, and in 1937 kicked up his heels in the lively *Something To Sing About*. The musical highspot of his film career came in 1942 with *Yankee Doodle Dandy*, in which Cagney's magnetic portrayal of the master-showman George M. Cohan won him an Academy Award. He played Cohan again in 1955 when he and Bob Hope (as Eddie Foy) combined in splendid fashion for 'Mary's A Grand Old Name' and 'Yankee Doodle Boy' in *The Seven Little Foys*. Also in the 50s he co-starred with Doris Day in two musicals, *West Point Story* and *Love Me Or Leave Me*. In the latter, the screen biography of torch singer Ruth Etting, Cagney gave a brilliant performance as Martin 'The Gimp' Snyder, Etting's jealous husband and Svengali. In 1960 Cagney retired from films, and despite repeated efforts to return (Jack Warner, head of Warner Brothers, is said to have pleaded with him to play Alfred P. Doolittle in the 1964 movie version of *My Fair Lady*) emerged only occasionally during the next 20 years to accept honours such as the second American Film Institute's Lifetime Achievement Award and a Kennedy Centre Lifetime Achievement Award. In 1981, at the age of 82, he was tempted back for *Ragtime*, a story of 1906 America in which he played (somewhat ironically in view of his early roles) a New York police commissioner. Parts of the film were shot in Britain and Cagney made a poignant appearance at a Royal Variety Show which was attended by the Queen Mother. He continued to play the occasional role on US television until shortly before his death in 1986.

Further reading: *Films Of James Cagney*, H. Dickens. *Cagney: The Actor As Auteur*, Patrick McGilligan. *James Cagney: The Authorized Biography*, Doug Warren. *Cagney By Cagney* (his autobiography).

Cahn, Sammy

b. Samuel Cohen, 18 June 1913, New York, USA, d. 15 January 1993, Los Angeles, California, USA. The son of Jewish immigrant parents from Galicia, Poland, Cahn grew up on Manhatten's Lower East Side. Encouraged by his mother, he learned to play the violin, joined a small orchestra that played at bar mitzvahs and other functions, and later worked as a violinist in Bowery burlesque houses. At the age of 16 he wrote his first lyric, 'Like Niagrara Falls, I'm Falling For You', and persuaded a fellow member of the orchestra, Saul Chaplin, to join him in a songwriting partnership. Their first published effort was 'Shake Your Head From Side To Side', and in the early 30s they wrote special material for vaudeville acts and bands. In 1935 they had their first big hit when the Jimmy Lunceford orchestra recorded their 'Rhythm Is Our Business'. The following year Andy Kirk topped the US Hit Parade with the duo's 'Until The Real Thing Comes Along', and Louis Armstrong featured their 'Shoe Shine Boy' in the Cotton Club Revue. In 1937 Cahn and Chaplin had their biggest success to date when they adapted the Yiddish folk song, 'Beir Mir Bist Du Schöen'. It became the top novelty song of the year and gave the Andrews Sisters their first million-seller. The team followed with 'Please Be Kind', a major seller for Bob Crosby, Red Norvo and Benny Goodman. During this time Cahn and Chaplin were also under contract to Warner Brothers, and soon after that commitment ended they decided to part company. In 1942, Cahn began his very productive partnership with Jule Styne, their first chart success, 'I've Heard That Song Before'. Just as significant was Cahn's renewed association with Frank Sinatra, whom he had known when the singer was with Tommy Dorsey. Cahn and Styne wrote the score for the Sinatra films *Step Lively* (1944), ('Come Out Wherever You Are' and 'As Long As There's Music'); *Anchors Aweigh* (1945), ('I Fall In Love Too Easily', 'The Charm Of You', and 'What Makes The Sunset?') and *It Happened In Brooklyn* (1947), ('Time After Time', 'It's The Same Old Dream' and 'It's Gotta Come From The Heart'). Sinatra also popularized several other 40s Cahn/Styne songs, including 'I'll Walk Alone', 'Saturday Night Is The Loneliest Night In The Week', 'The Things We Did Last Summer', 'Five Minutes More', and the bleak, 'Guess I'll Hang My Tears Out To Dry', which appeared on his 1958 album, *Only The Lonely*. Some of their other hits included 'It's Been A Long, Long Time', associated with Harry James and his vocalist Kitty Kallen, 'Let It Snow! Let It Snow! Let It Snow!' (Vaughan Monroe), and 'There Goes That Song Again' (Kay Kyser and Russ Morgan). Cahn and Styne wrote the score for several other films including *Tonight And Every Night* (1945), two Danny Kaye vehicles, *Wonder Man* (1945) and *The Kid From Brooklyn* (1946), and *West Point Story* (1950). They also provided the songs for *Romance On The High Seas* (1948), the film in which Doris Day shot to international stardom, singing 'It's Magic' and 'Put 'Em In A Box, Tie 'Em With A Ribbon'. The two songwriters also wrote the Broadway show, *High Button Shoes* (1947), starring Phil Silvers (later Sgt. Bilko) and Nanette Fabray, which ran for 727 performances and introduced songs such as 'I Still Get Jealous', 'You're My Girl' and 'Papa, Won't You Dance With Me'. After *High Button Shoes* Cahn went to California, while Styne stayed in New York. Cahn collaborated with Nicholas Brodsky for a while in the early 50s, writing movie songs for Mario Lanza, including 'Be My Love', 'Wonder Why', 'Because You're Mine', 'Serenade' and 'My Destiny'. The collaboration also composed 'I'll Never Stop Loving You' for the Doris Day film, *Love Me Or Leave Me* (1955). Cahn and Styne re-united briefly in 1954, ostensibly to write the score for the film, *Pink Tights*, to star Sinatra and Marilyn Monroe, but the project was shelved. Soon afterwards Cahn and Styne were asked to write the title song for the film, *Three Coins In The Fountain*. The result, a big hit for Sinatra and for the Four Aces, gained Cahn his first Academy Award. Cahn and Styne eventually worked with Monroe when they wrote the score for the comedy, *The Seven Year Itch* (1955). In the same year Cahn started his last major collaboration - with Jimmy Van Heusen and, some would say, with Frank Sinatra as well. They had immediate success with the title song of the Sinatra movie, *The Tender Trap* (1955), and won Academy Awards for songs in two of his movies, 'All The Way', from *The Joker Is Wild* (1957) and 'High Hopes', from *A Hole In The Head* (1959). A parody of 'High Hopes' was used as John F. Kennedy's presidential campaign song in 1960. Among the many other songs written especially for Sinatra were 'My Kind Of Town' (from *Robin And The Seven Hoods*)(1964) and the title songs for his best-selling albums, *Come Fly With Me, Only The Lonely, Come Dance With Me!, No One Cares, Ring-A-Ding-Ding!* and *September Of My Years*. Cahn and Van Heusen also produced his successful Timex television series during 1959-60. In the movies they won another Oscar for the song 'Call Me Irresponsible', (from *Papa's Delicate Condition*, 1963), Cahn's fourth Oscar from over 30 nominations, and contributed to many other films including 'The Second Time Around' (from *High Time*) and the title songs from *A Pocketful Of Miracles, Where Love Has Gone, Thoroughly Modern Millie* and *Star*. The songwriters also supplied the score for a television musical version of Thorton Wilder's play, *Our Town*, which introduced the songs, 'Love And Marriage' and 'The Impatient Years'. They also received critical approval for their score of the Broadway musical *Skyscraper* (1965), which included the songs, 'Everybody Has The Right To Be Wrong' and 'I'll Only Miss Her When I Think Of Her'. They also provided music and lyrics for the British musical *Walking Happy*, which opened on Broadway in 1966. In 1969 Cahn dissolved his partnership with Van Heusen and collaborated once more with Jule Styne on the Broadway musical, *Look To The Lilies*. His other collaborators included Axel Stordahl and Paul Weston ('Day By Day' and 'I Should Care'), Gene DePaul ('Teach Me Tonight'), Arthur Schwartz ('Relax-Ay-Voo'), George Barrie ('All That Love To Waste'), and Vernon Duke ('That's What Makes Paris Paree', and 'I'm Gonna Ring The Bell Tonight'). In 1972 Cahn was inducted into the Songwriters Hall Of Fame after claiming throughout his lifetime that he only wrote songs so that he could demonstrate them. In the same year he mounted his 'one man show', *Words And Music*, on Broadway, and despite his voice being described by a New York critic as that of 'a vain duck with a hangover', the nostalgic mixture of his songs, sprinkled with amusing anecdotes of the way they came about, won rave notices and the Outer Circle Critics Award for the best new talent on Broadway. He repeated his triumph in England two years later, and then re-mounted the whole thing all over again in 1987. After over six decades of 'putting *that* word to *that* note', as he termed it, he died in January 1993. His books include a songbook, *Words And Music* and *The Songwriter's Rhyming Dictionary*. Album: *I've Heard That Song Before* (1977). Further reading: *I Should Care - The Sammy Cahn Story*, Sammy Cahn.

Calamity Jane

Straying from her girl-next-door image, and employing all her substantial wisecracking and musical talents, Doris Day was the definitive Calamity Jane in this Warner Brothers' 1953 release. The story of one the most famous characters from the days of the Old West has been filmed several times over the years, but this version was as good as any of them. In James O'Hanlon's screenplay the residents of Deadwood, right in the heart of good ol' cowboy and Indian territory, drool over cigarette pictures of stage star Adelaide Adams. As a result, naive but good-hearted Calamity Jane takes the stagecoach to Chicago to persuade Adams to perform at Deadwood's humble theatre - but mistakenly returns with the star's maid instead. Rather conveniently, Katie Brown (Allyn McLerie) proves to be quite an entertainer and wins the hearts of the Deadwood people. Howard Keel is funny, and in fine voice as Wild Bill Hickock, a reminder of his performance in *Annie Get Your Gun* to which *Calamity Jane* was quite naturally compared. However, this film does not reach the excellence of that classic, although Day and Keel's wrangling on the song 'I Can Do Without You' was very reminiscent of Hutton and Keel's performance of 'Anything You Can Do' in the earlier film. Sammy Fain and Paul Francis Webster's refreshing score contained several effective comic uptempo moments such as 'The Deadwood Stage' and 'Just Blew In From The Windy City', along with other pleasant numbers including 'Higher Than A Hawk', ''Tis Harry I'm Planning To Marry', 'I've Got A Heart Full Of Honey', 'A Woman's Touch', and 'The Black Hills Of Dakota'. The tender 'Secret Love' won the Oscar for best song and went on to become a US number 1 for Doris Day. Also among the cast were Paul Harvey, Dick Wesson, Phil Carey, and Chubby Johnson. Jack Donohue staged the spirited dance sequences, and the wide open spaces gave Wilfred M. Cline ample scope for his superb Technicolor photography. The director was David Butler.

Call Me Madam

Ethel Merman enjoyed her greatest film triumph when she recreated her original role in this 1953 adaptation of Irving Berlin's hit Broadway show. Although she was never considered to be as effective on the screen as she was on stage, the part of the extrovert oil-heiress Sally Adams, the brand new Ambassador to the mythical Duchy of Lichtenburg, suited her down to the ground. In Arthur Sheekman's screenplay, which was faithfully based on Howard Lindsay and Russell Crouse's witty and sometimes satirical libretto, Merman flirted with one of the tiny Principality's highest officials, Cosmo Constantine (George Sanders), while enquiring 'Can You Use Any Money Today?'. That was just one of the charming and amusing numbers in a Berlin score which arrived in Hollywood from New York almost intact, although inevitably the reference to 'panties' in Merman's *tour de force*, 'The Hostess With The Mostes'', which had presumably been acceptable to Broadway theatregoers, was removed for worldwide consumption. Merman was also firing on all cylinders on 'That International Rag', 'You're Just In Love' (with Donald O'Connor, who played her press attaché Ken Gibson), and 'The Best Thing For You' (with Sanders). The latter artist was more than adequate on the gentle 'Marrying For Love', and O'Connor had his moments too on 'What Chance Have I With Love?', 'Something To Dance About' and the lively 'It's A Lovely Day Today', the last two with Vera-Ellen, whose singing was dubbed by Carole Richards. O'Connor and Vera-Ellen made a charming couple, and their dances together which were choreographed by Robert Alton, were sublime. The rest of the cast included the always watchable duo Walter Slezak and Billy De Wolfe. Musical Director Alfred Newman won an Oscar for his 'scoring of a musical picture' which was directed by Walter Lang and released by 20th Century-Fox.

Calloway, Cab

b. Cabell Calloway, 25 December 1907, Rochester, New York, USA. Involved in show business from an early age, vocalist Calloway was an occasional drummer and MC, working mostly in Baltimore, where he was raised, and Chicago, where he relocated in the late 20s. He worked with his sister Blanche, and then, in 1929, he became frontman for the Alabamians. Engagements with this band took him to New York; in the same year he fronted the Missourians, a band for which he had briefly worked a year earlier. The Missourians were hired for New York's Savoy Ballroom; although the band consisted of proficient musicians, there is no doubt that it was Calloway's flamboyant leadership that attracted most

attention. Dressing outlandishly in an eye-catching 'Zoot Suit' - knee-length drape jacket, voluminous trousers, huge wide-brimmed hat and a floor-trailing watch chain - he was the centre of attraction. His speech was peppered with hip phraseology and his catch-phrase 'Hi-De-Hi', echoed by the fans, became a permanent part of the language. The popularity of the band and of its leader led to changes. Renamed as Cab Calloway And His Orchestra, the band moved into the Cotton Club in 1931 as replacement for Duke Ellington, allegedly at the insistence of the club's Mafia-connected owners. The radio exposure this brought helped to establish Calloway as a national figure. As a singer Calloway proved difficult for jazz fans to swallow. His eccentricities of dress extended into his vocal style, which carried echoes of the blues, crass sentimentality and cantorial religiosity. At his best, however, as on 'Geechy Joe' and 'Sunday In Savannah', which he sang in the 1943 film *Stormy Weather*, he could be highly effective. His greatest popular hits were a succession of songs, the lyrics of which were replete with veiled references to drugs that, presumably, the record company executives failed to recognize. 'Minnie The Moocher' was the first of these, recorded in March 1931 with 'Kicking The Gong Around', an expression which means smoking opium, released in October the same year. Other hits, about sexual prowess, were Fats Waller's 'Six Or Seven Times' and the Harold Arlen-Ted Koehler song 'Triggeration'. For the more perceptive jazz fans who were patient enough to sit through the razzmatazz, and what one of his sidemen referred to as 'all that hooping and hollering', Calloway's chief contribution to the music came through the extraordinary calibre of the musicians he hired. In the earlier band he had the remarkable cornetist Reuben Reeves, trombonist Ed Swayzee, Doc Cheatham and Bennie Payne. As his popularity increased, Calloway began hiring the best men he could find, paying excellent salaries and allowing plenty of solo space, even if the records were usually heavily-orientated towards his singing. By the early 40s the band included outstanding players such as Chu Berry featured on 'Ghost Of A Chance' and 'Tappin' Off', Hilton Jefferson ('Willow Weep For Me'), Milt Hinton ('Pluckin' The Bass'), Cozy Cole ('Ratamacue' and 'Crescendo In Drums') and Jonah Jones ('Jonah Joins The Cab').

With such outstanding musicians including Ben Webster, Shad Collins, Garvin Bushell, Mario Bauza, Walter 'Foots' Thomas, Tyree Glenn, J.C. Heard and Dizzy Gillespie, the Calloway band was a force to be reckoned with and was one of the outstanding big bands of the swing era. In later years Cab worked on the stage in *Porgy And Bess* and *Hello, Dolly!*, and took acting roles in films such as *The Blues Brothers* (1980). His other films, over the years, included *The Big Broadcast* (1932), *International House*, *The Singing Kid*,

Manhattan Merry Go Round, *Sensations Of 1945*, *St. Louis Blues*, *The Cincinnati Kid*, and *A Man Called Adam* (1966). Calloway enjoyed a resurgence of popularity in the 70s with a Broadway appearance in *Bubbling Brown Sugar*. In the 80s he was seen and heard on stages and television screens in the USA and UK, sometimes as star, sometimes as support but always as the centre of attraction. Joe Jackson recorded Calloway's classic 'Jumpin' Jive' in 1981, proof that Cab's music will endure. In 1993 he appeared at London' Barbican Centre, and in the same year celebrated his honarary doctorate in fine arts at the University of Rochester in New York State by leading the 9,000 graduates and guests in a singalong to 'Minnie The Moocher'.

Selected compilations: *Club Zanzibar Broadcasts* (1981), *Kicking The Gong Around* (1982), *Cab & Co.* (1985), *Cab Calloway Collection - 20 Greatest Hits* (1986), *Missourians* (1986), *The Cab Calloway Story* (1989), *Hi-De-Hi* (1991), *Classics 1941-42* (1993).

Further reading: *Of Minnie The Moocher And Me* (his autobiography).

Camelot

This brave but financially unsuccessful attempt to bring Alan Jay Lerner and Frederick Loewe's underrated Broadway musical to the screen was produced by Jack L. Warner for Warner Brothers in 1967. Lerner's screenplay was adapted from his own stage libretto, which had been based on T.H. White's novel *The Once And Future King*. Richard Harris's portrayal of King Arthur, whose hopes and dreams are shattered when his Queen Guenevere (Vanessa Redgrave) is unfaithful with Sir Lancelot (Franco Nero), was far more sympathetic and less regal and arrogant than Richard Burton's original interpretation on Broadway. He also handled his songs in a most appealing way. Leonard Naismith as Merlin and David Hemmings as Mordred were in a supporting cast that also included Lionel Jeffries, Estelle Winwood, Pierre Olaf, Gary Marshall, and Anthony Rogers. Most of the songs in Lerner and Loewe's magnificent score were retained, including 'I Wonder What The King Is Doing Tonight', 'The Simple Joys Of Maidenhood', 'Camelot', 'Follow Me', 'C'est Moi', 'The Lusty Month Of May', 'Then You May Take Me To The Fair', 'How To Handle A Woman', 'If Ever I Would Leave You', 'What Do The Simple Folk Do?', 'I Loved You Once In Silence', and 'Guenevere'. Franco Nero's singing voice was dubbed by Gene Merlina. Joshua Logan directed, and *Camelot* received Academy Awards for its sumptuous costumes and art-set direction (John Truscott, Edward Carrere, and John W. Brown), and music scoring (Alfred Newman and Ken Darby). It was photographed in Technicolor and Panavision. Poorly received by the critics, the film went on to become one of the top box office attractions of the 60s, although with massive production cost of more than $15 million, it still lost money.

Can't Help Singing

War-weary cinema audiences experienced a welcome breath of fresh air with this 1944 Deanna Durbin vehicle in which she hits the trail to the wide open spaces of the Wild West. Lewis Foster and Frank Ryan's screenplay, set in 1847, finds Universal Studio's favourite female singing star aboard a wagon train bound for California and the man she loves. She fails to make the rendezvous after being waylaid by Robert Paige who is not only handsome - but he can sing as well. Durbin's own voice was as thrilling and spine-tingling as ever on a set of superior songs by Jerome Kern and E. Y. 'Yip' Harburg which included the lovely and lyrical 'Can't Help Singing', 'Californ-i-ay', 'Elbow Room', 'More And More', 'Any Moment Now', and 'Swing Your Sweetheart'. Ray Collins played the disgruntled and possessive father, with Akim Tamiroff and Leonid Kinskey as a pair of wandering adventurers. Also in the cast were Thomas Gomez, David Bruce, June Vincent, Olin Howlin, and Clara Blandick. This extremely good looking picture was photographed by Woody Bredell and W. Howard Greene in glorious Technicolor and directed by Frank Ryan.

Can-Can

This popular, but uninspired screen version of Cole Porter's smash hit Broadway musical was released by 20th Century-Fox in 1960. The all-star cast included Frank Sinatra as a lawyer who defends cabaret club owner Shirley MacLaine's constitutional right to present (and take part in) an immoral dance known as the can-can. He also takes a very personal interest in her welfare, in spite of opposition from Louis Jourdan, and even the judge (Maurice Chevalier), who is expected to protect the public virtue, but finds that his sympathies are most definitely with the attractive defendant. Several of Porter's Broadway songs survived, and a few were added from his other shows, in a score which included 'It's Alright With Me' (Sinatra), 'Come Along With Me' (MacLaine'), 'Live And Let Live' (Chevalier-Jourdan), 'You Do Something To Me' (Jourdan), 'Let's Do It', (Sinatra-MacLaine), 'Montmart' (Sinatra-Chevalier), 'C'est Magnifique' (Sinatra), 'Maidens Typical Of France' (chorus), 'Just One Of Those Things' (Chevalier), 'I Love Paris' (Sinatra-Chevalier), and 'Can-Can' (orchestral). One of the highest kickers in the business, Juliet Prowse, had her legs in the air and was displaying her frilly underwear, along with Shirley MacLaine and the rest of the chorus, when Russian premier Nikita Krushchev visited the film set - and departed somewhat disgusted. Those responsible for the 'shocking' display (which was shot in Technicolor and Todd-AO) - choreographer Hermes Pan,

Can't Help Singing

screenwriters Dorothy Kingsley and Charles Lederer, and director Walter Lang - were found not guilty of any moral offence, but were, perhaps, partly to blame for a fairly boring film.

Cantor, Eddie

b. Edward Israel Iskowitz, 31 January 1892, New York, USA, d. 10 October 1964, Hollywood, California, USA. An extremely popular comedian, singer and dancer. Highly animated in performance, jumping up and down, hands gesticulating, eyes popping and swivelling, giving rise to his nickname 'Banjo Eyes'. The son of Russian immigrants, Cantor was orphaned at an early age and reared by his grandmother. He sang on street corners before joining composer Gus Edwards' group of youngsters, and appearing in blackface for *Kid Cabaret* in 1912. George Jessel, another big star of the future, was in the same troupe. Cantor became a top performer in vaudeville before breaking into Broadway in Florenz Ziegfeld's *Midnight Frolics* (1916), leading to starring roles in the *Ziegfeld Follies* 1917-19. In the latter show, completely in character, he sang Irvin Berlin's saucy number, 'You'd Be Surprised', and it featured on what is considered to be the earliest 'original cast' album, on Smithsonian Records. After *Broadway Brevities* (1920) and *Make It Snappy* (1922), Cantor appeared in his two most successful Broadway shows. The first, *Kid Boots*, in 1923, ran for 479 performances, introduced two of his most popular songs, 'Alabamy Bound' and 'If You Knew Susie', and was filmed as a silent movie, three years later. The second, *Whoopee*, in 1928, teamed Cantor with a young Ruth Etting and was his biggest Broadway hit. The 1930 movie version only retained one song, 'Makin' Whoopee', from the original score, but it established Cantor as a Hollywood star, and was notable for the debut of dance-director Busby Berkeley and the use of two-colour technicolour. During the 30s and 40s, after reputedly losing heavily in the 1929 Wall Street Crash, he concentrated his efforts on films and radio. The extremely successful movies invariably featured him as the poor, timid little man, winning against all odds after wandering around some of Hollywood's most lavish settings, occasionally in blackface. They included *Glorifying The American Girl* (1929), *Palmy Days* (1931), *The Kid From Spain* (1932), *Roman Scandals* (1932), *Kid Millions* (1934), *Strike Me Pink* (1936), *Ali Baba Goes To Town* (1937), *40 Little Mothers* (1940), *Thank Your Lucky Stars* (1943), *Show Business* and *Hollywood Canteen* (both 1944). In the 30s he was reputed to be radio's highest-paid star via his *Chase & Sanborn* show with its famous theme, Richard Whiting's 'One Hour With You'. It is said that during this period Cantor had been responsible for helping Deanna Durbin, and later Dinah Shore and Eddie Fisher early in their careers. In 1941 Cantor made his last Broadway appearance in *Banjo Eyes* which ran for

126 performances and is remembered mainly for his version of 'We're Having A Baby'. After World War II he was on radio with his *Time To Smile* show and on early television in 1950 with the *Colgate Comedy Hour*. In the same year he played himself in the movie *The Story Of Will Rogers*. A heart attack in 1952 reduced his activities, eventually forcing him to retire, although he did appear in the occasional 'special'. He also dubbed the songs to the soundtrack of his bio-pic *The Eddie Cantor Story* in 1953, with Keefe Brasselle in the title role. The film contained some of the songs for which he was famous, such as 'Yes Sir, That's My Baby', 'How Ya Gonna Keep 'Em Down On The Farm', 'Oh, You Beautiful Doll', 'Margie', 'Ma (He's Making Eyes At Me)', and 'You Must Have Been A Beautiful Baby'. There were many others including 'My Baby Just Cares For Me', 'Everybody's Doing It', 'No, No Nora', Now's The Time To Fall In Love', 'Dinah', 'Keep Young And Beautiful' and 'Ida, Sweet As Apple Cider', which he always dedicated to his wife. He also wrote lyrics to some songs including 'Merrily We Roll Along' and 'There's Nothing Too Good For My Baby', and several books, including *Caught Short*, an account of his 1929 financial losses, and two volumes of his autobiography. He was awarded an Honorary Oscar in 1956, and died eight years later in Hollywood, California.
Selected compilations: *The Best Of Eddie Cantor* (1981), *Makin' Whoopee!* (1989).
Further reading: *Caught Short*, Eddie Cantor. *My Life Is In Your Hands*, Eddie Cantor. *Take My Life*, Eddie Cantor.

Cara, Irene

b. 18 March 1959, New York City, New York, USA. Having spent most of her childhood as a successful actor, singer and dancer, Cara's role as Coco Hernandez in the 1980 Alan Parker film *Fame*, was tailor-made. Based around the lives, loves and ambitions of students at the New York School of Performing Arts, Cara's rendition of the jubilant title song was an Oscar-winning international hit reaching the number 1 spot, belatedly, in the UK. This sparked off an entire 'Fame' industry and a world-wide boost to sales of leg warmers and a new generation of 'Mrs Worthingtons'. Another movie song, 'Flashdance...What A Feeling' from *Flashdance*, earned Irene a US number 1, a UK number 2 and and yet another Oscar for Best Song. Signing to Geffen Records, Cara scored further US hits with 'Why Me' (1983), a further movie hit with 'The Dream (Hold On To Your Dream)' from *DC Cab*, and the Top 10 hit 'Breakdance' (both 1984). Contractual disputes delayed her recording career in the mid-80s and Irene re-emerged with a new album in 1987 on Elektra Records.
Albums: *Anyone Can See* (1982), *What A Feelin'* (1983), *Carasmatic* (1987).

Carmen Jones (Dorothy Dandridge)

Carefree

After Ginger Rogers had a crack at straight acting and Fred Astaire had endured a rather unsatisfactory (professional) relationship with Joan Fontaine in *A Damsel In Distress*, the screen's all-time favourite dance team were reunited in 1938 for *Carefree*. Old stagers Allan Scott and Ernest Pagano set their story mostly in a plush country club, and cast Astaire as psychiatrist Tony Flagg, who, by means of hypnosis and food-induced dreams, convinces radio singer Amanda Cooper (Ginger Rogers) that she is crazy about him - and not her fiancé Stephen Arden (Ralph Bellamy) - who sent her for treatment in the first place! What Irving Berlin's score lacked in quantity - there were only five numbers, just three of which were sung - it made up for in quality. Astaire's reading of the gently chiding 'Change Partners' ('Must you dance, every dance, with the same fortunate man?') was alone worth the price of a ticket, and his version of 'I Used To Be Colour Blind' was just as good. The instrumental items consisted of two superb dance sequences, the romantic 'The Night Is Filled With Music', the joyfully energetic 'The Yam', along with 'Since They Turned Loch Lomond Into Swing'. The latter number accompanied one of the film's highspots in which Astaire consistently hit a considerable number of golf balls from tee to fairway in the style and manner of a US Masters champion. However, the box-office returns were not so spectacular, and in spite of the presence of regulars such as director Mark Sandrich and dance director Hermes Pan, *Carefree* turned out to be the first Astaire-Rogers movie to lose money.

Carmen Jones

This was at least the fifth manifestation of a story which started out as a novel by Frenchman Prosper Mérimeé, then became a grand opera by Bizet, Meilhac and Halévy, a 1943 Broadway musical, a 1948 film *The Loves Of Carmen* starring Rita Hayworth and Glenn Ford, and now this, a full-blown film musical which was produced and directed by Otto Preminger for 20th Century-Fox in 1954. Harry Kleiner's screenplay, which was based on Oscar Hammerstein II's libretto for that 1943 musical, follows the dramatic action of its operatic source, but changes the setting of the cigarette factory in Seville to a parachute factory in Chicago, and updates the story to World War II. Don José becomes Joe (Harry Belafonte), a young soldier destined for flying school before being ruined by Carmen (Dorothy Dandridge); Escamillo, the toreador, is now Husky Miller (Joe Adams), a champion heavyweight prizefighter; Micaëla, the village maid, is transformed into Cindy Lou (Olga James), a small-town maiden who always remains faithful to her Joe; and Frasquita and the smuggler friends of Carmen are now Frankie (Pearl Bailey), Myrt (Diahann Carroll), Dink (Nick Stewart), and Rum (Roy Glenn). The singing voices of Carmen, Joe, Husky, Myrt, Rum and Dink, are dubbed by Marilyn Horne, LeVerne Hutcherson, Marvin Hayes, Bernice Peterson, Brock Peters, and Joe Crawford respectively. The highly emotional score, with music by Georges Bizet and lyrics by Oscar Hammerstein, was comprised of 'Dat's Love', 'You Talk Jus' Like My Maw', 'Dere's A Cafe On De Corner', 'Dis Flower', 'Beat Out Dat Rhythm On A Drum', 'Stan' Up And Fight', 'Whizzin' Away Along De Track', 'Card Song', and 'My Joe'. Herbert Ross was the choreographer and *Carmen Jones* was photographed by Sam Leavitt in Delux Color and CinemaScope.

Carmichael, Hoagy

b. Hoagland Howard Carmichael, 22 November 1899, Bloomington, Indiana, USA, d. 27 December 1981. Growing up in a poor rural community, the young Carmichael was encouraged to play piano by his mother who accompanied silent films at a local movie theatre. Largely self taught, he continued to play despite ambitions for a career in law. In 1916 the Carmichaels moved to Indianapolis where he took lessons from Reginald DuValle, a ragtime pianist. While still at high school he formed a band and continued to lead bands during his time at Indiana University. In 1922 he met and became friendly with Bix Beiderbecke, then with the Wolverines for whom Carmichael composed 'Riverboat Shuffle', one of his first works. During the mid-20s he wrote occasionally, his music being published while he persisted with his law studies. In 1927 he chanced to hear a recording by Red Nichols of one of his tunes, 'Washboard Blues' (lyrics later added by Fred B. Callahan). This convinced Carmichael that he should quit law school and make a career in music. Also in 1927 he composed the tune which, with lyrics later added by Mitchell Parish, became his biggest seller and one of the most recorded songs of all time: 'Stardust'. In New York from 1929, the year 'Stardust' was published, Carmichael mixed with the jazz community, playing piano, singing and simply hanging out. For their part, the musicians, who included Louis Armstrong, Red Allen, Benny Goodman, Beiderbecke, Bud Freeman, Red Norvo, Glenn Miller, Joe Venuti, Gene Krupa, Tommy and Jimmy Dorsey, Pee Wee Russell, Jack Teagarden and many others, were happy to have him around and they recorded several of his compositions including 'Rockin' Chair', 'Georgia On My Mind' (lyrics by Stuart Gorrell), 'Lazy River' (with Sidney Arodin) and 'Lazybones' (lyrics by Johnny Mercer). By 1933, with Beiderbecke dead, Carmichael's interest in jazz waned although he never lost his affection for the music's early form and its performers. He began to concentrate on songwriting, redirecting his musical thought towards the mainstream of popular songs. In the mid-to-late 30s he collaborated with several lyricists on such songs as 'Little Old Lady', 'Small Fry' (lyrics by Frank Loesser), 'Two Sleepy People' (Loesser), 'Heart And Soul' (Loesser), 'I Get Along Without You Very Well', 'One Morning In May' (Parish), 'Blue Orchids', 'The Nearness Of You' (Ned Washington), 'Baltimore Oriole' (Paul Francis Webster) and another collaboration with Mercer which became a milestone in popular song, 'Skylark'. Some of the foregoing were written for the musical theatre, but many resulted from a stint in Hollywood, where he was a staff songwriter with Paramount. In the 40s Carmichael's involvement in films expanded to include acting roles on *To Have And Have Not* (1944), *Johnny Angel* (1945), *The Best Years Of Our Lives* (1946) and *Young Man With A Horn* (1950). He also published his memoirs, *The Stardust Road* (followed in 1965 by a second volume, *Sometimes I Wonder*). Songs he wrote in the 40s included 'Ole Buttermilk Sky' (with Jack Brooks), 'Doctor, Lawyer, Indian Chief' (lyrics by Webster), 'Memphis In June' (Webster) and 'Ivy'. In the 50s Carmichael's compositions included 'In The Cool, Cool, Cool Of The Evening' (Johnny Mercer), 'Winter Moon' (Harold Adamson) and 'My Resistance Is Low' (Adamson). Shifts in musical tastes gently shunted Carmichael onto the sidelines of contemporary popular music in the 60s and after the failure of two orchestral works, 'Brown County In Autumn' and 'Johnny Appleseed', he never resumed his role as an active composer. Nevertheless, his place as a major contributor to the Great American Song Book had long since become permanent. As a singer, Carmichael's intonation was uncertain and his vocal range decidedly limited (he referred to his frequently off-key voice as 'flatsy through the nose'). Nevertheless, as albums of his performances show, he sang with engaging simplicity and a delightful rhythmic gaiety. Carmichael spent the 70s in contented retirement, playing golf near his Palm Springs home. He died on 27 December 1981.

Albums: all as performer *Hoagy Sings Carmichael* (1956). Compilations: with Curtis Hitch *1923-28* (1979), *Hoagy* (1982), *16 Classic Tracks* (1982), *Ballads For Dancing* (1986), *1944-45 V-Discs* (1988), *The Hoagy Carmichael Songbook* (1988), *The Classic Hoagy Carmichael* (1989).

Further reading: *The Stardust Road*, Hoagy Carmichael. *Sometimes I Wonder: The Story Of Hoagy Carmichael*, Hoagy Carmichael with Stephen Longstreet.

Caron, Leslie

b. 1 July 1931, Paris, France. An elegant, captivating actress and dancer, Caron's mother was Margaret Petit, American ballet dancer, and her father, Claude Caron was a wealthy chemist with his own pharmacy in Paris. That is until France was occupied during World War II when the Caron family, like so many others, lost their fortune. Even so, Leslie Caron took ballet lessons, and had a ballet called *La Recontre* written especially for her. She was 17 and dancing professionally with the Ballet des Champs Elysées when she was seen by Gene Kelly who returned to Paris a year later to test her for the film *An American In Paris*. She accepted the ingenue role opposite him in Vincente Minnelli's charming film which won six Academy Awards, including one for best picture, following its release in 1951. She followed her enchanting performance in that film with others equally appealing in *Lili*, *The Glass Slipper*, *Daddy Long Legs*, and *Gigi* (1958). By the time she made the latter multi-Oscar winner, Caron was 27 and a mother, but she still managed to retain her fresh, gamin image. After her first marriage was dissolved in 1954, she married the British stage director Peter Hall two years later. He discouraged her from acting, although, having developed into a serious actress on the stage and screen in between her musical films, she did manage to do some work, including Jean Giraudoux's play *Ondine* for the RSC in 1961. A romantic relationship with the actor Warren Beatty precipitated her divorce from Hall in 1965, and she and Beatty lived together in the USA for two years. In 1969 she married the American producer Michael Laughlin who was six years her junior. During the 60s she returned to films, and although there were no more musicals among them, she was acclaimed for her dramatic performance in *The L-Shaped Room* (1962), and she and Cary Grant made an amusing couple in *Father Goose* (1964). Her most recent film to date is *Damage* with Jeremy Irons. She lives in Paris and New York, and continues to perform on stage, sometimes in plays she has written herself. In 1991 she learnt German so that she could play the role of the fading ballerina Grushinskaya in a stage production of the musical *Grand Hotel*. Two years later she opened her own restaurant in the Burgundy town of Villeneuve, having painstakingly converted a group of dilapidated 13th century houses over a period of five years.

Carousel

It took more than 10 years for Richard Rodgers and Oscar Hammerstein II's second musical to transfer from Broadway to Hollywood in 1956, but the wait was more than worthwhile. The story, with its inherent dark undertones, was always going to be tricky to film, but Henry Ephron and his wife Phoebe wrote a fine screenplay. It was based on the original stage libretto, which itself had been adapted from Ferenc Molnar's play *Liliom*. It was set in Maine, New England in 1873, and told of the tragic love affair between carousel barker Billy Bigelow (Gordon MacRae) and mill worker Julie Jordan (Shirley Jones). Out of work, and desperate to earn enough money to support his pregnant wife, Billy is persuaded by sly

Jigger Craigin (Cameron Mitchell) to take part in a robbery which goes awry. He is killed in the ensuing scuffle when he falls on his own knife. Fifteen years later he is allowed to return to earth for just one day so that he can make his peace with his lovely teenage daughter. An admirable supporting cast included Barbara Ruick and Robert Rounseville as the delightful Carrie Pipperidge and Enoch Snow, Claramae Turner, Susan Luckey, Audrey Christie, Gene Lockhart, and Jacques d'Amboise. The classic score remained more or less intact, from the majestic 'Carousel Waltz' through to the inspirational 'You'll Never Walk Alone'. Along the way there other memorable numbers such as 'You're A Queer One, Julie Jordan', 'If I Loved You', 'Mr. Snow', 'June Is Bustin' Out All Over', 'When The Children Are Asleep', 'Soliloquy', 'Stonecutters Cut It On Stone', 'What's The Use Of Wond'rin'?', and 'A Real Nice Clambake'. Roger Alexander and the legendary Agnes de Mille staged the dances, and the film, which was produced by Henry Ephron for 20th Century-Fox, was photographed by Charles Clarke in DeLuxe Color and CinemaScope. The director was Henry King. Frank Sinatra was the original choice to play Billy Bigelow but he withdrew soon after filming began. However, he did record an impressive version of 'Soliloquy' which stretched to both sides of a 12-inch 78 rpm record.

Castle, Vernon And Irene

Vernon Castle Blythe (b. Vernon Blyth, 1887, England, d. 1918) and Irene Foote (b. 1893, d. 1969) were the leading dance team pre-World War I. Influential as dancers and trend-setters in their way of life, fashions and coiffures. They were responsible for bringing an air of spontaneity to formal dancing (pre-empting the 'roaring 20s' 15 years early, in fact). Vernon was on Broadway in his teens and appeared in Victor Herbert's *Old Dutch*, where nine-year-old Helen Hayes made her debut. He and Irene met and teamed up in 1911 and had their first big success in Paris the following year, introducing various dancers including the Bunny Hug, Grizzly Bear, Turkey Trot, Maxixe, Fox Trot and the One-Step, later rechristened the Castle Walk. In 1914 alone they earned $31,000 on one-night-stands; starred on Broadway in *Sunshine Girl* and Irving Berlin's *Watch Your Step*; opened their own Sans Souci nightclub in Manhatten's Times Square, plus a chain of Castle House dance studios; and started work on their only joint film appearance, *The Whirl Of Life*. When Vernon, an Englishman, volunteered for the Royal Canadian Air Force, Irene co-starred with Vivienne Segal on Broadway in *Miss 1917* and appeared in several films, including *Patria* (1917), *The Hillcrest Mystery* (1918), *The Invisible Bond* (1919), *Broadway Bride* (1921 and *No Trespassing* (1922). With a fine combat record Vernon was promoted to Captain,

returned as an instructor, but was then killed in a training accident in Texas in 1918. Irene went into vaudeville but retired in the 30s, returning to create another dance, The World's Fair Hop, at the New York World's Fair in 1939. The Castles had been a great influence on a young Fred Astaire, so it was only logical that he, with Ginger Rogers, should recreate their lives in *The Story Of Vernon And Irene Castle* (1939). Irene, now Mrs McLaughlin, an early animal rights campaigner, finally retired to her pet sanctuary, Orphans Of The Storm, in Lake Forest, Illinois, where she died in 1969.

Cathcart, Dick

b. 6 November 1924, Michigan City, Indiana, USA, d. 8 November 1993. A fine trumpeter, his first major band appearance was with Ray McKinley. He later played in bands in the US Army during World War II and after the war was with Bob Crosby before a spell in the Hollywood studios. Among the film soundtracks on which he can be heard are *Dragnet* (1954), *Battle Stations* (1955), *Nightmare* (1956), in which he dubbed for the on-screen Billy May who was more than capable of blowing his own trumpet, and *The Five Pennies* (1959). Cathcart played in other name bands in the late 40s and 50s but became best known, by sound if not by name, when he played trumpet for the leading character in a 1952 USA radio series entitled *Pete Kelly's Blues*. When the programme also became a feature film in 1955 and transferred to television later in the decade, Cathcart again ghosted for the star (Jack Webb in the film, William Reynolds on television), although he also appeared on-camera in the small screen version. Cathcart made a series of successful small group jazz albums, not surprisingly taking the sound marketing step of naming his band 'Pete Kelly's Big Seven'. Apart from playing trumpet with a bell-like tone, Cathcart also sang; it was in this capacity that he was most active in the 60s and 70s. By the 80s he was back on jazz stages, playing trumpet as well as ever.

Selected albums: *Pete Kelly At Home* (1956), *Bix MCMLIX* (1959).

Champagne Charlie

Released by Ealing Studios in 1944, this film was set in the English musical halls of the 1860, and was packed full of traditional songs as well as specially composed items. The screenplay, by Austin Melford, Angus MacPhail, and John Dighton, concerns the rivalry between two of the most popular singers of the time, George Leybourne (Tommy Trinder) and the Great Vance (Stanley Holloway). Before they finally make their peace with each other they become involved in an attempted duel, and spectacular battle of drinking songs. The latter included 'Rum' and 'Old Ale', (both Ernest Irving-Frank Eyton), 'Little Drop Of Gin', 'Burgundy Claret And Port', 'Brandy And

Champagne Charlie (Tommy Trinder)

Seltzer Boys', 'Sherry Wine' (Billy Mayerl-Frank Eyton), and, of course, 'Champagne Charlie' (Alfred Lee-George Leybourne). Among the other featured numbers were 'Don't Bring Shame', 'It 'Im On The Boko', and 'Not In Front Of Baby' (Irving-Eyton), 'Arf Of Arf And Arf' (Una Bart), 'Norma' (Bellini-Ernest Irving), 'Perfection Polka' (J.H. White-Irving), 'Come On Algeron' (Lord Berners-T.E.B. Clark-Diana Morgan), 'Strolling In The Park' (Mayerl-Eyton), 'Polka' (Berners), 'Concerto' (Weber), 'Man On The Flying Trapeze', (Lee-Leybourne), 'By And By' (Noel Gay-Eyton), 'EE! But It's A Grand And Healthy Life' (George Formby-Harry Gifford-Frederick E. Cliffe), and 'Hunting After Dark' (Mayerl-Clarke-Morgan). However, it is not just the songs that make this film so appealing. It also had a fine supporting cast, which included Betty Warren, Austin Trevor, Jean Kent, Guy Middleton, Frederick Piper, Harry Fowler, Robert Wyndham, and Peter de Greef, and director Alberto Cavalacanti's sympathetic and skilful recreation of the period atmosphere was outstanding.

Champion, Gower

b. 22 June 1920, Geneva, Illinois, USA, d. 25 August 1980, New York City, New York, USA. One of the most distinguished and influential directors and choreographers in the American musical theatre. Champion was brought up in Los Angeles and took dancing lessons from an early age. When he was 15, he and his friend, Jeanne Tyler, toured nightclubs as 'Gower and Jeanne America's youngest dance team'. After serving in the US Coast Guard during World War II, Champion found another dance partner, Marge Belcher, and they were married in 1947. In the 50s they appeared together on numerous television variety programmes and in their own situation comedy, *The Marge And Gower Champion Show*. They also made several film musicals including *Mr. Music, Lovely To Look At, Give A Girl A Break, Jupiter's Darling, Three For The Show*, and the autobiographical *Everything I Have Is Yours*. Their exuberant dancing to 'I Might Fall Back On You' and 'Life Upon The Wicked Stage' were two of the highlights of the 1951 remake of *Show Boat* which starred Howard Keel and Kathryn Grayson. During the late 30s and 40s Champion worked on Broadway as a solo dancer and choreographer. In 1948 he began to direct as well, and won a Tony Award for his staging of the musical *Lend An Ear*, the show which introduced Carol Channing to New York theatre audiences. From then on he choreographed and directed a mixture of smash hits and dismal flops in a list which included *Three For Tonight, Bye By Birdie, Carnival, Hello, Dolly!, I Do! I Do!, The Happy Time, Sugar, Irene, Mack And Mabel* (1974), and *Rockabye Hamlet* (1976). They earned him another three Tonys and New York Critics and Donaldson Awards. After some years away from the

Broadway he returned (uncredited) to 'doctor' *The Act* (1977), but could do nothing to prevent *A Broadway Musical* (1978) folding after only one night. He finished with a smash-hit though, when he choreographed and directed a 1980 stage adaptation of the movie classic *42nd Street*. During the show's tryout in Washington Champion learnt that he had a rare form of blood cancer, and after the first curtain call on the New York opening night, producer David Merrick told the cast and the audience that Gower Champion had died that afternoon.

Charisse, Cyd

b. Tulla Ellice Finklea, 8 March 1923, Amarillo, Texas, USA. An elegant, long-legged dancer who appeared in several outstanding film musicals of the 40s and 50s. She took ballet classes from an early age, and was enrolled in the renowned Fanchon and Marco Dance Studio in Hollywood at the age of 12. One of the teachers there was Frenchman Nico Charisse, and four years later, during which time she performed at intervals with the famed Ballet Russes, they were married. Her connections with the Ballet Russes gained Charisse a part in the Columbia film *Something To Shout About* (1943), which led to a contract with MGM. One of the studio's top producers, Arthur Freed, is said to have been responsible for changing her name to Cyd (she had been known as Sid by her friends since childhood). During the late 40s and early 50s she made effective contributions to several straight films, and a number of musicals which included *Ziegfeld Follies, The Harvey Girls, Till The Clouds Roll By, Fiesta* (in which Ricardo Montalban made his debut), *The Unfinished Dance, On An Island With You, Words And Music, The Kissing Bandit, Singin' In The Rain* (with Gene Kelly), and *Easy To Love* (1953). Also in 1953 she had what was arguably her best role in *The Band Wagon* with Fred Astaire and Jack Buchanan. By this time she was at her peak both as an actress and a dancer, and her excellent work during the remaining years of the 50s included *Brigadoon, It's Always Fair Weather* and *Invitation To The Dance*, (all with Kelly), *Meet Me In Las Vegas* (with Dan Dailey), and *Silk Stockings* (with Astaire). The latter was her last musical although she did appear in the occasional dance sequence in films such as *Black Tights* (1960) and *The Silencers* (1966). Her screen work since then has been confined to guest appearances and television features. After the breakup of her first marriage in the early 40s, she married the popular singer Tony Martin in 1948, and he travelled with her to London in 1986 when she played the role of Lady Hadwell in a new production of David Heneker's musical *Charlie Girl*. Even then, when she was in her 60s, those famous legs were still the main subject of discussion. Impresario Harold Fielding said: 'They are her trademark, so we're going to insure them for a million, maybe two.' A

substantial sum of money must also have changed hands in 1988 when Cyd Charisse agreed to appear in a video to promote a pop single by the two-man group the Blue Mercedes. Their record of 'I Want To Be Your Property' reached the top of the US dance charts. In rather a different vein, four years later Miss Charisse made her Broadway debut when she took over the role of fading ballerina Grushinskaya in the hit musical *Grand Hotel*. Asked about her age, which has always been a subject of some dispute (born 1921 or 1923), she would only say: 'Oh, I feel young!'
Further reading: *The Two Of Us*, Tony Martin and Cyd Charisse.

Charles Lloyd - Journey Within
Tenor saxophonist Charles Lloyd formed a quartet in 1965 and after various personnel changes settled in with Keith Jarrett, Ron McClure and Jack DeJohnette. Aggressively marketed, the group enjoyed huge success in jazz-rock circles despite having its roots in bop and the blues. This documentary made in 1968 captures the band at the height of its popularity.

Chevalier, Maurice
b. Maurice Auguste Chevalier, 12 September 1888, Menilmontant, nr. Paris, France, d. 1 January 1972, Paris, France. The ninth of 10 children eventually reduced by death to three males, Chevalier's early ambitions to become an acrobat were thwarted by injury. He toured local cafes and music halls as a singer and broad comedian, and later performed at the Eldorado in Paris. His big break came when he signed a three-year contract with the Folies Bergere, and worked with his idol, Mistinguett. In 1913 he was drafted into the French Army, was captured, and sent to Alten Grabow prisoner-of-war camp where he learnt to speak English. After the war he developed a more sophisticated act, wearing a tuxedo for his solo spot, and the straw boater which soon became his trademark. In between the triumphs at the Folies Bergere, Casino de Paris and the Empire in Paris, Chevalier suffered a serious mental breakdown. When he recovered he went to England in 1927 and appeared in the revue *White Birds*. Two years later he made his first Hollywood film, *Innocents Of Paris*, in which he introduced 'Louise', a song forever associated with him ('every little breeze seems to whisper Louise'). He also sang his famous French version of 'Yes, We Have No Bananas'. He then starred in several films, directed by Ernst Lubitsch including Lubitsch's first talkie, *The Love Parade* (1929). It was also the first of four films that Chevalier made with Jeanette MacDonald. Following *The Smiling Lieutenant* (1931) with Claudette Colbert, and *One Hour With You* (1932), Chevalier made what has been described as 'one of the great films of the decade'. *Love Me Tonight*, directed by Rouben Mamoulian, and co-starring Jeanette MacDonald, was innovative in several ways, especially in its integration of plot and music. It also contained 'Mimi', another special Chevalier song. After Paramount, Chevalier made *The Merry Widow* (1934, MGM) and *Follies Bergère* (1935, United Artists) in 1935 before returning to France, as one of the world's leading entertainers. During World War II Chevalier lived mostly in seclusion, emerging twice to perform in response to German demands, once in exchange for the release of 10 French prisoners. Rumours and accusations of collaboration with the enemy were emphatically disproved. After the war he projected a more mature image in the film *Le Silence Est D'or* (*Man About Town* 1947) directed by René Clair, which won the Grand Prize at the Brussels Film Festival. During the same period, Chevalier toured Europe and the USA with his 'one man show'. Semi-retired during the early 50s, he returned to Hollywood to play a series of character roles in films such as *Love In The Afternoon* (1957), *Gigi* (1958), *Can-Can* (1959), *Fanny* (1961), *In Search Of The Castaways* (1962) and *I'd Rather Be Rich* (1964). *Gigi* was one of the highlights of Chevalier's career. His idiosyncratic versions of 'Thank Heaven For Little Girls', 'I'm Glad I'm Not Young Any More', and a duet with Hermione Gingold, 'I Remember It Well', charmed the Academy of MPAS into awarding *Gigi* the Oscar for Best Picture. At the age of 70, Chevalier received a special Academy Award for his contribution to the world of entertainment for over half a century. During the 60s he appeared frequently on US television with his own 'specials' such as *The World Of Maurice Chevalier*, and travelled widely with his 'one man show' until 1968, when, from the stage of the Theatre des Champs Elysees in Paris, he announced his retirement. His honours included the Croix de Guerre (1917), the Belgian Order of Leopold (1943), the Legion d'Honneur (1938) and the Order Merite National (1964).
Compilations: *Sings* (1969), *The World Of Maurice Chevalier* (1971), *You Brought A New Kind Of Love To Me* (1979), *Encore Maurice* (1982), *Bonjour D'Amour* (1982), *Ma Pomme* (1982), *The Golden Age Of Maurice Chevalier* (1984), *Brava Maurice* (1986), *The Maurice Chevalier Collection* (1987), *Maurice Chevalier's Paris* (1988, CD only).
Further reading: *The Man In The Straw Hat*, Maurice Chevalier. *With Love*, Maurice Chevalier. *I Remember It Well*, Maurice Chevalier.

Chitty Chitty Bang Bang
Made in Britain, this highly successful, but critically derided children's musical is about a more than usually eccentric inventor, Caractacus Potts (Dick Van Dyke), whose crowning achievement is a flying car. This airy form of transportation conveys his two children, Jemina and Jeremy (Heather Ripley and Adrian Hall),

and their mutual friend, Truly Scrumptious (Sally Ann Howes), on their mission to bring down the authoritarian regime of a country that does not like children. On their travels they are surrounded by a host of familiar and much-loved characters from UK show business, including Lionel Jeffries, Benny Hill, Anna Quayle, Robert Helpmann, James Robertson Justice, Max Wall, Bernard Spear, Davy Kaye, Barbara Windsor, Stanley Unwin, Victor Maddern, Max Bacon, Richard Wattis, and Peter Arne. Gert Frobe, the German actor who made such as impact in Goldfinger a few years earlier, was in it too. Richard M. Sherman and Robert B. Sherman's score was nothing special, and included 'Lovely Lonely Man', 'Hushabye Mountain', 'Toot Sweet', 'Truly Scrumptious', 'Posh!', 'Chu-Chi Face', and the title song. One of the most appealing moments comes when Van Dyke gets caught up with a folk dance group at a fairground. The ensuing number, 'The 'Ole Bamboo', which involves the dextrous use of white bowler hats and lengthy individual poles, is a delight. Comparisons with the blockbuster *Mary Poppins* were inevitable, especially as Dick Van Dyke was in it, and Sally Ann Howes' 'terribly British' image is similar to that of Julie Andrews. However, this film is just not in that class. Roald Dahl and Ken Hughes' sugary screenplay was based on a novel by Ian Fleming, and Hughes also directed. The choreographers were March Breaux and DeeDee Wood, and the film was produced by Albert R. Broccoli and released by United Artists.

Chorus Line, A

Richard Attenborough was the controversial choice of director to attempt the transfer of the longest-running (to date) Broadway production from stage to screen in 1985. General opinion seemed to be that the outcome was unsatisfactory, but then the task was an extremely difficult one. Even Michael Bennett, who conceived the show and was its director-choreographer, declined 'to spend three more years of his life' on a film version. Screenwriter Arnold Shulman adapted the original story of a group of chorus dancers auditioning on a bare stage in an empty theatre for the show's volatile director, Zach (Michael Douglas). One by one they step forward to push their claims to be one of the lucky final eight, revealing more about themselves than they probably realise. One of them, Cassie (Alyson Reed), is an ex-girlfriend of Zach's who is trying to make a comeback as a dancer - despite his opposition. The rest of the hopefuls included Gregg Burke, Cameron English, Vicki Frederick, Audrey Landers, Nicole Fosse, and Janet Jones. Most of Marvin Hamlisch and Edward Kleban's original numbers were retained, and two added, in a score which consisted of 'I Hope I Get It', 'I Can Do That', 'Surprise, Surprise', 'At The Ballet', 'Nothing', 'Dance: Ten, Looks: Three', 'Let Me Dance For

You', 'One', and 'What I Did For Love'. Jeffrey Hornaday created the 'lacklustre' choreography and the film was produced by Embassy and Polygram in Technicolor and Panavision.

Clark, Petula

b. 15 November 1932, Epsom, Surrey, England. Her Welsh mother, a soprano, taught Petula to sing, which enabled her to commence a stage career at the age of seven and in broadcasting two years later. Her youthful image and crystal-clear enunciation were ideal for radio and by 1943, she had her own programme with the accent on wartime, morale-building songs. She made her first film, *Medal For The General*, in 1944 and then signed for the J. Arthur Rank Organization appearing in over 20 feature films, including the *Huggett* series, alongside other young hopefuls such as Anthony Newley and Alec Guinness. By 1949 she was recording, and throughout the 50s had several hits including 'The Little Shoemaker', 'Suddenly There's A Valley' 'With All My Heart' and 'Alone'. Around this period, Petula's success in France led to many concert appearances in Paris and recording, in French, for the Vogue label. Eventually, in 1959, at the age of 27 and unhappy with the British audiences' reluctance to see her as anything but a sweet adolescent, she moved to France, where she married Vogue's PR representative, Cluade Wolff. At the Olympia Theatre, Paris in 1960 she introduced her new sound, retaining the ultra-clear vocals, but adding to them electronic effects and a hefty beat. Almost immediately her career took off. She had a massive hit with 'Ya-Ya Twist', for which she received the Grand Prix du Disque, and by 1962 was France's favourite female vocalist, ahead even of the legendary Edith Piaf. Meanwhile, in Britain, Petula's versions of 'Romeo', 'My Friend The Sea' and 'Sailor', were chasing Elvis Presley up the charts. Her international breakthrough began in 1964 when the British songwriter/arranger Tony Hatch presented Petula with 'Downtown'. It became a big hit in western Europe, and a year later climbed to the top of the US charts, clinching her popularity in a country where she was previously unknown. The record sold over three million copies worldwide and gained a Grammy Award in the USA as the best rock 'n' roll single. Petula's subsequent recordings of other Hatch songs, written sometimes with his lyricist wife, Jackie Trent, including 'Don't Sleep In The Subway', 'The Other Man's Grass', 'I Couldn't Live Without Your Love', 'My Love', and 'I Know A Place' all made the US Top 10. Her recording of 'This Is My Song', written by Charles Chaplin for the Marlon Brando/Sophia Loren epic, *A Countess From Hong Kong* (1967) reached number 1 in the UK charts. Tours of the USA and television guest shots followed. As well as hosting her own BBC television series, she was given her own US NBC television special *Petula*, in 1968. This was marred by the programme sponsor's request that a sequence in which she touched the arm of black guest Harry Belafonte, should be removed in deference to the southern States. The show was eventually transmitted complete. That same year Petula revived her film career when she appeared as Sharon, the 'Glocca Morra' girl in E.Y. 'Yip' Harburg and Burton Lane's *Finian's Rainbow*, co-starring with Fred Astaire and Tommy Steele. While the film was generally regarded as too old fashioned for 60s audiences, Petula's performance, with just a touch of the blarney, was well received, as was her partnership with Peter O'Toole in MGM's 1969 re-make of *Goodbye, Mr. Chips*, marking her 30 years in show business. She was, by now, not only a major recording star, but an international personality, able to play all over the world, in cabaret and concerts. Between 1981 and 1982 she played the part of Maria in the London revival of Richard Rodgers/Oscar Hammerstein II's *The Sound Of Music*. It ran for 14 months, and was a great personal success. In 1989 PYS Records issued a 'radically remixed' version of her 60s hit, 'Downtown', with the original vocal accompanied by 'acid house' backing. It went to number 10 in the UK chart. To date she has sold over 30 million records worldwide and has been awarded more gold discs than any other British female singer. From early in her career she has written songs, sometimes under the pseudonym of Al Grant. So it was especially pleasing for Clark, in 1990, to write the music, and appear in the London West End musical, *Someone Like You*. The show opened in March to mixed reviews, and had only a brief run. In 1992, Clark made her first concert tour of the UK for 10 years.

Albums: *Petula Clark Sings* (1956), *A Date With Pet* (1956), *You Are My Lucky Star* (1957), *Pet Clark* (1959), *Petula Clark In Hollywood* (1959), *In Other Words* (1962), *Petula* (1962), *Les James Dean* (1962), *Downtown* (1964), *I Know A Place* (1965), *The World's Greatest International Hits!* (1965), *The New Petula Clark Album* (1965), *Uptown With Petula Clark* (1965), *In Love* (1965), *Petula '65* (1965), *My Love* (1966), *Petula '66* (1966), *My Love* (1966), *Hello Paris, Vol. I* (1966), *Hello Paris, Vol. II* (1966), *Petula Clark Sings For Everybody* (1966), *I Couldn't Live Without Your Love* (1966), *Hit Parade* (1967), *Colour My World/Who Am I?* (1967), *These Are My Songs* (1967), *The Other Man's Grass Is Always Greener* (1968), *Petula* (1968), *Portrait Of Petula* (1969), *Just Pet* (1969), *Memphis* (1970), *The Song Of My Life* (1971), *Wonderland Of Sound* (1971), *Today* (1971), *Petula '71* (1971), *Warm And Tender* (1971), *Live At The Royal Albert Hall* (1972), *Now* (1972), *Live In London* (1974), *Come On Home* (1974), *C'est Le Befrain De Ma Vie* (1975), *La Chanson De Marie-Madeleine* (1975), *I'm The Woman You Need* (1975), *Just Petula* (1975), *Noel* (1975), *Beautiful Sounds* (1976), *Destiny* (1978), *An Hour In Concert With Petula*

Clark (1983). Compilations: *Petula's Greatest Hits, Volume 1* (1968), *Petula Clark's 20 All Time Greatest* (1977), *Spotlight On Petula Clark* (1980), *100 Minutes Of Petula Clark* (1982), *Early Years* (1986), *The Hit Singles Collection* (1987), *My Greatest* (1989), *Downtown* (1989), *Treasures Vol. 1* (1992), *Jumble Sale: Rarities And Obscurities 1959-64*, 2 CD-set (1992).

Clooney, Rosemary

b. 23 May 1928, Maysville, Kentucky, USA. While very young, Rosemary and her sister Betty sang at political rallies in support of their paternal grandfather. When Rosemary was 13 the Clooney children moved to Cincinnati, Ohio and appeared on radio station WLW. In 1945 they auditioned successfully for tenor saxophonist Tony Pastor and joined his band as featured vocalists, travelling the country doing mainly one-night stands. Rosemary made her first solo record in 1946 with 'I'm Sorry I Didn't Say I'm Sorry When I Made You Cry Last Night'. After about three years of touring Betty quit, and Rosemary stayed on as a soloist with the band. She signed for Columbia Records in 1950 and had some success with children's songs such as 'Me And My Teddy Bear' and 'Little Johnny Chickadee' before coming under the influence of A&R manager Mitch Miller who had a penchant for folksy, novelty dialect songs. In 1951 Clooney's warm, husky melodious voice registered well on minor hits, 'You're Just In Love', a duet with Guy Mitchell, and 'Beautiful Brown Eyes'. Later that year she topped the US chart with 'Come On-My House', from the off-Broadway musical, 'The Son', with a catchy harpsichord accompaniment by Stan Freeman. During the next four years Clooney had a string of US hits including 'Tenderly', which became her theme tune, 'Half As Much' (number 1), 'Botcha-Me', 'Too Old To Cut The Mustard' (a duet with Marlene Dietrich), 'The Night Before Christmas Song' (with Gene Autrey), 'Hey There' and 'This Ole House' (both number 1 hits), and 'Mambo Italiano'. UK hits included 'Man', with the b-side, 'Woman', sung by her husband, actor/producer/director Jose Ferrer, and the novelty, 'Where Will The Dimple Be'. Her last singles hit was 'Mangos', in 1957. Her own US television series regularly featured close harmony vocal group the Hi-Lo's, leading to their communal album *Ring Around Rosie*. Clooney's film career started in 1953 with *The Stars Are Singing* and was followed by three films the next year, *Here Come The Girls* with Bob Hope, *Red Garters* (1954) with Guy Mitchell and the Sigmund Romberg bio-pic, *Deep In My Heart* in which she sang 'Mr And Mrs' with Jose Ferrer. In the same year she teamed with Bing Crosby in *White Christmas*. Highly compatible, with friendly, easy-going styles, their professional association was to last until Crosby died, and included, in 1958, the highly regarded album *Fancy Meeting You Here*, a musical travelogue with special material by

Sammy Cahn and James Van Heusen, arranged and conducted by Billy May. Semi-retired in the 60s, her psychiatric problems were chronicled in her autobiography, *This For Remembrance*, later dramatized on television as *Escape From Madness*. Her more recent work has been jazz-based, including a series of tributes to the 'great' songwriters such as Harold Arlen, Cole Porter and Duke Ellington, released on the Concorde Jazz label. In 1991 Clooney gave an 'assured performance' in concert at Carnegie Hall, and duetted with her guest artist, Linda Ronstadt. Two years later she was still playing clubs in New York.

Albums: *Deep In My Heart* (1954, film soundtrack), *Hollywood's Best* (1955), *Blue Rose* (1956), *Clooney Times* (1957), with the Hi-Lo's *Ring A Round Rosie* (1957), *Swing Around Rosie* (1958), with Bing Crosby *Fancy Meeting You Here* (1958), *The Ferrers At Home* (1958), *Hymns From The Heart* (1959), *Rosemary Clooney Swings Softly* (1960), *A Touch Of Tobasco* (1960), *Clap Hands, Here Comes Rosie* (1960), *Rosie Solves The Swingin' Riddle* (1961), *Country Hits From The Past* (1963), *Love* (1963), *Thanks For Nothing* (1964), with Crosby *That Travelin' Two Beat* (1965), *Look My Way* (1976), *Nice To Be Around* (1977), *Here's To My Lady* (1979), *Rosemary Clooney Sings The Music Of Cole Porter* (1982), *Rosemary Clooney Sings Harold Arlen* (1983), *My Buddy* (1983), *Rosemary Clooney Sings The Music Of Irving Berlin* (1984), *Sings Ballads* (1985), *Our Favourite Things* (1986), *Mixed Emotions* (1986), *Rosemary Clooney Sings The Lyrics Of Johnny Mercer* (1987), *Rosemary Clooney Sings The Music Of Jimmy Van Heusen* (1987), *Show Tunes* (1989), *Everything's Coming Up Rosie* (1989), *Girl Singer* (1992). Compilations: *Rosie's Greatest Hits* (1957), *Rosemary Clooney Showcase Of Hits* (1959), *Greatest Hits* (1983), *The Best Of Rosemary Clooney* (1984), *The Rosemary Clooney Songbook* (1984).

Further reading: *This For Remembrance*, Rosemary Clooney.

Comden, Betty

b. 3 May 1915, New York City, New York, USA. After graduating with a degree in science, Comden strove to find work as an actress. During this period, the late 30s, she met Adolph Green who was also seeking work in the theatre. Unsuccessful in their attempts to find acting jobs, Comden and Green formed their own troupe, together with another struggling actress, Judy Holliday. In the absence of suitable material, Comden and Green began creating their own and discovered an ability to write librettos and lyrics. At first their success was only limited, but in the early 40s they were invited by a mutual friend, Leonard Bernstein, to work on the book and lyrics of a musical he planned to adapt from his ballet score, *Fancy Free*. The show, retitled *On The Town* (1944), was a huge success and Comden and Green never looked back. This show was followed by *Billion Dollar Baby* (1945, music by Morton Gould) and an assignment in Hollywood for the musical films *Good News* (1947), *The Barkleys Of Broadway* (1949), *On The Town* and *Take Me Out To The Ball Game* (both 1949). In the early 50s Comden and Green were back on Broadway, collaborating with Bernstein again, on *Wonderful Town* (1953), and with Jule Styne on several occasions, most notably with *Bells Are Ringing* (1956) in which the leading role was played by their former associate Judy Holliday. Throughout the 50s Comden and Green worked steadily on Broadway and in Hollywood. Among their films were *Singing In The Rain* (1952), for which they wrote the screenplay, incorporating the songs of Herb Nacio Brown and *The Band Wagon* (1953), again contributing the screenplay which was peppered with the songs of Arthur Schwartz and Howard Dietz. For *It's Always Fair Weather* (1955) they wrote screenplay and lyrics (music by André Previn) and later in the 50s and into the 60s wrote screenplays for *Auntie Mame* (1958) and *Bells Are Ringing* (1960), among others. In the late 50s they also performed their own two-person stage show. After writing the libretto for *Applause* (1970) they rested on their remarkable laurels but continued to make sporadic returns to the musical stage with *On The Twentieth Century* (1978) and *A Doll's Life* (1982), and occasional revivals of their personal-appearance show both on the stage and on television.

Coney Island

With her legs insured for astronomical sums, and that famous pin-up picture pinned on a million or more US (and UK) servicemen's bedside cupboard doors, Betty Grable was box office dynamite in films such as this one which was released by 20th Century-Fox in 1943. With her appeal, any showcase for her shapely song-and-dance talent could get away with the slightest of stories. In this case, George Seaton's screenplay was set at the turn-of-the-century and concerned the efforts of two pleasure park owners, played by George Montgomery and Cesar Romero, to boost their takings by having Miss Grable strut her gaudy stuff in front of their own particular audiences. However, the lady has loftier ambitions - for instance, on Broadway - and eventually, with a touch of class, makes it to the big time. The always amusing Charles Winninger and Phil Silvers were also in the film, along with Matt Briggs, Paul Hurst, Frank Orth, Carmen D'Antonio, Phyllis Kennedy, Hal K. Dawson, and Andrew Tombes. Grable's big number was Karl Hoschna and Otto Harbach's 'Cuddle Up A Little Closer', and the film was jam-packed with several other warm and wonderful songs such as 'Pretty Baby', (Egbert Van Alstyne-Gus Kahn-Tony Jackson), 'The Darktown Strutters' Ball' (Shelton Brooks), 'When Irish Eyes Are Smiling' (George Graff-Ernest Ball-Chauncey Olcott), 'Put Your Arms Around Me, Honey' (Albert Von Tilzer-Junie

McCree), 'Let Me Call You Sweetheart' (Beth Slater Whitson-Leo Friedman), and several by Ralph Rainger and Leo Robin, including 'Beautiful Coney Island', 'Lulu From Louisville', 'Take It From There', 'There's Danger In A Dance', 'Get The Money', and 'Old Demon Rum'. Hermes Pan staged the dances, and Walter Lang directed a typical Technicolor mélange of colourful song and dance. Betty Grable reprised her role in the 1950 remake which was entitled *Wabash Avenue*, along with co-stars Victor Mature, Phil Harris, James Barton, and Reginald Gardiner. Once again there were some good songs, including 'Wilhelmina', 'Baby, Won't You Say You Love Me?', and 'Walking Along With Billy', all by Mack Gordon and Josef Myrow.

Conti, Bill

b. 13 April 1942, Providence, Rhode Island, USA. A composer, conductor and musical director for television and films, Conti was taught to play the piano by his father from the age of seven, and later, after the family had moved to Miami, Florida, took up the bassoon. After leaving high school he studied composition at Louisiana State University, and played in its symphony orchestra, while also playing jazz in local nightspots to defray educational expenses. Subsequently, he gained honours at the Juilliard School Of Music, New York, including a master's degree. Influenced by his major professor at Juilliard, composer Hugo Weisgall, Conti and his wife moved to Italy in 1967. During his seven year stay, he broke into films, arranging, composing and conducting for productions such as *Juliette De Sade*, *Candidate Per Un Assassino (Candidate For Killing)*, *Liquid Subway*, and *Blume In Love* (1973). On his return to the USA in 1974, he settled in California, and, aided by established film composer Lionel Newman, began to make his name all over again. Success was just around the corner, for, after scoring *Harry And Tonto*; *Next Stop, Greenwich Village*, and the documentary, *Pacific Challenge*, Conti hit the big time with his music for *Rocky* (1976). The soundtrack album went platinum, and one of the numbers, 'Gonna Fly Now' (lyric by Carol Connors and Ayn Robbins), was nominated for an Oscar and, in an instrumental version by Conti, topped the US singles chart. He also scored the *Rocky* sequels, II, III (gold album), and V (1990). The composer's projects in the late 70s included two more Stallone vehicles, *F.I.S.T*; and *Paradise Alley*; plus others, such as *Citizens' Band (Handle With Care)*, *An Unmarried Woman*, *The Big Fix*, *A Man, A Woman, And A Bank*, *Goldengirl*, and *The Seduction Of Joe Tynan*. In 1981 Conti provided the score for 'one of the best' James Bond movies, *For Your Eyes Only*, starring Roger Moore. UK expatriate, Sheena Easton sang Conti's title song (written with Mick Leeson), and her record made the US Top 5. It gained Conti his second Oscar nomination and, two years later, he finally won an Academy Award for his music to *The Right Stuff*, 'an off-beat story about America's space programme'. Throughout the rest of the 80s, and early 90s, Conti's music continued to pour out, for films such as *Unfaithfully Yours*, *Mass Appeal*, *The Karate Kid* and its two sequels; *The Bear*, *Nomads* (his first all-electronic score), *Gotcha*, *FIX*, *Masters Of The Universe*, *Baby Boom*, *Broadcast News*, *Lean On Me*, *The Fourth War*, *Year Of The Gun*, *Necessary Roughness*, *Blood In Blood Out*, *The Adventures Of Huck Finn*, and *Rookie Of The Year* (1993). Conti by no means concentrated on composing for the big screen - his television credits are formidable. He gained two Emmys as 'creative concept and composer' for the New York City Marathon (1990), and nominations for his music for the popular mini-series *North And South II* (1985). His themes for the small screen include *Dallas*, *Falcon Crest*, *Lifestyles Of The Rich And Famous*, *Cagney And Lacey*, *The Colbys*, *O'Hara*, *Our World*, and *Mariah*; he also composed the complete scores for several television movies. On several occasions, between 1977 and 1993, Conti served as arranger and musical director for the Academy Awards ceremony. In 1983 he had to relinquish the baton, and go on stage to receive the Oscar for his work on *The Right Stuff*.

Cotton Club, The

Made in 1984 this was one of the most expensive films ever produced (reputedly $47 million), it is hard to see just where the money went. Producer Robert Evans and writer-director Francis Ford Coppola lavished everything except sensitivity and foresight on the project. In retrospect, one of their best decisions was to hire Bob Wilber as arranger for the jazz sequences. Given the film's premise - the gangsters, molls and, almost an afterthought, entertainers associated with Harlem's most celebrated uptown nightclub - it is hard to see how it could miss. Yet, somehow, it did. Up front dramatics surrounding a (white, of course!) trumpet player, Richard Gere, were inappropriate, so too were the jokey gangsters, Bob Hoskins and Fred Gwynne. Dancer Gregory Hines did his considerable best but only some aspects of the soundtrack can be treated with unreserved praise. Masterminded by Wilber (who was living and working in the UK at the time and commuted to Los Angeles every few weeks), the arrangements and sound he created for the club's resident orchestra, theoretically Duke Ellington's, were an extraordinary achievement as can be heard on soundtrack albums. Gere's on-screen cornet playing was ostensibly his own, although he was, at least, coached by Warren Vaché Jnr.

Court Jester, The

Regarded by many as the best film Danny Kaye ever made, this 1956 Paramount release is the one in which

The Cotton Club

he is perpetually puzzled as to the contents of the 'chalice from the palace' ('the pellet with the poison is in the vessel with the pestle'). The rest of this hilarious mediaeval story is just as complicated, with the red-headed clown getting mixed up with a gang of Robin Hood-style outlaws led by the Black Fox, inveigling himself into the English court of the evil King (Basil Rathbone), and assisting in the royal downfall. In less hectic moments he finds time to fall for the lovely Maid Jean played by Glynis Johns. She headed a particularly strong supporting cast which included Angela Lansbury, Cecil Parker, Mildred Natwick, Michael Pate, John Carradine, Robert Middleton, and Alan Napier. Danny Kaye's wife, Sylvia Fine, who wrote so many excellent songs for the comedian throughout his career, contributed one clever number 'The Maladjusted Jester', and collaborated with Sammy Cahn on the remaining 'They'll Never Outfox The Fox', 'Life Could Not Be Better', 'My Heart Knows A Love Song', and 'Baby, Let Me Take You Dreaming'. James Starbuck staged the dances and Ray June was responsible for the photography in Technicolor and VistaVision. The witty screenplay was written by producer-directors Norman Panama and Melvyn Frank, and just went to prove that, when Kaye was in the mood, and with material like this, he was unbeatable.

Courtneidge, Cicely

b. Esmeralda Cicely Courtneidge, 1 April 1893, Sydney, Australia. Her father, actor/producer/writer Robert Courtneidge was appearing in the operetta *Esmeralda* when she was born, hence the name. Back in Britain she trained for the stage and at the age of 10 appeared as Fairy Peaseblossom in *Midsummer Night's Dream*, followed by her father's production of *The Arcadians* in 1909. She made her first records in 1911, singing selections from the show in which she was appearing, *(The) Mousme*. Courtneidge married musical comedy star Jack Hulbert in 1914, and while he was engaged in World War I she toured the music halls as a male impersonator and somewhat *risqué* comedienne. After appearing in several shows together Courtneidge and Hulbert made their first big impact as a team in the 1925 revue *By The Way*, with music by Vivian Ellis. It ran for over 300 performances before transferring to New York. *Lido Lady*, in 1926, with a Richard Rodgers/Lorenz Hart score, and *Clowns In Clover*, which opened in 1927 and ran for two years, confirmed their enormous popularity in London's West End. By now, Hulbert was also writing and producing. The team split up temporarily, and while he was appearing with Sophie Tucker in the musical play *Follow A Star*, Courtneidge was considered to be at her best in the Vivian Ellis revue *Folly To Be Wise*. For most of the 30s

Courtneidge concentrated on making films such as *Ghost Train*, *Jack's The Boy*, *Aunt Sally*, *Soldiers Of The King*, *Me And Marlborough* and *Take My Tip*. She returned to the stage in 1937 in *Hide And Seek* and in the following year the Hulberts reunited for one of their biggest successes, *Under Your Hat*, yet again with music and lyrics by Vivian Ellis. It ran for over two years and was filmed in 1940. During World War II the team had substantial runs in *Full Swing* and their last show on the London stage together, *Something In The Air*, as well as undertaking extensive ENSA tours. After the war Courtneidge starred in *Your Excellency*, and *Under The Counter* in London and New York where it attracted extremely hostile reviews. In 1951 she undertook probably the best role of her career, playing Gay Davenport in the satirical backstage musical play, *Gay's The Word* by Ivor Novello and Alan Melville. It gave her several good songs including 'Guards Are On Parade', 'It's Bound To Be Right On The Night', and 'Vitality', a number that epitomized her stage persona throughout her long career. The show ran at the Saville Theatre for 504 performances, and was Novello's last - he died three weeks after the opening. Courtneidge's final West End show was *High Spirits*, in 1963, a musical version of Noel Coward's 1941 play *Blithe Spirit*. Its songs did not suit her as well as others she had introduced over the years such as 'The King's Horses', 'Home',

'There's Something About A Soldier', 'We'll All Go Riding On A Rainbow' and 'I Was Anything But Sentimental'. During the 60s and 70s she toured in plays and revues including, with Hulbert, the semi-autobiographical *Once More With Music*. She also made several more films including a critically-acclaimed character part in Bryan Forbes's *The L-Shaped Room* (1963), and cameos in *Those Magnificent Men In Their Flying Machines* (1965), *The Wrong Box* (1966) and *Not Now Darling* (1972). The latter was released when she was aged 80. In the same year she was created a Dame of the British Empire. Cicely Courtneidge died on 26 April 1980, two years after Hulbert. In 1986, Courtneidge's history reached a new generation when her 'Take Me Back To Dear Old Blighty' was used as the opening for the Smiths' album *The Queen Is Dead*. Further reading: *Cicely*, Cicely Courtneidge.

Cover Girl

Although Gene Kelly made an impressive debut in *For Me And My Gal* two years earlier, it is well recorded that he was by no means Columbia studio boss Harry Cohn's first choice to play the lead in this film which was released in 1944. However, his decision to borrow the rising star from MGM proved to be a winner. In Virginia Van Upp's screenplay, Kelly plays Danny McGuire, a performer who owns a nightclub in Brooklyn. The McGuire philosophy towards life,

Cover Girl

explains one of his chorus girls, is 'that you get to the top on your feet, not your face'. So, when Danny's girlfriend, Rusty Parker (Rita Hayworth), enters a *Vanity* magazine competition to become a cover girl, he feels hurt and betrayed, and even more so when she wins and the club is besieged by her new fans, with Kelly being pushed into the background. What Parker does not realise is that *Vanity's* ageing publisher (Otto Kruger) (who is ably assisted by Eve Arden) was once in love with her grandmother, a great music hall performer. However, he and his money could not tempt her away from her impoverished piano playing lover - just as many years later Parker eschews her own fame and fortune and returns to McGuire. Kruger remembers Parker's grandmother in flashback, with Hayworth playing both parts of Parker and her grandmother. While *Cover Girl* may not be quite as sophisticated as Kelly's later work at MGM, some of the musical sequences are very entertaining, and provide a foretaste of his innovative and inspired later work. Jerome Kern and Ira Gershwin's score contained the exquisite ballad 'Long Ago And Far Away' (Kelly), as well as 'Make Way For Tomorrow' (lyric: Gershwin-E.Y. 'Yip' Harburg), during which Hayworth, Kelly and Phil Silvers (as amusing as ever) dance through the streets of Brooklyn improvising dance with anything that comes to hand along the way. The film is also remembered for Kelly's 'alter-ego' dance as he tussles with both sides of his conscience. Walking home one night, confused and unhappy, he begins to argue with his reflection in a shop window. The reflection answers back and then jumps out of the window to join him for a frenetic dance. A clever and innovative sequence, it has Kelly and Stanley Donen's stamp on it, despite Val Raset and Seymour Felix being credited for the film's overall choreography. The other numbers included 'Sure Thing' (Hayworth), 'Put Me To The Test' (Hayworth-Kelly), and 'Who's Complaining?' (Silvers). Also in the cast were Lee Bowman, Jinx Falkenburg, Jess Barker, Leslie Brooks, Curt Bois, Thurston Hall, and Ed Brophy. Charles Victor was the director, and the film was photographed in Technicolor and produced by Arthur Schwartz.

Crimson Canary, The

Amongst the ingredients of *film noir* was jazz-inflected music as background to shady on-screen happenings. A low-budget, generally ineffective, and decidedly borderline entry for the genre, this 1945 film went one better by setting the plot in the jazz world. When a band singer is found beaten to death with a trumpet ('how I wish' many trumpet-section members must have cried), two of the band's sidemen are suspected. The detective in charge of the investigation is a jazz fan and digs into the case with finger-snapping enthusiasm. In keeping with Hollywood's tradition of hiring the band for filming one day and the band for

the recording another, who you see does not often, if ever, match who you hear. Amongst those you see are Denzil De Costa Best, Coleman Hawkins, Howard McGhee, Oscar Pettiford and Sir Charles Thompson (current winners in the *Esquire* poll). Josh White performs his hit song, 'One Meat Ball'. Oh, yes, the club owner did it.

Crosby, Bing

b. Harry Lillis Crosby, 3 May 1903, Tacoma, Washington, USA, d. 14 October 1977. Crosby picked up his nickname through a childhood addiction to a strip cartoon character in a local newspaper. After first singing with a jazz band at high school, he sang at university with a friend, Al Rinker. The duo decided to take a chance on showbiz success, quit school and called on Rinker's sister, Mildred Bailey, in the hope that she could help them find work. Their hopes were fulfilled and they were soon hired by Paul Whiteman. With the addition of Harry Barris they formed the singing trio, the Rhythm Boys, and quickly became one of the major attractions of the Whiteman entertainment package. The popularity of the trio on such recordings as 'Mississippi Mud' and 'I'm Coming Virginia' and an appearance in the film, *The King Of Jazz* (1930), gave Crosby an edge when he chose to begin a solo career. The late 20s saw a great increase in the use of microphones in public auditoriums and the widespread use of more sophisticated microphones in recording studios. This allowed singers to adopt a more confidential singing style, which became known as 'crooning'. Of all the new breed of crooners, Crosby was by far the most popular and successful. Although never a jazz singer, Crosby worked with many jazzmen, especially during his stint with Whiteman, when his accompanists might include Jimmy and Tommy Dorsey, Joe Venuti and Bix Beiderbecke. This early experience, and a sharp awareness of the rhythmic advances of Louis Armstrong, brought Crosby to the forefront of popular American singers in an era when jazz styles were beginning to reshape popular music. Also contributing to his rise was the fact that the new singing style was very well suited to radio, which currently dominated the entertainment industry. He made numerous film appearances and many hundreds of records, several of them massive hits. Indeed, sales of his records eclipsed every recording artist who had gone before and by the 40s these had helped build Crosby into the world's biggest singing star. In contrast, his films were usually frothy affairs and he displayed only limited acting ability. In the 30s these included *The Big Broadcast*, *Going Hollywood*, *We're Not Dressing*, *Mississippi*, *Two For Tonight*, *The Big Broadcast Of 1936*, *Anything Goes*, *Rhythm On The Range*, *Pennies From Heaven*, and *Sing You Sinners*. In the early 40s his film career took an upswing after he appeared with with Bob Hope and Dorothy Lamour in *The Road To Singapore*, the first of seven enormously popular 'Road' journeys to Zanzibar, Morocco, Utopia, Rio, Bali, and Hong Kong. Some good light dramatic roles advanced his career still further. In 1944 he won an Academy Award for his sympathetic performance in *Going My Way*, and continued to excel throughout the decade in highly enjoyable pictures such as *Rhythm On The River, Birth Of The Blues, Holiday Inn, The Bells Of St. Mary's, Blue Skies*, and *A Connecticut Yankee In King Arthur's Court*. In the 50s Crosby made only a few film musicals, but two of them, *White Christmas* and *High Society*, were among the most popular movies of the decade. At the same time he continued to work in radio and television, and made regular concert appearances and still more records. During his radio and television career Crosby often worked with other leading entertainers, among them Al Jolson, Connee Boswell, Dinah Shore, Judy Garland, Armstrong, Hope and his brother, Bob Crosby. By the mid-60s he was content to take things a little easier, although he still made records and personal appearances. Despite his carefree public persona, Crosby was a complex man, difficult to know and understand. As a singer, his seemingly lazy intonation often gave the impression that anyone could sing the way he did, itself a possible factor in his popularity. Nevertheless, his distinctive phrasing was achieved by a good ear, selective taste in building his repertoire, and an acute awareness of what the public wanted. Although his countless fans may well regard it as heresy, Crosby's way with a song was not always what songwriters might have wanted. Indeed, some of Crosby's recordings indicate scant regard for the meaning of lyrics and unlike, say, Frank Sinatra, he was never a major interpreter of songs. Despite this casual disregard for the niceties of music and lyrics, many of Crosby's best-known recordings remain definitive by virtue of the highly personal stylistic stamp he placed upon them. Songs such as 'Pennies From Heaven', 'Blue Skies', 'White Christmas', 'The Bells Of St Mary's', 'Moonlight Becomes You', 'Love In Bloom', 'How Deep Is The Ocean', 'The Blue Of The Night' and 'Temptation' became his. Although Sinatra is the major male song-stylist of American popular music, and also the one who most influenced other singers, every vocalist who followed Crosby owes him a debt for the manner in which his casual, relaxed approach completely altered audience perceptions of how a singer should behave. Towards the end of his life Crosby's star had waned but he was still capable of pulling in sell-out crowds for his occasional public appearances, even though he preferred to spend as much time as he could on the golf course. It was while playing golf in Spain that he collapsed and died.

Selected albums: *Merry Christmas* (1945), *Going My Way* (1945), *The Bell's Of St. Mary's* (1946), *Don't Fence Me In* (1946), *The Happy Prince* (1946), *Road To Utopia* (1946), *Stephen Foster Songs* (1946), *What So Proudly We Hail* (1946), *Favorite Hawaiian Songs Vols. 1 & 2* (1946), *Blue Skies* (1946), *St. Patrick's Day* (1947), *Merry Christmas* (1948), *Emporer Waltz* (1948), *St. Valentine's Day* (1948), *Stardust* (1948), *A Connecticut Yankee* (1949), *South Pacific* (1949), *Christmas Greetings* (1949), *Hits From Musical Comedies* (1949), *Jerome Kern Songs* (1949), with Andrews Sisters *Merry Christmas* (1949), *Crosby Classics, Vol. 1* (1949), *El Bingo* (1950), *Drifting And Dreaming* (1950), *Auld Lang Syne* (1950), *The Bells Of St. Mary's* (1950, film soundtrack), *Showboat Selections* (1950), *Cole Porter Songs* (1950), *Songs By Gershwin* (1950), *Holiday Inn* (1950, film soundtrack), *Blue Of The Night* (1950), *Cowboy Songs* (1950), *Cowboy Songs, Volume 2* (1950), *Bing Sings Hits* (1950), *Top O' The Morning* (1950), *Mr. Music* (1950), *The Small One / The Happy Prince* (1950), *Crosby Classics, Vol. 2* (1950), with Connee Boswell *Bing And Connee* (1951), *Hits From Broadway Shows* (1951), *Bing Crosby Vols. 1 & 2* (1950), *Go West, Young Man* (1951), *Way Back Home* (1951), *Bing Crosby* (1951), *Bing And The Dixieland Bands* (1951), *Yours Is My Heart Alone* (1951), *Country Style* (1951), *Down Memory Lane* (1951), *Down Memory Lane, Volume 2* (1951), *Beloved Hymns* (1951), *Bing Sings Victor Herbert* (1951), *Ichabod Crane* (1955), *Collector's Classics* (1951), *Two For Tonight* (1951), *Rhythm Of The Range* (1951, film soundtrack), *Waikiki Wedding* (1951, film soundtrack), *The Star Maker* (1951), *The Road To Singapore* (1951), *When Irish Eyes Are Smiling* (1952), *Just For You* (1952), *The Road To Bali* (1952, film soundtrack), *Song Hits Of Paris / Le Bing* (1953), *Country Girl* (1953), *Some Fine Old Chestnuts* (1954), *Bing - A Musical Autobiography* (1954), *Old Masters* (1954), *A Man Without A Country* (1954), *White Christmas* (1954, film soundtrack), *Lullabye Time* (1955), *The Voice Of Bing In The 30s* (1955), *Crosby Classics* (1955), *Shillelaghs And Shamrocks* (1956), *Home On The Range* (1956), *Blue Hawaii* (1956), *High Tor* (1956, television soundtrack), *Anything Goes* (1956, film soundtrack), *Songs I Wish I Had Sung The First Time Around* (1956), *Twilight On The Trail* (1956), *A Christmas Sing With Bing Around The World* (1956), *High Society* (1956, film soundtrack), *Bing Crosby Sings While Bregman Swings* (1956), with Rosemary Clooney *That Travellin' Two-Beat* (1956), *New Tricks* (1957), *Ali Baba And The Forty Thieves* (1957), *Christmas Story* (1957), *Bing With A Beat* (RCA 1957), *Around The World* (1958), *A Musical Autobiography Of Bing Crosby 1927-34 / 1934-41 / 1941-44 / 1944-47 / 1947-53* (all 1958), *Bing In Paris* (1958), *That Christmas Feeling* (1958), with Clooney *Fancy Meeting You Here* (1958), *Paris Holiday* (1958, film soundtrack), *In A Little Spanish Town* (1959), *Ichabod* (1959), *Young Bing Crosby* (1959), *Bing And Satchmo* (1960), *High Time* (RCA 1960, film soundtrack), *Join Bing And Sing Along: 33 Great Songs* (1960), *Join Bing And Sing Along: 101 Gang Songs* (960), *Join Bing In A Gang Sing*

Along (1961), *My Golden Favorites* (1961), *Easy To Remember* (1962), *Pennies From Heaven* (1962), *Pocket Full Of Dreams* (1962), *East Side Of Heaven* (1962), *The Road Begins* (1962), *Only Forever* (1962), *Swinging On A Star* (1962), *Accentuate The Positive* (1962), *But Beautiful* (1962), *Sunshine Cake* (1962), *Cool Of The Evening* (1962), *Zing A Little Zong* (1962), *Anything Goes* (1962), *Holiday In Europe* (1962), *The Small One* (1962), *The Road To Hong Kong* (1962, film soundtrack), *A Southern Memoir* (1962), *Join Bing And Sing Along: 51 Good Time Songs* (1962), *On The Happy Side* (1962), *I Wish You A Merry Christmas* (1962), *Bing Sings The Great Standards* (1963), *Songs Everybody Knows* (1964), *The Very Best Of* (1964), *Return To Paradise Islands* (1964), with Frank Sinatra, Fred Waring *America, I Hear You Singing* (1964), *Robin And The Seven Hoods* (1964, film soundtrack), *The Best Of* (1965), *Bing Crosby* (1965), *Great Country Hits* (1965), *Thoroughly Modern Bing* (1968), *The Bing Crosby Story - Vol. 1: Early Jazz Years 1928-32* (1968), *Hey Jude/Hey Bing!!* (1969), *Wrap Your Troubles In Dreams* (1972), *Bingo Viejo* (1975), *The Dinah Shore-Bing Crosby Shows* (1975), *That's What Life Is All About* (1975), *Feels Good, Feels Right* (1976), *Live At The London Palladium* (1976), *"On The Air"* (1976), with Fred Astaire *A Couple Of Song And Dance Men* (1975), *At My Time Of Life* (1976), *Beautiful Memories* (1976), *Bing Crosby Remembered: A CSP Treasury* (1977), *The Best Of Bing* (1977), *Seasons* (1977), *A Legendary Performer* (1977), *Crosby Classics Volume 3* (1977), *Kraft Music Hall December 24, 1942* (1978), *A Bing Crosby Collection Vols. 1 & 2* (1978), *Christmas With Bing* (1980), *Bing In The Hall* (1980), *Music Hall Highlights* (1981), *Rare 1930-31 Brunswick Recordings* (1982), *Bing In The Thirties Volumes 1-8* (1984-88), *The Radio Years Volumes 1-4* (Cresendo 1985-87), *Bing Crosby Sings Again* (1986), *10th Anniversary Album* (1987), *Bing Crosby 1929-34, Classic Years Volume 1* (1987), *Chronological Bing Crosby Vols 1-10* (1985-88), *The Crooner: The Columbia Years 1928-34* (1988), *The Victor Masters Featuring Bing Crosby (Paul Whiteman And His Orchestra)* (1989), *The All Time Best Of* (1990), *Bing Crosby And Some Jazz Friends* (1991), *The Jazzin' Bing Crosby* (1992), *16 Most Requested Songs Legacy* (1992), *The Quintessential Bing Crosby* (1993), *The EP Collection* (1993), *Bing Crosby And Friends* (1993).

Further reading: *Call Me Lucky!* (his autobiography), *The Incredible Crosby*, B. Ulanov. *Bing: The Authorised Biography*, C .Thompson. *The Films Of Bing Crosby*, Robert Bookbinder. *My Life With Bing*, Kathryn Crosby. *The Hollow Man*, Robert F. Slatzer.

Cugat, Xavier

b. Francisco de Asis Javier Cugat Mingall de Bru y Deluefeo, 1 January 1900, Gerona, Spain, d. 27 October 1990, Barcelona, Spain. Cugat grew up in Cuba where he learned violin and played in both cafes and concert halls before moving to the USA in 1921. Based in California, he formed Xavier Cugat And His Gigolos to provide music for the tango dance fashion and appeared in several films during the early 30s. Cugat widened his repertoire to include waltzes and current hits which he performed with his Waldorf Astoria Orchestra from the mid-30s. However, the exotic Latin elements, supplemented by singers and dancers who included the young Rita Hayworth, brought the greatest audience response. Cugat recorded regularly for RCA Victor, having his biggest successes with 'The Breeze And I' (sung by Dinah Shore in 1940) and 'Brazil' in 1943. During the 40s and 50s he appeared frequently in films such as *You Were Never Lovelier* (1942), *Stage Door Canteen, The Heat's On, Bathing Beauty, Two Girls And A Sailor, Holiday In Mexico, This Time For Keeps, A Date With Judy, Luxury Liner, Neptune's Daughter* (1949), and also on television. Although Cugat's arrangements could not stand comparison with the more authentic Afro-Cuban sound of Tito Puente, it was widely accepted by mainstream audiences as the essence of Latin-American music. Among the later singers with his band was Abbe Lane, whom he married. Cugat was forced to retire through ill-health in 1971, but he continued to invest his considerable fortune in projects such as Brazilan films and American nougat bars. He died in October 1990.

Selected albums: *Viva Cugat* (1958), *Continental Hits* (1959, rec 1944-45 reissue 1984), *To All My Friends* (reissue 1986).

Further reading: *Rumba Is My Life* (his autobiography).

D

Daddy Long Legs

Previously filmed in 1919, 1931, and 1935, this 1955 adaptatation of Jean Webster's classic novel, by Phoebe and Henry Ephron, strayed somewhat from the original because of the presence of the delightful French actress Leslie Caron. In this version of the story, a wealthy US businessman played by Fred Astaire, sponsors the education of a French orphan-girl (Caron) - on the strict understanding that he remains anonymous. After his office receives fulsome letters of gratitude from her school, his secretary (a beautifully 'hard-bitten' performance by Thelma Ritter) persuades him to go and see her. He is

Daddy Long Legs

captivated by the charming young woman and they fall in love, although she still has no idea that he is her mysterious benefactor, even when she continues her eduation in the USA. Their romance blossoms, and Astaire and Caron proved to be a perfect dancing team, accompanied by a score by Johnny Mercer which contained two songs that went on to become standards, 'Something's Gotta Give' and 'Dream'. The former gave Astaire the opportunity to convey a perfect lyrical illustration of the difficulties inherent in the 'generation gap' . . . 'When an irresistible force such as you/Meets an old immovable object like me' . . . and the latter, a lovely ethereal ballad which enhanced the film's dream sequences, and was subsequently used for many years by Frank Sinatra as his closing theme. One of the many highlights in *Daddy Long Legs* came when Astaire demonstrated to a bunch of college kids how this dance business really should be done in 'Sluefoot', which featured trumpeter Ray Anthony And His Orchestra. Astaire also gave a good acount of himself on the drums. The rest of a lively and highly entertaining set of songs included 'History Of The Beat', 'C-A-T Spells Cat', and 'Welcome Egghead'. Legendary film composer Alex North was responsible for much of the film's orchestral music. Also in the cast were Terry Moore, Fred Clark, Ralph Dumke, and Larry Keating. The film, which was choreographed by David Robel and Roland Petit, and directed by Jean Negulesco, was photographed in DeLuxe Color and CinemaScope and released by 20th Century-Fox. In the early 90s the company announced that it was planning a re-make of *Daddy Long Legs* starring the popular singer Whitney Houston.

Dailey, Dan

b. 14 December 1914 (or 1917), New York City, New York, USA, d. 1978. An elegant and versatile song-and-dance-man with a genial personality, who starred in some of the most entertaining musicals of the 40s and 50s, often as a vaudeville performer or similar. As a youngster, Dailey worked in minstrel shows and vaudeville. In 1937 he got a job in the chorus of Richard Rodgers and Lorenz Hart's Broadway show *Babes In Arms*, and, two years later, played a supporting role in another stage musical, *Stars In Your Eyes*, which starred Ethel Merman and Jimmy Durante. His first appearance in a movie musical came in 1941 with the lavish *Ziegfeld Girl*, which was followed by *Lady Be Good* and *Panama Hattie*. After service in World War II, Dailey signed for 20th Century-Fox and began to play the lead in films such as *Mother Wore Tights* (the first of several he made with Betty Grable), *You Were Meant For Me*, *Give My Regards To Broadway*, *When My Baby Smiles At Me* (for which he was nominated for the best actor Oscar, only to be beaten by Laurence Olivier!), *You're My Everything*, *I'll Get By*, *My Blue Heaven*, and *Call Me Mister* (1951). In 1952 his portrayal of baseball star Dizzy Dean in *The Pride Of St. Louis* was highly acclaimed. As well as these occasional, but skilfully played straight roles, he continued to devote most of his time to musicals such as *The Girl Next Door, There's No Business Like Show Business, It's Always Fair Weather, The Best Things In Life Are Free, Meet Me In Las Vegas*, and *Pepe* (1960). By then, the lavish, big budget musicals had become old fashioned, and Dailey subsequently worked on stage and in the big US cabaret rooms. In the late 50s he co-starred with Vittorio De Sica, Jack Hawkins and Richard Conte in *The Four Just Men*, a television series which was popular in the US and UK, and his other small screen work included *The Governor And J.J.* in the 60s, and *Faraday And Company* in the 70s.
Selected album: *Dan Dailey* (c.50s), and film soundtracks.

Dames

Following their triumphs in *42nd Street, Gold Diggers Of 1933*, and *Footlight Parade*, Dick Powell, Ruby Keeler, Busby Berkeley and songwriters Harry Warren and Al Dubin reconvened for more of the same in this Warner release of 1934. The dramatic backstage events this particular time concern the efforts of a wealthy philanthropist (Hugh Herbert) to give away his money, while his cousin (Guy Kibbee) is practically given the 'third degree' by Joan Blondell in an effort to extract cash from him so that Dick Powell can put on his show. In any event, Delmar Daves's screenplay is simply an excuse for Warren and Dubin's marvellous songs and Busby Berkeley's imaginative and spectacular dance sequences. Perhaps the most memorable is the one built around 'I Only Have Eyes For You', which begins with Powell and Keeler on a street corner, and then moves to the subway where, aided by the train's motion, the couple fall asleep. In the dream sequence that follows, every advertisement bears Ruby's face, as does a whole screenful of faces which is transposed into an enormous jigsaw puzzle. Finally, a set consisting of huge revolving ferris-type wheels and connecting staircases is filled with a host of Berkeley's beauties - all dressed and made-up to look exactly like Ruby Keeler. Dick Powell gives a spirited rendition of the title song, and Joan Blondell has her big moment too with the endearing 'The Girl At The Ironing Board'. The score was supplemented by Sammy Fain and Irving Kahal's 'When You Were A Smile On Your Mother's Lips' and 'Try To See It My Way' by Allie Wrubel and Mort Dixon. The popular comedienne ZaSu Pitts made a significant contribution to a film that was fast moving, funny, enterertaining, and a sumptuous feast for the ear and eye.

Damn Yankees

Although the original 1955 Broadway show kept that

title for the London stage production, the 1958 film version was released in the UK as *What Lola Wants*. Whatever it was called, this story of Joe Boyd (Robert Shafer), an ageing American baseball fan, whose frustration with his team, the Washington Senators, leads him to make a *Faustian* pact with the Devil, turned out to be a highly entertaining movie musical. Joe's musings along the lines of 'I'd sell my soul for just one long-ball hitter' bring forth a Mr. Applegate (Ray Walston), who, after casually flashing his red socks and lighting a cigarette by spontaneous combustion ('I'm handy with fire'), agrees to turn Joe into a young athlete for one season in return for his soul. The deal is done, and, sure enough, as the Senators' amazing new discovery Joe Hardy (Tab Hunter), he galvanizes the team to action and leads them to glory, after which he reverts to his former self (his contract with Applegate contains an escape clause) and returns to his humdrum life and wife Meg (Shannon Bolin). Walston was marvellous, as always, and former pop heart-throb Hunter gave an appealing performance, too. However, the star of the film without any doubt was red-headed and long-legged dancer, Gwen Verdon. She plays Lola, Applegate's apprentice, whose mission is to retain Joe's soul forever. Her attempt to seduce him in the locker room to the sexy strains of 'Whatever Lola Wants', was an hilarious send-up of every vamp scene in the history of the stage or screen. Verdon was one of the original Broadway team - not including Hunter - who recreated their roles for the screen. Russ Brown, as the Senators' coach, and Rae Allen, in the role of Gloria the nosy, hard-bitten newspaper reporter, were also in the film cast, along with Nathaniel Frey, Jimmie Komack, Jean Stapleton, and Albert Linville. Richard Adler and Jerry Ross's splendid score included 'Goodbye, Old Girl', 'Heart' ('You gotta have . . .'), 'Shoeless Jo From Hannibal, Mo', 'A Little Brains, A Little Talent', 'There's Something About An Empty Chair', 'Two Lost Souls', 'Those Were The Good Old Days', and 'Six Months Out Of Every Year'. Bob Fosse was again responsible for the brilliant choreography, and he also joined Gwen Verdon for the mambo-styled 'Who's Got The Pain?'. George Abbott's screenplay was based on his own stage libretto which was adapted from the novel *The Year The Yankees Lost The Pennant* by Douglass Wallop. Abbott also co-directed the film with Stanley Donen. It was shot in Technicolor for Warner Brothers.

Damsel In Distress, A

Following Ginger Rogers' reported desire to take a rest from musicals, the British-born actress Joan Fontaine became Fred Astaire's new partner in this 1937 RKO release - and proved to be a somewhat disappointing choice. In the screenplay by P.G. Wodehouse, Ernest Pagano and S.K. Lauren, which was adapted from Wodehouse's 1919 novel, Fontaine was cast as a society lady incarcerated in 'Ye olde English castle' complete with a scheming butler (Reginald Gardiner). A swashbuckling dancer (Astaire) -from the 'new' country - goes to the maiden's rescue, and would probably have swept her off into the sunset, singing and dancing - except that Joan Fontaine was not much good at either. The comedy team of George Burns and Gracie Allan (as Astaire's press agent and scatty secretary) were pretty nifty though, and Astaire's best dance moments came with them. As usual with these 30s musicals, the inadequacies of the plot were overcome, and more than compensated for by the marvellous music. The score this time was by George and Ira Gershwin, and included two of their enduring standards, 'A Foggy Day' and 'Nice Work If You Get It', as well as others just as good but not as popular, such as 'I Can't Be Bothered Now', 'The Jolly Tar And The Milkmaid', 'Put Me To The Test', 'Stiff Upper Lip', 'Sing Of Spring', and 'Things Are Looking Up'. Also included was another musical piece, 'Ah, Che A Voi Perdoni Iddio' (from Flowtow's *Marta*). George Stevens directed, and dance director Hermes Pan won an Academy Award for his contribution to a movie which, although vastly entertaining, proved to be Fred Astaire's first box-office failure.

Dance Band

The American actor, singer and band leader Charles 'Buddy' Rogers added some welcome authenticity to this amusing comedy of misunderstandings which was produced by British International Pictures (BIP) in 1935. A competition for dance bands with big prize money and a year's recording contract draws Buddy Milton (Rogers) to London. Blonde and beautiful Pat Shelley (June Clyde) and her all-female orchestra are also entered in the contest, but her pianist is injured in an accident and Buddy deputises for him - under an alias. When she finds out who Buddy really is Pat is furious and accuses him of foul play. The happy ending arrives after Buddy's boys come to the rescue when the girls lose their instruments, and the result of the competition is, of course, a tie - with the inevitable romance to follow. The 'scenario and dialogue' by Roger Burford, Jack Davies Jnr., and Denis Waldock, provides plenty of opportunities for some smart set pieces and snappy musical numbers. The dance team of Jack Holland and June Hart introduced what was intended to be the newest dance sensation, 'The Valparaiso', and the three other catchy songs by Mabel Wayne, Desmond Carter, Arthur Young, Sonny Miller, and Jack Shirley were 'Turtle-Dovey', 'I Hate To Say Goodnight', and 'Gypsy Love'. Steve Geray and the Hungarian actress Magda Kun provided the secondary love interest, and other roles went to Fred Duprez, Leon Sherkot, Richard Hearne (as a drunk), Hal Gordon, and Albert Whelan (the music hall favourite). The musical director was

Harry Acres, and this light but entertaining film was directed by Marcel Varnel.

Dancing Lady

Backstage musicals in which the young chorus girl saves the show by 'going out there on stage a youngster and coming back a star' proliferated in Hollywood in the early 30s, and this one, which was released by MGM in 1933, was really only significant because it marked the film debut of Fred Astaire - complete with his trade-mark top hat, white tie and tails. He played himself, and danced with Joan Crawford to 'Heigh-Ho, The Gang's All Here' and 'Let's Go Bavarian'. Those two numbers and the lovely ballad 'Everything I Have Is Yours', were written by Harold Adamson and Burton Lane. Fresh from their Broadway success, Richard Rodgers and Lorenz Hart, contributed the lively 'That's The Rhythm Of The Day', which was sung by Nelson Eddy, and the always reliable team of Dorothy Fields and Jimmy McHugh provided 'My Dancing Lady', 'Close Your Old Umbrella', and 'Hey, Young Fella'. Clark Gable was perfectly cast as the hard-hearted director who pushed Crawford into the limelight, and Franchot Tone, on the brink of a distinguished film career, was in a cast which also included Al Jarrett, May Robson, Robert Benchley, Winnie Lightner,

and the Three Stooges. The screenplay was written by Allen Rivkin and P.J. Wolfson, the choreographers were Sammy Lee and Eddie Prinz, and the picture was directed by Robert Z. Leonard. Although their subsequent careers were in completely different areas of the movie business, Gable and Astaire are both indelibly associated with one particular song - 'Puttin' On the Ritz'. It provided the accompaniment for one of Fred's most memorable moments in *Blue Skies* (1946), and was also used to great effect in Clark Gable's snappy song-and-dance routine in *Idiot's Delight* (1939).

Dangerous When Wet

The clue is in the title - this was a vehicle - or a vessel - for Esther Williams, the aquatic queen herself. Whilst on dry land, Esther is member of an Arkansas farming family of keep-fit fanatics, consisting of Ma (Charlotte Greenwood), Pa (William Demarest), and two sisters played by Barbara Whiting and Donna Corcoran. One fine day, a travelling salesman in a body-enhancing elixir named Liquapep, (Jack Carson) shows up, and his marketing skills come in handy when Esther to decides to take the plunge and engage in a sponsored swim of the English channel in order to raise money so that Pa can add a prize Jersey bull to the herd. Seriously handsome Fernando Lamas

Dancing Lady

provides Esther's love interest, and serenades her with the attractive ballad, 'In My Wildest Dreams', Arthur Schwartz and Johnny Mercer wrote that one, and the rest of the songs, including the vigorous 'I Got Out Of Bed On The Right Side', 'Ain't Nature Grand?', and 'I Like Men'. The latter number was sung appealingly by Esther's sister Susie who was played Barbara Whiting, the real-life sister of popular singer Margaret Whiting, and the daughter of composer Richard Whiting. Esther was involved in a couple other underwater escapades, and was joined in one of them - a clever dream sequence - by the animated duo Tom And Jerry. Also in the cast were Denise Darcel, Paul Bryer, Henri Letondel, Bunny Waters, and Richard Alexander. Dorothy Kingsley wrote the amusing screenplay and Charles Walters directed this entertaining film which was shot in Technicolor.

Darin, Bobby

b. Walden Robert Cassotto, 14 May 1936, New York, USA, d. 20 December 1973. Darin's entry to the music business occurred during the mid-50s following a period playing in New York coffee houses. His friendship with co-writer/entrepreneur Don Kirshner resulted in his first single, 'My First Love'. A meeting with Connie Francis' manager George Scheck led to a prestigious television appearance on the Tommy Dorsey television show and a contract with Decca. An unsuccessful attempt to score a hit with a cover of Lonnie Donegan's 'Rock Island Line' was followed by a move towards pop novelty with 'Splish Splash'. Darin's quirky vocal ensured that his song was a worldwide hit, although he was outsold in Britain by a rival version from comedian Charlie Drake. During this period, Darin also recorded in a group called the Ding Dongs, which prompted a dispute between Atco and Brunswick Records, culminating in the creation of a new group, the Rinky Dinks who were credited as the backing artists on his next single, 'Early In The Morning'. Neither that, nor its successor, 'Mighty Mighty', proved commercially viable, but the intervening Darin solo release, 'Queen Of The Hop', sold a million. The period charm of 'Plain Jane' presaged one of Darin's finest moments - the exceptional 'Dream Lover'. An enticing vocal performance allied to strong production took the song to number 1 in the UK and number 2 in the USA. Already assured of considerable status as a pop artist, Darin dramatically changed direction with his next recording and emerged as a finger-clicking master of the supper club circuit. 'Mack The Knife', composed by Bertolt Brecht and Kurt Weill for the celebrated *Threepenny Opera*, proved a million-seller and effectively raised Darin to new status as a 'serious singer' - he even compared himself favourably with Frank Sinatra, in what was a classic example of pop hubris. Darin's hit treatments of 'La Mer (Beyond The

Sea)', 'Clementine', 'Won't You Come Home Bill Bailey?' and 'You Must Have Been A Beautiful Baby' revealed his ability to tackle variety material and transform it to his own ends.

In 1960, Darin adeptly moved into film and was highly praised for his roles in *Come September* (whose star Sandra Dee he later married), *State Fair*, *Too Late Blues*, *If A Man Answers*, *Pressure Point*, *Hell Is For Heroes* and *Captain Newman MD*. He returned to form as a pop performer with the lyrically witty 'Multiplication' and the equally clever 'Things'. In the meantime, he had recorded an album of Ray Charles' songs, including the standard 'What'd I Say'. During the beat boom era Darin briefly reverted to show tunes such as 'Baby Face' and 'Hello Dolly', but a further change of style beckoned with the folk-rock boom of 1965. Suddenly, Darin was a protest singer, summing up the woes of a generation with the surly 'We Didn't Ask To Be Brought Here'. Successful readings of Tim Hardin songs, including 'If I Were A Carpenter' and 'The Lady Came From Baltimore', and John Sebastian's 'Lovin' You' and 'Darling Be Home Soon' demonstrate his potential as a cover artist of seemingly limitless range. A more contemporary poet/political direction was evident on the album *Born Walden Robert Cassotto*, and its serious follow-up *Commitment*. As the 60s ended Darin was more actively involved in related business interests, although he still appeared regularly on television. One of the great vocal chameleons of pop music, Darin suffered from a weak heart and after several operations time finally caught up with the singer at Hollywood's Cedars of Lebanon Hospital in December 1973.

Albums: *Bobby Darin* (1959), *That's All* (1959), *This Is Darin* (1960), *Darin At The Copa* (1960), *For Teenagers Only* (1960), with Johnny Mercer *Two Of A Kind* (1961), *Love Swings* (1961), *Twist With Bobby Darin* (1962), *Darin Sings Ray Charles* (1962), *It's You Or No-One* (1962), *Oh Look At Me Now* (1962), *Earthy* (1962), *You're The Reason I'm Leaving* (1963), *Eighteen Yellow Roses* (1963), *From Hello Dolly To Goodbye Charlie* (1964), *Venice Blues* (1965), *In A Broadway Bag (Mame)* (1966), *If I Were A Carpenter* (1967), *Bobby Darin Something Special* (1967), *Born Walden Robert Cassotto* (1968), *Commitment* (1969). Compilations: *The Bobby Darin Story* (1961), *Things And Other Things* (1962), *The Versatile Bobby Darin* (1985), *The Legend Of Bobby Darin* (1985), *His Greatest Hits* (1985).

Darren, James

b. James Ercolani, 3 October 1936, Philadelphia, Pennsylvania, USA. The photogenic actor/singer was signed to Columbia Pictures in the mid-50s, his first film being *Rumble On The Docks* in 1956. He first sang in the film *Gidget* in 1959 and the title song made the US chart. He starred in *Because They're Young* in 1960 and the epic *The Guns Of Navarone* in 1961. In 1962 he debuted in the US Top 20 with his lucky 13th single 'Goodbye Cruel World' and followed it with two more US Top 20 and UK Top 40 hits 'Her Royal Majesty', a Carole King song and 'Conscience', written by Barry Mann. Darren later recorded with little success on Warner Brothers in 1965, Kirshner in 1969, Buddah in 1970, MGM in 1973, Private Stock in 1975 (where he returned briefly to the US Top 100 in 1977) and RCA in 1978. This distinctively-voiced pop/MOR singer is perhaps now best remembered for playing the role of Tony Newman in the popular and often re-run 60s television series *The Time Tunnel*, although the memorable fairground atmosphere of 'Goodbye Cruel World' probably was his finest moment on record.

Albums: *Gidget Goes Hawaiian* (1961), *James Darren Vol 1* (c.60s), *Teenage Triangle* (1963), *Love Among the Young* (1962), *All* (1967).

David, Mack

b. 5 July 1912, New York City, New York, USA, d. 30 December 1993, Rancho Mirage, California, USA. An outstanding lyricist mainly for films, whose career stretched for more than 30 years. He was the older brother of Hal David, who wrote the lyrics for so many hits with composer Burt Bacharach. After studying law for a time, Mack David himself collaborated with Bacharach on 'Baby, It's You' which was a US Top 10 hit for the Shirelles in 1962. Many years before that - in 1939, he had his first hit with 'Moon Love' which he, Mack Davis and André Kostelanetz adapted from a part of Tchaikovsky's Fifth Symphony. It became successful for Glenn Miller, amongst others, and the next year David and Kostelanetz turned to Tchaikovsky again for inspiration on the Connee Boswell favourite 'On The Isle Of May'. In 1941 David and Vee Lawnhurst contributed 'Do You Believe In Fairy Tales?' to the movie *Pot 'O Gold*, and the rest of the 40s found David writing lyrics for mostly popular songs such as 'A Sinner Kissed An Angel', 'Sweet Eloise', 'Take Me', 'Candy', 'Don't You Know I Care?', 'I'm Just A Lucky So And So', 'I Don't Care If The Sun Don't Shine', and the delightfully nonsensical 'Chi-Baba, Chi-Baba' which was a US chart-topper for Perry Como in 1947. A year later another top crooner of the day, Frank Sinatra, did well with 'Sunflower' (words and music by Mack David), as did Russ Morgan And His Orchestra. In 1950 David received his first Oscar nomination for another catchy nonsense song, 'Bibbidi-Bobbidi-Boo', which was part of the score which he, Jerry Livingston and Al Hoffman wrote for the Walt Disney animated feature *Cinderella*. The other numbers included 'A Dream Is A Wish Your Heart Makes', 'The Work Song', and 'So This Is Love'. During the 60s David was nominated on a further seven occasions for the film title songs *The Hanging Tree*, *Bachelor In Paradise*, *Walk On The Wild Side*, *It's A Mad, Mad, Mad World*, *Hush, Hush Sweet*

Charlotte, and for 'The Ballad Of Cat Ballou', and 'My Wishing Doll' from *Hawaii*. The 50s had seen him working on pictures such as *At War With The Army* ('The Navy Gets The Gravy But The Army Gets The Beans'), *Sailor Beware* ('Never Before' and 'Merci Beaucoup'), and *Those Readheads From Seattle* ('I Guess It Was You All The Time' and 'Baby, Baby, Baby'). He also contributed theme songs to *Shane*, *The Hanging Tree*, *To Kill A Mocking Bird*, *Bachelor In Paradise*, *Hud*, and *The Dirty Dozen* (1967), and added a lyric to Max Steiner's 'Tara's Theme' from *Gone With The Wind*, turning it into 'My Own True Love'. The new version was popularised by Leroy Holmes And His Chorus And Orchestra. David's other notable songs over the years included 'La Vie En Rose', 'Cherry Pink And Apple Blossom White', 'It Must Be Him' (a US and UK hit for Vikki Carr), 'Falling Leaves', 'At The Candlelight Café', 'Johnny Zero', and 'It's Love, Love, Love'. He also wrote the words to several popular television themes, such as 77 *Sunset Strip*, *Hawaiin Eye*, *The Roaring Twenties*, *Caspar And The Friendly Ghost*, and *Surfside 6*. Apart from those already mentioned, his collaborators included Duke Ellington, Joan Whitney, Frankie Carle, Count Basie, Alex Kramer, Henry Mancini, Elmer Bernstein, and Frank DeVol. He was a long-time member of ASCAP and was also inducted into the US Songwriters Hall of Fame.

Davis, Carl

b 28 October 1936, Brooklyn, New York, USA. A conductor, and composer, Davis moved to England in 1961, and, after an initial struggle, became a respected figure in films and television during the next 30 years. From 1962, he contributed music to television programmes such as *The Right Prospectus*, *Mad Jack*, *The World Of Coppard*, *Edward II*, *The Arrangement* (television opera), *The Snowgoose*, *The Grievance*, *Hells Angels*, *Arturo Ui*, *Catholics*, *The Merchant Of Venice* (A National Theatre production), *The World At War* (series), *The Pickwick Paper*, *Prince Regent*, *Late Starter*, *The Naked Civil Servant*, *The Day The Universe Changed*, *Oscar*, *Why Lockerbie*, *The Secret Life Of Ian Fleming*, *The Accountant*, *Somewhere To Run*, *The Far Pavilions*, *Silas Marner*, *Hotel Du Lac*, *Winston Churchill - The Wilderness Years*, *The Last Romantics*, *Seperate But Equal* (Parts I & II), *The Crucifer Of Blood*, *Covington Cross*, *A Very Polish Practice*, *Clive James - Fame In The Twentieth Century*, and *A Year In Provence* (1993). Davis' most memorable work for television, however, is probably his complementary music to *Hollywood*, a major documentary series on the motion picture's formative silent era. His other work in that area included a music score for the 1927 silent *Napoleon*, and 10 more musical pieces to accompany short films made between 1919 and 1924, and released on *The Silents*. He began composing for the talkies in 1967, and his credits included *The Bofors Gun*, *Praise Marx*

And Pass The Ammunition, Up Pompeii, Up The Chastity Belt, What Became Of Jack And Jill, Rentadick, The Lovers, The National Health, The French Lieutenant's Woman (British Film Academy Award for Davis in 1981), *Champions, King David, The Rainbow, The Girl In A Swing, Scandal* and Roger Corman's *Frankenstein Unbound* (1990). In 1985 Davis toured the UK, conducting the Halle Orchestra, the Liverpool Philharmonic, and various other orchestras, in a series of concerts to commemorate the 40th anniversary of VE and VJ days (Victory in Europe and Victory in Japan). The programmes included music composed by Sir William Walton for the film *The Battle Of Britain*, which did not make the final cut. In 1989, Davis provided the incidental music for the London version of the Off-Broadway hit play *Steel Magnolias*, and, around the same time, he began collaborating with the world's best known left-handed guitarist, to create 'Paul McCartney's Liverpool Oratorio, to mark the 150th anniversary of the Royal Liverpool Philharmonic Society. The piece had its world premiere in the Liverpool Anglican Cathedral in 1991, and featured soloists, Dame Kiri Te Kanawa, Jerry Hadley, Sally Burgess and Williard White. Also in 1991, Davis's music accompanied the 'absorbing persuasive' US telefilm, *Separate But Equal Parts I & II*, and *The Crucifer Of Blood*, in which Charlton Heston was cast, somewhat intriguingly, as Sherlock Holmes.

Davis, Sammy, Jnr.

b. 8 December 1925, Harlem, New York, USA, d. 16 May 1990, Los Angeles, California, USA. A dynamic and versatile all-round entertainer - a trouper in the old-fashioned tradition. The only son of two dancers in a black vaudeville troupe, called Will Mastin's Holiday In Dixieland, Davis Jnr. made his professional debut with the group at the age of three, as 'Silent Sam, The Dancing Midget'. While still young he was coached by the legendary tap-dancer, Bill 'Bojangles' Robinson. Davis left the group in 1943 to serve in the US Army, where he encountered severe racial prejudice for the first, but not the last, time. After the war he rejoined his father and adopted uncle in the Will Mastin Trio. By 1950 the Trio were headlining at venues such as the Capitol in New York and Ciro's in Hollywood with stars including Jack Benny and Bob Hope, but it was Davis who was receiving the standing ovations for his singing, dancing, drumming, comedy and apparently inexhaustible energy. In 1954 he signed for Decca Records, and released two albums, *Starring Sammy Davis Jr*, (number 1 in the US chart), featuring his impressions of stars such as Dean Martin and Jerry Lewis, Johnnie Ray and Jimmy Durante; and *Just For Lovers*. He also made the US singles chart with 'Hey There', from *The Pajama Game* and in the same year he lost his left eye in a road accident. When he returned to performing in January 1955 wearing an eyepatch he was greeted even more enthusiastically than before. During that year he continued to reach the US Top 20 with 'Something's Gotta Give', 'Love Me Or Leave Me' and 'That Old Black Magic'. In 1956 he made his Broadway debut in the musical *Mr Wonderful*, music and lyrics by Jerry Bock, Larry Holofiener and George Weiss. Also in the show were the rest of the Will Mastin Trio, Sammy's uncle and Davis Snr. The show ran for nearly 400 performances and produced two hits, 'Too Close For Comfort', and the title song, which was very successful for Peggy Lee. Although generally regarded as the first popular American black performer to become acceptable to both black and white audiences, Davis attracted heavy criticism in 1956 over his conversion to Judaism, and later for his marriage to Swedish actress Mai Britt. He described himself as a 'one-eyed Jewish nigger'. Apart from a few brief appearances when he was very young, Davis started his film career in 1958 with *Anna Lucasta*, and was critically acclaimed in the following year for his performance as Sporting Life in *Porgy And Bess*. By this time Davis was a leading member of Frank Sinatra's 'inner circle', called variously, the 'Clan', or the 'Rat Pack'. He appeared with Sinatra in three movies, *Ocean's Eleven* (1960), *Sergeants 3* (1962), and *Robin And The Seven Hoods* (1964), but made, perhaps, a greater impact when he co-starred with another member of the 'Clan', Shirley MacLaine, in the Cy Coleman and Dorothy Fields' film musical, *Sweet Charity*. The 60s were good times for Davis, who was enormously popular on records and television, but especially 'live', at Las Vegas and in concert. In 1962 he made the US chart with the Anthony Newley/Leslie Bricusse number, 'What Kind Of Fool Am I?', and thereafter featured several of the their songs in his act. He sang Bricusse's nominated song, 'Talk To The Animals', at the 1967 Academy Awards ceremony, and collected the Oscar, on behalf of the songwriter, when it won. And in 1972, he had a million-selling hit record with the Newley/Bricusse song, 'The Candy Man', from the film, *Willy Wonka And The Chocolate Factory*. He appeared again on Broadway in 1964 in *Golden Boy*, Charles Strouse and Lee Adams' musical adaptation of Clifford Odet's 1937 drama of a young man torn between the boxing ring and his violin. Also in the cast was Billy Daniels. The show ran for 569 performances in New York, and went to London in 1968. During the 70s he worked less, suffering, it is said, as a result of previous alcohol and drug abuse. He entertained US troops in the Lebanon in 1983, and five years later undertook an arduous comeback tour of the USA and Canada with Sinatra and Dean Martin. In 1989 he travelled further, touring Europe with the show, *The Ultimate Event*, along with Liza Minnelli and Sinatra. While he was giving everything to career favourites such as 'Birth Of The Blues', 'Mr Bojangles' and 'Old Black Magic' he was already ill, although he did not let it show. After his death in 1990 it was revealed that his estate was almost worthless. In 1992, an all-star tribute, led by Liza Minnelli, was mounted at the Royal Albert Hall in London, the city that had always welcomed him. Proceeds from the concert went to the Royal Marsden Cancer Appeal.

Selected albums: *Starring Sammy Davis Jr* (1955), *Just For Lovers* (1955), *Mr. Wonderful* (1956, film soundtrack), *Here's Looking At You* (late 50s), with Carmen McRae *Boy Meets Girl* (late 50s), *It's All Over But The Swingin'* (late 50s), *Mood To Be Wooed* (late 50s), *All The Way And Then Some* (late 50s), *Sammy Davis Jr. At Town Hall* (1959), *Porgy And Bess* (1959), *Sammy Awards* (1960), *I Got A Right To Swing* (1960), *What Kind Of Fool Am I And Other Show-Stoppers* (1962), *Sammy Davis Jr. At The Cocoanut Grove* (1963), *As Long As She Needs Me* (1963), *Sammy Davis Jr. Salutes The Stars Of The London Palladium* (1964), *The Shelter Of Your Arms* (1964), with Count Basie *Our Shining Hour* (1965), *Sammy's Back On Broadway* (1965), *I've Gotta Be Me* (1969), *Sammy Davis Jr. Now* (1972), *Portrait Of Sammy Davis Jr.* (1972), *It's A Musical World* (1976), *The Song And Dance Man* (1977), *Sammy Davis Jr. In Person 1977* (1983), *Closest Of Friends* (1984). Compilations: *The Best Of Sammy Davis Jr.* (1982), *Collection* (1989), *The Great Sammy Davis Jr.* (1989), *Sammy Davis Jr Capitol Collectors Series* (1990).

Further reading: *Yes I Can*, Sammy Davis Jnr. *Why Me?*, Sammy Davis Jnr.

Day, Doris

b. Doris Von Kappelhoff, 3 April 1922, Cincinnati, Ohio, USA. One of popular music's premier post-war vocalists and biggest names, Kappelhoff originally trained as a dancer, before turning to singing at the age of 16. After changing her surname to Day, she became the featured singer with the Bob Crosby Band. A similarly successful period with the Les Brown Band saw her record her single for Columbia, 'Sentimental Journey', which sold in excess of a million copies. Already an accomplished businesswoman, it was rumoured that she held a substantial shareholding in her record company. After securing the female lead in the 1948 film, *Romance On The High Sea*, in which she introduced Sammy Cahn and Jule Styne's 'It's Magic', she enjoyed a stupendous movie career. Her striking looks, crystal clear singing voice and willingness to play tomboy heroines, as well as romantic figures, brought her a huge following. In common with other female singers of the period, she was occasionally teamed with the stars of the day and enjoyed collaborative hits with Frankie Laine ('Sugarbush') and Johnnie Ray ('Let's Walk That A-Way'). She appeared in nearly 40 movies over two decades, which included *It's A Great Feeling* (1949), *Young Man With A Horn* (1950), *Tea For Two* (1950), *West Point Story* (1950), *Lullaby Of Broadway* (1951),

On Moonlight Bay (1951), *Starlift* (1951), *I'll See You In My Dreams* (1951), *April In Paris* (1952), *By The Light Of The Silvery Moon* (1953), *Calamity Jane* (1953), *Young At Heart* (1954), *Love Me Or Leave Me* (1955), *The Man Who Knew Too Much* (1956), *The Pajama Game, Pillow Talk* (1959) and *Jumbo* (1962). These films featured some of her most well known hits. Her finest performance undoubtedly occurred in the uproarious romantic western, *Calamity Jane*, which featured her enduringly vivacious versions of 'The Deadwood Stage' and 'Black Hills Of Dakota'. The movie also gave her a US/UK number 1 single with the yearningly sensual 'Secret Love' (later a lesser hit for Kathy Kirby). Day enjoyed a further UK chart topper with the romantically uplifting 'Whatever Will Be Will Be (Que Sera, Sera)'. After a gap of nearly six years, she returned to the charts with the sexually inviting movie theme 'Move Over Darling', co-written by her producer son Terry Melcher. Her Hollywood career ended in the late 60s and thereafter she was known for her reclusiveness. After more than 20 years away from the public's gaze, she emerged into the limelight in 1993 for a charity screening of *Calamity Jane* in her home town of Carmel, California. History has made her an icon, whose fresh-faced looks, sensual innocence and strikingly pure vocal style effectively summed up an era of American music.

Albums: *Young At Heart* (1955), *Love Me Or Leave Me* (1955), *Day By Day* (1957), *Day By Night* (1957), *Hooray For Hollywood* (1958), *Cuttin' Capers* (1959), *Show Time* (1960), *What Every Girl Should Know* (1960), *Listen To Day* (1960), *Bright & Shiny* (1961), *I Have Dreamed* (1961), with Andre Previn *Duet* (1962), *Love Him* (1964) *Sentimental Journey* (1965), *Latin For Lovers* (1965), *It's Magic* (1993). Various soundtrack albums and compilations have also been issued.

Further reading: *Doris Day: Her Own Story*, Doris Day and A.E. Hotcher. *Doris Day*, Eric Braun.

De Haven, Gloria

b. 23 July 1924, Los Angeles, California, USA. An accomplished actress and singer, with a fine voice and style and a glamorous personality who appeared in several movie musicals in the 40s and 50s. Her parents were the popular stage entertainers the Carter De Havens, and Gloria entered show business while she was quite young. In the early 40s she sang with acclaimed dancebands lead by names such as Jan Savitt, and was employed as an extra in the Charlie Chaplin films *Modern Times* and *The Great Dictator*. After playing some bit parts, she signed to MGM and made her first impression in *Best Foot Forward* (1943), and, in the same year, took part in the all-star extravaganza *Thousands Cheer*. During the rest of the 40s she had mostly good roles in musicals such as *Broadway Rhythm, Two Girls And A Sailor, Step Lively, Summer Holiday*, and *Yes Sir That's My Baby* (1949), as well as playing several solely dramatic parts. In 1950 Gloria De Haven portrayed her mother and sang 'Who's Sorry Now' in the bio-pic of songwriters Bert Kalmar and Harry Ruby, and followed that with appearances in *Summer Stock*, *I'll Get By*, *Two Tickets To Broadway*, *Down Among The Sheltering Palms, So This Is Paris*, and *The Girl Rush* (1955). With the advent of rock 'n' roll, musical films underwent some radical changes in the late 50s, so De Haven turned to television and stage work. In 1955 she co-starred with Ricardo Montalban on Broadway in *Seventh Heaven*, a musical version of the 1927 Janet Gaynor-Charles Farrell silent film classic. In the 70s she was still appearing in dramatic parts in films and US television series. In 1989 she re-launched her career as a cabaret singer at the Rainbow & Stars in New York, where she sang saloon songs and talked of her vaudevillian parents who launched her career so many years ago. It is not reported if she dwelt on the subject of her several husbands, one of whom was another film star of the golden era of movie musicals, John Payne.

De Paul, Gene

b. Gene Vincent De Paul, 17 June 1919, New York, USA, d. 27 February 1988, Northridge, California, USA. De Paul was a pianist, arranger and composer for films, during the 40s and 50s. Early in his career he performed as a pianist-singer, and also wrote arrangements for vocal groups, before starting to compose in 1940. One of his first published songs was 'Your Red Wagon', written in collaboration with lyricist Don Raye and Richard M. Jones, and based on an instrumental blues theme by Jones. It was sung by Marie Bryant in the RKO film, *They Live By Night* (1949), and became a hit for the Andrews Sisters and Ray McKinley. Some years before that, in 1941, the Andrews Sisters, together with Abbott And Costello, and singers Dick Powell and Dick Foran, were the stars of *In The Navy*, the first of many, mostly small-scale, musical movies to which De Paul and Raye contributed songs during the 40s. *In The Navy*, featured songs such as 'Starlight, Starbright', 'A Sailor's Life For Me', 'You're Off To See The World' and 'Hu Ba Lua'. This was immediately followed by *San Antonio Rose* ('Mexican Jumping Beat' and 'You've Got What It Takes'), *Moonlight In Hawaii* ('Aloha Low Down' and 'It's People Like You') and *Keep 'Em Flying* ('You Don't Know What Love Is' and 'Pig Foot Pete'). In the following year, *Hellzapoppin'*, the film adaptation of Olsen and Johnson's successful Broadway musical, included the zany 'Watch The Birdie'. The film's other new songs from De Paul and Raye included 'Putting On The Dog', 'What Kind Of Love Is This?' and 'You Were There'. Also in 1942, De Paul and Raye contributed numbers to *Get Hep To Love* ('Heaven For Two'); *What's Cookin'* ('If' and 'Love Laughs At Anything'), featuring Woody Herman's Band and the Andrews Sisters; *Ride 'Em*

Cowboy, one of the top Abbott and Costello movies which included 'Wake Up Jacob', 'Beside The River Tonto', 'Rockin' and Reelin'' and 'I'll Remember April'. The co-writer on the latter was teenager Patricia Johnston, who died in 1953. The song later became a much-recorded number by artists such as June Christy and Julie London. Other De Paul projects around this time included *Almost Married* ('Just To Be Near You' and 'Mister Five By Five', a novelty number said to have been inspired by the generously built blues singer, Jimmy Rushing); *Pardon My Sarong*, another Abbott and Costello vehicle, ('Island Of The Moon', 'Lovely Luana' and 'Vingo Jingo') and *Behind The Eight Ball* ('Don't You Think We Ought To Dance?', 'Riverboat Jamboree' and 'Wasn't It Wonderful?'). After writing 'He's My Guy', a hit for Harry James, which was included in *Hi Ya Chum* (1943), De Paul and Raye briefly turned their attention to World War II with *When Johnny Comes Marching Home* ('This Is It', and 'Say It With Dancing') and *Hi Buddy* ('We're In The Navy'). Another film with a wartime theme was *Reveille With Beverly* (1943), which starred Frank Sinatra, and featured several musical stars such as the Mills Brothers, Freddie Slack, Bob Crosby and Count Basie. Also, Ella Mae Morse sang 'Cow-Cow Boogie', written by De Paul, Raye and Benny Carter, and her version became the first release for the newly-formed Capitol label. Other 1943 songs by De Paul and Raye included 'Ain't That Just Like A Man' and 'Short, Fat and 4F' for *What's Buzzin' Cousin?*; 'They Died With Their Boots Laced' and 'Do You Hear Music? for *Larceny With Music*; 'Get On Board Little Children' *Crazy House*, and 'Star Eyes', one of the songwriters' most enduring numbers, sung in *I Dood It* by Bob Everly and Helen O'Connell with Jimmy Dorsey's Orchestra. In 1944 De Paul and Raye contributed 'I Won't Forget The Dawn' to *Hi Good Lookin'* and 'Where Am I Without You' to *Stars On Parade*. They also enjoyed success with 'Who's That In Your Love Life?', 'Irresistible You' and 'Solid Potato Salad'. 'Milkman, Keep Those Bottles Quiet' (from *Broadway Rhythm*) became a hit for Ella Mae Morse, Woody Herman and the King Sisters. Towards the end of World War II, De Paul spent two years in the Armed Forces. He and Don Raye resumed writing their movie songs in 1947 with 'Who Knows?' for *Wake Up And Dream* and 'Judaline' for *A Date With Judy*. In 1948 they contributed to *A Song Is Born*, Danny Kaye's last film for Samuel Goldwyn, and also wrote 'It's Whatcha Do With Whatcha Got' for the Walt Disney live-action feature, *So Dear To My Heart*. De Paul and Raye's last film work together was in 1949, for another Disney project, the highly acclaimed cartoon, *The Adventures Of Ichabod And Mr Toad*. Bing Crosby was one of the narrators and the songs included 'Ichabod', 'Katrina' and 'The Headless Horseman'. De Paul returned to movie musicals in

1954 with the celebrated *Seven Brides For Seven Brothers*, an exhilarating, dance-orientated musical, on a par with the best of that genre. The choreography was by Michael Kidd, and Johnny Mercer supplied the lyrics for the songs which included 'Bless Your Beautiful Hide', 'Goin' Courtin'', 'June Bride', 'Spring, Spring, Spring', 'Sobbin' Women', 'When You're In Love', 'Wonderful Day' and 'Lonesome Polecat (Lament)'. In 1956 De Paul and Mercer combined again, on the songs for *You Can't Run Away From It*, based on the 1934 Oscar-winning comedy, *It Happened One Night*. The film included numbers such as 'Howdy Friends And Neighbours', 'Temporarily', 'Thumbing a Ride' and 'Scarecrow Ballet'. In the same year, De Paul and Mercer were back on Broadway with the smash hit, *Li'l Abner*, based on Al Capp's famous cartoon character, and his life in Dogpatch, a town designated by the Government as 'the most useless piece of real estate in the USA'. The population's efforts to reverse that decision, and Daisy Mae's persistent pursuit of Abner Yokum, were accompanied by songs such as 'If I Had My Druthers', 'The Country's In The Very Best Of Hands', 'Oh, Happy Day' and 'Jubilation T. Cornpone', with which the ever ebullient Stubby Kaye, regularly stopped the show. Another number, 'Namely You', became popular outside the show, which ran for nearly 700 performances, and was transferred to the screen in 1959 with most of its original players. In later years, De Paul composed a good deal for television, including music for the popular *Sesame Street* series. His other songs included 'Your Eyes', 'I'm In Love With You', 'I Love To Hear A Choo Choo Train' and 'Teach Me Tonight', which he wrote with Sammy Cahn. The latter was a hit for the De Castro Sisters, Jo Stafford and Dinah Washington. De Paul was inducted to the Songwriters' Hall of Fame in 1985, and died three years later, following a long illness.

De Sylva, Buddy

b. George G. De Sylva, 27 January 1895, New York City, New York, USA, d. 11 July 1950. Growing up in Los Angeles, De Sylva worked briefly in vaudeville while still a small child. In school and college he was active in theatrical pursuits, played in bands and wrote song lyrics. In his early 20s, De Sylva began a mutually profitable association with Al Jolson, who sang and recorded songs for which De Sylva wrote the lyrics. He collaborated with several composers including Jolson, George Gershwin, Rudolf Friml and Jerome Kern. His first hit was with Kern, 'Look For The Silver Lining', published in 1920. The following year Jolson introduced De Sylva's 'April Showers' (music by Louis Silvers) and in 1924, in his show, *Bombo*, Jolson sang 'California, Here I Come' (Jolson as co-lyricist, music by Joseph Meyer). Again with Jolson and Meyer, De Sylva wrote 'If You Knew

Susie', and another popular success of the mid-20s was 'Keep Smiling At Trouble' (Jolson and Lewis E. Gensler). This same period saw De Sylva writing lyrics, often with other lyricists, to many of George Gershwin's compositions. These included 'I'll Build A Stairway To Paradise' (co-lyricist Ira Gershwin), 'Somebody Loves Me' (Ballard MacDonald), 'Why Do I Love You?' (Ira Gershwin) and 'Do It Again'. He also wrote lyrics to music by Victor Herbert, ('A Kiss In The Dark') and James F. Hanley, ('Just A Cottage Small By A Waterfall'). In 1925 De Sylva began his most fruitful association when he teamed up with composer Ray Henderson and lyricist Lew Brown. Their first success, again introduced by Jolson, was 'It All Depends On You'. Following this, and mostly written for the popular Broadway shows such as *Good News*, *Hold Everything*, *Follow Through*, *Flying High*, and some of the annual editions of *George White's Scandals*, came 'The Birth Of The Blues', 'Black Bottom', 'Life Is Just A Bowl Of Cherries', 'Good News', 'The Best Things In Life Are Free', 'The Varsity Drag', 'Luck In Love', 'Broadway', 'You're The Cream In My Coffee', 'Button Up Your Overcoat', 'My Lucky Star', 'Sonny Boy' (written for Jolson's 1928 early talkie, *The Singing Fool*), 'Aren't We All', 'An Old-fashioned Girl', 'My Sin' and 'If I Had A Talking Picture Of You.' The trio's involvement with talking pictures grew, and from 1929-31 they wrote songs for *Sunny Side Up*, *Say It With Songs*, *In Old Arizona*, *Just Imagine*, *Show Girl In Hollywood*, and *Indiscreet*. They also formed a music publishing house to market their own compositions and those of other songwriters. In 1931 De Sylva split from Brown and Henderson, opting to continue working in films while they wanted to concentrate on writing for the New York stage. The careers of the three songwriters was the subject of *The Best Things In Life Are Free*, a Hollywood bio-pic released in 1956. After the split, De Sylva became involved in motion picture production, being successful with a string of musicals featuring child-star Shirley Temple.. During the years he was involved in production he still wrote lyrics, but inevitably with much less frequency. At the end of the 30s, De Sylva, too, was in New York, where he engaged in theatrical production, enjoying considerable success with several hit musicals. In addition to producing, De Sylva also co-wrote the books for some of the shows, including Cole Porter's *Du Barry Was A Lady* (1939) and *Panama Hattie* (1940). In the early 40s De Sylva returned to film production in Hollywood. In 1942 he teamed up with Glen Wallichs and Johnny Mercer to found Capitol Records. He died, eight years later, in July 1950.

Deep In My Heart

This film biography of Sigmund Romberg, the composer of more than 50 American stage musicals was released by MGM in 1954. José Ferrer, who had distinguished himself in movies such as *Joan Of Arc*, *Cyrano De Bergerac*, and *Moulin Rouge*, played Romberg with Doe Avedon as his wife. The screenplay, by Leonard Spigelgass, traced the composer's life from his early days as a musician in a New York café run by Anna Mueller (Helen Traubel), through to his many and varied Broadway triumphs. Among the cast were Walter Pidgeon as J.J. Shubert, the youngest brother of the powerful trio of theatrical producers, Merle Oberon as lyricist Dorothy Donnelly, one of Romberg's principal collaborators, and Paul Henreid who played impresario Florenz Ziegfeld. Other parts were taken by Tamara Toumanova, Jim Backus, and Paul Stewart. What must have been an almost impossible task of selecting musical highlights from such a prolific output, resulted in sequences in which Gene Kelly and his brother, Fred, dance together for the first time on film in 'I Love To Go Swimmin' With Wimmen''; Ann Miller's scintillating dance to 'It'; Ferrer and his real-life wife, actress-singer Rosemary Clooney, with 'Mr. And Mrs.'; Ferrer again in another duet, this time with Helen Traubel, on 'Leg Of Mutton'; and Tony Martin and Joan Weldon's lovely version of 'Lover, Come Back To Me'. One particularly memorable scene had Ferrer taking all the roles in an hilarious musical comedy spoof, *Jazz A Doo*. Squeezed into the film's running time of more than two hours, were many more of Romberg's wonderful songs, including 'The Road To Paradise', 'Softly, As In a Morning Sunrise', 'Stouthearted Men', 'Serenade', 'One Alone', 'Your Land And My Land', 'You Will Remember Vienna', 'When I Grow Too Old To Old To Dream', 'One Kiss', 'Auf Wiedersehn', and of course, 'Deep In My Heart'. The list of guest artists contained such illustrious names as Howard Keel, Vic Damone, Jane Powell, Cyd Charisse, James Mitchell, and William Ovis. The choreographer was Eugene Loring, and the film, which was shot in Eastman Color, was directed by Stanley Donen. Not a box-office blockbuster by any means, but a diverting film for all that.

Delerue, Georges

b. 12 March 1925, Roubaix, France, d. 20 March 1992, Los Angeles, Calfornia, USA. An important composer of film music for well over 150 features, from the early 50s through to the 90s. Delerue won a scholarship to the prestigious Paris Conservatoire, where he was encouraged to develop his interest in music for the screen. In 1952 Delerue composed new scores for two early 20s silent films, *Le Chapeau De Paille De'Italie* and *Les Deux Timides*, and, in 1956, he served as musical director for a series of short films by Alain Resnais, and then for Raymond Rouleau's *The Witches Of Salem* (1957). Two years later he co-composed the scores for *Le Bel Age* (with Alain Goraguer), and *Hiroshima Mon Amour* (with Giovanni

Fusco). In 1960 Delerue made *Shoot The Piano Player*, the first of a celebrated series of films with Francois Truffaut, one of France's premier 'new wave' directors. Their other collaborations included *Jules And Jim*; *Love At Twenty*; *The Soft Skin*; *Two English Girls* (in which Delerue made a cameo appearance); *Such A Gorgeous Kid Like Me*; *Day For Night* (Oscar for Best Foreign Language Film (1973)); *Love On The Run*; *The Last Metro*; *The Woman Next Door*; and *Confidentially Yours* (1983). In 1961 Delerue began another important association with director Philippe De Broca, lasting some 16 films. These included *Five Day Lover (Time Out For Love)*; *The Joker*; *Cartouche*; *That Man From Rio*; *Up To His Ears*; *King Of Hearts*, which became a cult item); *Practice Makes Perfect* (1978).

In the early 60s Delerue's career developed further with his involvement in British films. In 1963 he scored *French Dressing*, controversial director Ken Russell's feature debut, and also Russell's *Women In Love* (1969), with its famous nude wrestling sequence. Delerue's other scores for British films included *The Pumpkin Eater*; *It Began In Brighton*; *A Man For All Seasons*; *Our Mother's House*; *Interlude*; *Anne Of The Thousand Days* (the first of his five Oscar nominations); *The Lonely Passion Of Judith Hearne*; *A Summer Story*; and *Paris By Night* (1988). By the early 70s, after completing one of his best scores for *The Conformist*, an Italian-French-West German production, Delerue broke into Hollywood, and subsequently lived in Los Angeles for several years. Even so, for the majority of the time he continued to work in France. His initial US scores included Frankenheimer's *The Horsemen*; *The Day Of The Dolphin*; Fred Zinnemann's *Julia*; and *A Little Romance* (1979), for which Delerue received an Academy Award. During the 80s scores for English-language movies included *Rich And Famous*; *True Confessions*; *A Little Sex*; *The Escape Artist*; *Exposed*; *Man, Woman And Child*; *Agnes Of God*; *Maxie*; *Salvador*; *Maid To Order*; *A Man In Love*; *The House On Carroll Street*; *Memories Of Me*; *Heartbreak Hotel*; and such box-office hits as Mike Nichols' *Silkwood* and *Biloxi Blues*; Oliver Stone's *Platoon* and *Twins* (Schwarzenegger and De Vito); *Beaches* ('Bette Midler is dynamite'); and *Steel Magnolias* (1989).

In 1985, he composed a new score for Alexander Volkov's 1927 silent film *Casanova*. His last few scores, in the early 90s, included *Black Robe*; *Curly Sue*; *Count A Lonely Cadence*; *Mister Johnson*; *American Friends*; and the French production *Dien Bien Phu* (1992). Delerue died shortly after the latter film had been previewed at the Berlin Festival. Besides his work for feature films, he wrote a great deal of music for television, for shows such as *Love Thy Neighbour*; *Silence Of The Heart*; *Aurora*; *Arch Of Triumph*; *The Execution*; *Amos*; *Deadly Intentions*; *Stone Pillow*; *A Time To Live*; *Sin Of Innocence*; *Women Of Valour*; *Her Secret*

Life; *Escape From Sobibor*; and *Queenie* (mini-series). His last few projects for the small screen were *The Josephine Baker Story*; *Without Warning: The James Brady Story*; and *Momento Mori*, based on Muriel Spark's 1958 novel, which received rave reviews when it was shown in Britain in April 1992. Representative recordings include: *The London Sessions* volumes 1-3. Delerue was a Commander of Arts and Letters, one of France's highest honours.

Deutsch, Adolph

b. 20 October 1897, London, England, d. 1 January 1980, Palm Desert, California, USA. A composer, arranger and musical director for films from the 30s to the 60s. Deutsch began to learn music at the age of five, and, while still a schoolboy, studied composition and piano at the Royal College of Music in London. At the age of 13 he was taken to the USA by his uncle and settled in Buffalo. He became a US citizen in 1920. After high school he worked in the accessory department at the Ford Motor Company, at the same time submitting arrangements to various entertainment organizations. He moved to New York, and during the 20s and early 30s, scored and arranged for musical shows, including those of Irving Berlin and George Gershwin; worked in radio, with a three year stint on *Paul Whiteman's Music Hall;* and served as musical director on a few films, such as *The Smiling Lieutenant* (1931). In 1937 he began to score films, initially for Warner Brothers, such as *They Won't Forget Him*, *The Great Garrick*, *Cowboy From Brooklyn*, *Indianapolis Speedway*, *Three Cheers For The Irish*, *The Fighting 69th*, *They Drive By Night*, *High Sierra*, *The Maltese Falcon*, *Across The Pacific*, *The Great Mr Nobody*, *Action In The North Atlantic*, *Northern Pursuit*, *Uncertain Glory*, *The Mask Of Dimitrios*, and *Three Strangers*. In 1939, Deutsch spent 12 weeks assisting Max Steiner with his score for *Gone With The Wind*. In 1948 he joined MGM, already well into their golden age of musical movies, and was associated with the a studio until 1962. He won Academy Awards for his scores for *Annie Get Your Gun* (1950) (with Roger Edens), *Seven Brides For Seven Brothers* (1954) (with Saul Chaplin), *Oklahoma!* (1955) (with Robert Russell Bennett and Jay Blackton). His Oscar nominations included *Showboat*, *The Band Wagon*, *Deep In My Heart*, *Some Like It Hot* and *The Apartment* (1960). His other background scores through the 50s, included *Father Of The Bride*, *Mrs O'Malley And Mr Malone*, *The Long Long Trailer*, *The Rack*, *Tea And Sympathy*, *Funny Face*, *The Matchmaker*, *Les Girls* and many others. Deutsch also wrote a symphonic piece, the 'Scottish Suite', which was performed by US classical orchestras, and a number of other instrumental works, such as 'March Of The United Nations', 'Clarabelle', 'Three Sister's', 'Piano Echoes', 'Skyride', 'March Eccentrique' 'Margo', 'Stairway' and 'Lonely Room' (theme from *The Apartment*). In

1943 Deutsch formed the Screen Composers Association and was its President Emeritus from 1955 until his death.

Diamond Horseshoe (see **Billy Rose's Diamond Horseshoe**)

Dietrich, Marlene

b. Maria Magdelene Dietrich, 27 December 1901, Berlin, Germany, d. 6 May 1992, Paris, France. Dietrich's heavily accented, half-spoken vocal style made her a *femme fatale* for nearly half a century. She studied acting with director Max Reinhardt, appearing in Germany on stage and in films during the 20s. Her first major role was in *The Blue Angel*, in which she sang what was to become her theme tune, 'Falling In Love Again'. The international success of the film led to a career in Hollywood, where Dietrich starred as a cabaret singer or bar-girl in numerous movies. Among them were *Morocco* (1930), *The Blonde Venus* (1932), *Song Of Songs* (1933), *Destry Rides Again* (in which she performed 'The Boys In The Back Room'), *Follow The Boys* (1944), *A Foreign Affair* (1948) and *Stagefright* from 1950. After becoming a US citizen in 1939, Dietrich joined the American war effort in 1941, and became associated with the song 'Lilli Marlene'. Originally a German poem written in World War II, it had been recorded in 1939 by Lale Anderson, whose version was extremely popular in Nazi Germany. In turn, Dietrich's Brunswick recording was a big hit in the USA.

In the 50s, she began a new career as one of the world's most highly paid cabaret artists. With musical direction by Burt Bacharach, Dietrich sang in three languages and performed a wide variety of songs ranging from 'Miss Otis Regrets' to the Pete Seeger anti-war composition 'Where Have All The Flowers Gone ?' In translation, this song was a German hit in 1968.

In 1963 Dietrich appeared with the Beatles at the Royal Variety Performance. She came out of retirement in 1979 for her final film role with David Bowie in *Just A Gigolo*, in which she sang the title song. After almost a decade as a virtual recluse, she died in 1992. A year later, a new musical about her life, *Sag Mir Wo Die Blumen Sind* (Where Have All The Flowers Gone), opened in Berlin.

Albums: *Dietrich Returns To Germany* (1962), *At The Café De Paris* (1964), *Mythos* (1968), *The Legendary, Lovely Marlene* (1972), *Lilli Marlene* (1983).

Further reading: *Dietrich*, Donald Spoto. *Marlene Dietrich: Life And Legend*, Steven Bach.

Dirty Dancing

If films that adhered to a conventional musical formula could be counted on the fingers of one hand in the 80s, the excitement of dance never ceased to attract enthusiastic audiences. Following in the dance steps of the success of *Footloose* and *Flashdance*, *Dirty Dancing*, released in 1987, caught the imagination of many with its combination of raunchy dancing, romance and upbeat soundtrack. Directed by Emile Ardolino, with a screenplay by Eleanor Bergstein, it tells the story of Baby (Jennifer Grey), her father's favourite daughter, who suffers the ups-and-downs of growing up while on a family holiday at a Catskills resort in the summer of 1963. Baby is an idealistic girl, soon to begin at college, who thinks she can right any problem, and help anyone, whatever the situation. These are all characteristics which one of the resort's leading dancers, Johnny (Patrick Swayze), finds refreshing and attractive. When someone is desperately needed to fill the shoes of Johnny's dancing partner, Penny (Cynthia Rhodes), it's hardly surprising that Baby is chosen to substitute, learning all the steps from scratch - almost a mild modern variation of the chorus girl becomes star routine. It's at this point that Baby and Johnny begin to fall in love, and despite the protestations of most of the adults around them - particularly Baby's father (Jerry Orbach) - the young lovers are isolated for a time before the inevitable happy ending. The uplifting finalé features the film's biggest song hit, '(I've) Had The Time Of My Life' sung by Bill Medley and Jennifer Warnes, which won an Oscar and a Grammy, and topped the US chart. Many of the other tracks reflect the film's theme of 60s nostalgia with contributions from Frankie Valli, the Four Seasons, Otis Redding, the Shirelles and Mickey And Sylvia. There is even one song on the soundtrack, 'She's Like The Wind', performed and written by Swayze (with Stacy Widelitz). *Dirty Dancing* was the first feature release for the home video company Vestron Pictures. While its plot is simplistic, it's a sensitive and original portrayal of a young girl's coming of age, helped along by fine performances and some great frenetic and exciting dancing.

Disney, Walt

b. 23 August 1901, Chicago, Illinois, USA, d. 15 December 1966, New York, USA. Apart from creating legendary cartoon characters such as Mickey and Minnie Mouse, Donald Duck, Goofy and Pluto, the Walt Disney Studio was responsible for a series of phenomenally successful full-length animated feature films, the first of which, *Snow White And The Seven Dwarfs*, was released in December 1937. It was three years in the making, with 600 artists producing more than two million Technicolor drawings, only about an eighth of which were used. The ravishing fairy story by the brothers Grimm was adapted for the screen by Ted Sears, Dorothy Ann Blank, Otto Englander, Earl Hurd, Richard Creedon, Dick Richard, Merrill de

Dirty Dancing

Maris, and Webb Smith. All the dwarfs, Grumpy, Doc, Sleepy, Happy, Sneezy, Bashful, and Dopey (who Charlie Chaplin said was one of the greatest comedians of all time), were given their own delightful personalities, and the soundtrack voices of Andriana Caselotti, Harry Stockwell, Lucille LaVerne, Roy Atwell, Pinto Colvig, Otis Harlan, Billy Gilbert, Scot Mattraw, and Moroni Olsen were perfectly matched to them and the rest of the characters including the handsome Prince whose kiss brings Snow White back to life after the evil Queen has tried to get rid of her. All this was supplemented by some marvellous songs by Frank Churchill (music) and Larry Morey (lyrics), which included 'Whistle While You Work', 'Heigh-Ho', 'Some Day My Prince Will Come', 'With A Smile And A Song', 'I'm Wishing', 'One Song', and 'Isn't This A Silly Song?'. David Hand was the supervising editor, and, although *Snow White And The Seven Dwarfs* was released late in the 30s, it went on to take more money than any other film at the US box-office during the decade, with the exception of *Gone With The Wind*. In 1938 Walt Disney received a special Academy Award 'in recognition of a significant screen innovation which has charmed millions and pioneered a great new entertainment field for the motion picture cartoon' (one statuette and seven minature statuettes). More than 50 years later, in 1993, the picture's overall earnings were estimated at £92 million, a record for any animated film until Disney's own *Aladdin* overtook it (with the help of inflation) after being screened for just 11 incredible weeks in the world's cinemas. As just one more example of the enduring interest in this historic picture, in 1992 an original production cel (a hand-painted celluloid still) from the film fetched £115,000 at Sotheby's auction house in New York, three times its estimated price. A digitally restored version of *Snow White* was set for UK release in July 1994, and around the same time the film was due to appear in the USA on homevideo for the first time. Most of Disney's other full-length animated features have already been made available in that form although usually only for a strictly limited period of time before being withdrawn. In May 1994 it was reported that nine out of ten of all homevideos sold have been Disney films. These included:

Pinocchio (1940). Inspired by the stories of 19th century author, Carlo Collodi, this film concerns a wilful puppet whose habitual 'economy with the truth' results in his nose growing longer and longer. However, by listening to his conscience, in the shape of the loveable character Jiminy Cricket, he mends his ways, bravely rescues his personal Svengali, Geppetto the wood carver from inside Monstro the whale, and eventually achieves his ambition, and is turned into a real live boy by the Blue Fairy. Cliff Edwards, the puckish entertainer, provided the voice for Jiminy Cricket, and he had two of Leigh Harline and Ned

Washington's most endearing and enduring songs, 'Give A Little Whistle' and 'When You Wish Upon A Star'. The latter number won an Academy Award, and the two songwriters, together with P. J. Smith, won another Oscar for their original score. The remaining songs were 'Hi-Diddle-Dee-Dee (An Actor's Life For Me)', 'I've Got No Strings', 'Three Cheers For Anything', 'As I Was Say'n' To The Duchess', and 'Turn On The Old Music Box'. Some of the other voices which, together with the brilliant animation, brought the various characters to life with startling effect, were provided by Dickie Jones (Pinocchio), Christian Rub (Geppetto), Evelyn Venable (the Blue Fairy), Walter Catlett (J. Worthington Foulfellow), Charles Judels (Stromboli), and Frankie Darrow (Lampwick). Ben Sharpsteen and Hamilton Luske were the supervising editors, and the film, which was photographed in Technicolor, took over $40 million in the USA and Canada, becoming the fourth-highest-grossing film of the decade.

Fantasia (1940). This was an astonishingly successful blending of cartoon characters and classical music which featured Leopold Stokowski and the Philadelphia Orchestra. It was narrated by Deems Taylor, and contained eight pieces, 'Toccato And Fugue In D Minor' (Bach), 'The Nutcracker Suite' (Tchaikovsky), 'The Sorcerer's Apprentice' (Dukas), 'The Rite Of Spring' (Stravinsky), 'Pastoral Symphony' (Beethoven), 'Dance Of The Hours' (Ponchielli), 'Night On The Bald Mountain' (Mussorgsky), and 'Ave Maria' (Schubert). Amidst all this wonderful music, there cavorted Mickey Mouse and any number of other animals, including hippopotami, dinosaurs, alligators, elephants, and ostriches, along with nymphs, satyrs, the Goddess of Night, and many more strange and fantastic creations. Ben Sharpsteen was the production supervisor, and this incredible piece of entertainment was filmed in Technicolor and Fantasound. It was the second-highest-grossing 40s picture in the USA. Fifty years after it burst gloriously upon the scene, *Fantasia* was subjected to the currently fashionable desire for 'political correctness' which prevailed in the early 90s. Prior to its video release, and at a reputed cost of hundreds of thousands of pounds, a black 'piccaninny centaurette' seen polishing the hooves of a preening blonde figure was removed from all prints.

Bambi (1942). The general consensus of opinion seems to be that this is the most naturalistic of all Walt Disney's full-length animated features. The animators' skill in their drawing of the animals' graceful movements and charming facial expressions gave the tender, exquisite story of a young deer growing up in a world of changing seasons an awesome sense of reality. Apart from Bambi himself, another star to emerge was Thumper the rabbit, whose amusing voice was dubbed by Peter Behn. Frank Churchill and Larry Morey wrote the score, which included 'Love Is

A Song', 'The Thumper Song', 'Let's Sing A Gay Little Spring Song', 'Twitterpated', and 'Little April Show'. David Hand was the production supervisor, and the screenplay was adapted from a book by Felix Salten. By 1993, according to the *Variety* trade newspaper, *Bambi* was at the head of the US money-earning list of films made in the 40s.

Cinderella (1950). Based on Charles Perrault's traditional fairytale, this was another triumph for the Disney Studio. Once again, as in previous features, the animators came up with some more endearing creatures. This time they were two resourceful rodents, Jaq and Gus, who enlist the help of their friends to make a gorgeous gown so that Cinderella can finally go to the Ball. The dynamic duo were dubbed by James Mcdonald, and the rest of the soundtrack voices were just about perfect, including Ilene Woods as the lovely Cinderella, William Phipps (Prince Charming), Eleanor Audley (wicked stepmother), Verna Felton (fairy godmother), and Luis Van Ruten (King and Grand Duke). Rhoda Williams and Lucille Bliss voiced the ugly stepsisters and were suitably disagreeable on the incongruously titled 'Sing Sweet Nightingale'. The remainder of Mack Gordon, Jerry Livingston and Al Hoffman's score was first-rate, and included 'A Dream Is A Wish Your Heart Makes', 'Bibbidi-Bobbidi-Boo', 'The Work Song', 'So This Is Love', and 'Cinderella'. The Technicolor production was supervised by Ben Sharpsteen, and directed by Wilfred Jackson, Hamilton Luske, and Clyde Geronomi. Some sources, including *Variety*, regard *Cinderella* as a 1949 film because it is said to have been released in December of that year. The newspaper places it third in domestic rental earners during that decade.

Peter Pan (1953) Not regarded as one of the best of Disney's animated features at the time, although it was still an outstanding piece of work. John M. Barrie's classic story was ideal material from which the studio's artists crafted a magical picture. All the much-loved, characters were on hand, including Peter himself (dubbed by Bobby Driscoll), Wendy (Kathy Beaumont), the deliciously evil Captain Hook (Hans Conreid), Mrs. Darling (Heather Angel), Mr. Darling ((Paul Collins), Smee (Bill Thompson), John (Tommy Luske), and Tom Conway (narrator) - not forgetting Tinkerbell and the animal that Frank Churchill and Jack Lawrence warned about in their amusing song, 'Never Smile At A Crocodile'. Sammy Cahn and Sammy Fain wrote most of the remaining numbers, including the popular 'You Can Fly', 'Your Mother And Mine', 'The Elegant Captain Hook', and 'What Makes The Red Man Red?', and there were also contributions from Oliver Wallace and Erdman Penner ('A Pirate's Life') and Wallace also collaborated with Winston Hibler and Ted Sears on 'Tee Dum-Tee Dee'. The production and direction credits were the same as *Cinderella*. *Peter Pan* is third in the line of 50s top money-spinners in the USA, just behind the next listed film.

Lady And The Tramp (1955). The first of these full-length animated features to be photographed in Cinemascope was based on Ward Green's waggish tale about a mongrel called Tramp who falls in a big way for Lady, a spoilt pedigree cocker spaniel, while he is helping her to come to terms with the changes that are taking place (such as the arrival of a new baby) in her owners' family. Getting in on the act are Trusty the bloodhound, Lady's owners Jim Dear and Darling, and a sundry collection of hounds such as Toughy, Bull, Boris, Pedro, and an ex-show dog called Peg. Erdman Penner, Joe Rinaldi, Ralph White and Donald Da Gradi wrote the screenplay, while Sonny Burke and Peggy Lee came up with some charming songs which included 'He's A Tramp', 'Siamese Cat Song', 'Bella Notte', 'Peace On Earth', and 'La La Lu'. Lee herself provided the voices for Peg (an ex-show dog), two naughty Siamese cats, and Darling, and other characters were dubbed by Barbara Luddy (Lady), Larry Roberts (Tramp), George Givot, Bill Thompson, Stan Freberg, Bill Baucon, Verna Felton, and Alan Reed. Production and direction credits as for *Cinderella* and *Peter Pan*. A sad aspect of this production is that, nearly 40 years after it was made, Peggy Lee was locked in litigation with the Disney organization over disputed amounts of homevideo royalties.

Sleeping Beauty (1959). The Disney Studio's preoccupation with live-action feature films, beginning with *Treasure Island* in 1950 and leading to 60s classics such as *Mary Poppins*, meant that this was one of their last animated fairytales - for some time, at least. Extremely expensive to make, it was a box-office failure following its original release, although subsequent re-valuation of the film's outstanding qualities have resulted in substantial earnings from reissues, pushing it into the 50s US Top 6 in more recent times. Like *Cinderella*, the film was based on a Charles Perrault fairytale in which the three good fairies, Flaura, Fauna and Merryweather, care for the Princess Aurora after the wicked fairy, Maleficent, has put a spell on her. After many exciting adventures involving some superb animation and special effects, the seriously handsome Prince Philip ensures that, as always with Disney, good triumphs over evil. Opera singer Mary Costa voiced the Princess, with Bill Shirley (Prince), Eleanor Audley (Maleficent), Verna Felton, Barbara Luddy, Candy Candido, and Bill Thompson as the other main characters. The songs included 'Once Upon A Dream' (Sammy Fain-Jack Lawrence), 'Hail The Princess Aurora' and The Sleeping Beauty Song' (both Tom Adair-George Bruns), 'I Wonder' (Winston Hibler-Ted Sears-Bruns), 'The Skump Song' (Adair-Erdman Penner-Bruns), and excerpts from Tchaikovsky's *Sleeping Beauty*. This production, which was supervised by

Don da Gradi and Ken Anderson and directed by Clyde Geronomi, was shot in Technicolor and the wide-screen process Super Technirama 70. A combination which enhanced the proceedings for some viewers, but was a disturbing influence for others.

The Jungle Book (1967). After a lean spell - and Walt Disney's death the year before - the Studio was back on top form with this captivating film which was inspired by Rudyard Kipling's *Mowgli* stories. It tells of the boy Mowgli who was raised by wolves in the jungle until he was 10 years old. After it is learned that Shere Khan the tiger intends to kill him, Bagheera the panther undertakes to return the youngster to the safety of the man village. After some scrapes along the way involving Baloo the bear, a band of monkeys led by King Louie of the Apes, and Shere Khan himself, the youngster reaches the village where he really belongs. Major features of this production are the inspired choice of actors to voice these marvellous characters, such as Phil Harris (Balloo), Louis Prima (King Louie), Sebastion Cabot (Bagheera), George Sanders (Shere Khan), and Sterling Holloway (Kaa the Snake), and the jazzy score which consisted of 'Colonel Hathi's March', 'Trust In Me', 'I Wan'na Be Like You', 'That's What Friends Are For', and 'My Own Home' (all by Richard M. Sherman and Robert B. Sherman), and 'The Bare Necessities' (Terry Gilkyson). This joyous and immensely entertaining Technicolor film had a screenplay by Larry Clemmons, Ralph Wright, Ken Anderson and Vance Gerry, and was directed by Wolfgan Reitherman. In 1994 it was reported that a £20 million film version of *The Jungle Book* was planned using real-live actors such as Anthony Hopkins, Jason Lee and Len Headey. In the 70s Disney released further full-length animated features, *The Aristocats*, *Robin Hood*, and *The Rescuers*, which, although fine in their way, were not in the same class as many of the Studio's earlier efforts. It was not until 1989 that the great Disney comeback began with *The Little Mermaid*, and continued with *Beauty And The Beast*, and *Aladdin*. Each of those incredibly successful pictures has its own entry in this book.

Walt Disney's latest animated movie to date, *The Lion King*, is due to open worldwide in 1994. It is set once again in the jungle, and has 'lions dancing with zebras, monkeys aping around with warthogs and ostriches, and giraffes performing as in the *Folies Bergere*'. It also has songs by Elton John and Tim Rice, and features the voices of Whoopi Goldberg, Rowan Atkinson, James Earl Jones, Matthew Broderick and Jeremy Irons.

Further reading: *Walt Disney*, Diane Disney Miller. *The Disney Version*, Richard Schickel. *The Art Of Walt*

Jungle Book

Disney, Christopher Finch. *Walt Disney: Hollywood's Dark Prince*, Marc Eliot. *Walt Disney's Snow White And The Seven Dwarfs*, Jack Solomon. *Disney Animation: The Illusion Of Life*, Frank Thomas and Ollie Johnston. *The Disney Studio Story*, Richard Hollis and Brian Sibley. *Walt Disney - Hollywood's Dark Prince*, Marc Eliot.

Dixon, Mort

b. 20 March 1892, New York, USA, d. 23 March 1956, Bronxville, New York, USA. Dixon was a leading lyricist for popular songs during the 20s and 30s. As a young man, he became an actor in vaudeville and then served in France during World War I. After the war, he directed the famous army show, *Whiz Bang*, in France. He began to write songs in the early 20s and, in 1923, collaborated with Ray Henderson on 'That Old Gang Of Mine', which became a big hit for Billy Murray and Ed Smalle, and Benny Krueger, among others. Throughout the decade, Dixon had more success with 'Wonder Who's Kissing Her Tonight?' and 'If I Had A Girl Like You' (both Krueger), 'Follow The Swallow' (Al Jolson), 'Bam, Bam, Bamy Shore' (Ted Lewis), 'Bye Bye Blackbird' (written with Henderson, and one of Dixon's biggest hits, for Nick Lucas and Gene Austin, and revived later by Helen Merrill), 'I'm Looking Over A Four-Leaf Clover' (written with Harry Woods, and another of Dixon's most enduring numbers, especially in the Al Jolson version), 'Just Like A Butterfly' (Ipana Troubadors), 'Nagasaki' (written with Warren, and a song which epitomized the whole 20s flappers scene) and 'Where The Wild Flowers Grow'. In 1928, 'If You Want A Rainbow (You Must Have The Rain)' (written by Dixon, Billy Rose and Oscar Levant) was included in the early talkie, *My Man*. This was followed by Billy Rose's Broadway revue, *Sweet And Low* (1930), for which Dixon, Harry Warren and Rose wrote 'Would You Like To Take A Walk?'. When the show was re-staged the following year under the title, *Crazy Quilt*, 'I Found A Million Dollar Baby (In A Five And Ten Cent Store)' was added. Later it was associated mostly with Nat 'King' Cole, and was featured in the Barbra Streisand vehicle, *Funny Girl* (1975). Also in 1931, Morton, together with Joe Young and Warren, wrote 'Ooh! That Kiss', 'The Torch Song' and 'You're My Everything'. The latter became the title song of the 1949 movie starring Dan Dailey and Anne Baxter, and was used even later by the popular UK entertainer, Max Bygraves, as the signature tune for his *Sing-Along-A-Max* television series. In the early 30s, Dixon collaborated with composer Allie Wrubel on the songs for several Warner Brothers movies. For the spectacular *Dames* (1934), they merely added 'Try To See It My Way' to the existing Warren-Dubin score, but for *Flirtation Walk*, they wrote 'Mr And Mrs Is The Name', 'I See Two Lovers', 'When Do We Eat?'

and the title song. Other Dixon-Wrubel scores included *Happiness Ahead* ('Pop! Goes Your Heart', 'All On Account Of A Strawberry Sundae' and the title song *Sweet Music*, starring Rudy Vallée ('Fare thee Well Annabelle', 'The Snake Charmer'), *In Calient* ('To Call My Own', the title song and 'The Lady In Red', *I Live For Love* ('Mine Alone', 'Silver Wings', 'I Wanna Play House', 'A Man Must Shave', and the title song), and *Broadway Hostess* ('He Was Her Man', 'Let It Be Me', 'Weary', 'Who But You' and 'Playboy Of Paris'). His other songs included 'Under The Ukelele Tree', 'I'm In Love With You, That's Why', 'Is It Possible?', 'Moonbeam', 'In The Sing Song Sycamore Tree', 'Where The Forget-Me-Nots Remember', 'River Stay Way From My Door' (a hit in 1931 for Ethel Waters and Kate Smith, and revived by Frank Sinatra over 20 years later), 'Pink Elephants' (George Olsen and Guy Lombardo), 'I Raised My Hat', 'Marching Along Together', 'So Nice Seeing You Again', 'Toddlin' Along With You', 'Did You Mean It?', 'Every Once In A While' and 'Tears From My Inkwell'. In the late 30s, Dixon's output declined, and he retired early to live in Westchester County, New York. He died in March 1956.

Django Reinhardt

A good exploration of the work of the first European to achieve international status in jazz. Directed by Paul Paviot, this 1958 film features several musicians associated with Reinhardt, including his brother, Joseph, and Stéphane Grappelli.

Doctor Dolittle

A disaster movie of the wrong kind - this lavish and expensive musical about animals was released from captivity in 1968 by 20th Century-Fox, and quietly crawled into a corner and died. Rex Harrison, just a few years after his triumph in the screen version of *My Fair Lady*, played the good Doctor who could talk to the animals in more than 400 different languages, and whose house in the English village Puddleby-on-the-Marsh, resembled the London Zoo - only more so. Samantha Eggar and Anthony Newley tried to inject some life into the proceedings, and Richard Attenborough, as a circus promotor confronted by a double-headed llama (one at each end), was suitably incredulous on 'I've Never Seen Anything Like It'. That song was part of an engaging score by Leslie Bricusse which also included 'My Friend The Doctor', 'Beautiful Things', 'When I Look In Your Eyes', 'After Today', 'Fabulous Places', 'I Think I Like You', 'Where Are The Words?', 'Something In Your Smile', and 'Doctor Dolittle'. Harrison's best number, 'Talk To The Animals', won the Academy Award for best song, and the film also picked up another Oscar for special effects (L.B. Abbott), the most impressive of these being the Great Pink Sea Snail which roamed the high seas. Other, more

The Dolly Sisters

human roles, were taken by Peter Bull, William Dix, Geoffrey Holder, Norma Varden, Muriel Landers, and Portia Nelson. Leslie Bricusse was responsible for the screenplay which was based on Hugh Lofting's book, and Herbert Ross designed the choreography. Richard Fleischer was the director and the film, which was not nearly as bad as it was made out to be - in fact it was rather charming - was shot in DeLuxe Color and Todd AO.

Dolly Sisters, The

The real-life Hungarian Dolly Sisters, Jenny and Rosie, started in American vaudeville before graduating to Broadway musicals and revues such as the *Ziegfeld Follies* (1911) and the *Greenwich Village Follies* of 1924. In the latter production they introduced Cole Porter's 'I'm In Love Again', and they were always surrounded by good songs. There were plenty of those, too, in this 1945 film biography which had a screenplay by John Larkin and Marion Spitzer based on John Kenyon Nicholson's story. Betty Grable and June Haver portray the song-and-dance sister act which, after playing small-time clubs and theatres, catch the attention of producer Oscar Hammerstein (grandfather of Oscar Hammerstein II) played by Frank Middlemass, and zooms right to the top. Along the way - in the film, at least - Haver falls for Frank Latimore, and Grable gets John Payne at last - something she failed to do in *Tin Pan Alley* (1940). Also in the cast were S.Z. Sakall, Reginald Gardiner, Gene Sheldon, Andre Charlot, Sig Ruman, Colette Lyons, and Lester Allen. As for the songs, they were a mixture of old and new. Grable, Payne and Haver all had a crack at the best of the newcomers, 'I Can't Begin To Tell You' (Jimmy Monaco-Mack Gordon), and the trio shared the honours on the remainder which included 'I'm Always Chasing Rainbows' (Harry Carroll-Joseph McCarthy, adapted from Chopin), 'Give Me The Moonlight, Give Me The Girl' (Albert Von Tilzer-Lew Brown), 'Darktown Strutters' Ball' (Shelton Brooks), 'The Sidewalks Of New York' (James Blake-Charles Lawlor), 'Powder, Lipstick And Rouge' (Harry Revel-Mack Gordon), 'Carolina In The Morning' (Walter Donaldson-Gus Kahn), 'We Have Been Around' (Gordon-Charles Henderson), and 'The Vamp' (Byron Gay). This lively, colourful and thoroughly enjoyable film - it grossed nearly $4 million and became one of the hit musicals of the 40s - was choreographed by Ernest Palmer and directed by Irving Cummings. It was photographed in Technicolor and produced by 20th Century-Fox.

Donaldson, Walter

b. 15 February 1893, New York City, New York, USA, d. 15 July 1947. A self-taught pianist, despite his mother being a piano teacher, Donaldson began composing while still attending school. After leaving school he worked in various finance companies, but also held down jobs as a song plugger and piano demonstrator. He had his first small successes in 1915 with 'Back Home In Tennessee' (lyrics by William Jerome), 'You'd Never Know The Old Town Of Mine' (Howard Johnson) and other songs popularizing places and regions. Donaldson's first major success was 'The Daughter Of Rosie O'Grady' in 1918, just before he began a period entertaining at US army camps. After the war he had some minor successes with songs used in Broadway shows, the best known of which was 'How Ya Gonna Keep 'Em Down On The Farm' (Sam M. Lewis and Joe Young). It was another song, written by Donaldson with Lewis and Young, that established him as a major songwriter of the 20s. This was 'My Mammy', popularized by Al Jolson and which ever afterwards became synonymous with the blackface entertainer. Jolson also sang other Donaldson compositions, including 'My Buddy' and 'Carolina In The Morning' (both with Gus Kahn). With Kahn, Donaldson also wrote 'I'll See You In My Dreams', 'Yes Sir, That's My Baby', 'I Wonder Where My Baby Is Tonight', 'That Certain Party', 'Makin' Whoopee' and 'Love Me Or Leave Me'. These last two songs came from the Broadway show, *Whoopee*, written by Donaldson and Kahn in 1928, where they were sung respectively by Eddie Cantor and Ruth Etting. When the Hollywood version of the show was filmed, in 1930, among additional songs Donaldson and Kahn wrote was 'My Baby Just Cares For Me'. In the 30s Donaldson also contributed numbers to films such as *Hollywood Party*, *Kid Millions*, *The Great Ziegfeld*, *Suzy*, *Sinner Take All*, *After The Thin Man*, *Saratoga*, and *That's Right-You're Wrong*. Although his collaboration with Kahn was enormously successful, Donaldson sometimes worked with other lyricists, including George Whiting ('My Blue Heaven'), Howard Johnson ('Georgia'), Cliff Friend ('Let It Rain, Let It Pour') and Abe Lyman ('What Can I Say After I Say I'm Sorry'). On occasions he also wrote lyrics to his own music, notably on 'At Sundown', 'You're Driving Me Crazy' and 'Little White Lies'. In the 30s, Donaldson wrote many songs for films with such collaborators as Kahn and Howard Dietz, and he also worked with Johnny Mercer.

Donen, Stanley

b. 13 April 1924, Columbia, South Carolina, USA. The director and choreographer for a string of classic MGM musicals of the 50s, Donen was fascinated by film and theatre from an early age. After graduating from high school he worked on Broadway in the chorus of the Richard Rodgers and Lorenz Hart musical *Pal Joey* (1940) which starred Gene Kelly, and he assisted Kelly on the choreography for *Best Foot Forward* (1941) and also appeared in the chorus. Signed to MGM, during the 40s he worked as choreographer, co-choreographer and/or co-director of occasional sequences (often uncredited) on musicals such as *Cover Girl, Hey Rookie, Jam Session, Kansas City Kitty, Anchors Aweigh, Holiday In Mexico, No Leave, No Love, Living In A Big Way, This Time For Keeps, A Date With Judy, The Kissing Bandit,* and *Take Me Out To The Ball Game.* In 1949 Donen made his official directorial debut as Gene Kelly's co-director on the acclaimed, ground-breaking musical *On The Town,* and they worked together on several more memorable films, including *Singin' In The Rain, It's Always Fair Weather,* and *The Pajama Game.* Donen also brought his skill as a director of breathtakingly fresh and exuberant sequences to pictures such as *Wedding Bells, Give A Girl A Break* (also choreographed with Gower Champion), *Deep In My Heart, Seven Brides For Seven Brothers, Funny Face,* and *Damn Yankees* (1958). By then the golden age of movie musicals was over, and, with the exception of *The Little Prince* (1974), Donen concentrated on directing (and producing) dramatic and light-comedy films such as *Indiscreet, The Grass Is Greener, Arabesque, Two For The Road, Bedazzled, Staircase, Lucky Lady, Movie, Movie, Saturn 3,* and *Blame It On Rio* (1984). Since then, Donen has been rumoured to be trying to bring biographies of Judy Garland and Marlene Dietrich to the screen, but to date nothing has materialized. In 1988 he produced the Academy Awards show, and five years later made his directorial debut on Broadway in the Jule Styne musical *The Red Shoes.* After the original director, Susan Schulman, bowed out in the early stages of production, Donen took over. Unfortunately, unlike those earlier MGM musicals, there was no happy ending and the show closed after three days.

Down Argentine Way

Don Ameche and Betty Grable were the headliners in this 1940 20th Century-Fox musical, but, as the opening titles gave way to the action, the first impression was made by Brazilian bombshell Carmen Miranda who began her American film debut with a dynamic interpretation of Jimmy McHugh and Al Dubin's 'South American Way' - or as she insisted on singing it, 'Souse American Way'. Miranda was also involved in two other numbers, which was rather fortunate because there was not a lot to the plot. It concerned a Buenos Aires horsebreeder, played by Don Ameche, who is prevented from selling one of his prized specimens to wealthy New Yorker Glenda Crawford (Betty Grable), because she is the daughter of his father's worst enemy. This is an obstacle that true romance eventually surmounts, and the two lovers, Ameche and Gable - and their respective families - settle their differences with the help of some agreeable locations and an attractive bunch of songs, most of which were written by Harry Warren and Mack Gordon. These included a lovely ballad, 'Two

Dreams Met', along with 'Sing To Your Senorita', 'Nenita', and 'Down Argentina Way' which is sung by practically everyone in the film including the Nicholas Brothers who use it as the setting for one of their scintillating acrobatic dance routines. The other songs were 'Mama Yo Quiero' (Jaraca and Vincente Paiva) and 'Doin' The Conga' (Gene Rose). Also in the cast were J. Carroll Naish, Henry Stephenson, Katharine Aldridge, Leonid Kinskey, Chris-Pin Martin, and the ubiquitous Charlotte Greenwood, whose wise-cracking and high-kicking was a joy, as ever. Darrell Ware and Karl Tunberg's screenplay was based on a story by Rian James and Ralph Spencer, and the bright and attractive dances were staged by Nick Castle and Geneva Sawyer. Irving Cummings was the director, and this diverting and tuneful film was photographed in Technicolor.

Dubin, Al

b. Alexander Dubin, 10 June 1891, Zurich, Switzerland, d. 11 February 1945. Brought by his parents to the USA when still a small child, Dubin grew up in Philadelphia. He wrote poetry and song lyrics while attending school, but his aspiration to become a professional songwriter was obstructed by parental hopes that he would follow in his father's footsteps as a surgeon. His education came to an abrupt halt in 1911 when he was expelled for neglecting his studies in favour of hanging out with musicians, gamblers and drunks, and he promptly headed for New York, and a career in music. A number of moderately successful songs were published in the years before World War I. During the war Dubin was gassed while serving in France, and soon afterwards he was back in New York writing songs. His work still met with only mild success until he had the idea of writing lyrics to several popular instrumentals, some of them from the classical field. The resulting songs included 'Humoresque' (music by Anton Dvorak) and 'Song Of India' (Rimsky-Korsakov). More orthodoxly, he wrote lyrics for 'The Lonesomest Gal In Town' (Jimmy McHugh and Irving Mills). By the late 20s Dubin was in Hollywood where he was teamed with Joe Burke, with such popular results as 'Tip Toe Through The Tulips', 'Painting The Clouds With Sunshine', 'Sally', 'Love Will Find A Way' and 'Dancing With Tears In My Eyes'. During the 30s, now collaborating with Harry Warren, Dubin enjoyed his most prolific and creative period, writing for films such as *The Crooner, Roman Scandals, 42nd Street, Gold Diggers Of 1933, Footlight Parade, Wonder Bar, Moulin Rouge, Twenty Million Sweethearts, Dames, Go Into Your Dance, Gold Diggers Of 1935, Broadway Gondolier, Shipmates Forever, Page Miss Glory, Sweet Music, Stars Over Broadway, Colleen, Hearts Divided, Sing Me A Love Song, Cain And Mabel, Melody For Two, Gold Diggers Of 1937, The Singing Marine, Mr. Dodd Takes The Air,* and *Gold*

Diggers In Paris (1939). Among the many successes the duo enjoyed over a five-year period were 'You're Getting To Be A Habit With Me', 'Young And Healthy', 'We're In The Money', 'Shanghai Lil', 'Honeymoon Hotel', 'The Boulevard Of Broken Dreams', 'I'll String Along With You', 'I Only Have Eyes For You', 'Keep Young And Beautiful', Lulu's Back In Town', 'With Plenty Of Money And You', 'Confidentially', 'Lullaby Of Broadway', which won an Oscar, and 'Love Is Where You Find It' (co-lyricist with Johnny Mercer). Dubin's hits with other collaborators included 'Nobody Knows What A Red Headed Mama Can Do' (Sammy Fain and Irving Mills); 'Dancing With Tears In My Eyes', and 'For You' (Joe Burke) and 'South American Way' (Jimmy McHugh). Despite a lifestyle in which he indulged in excesses of eating, drinking, womanizing and drug-taking, Dubin wrote with enormous flair and speed. In addition to the foregoing collaborations with Warren, Dubin also wrote 'South American Way' (with McHugh), 'Indian Summer' (Victor Herbert), 'Along The Santa Fe Trail' (Will Grosz) and 'I Never Felt This Way Before' (Duke Ellington). By the end of the 30s, Dubin's lifestyle began to catch up with him and in the early 40s he suffered severe illness, the break-up of two marriages and a final collapse brought on by a drugs overdose. He died in February 1945.

Duning, George

b. 25 February 1908, Richmond, Indiana, USA. A composer and conductor for films, from the 40s through to the 80s. Duning studied at the University of Cincinnati, and the Cincinnati Conservatory Of Music, becoming a jazz and symphonic trumpet player. He was a sideman and chief arranger for the Kay Kyser Band in the early 40s when Kyser was one of the biggest attractions in the business. Around the same time, he began to arrange and orchestrate music for films, and in 1946 he collaborated with Irving Gertz to write the score for *The Devil's Mask*. Between then and 1950, he scored some 21 features for Columbia, a mixture of thrillers, melodramas, westerns, 'private eyes', and comedies. These included *Mysterious Intruder*; *Johnny O'Clock* and *To The Ends Of Earth*, both starring Dick Powell; *The Guilt Of Janet James*; *I Love Trouble*; *The Man From Colorado*; *Shockproof*; *The Dark Past*; *The Undercover Man*; and *And Baby Makes Three*. Duning also scored *Down To Earth* and *The Gallant Blade*, both starring Larry Parks, and it was Parks once more in *Jolson Sings Again*, for which Duning gained the first of five Oscar nominations. Three of the others came to Duning in the 50s for his work on *From Here To Eternity*; *The Eddie Duchin Story*; and *Picnic* (1955). The last film's theme music, used extremely effectively on the soundtrack in conjunction with the 1934 melody, 'Moonglow', became a US number 1 for Morris Stolloff and his orchestra, and a substantial hit for pianist George Cates. A lyric was added by Steve Allen. Duning's other scores during the 50s and 60s included *Lorna Doone, Man In The Saddle, Scandal Sheet; Last Of The Commanches, Salome, Houseboat; Bell, Book And Candle, Cowboy, The World Of Suzie Wong, The Devil At 4 O'Clock, Toys In The Attic, My Blood Runs Cold*, and *Any Wednesday*. In the 60s and 70s, apart from the occasional feature such as *Arnold* (1973), *Terror In The Wax Museum* (1976), and *The Man With Bogart's Face* (1980), which was George Raft's last film, Duning concentrated on writing for television. He scored several films such as *Then Came Bronson, Quarantined, But I Don't Want To Get Married!, Yuma, Black Noon, Climb An Angry Mountain, The Woman Hunter, Honour Thy Father, The Abduction Of Saint Anne, The Top Of The Hill, The Dream Merchants*, and *Goliath Waits* (1981); and contributed music to numerous television series, including *Star Trek, The Partridge Family*, and *Houseboat*.

Durante, Jimmy

b. James Francis Durante, 10 February 1893, New York City, New York, USA, d. 29 January 1980, Santa Monica, California, USA. A unique entertainer: a comedian, actor and singer whose straight-legged strut, outsize nose (which brought him the nickname 'Schnozzola') and a penchant for mangling the English language ('Da hours I worked were 8 to unconscious') made him a much-loved character throughout the world. The son of immigrant French-Italian parents, Durante taught himself to play ragtime on a piano his father bought him when he was 12. While in his teens he played in New York clubs and gangster hangouts, and later had his own six-piece jazz band in New Orleans. In the early 20s he ran his own speakeasy, the Club Durant, with his partners, dancer and businessman Lou Clayton and song-and-dance-man Eddie Jackson. When the trio began to receive 'offers that they couldn't refuse' from certain shady characters, they gave up the club and toured as a vaudeville act. They also appeared in the Broadway musicals *Show Girl* and *The New Yorkers* (1930). In 1931 the partnership split up and Durante signed a contract with MGM, going on to make nearly 40 films. In the 30s these included musicals such as *Roadhouse Nights, The Cuban Love Song, The Phantom President, Blondie Of The Follies, Broadway To Hollywood, George White's Scandals, Palooka, Strictly Dynamite, Hollywood Party, She Learned About Sailors, Sally, Irene And Mary, Little Miss Broadway*, and *Start Cheering* (1938). During that period Durante also starred in several Broadway musicals, *Strike Me Pink, Jumbo, Red, Hot And Blue!, Stars In Your Eyes*, and *Keep Off the Grass* (1940), as well as performing his comedy act at the London Palladium. He was successful on radio, too, and was teamed with straight man Garry Moore in *The Camel Comedy Hour* from 1943-47. After that Durante had his own show for

three years before he moved into television with the comedy-variety *All Star Revue* (they called him 'TV's newest and freshest face' - he was 57), and, later, *The Jimmy Durante Show* in a nightclub setting similar to the old Club Durant with his old friend Eddie Jackson. In 1952 he was back at the London Palladium and played other theatres and important clubs. Throughout the 40s and 50s he continued to appear in film musicals such as *Melody Ranch*, *This Time For Keeps*, *Two Girls And A Sailor*, *Music For Millions*, *Ziegfeld Follies*, *Two Sisters From Boston*, *It Happened In Brooklyn*, and *On An Island With You*. In 1960 Durante was one of the guest stars in *Pepe*, and, two years later, co-starred with Doris Day in *Billy Rose's Jumbo*. His final film appearance was a cameo role in that orgy of slapstick (or slapschtik), *It's A Mad Mad Mad Mad World* (1963), but he remained popular on US television shows in such as *Jimmy Durante Meets The Seven Lively Arts*, *Jimmy Durante Presents The Lennon Sisters* and *The Hollywood Palace*. In 1960, at the age of 67, he was married for the second time (his first wife died in 1943) to the actress Margaret Alice Little, an actress he had been dating for 16 years. Four years later he was honoured for his 50 years in show business with a lavish ceremony at the Hollywood Roosevelt Hotel. His other awards included Best TV Performer (Motion Picture Daily 1951), George Foster Peabody Award (1951), and Citation Of Merit, City Of New York (1956), and Special Page One Award (1962). He was the composer or co-composer of several of his most popular numbers, including his trademark 'Inka Dinka Doo', and others such as 'Umbriago', 'So I Ups To Him', 'Start Off Each Day With A Song', 'Can Broadway Do Without Me?', and 'Jimmy, The Well Dressed Man'. Several of these, and others that he did not write but are indelibly associated with him such as 'September Song', were featured in two tribute shows, both entitled *Durante*, which played in Hollywood and San Francisco in 1982 and 1989. No doubt Durante's immortal protest 'Everybody wants to get into the act' and his closing message 'Goodnight, Mrs, Calabash, wherever you are', also cropped up in these celebrations of this loveable clown who was much-missed after he died in 1980 following several years of ill health.
Selected albums: *Club Durant* (c.50s), *At The Piano* (1959), *At The Copacabana* (1961), *September Songs* (1963), *Very Best Of* (1964), *One Of Those Songs* (1965), *Songs For Sunday* (1967), *The Special Magic Of Jimmy Durante* (1973), *Bing Crosby With Spike Jones And Jimmy Durante* (1989), *On the Radio* (1989).
Further reading: *Schnozzola*, Gene Fowler. *Goodnight Mrs. Calabash: The Secret Life Of Jimmy Durante*, William Cahn. *Inka Dinka Doo: The Life Of Jimmy Durante*, Jhan Robbins.

Durbin, Deanna

b. Edna Mae Durbin, 4 December 1921, Winnipeg, Canada. A refreshingly natural and spirited actress and singer, with a clear, thrilling soprano voice, who was one of the top box-office stars in film musicals of the late 30s and 40s. The Durbin family moved to Los Angeles, California when Deanna was a baby, and she received voice training from the age of eight. After being spotted by an MGM agent singing at a recital, she was set to portray the opera singer Eva Schumann-Heink as a child in a picture based on the diva's life, but that fell through and instead she co-starred with Judy Garland in the musical short film *Every Sunday* (1936). When MGM boss Louis B. Mayer decided to drop Durbin and keep Garland, she was immediately snapped up for Universal by producer Joe Pasternak. The public's response to her performance in *Three Smart Girls* (1936) was rapturous, and the film's receipts of $2 million saved the studio from bankruptcy. Just before it was released she had made several highly impressive appearances on the Eddie Cantor Radio Hour, so a great many Americans were already familiar with this enchanting 15-year-old with the mature voice and style. During the rest of the 30s, with Pasternak's guidance and skill, audiences were able to follow her gradual evolving from a precocious teenager into a lovely woman in films such as *100 Men And A Girl*, *Mad About Music*, *That Certain Age*, *Three Smart Girls Grow Up*, *First Love*, (in which she had her first screen kiss with Robert Stack), *It's A Date*, and *Spring Parade* (1940). In 1938 she and that other fine young star, Mickey Rooney, were awarded special Oscars 'for their significant contribution in bringing to the screen the spirit and personification of youth, and as juvenile players setting a high standard of ability and achievement'. For most of the 40s she was still Hollywood's top female attraction, via the musicals *Nice Girl?*, *It Started With Eve*, *Hers To Hold*, *Can't Help Singing* (her only film in colour), *I'll Be Yours*, *Something In The Wind*, and *Up In Central Park* (1948). She tried to change her girl-next-door image by accepting straight parts in pictures such as *Christmas Holiday* and *Lady In A Train*, but Universal, who made all her 22 pictures, were not interested in grooming her for sophisticated dramatic roles, so in 1948 she quit Hollywood for good. With two failed marriages behind her (to producer Vaughn Paul when she was 19, and German-born producer Felix Jackson in 1945), she retired with her third husband, French film director Charles David, to the French village of Neauphle-le-Château near Paris where they still live to this day. Despite the repeated efforts of Pasternak she refused to return, saying 'I can't run around being a Little Miss Fix-it who bursts into song - the highest paid star with the poorest material'. She did have the pick of the leading men, though, including Robert Cummings, Walter Pidgeon, Franchot Tone, and Melvyn Douglas. While refusing to make public appearances, she apparently works tirelessly for

Deanna Durbin

UNICEF and remains particularly popular in the UK where the BBC still receives more requests for her films than for any other film star of the 30s and 40s.

Selected albums: *Best Of* (1981), *Can't Help Singing* (1982), *Best Of Volume 2* (1983), *Songs Of The Silver Screen* (1986), *20 Golden Greats* (1987), *Movie Songs* (1988), *Favourites* (1989), *The Legendary* (1990), *With A Song In My Heart* (1993).

E

Easter Parade

It is fascinating to think how it would all have turned out if Gene Kelly had not broken his ankle and therefore been able to partner Judy Garland in this 1948 musical. As it was, MGM tempted Fred Astaire out of retirement - and the rest is history. Astaire played Don Hewes, whose partner in a successful dance act, Nadine (Ann Miller), gets the urge to go solo and leaves him in the lurch. More than slightly miffed, especially as he had hoped to marry the lady, Don plucks Hannah Brown (Judy Garland) from the chorus of a small club, and together they form a happy and prosperous relationship - on stage and off. Irving Berlin's wonderful songs - a mixture of the old and the new - revealed the incredible range of his writing as one musical highlight followed another. Astaire, at nearly twice the age of Garland, was singing and dancing as well as ever in numbers such as 'Drum Crazy', 'Steppin' Out With My Baby', and 'It Only Happens When I Dance With You' (with Ann Miller). His moments with Garland were a joy, and included a ragtime vaudeville medley, 'When The Midnight Choo-Choo Leaves For Alabam', 'Snooky Ookums', 'Ragtime Violin', 'I Love A Piano', and, of course 'Easter Parade'. However, their most memorable number was surely 'A Couple Of Swells', in which, dressed as two social-climbing tramps, they mused: 'The Vanderbilts have asked us out to tea/We don't know how to get there, no siree.' Garland had the poignant 'Better Luck Next Time' and 'I Want to Go Back To Michigan', and Miller was scintillating and sizzling on 'Shaking The Blues Away'. Peter Lawford too, as Astaire's best friend 'The Professor', displayed a pleasant light vocal touch with 'A Fella With An Umbrella'. The supporting cast was particularly fine, and included Clinton Sundberg as Mike, the philosophical barman, and Jules Munshin in the role of frustrated head waiter. All in all, a triumph for all concerned, including producer Arthur Freed, director Charles Walters, dance director Robert Alton, and screenwriters Sidney Sheldon, Frances Goodrich, and Albert Hackett. Roger Edens and Johnny Green won Academy Awards for 'scoring of a musical picture'. In 1992, *Easter Parade* was issued on a laserdisc in a 'Technicolor restoration' from the original nitrate camera negative, with improved digital sound. The disc also included Judy Garland's performance of 'Mr. Monotony', a number which was cut from the original release.

Eddy, Nelson, And Jeanette MacDonald

Nelson Eddy (b. 29 June 1901, Providence, Rhode Island, USA, d. 6 March 1967) and Jeanette MacDonald (b. 18 June 1901, Philadelphia, Pennsylvania, USA, d. 14 January 1965, Houston, Texas, USA). Often called the most successful singing partnership in the history of the cinema, their series of eight operetta-style films vividly caught the imagination of 30s audiences. Eddy came from a musical family and learned to sing by continually listening to operatic records. After the family moved to Philadelphia, he worked at a variety of jobs including telephone operator, advertising salesman and copy-writer. He played several leading roles in Gilbert and Sullivan operettas presented by the Savoy Company of Philadelphia, before travelling to Europe for music studies. On his return in 1924, he had minor parts at the Metropolitan Opera House, in New York, and other concert halls, and appeared on radio. In 1933, he made a brief appearance singing 'In the Garden Of My Heart', in the film, *Broadway To Hollywood*, which featured 10-year-old Mickey Rooney. This was followed by small roles in *Dancing Lady* (1933), (in which Fred Astaire made his debut) and *Student Tour* (1934) after which he attained star status with MacDonald in 1935.

MacDonald took singing and dancing lessons as a child, before moving to New York to study, and in 1920 her tap dancing ability gained her a place in the chorus of the Broadway show *The Night Boat*, one of the year's best musicals, with a score by Jerome Kern. In the same year she served as a replacement in *Irene*, a fondly remembered all-time favourite of the US theatre. Harry Tierney and Joseph McCarthy were responsible for the show's score, which contained the big hit, 'Alice Blue Gown'. MacDonald's other 20s shows included *Tangerine, A Fantastic Fricassee, The Magic Ring, Sunny Days*, and the title roles in *Yes, Yes, Yvette* and *Angela*. However, she appeared in only one real hit, the George and Ira Gershwin's *Tip-Toes* (1925), in which she co-starred with Queenie Smith. In 1929 she was teamed with Maurice Chevalier for her film debut in director Ernst Lubitsch's first sound picture, *The Love Parade*. The musical score, by Victor Schertzinger and Clifford Grey, included 'Dream Lover', 'March Of The Grenadiers' and 'My Love

Nelson Eddy and Jeanette MacDonald (*Maytime*)

Parade'. It was a great success and prompted MacDonald and Chevalier to make three more similar operetta-style films together: *One Hour With You*, (1932), (the Oscar Strauss-Richard Whiting-Leo Robin songs included 'We Will Always Be Sweethearts' and the title song); *Love Me Tonight* (1932), one of the most innovative of all movie musicals, directed by Rouben Mamoulian, with a Richard Rodgers and Lorenz Hart score which included 'Lover', 'Isn't It Romantic?', 'Mimi'; and a lavish production of *The Merry Widow* (1934), (with Franz Lehar's enduring score being aided by some occasional Lorenz Hart lyrics). MacDonald's other movies during the early 30s were a mixture of musicals and comedies, including *The Lottery Bride*, *Monte Carlo* (both 1930) and *The Cat And The Fiddle* (1934). The latter was another outstanding Lubitsch musical which teamed MacDonald with UK song and dance man, Jack Buchanan, and included 'Beyond The Blue Horizon', one of her first hit recordings.

It was in 1935 that MGM brought Eddy and MacDonald together for the first time in *Naughty Marietta*. They were not at first sight an ideal combination, MacDonald's infectious personality and soprano voice, ideal for operetta, coupled with Eddy, whose acting occasionally lacked animation. Despite being known in some quarters as 'The Singing Capon And The Iron Butterfly', the duo's impact was immediate and enormous. *Naughty Marietta*'s score, by Victor Herbert, included 'Tramp, Tramp, Tramp', 'The Italian Street Song', and the big duet, 'Ah, Sweet Mystery Of Life'. Rudolph Friml's *Rose Marie* (1936) followed, and was equally successful. Sometimes called the quintessential operetta, the original play's plot underwent severe changes to enable MacDonald to play a renowned Canadian opera singer, while Eddy became an extremely heroic mountie. Two of the most popular Friml-Oscar Hammerstein II-Harbach songs were the evergreen 'Rose Marie', and the duet, 'Indian Love Call', which proved to be a major US record hit. Both stars made other films during the 30s besides their mutual projects. In 1936, MGM starred MacDonald in the highly regarded melodramatic musical *San Francisco*, with Clark Gable and Spencer Tracy. The movie's earthquake climax was lampooned by Judy Garland in her legendary 1961 Carnegie Hall Concert, when she sang the film's title song, with a special verse which ran: 'I never will forget Jeanette MacDonald/Just to think of her, it gives my heart a pang/I never will forget, how that brave Jeanette, just stood there in the ruins, and sang - aaaand sang!' Meanwhile, Eddy was somewhat mis- cast as an American football hero in *Rosalie*, with Eleanor Powell as Princess Rosalie of Romanza. However, he did introduce a Cole Porter classic, 'In The Still Of The Night', the song that is supposed to have moved MGM boss Louis B. Mayer to tears, the first time he heard it. Noël Coward is said also to have wept, albeit for a different reason, when he saw MacDonald optimistically playing a girl of 18, and Eddy as a starving Viennese singing teacher in the film version of Coward's *Bitter Sweet* (1940). Several songs from the original stage show were retained including 'Zigeuner' and 'I'll See You Again'. The MacDonald- Eddy partnership attracted much criticism for being over-romantic and far too saccharine. However, 30s audiences loved their films such as *Maytime* (1937), *The Girl Of The Golden West* (1938), *Sweethearts* (1938, MGM's first three-colour technicolour picture); and *New Moon* (1940), one of their biggest box-office hits, with a Sigmund Romberg-Oscar Hammerstein II score, which included the memorable 'Lover Come Back To Me', 'Softly As In A Morning Sunrise' and 'Stout-Hearted Men'. In 1941, MacDonald appeared in *Smilin' Through*, with her husband Gene Raymond, while Eddy's performance that same year in *The Chocolate Soldier* was generally thought to be his best acting on film. By 1942, the team had run out of steam. With the onset of World War II, moviegoers' tastes had changed. Their last film together, *I Married An Angel*, even with songs by Rodgers and Hart, was the least successful of the series. In 1942, MacDonald made her final film at MGM, *Cairo*, with Robert Young. This was followed, later in the 40s, by a brief appearance in *Follow The Boys* (1944) and a starring role in *Three Daring Daughters*, in which, with the trio, she sang an appealing version of 'The Dickey Bird Song', by Sammy Fain and Howard Dietz. In 1949, after a career which had teamed her with many of Hollywood's leading men, she made her last film, *The Sun Comes Up*, with another big star, the wonder dog, Lassie! For several years MacDonald also returned to the concert stage and appeared in operettas, and on television, before eventually disappearing from the limelight. She died from a heart attack in January 1965. After their break-up, Nelson Eddy appeared in the horror-musical, *Phantom Of The Opera* (1943) and *Knickerbocker Holiday* (1944), in which he sang 'There's Nowhere To Go But Up'. His final movie appearance was with Ilona Massey in the Rudolph Friml operetta, *Northwest Outpost*, in 1947. He returned to the stage, played in nightclubs and stock musicals and on radio, and occasionally television. He was appearing at the Miami Beach Hotel in Florida when he became ill and was taken to hospital. He died shortly afterwards, on 6 March 1967.

Compilations: *Favourites In Hi-Fi* (1959), *Favourites* (1976), *Legendary* (1978), *Jeanette MacDonald And Nelson Eddy* (1980), *20 Golden Hits* (1985), *Together Again 1948* (1989). Solo compilations: Nelson Eddy *World Favourite Love Songs* (1972), *Isn't It Romantic* (1974), *Love's Old Sweet Song* (1988); Jeanette MacDonald *'San Francisco' And Other Silver Screen Favourites* (1983), *Dream Lover* (1988).

Further reading: *The Films Of Jeanette MacDonald And Nelson Eddy*, E. Knowles. *Jeanette MacDonald: A*

Pictorial History, S. Rich. *The Jeanette MacDonald Story*, J.R. Parish. *Jeanette MacDonald*, L.E. Stern.

Edelman, Randy

This US vocalist won his audience by writing and performing some classic love songs. He made his debut in 1972, with a self-titled album that went largely unnoticed. During the 70s, however, he slowly built up his reputation and finally reached the big time with the worldwide smash 'Uptown Uptempo Woman'. His highest chart entry in the UK came with a revival of Unit Four Plus Two's 1965 hit 'Concrete And Clay'. By 1978 his singles career had ground to a halt. During this period one of his songs 'Weekend In New England' was covered and made into a million selling record by Barry Manilow. An attempted comeback in 1982 failed, but a new career was found when he was invited to provide the music for a new animated feature *The Care Bears*. He went on to write and perform the soundtrack for a number of movies and by 1988 was in the big league writing scores for movies including *Parenthood* and *Kindergarten Cop*. His other credits in the late 80s and early 90s included *Twins* (with George Delarue), *Troop Beverly Hills*, *Ghostbusters II*, *Come See The Paradise*, *Quick Change*, *Drop Dead Fred*, *V.I. Warshawski*, *Beethoven*, *The Last Of The Mohicans*, *The Distinguished Gentlemen*, *Dragon: The Bruce Lee Story*, and *Beethoven's Second* (1993).
Albums: *Randy Edelman* (1972), *Laughter And Tears* (1973), *Prime Cuts* (1975), *Fairwell Fairbanks* (1976), *If Love Is Real* (1977), *You're The One* (1979), *On Time* (1982), *... And His Piano* (1984), *The Distinguished Gentlemen* (1993). Compilation: *Best Of* (1979).

Edens, Roger

b. 9 November 1905, Hillsboro, Texas, USA, d. 13 July 1970, Hollywood, California, USA. An important arranger, songwriter - and later - producer, who was a close associate of MGM producer Arthur Freed from the 30s through to the 50s, when the legendary Freed Unit was turning out one magnificent film musical after another. Edens first came to notice on Broadway in *Girl Crazy* (1930) when he stepped out of the pit orchestra and took over as Ethel Merman's pianist when her regular man became ill. He subsequently became Merman's arranger and accompanist for some time before joining MGM in 1934. After serving as musical supervisor on the Jean Harlow picture *Reckless*, he adapted Freed and Nacio Herb Brown's songs for the studio's big-budget *Broadway Melody Of 1936*, which was released in 1935. In the same year, Edens arranged the music for a party to celebrate the 36th birthday of one of MGM's biggest stars, Clark Gable. The highlight of the affair was 15-year-old Judy Garland's tender version of 'You Made Me Love You', which she prefaced with the 'fan letter' 'Dear Mr. Gable',

written by Edens. The response was sensational and Garland reprised the sequence in *Broadway Melody Of 1938*. From then on Edens scored numerous films, winning Academy Awards for his work on *Easter Parade* (with Johnny Green), *On The Town* (with Lennie Hayton), and *Annie Get Your Gun* (with Adolph Deutsch). He also contributed songs to numerous pictures including *Love Finds Any Hardy*, *Babes In Arms*, *Little Nellie Kelly*, *Strike Up The Band*, *Two Girls On Broadway*, *Lady Be Good*, *Ziegfeld Girl*, *Babes On Broadway*, *Girl Crazy*, *Thousands Cheer*, *Good News*, *On The Town*, *Take Me Out To The Ball Game*, *Singin' In The Rain*, *Funny Face*, and *Billy Rose's Jumbo*. Out of these came numbers such as 'In-Between', 'It's A Great Day For The Irish', 'Our Love Affair', 'Nobody', 'Do The Conga', 'My Wonderful One', 'Minnie From Trinidad', 'Caribbean Love Song', 'Carnegie Hall', 'Hoe Down', 'Here's To The Girls', 'Pass That Peace Pipe', 'You're Awful', 'The Right Girl For Me', 'Strictly USA', 'Moses Supposes', 'Sawdust, Spangles And Dreams', and 'Think Pink', 'Bonjour Paris', 'On How To Be Loved' (the last three for *Funny Face*). For much of the time Edens wrote both words and music, but on other occasions his main collaborators were Arthur Freed, Ralph Freed, Hugh Martin, Betty Comden and Adolph Green, Sigmund Romberg and Jimmy Monaco. He was associate producer on *The Harvey Girls* (1946) and many other Freed musicals, but it was not until several years later that he took full producer credit on the Sigmund Romberg bio-pic *Deep In My Heart* (1954), and *Funny Face* (1957) for which MGM loaned him to Paramount. His last major assignment was as associate producer on *Hello Dolly!* for 20th Century-Fox in 1967, although he was also involved in the preliminary work on Irving Berlin's *Say It With Music*, which was to have been made in 1969, but never materialized due to upheavals in Metro's top management. One of the most important aspect of Edens' work was his ability to discover and nurture fresh talent. He gave Lena Horne her break in films which led to appearances in *Cabin In The Sky* and *Stormy Weather*, and he befriended and nurtured Judy Garland through some well-documented difficult times, as well as writing special material for her concerts. According to the trade paper *Variety*, he coached Katharine Hepburn for her starring role in *Coco* which opened on Broadway in December 1969. He died a few months later of lung cancer.
Further reading: *The Movies' Greatest Musicals-Produced In Hollywood USA By The Freed Unit*, Hugh Fordin.

Edwards, Cliff

b. 14 June 1895, Hannibal, Missouri, USA, d. 18 July 1972, Los Angeles, California, USA. This diminutive soft-voiced singer became universally known as 'Ukelele Ike', and popularized that instrument during his successful vaudeville career in the early 20s. Before

that he had worked in carnivals, St. Louis saloons, and in Chicago with comedian Joe Frisco. As well as vaudeville, Edwards appeared in several Broadway musicals including *Lady Be Good* (1924), with Adele and Fred Astaire, (in which he sang 'Fascinating Rhythm'), *Sunny* (1925), *Ziegfeld Follies Of 1927* and *George White's Scandals Of 1931*. The beginning of his film career coincided with the transition from silent to 'talkies', and he is reputed to have made over 60 films which included musicals, romantic comedies and dramas such as *Hollywood Revue Of 1929* (1929) in which he introduced the Arthur Freed/Nacio Herb Brown song, 'Singin' In The Rain', *Parlor, Bedroom And Bath* (1931) with Buster Keaton, *Hell Divers* (1932), *Take A Chance* (1933) in which he sang 'It's Only A Paper Moon', *George White's Scandals* (1934) and *George White's 1935 Scandals* (1935). He had a string of hits between 1924 and 1933 with songs such as 'It Had To Be You', 'All Alone', 'Who Takes Care Of The Caretaker's Daughter?', 'If You Knew Susie (Like I Know Susie)', 'Paddlin' Madelin' Home', 'Remember', 'Dinah', 'Sunday', 'I'm Tellin' The Birds And Bees (How I Love You)', 'Together', 'Mary Ann' and 'I Can't Give You Anything But Love'. On many records he was joined by top instrumentalists such as Jimmy Dorsey, Miff Mole and Red Nichols, and was credited with playing the kazoo, though it is fairly certain that it was a vocal effect, unaided by any instrument. In the early 30s Edwards' career waned, but was revived in 1940 when he provided the voice of Jiminy Cricket in Walt Disney's animated classic, *Pinocchio*. Two of the movie's most popular numbers, 'Give A Little Whistle' and 'When You Wish Upon A Star' (which won an Oscar for 'Best Song'), were Edwards' first hits for seven years, and his last US chart entries. In 1941 he became the voice of another Disney cartoon character, Jim Crow, in *Dumbo*, and despite poor health and alcohol problems, continued to work for the studio, recording children's songs, and making appearances in the television series, *Mickey Mouse Club*. He died from a heart attack in a nursing home in 1972.
Compilations: *I Want A Girl* (1978), *Cliff Edwards And His Hot Combination* (1979), *The Hottest Man In Town* (1981), *Fascinatin' Rhythm* (1988), *Shakin' The Blues Away* (1988).

Elstree Calling

This 'all-star vaudeville and revue entertainment' which was compered by the popular radio comedian Tommy Handley and produced by British International Pictures (BIP) at Elstree Studios in 1930, is reputed to be the first British film musical. A variety of artists, most of whom were drawn from London shows, performed a series of sketches and musical numbers which included 'Ain't Misbehavin'' (Thomas 'Fats' Waller-Harry Brooks-Andy Razaf) performed

by Teddy Brown with his xylophone and Orchestra; 'My Heart Is Singing' (Ivor Novello-Donovan Parsons, from the current show *The House That Jack Built*) sung by Helen Burnell with the Adelphi Girls; 'Why Am I Always The Bridesmaid' (Fred W. Leigh-Charles Collins) and 'He's Only A Working Man' sung by Lily Morris; 'The Ladies Maid Is Always In The Know' sung by the Charlot Girls; 'The Thought Never Entered My Head' (Novello-Parsons from *The House That Jack Built*) sung by Helen Burnell and Jack Hulbert; 'I've Fallen In Love' sung by Cicely Courtneidge; 'It's Twelve and A Tanner A Bottle' sung by Will Fyffe; and 'Dance Around In Your Bones' which was tap-danced by the Three Eddies dressed as skeletons. The remainder of the music was composed by Vivian Ellis, Reginald Casson, Jack Strachey, and Chick Endor. Others taking part were Anna May Wong, Bobbie Comber, Hannah Jones, Jameson Thomas, John Longden, Ivor McLaren, Lawrence Green, the Berkoff Dancers, the Kasbeck Singers, and the Balalaika Choral Orchestra. During the proceedings, funny-man Gordon Harker is constantly trying to receive the show on a home-made television set. The screenplay was written by Val Valentine, Walter Mycroft, and Adrian Brunel, who, in his dual role as director, skilfully assembled the whole affair. The sketches and other interpolated items were staged by the 31-year-old Alfred Hitchcock. *Elstree Calling* was photographed by John Maxwell, with some of the sequences in colour including those featuring the Charlot Girls, the Adelphi Girls, and Cicely Courtneidge.

Ennis, Skinnay

b. Robert Ennis, 13 August 1909, Salisbury, North Carolina, USA, d. 3 June 1963, Beverley Hills, California, USA. Ennis joined the Hal Kemp band as a singer/drummer in the late 20s while still at the University of North Carolina He became the band's leading attraction because of his unique 'out of breath' vocal style. Ennis left Kemp in 1938 and, after working with Gil Evans and Claude Thornhill, formed his own band popularizing their theme song 'Got A Date With An Angel', and gained maximum exposure with a prestigious residency on Bob Hope's *Pepsodent Show*. Ennis also featured in the show's comedy routines and became a personality in his own right. After World War II, during which he led a service band, Ennis rejoined Hope until 1946, and then worked on radio with Abbott And Costello in the late 40s. He made several diverting appearances in films including *College Swing* (with Bob Hope), *Follow The Band*, *Swing It Soldier*, *Sleepytime Gal*, *Let's Go Steady*, and *Radio Stars On Parade*. During the 50s his band toured the USA, playing the hotel circuit, including, from 1958, a five-year residency at the Statler-Hilton, Los Angeles. During the early 60s he recorded the album, *Skinnay Ennis Salutes Hal Kemp*,

Evergreen

using many of the musicians who had played in the original Kemp band. He died from choking on a bone while dining in a restaurant.

Evensong

Evelyn Laye, who was one of the most enchanting leading ladies of the London musical theatre, especially during the 20s, only made a few films, and this was arguably the best of them. In the poignant and tragic story she plays the young and lovely Maggie O'Neil who leaves her home in England, against her parents' wishes, and runs away to Paris in the hope of becoming a famous opera star. Changing her name to Mm. Irela, she is warned by her manager, Kober (Fritz Kortner), that she cannot have both romance and career. She chooses the latter course, and so loses her first love, George Murray (Emlyn Williams), who is killed in World War I. Many years later she realises that it was the wrong decision, but by then her constant admirer, Archduke Theodore (Carl Esmond), is an old man, and she herself is embittered. After being up-staged by the young pretender, Baba (Conchita Supervia), she dies in her dressing room while listening to an early recording of her voice on a gramophone record. A particularly fine supporting cast included Muriel Aked, Patrick O'Moore, Dennis Van Norton, Arthur Sinclair, and Browning Mummary. The film was full of music, with both Evelyn Laye and Supervia in superb voice with operatic excerpts such as 'Mimi's Song' and 'Musetta's Song' (from *La Boheme*), the 'Drinking Song' (from *La Traviata*), and 'Carceleras' (from *Las Hijas Del Zebado*). Laye also sings a medley of old favourites which were popular during the 1914-18 war years, such as 'A Perfect Day' (Carrie Jacobs-Bond), 'There's A Long, Long Trail' (Stoddard King-Joe Elliot), 'Keep The Home Fires Burning' (Ivor Novello-Lena Guilbert-Ford), 'I Love The Moon' (Paul Rubens), and 'Love's Old Sweet Song' (G. Clifton Bingham-James L. Molloy). In addition there were two new numbers by M. Spoliansky and Edward Knoblock, 'Irela Valse' and 'I'll Wait For You'. In the final analysis, though, as one critic pointed out at the time, this is a tensely dramatic picture which has drama, romance, opera, comedy, tears and all the other surefire ingredients that make a success in show business. It also had a magnificent central performance from Evelyn Laye, whose portrayal of the prima donna from girlhood to her eventual eclipse, in dramatic terms surpassed anything she had done previously. The screenplay, by Edward Knoblock and Dorothy Farnum, was adapted from Beverley Nichols' novel, which he and Knoblock turned into a successful West End play. This memorable film was photographed by Mutz Greenbaum and impressively directed by Victor Saville.

Evergreen

After delighting West End audiences with her scintillating singing and dancing in the stage musical *Ever Green* (1930), Jessie Matthews recreated her role for this film version (with its slightly different title) in 1934. In the screenplay, which was written by the celebrated actor and playwright Emlyn Williams and Majorie Gaffney, Miss Matthews plays Harriet Green, the daughter of an Edwardian music-hall singing star, who secretly takes her mother's place after she has gone missing, and triumphs in her own right. Most of the songs from the stage show were dispensed with, but three survived the trip to the Gaumont British Studios at Shepherd's Bush: 'Dear Dear', 'If I Give In To You', and the big hit, 'Dancing On The Ceiling', which gave Jessie Matthews a wonderful opportunity for a fine solo dance which she is reputed to have choreographed herself. Harry Woods contributed two songs which the leading lady immediately made her own: 'When You've Got A Little Springtime In Your Heart', and the lively 'Over My Shoulder' which accompanied a spectacular production number atop a 'wedding cake'. Jessie's husband, Sonnie Hale, played stage director Leslie Benn, and also in the cast were Betty Balfour, Barry Mackay, Ivor McLaren, Hartley Power, Patrick Ludlow, Betty Shale, and Marjorie Brooks. Buddy Bradley staged the imaginative dance sequences, and *Evergreen*, which was its leading lady's most successful film, was produced by Michael Balcon and directed by Victor Saville.

Everybody's Cheering

(see *Take Me Out To The Ball Game*)

F

Fabulous Dorseys, The

The first jazz-related bio-pic, this 1947 film also has the dubious distinction of casting its subjects as themselves. Although both Jimmy and Tommy Dorsey managed to avoid appearing too embarrassed by the shaky plot (much of which centred on pleasing Ma and Pa Dorsey), their acting was understandably wooden. Their playing was, of course, excellent as both men, then still in their prime, were amongst the outstanding technicians on their respective instruments. For jazz fans the best moment comes in a cornily-contrived nightclub scene in which a jam session occurs. Apart from Jimmy and Tommy, the mismatched musicians include Charlie Barnet, Ray Bauduc and Ziggy Elman, all of whom get in the way of the superb Art Tatum.

Fain, Sammy

b. Samuel Feinberg, 17 June 1902, New York, USA, d. 6 December 1989, Los Angeles, California, USA. Fain was a prolific composer of Broadway shows and films for over 40 years, winning two Oscars, and nine nominations. Early in his career he worked for music publisher Jack Mills, and as a singer/pianist in vaudeville and radio. His first published song, with a lyric by Irving Mills and Al Dubin in 1925, was 'Nobody Knows What A Red-Haired Mamma Can Do', and was recorded, appropriately, by Sophie Tucker. In 1926 he met Irving Kahal (b. 5 March 1903, Houtzdale, Pennsylvania, USA), who was to be his main collaborator until Kahal's death in 1942. Almost immediately they had hits with 'Let A Smile Be Your Umbrella' and 'I Left My Sugar Standing In The Rain'. In 1929 their song, 'Wedding Bells Are Breaking Up That Old Gang Of Mine' was a hit for another singer/pianist, Gene Austin, and surfaced again 25 years later, sung by the Four Aces. Fain contributed songs to several early musical films including The Big Pond (1930) in which Maurice Chevalier introduced 'You Brought A New Kind Of Love To Me', the Marx Brothers' comedy, Monkey Business (1931) 'When I Take My Sugar To Tea', Footlight Parade (1933) 'By A Waterfall', Goin' To Town (1935) in which Mae West sang 'Now I'm A Lady' and 'He's A Bad, Bad Man But He's Good Enough For Me' and Dames (1934) which featured the song 'When You Were A Smile On Your Mother's Lips And A Twinkle In Your Daddy's Eye' – and in which Fain actually appeared as a songwriter. Fain's 30s Broadway credits included Everybody's Welcome, Right This Way (featuring 'I'll Be Seeing You' and 'I Can Dream Can't I'), Hellzapoppin' (reputedly the most popular musical of the 30s) and George White's Scandals Of 1939 ('Are You Havin' Any Fun?' and 'Something I Dreamed Last Night'). During the 40s and 50s Fain collaborated with several lyricists including Lew Brown, Jack Yellen, Mitchell Parish, Harold Adamson, E.Y. 'Yip' Harburg, Bob Hilliard and Paul Francis Webster. In 1945 Fain worked with Ralph Freed, brother of the more famous lyricist and movie producer, Arthur Freed. Fain and Freed's 'The Worry Song' was interpolated into the Sammy Cahn/Jule Styne score for the Frank Sinatra/Gene Kelly movie Anchors Aweigh (1945), to accompany Kelly's famous dance sequence with the animated Jerry the mouse. Fain's greatest Hollywood success was in the 50s. He wrote the scores for two Disney classics: Alice In Wonderland (1951), 'I'm Late' with Bob Hilliard; and Peter Pan (1953), 'Your Mother And Mine' and 'Second Star To the Right' with Sammy Cahn. Also with Cahn, Fain wrote some songs for the Three Sailors And a Girl (1953) movie ('The Lately Song' and 'Show Me A Happy Woman And I'll Show You A Miserable Man'). In 1953 Fain, in collaboration with Paul Francis Webster, won his first Academy Award for the song, 'Secret Love', from their score for the Doris Day/Howard Keel movie, Calamity Jane. His second Oscar, the title song for the film, Love Is A Many Splendored Thing (1955), was also written in partnership with Webster, as were several other film title songs including 'A Certain Smile', 'April Love', and 'Tender Is The Night' which were all nominated for Academy Awards. Other Fain/Webster movie songs included 'There's A Rising Moon (For Every Falling Star)', from Young At Heart (1954) and 'A Very Precious Love', from Marjorie Morningstar (1958), both sung by Doris Day. Fain's last four Broadway musicals were Flahooley (1951) written with Harburg ('Here's To Your Illusions' and 'He's Only Wonderful'), Ankles Aweigh (1955) written with Dan Shapiro, Christine (1960), with Webster, and Something More (1964) with Alan and Marilyn Bergman. Fain continued to write films songs through to the 70s. He also made some vocal records, and had a US chart entry as early as 1926 with Al Dubin and Joe Burke's, 'Painting The Clouds With Sunshine'. He was voted into the Songwriters Hall Of Fame in 1971, and served on the board of directors of ASCAP from 1979 until his death from a heart attack on 6 December 1989. His main lyricist during the 50s, Paul Francis Webster (b. 20 December 1907, New York, USA), also wrote lyrics for other composers including Duke Ellington ('I Got It Bad And That Ain't Good'), Hoagy Carmichael ('Baltimore Oriole', 'Doctor, Lawyer, Or Indian Chief', and 'Memphis In June'), and for Dmitri Tiomkin film themes including Rio Bravo (1959), The Alamo (1960), The Guns Of Navarone (1961), 55 Days At Peking (1963) and the title song for Friendly Persuasion (1956). Webster, partnered by Johnny Mandel, also won an Oscar in 1965 for the song, 'The Shadow Of Your Smile', from the film The Sandpiper.

Faith, Percy

b. 7 April 1908, Toronto, Ontario Canada, d. 9 February 1976, Ericino, California, USA. During the 30s Faith worked extensively on radio in Canada. He moved to the USA in 1940 to take up a post with NBC. During the 50s he was musical director for Columbia Records, for whom he made a number of popular albums, mostly of mood music. He worked with Tony Bennett, with whom he had three million-selling singles, and, from 1950, also had several hits in his own right, including 'Cross My Fingers', 'All My Love', 'On Top Of Old Smoky' (vocal by Burl Ives), 'Delicado', 'Song From The Moulin Rouge (Where Is Your Heart)' (US number 1 in 1953), 'Return To Paradise' (1953), and 'Theme From A Summer Place', which reached number 1 in the US and number 2 in the UK charts in 1960. In Hollywood in the 50s, Faith had written several background film scores, including *Love Me Or Leave Me* (1955), a bio-pic about Ruth Etting which starred Doris Day. His film credits in the 60s included *Tammy Tell Me True* (1961), *I'd Rather Be Rich* (1964), *The Third Day,* (1965), and *The Oscar* (1966). For *The Love Goddesses,* Faith wrote the title song, with Mack David. His other compositions included 'My Heart Cries For You' (with Carl Sigman), which was a big hit for Guy Mitchell, Dinah Shore, Vic Damone and others in 1951.

Selected albums: *Continental Music* (1956), *Passport To Romance* (1958), *Touchdown!* (1958), *North & South Of The Border* (1958), *Music From My Fair Lady* (1959), *Viva!* (1959), *Hallelujah* (1959), *Music Of George Gershwin* (1959), *Malaguena* (1959), *Music From South Pacific* (1960), *Music Of Victor Herbert* (1958), *A Night With Sigmund Romberg* (1959), *Bouquet* (1959), *Porgy And Bess* (1960), *Bon Voyage!* (1960), *Continental Souvenirs* (1960), *Jealousy* (1960), *A Night With Jerome Kern* (1960), *Camelot* (1961), *Carefree* (1961), *Mucho Gusto!* (1961), *Tara's Theme* (1961), *Bouquet Of Love* (1962), *Subways Are For Sleeping* (1962), *Music Of Brazil* (1962), *Hollywood's Themes* (1963), *American Serenade* (1963), *Exotic Strings* (1963), *Shangra-La!* (1963), *More* (1964), *Great Folk Themes* (1964), *Latin Themes* (1965), *Broadway Bouquet* (1965), *Themes For The 'In' Crowd* (1966), *Today's Themes* (1967), *Forever Young* (1970).

Fantasia (see **Disney, Walt**)

Farnon, Robert

b. 24 July 1917, Toronto, Ontario, Canada. Gifted with a prodigious musical talent, Farnon was skilled on several instruments and at the age of 11 was playing with the Toronto Junior Symphony Orchestra. In 1932 he joined the Canadian Broadcasting Corporation Orchestra where the musical director, Percy Faith, made him responsible for many of the choral arrangements. During the 30s Farnon's First Symphony was performed by the Philadelphia Symphony Orchestra under Eugene Ormandy. At the start of World War II Farnon enlisted in the Canadian army and was sent to Europe as leader of the Canadian Band of the American Expeditionary Force. After the war, he remained in the UK, writing arrangements for popular bands such as those of Ted Heath and Geraldo. He formed and led a studio orchestra for a long-running BBC radio series and many of his light orchestral compositions became popular most notably, 'Jumping Bean', 'Portrait Of A Flirt', 'The Westminster Waltz' and

Alice Faye with John Payne

'The Colditz March'. In the late 40s and early 50s he wrote scores for several films including *I Live In Grosvenor Square* (1946), *Spring In Park Lane* (1948), *Maytime In Mayfair* (1949), *Lilacs In The Spring* (1949), and *Captain Horation Hornblower RN* (1951). In 1962, Farnon arranged and conducted for Frank Sinatra's *Great Songs From Great Britain*, the first album the singer had recorded in the UK. Subsequently, Farnon worked in television, still making occasional radio broadcasts and assembling orchestras for special concerts and recording dates. By the late 80s he was living in semi-retirement.

Faye, Alice

b. Alice Jeanne Leppert, 5 May 1912, New York City, New York, USA. The actress/singer Faye was noticed by Rudy Vallee in the Broadway chorus of *George White's Scandals Of 1931*. After touring and recording with his Connecticut Yankees, she starred with Vallee in the movie, *George White's Scandals* (1934), making a strong impression with her version of 'Nasty Man'. Over the next 11 years she made more than 30 films, mostly very appealing musicals such as *On The Avenue* (1937), *In Old Chicago* (1938), *Alexander's Ragtime Band* (1938), *Rose Of Washington Square* (1939), *Hollywood Cavalcade* (1939), *Hello, Frisco, Hello* (1943) and *Lillian Russell* (1940), a bio-pic of the Broadway star. With her deep-throated, sexy voice Faye serenaded her glamorous leading men, Dick Powell, Tyrone Power, Don Ameche and John Payne with songs that included 'Goodnight My Love', 'No Love, No Nothing', 'Sing, Baby, Sing', 'You're A Sweetheart', and 'You'll Never Know' the Academy Award winning song for 1943. By this time she was a major star, together with her friend Betty Grable, with an equally loyal following. Faye retired from movies in 1945 following a much-publicized rift with 20th Century-Fox boss Darryl F. Zanuck, but she returned in 1962 for the second re-make of *State Fair*. Following a first marriage to singer Tony Martin, she re-married in 1941 to bandleader/singer/actor Phil Harris, famous for his delivery of novelty songs such as 'Woodman, Spare That Tree', 'The Darktown Poker Club' and 'That's What I Like About The South'. From 1946-54 they appeared together on a top rated US radio series, and thereafter Faye starred in her own television specials and continued to record, mostly songs forever associated with her.
Compilations: *Alice Faye And The Songs Of Harry Warren* (1979), *On The Air, Volume One* (1979), *On The Air, Volume Two* (1979), *In Hollywood* (1983), *All The Gang's Here* (1988), *This Year's Kisses* (1989).

Fenton, George

b. 19 October 1949, England. An important composer for the British theatre, films and television, from the 70s through to the 90s. After working on minor films in the 70s and early 80s, such as *What Became Of Jack*

And Jill, You're A Big Girl Now and *Hussy*, Fenton got his big break in 1982, when he collaborated with Ravi Shankar on the score for Richard Attenborough's *Gandhi*. It was nominated for a Grammy and an Oscar, and the theme, 'For All Mankind', won an Ivor Novello Award. Five years later, Fenton, in association with Jonas Gwangwa, won another 'Ivor', and two Oscar nominations (score and title song), for his work on another Attenborough project, *Cry Freedom*. Around the same time, Fenton scored several other superior British productions, such as *Runners, The Company Of Wolves, Clockwise, White Of The Eye, 84 Charing Cross Road, High Spirits, The Dressmaker, A Handful Of Dust*, and *White Mischief*. In the late 80s and early 90s, Fenton worked a good deal in the USA, and won another Academy Award nomination for his score to the Glenn Close-John Malkovich drama, *Dangerous Liaisons* (1988). Apart from *Memphis Belle*, which told an American World War II story, but was actually a UK production, Fenton's other US movies included *We're No Angels, The Long Walk Home, White Palace, China Moon* and *The Fisher King, Hero (Accidental Hero* in UK), *Groundhog Day, Born Yesterday*, and *Shadowlands* (1993). In 1991, his score for the Richard Gere-Kim Basinger thriller, *Final Analysis*, was compared favourably to 'nearly everything Bernard Herrmann and Miklos Rozsa ever did'. As well as feature films, the composer worked prolifically in television, on some of the most popular and critically acclaimed programmes of their time. By the early 90s these totalled a staggering 80 productions, and included *Shoestring, Fox, The History Man, Going Gently, No Country For Old Men, Bergerac, A Woman Of No Importance, Outside Edge, Natural World, An Englishman Abroad, Saigon-Year Of The Cat, Village Earth, Walter, The Ghost Writer, The Jewel In The Crown, The Monocled Mutineer, The Trials Of Life*, and two sets of six plays and six monologues (*Talking Heads*), by Alan Bennett. He won the BAFTA Award for the best original television music in 1981, 1983 and 1986, and cornered the market in jingles for various daily news bulletins in the BBC's domestic and World Service. From the early 70s he also worked in provincial theatres, with the Royal Shakespeare Company, and at the National Theatre, composing music and serving as musical director for a variety of productions including *Rosencrantz And Guildenstern Are Dead, A Month In The Country, Don Juan, Bengal Lancer, Kafka's Dick, High Society, Racing Demon, Saki* (1991), and many more. He also composed a children's opera, *Birthday*. Much of his music has been released on records.

Fiddler On The Roof

This generally satisfactory screen version of the record-breaking Broadway musical came to the screen in 1971. The Israeli actor Topol, who had enjoyed much success in the London stage production, was chosen to play the role of Tevye, the Jewish milkman in the small town of Anatevka in Russia, who is forever trying to come to terms with his daughters (played by Michele Marsh, Rosalind Harris, and Neva Small) and the lives they are making for themselves, whilst also fighting to retain the traditions that have, for centuries, existed amongst his people. Topol gave a fine charismatic performance, and had excellent support form Norma Crane as his wife, and the celebrated American stage actress Molly Picon in the key role of the Matchmaker. Also in the cast were Zvee Scooler, Michael Glaser, Paul Mann, and Leonard Frey as Motel the tailor, the role he played in the original Broadway production. Swedish actor Tutte Lemkow appeared as the Fiddler, and his playing was dubbed by Isaac Stern. Jerry Bock and Sheldon Harnick's magnificent stage score was mostly retained, and included 'Tradition', 'Matchmaker, Matchmaker', 'If I Were A Rich Man', 'Sabbath Prayer', 'To Life', 'Miracle Of Miracles', 'Tevye's Dream', 'Sunrise, Sunset', 'Wedding And The Bottle Dance', 'Do You Love Me', 'Far From The Home I Love', 'Chava Ballet Sequence', and 'Anatevka'. Tom Abbott based his choreography on Jerome Robbins's Tony Award-winning original work and Joseph Stein's screenplay was adapted from his Broadway

libretto. Norman Jewison was the producer-director, and the film won Academy Awards for Oswald Morris's cinematography (DeLuxe Color and Panavision), sound (Gordon K. McCallum and David Hildyard), and adaptation and music scoring (John Williams). According to *Variety*, the film, which grossed nearly $40 million, was one of the hit movies of the decade.

Fields, Gracie

b. Grace Stansfield, 9 January 1898, Rochdale, Lancashire, England, d. 27 September 1979. A singer and comedienne, so popular in the UK during the 30s and 40s that she was its most famous person next to Royalty. Educated occasionally, in-between work in a cotton mill and playing in juvenile troupes, pierrot shows and revues, she took her first big step in 1918 when she won the part of Sally Perkins in the musical *Mr Tower Of London*, which ran for over seven years. Her career took off after she married the show's producer/comedian Archie Pitt. She started recording in 1928, and by 1933 was celebrating the sale of four million records. Guided by stage producer Basil Dean, Fields made her film debut in 1931 with *Sally In Our Alley*, from which came 'Sally', her famous theme song. In other movies such as, *Looking On The Bright Side*, *This Week Of Grace*, *Love, Life And Laughter*, *Sing*

Gracie Fields (*Sally In Our Alley*)

As We Go, Look Up And Laugh, Queen Of Hearts, The Show Goes On, We're Going To Be Rich, Keep Smiling, and *Shipyard Sally* (1939), her vitality and spirit of determination, cheerfulness and courage, endeared her particularly to working-class people during the dark years of the 30s. After divorcing Pitt, she married Italian comedian/dancer Monte Banks in 1940. When she subsequently moved to the USA, taking with her substantial assets, questions were asked in Parliament. The once supportive UK Press even went as far as branding her a traitor. During World War II she toured extensively, entertaining troops and appearing in USA stage shows, nightclubs, some films, including *Hollywood Canteen* (1944), and on her own radio programmes. After the War she was welcomed back to the UK and featured in a series of morale-building radio shows, *Gracie's Working Party*, but still retained her popularity in the USA during the 40s with chart hits 'Forever And Ever' and the Maori song, 'Now Is The Hour'. As early as 1933 she had bought a villa on the Isle of Capri, and during the 50s she went into semi-retirement there with her third husband, Boris Alperovic, emerging only for the occasional concert or record date. She made her final London appearance at her 10th Royal Command Performance in 1978. Her song hits, sung in a fine soprano voice, varied from the comic 'In My Little Bottom Drawer', 'Walter, Walter', 'I Took My Harp To A Party', 'Fred Fannakapan', and 'The Biggest Aspidistra In The World', through the spirited 'Sing As We Go' and 'Wish Me Luck As You Wave Me Goodbye', to the ballads 'Around The World', 'Pedro The Fisherman', 'Little Donkey', 'La Vie En Rose', and 'Ave Maria'. Some of her more personalized material was studied, as social documents, by the Department of Social History at the University of Lancaster. Throughout her life she worked hard for charities, including the Gracie Fields Orphanage, and was awarded the CBE in 1938. Fields was made Dame Commander of the British Empire shortly before her death in September 1979.

Compilations: *The World Of Gracie Fields* (1970), *Stage And Screen* (1972), *The Golden Years Of Gracie Fields* (1975), *Focus On Gracie Fields* (1977), *The Gracie Fields Story* (1979), *Amazing Gracie Fields* (1979), *Gracie Fields - Best Of Her BBC Broadcasts* (1980), *Life Is A Song* (1983), *The Biggest Aspidistra In The World* (1985), *Incomparable* (1985), *Isle Of Capri* (1987), *Laughter And Song* (1987), *Sally* (1988), *Queen Of Hearts* (1989), *Last Concert In America* (1989), *That Old Feeling* (1989).

Further reading: *Sing As We Go*, Gracie Fields.

Finian's Rainbow

Some Broadway musicals defy even the most determined attempts to transform them into successful movies, and *Finian's Rainbow* falls very much in that category. Twenty one years after the show made its

debut at the 46th Street in New York, E.Y. 'Yip Harburg' and Fred Saidy finally adapted their whimsical stage libretto for this film which was released by Warner Brothers in 1968. Their moralistic story told of simple Irishman Finian McLonergan (Fred Astaire), who travels to Rainbow Valley, Missitucky, USA with his daughter Sonia (Petula Clark) and a crock of gold which he has stolen from a leprechaun (Tommy Steele). Finian believes that if he buries the gold in the ground it will increase in value just as it does at Fort Knox. It does not quite work out that way, and the crock causes a heap of trouble - especially to a bigoted Southern Senator (Keenan Wynn) who turns black after tinkering with its 'three wish factor' - before Sonia falls for the leprechaun - who gets his gold back - and Finian takes off by himself to pastures new. The principle of people over profit has by then been clearly established. Most of the engaging and melodic songs from the show, by Burton Lane and Harburg, were retained for the screen version. They included 'How Are Things In Glocca Morra?', 'If This Isn't Love', 'Look To The Rainbow', 'Something Sort Of Grandish', 'That Great Come-And-Get-It Day', 'Old Devil Moon', 'When The Idle Poor Become The Idle Rich', 'When I'm Not Near The Girl I Love', 'Rain Dance', and 'The Begat'. The film, which was Fred Astaire's last musical, was directed by Francis Ford Coppola, with choreography by Hermes Pan, and was photographed in Technicolor and Panavision.

Firefly, The

Remembered particularly for one of Allan Jones's finest film performances and his thrilling rendition of 'The Donkey Serenade', *The Firefly* was released by MGM in 1937. The song itself was based on Rudolph Friml's 'Chanson', a solo piano piece written in 1920, which was arranged for the picture by Herbert Stothart, with a lyric by Robert Wright and Chet Forrest. Most of the songs from the 1912 Broadway show were discarded, and Frances Goodrich and Albert Hackett came up with a new story which was set in Spain at the time of the Napoleonic war. Jones and his co-star, Jeanette MacDonald, were both involved in espionage work during the hostilities, while their personal relationship flourished. The songs that survived from the original stage musical, with music by Rudolph Friml, were 'Giannina Mia' (lyric by Otto Harbach), 'When A Maid Comes Knocking At Your Heart' (lyric Harbach-Robert Wright-Chet Forrest), 'Love Is Like A Firefly' (lyric Wright-Forrest), and 'Sympathy' (lyric Gus Kahn-Harbach), were supplemented by several others including 'He Who Loves And Runs Away' (Friml-Kahn). Also in the cast were Henry Daniell, Warren William, Leonard Penn, Douglas Dumbrille, Billy Gilbert, and George Zucco. The choreographer was Albertina Rasch, and the opulent and entertaining Hunt

The Firefly

Stromberg production, which was photographed by Oliver T. Marsh in a sepia tint, was directed by Robert Z. Leonard.

Five Pennies, The

If they gave Oscars for embarrassment, this 1959 biopic would be a winner. The subject, Red Nichols, is caricatured by Danny Kaye and if eyes are closed, and ears to the dialogue, much of the music is fine. On-screen musicians include Shelly Manne (in the role of Dave Tough, the second time in the same year he played the part of the drummer), Bobby Troup, Ray Anthony (in the role of Jimmy Dorsey, despite his being a trumpet player), and Louis Armstrong and his current All Stars who include Peanuts Hucko, Billy Kyle and Trummy Young. Kaye and Armstrong mug their way through a vocal and trumpet duet, with Nichols himself dubbing for Kaye. Annoying cutaways relegate some of Armstrong's playing to background music behind vapid chattering by the cast. The soundtrack orchestra includes many top-flight musicians and the score, for which Leith Stevens was nominated for an Oscar, includes numerous arrangements by Heinie Beau. The scene in which Kaye/Nichols dances with his crippled daughter should be avoided at all costs.

Fleet's In, The

Blonde bombshell Betty Hutton made her screen debut in this lively, amusing and typically wartime musical which was produced by Paramount in 1942. She plays the best friend of the Countess of Swingland (Dorothy Lamour), a nightclub singer whose methods of dealing with troublesome customers ensure that she does not meet with much aggravation. One of a bunch of visiting sailors, the shy and retiring Casey Kirby (William Holden), is urged by his friends to try to make a breakthrough on behalf of the Navy, which he does - and ends up marrying her. Victor Schertzinger and Johnny Mercer provided a bunch of terrific numbers such as 'Tangerine', which was introduced by vocalists Bob Eberly and Helen O'Connell with the popular Jimmy Dorsey Orchestra, and subsequently proved to be an enormous hit for them. The rest of the songs included 'It's Somebody Else's Moon', 'When You Hear The Time Signal', and 'I Remember You' (all Lamour), 'The Fleet's In' (Betty Jane Rhodes), 'Not Mine' (Hutton and Lamour), and 'If You Build A Better Mousetrap', and 'Arthur Murray Taught Me Dancing In A Hurry' ('To my way of thinkin', it came out stinkin'/I don't know my left from my right') (both Hutton). The other songs were 'Tomorrow You Belong To Uncle Sam' and 'Conga From Honga', Also in the cast were comedian Eddie Bracken (who winds up with Hutton), Leif Erickson, Cass Daley ('an osteopathic soprano-she sings in the joints'), Barbara Brittan, Gil Lamb, and Rod Cameron. Jack Donahue staged the dances and the director was Victor Schertzinger. Walter DeLeon and Sid Silvers' screenplay was the third time the original story by Walter de Leon had been filmed. Previous efforts in the 30s starred Clara Bow and Mary Carlisle, and there was yet another remake in 1915, entitled *Sailor Beware*, with Dean Martin and Jerry Lewis.

Flight From Folly

This bright and breezy musical, one of the last films to be made at Teddington Studios in England, was released by Warner Brothers-First National in 1945. It starred one of the West End's favourite leading ladies, Pat Kirkwood. She plays showgirl Sue Brown who poses as a nurse in order to impress playwright Clinton Clay (Hugh Sinclair) while he is suffering from amnesia. The celebrated British composer Michael Carr contributed the appealing 'Never Like This Before', 'Miss Brown', and collaborated with Benjamin Frankel on the impressive 'Dream Sequence' during which Sue and Clinton 'find' each other. Frankel composed most of the film's instrumental themes such as 'Symphonic Jazz', 'Harem

Dance' and 'Fiesta Dance'. Eric Spear, too, provided much of the film's music, including 'The Sultan', 'Cuban Song', and the spectacular 'The Majorca' song-and-dance finalé. Basil Woon, Lesley Storm, and Katherine Strueby wrote the screenplay which involved chubby comedian Sydney Howard (in his last film role), Marian Spencer, Tamara Desni, A.E. Matthews, Jean Gillie, Charles Goldner and dancers Halama and Konarski. Also taking part were the bands of Edmundo Ros and Don Marino Barreto. The director of this tuneful - and, at time, quite hilarious - feature was Herbert Mason.

Flower Drum Song

Whilst being perfectly agreeable - and successful - in the form of the stage musical which opened on Broadway in 1958, this screen version which was released three years later, seemed somewhat precious and quaint, particularly in comparison with the dynamic *West Side Story* which arrived in US cinemas at round the same time. Joseph Fields and Oscar Hammerstein II were responsible for the stage libretto which was based on a novel by Chin Y. Lee. Fields' screenplay for the film, followed the original closely, telling of the mail-order bride, played by Miyoshi Umeki, who travels from Hong Kong to San Francisco for the sole purpose of marrying nightclub

Flying Down To Rio

owner Sammy Fong (Jack Soo). Things do not quite work out that way, and she finally finds happiness with student Wang Ta (James Shigeta), while Fong stays true to his longtime girlfriend, Linda Low (Nancy Kwan). Umeki was in the original Broadway cast, and so was Juanita Hall, who gave a delicious performance in the role of Madam Liang. There were several memorable numbers in Richard Rodgers and Oscar Hammerstein's score which included 'I Enjoy Being A Girl' (Kwan), 'You Are Beautiful' (Shigeta), 'Sunday' (Kwan-Soo), 'Love, Look Away' (Sato), 'Chop Suey' (Hall), 'A Hundred Million Miracles' (Umeki-Kam Tong), 'I Am Going To Like It Here' (Umeki), 'Don't Marry Me' (Umeki-Soo), 'Grant Avenue' (Kwan), and 'The Other Generation' (Fong-Hall-Adiarte). As usual, Hermes Pan's choreography was singled out for praise, as was Russell Metty's photography in Eastman Color and Panavision. Henry Koster was the director for this Universal picture, which, although pleasantly entertaining, dealt with a subject - the problems of adjustment between different generations of the Chinese-American community in the USA - that did not appeal to a wide range of cinema-goers in the early 60s.

Flying Down To Rio

It is not recorded whether the earth moved, but it certainly should have done when Fred Astaire and Ginger Rogers teamed for the first time in this film which was released in 1933 by RKO. Dolores Del Rio, as the sultry Belinha De Rezende, was supposed to be the star of a story by Cyril Hume, H.W. Hanemann and Erwin Gelsey (from a play by Anne Caldwell), in which she has to choose between the charms of the glamorous American bandleader-aviator Roger Bond (Gene Raymond) and her Brazilian boyfriend Julio Rubeire (Raul Roulien), but Astaire and Rogers stole the film away. The seven white grand pianos on which they danced 'The Carioca', proved to be the launching pad to a glittering future. That number was part of a score by Vincent Youmans (music) and Edward Eliscu and Gus Kahn (lyrics), which also included 'Orchids In The Moonlight' and 'Music Makes Me'. The spectacular 'Flying Down To Rio' sequence featured a bevy of beautiful girls clad in various modes of dress (and undress), performing a series of formation dances while balanced on the wings of biplanes apparently several thousand feet above the city. The choreography for that and the rest of the splendid dance scenes, was by Dave Gould and Hermes Pan, and the film was directed by Thorton Freedland.

Folies Bergère De Paris

From the moment when the opening titles fade and Maurice Chevalier, complete with familiar straw boater, launches into the jaunty 'Valentine' (Herbert Reynolds-Henri Christine), all sense of belief is necessarily suspended while he plays an entertainer who is hired by a wealthy businessman to substitute for him at a swanky social occasion. He fools all the guests except for the busy executive's wife (Merle Oberon) who would know her husband anywhere, or would she? Chevalier played both leading male roles, of course, and Ann Sothern was his feisty mistress. Also in the cast were Walter Byron, Eric Blore, and Lumsden Hare. Jack Stern and Jack Meskill wrote most of the songs which included 'Rhythm Of The Rain' (with Chevalier and Sothern plus lots of girls and umbrellas), 'I Was Lucky', 'Singing A Happy Song', and 'Au Revoir, L'Amour'. The best of the rest was Burton Lane and Harold Adamson's 'You Took The Words Right Out Of My Mouth'. Bess Meredyth and Hal Long wrote the screenplay which was adapted from a play by Rudolph Lothar and Hans Adler by Jessie Enst, which was also used as the basis for two other movies, *That Night In Rio* (1941) and *On The Riviera* (1951). Roy Del Routh directed *Folies Bergère De Paris*, and dance director Dave Gould won an Oscar for his staging of the spectacular 'Straw Hat' finalé.

Follow The Fleet

After their triumph in *Top Hat* in 1935, Fred Astaire and Ginger Rogers did it again with more or less the same artistic team a year later in *Follow The Fleet*. Mark Sandrich (director), Hermes Pan (dance director) and songwriter Irving Berlin, all combined for another feast of song and dance. Apart from one number, 'Let's Face The Music And Dance', Fred traded in his top hat, white tie and tails for a sailor suit in Dwight Taylor and Allan Scott's screenplay which was based on Hubert Osborne's Broadway play *Shore Leave*. The central love story concerns spinster Connie Martin (Harriet Hilliard) who falls for Bilge Smith (Randolph Scott) in such a big way that she arranges for a ship to be salvaged for him after his discharge from the US Navy. Harriet reveals the depths of her love for Bilge via two beautiful but surprisingly melancholy ballads 'Get Thee Behind Me, Satan' and 'But Where Are You?', but that is where the film's heartaches began and ended. On a much brighter note, Fred and Ginger, as Bake Baker and Sherry Martin the former dance team which split up when Bake enlisted in the navy, meet again at the Paradise Ballroom in San Francisco, and rekindle the old magic in an effort to raise money to salvage the ship. They dance everybody's cares away to glorious Berlin numbers such as 'We Saw The Sea', 'I'd Rather Lead A Band', 'Let Yourself Go', and 'I'm Putting All My Eggs In One Basket'. Future stars Tony Martin, Lucille Ball, and Betty Grable made brief but effective appearances in this RKO release which some critics thought was too long at 110 minutes. The public did not seem to agree and flocked to see *Follow The Fleet* in great numbers.

Footlight Parade

Following their highly successful teaming in *42nd Street* and *Gold Diggers Of 1932*, Dick Powell and Ruby Keeler were joined by a new boy to musicals - James Cagney - in this backstage saga which was released by Warner Brothers in 1933. Cagney plays a slick, hyperactive dance director of 'prologues', those miniature 'live' productions which were inserted between showings of main feature movies in the early days of the talkies. In Manuel Seff and James Seymour's screenplay for *Footlight Parade*, Chester Kent (Cagney) stages three of these creations, each of which has its own title song. The first, a somewhat saucy piece entitled 'Honeymoon Hotel' (Harry Warren-Al Dubin), is thought to be a follow-up from the 'Shuffle Off To Buffalo' number in *42nd Street*. Just married Powell and Keeler arrive at the hotel (where every guest's name is 'Smith'!), only to find their entire family is there to greet them. 'By A Waterfall' (Sammy Fain-Irving Kahal) is a dream sequence during which Powell and Keeler 'imagine' scores of beautiful girls swimming and relaxing in a gigantic pool which had glass sides so that head of photography George Barnes could shoot the scene from all angles. The 'five tier' finalé rounds off one of the most spectacular production numbers of any film musical. The final 'prologue', the dramatic 'Shanghai Lil' (Warren-Dubin), sees Cagney, as a sailor, scouring Shanghai saloons and opium dens for his Lil (Keeler). When he finds her in a sleazy club they perform a tap dance atop the bar before he is called back to his ship, accompanied by a sailor who looks remarkably like . . . Shanghai Lil. Fain and Kahal also contributed 'Sittin' On A Backyard Fence', and 'Ah, The Moon Is Here'. Among the rest of the cast were Joan Blondell, Guy Kibbee, Frank McHugh, Claire Dodd, Ruth Donnelly, and Hugh Herbert. *Footlight Parade*, which was directed by Lloyd Bacon and choreographed by Busby Berkeley in his own highly innovative style, remains one of the most memorable of all movie musicals.

For Me And My Gal

If asked to name Judy Garland's most famous movie partner, most people would plump for Mickey Rooney, but her partnership with Gene Kelly in films like this one, together with *Summer Stock* and *The Pirate*, were just as endearing in their way. *For Me And My Gal*, released by MGM in 1942, was Kelly's first film appearance, although he arrived on set at the age of 30 direct from his success in the title role of Richard Rodgers and Lorenz Hart's Broadway musical *Pal Joey*. In this film, which had a screenplay by Richard Sherman, Fred Finklehoffe, and Sid Silvers, Kelly is cast as Harry Palmer, an ambitious vaudeville song-and-dance-man who falls for Jo Hayden (Garland). They form a double act and dream of winning the ultimate prize - a chance to perform at the Palace Theatre. However, when they eventually achieve their goal, World War I looms large and Kelly receives his draft notice. Desperate not to miss his big career chance, he deliberately cripples his hand. His actions help him to avoid the draft but appall Garland and they split up. After suffering a crisis of conscience, Kelly travels overseas to entertain the troops, and while there becomes something of a hero. His moral transformation complete, the couple are reunited on the stage of the Palace Theatre after the war. George Murphy co-starred, and also featured were Marta Eggerth, Ben Blue, Horace (later Stephen) McNally, Keenan Wynn, and Richard Quine. Garland and Kelly sang a delightful version of 'For Me And My Gal' (Edgar Leslie-Ray Goetz-George W. Meyer), and the rest of the score - a substantial collection of memorable old numbers - included 'When You Wore A Tulip' (Jack Mahoney-Percy Wenrich), 'After You've Gone' (Turner Layton-Henry Creamer), 'Ballin' The Jack' (Jim Burris-Chris Smith), 'Oh You Beautiful Doll' (Seymour Brown-Nat D. Ayer), 'How Ya Gonna Keep 'Em Down On The Farm?' (Walter Donaldson-Sam M. Lewis-Joe Young), and 'It's A Long Way To Tipperary' (Harry Williams-Jack Judge). The many dance sequences were staged by Bobby Connelly (with uncredited assistance from Kelly), and the film, which was a product of Arthur Freed's legendary MGM unit, was directed by Busby Berkeley.

Formby, George

b. George Hoy Booth, 26 May 1904, Wigan, Lancashire, England, d. 6 March 1961, Penwortham, Lancashire, England. The son of a successful Edwardian Music Hall comedian, George Formby Snr., George Jnr. was a horse jockey before following in his father's footsteps when he died in 1921, initially doing the same comedy/song act. At first, he worked under the name of George Hoy, later changing to his father's stage name, Formby. He discarded his father's image when he introduced a ukulele into to his act and, just as significantly, married a dancer, Beryl Ingham. The lady was to mastermind, some would say dominate, the rest of his career. In the late 20s he developed a stage personality that was described variously as: 'the beloved imbecile', 'the modern minstrel' and, 'with a carp-like face, a mouth outrageously full of teeth, a walk that seems normally to be that of a flustered hen and a smile of perpetual wonder at the joyous incomprehensibility of the universe'. Self-taught on the ukulele, he developed an individual style, that even years later, was difficult to copy. Apart from a small part in a silent movie in 1915, Formby's film career started in 1934 with *Boots, Boots*, and continued until 1946 with such films as *No Limit* (1935), *Keep Your Seats Please* (1935), *Feather Your Nest* (1937), *Trouble Brewing* (1939), *Turned Out Nice Again* (1940 - his catchphrase), *Spare A Copper*

(1941), and *George In Civvy Street* (1946). As with his music hall act, the films featured a series of saucy songs such as 'With My Little Ukulele In My Hand', 'When I'm Cleaning Windows', 'Fanlight Fanny', 'Auntie Maggie's Remedy', 'She's Got Two Of Everything', 'You Don't Need A Licence For That' and 'Grandad's Flannelette Nightshirt'. Besides his other 'identity' songs such as 'Leaning On A Lamp Post', 'Chinese Laundry Blues' and 'Mr. Wu's A Window Cleaner Now'. His film image was that of a little man, with a very attractive girl friend, fighting evil in the shape of crooks or the Germans, and coming out on top in the end, to the sheer delight of cinema audiences: 'Our George has done it again!' During the 30s and 40s Formby was, along with Gracie Fields, one of the most popular entertainers in the UK. Even in the early 30s his annual earnings were estimated at around £85,000. During World War II Formby toured extensively with ENSA, entertaining troops in Europe, the Middle East and North Africa. In 1946 he was awarded the OBE for his war efforts. In 1951 he appeared in his first 'book' musical at the Palace Theatre in London's West End. The show was *Zip Goes A Million*, a musical adaptation of the George Barr McCutcheon novel, *Brewster's Millions*. It gave Formby the biggest success of his career, but six months into the run he had to withdraw after suffering a heart attack, to be replaced by comedian Reg Dixon. A year later he returned to work in the usual round of revues and summer shows, but throughout the 50s he was plagued by recurring illness. In 1960 he made his first record for 15 years. The single, 'Happy Go Lucky Me'/'Banjo Boy', was also his first to make the UK Top 40. On Christmas Day of that year his wife and manager, Beryl, died. About two months later, his fans, and especially his family, were startled when he announced his engagement to a 36-year-old schoolteacher, Pat Howson. The marriage was arranged for May, but never took place. George Formby died 6 March 1961. He left most of his fortune to his fiancée, a situation which led to a lengthy period of litigation when his relations decided to contest the will. A musical play, *Turned Out Nice Again*, set in the period just before he died, written by Alan Randall and Vince Powell, and starring Randall, was presented in 1992.

Compilations: *The World Of George Formby* (1969), *George Formby* (1970), *The Best Of George Formby* (1975), *The World Of George Formby, Volume Two* (1976), *With My Ukulele* (1981), with George Formby Snr. *A Chip Off The Old Block* (1981), *Leaning On A Lamp Post* (1986), *Easy Going Chap* (1989).

Further reading: *George Formby*, Alan Randall and Ray Seaton.

42nd Street

42nd Street

The definitive backstage musical, renowned for the director's instruction to the young understudy Peggy Sawyer (Ruby Keeler): 'Sawyer, you're going out a youngster, but you've got to come back a star!' Warner Baxter played tough guy Julian Marsh who utters those immortal words as he gives her a push into the spotlight after his has-been star Dorothy Brock (Bebe Daniels) hits the bottle and accidentally descends a long flight of stairs. Tommy Lawer (Dick Powell) is the show's juvenile lead and Peggy's biggest fan, but Ginger Rogers, as Anytime Annie, almost steals the film away from everyone. The screenplay was by James Seymour and Rian James, and Harry Warren and Al Dubin contributed some memorable songs, including 'Young And Healthy', 'Shuffle Off To Buffalo', 'You're Getting To Be A Habit With Me', 'It Must Be June', and 'Forty-Second Street'. That score, and the sensational dance routines of Busby Berkeley, make this one of the all-time great screen musicals, and are the reasons why it still sounds and looks so good more than 60 years later. Also in the cast were George Brent, Ned Sparks, Guy Kibbee, Allen Jenkins, George E. Stone, and Una Merkel. Warren and Dubin also made brief appearances, as did another well-known songwriter, Harry Akst. *42nd Street* was produced for Warner Brothers by Darryl F. Zanuck and directed by Lloyd Bacon. In 1980, a stage version began a run of more than eight years on Broadway, and, four years later, a successful production opened in London.

Fosse, Bob

b. Robert Louis Fosse, 23 June 1927, Chicago, Illinois, USA, d. 23 September 1987, Washington DC, USA. A director, choreographer, dancer, and actor for films and stage, Fosse was renowned particularly for his innovative and spectacular staging, with the emphasis very firmly on the exhilarating dance sequences. He studied ballet, tap and acrobatic dance from an early age, and, while still a youngster, performed with a partner as the Riff Brothers in vaudeville and burlesque houses. After graduating from high school in 1945, he spent two years in the US Navy before moving to New York and studying acting at the American Theatre Wing. He then toured in the chorus of various productions before making his Broadway debut as a dancer in the revue *Dance Me A Song* (1950). He worked on television and in theatres and clubs for a time until Hollywood beckoned and he moved to the west coast to appear in three films, *Give A Girl A Break*, *The Affairs Of Dobie Gillis*, and *Kiss Me, Kate* (1953). On his return to New York, he got his big break when author and director George Abbott hired him as a choreographer for *The Pajama Game* (1954). The show was a massive hit, and Fosse was much in demand - for a time at least. He met Gwen Verdon while working on *Damn Yankees* in 1955, and they were married in 1960. He choreographed *Bells Are Ringing* in 1956, and worked with Verdon again on *New Girl In Town* a year later. From then on, with the exception of *How To Succeed In Business Without Really Trying* (1961), he directed his shows as well as staging the dancing. Fosse's dual role is considered by critics to be a major factor in the success of highly successful productions such as *Redhead* (1959), *Little Me* (1962), *Sweet Charity* (1966), *Pippin* (1972), *Chicago* (1975) and *Dancin'* (1978). All the time he was back and forth to Hollywood, working on films such as *My Sister Eileen* (1955), *The Pajama Game* (1957), and *Damn Yankees* (1958), all three of which were well-received. However, *Sweet Charity* (1968), which Fosse controlled completely in his role as director and choreographer, was hammered by many critics for Shirley MacLaine's over-the-top performance, and particularly for the director's self-indulgent cinematography with its looming closeups, zooms, blurred focus effects. Fosse was in the wilderness for some time, but all was forgiven four years later when *Cabaret*, starring Liza Minnelli and Joel Grey, won eight Academy Awards, one of which went to Fosse. It was a box-office smash, and Fosse also satisfied most of the purists by confining the dance sequences to appropriate locations such as beer garden and a nightclub, rather than flooding the streets of Berlin with terpsichorean tourists. In the early 70s Fosse was applauded for his direction of *Lenny*, a film biography of the comedian Lennie Bruce, which starred Dustin Hoffman. In the light of Fosse's recent heart problems, his record as a workaholic, and his life-long obsession with perfection, many observers thought that *All That Jazz* (1979) was intended to be Fosse's own film biography with it's ghoulish, self-indulgent examination of life and death. However, no one denied the brilliance of the dance routines or the outstanding performance of Roy Schneider in the leading role. In 1983 Fosse wrote and directed his last movie, *Star 80*, which also had a lurid, tragic theme. Three years later, he wrote, staged, and choreographed his final Broadway musical, *Big Deal* - which definitely was not. Neither was it a fitting end to a brilliant career in which Fosse had created some of the most imaginative and thrilling dance routines ever seen on Broadway or in Hollywood - and won eight Tony Awards in the process. In 1987 he revived one of his most successful shows, *Sweet Charity*, and died shortly before the curtain went up on the night of 23 September.

Freed, Arthur

b. 9 September 1894, Charleston, South Carolina, USA, d. 12 April 1973. While still at school Freed began to write song lyrics. He was already an accomplished pianist and was determined to make his way as a songwriter. His first job was as a demonstrator in a Chicago music shop where he met

Minnie Marx, mother of the Marx Brothers. With her encouragement he quit his job and joined her sons' show as a singer. He later teamed up with Gus Edwards as a musical act in vaudeville. During this period he wrote many songs with different collaborators and had his first big success in 1923 with 'I Cried For You', written with Gus Arnheim and Abe Lyman. By the end of the 20s Freed was in Hollywood where he contributed the score to *The Broadway Melody* (1929) and *The Hollywood Revue Of 1929*, amongst others. Throughout the 30s he continued to write songs for films such as *Montana Moon*, *Lord Byron Of Broadway*, *Those Three French Girls*, *The Big Broadcast*, *The Barbarian*, *Going Hollywood*, *Sadie McKee*, *Student Tour*, *A Night At The Opera*, *Broadway Melody Of 1936*, *San Francisco*, *Broadway Melody Of 1938*, and *Babes In Arms* (1939). As well as being a hit for all concerned, including its stars, Judy Garland and Mickey Rooney, the latter picture was significant in that it marked the beginning of Arthur Freed's second career, that of a producer. During the next two decades the legendary Freed Unit produced most of MGM's outstanding musicals, including *The Wizard Of Oz*, *Strike Up The Band*, *Lady Be Good*, *Cabin In the Sky*, *Meet Me In St. Louis*, *The Ziegfeld Follies*, *The Pirate*, *The Barkleys Of Broadway*, *Easter Parade*, *Take Me Out To The Ball Game*, *Words And Music*, *Annie Get Your Gun*, *On The Town*, *An American In Paris* (1951 Oscar for best film), *Show Boat*, *Singin' In The Rain*, *The Band Wagon*, *Brigadoon*, *Kismet*, *Silk Stockings*, and *Gigi*, (1958 Oscar for best film). During his long stay at MGM Freed's closest associate was musical arranger and songwriter Roger Edens. However, his chief composing partner was Nacio Herb Brown, with whom he wrote 'After Sundown', 'Alone', 'The Boy Friend,' Broadway Rhythm', 'You Were Meant For Me', 'The Wedding Of The Painted Doll', 'The Broadway Melody', 'Singin' In The Rain', 'Should I?', 'Temptation', 'Fit As A Fiddle', 'Pagan Love Song', 'Alone', 'I Got A Feelin' You're Foolin', 'You Are My Lucky Star', ' Lovely Lady', 'Good Morning', 'All I Do Is Dream Of You', and many others. These were all written for various films before Freed devoted himself to producing, although several of their most popular numbers were reprised in *Singin' In The Rain* (1951), including the title song which was originally introduced in *Hollywood Revue Of 1929*. For *Singin' In The Rain* Freed and Brown wrote a new song, 'Make 'Em Laugh', which Donald O'Connor immediately made his own. Freed's other collaborators included Al Hoffman, Harry Warren, and Burton Lane. For a number of years in the 60s Freed was president of the American Academy of Motion Picture Arts and Sciences, from whom he received the Irving Thalberg Award in 1951 and a further award in 1967 'for distinguished service to the Academy and the production of six top-rated Awards telecasts'. Arthur

Freed's brother, Ralph Freed (b. 1 May 1907, Vancouver, Canada, d. 13 February 1973, California, USA), was also a lyricist, and contributed songs, written mainly with composers Burton Lane and Sammy Fain, to several movies during the 30s and 40s. These included *Champagne Waltz* (1937), *College Holiday*, *Double Or Nothing*, *Swing High, Swing Low*, *Cocoanut Grove*, *She Married A Cop*, *Babes On Broadway*, *Ziegfeld Girl*, *Dubarry Was A Lady*, *Thousands Cheer*, *Thrill Of Romance*, *No Leave, No Love*, *Two Sisters From Boston*, and *Ziegfeld Follies* (1946). One of his numbers, 'The Worry Song' (with Fain), was featured in the renowned live/action sequence in *Anchors Aweigh* in which Gene Kelly danced with Jerry the cartoon mouse. His other songs included 'How About You?', 'You Leave Me Breathless', 'Love Lies', 'Smarty', 'Little Dutch Mill', 'Hawaiian War Chant', and 'Who Walks In When I Walk Out?'.
Further reading: *The Movies' Greatest Musicals-Produced In Hollywood USA By The Freed Unit*, Hugh Fordin.

Friedhofer, Hugo Wilhelm

b. 3 May 1901, San Francisco, California, USA, d. 17 May 1981. After an early career as a painter, Friedhofer turned to another branch of the arts, taking up the cello and studying composition under Domenico Brescia. He wrote music to accompany silent films and in 1929 went to Hollywood to arrange and direct music for the new sound films. When procedures changed and composers were hired to write specifically for films, Friedhofer was well-suited for a new role, and was called upon to orchestrate the music for *Keep Your Sunny Side Up*. He later orchestrated music composed by acclaimed and much better-known people such as Erich Wolfgang Korngold, Max Steiner and Franz Waxman. The films on which he worked for these composers are numerous and his contribution to their success undoubted, if undervalued. As a film composer in his own right, Friedhofer's first complete score was for the 1938 film, *The Adventures Of Marco Polo*. He also composed for films such as *Brewster's Millions*, *Joan Of Arc*, *Body And Soul*, *No Man Of Her Own*, *Hondo*, *Vera Cruz*, *Young Lions* and *The Best Years Of Our Lives* (for which he won an Oscar), and *One-Eyed Jacks* - just a few of a very long list. Greatly admired by fellow musicians as diverse as Paul Glass and John Lewis, Friedhofer remained almost unknown to the world outside. Gene Lees, a longtime friend, wrote movingly of him in his book, *Singers And The Song*.

Friml, Rudolph

b. 8 December 1879, Prague, Bohemia, d. 12 November 1972, Hollywood, California, USA. An important composer who helped to perpetuate the romantic operetta-style of musical which was so popular in America at the turn of the century. After studying at Prague University, Friml toured Europe and America as a concert pianist and settled in the US in 1906. As a composer his first opportunity came when he took over from Victor Herbert on the score for *The Firefly* (1912) from which came 'Gionnina Mia' and 'Sympathy'. His collaborator for that show was Otto Harbach, and the two men worked together on a further nine productions. Throughout his career Friml's other lyricists and librettists included P.G. Wodehouse, Herbert Reynolds, Harold Atteridge, Rida Johnson Young, Oscar Hammerstein II, Brian Hooker, Clifford Grey, Dailey Paskman, Edward Clark, Chisholm Cushing, and Rowland Leigh. He composed the music for some of the most popular songs of the time in a list of shows which includes *High Jinks* ('The Bubble'; 'Love's Own Kiss'; 'Not Now But Later'), *The Peasant Girl* ('Love Is Like A Butterfly'; 'Listen, Dear'; 'And The Dream Came True'), *Katinka* ('Allah's Holiday'; 'I Want to Marry A Male Quartet'; 'Katinka'), *You're In Love* ('I'm Only Dreaming'; 'You're In Love'), *Glorianna* ('My Climbing Rose'; 'Toodle-oo'), *Sometime* ('Sometime'; 'Keep On Smiling') *Tumble Inn* ('Snuggle And Dream'; 'I've Told My Love'), *The Little Whopper* ('You'll Dream And I'll Dream'; ''Round The Corner'), *June Love* ('June Love'; 'The Flapper And The Vamp'; 'Don't Keep Calling Me Dearie'), *Ziegfeld Follies Of 1921* ('Bring Back My Blushing Rose'; 'Every Time I Hear The Band Play'), *The Blue Kitten* ('When I Waltz With You'; 'Cutie'; 'Blue Kitten Blues'), *Cinders* ('Belle Of The Bronx'; 'I'm Simply Mad About The Boys'), *Rose-Marie* ('Rose-Marie'; 'Indian Love Call'; 'Totem Tom-Tom'; 'Song Of The Mounties'), *The Vagabond King* ('Only A Rose'; 'Song Of The Vagabonds'; 'Some Day'), *The Wild Rose* ('Brown Eyes'; 'One Golden Hour'), *No Foolin'* ('Wasn't It Nice?'; 'Florida, The Moon And You'), *The Three Musketeers* ('March Of The Musketeers'; 'Ma Belle'; 'Queen Of My Heart'; 'Heart Of Mine'), *The White Eagle* ('Gather The Rose'; 'Give Me One Hour'), *Luana* ('My Bird of Paradise'; 'Aloha'), and *Music Hath Charms* (1934) ('My Heart Is Yours'; 'Sweet Fool'). In the lavish 1935 film version of Friml's first show, *The Firefly*, Allan Jones had a big hit with 'The Donkey Serenade' which was adapted from Friml's composition 'Chansonette', a piece he had originally written for the *Ziegfeld Follies Of 1923*. Some of his other shows were filmed and he also wrote the music for the 1947 movie *Northwest Outpost*. Friml's last two shows, *Luana* and *Music Hath Charms*, only ran for some 20-odd performances each and he appeared unable or unwilling to adapt his music to the ever-growing American-style of musical comedy, although he remained active in his later years and appeared frequently on US television.

Funicello, Annette (see **Annette**)

Funny Face

George and Ira Gershwin's 1927 Broadway hit, *Funny Face*, took 30 years to travel from New York to Hollywood, but the wait was well worthwhile. Screenwriter Leonard Gershe discarded the orginal story entirely and adapted the plot from his own unproduced musical *Wedding Day*. Five songs survived the trip - and so did Fred Astaire who had co-starred with his sister Adele in *Funny Face* in both New York and London. In this new scenario Fred plays a fashion photographer who transforms a shy, intellectual Greenwich Village librarian (Audrey Hepburn) into a cover girl for a sophisticated magazine. She agrees to go with him to Paris for the photo-shoot so that she can meet her intellectual mentor who is portrayed in the film in the manner of Jean-Paul Sartre, the founder of the currently popular Existentialist movement. However, he and his philosophies are soon forgotten shortly after the elegant Astaire takes her in his arms and the magical music begins. Although Astaire was in his late 50s, the years just seemed to fall away as he recreated those wonderful numbers from 30 years ago, such as 'Funny Face', ''S Wonderful', 'He Loves And She Loves', and 'Let's Kiss And Make Up'. Hepburn, too, was charming on 'How Long Has This Been Going On?', which had been written for the original show but was cut before the New York opening night. Kay Thompson gave an outstanding performance as the magazine editor with lots of pizzazz, and duetted with Astaire on another Gershwin song, 'Clap Yo' Hands', which had been used previously in the musical *Oh, Kay!* (1926). Leonard Gershe and Roger Edens contributed 'Bonjour Paris', 'On How To Be Lovely', and 'Think Pink' which was the opening number in what is generally regarded as a visually gorgeous movie. Much of the credit for that aspect of the production is said to be due to fashion photographer Richard Avedon's work as visual consultant. Ray June photographed the film in Technicolor and VistaVision. *Funny Face* was originally conceived by the Arthur Freed Unit at MGM, who, for various reasons, decided not to proceed with it themselves and sold it to Paramount, along with the services of MGM stalwarts such as Edens, Gershe, director Stanley Donen, dance director Eugene Loring, and music arranger Adolph Deutsch. In 1992 *Funny Face* was released on laserdisc with its colour enhanced and in a slightly 'letterboxed' format.

Funny Girl

Youth and experience were celebrated by the Academy Awards committee in April 1969, when Barbra Streisand and Katharine Hepburn tied for the best actress Oscar. It was Hepburn's third Award, for her 36th film, while Streisand was making her movie debut in what proved to the role-of-a-lifetime as comedienne Fanny Brice, the most famous star of the *Ziegfeld Follies*. Streisand had already enjoyed much

Funny Girl

success on Broadway and in London with this saga of Fanny's on-stage triumphs and her turbulent marriage to compulsive gambler Nicky Arnstein (Omar Sharif). Kay Medford, who was in the original Broadway cast, recreated her fine and funny performance as Fanny's typically Jewish mother, and some of the other parts went to Walter Pidgeon (as Florenz Ziegfeld), Anne Francis, Ma Questel, Lee Allen, Tommy Rall, and Gerald Mohr. Three of Brice's genuine hit songs, 'My Man' (Channing Pollock-Maurice Yvain), 'I'd Rather Be Blue Over You (Than Be Happy With Somebody Else)' (Billy Rose-Fred Fisher), and 'Second Hand Rose' (Grant Clarke-James F. Hanley), were added to what remained of Jule Styne and Bob Merrill's splendid stage score and some additional songs they wrote especially for the film. Streisand's big emotional numbers such as 'People', 'His Love Makes Me Beautiful', and 'Don't Rain On My Parade', were all retained, and the rest of the songs, including several comedy items which fitted the 'funny girl' like a glove, were 'I'm The Greatest Star' (Streisand), 'If A Girl Isn't Pretty' (Streisand-Medford-Questel), 'Roller Skate Rag' (Streisand), 'You Are Woman, I Am Man' (Streisand-Sharif), 'Sadie, Sadie' (Streisand), 'The Swan' (orchestral ballet parody), and 'Funny Girl' (Streisand). Styne and Merrill wrote at least one more title song, a lively, up-tempo number which Streisand

released on record but was not included in the film. Isobel Lennart, adapted her own witty stage libretto for the screenplay, and Herbert Ross designed the often hilarious choreography. He is also said to have collaborated with director William Wyler on some of the film's spectacular sequences, including the 'Don't Rain On My Parade' number which Streisand performed while tearing around on various modes of transport, ending up on a tugboat in New York harbour. *Funny Girl* was photographed by Harry Stradling in Technicolor and Panavision and released by Columbia in 1968. According to *Variety*, it went on to become the 10th highest-grossing film of the decade.

Barbra Streisand starred in the 1975 sequel, *Funny Lady*, in which Fanny marries producer Billy Rose (James Caan), but is still unable to find enduring happiness. John Kander and Fred Ebb provided most of the songs, including the appealing 'How Lucky Can You Get?', 'Isn't It Better?', 'Blind Date', 'Let's Hear It For Me', and 'So Long, Honey Lamb', and there were also several oldies such as 'More Than You Know' (Billy Rose-Edward Eliscu-Vincent Youmans), 'I Found A Million Dollar Baby' (Rose-Mort Dixon-Harry Warren), and 'Great Day' (Rose-Eliscu-Youmans). Roddy McDowall, Ben Vereen, and Carole Wells were also in the cast, along with

Omar Sharif, who made a brief appearance as Fanny's ex-husband who passes briefly through her life again. The screenplay was by Jay Presson Allen and Arnold Shulman, and Herbert Ross was present again, this time as choreographer-director.

Funny Lady (see **Funny Girl**)

G

Gang's All Here, The

Although Alice Faye, Carmen Miranda, Phil Baker and Benny Goodman And His Orchestra were top-billed in this 1943 20th Century-Fox release, the real star, by general consent, was director-choreographer Busby Berkeley. Taking full advantage of Edward Cronjager's photography and the Technicolor process, early in the film Berkeley created the famous 'The Lady In The Tutti-Frutti Hat' sequence during which dozens of girls manipulating gigantic bananas dance around Carmen Miranda who is topped by her basket of fruit *chapeau*. Later on, Alice Faye joins a group of snazzily dressed children in the spectacular finalé based on 'The Polka Dot Polka', in which Berkely added a display of pink and other delicately coloured discs and fluorescent rings to his trade-mark kaleidoscopic patterns. In between those two quite stunning set pieces, there was a slight story by Walter Bullock which involved a US Army sergeant (James Ellison) who finds it impossible to resist a nightclub singer (Faye), especially when she sings Harry Warren and Leo Robin's tearful 'No Love, No Nothin'' and 'A Journey To A Star': millions of real-life American (and British) servicemen and civilians knew exactly how he felt. As for the rest, the slim and sassy Charlotte Greenwood's high-kicks were well up to her usual standard, clarinettist Benny Goodman's vocals on 'Minnie's In The Money' and 'Paducah' (with Miranda) were not in the least offensive, and Miranda combined with Baker (and others) for the lively 'You Discover You're In New York'. Among a strong supporting cast were the always amusing Edward Everett Horton, Sheila Ryan, Eugene Pallette, Tony DeMarco, and Dave Willock. Two future movie favourites, Jeanne Crain and June Haver, also made brief appearances.

Garland, Judy

b. Frances Gumm, 10 June 1922, Grand Rapids, Minnesota, USA, d. 22 June 1969. The Gumms were a theatrical family. Parents, Frank and Ethel, had appeared in vaudeville as Jack and Virginia Lee and, later, with the addition of their first two daughters, Mary Jane and Virginia, appeared locally as 'The Four Gumms'. 'Baby Frances' joined the troupe when she was a little over two years of age and it was quickly apparent that with her arrival, even at that early age, the Gumm family had outgrown their locale. The family moved to Los Angeles, where all three girls were enrolled in a dance school. When Frank Gumm bought a run-down theatre in Lancaster, a desert town north of Los Angeles, the family moved again. Domestic problems beset the Gumm family throughout this period and Frances's life was further disrupted by Ethel Gumm's determined belief in her youngest daughter's show-business potential. The act had become the Gumm Sisters, although Baby Frances was clearly the one audiences wanted to see and hear. In 1933 Ethel Gumm returned to Los Angeles, taking the girls with her. Frances was again enrolled in a theatrical school. A visit to Chicago was an important step for the girls, with the youngest once more attracting the most attention; here too, at the urging of comedian George Jessell, they changed their name to the Garland Sisters. On their return to Los Angeles in 1934 the sisters played a successful engagement at Grauman's Chinese Theater in Hollywood. Soon afterwards Frances was personally auditioned by Louis B. Mayer, head of MGM. Deeply impressed by what he saw and heard, Mayer signed the girl before she had even taken a screen test. With another adjustment to her name, Frances now became Judy Garland. She made her first film appearance in *Every Sunday* (1936), a short musical film which also featured Deanna Durbin. Her first major impact on audiences came with her third film, *Broadway Melody Of 1938*, in which she sang 'Dear Mr Gable' (to a photograph of Clark Gable), seguing into 'You Made Me Love You'. She was then teamed with MGM's established child star, Mickey Rooney, a partnership which brought a succession of popular films in the 'Andy Hardy' series. By now, everyone at MGM knew that they had a star on their hands. This fact was triumphantly confirmed with her appearance in *The Wizard Of Oz* (1939), in which she sang 'Somewhere Over The Rainbow', the song with which she would subsequently always be associated. Unfortunately, this period of frenzied activity came at a time when she was still developing physically. Like many young teenagers, she tended to put on weight and this was something film-makers could not tolerate. On the one hand they did not want a pudgy celebrity; on the other it was the practical effect of not wanting their star to change appearance during the course of a film. Whatever the reason, she was prescribed some drugs for weight control, others to ensure she was bright and perky for the long hours of shooting, and still more to bring her down at the end of the day so that she could sleep. These were the days before the side effects of amphetamines (which she took to suppress her appetite) were understood, and no one at the time knew that the pills she was taking in such huge quantities were habit-forming. Adding to the growing girl's problems were emotional difficulties which had begun during her parents' stormy relationship, and which were exacerbated by the high pressure of her new life. In 1941, against the wishes and advice of her mother and the studio, she married David Rose and soon afterwards became pregnant but was persuaded, by her mother and Mayer, to have an abortion. With her personal life firmly on the downward slide towards later disasters, Garland's successful film career now took a further upswing. In 1942 she appeared in *For Me And My Gal*, then made *Presenting Lily Mars*, *Thousands Cheer*, *Girl Crazy* (all 1943), *Meet Me In St Louis* (1944), *The Harvey Girls*, *Ziegfeld Follies* and *Till The Clouds Roll By* (all 1946). Garland's popularity extended beyond films into radio and records, but her private life was still in disarray. In 1945 she divorced Rose and married Vincente Minnelli, who had directed her in *Meet Me In St Louis*. In 1946 her daughter, Liza Minnelli, was born. The late 40s brought more film successes with *The Pirate*, *Easter Parade*, *Words And Music* (all 1948) and *In The Good Old Summertime* (1949). Although Garland's career appeared to be in splendid shape, in 1950 her private life was fast deteriorating. Pills and alcohol and severe emotional disturbances led to her failing to appear before the cameras on several occasions and resulted in the ending of her contract with MGM. In 1951 her marriage to Minnelli also finished and she attempted suicide. Her subsequent marriage to Sid Luft and his handling of her career brought an upturn both emotionally and professionally. She made a trip to Europe, appearing at the London Palladium to great acclaim. On her return to the USA she played the Palace Theater in New York for a hugely successful 19-week run. Her film career resumed with a dramatic/singing role in *A Star Is Born* (1954), for which she was unsuccessfully nominated for an Oscar. By the late 50s all the problems were back, and in some cases had worsened. She suffered nervous and emotional breakdowns, her marriage was on the rocks, and she made further suicide attempts. A straight dramatic role, in *Judgement At Nuremberg* (1961), for which she was again nominated for an Oscar, enhanced her reputation. However, her marriage was still in trouble, although she and Luft made repeated attempts to hold it together (they had two children, Lorna and Joey). Despite the personal traumas and the professional ups and downs, Garland achieved another huge success with a personal appearance at New York's Carnegie Hall on 23 April 1961, the subsequent album of the concert winning five Grammy Awards. A 1963 television series was

disappointing and, despite another good film performance in a dramatic role, in *A Child Is Waiting* and a fair dramatic/singing appearance in *I Could Go On Singing* (both 1963), her career remained plagued with inconsistencies. The marriage with Luft ended in divorce, as did a subsequent marriage. Remarried again in 1968, Garland attempted a comeback with a club appearance in London but suffered the indignity of a major flop. On 22 June 1969 she was found dead, apparently from an overdose of sleeping pills. She was at her best in such films as *Meet Me In St Louis* and *The Wizard Of Oz* and on stage for the superb Carnegie Hall concert, and had she done nothing else, she would have earned a substantial reputation as a major singing star. To her powerful singing voice she added great emotional depths, which came not only through artifice but from the sometimes cruel reality of her life. When the catalogue of personal tragedies was added to Garland's performing talent she became something else, a cult figure, a show business legend. She was a figure that only Hollywood could have created and yet, had she been a character in a melodrama, no one would have believed such a life was possible.

Selected albums: *Judy* (1956) *Judy In Love* (1958), *Garland At The Grove* (1959), with John Ireland *The Letter* (1959), *Judy At Carnegie Hall* (1961, 2-LP set), *Judy! That's Entertainment* (1961), *Star Years* (1961), *Magic* (1961), *Our Love Letter* (1963), *Alone* (1963), *Miss Show Business* (1963), *Just For Openers* (1964), with Liza Minnelli *Live At The London Palladium* (1965), *Judy Garland* (1965), *The Last Concert 20-7-68* (1968). Compilations: *The Young Judy Garland* (c.1938-42), *The Beginning* (1979).

Further reading: *Judy Garland*, Anne Edwards. *Judy and Liza*, James Spada with Karen Swenson. *The Other Side Of The Rainbow: With Judy Garland On The Dawn Patrol*, Mel Torme. *Judy Garland*, David Shipman. *World's Greatest Entertainer,* John Fricke.

Garrett, Betty

b. 23 May 1919, St. Joseph, Missouri, USA. After winning a scholarship to a New York theatre company, Garrett enjoyed some success on the stage. She was an accomplished dancer, working with the celebrated Martha Graham troupe, and she also sang in clubs and hotel lounges. She made her Broadway debut in 1942 in the revue *Let Freedom Ring*, and had supporting roles in other stage shows such as *Something For The Boys*, *Jackpot*, and *Laffing Room Only*. After starring in *Call Me Mister* (1946) in which she introduced Harold Rome's 'South America, Take It Away', she was signed to a film contract. In the late 40s she sang and danced with immense zest and vitality in popular movie musicals such as *Anchors Aweigh*, *Big City*, *Words And Music*, *Take Me Out To The Ball Game*, *On the Town*, and *Neptune's Daughter*. After retiring to have children she attempted a

The Gay Divorcee

comeback but her husband, Larry Parks, who had starred in two bio-pics about Al Jolson, had been blacklisted for refusing to testify before the House Un-American Activities Committee, and her career, too, was severely damaged. Later, Garrett and Parks developed a nightclub act and, later still, they worked in repertory theatres. She made one more film musical in the 50s, *My Sister Eileen*, but was reluctant to be parted from Parks and dropped out of that area of show business. She did appear on television, however, with roles in the long-running comedy *All In The Family*, and *Laverne And Shirley* (1976). In the 80s she toured with Sheree North and Gale Storm in the comedy *Breaking Up The Act*, and returned to Broadway in the short-lived stage adaptation of the hit film musical *Meet Me In St. Louis*. In 1990 her one-woman show, *Betty Garrett And Other Songs*, was acclaimed at the Ballroom in New York, and in the early 90s she presented her cabaret act, which includes Broadway and Hollwood songs old and new - plus a little Jacques Brel - at London's Pizza On The Park.

Gay Divorcee, The

It was not just the title that was changed when Cole Porter's 1932 hit Broadway show, *The Gay Divorce*, was transferred to the screen two years later. The title itself was not seen to be fit for wider consumption in America, and only one song, the incomparable 'Night And Day', survived from the smart and sophisticated stage score. Fortunately, Fred Astaire also made the trip from New York to Hollywood, and the screenplay, by George Marion Jnr., Dorothy Yost and Edward Kaufman, remained reasonably true to the original book. After the plot, which was set in an English seaside town and involved Guy Holden (Astaire) being mistaken for the professional co-respondent hired by Mimi Glossop (Ginger Rogers) in an effort to facilitate her divorce, had got under way, delighted audiences were able to sit back and enjoy the sublime dancing of Astaire and Rogers in their first starring role together. 'Night And Day' would dominate any film musical, especially when it accompanied dancing of this style and grace, *The Gay Divorcee* was no exception, but there were several other engaging numbers by a variety of composers, including 'A Needle In A Haystack' (Con Conrad-Herb Magidson), and two by Mack Gordon and Harry Revel - 'Don't Let It Bother You' and 'Let's K-nock K-nees'. The latter was punched out with a great deal of zest by Betty Grable, whose 'pin-up' image during the 40s neccessitated her own legs being insured for many thousands of dollars. 'Night And Day' may have been the film's major romantic moment, but *The Gay Divorcee* is probably best-remembered for another song, 'The Continental' (Conrad-Magidson), which was introduced by Fred and Ginger in a spectacular 17-minute sequence, and went on to become all the rage of dance floors everywhere. It also has the distinction of being the first song to win an Academy Award. Meanwhile, back to the plot. As for the details of the prospective divorce, a character by the name of Rodolfo Tonetti (Erik Rhodes) turned out to be the real co-respondent, and the rest of the cast was made up of always reliable and amusing supporting players such as Edward Everett Horton and Alice Brady. Dave Gould and Hermes Pan were responsible for the innovative choreography, and the film, which was released by RKO, was directed by Mark Sandrich. In view of the film's title change, which was apparently demanded by the US censor, it is interesting that his UK equivalent had no such problems, and both the original British cinema and subsequent video release bear the title: *The Gay Divorce*.

Gay, Noel

b. Richard Moxon Armitage, 3 March 1898, Wakefield, Yorkshire, England, d. 3 March 1954, London England. A prolific composer and lyricist, Gay was responsible for many of the most popular and memorable songs in the UK during the 30s and 40s. A child prodigy, he was educated at Wakefield Cathedral School, and often deputized for the Cathedral organist. In 1913 he moved to London to study at the Royal College of Music, and later became the director of music and organist at St Anne's Church in Soho. After four years studying for his MA and B.Mus. at Christ's Church College, Cambridge, he seemed destined for a career in a university or cathedral. While at Cambridge he became interested in the world of musical comedy, and started to write songs. After contributing to the revue, *Stop Press*, he was commissioned to write the complete score for the *Charlot Show Of 1926*. He was also the principal composer for *Clowns In Clover*, which starred Jack Hulbert and Cecily Courtneidge, and ran for over 500 performances. Around this time he took the name of Noel Gay for his popular work to avoid embarrassment to the church authorities. In 1930, Gay, with Harry Graham, wrote his most successful song to date, 'The King's Horses', which was sung in another Charlot revue, *Folly To Be Wise*. He then collaborated with lyricist Desmond Carter for the score of his first musical show, *Hold My Hand* (1931). Starring Jessie Matthews, Sonnie Hale and Stanley Lupino, the songs included 'Pied Piper', 'What's In A Kiss', 'Hold My Hand' and 'Turn On The Music'. During the 30s Gay wrote complete, or contributed to, scores for popular shows such as *She Couldn't Say No*, *That's A Pretty Thing*, *Jack O'Diamonds*, *Love Laughs!*, *O-Kay For Sound* (the first of the famous Crazy Gang Music Hall-type revues at the London Palladium, in which Bud Flanagan sang Gay's 'The Fleet's In Port Again'), *Wild Oats* and *Me And My Girl* (1937). The latter show, with a book and lyrics by L. Arthur Rose, and starring Lupino Lane in the central role of Bill Sibson, ran for over 1,600 performances and featured 'The Lambeth Walk', which became an enormously popular sequence dance craze - so popular, in fact, that when the show was filmed in 1939, it was titled *The Lambeth Walk*. In the same year, with Ralph Butler, Gay gave Bud Flanagan the big song, 'Run Rabbit Run', in another Crazy Gang revue, *The Little Dog Laughed*. During the 40s, Gay wrote for several shows with lyrics mostly by Frank Eyton, including *Lights Up* ('Let The People Sing'), 'Only A Glass Of Champagne' and 'You've Done Something To My Heart'); *Present Arms*; *La-Di-Di-Di-Da'*; *The Love Racket*; *Meet Me Victoria*; *Sweetheart Mine*; and *Bob's Your Uncle* (1948). His songs for films included 'All For A Shilling A Day' and 'There's Something About A Soldier' Sung by Courtneidge in *Me And Marlborough* (1935); 'Leaning On A Lamp Post' introduced by comedian George Formby in *Feather Your Nest*; 'Who's Been Polishing The Sun', sung by Jack Hulbert in *The Camels Are Coming*; 'I Don't Want To Go to Bed' (Lupino in *Sleepless Nights*); and 'All Over The Place' (*Sailors Three*). Gay also composed 'Tondeleyo', the first song to be synchronized into a British talking picture (*White Cargo*). His other songs included 'Round The Marble Arch', 'All For The Love Of A Lady', 'I Took My Harp To A Party' (a hit for Gracie Fields), 'Let's Have A Tiddley At The Milk Bar', 'Red, White And Blue', 'Love Makes The World Go Round', 'The Moon Remembered, But You Forgot', 'The Girl Who Loves A Soldier', 'The Birthday Of The Little Princess', 'Are We Downhearted? - No!', 'Hey Little Hen', 'Happy Days Happy Months', 'I'll Always Love You', 'Just A Little Fond Affection', 'When Alice Blue Gown Met Little Boy Blue', 'I Was Much Better Off In The Army' and 'My Thanks To You' (co-written with Norman Newell). His other collaborators included Archie Gottler, Clifford Grey, Dion Titheradge, Donavan Parsons and Ian Grant. In the early 50s, Gay wrote very little, just a few songs such as 'I Was Much Better Off In The Army' and 'You Smile At Everyone But Me'. He had been going deaf for some years, and had to wear a hearing aid. After his death in March 1954, his publishing company, Noel Gay Music, which he had formed in 1938, published one more song, 'Love Me Now'. His son, Richard Armitage (b. 12 August 1928, Wakefield, England, d. 17 November 1986), a successful impresario and agent, took over the company, and extended and developed the organization into one of the biggest television and representational agencies in Europe. His clients included David Frost, Rowan Atkinson, Esther Rantzen, Russ Conway, Russell Harty, Jonathan Miller, John Cleese, the King's Singers and many more. The publishing side had several hit copyrights, including the Scaffold's 'Thank U Very Much'. After mounting several minor productions, Armitage revived his father's most popular show, *Me And My Girl*, in London in February 1985. With the versatile actor, Robert Lindsay as Sibson, a revised book, and two other Gay hits, 'The Sun Has Got His Hat On' and 'Leaning On A Lamp Post' interpolated into the score, it was an immediate success, and closed in 1993 after a stay of eight years, shortly after *Radio Times*, another production featuring Noel Gay's music, had enjoyed a brief West End run. Opening on Broadway in 1986, *Me And My Girl* ran for over 1,500 performances, New York's biggest hit for years. Armitage died three months after the show's Broadway debut.

Gaynor, Mitzi

b. Francesca Mitzi Gerber, 4 September 1930, Chicago, Illinois. USA. A vivacious and extremely talented actress, singer and dancer, reputedly of Hungarian descent, who graced several good movie musicals in the 50s, and is probably best-remembered as the girl who tried to 'wash that man (Rossano Brazzi) right out of her hair' in *South Pacific* (1958). After taking ballet lessons from an early age, Gaynor danced with the Los Angeles Civic Light Opera while in her early teens, and made a strong impression with Betty Grable and Dan Dailey in her first movie, *My Blue Heaven* (1950). This was followed by one or two straight parts, and a few musicals such as *Golden Girl*, *Bloodhounds Of Broadway*, *Down Among The Sheltering Palms*, and *The 'I Don't Care' Girl* (1953), which were not so satisfying. The situation improved as the 50s progressed and she had excellent roles in *There's No Business Like Show Business*, *Anything Goes*, *The Birds And The Bees*, *The Joker Is Wild*, and *Les Girls* (1957). She was fine, too, in *South Pacific*, but although it remains, to date, the fourth highest-grossing screen musical of the 60s in the USA, she was reportedly personally disaffected with the experience. Her kind of film musicals were becoming extinct, anyway, and, like so many others, she worked more and more in television and had her own top-rated specials during the 60s. She also toured in stage musical revivals, and, as an accomplished actress, continued to play the occasional comedy or dramatic movie role. Gaynor also built up a skilful and highly regarded concert and cabaret act. As recently as 1987 she was acclaimed for her nightclub performances which included a section devoted to Irving Berlin and Fred Astaire, a satirical version of Harry Von Tilzer and Arthur Lamb's 19th century song 'A Bird In A Gilded Cage', and a rousing singalong 'God Bless America' finalé. Two years later she embarked on an 11-month, 36-city tour of the USA in a revival of Cole Porter's 1934 show *Anything Goes*, the first time in her long career that she had been on the road in a book musical.
Selected album: *Sings The Lyrics Of Ira Gershwin* (1959), and soundtrack recordings.

Mitzi Gaynor with Ray Walston (*South Pacific*)

Gene Krupa Story, The

This film made in 1959 is another jazz bio-pic that misses its target by a mile. Sal Mineo portrays Gene Krupa as a sulky rebel, which the real-life drummer was not although Mineo probably was. Despite other shortcomings, Mineo convincingly played on-screen drums to Krupa's ghosted backing; and, to his credit, the actor later acknowledged the film's mediocrity. From this telling of Krupa's tale no one could imagine that he was a heart-throb idol of millions and one of the greatest showbiz attractions of his era. But, then, any film on Krupa which manages to miss out Benny Goodman is more than a little short on veracity. Shot in black and white, the film's director was Don Weis. Musically, there are low and high points. Amongst the former is a scrappy jam session with Red Nichols; the best of the latter is a wonderful version of 'Memories Of You' sung by Anita O'Day. Shelly Manne appears as Dave Tough (he also played the late drummer in *The Five Pennies*). Krupa's return to the stage after drugs bust that put him in jail and cost him his highly popular band is quite well represented with Tommy Pederson playing the role of Tommy Dorsey who hired Krupa in 1944. In 1989 a projected remake was abandoned when a leading Hollywood star, interested in the role of Krupa, had to bow out to meet other obligations. (Alternative title: *Drum Crazy*).

Gentlemen Marry Brunettes (see *Gentlemen Prefer Blondes*)

Gentlemen Prefer Blondes

Carol Channing really started something in 1949 when she created the role of diamond-loving Lorelei Lee in the hit Broadway musical *Gentlemen Prefer Blondes*. Ever since then - even into the early 90s - actresses all over the world have endeavoured to purvey the mixture of sexiness and vulnerability that was Lorelei, and one of them who got it just about right, in this 1953 screen version, was Marilyn Monroe. It all started with Anita Loos' novel which she turned into the stage show with the help of Joseph Fields. Charles Lederer's screenplay followed the same familiar path: thoroughly modern 20s girls Lorelei and her best friend, Dorothy Shaw (Jane Russell), travel to Paris with the intention of improving Lorelei's finances and Dorothy's marriage prospects. After causing a certain amount of havoc among the city's male population, they return to New York having accomplished their aims (and celebrate with a double wedding). The supporting cast was exceptionally fine, and included Charles Coburn, Tommy Noonan, Elliot Reid, Taylor Holmes, Norma Varden, Steven Geray, the seven-years-old 'frog-voiced' George Winslow, and the 20-year-old George (*West Side*

Story) Chakiris. Only three of Jule Styne and Leo Robin's songs survived from the original show: the delicious 'Diamonds Are A Girl's Best Friend' (Monroe), 'A Little Girl From Little Rock' - or rather, 'Two Girls From Little Rock' (Monroe-Russell) - and 'Bye, Bye Baby'. Hoagy Carmichael and Harold Adamson contributed two more: 'Ain't There Anyone Here For Love?', Jane Russell's touching plea to a gymnasium full of muscular males, and the reflective 'When Love Goes Wrong' (Monroe-Russell). The whole affair was a delight, with Monroe and Russell, who were really so different in style, both giving marvellous performances. Jack Cole designed the spirited choreography, and the director was Howard Hawks. Sol C. Seigel produced the film in Technicolor for 20th Century-Fox.

A sequel, *Gentlemen Marry Brunettes*, was released in 1955. Jeanne Crain replaced Marilyn Monroe and played Jane Russell's sister in a lacklustre, pale shadow of the original which, apart from the title song by Herbert Spencer and Earle Hagen, had a score consisting of old standards.

Gershwin, George

b. 26 September 1898, New York City, New York, USA, d. 11 June 1937. Although a poor student, and happy to spend his days playing in the streets, Gershwin took up piano when the family bought an instrument for his older brother, Ira Gershwin. He quickly showed enormous enthusiasm for music, taking lessons and studying harmony and theory. His musical taste was eclectic; he listened to classical music and to the popular music of the day, in particular the music of black Americans which was then gaining a widespread appeal. He became a professional musician in 1912, playing piano at holiday resorts in upstate New York and then working as a song plugger. He continued with his studies and began to write music. His first songs were undistinguished, but attracted the attention of important figures such as Sophie Tucker, Harry Von Tilzer and Sigmund Romberg. Some of his early compositions were influenced by ragtime - 'Rialto Ripples' (1916, with Will Donaldson) was one such example - and he also continued to gain a reputation as a performer. In 1917 he was hired as rehearsal pianist for a Jerome Kern - Victor Herbert Broadway show. His compositions continued to appear, some with lyrics by his brother Ira and others by Irving Caesar. It was a 1919 collaboration with Caesar that gave Gershwin his first hit: 'Swanee' had originally been played by the popular Arthur Pryor band, but it was when Al Jolson sang it in *Sinbad* (1919) that it became a success. Also in 1919, Gershwin was commissioned to write the music for *George White's Scandals Of 1919*. The score included such milestones in American popular music as 'I'll Build A Stairway To Paradise' (lyrics by Buddy De Sylva and Ira Gershwin) and 'Somebody Loves Me' (lyrics by De Sylva and Ballard MacDonald). In the early 20s Gershwin continued to write successful songs, including 'Do It Again' (with De Sylva), 'Oh, Lady, Be Good', 'Fascinating Rhythm' and 'The Man I Love' (with Ira). This same period saw his first success in an area of music removed from the popular song and the Broadway stage. An unsuccessful song from George White's *Scandals Of 1922*, 'Blue Monday Blues' (unsuccessful because it was dropped as being too downbeat), had attracted the attention of Paul Whiteman, who commissioned George to write an extended piece that was to be classical in structure but which would use the jazz idiom. The result was 'Rhapsody In Blue', first performed by Whiteman, with the composer at the piano, in 1924. The joint successes of the Gershwin brothers continued into the late 20s with 'That Certain Feeling', 'Someone To Watch Over Me', 'Clap Yo' Hands', 'Fidgety Feet', 'Do, Do, Do', 'Maybe', ''Swonderful', 'How Long Has This Been Going On', 'I've Got A Crush On You' and 'Liza' (the last with lyrics by Ira and Gus Kahn).

Many of the foregoing songs first appeared in shows for which the Gershwin brothers wrote complete scores, among them *Oh, Kay!* (1926), *Funny Face* (1927, which starred Adele and Fred Astaire) and *Rosalie* (1928 which also had contributions from P.G. Wodehouse and Romberg. The Gershwins' celebrity was maintained in the early 30s with *Strike Up The Band* (1930) with its popular title song, and *Girl Crazy* (1930), which starred Ethel Merman whose big number was 'I Got Rhythm' and which had Ginger Rogers in the ingenue role, singing 'But Not For Me' and duetting on 'Embraceable You'. In the pit band for *Girl Crazy* were up-and-coming musicians such as Benny Goodman, Glenn Miller and Gene Krupa. *Of Thee I Sing* (1931) was another hit, but the next two Broadway shows were flops. After the success of 'Rhapsody In Blue' Gershwin had again written music in classical form with his 'Concert In F' (1925), a tone poem, 'An American In Paris' (1928) and his 'Second Rhapsody' (1930). In 1935 his folk opera *Porgy And Bess* opened in Boston, Massachusetts, and despite early critical disapproval and audience disinterest, it became one of his most performed works, with songs such as 'It Ain't Necessarily So', 'Bess, You Is My Woman Now', 'Loves You, Porgy', 'I Got Plenty Of Nuttin'' and 'Summertime'. Having seen the possible end of their success story on Broadway, the Gershwin brothers went to Hollywood in 1936, which they had visited a few years earlier with only modest results. Now they entered into a new phase of creativity, writing 'They All Laughed', 'Let's Call The Whole Thing Off' and 'They Can't Take That Away From Me' for *Shall We Dance* (1937), which starred Astaire and Rogers, and 'Nice Work If You Can Get It' and 'A Foggy Day' for *A Damsel In Distress* (1937), in which Astaire again starred. It was while he was working on the next film, *The Goldwyn Follies* (1938), that George Gershwin was taken ill. A brain tumour was discovered and he died in June 1937. Despite the severity of his illness, Gershwin's songs for the film, 'Love Walked In' and 'Love Is Here To Stay' were among his best work. Although his lifespan was relatively short, Gershwin's work was not merely extensive but was also imperishable and provides a substantial contribution to the Great American Song Book. Little of his work has dated and it is performed as much, if not more, in the 80s and 90s as it ever was in his lifetime. As with so many of his contemporaries, Gershwin's popular songs adapted to the latest musical developments, in particular incorporating concepts from the jazz world and, not surprisingly, his work is especially popular among jazz instrumentalists. It is, however, with singers that the full glory of Gershwin's music emerges and he remains a key and influential figure in the story of American popular song. In 1992 the musical, *Crazy For You*, opened on Broadway. It was 'very loosely based' on the Gershwins' 1930 show, *Girl Crazy*, with several additional numbers, and was still running in the summer of 1993. In the same year, a West End production opened to rave notices, and looked set for long residency.

Further reading: *Gershwin*, Edward Jablonski. *The Memory Of All That: The Life Of George Gershwin*, Joan Peyser.

Gershwin, Ira

b. 6 December 1896, New York City, New York, USA, d. 17 August 1983. Like his younger brother, George Gershwin, Ira was an indifferent student but became fascinated by popular music and in particular by the lyrics of songs. He began writing seriously in 1917 and had a number of minor successes, sometimes using the pseudonym 'Arthur Francis'. In the 20s and 30s he was closely associated with his brother, George, collaborating on Broadway shows such as *Tip Toes*, *Lady, Be Good!*, *Oh, Kay!*, *Funny Face*, *Rosalie*, *Strike Up The Band*, *Girl Crazy*, *Let 'Em Eat Cake*, and *Porgy And Bess*. From those productions came some of the perennial standards of American popular song. Despite the high level of productivity the brothers maintained, and which produced such hits as 'That Certain Feeling', 'Someone To Watch Over Me', 'Do, Do, Do', ''S Wonderful', 'How Long Has This Been Going On?', 'I've Got A Crush On You', 'I Got Rhythm', 'But Not For Me', 'It Ain't Necessarily So', and 'Embraceable You', Ira Gershwin found time to write lyrics for other composers. Among these other songs were 'Cheerful Little Earful' (with Billy Rose and Harry Warren), 'Let's Take A Walk Around The Park' (with Warren and E.Y. 'Yip' Harburg) and 'I Can't Get Started' (with Vernon Duke). In 1931, the brothers' collaboration on the Broadway show, *Of Thee I Sing*, resulted in an unprecedented honour when it became the first musical to be awarded a Pulitzer Prize. Just before George died in 1937, he worked with Ira on the movies *A Damsel In Distress* ('A Foggy Day', 'Nice Work If You Can Get It') and *Shall We Dance?* ('Let's Call The Whole Thing Off', 'They All Laughed', 'They Can't Take That Away From Me'). In the years immediately after his brother's tragically early death, Ira Gershwin wrote little but eventually resumed work, collaborating with Kurt Weill on the Broadway musical *Lady In The Dark*. He also wrote for films with Jerome Kern (Cover Girl), Harold Arlen (A Star is Born), and Harry Warren (The Barkleys of Broadway). Several of his and George's stage shows were adapted for the screen, and a collection of their old numbers formed the score for the Oscar-winning An American In Paris (1951). In 1959 Ira published a delightful collection of his works entitled *Lyrics On Several Occasions*. He retired the following year, occasionally working on lyrics of past successes when they needed refining or updating for revivals of the most popular Gershwin shows. He died in August 1983. Ten years later some of his most popular lyrics were still being heard in New York and London in productions of *Crazy For You*, a re-hash of the Gershwins' 1930 hit, *Girl Crazy*. Further reading: *Lyrics On Several Occasions*, Ira Gershwin. *The Complete Lyrics Of Ira Gershwin*.

Gigi

The golden era of MGM films musicals was drawing to a close when this most delightful of films was released in 1958. The original story, by the French novelist Colette, had previously been adapted into a non-musical film in 1948 starring Daniele Delormé and Gaby Morlay, and a play which was subsequently presented in New York and London. Alan Jay Lerner's screenplay for this musical treatment was set in Paris at the turn-of-the-century and tells of the young, strong-willed Gigi (Leslie Caron), who is being brought up by her grandmother, Mamita (Hermione Gingold) and her great-aunt Alicia (Isabel Jeans) to be a courtesan, but breaks with that family tradition – and actually marries her suitor, Gaston Lachailles (Louis Jourdan). Watching over this somewhat shocking situation is Honoré Lachailles (Maurice Chevalier), Gaston's grandfather and a good friend of Mamita. He is also a gentleman with much experience in the delights of romance, and so is appalled when Gaston, his well-heeled grandson, who, permanently surrounded by lovely ladies and all the other good things in life, declares that 'It's A Bore'. That was just one of Alan Jay Lerner and Frederick Loewe's memorable songs which were so skilfully integrated into the charming story. Other highlights included Chevalier's 'Thank Heaven For Little Girls' ('Those little eyes so helpless and appealing/One day will flash, and send you crashing through the ceiling'), 'The Parisians' (Caron), 'Waltz

At Maxim's (She Is Not Thinking Of Me)' (Jordan), 'The Night They Invented Champagne' (Caron-Jourdan-Mamita), 'Say A Prayer For Me Tonight' (Caron), 'I'm Glad I'm Not Young Anymore' (Chevalier), and 'Gigi (Gaston's Soliloquy)' (Jourdan). For many, the most endearing moment came when Honoré and Mamita reminisced about old times with 'I Remember It Well' (He: 'You wore a gown of gold.'/She: 'I was all in blue.'/He: 'Am I getting old?'/She: 'Oh, no - not you.'). Vincente Minnelli directed the film which was mostly shot on location in Paris, and the producer was Arthur Freed. It was magnificently photographed in Metrocolor and CinemaScope by Joseph Ruttenberg, and he won one of the picture's Academy Awards, along with those for Cecil Beaton's sumptous costumes and best picture, director, writer (Lerner), art direction-set direction (William A. Horning and Preston Ames; Henry Grace and Keogh Gleason), film editing (Adrienne Fazan), best song ('Gigi'), and scoring of a musical picture (André Previn). At the same awards ceremony Maurice Chevalier received a special Oscar 'for his contributions to the world of entertainment for more than half a century'. Gigi was one of the Top 10 highest-grossing films of the 50s in the USA, but subsequent stage productions did not appeal. The 1973 Broadway production starring Alfred Drake, Agnes Moorhead, Maria Karnilova and Daniel Massey only ran for three months, and West End audiences saw Gigi for seven months in 1985-86.

Girl Crazy (see Babes In Arms)

Glamorous Night

When Ivor Novello's hit show opened at the Drury Lane Theatre in London in 1935, critics were quick to compare its story of the king who is so infatuated with a gypsy girl that he is willing to give up his throne, with a similar state of affairs between the King of Rumania and Mme. Lupesco. Two years later, when this film version was released by the Associated British Picture Corporation, a situation much nearer home - the abdication of King Edward owing to his relationship with the American Mrs. Simpson - was still very fresh in the British people's minds. Mary Ellis recreated her stage role as the fiery gypsy, and Otto Kruger gave a fine performance as the weak and confused king. Barry Mackay, in the role originally played by Ivor Novello, was suitably macho as the young Englishman who saves the Romany girl's life, and the villainy and comedy aspects were handled by Victor Jory and Finlay Currie respectively. Other roles went to Trefor Jones, Anthony Holles, Maire O'Neill, Charles Carson, and Felix Aylmer. Most of Ivor Novello and Christopher Hassall's lovely stage score survived, including four of the most popular pieces, 'Shine Through Your Dreams', 'Fold Your Wings', 'When A Gypsy Played', and 'Glamorous Night'. The

screenplay was adapted from Novello's original play by Dudley Leslie, Hugh Brooke, and William Freshman. Fritz Arno Wagner photographed this lavish and good-looking production which was directed by Brian Desmond Hurst.

Glenn Miller Story, The

Well directed by Anthony Mann, and with James Stewart very good as Miller (but much warmer-hearted than the real man), this 1953 bio-pic does not let a cliche go by. Miller's search for a 'new sound' is hounded to death (scratch any ex-sideman of Miller and you get a different version of how he achieved it) but omits the obvious, if dull, solution that it was all a matter of workmanlike arranger sticking to his trade. The cross-country slogs on a tour of one-night stands is well shown and the studio-assembled band accurately recreates Miller's music. Stewart copes well with his on-screen trombone miming and off-screen Joe Yukl (and possibly Murray McEachern) provide the sound. Miller's disappearance, just before Christmas 1944, is tied into a mythical 'gift' to his wife of an arrangement of her favourite tune, 'Little Brown Jug'. In fact, Miller's hit recording of this tune came some years before but, no matter, this way the film can end without a dry eye in the house. In a jazz club sequence, the 1953 edition of the Louis Armstrong All Stars, including Barney Bigard, William 'Cozy' Cole and Trummy Young, teams up with a handful of 30s swing stars, including Gene Krupa and Babe Russin, to knock spots off 'Basin Street Blues'.

Go Into Your Dance

The only film in which Al Jolson and his wife, Ruby Keeler, starred together was released by Warner Brothers in 1935. Al plays a woman-chasing entertainer on the loose in Chicago, hanging around clubs such as La Cucaracha (complete with sombrero and Mexican shawl), before Keeler is persuaded by a mutual friend to look after him. After surviving being framed for a murder he probably is not even capable (mostly too drunk) of committing, he and Keeler celebrate the happy ending in their own nightspot. The songs, by Harry Warren and Al Dubin, included a smart little floor-show number for Keeler called 'A Good Old-Fashioned Cocktail', and there were several attractive items for Jolson such as 'She's A Latin From Manhattan', 'Mammy, I'll Sing About You', and 'Go Into Your Dance'. He also strutted with Keeler in the film's highspot, a spectacular production number constructed around the spirited 'A Quarter To Nine', in which, after a brief and slightly incongruous segue into 'Way Down Upon The Swanee River', the faces of Jolson and the male chorus turn black, while their top hats become white. It was almost as if the film was being shown in negative, except that Keeler's face and costume remained white all the time. Torch singer Helen

The Glenn Miller Story

Morgan, who was to make such an impact as Julie in the film of *Show Boat* in 1936, also brought a touch of class to *Go Into Your Dance* with a lovely version of 'The Little Things You Used To Do'. Earl Baldwin wrote the screenplay, Bobby Connolly created the lively and enterprising choreography, and the film was directed by Archie Mayo.

Going Hollywood

Bing Crosby was on temporary loan from Paramount for this 1933 MGM release which teamed him with Marion Davies, who, despite being a talented actress, is best-known for her friendship with millionaire newspaper tycoon William Randolph Hearst. Screenwriter Donald Ogden Stewart's slight story concerns a young teacher (Davies), who follows her crooning idol (Crosby) to Hollywood, and masquerades as a maid before playing a starring role in Bing's latest movie (and his subsequent personal life) when his leading lady (Fifi D'Orsay) hits the bottle. Generously built comedienne Patsy Kelly, who had enjoyed success in Broadway revues, made a big impression in her screen debut, and the cast also included Stuart Erwin, Bobby Watson, Ned Sparks and Sterling Holloway. Nacio Herb Brown and Arthur Freed wrote songs, and one of them, the powerful 'Temptation', became popular for Crosby at

the time of the picture's release, and was revived by Perry Como some 10 years later. The other songs included the spirited 'Going Hollywood', 'Beautiful Girl', 'After Sundown', 'Our Big Love Scene', and 'We'll Make Hay While The Sun Shines' which became a record hit for Crosby and was also popular with the British dance bands of the period, particularly Billy Merrin And His Commanders. *Going Hollywood* was directed by Raoul Walsh and the choreographer was Albertina Rasch. Bing Crosby did not appear in another film for MGM until *High Society* in 1956.

Going My Way

This enormously successful light-comedy musical was released by Paramount in 1944. It starred Bing Crosby as Father Chuck O'Malley, a young priest whose attempts to introduce order to the run-down St. Dominick's Church in a tough area of New York. bring him into conflict with the crotchety long-time incumbent, Father Fitzgibbon (Barry Fitzgerald). Frank Butler and Frank Cavett's screenplay (from an original story by producer-director Leo McCarey) was warm and tender, without being maudlin, but there was not a dry eye in the house when, towards the end, the two men resolve their differences and Father Fitzgibbon is reunited with his aged mother (Adeline DeWalt Reynolds). Crosby and Fitzgerald were

Going My Way

splendid together, and the admirable supporting cast included Risë Stevens, Jean Heather, Frank McHugh, Gene Lockhart, William Frawley, Carl Switzer, Stanley Clements, James Brown, and the Robert Mitchell Boys' Choir. Jimmy Van Heusen and Johnny Burke wrote three of the songs: 'The Day After Forever' (Crosby-Heather), 'Going My Way' (Crosby-Stevens), and the lively 'Swinging On A Star', which Crosby performed in beguiling style at the piano, surrounded by a group of youngsters. He also gave a memorable reading of the lovely 1914 ballad 'Too-Ra-Loo-Ra-Loo-Ral' (J. R. Shannon). The rest of the score consisted of 'Silent Night' (Franz Gruber), 'Ave Maria' (Schubert), and 'Haberna' (Bizet). Not only was *Going My Way* one of the top money-spinners of the decade, it also scooped the Oscars for 1944, winning for best picture, actor (Crosby), supporting actor (Fitzgerald), director (McCarey), original story (McCarey), and song ('Swinging On A Star').

Bing Crosby reprised his role of Father O'Malley in *The Bells Of St. Mary's* which was released by RKO in 1945. This time he was called upon to win over Sister Benedict (Ingrid Bergman) at the local Catholic school, but still found the time to sing 'Aren't You Glad You're You?' (Van Heusen-Burke). *The Bells Of St. Mary's* was even more successful at the box-office than *Going My Way*.

Gold Diggers Of Broadway

This film, the first in a series of popular backstage musicals produced by Warner Brothers in the early days of sound, was released in 1929. It was adapted from Avery Hopwood's 1919 play *The Gold Diggers*, which the studio orginally filmed as a silent in 1923. Robert Lord's charming and amusing screenplay was all about a trio of chorus girls played by Winnie Lightner, Nancy Welford and Anne Pennington, whose feminine charms break down all social barriers in their quest for well-heeled husbands. Al Dubin and Joe Burke's tuneful score contained two enduring numbers, 'Painting The Clouds With Sunshine' and 'Tip Toe Through The Tulips', which were introduced by Nick Lucas, a singer with an appealing, easy-going style. He had enormous record hits with both of them. The rest of the songs included 'What Will I Do Without You?', 'And They Still Fall In Love', 'Go To Bed', 'In A Kitchenette', 'Song Of The Gold Diggers', and 'Mechanical Man'. Also in the cast were Conrad Tearle, Lilyan Tashman, William Blakewell, and Helen Foster. The lively dance sequences were staged by Larry Ceballos, and the director was Roy Del Ruth. It was filmed in two-colour Technicolor, a process which, at times, could be surprisingly effective. Even as early as this in the evolvement of movie musicals, different studios were beginning to specialise in their own particular aspects of the genre: Universal had their operettas with Maurice Chevalier and Jeanette MacDonald, MGM pioneered revue-type features, RKO were to enjoy tremendous success with the Fred Astaire and Ginger Rogers dance diversions, and Warners soon led the way (with MGM in hot pursuit) in memorable backstage sagas such as *42nd Street* and *Footlight Parade* and others in the same vein:

Gold Diggers Of 1933. Dick Powell and Ruby Keeler, who had made such a favourable impression in the aforementioned *42nd Street*, were reunited for this film whose screenplay, by Erwin Gelsey, James Seymour, David Boehm, and Ben Markson, was again based on that Avery Hopwood play. Harry Warren and Al Dubin's songs provided the inspiration for choreographer Busby Berkeley's memorable production numbers, complete with his trademark 'top shots': 'We're In The Money', in which Ginger Rogers, her fellow chorus girls, and the stage on which they are performing, are completely clad in various-sized models of silver dollars (an ironic touch considering America was still in the midst of its worst Depression); 'Shadow Waltz', and a spectacular array of white-wigged girls in double-hooped dresses 'playing' neon-edged violins; and 'Pettin' In The Park', a risqué sequence, during which several apparently nude female forms are tantalisingly silhouetted behind flimsy roller blinds. When the blinds are raised the girls emerge dressed in *metal* costumes, and the scene ends with Dick Powell hard at work with a can opener! The most poignant sequence, though, is 'Remember My Forgotten Man', a powerful portrait of post-World War I disillusionment with the American Dream, which culminates in three sets of armed soldiers marching over a curved bridge set, while, in the foreground, Joan Blondell sings the heart-rending lyric. All in all, with its persistent emphasis on the scarcity of money, the picture was as much a social document as a lively and entertaining musical. Also among the cast were Warren William, Aline MacMahon, Guy Kibbee, Ned Sparks, Sterling Holloway, and Dennis O'Keefe. Mervyn LeRoy directed, and this edition, and the rest of the series, was shot in more conventional black and white.

Gold Diggers Of 1935. Busby Berkeley served as director as well as choreographer, and this picture is mainly remembered for his creation of one of the most outstanding sequences in movie musical history based on the Oscar-winning song 'Lullaby Of Broadway'. It begins as dawn breaks, and ends 24 hours later. The spectacular climax comes when Dick Powell and Wini Shaw, a couple of good-time pleasure seekers, are seated high up in a nightclub looking down on a sensational orgy of power tap dancing, after which the girl falls to her death from a window. Another memorable number is 'The Words Are In My Heart', during which more than 50 girls

seated at white pianos are slickly manoeuvred around in time with the music - by very small men, if you look closely enough. Harry Warren and Al Dubin also contributed the appealing 'I'm Going Shopping With You'. Manuel Seff and Peter Milne's slight screenplay (adapted from a story by Robert Lord and Peter Milne), concerns the efforts of the wealthy set to put on a lavish musical show at a country house (makes a change from a barn). Also involved were Adolph Menjou, Frank McHugh, Gloria Stuart, Glenda Farrell, Alice Brady, Joseph Cawthorn, Hugh Herbert, Grant Mitchell, and Virginia Grey.

Gold Diggers Of 1937. Dick Powell's last '*Gold Diggers*' outing found him cast as an insurance salesman who sells a $1 million life-insurance policy to a Broadway producer (Victor Moore)- and ends up starring in the (still healthy) impresario's lavish show. Yet again Busby Berkeley came up with some marvellous production numbers including 'Let's Put Our Heads Together' (Harold Arlen-E.Y. 'Yip' Harburg) with its bevy of girls on rocking chairs, and the razzamatazz finalé, 'All's Fair In Love And War' (Warren-Dubin), in which Joan Blondell puts a kind of all-girl military band, some 70 strong, through their paces, predating the 'Seventy-Six Trombones' sequence in *The Music Man* by some 25 years. Powell also introduced the delightful 'With Plenty Of Money And You' (Warren-Dubin), and the score was completed by 'Life Insurance Song', 'Speaking Of The Weather', and 'Hush Ma Mouth' (Arlen-Harburg). Also cast were Glenda Farrell, Lee Dixon, Osgood Perkins, and Rosalind Marquis. Warren Duff wrote the screenplay and the director was Lloyd Bacon.

Gold Diggers In Paris (1938). Rudy Vallee takes a three-girl dance act to Europe where they are mistaken for a classical troupe - with the inevitable complications. Earl Baldwin and Warren Duff's slight story was just an excuse for more of Berkeley's ingenious ideas based around such numbers as 'I Wanna Go Back To Bali', 'The Latin Quarter', 'Put That Down In Writing', and 'A Stranger In Paree' (all Warren-Dubin), and 'Day Dreaming All Night Long', 'Waltz Of The Flowers' and 'My Adventure' (Warren-Mercer). Rosemary Lane was Vallee's love interest, and supporting the couple were Hugh Herbert, Allen Jenkins, and Gloria Dickson. Ray Enright directed, but the *Gold Diggers* concept was worn out. However, it resurfaced once more (to date) in:

Painting The Clouds With Sunshine (1951). Named after one of the hit songs in the original 1929 film, it was loosely based on Avery Hopwood's story, only this time the girls (Virginia Mayo, Virginia Gibson and Lucille Norman) are sisters, and Las Vegas is the base for the male chase. Most of the songs were old standards, and the creaky screenplay was by Harry Clark, Roland Kibbee, and Peter Milne. Gene Nelson, Dennis Morgan, S.Z. Sakall, Tom Conway,

Gold Diggers Of 1935

and Wallace Ford tried their best to put some life in it, as did choreographer LeRoy Prince and director David Butler. It was photographed in Technicolor by William Jacobs, and, like the rest of what is regarded as an historic series, produced by Warner brothers.

Goldsmith, Jerry

b. Jerrald Goldsmith, 10 February 1929, Los Angeles, California, USA. Goldsmith is a prolific composer for films and television, from the late 50s through to the 90s. Besides studying music at the University of South Carolina, Goldsmith also took lessons in office practice, and secured a job as a clerk/typist with CBS Television, before moving to the company's music department in Los Angeles in 1950. During the 50s, first as a staffer, and then as a freelancer, he wrote theme music for popular television series such as *Gunsmoke, Perry Mason, Have Gun Will Travel, The Twilight Zone, The Man From U.N.C.L.E., Doctor Kildare*, and several more. In the late 50s, Goldsmith started to compose for films such as *Black Patch* and *City Of Fear* and, through the good auspices of film composer Alfred Newman, he came to prominence with his score for *Lonely Are The Brave* (1962). It was the start of a career in which he composed the music for over 150 films, ranging from westerns such as *Rio Conchos, Bandolero!* and a re-make of *Stagecoach* to the 'schockers', *Poltergeist, The Omen, Damien: Omen II,*

The Final Conflict, Psycho II and *Seconds*. He was also involved in *Star Trek, Gremlins, Total Recall, Rambo, Patton, Tora! Tora! Tora!, Chinatown, Freud, Seven Days In May, The Secret Of Nimh* and *Islands In The Stream*. The latter film was one of several that he made with his favourite director, Franklin Schaffner. The others included *The Boys From Brazil, The Stripper, Papillon, Planet Of The Apes* and *Patton*. During the 60s it was estimated that Goldsmith was averaging about six films a year. These included *The Prize, Seven Days In May, The Spiral Road, Lilies Of The Field, In Harm's Way, The Trouble With Angels, The Sand Pebbles, The Blue Max, In Like Flint, To Trap A Spy, A Patch Of Blue, Von Ryan's Express, The Satan Bug, The Flim-Flam Man, The Detective* and *Justine*. Throughout the 70s, 80s and early 90s, he was still one of the busiest film composers, contributing to movies such as *The Mephbisto Waltz, The Reincarnation Of Peter Proud, MacArthur, Capricorn One, Coma, Magic, The First Great Train Robbery, Outland, Raggedy Man, Under Fire, King Solomon's Mines, Hoosiers, Extreme Prejudice, Best Shot, Innerspace, Warlock, Rambo III, Gremlins: The New Batch, Star Trek V The Final Frontier, The Russia House, Sleeping With The Enemy, Not Without My Daughter, Total Recall, Basic Instinct, Mom And Dad Save The World, Forever Young, Love Field, Matinee, The Vanishing, Dennis,* and *Malice* (1993). By this stage, 16 of his scores had been nominated for an Academy

Award, but only *The Omen* (1976) received an Oscar. In addition to composing, Goldsmith conducted orchestras such as the San Diego Symphony and Britain's Royal Philharmonic, playing his music in concert halls around the world.

Good News

Twenty years after it became a smash-hit Broadway musical, *Good News* came to the screen in 1947 courtesy of MGM. It was one of songwriters' De Sylva, Brown And Henderson's 'fad' musicals - and the fad this time was US football. Star player Tommy Marlowe (Peter Lawford) might not be able to play for Tait college in the big game because he has been neglecting his studies and concentrating on having fun and games with Pat McClellan (Patricia Marshall). However, after Connie Lane (June Allyson) has helped him to swot, Tommy wins the game and Connie as well. Classy singer Mel Tormé was in the admirable supporting cast, along with Joan McCracken, Donald MacBride, Ray McDonald, Robert Strickland, Tommy Dugan, Clinton Sundberg, and Loren Tindall. The lively and hugely enjoyable 'Varsity Drag' and 'Good News' were two of the songs retained from the original stage production in a score which included 'He's A Ladies Man', 'Lucky In Love', 'The Best Things In Life Are Free', 'Just Imagine' (all De Sylva, Brown And Henderson), 'The French Lesson' (Roger Edens-Kay Thompson), and 'Pass That Peace Pipe' (Edens-Ralph Blane-Hugh Martin) which accompanied just one of the entertaining and energetic dance numbers staged by Robert Alton and Charles Walters. Betty Comden and Adolph Green's screenplay (their first) was adapted from De Sylva and Laurence Schwab's Broadway libretto, and film was produced by Arthur Freed. The director, Charles Walters, was also making his film debut. A previous version of *Good News* had been made in 1930 as an early talkie. It starred Bessie Love, Stanley Smith, Gus Shy and Mary Lawlor, and used more songs from the stage show than this 1947 version did.

Goodnight Vienna

After a brief foray to Hollywood in 1930 to co-star with Jeanette MacDonald in Ernst Lubitsch's *Monte Carlo*, Jack Buchanan returned to England for this popular film which was released by the British Dominions company two years later. Set in Vienna in 1914, it concerns a bachelor gay, Captain Maximilian Schlettoff (Buchanan), who falls in love with Viki (Anna Neagle), a pretty young assistant in a flower shop. On the night they are due to elope the gallant Captain is ordered to leave for the war front immediately, and the note he sends to Viki is never delivered. She is distraught when she receives a letter from Maximilian's father (Clive Currie) telling her that his son has entered into an arranged marriage

with Countess Helga (Joyce Bland). After the war has ended, the Captain returns to Vienna in reduced financial circumstances and gets a job in a shoe shop where one of his first customers is Viki - now a famous opera star. She is initially aloof, but eventually, according to the film's publicity hand-out at the time, 'they meet again in a charming café set amidst flowering trees, where in the old days they had laughed and sung with carefree joyousness, and their favourite song re-unites them.' All four of the songs in the film, 'Just Heaven', 'Living In Clover', 'Marching Song', and 'Goodnight Vienna', were the work of Eric Maschwitz and George Posford, who also adapted the screenplay from the original radio play. Buchanan gave his usual engaging performance, and Anna Neagle, who had come to prominence only the year before in Buchanan's musical comedy *Stand Up And Sing*, was delightful and obviously a star in the making. Gina Malo as Frieda, headed a supporting cast which included William Kendall, Herbert Carrick, Gibb McLaughlin, Clifford Heatherley, O.B. Clarence, Aubrey Fitzgerald, Peggy Cartwright, and Muriel Akred. The producer-director was Herbert Wilcox. For its release in the USA the film was re-titled *Magic Night*.

Goodwin, Ron

b. 17 February 1925, Plymouth, Devon, England. Although deeply interested in all things musical, Goodwin began his working life outside music. Eventually, he took a job as a music copier with a firm of music publishers. He also studied trumpet and arranging at the Guildhall School of Music in London. He played trumpet professionally with Harry Gold and wrote arrangements for the bands of Ted Heath and Geraldo. Goodwin made several records, arranging and conducting the backing music for singers, including Petula Clark, and also worked in radio. He has written music in the classical form, including his 'Drake 400 Concert Suite' and 'New Zealand Suite', but it is as a writer for films that he made his greatest impact. After first writing for documentaries, he went on to provide scores for a succession of British feature films including *I'm All Right, Jack* (1960), *The Day Of The Triffids* (1963), *633 Squadron* (1964), *Those Magnificent Men In Their Flying Machines* (1965), *Battle Of Britain* (1969), *Where Eagles Dare* (1969) and *Frenzy* (1972). In the 70s Goodwin made concert tours of the UK with an orchestra performing his own film scores. He continued to broadcast on the radio and has also worked extensively in Canada.

Selected albums: *Adventure And Excitement/Music For An Arabian Night* (1959), *Legend Of The Glass Mountain* (1970), *Spellbound* (1973), *Drake 400 Concert Suite* (1980), *Projections* (1983), *Fire And Romance* (1984), *New Zealand Suite* (1984), *Christmas Wonderland* (1985), *Love Album* (1985).

Gordon, Mack

b. Morris Gittler, 21 June 1904, Warsaw, Poland, d. 1
March 1959, New York, USA. This prolific lyricist
composed mainly for movie songs during the 30s and
40s. Gordon was taken to the USA at an early age,and
grew up in the Brooklyn area of New York. He
toured with minstrel shows as a boy soprano, and later
became a singer-comedian in vaudeville, before
starting to write songs in the late 20s. His 'Aintcha',
with music by Max Rich, was featured in the 1929
movie, *Painted Heels*, and he also contributed to *The
Song Of Love* and *Swing High* (1930). In the same year
he teamed with Harold Adamson and Vincent
Youmans for 'Time On My Hands', which was
performed by Marilyn Miller and Paul Gregory in the
Broadway revue, *Smiles*. In 1931, Gordon began a
collaboration with composer Harry Revel which
lasted until 1939. Initially they contributed songs to
stage shows such as the *Ziegfeld Follies Of 1931* ('Help
Yourself To Happiness' and 'Cigarettes, Cigars') and
Everybody's Welcome ('All Wrapped Up In You') but,
from 1933 onwards, they wrote mainly for the movies
- over 30 of them. These included *Broadway Thru A
Keyhole*, starring Russ Columbo and Constance
Cummings, and featuring 'Doin' The Uptown
Lowdown'; *Shoot The Works* ('With My Eyes Wide
Open I'm Dreaming'); *Sitting Pretty* ('Did You Ever
See A Dream Walking?'); *We're Not Dressing*, with
Bing Crosby and Carole Lombard ('May I?', 'Love
Thy Neighbour' and 'She Reminds Me Of You');
The Gay Divorcée, ('Don't Let It Bother You', sung by
Fred Astaire); *College Rhythm* ('Stay As Sweet As You
Are'); *Love In Bloom* ('Here Comes Cookie' and 'My
Heart Is An Open Book'); *Two For Tonight*, with
Crosby and Joan Bennett ('Without A Word Of
Warning' and 'From The Top Of Your Head');
Collegiate ('I Feel Like A Feather In The Breeze' and
'You Hit The Spot'); *Stowaway* starring Shirley
Temple, Alice Faye and Robert Young ('Goodnight
My Love' and 'One Never Knows, Does One?');
Wake Up And Live ('Never In A Million Years' and
'There's A Lull In My Life'); *You Can't Have
Everything* (title song); *Love Finds Andy Hardy*, with
Judy Garland and Mickey Rooney ('What Do You
Know About Love?' and 'Meet The Beat Of My
Heart'); *Thanks For Everything* (title song) and *My
Lucky Star* ('I've Got A Date With A Dream'). In
1940, Gordon teamed up with Harry Warren, fresh
from his Warner Brothers triumphs with Al Dubin.
During the next 10 years, they wrote some of
America's most memorable popular songs, for films
such as *Down Argentine Way* (title song and 'When
Two Dreams Met'); *Tin Pan Alley* ('You Say The
Sweetest Things, Baby'); *That Night In Rio* ('Chica
Chica Boom Chic', 'Boa Noite' and 'I, Yi, Yi, Yi, Yi,
I Like You Very Much'); *The Great American Broadcast*
('Where You Are' and 'Long Ago Last Night'); and
Weekend In Havana ('When I Love I Love' and

'Tropical Magic'). They featured some of the biggest
stars of the day, including Alice Faye, John Payne,
Carmen Miranda, Betty Grable, Don Ameche, the
Nicholas Brothers, and many more. In 1941/2,
Gordon and Warren contributed perhaps their best
known songs to *Sun Valley Serenade* and *Orchestra
Wives*, starring the enormously popular Glenn Miller
And His Orchestra. They included 'I Know Why',
'Chattanooga Choo Choo', 'It Happened In Sun
Valley', 'The Kiss Polka', 'At Last', 'I've Got A Girl In
Kalamazoo' and 'People Like You And Me'. Miller's
million-selling record of 'Chattanooga Choo Choo'
was the first to be awarded a gold disc. Gordon and
Warren continued throughout the 40s, with films
such as *Iceland* ('There Will Never Be Another You');
Sweet Rosie O'Grady ('My Heart Tells Me' and 'The
Wishing Waltz'); *Hello, Frisco, Hello* ('You'll Never
Know', the Academy Award-winning song of 1943);
Billy Rose's Diamond Horseshoe, with Dick Haymes ('I
Wish I Knew' and 'The More I See You'); and
Summer Stock (1950), with Judy Garland ('If You Feel
Like Singing, Sing'). Even during the period of almost
20 years with Revel and Warren, Gordon found the
time to collaborate with several other composers on
songs such as 'Mamselle', 'Time Alone Will Tell', 'I
Can't Begin To Tell You', 'Somewhere In The
Night', 'This Is Always', 'You Make Me Feel So
Young' (with Joseph Myrow), 'You Do', 'Baby,
Won't You Say You Love Me?' and 'A Lady Loves
To Love'. His last film score, with Myrow, was for
Bundle Of Joy, starring Eddie Fisher and Debbie
Reynolds, in 1956. He died, three years later, in
March 1959. His other collaborators included Ray
Henderson, Jimmy Van Heusen, James V. Monaco,
Max Rich, Maurice Abrahams, Ted Snyder, Abner
Silver and George Weist.

Grable, Betty

b. Ruth Elizabeth Grable, 18 December 1916, St.
Louis Missouri, USA, d. 2 July 1973, Santa Monica,
California, USA. An actress, singer and dancer in
movie musicals of the 30s, 40s and early 50s. A
beautiful blonde with a peaches-and-cream
complexion, during World War II the famous picture
of her wearing a white bathing suit displaying her
shapely legs (which were reportedly insured for a
million dollars) and looking over her right shoulder,
was pinned up on servicemen's lockers the world
over. Encouraged by her mother, Grable began to
take singing and dancing lessons while she was still
very young, and she was part of the chorus in musical
films such as *Let's Go Places*, *New Movietone Follies Of
1930*, and *Whoopee!* while still in her early teens.
During the 30s, sometimes under the name of Frances
Dean, she played roles of varying importance (but
never starring ones) in a several comedies such as *Hold
'Em Jail* and *The Nitwits*, and musicals which included
Palmy Days, *The Kid From Spain*, *Student Tour*, *The*

Gay Divorcee, Old Man Rhythm, Collegiate, Follow The Fleet, Pigskin Parade, This Way Please, College Swing, Give Me A Sailor, and Million Dollar Legs (1939). Also in 1939 she had a good role in the Broadway musical Panama Hattie in which she introduced Cole Porter's famous song of 'social scandal', 'Well, Did You Evah?' with Charles Walters. In 1937 Grable had married former child star Jackie Coogan, and their divorce in 1940 coincided with her elevation to star status when she signed for 20th-Century Fox. After co-starring with Don Ameche in Down Argentine Way, she worked with several other handsome leading men of the day, such as John Payne, Victor Mature, Dan Dailey, George Montgomery, Cesar Romero, Robert Cummings, and Dick Haymes in a string of mostly entertaining and tuneful musicals such as Tin Pan Alley, Moon Over Miami, Footlight Serenade, Song Of The Islands, Springtime In The Rockies, Coney Island, Sweet Rosie O'Grady, Four Jills In A Jeep, Pin-Up Girl, Billy Rose's Diamond Horseshoe, The Dolly Sisters, The Shocking Miss Pilgrim, Mother Wore Tights, That Lady In Ermine, When My Baby Smiles At Me, The Beautiful Blonde From Bashful Bend, Wabash Avenue, My Blue Heaven, Call Me Mister, Meet Me After The Show, The Farmer Takes A Wife, and Three For The Show (1955). Several of those were set at the turn of the century, and, by the late 50s, Grable's kind of movie musical was itself a period piece. She played nightclubs, appeared on television, and also worked with her husband, bandleader Harry James, before they divorced in 1964. In 1967 she took over the leading role from Carol Channing in the Broadway production of Hello, Dolly!, and subsequently headed a road tour of the show. In 1989 she travelled to England for a brief appearance in the spectacular flop American musical Belle Starr at the Palace Theatre in London. She continued to work on US television and in provincial theatres until her death from cancer in 1973 at the age of 56.
Further reading: Betty Grable: The Reluctant Movie Queen, D. Warren.

Grainer, Ron

b. 1922, Australia, d. 22 February 1981, Sussex, England. Grainer was a musical director and extremely successful composer for television, films and the stage. He trained as a musician in Australia before moving to England in 1952 with the intention of working as a pianist and writing classical music. Instead, at first he became part of a knockabout variety act, the Allen Brothers And June, and toured the UK music halls, staying in touch with music by being hit on the head every night by the lid of a grand piano! Later in the 50s, he served as musical director for London's West End musical comedy, Zuleika, and spent some time as a rehearsal pianist for television, which led to his contributing music for a few plays. His big break came when he wrote the theme music

for the highly popular BBC detective series, Maigret. This won him an Ivor Novello Award in 1961, and he also received 'Ivors' for his themes for Steptoe And Son (1962); and the satirical Not So Much A Programme, More A Way Of Life, in collaboration with writer-director Ned Sherrin and his oft-time partner Caryl Brahms. Grainer's other television music included, Comedy Playhouse, Dr Who (on which he pioneered the use of electronic music in the medium as Ray Cathode), Panorama, Five O'Clock Club, That Was The Week That Was, Oliver Twist, Boy Meets Girl, The Flying Swan, Man In A Suitcase, The Prisoner, Thief, For The Love Of Ada, Paul Temple, South Riding, Kim The Detective, Edward And Mrs Simpson, Malice Aforethought, Rebecca and Tales Of The Unexpected. Grainer's enormous success in television led to continuous film work during the 60s and 70s. His film scores included, A Kind Of Loving (1962), The Moonspinners (1964), Night Must Fall (1964), The Caretaker (1964), Nothing But The Best (1964), Station Six-Sahara (1964), To Sir With Love (1967), Only When I Larf (1968), The Assassination Bureau (1969), Before Winter Comes (1969), Hoffman (1970), In Search Of Gregory (1970), The Omega Man (1971), Cat And Mouse (1974), I Don't Want To Be Born (1975) and The Bawdy Adventures Of Tom Jones (1976). For the stage, Grainer contributed some songs for the pasticcio, Cindy-Ella in 1962, a Sherrin/Brahms all-black production of the traditional English pantomime, Cinderella. Two years later, he wrote the music, with Ronald Millar's lyrics, for Robert And Elizabeth, a musical adaptation of The Barretts Of Wimpole Street, by Rudolph Besier. It was a great success, running for over 900 performances in the West End, and winning another Ivor Novello Award in 1964, for 'The Year's Outstanding Score Of A Stage Musical'. Grainer's other music for the London theatre included On The Level, also with Millar, a tale of contemporary education, which featured an amusing number entitled, 'Thermodynamically Yours'; Sing A Rude Song, a musical biography of legendary British Music Hall star, Marie Lloyd; and Nickleby And Me, a musical play-within-a-play about the famous Dickens' character. Grainer's orchestral albums, mainly of film and television music, included Tales Of The Unexpected, which contained the insinuating, 'I've Danced With The Man', sung by Jenny Wren over the titles of Edward And Mrs. Simpson; and 'A Touch Of Velvet, A Sting Of Brass', which was a minor chart hit in 1978 for Ron Grainer and his Orchestra.
Albums: Edward And Mrs. Simpson (1978, television soundtrack), Tales Of The Unexpected And Other Themes (1980).

Grayson, Kathryn

b. Zelma Kathryn Hedrick, 9 February 1922, Winston-Salem, North Carolina, USA. An actress and singer with a spectacular soprano voice and a

charming and ingenuous personality who was popular in MGM musicals in the 40s and 50s. She is said to have been discovered while singing on Eddie Cantor's radio show in the late 30s, and made her film debut in 1941 with Mickey Rooney in *Andy Hardy's Private Secretary*. After being teamed with the comedy duo Bud Abbott and Lou Costello in *Rio Rita* (1942), during the rest of the 40s, and in the 50s, she co-starred with major stars such as Frank Sinatra, Mario Lanza, and Howard Keel in a string of musicals which included *Seven Sweethearts, Thousands Cheer, Two Sisters From Boston, Ziegfeld Follies, Till The Clouds Roll By, It Happened In Brooklyn, The Toast Of New Orleans, Show Boat, Lovely To Look At, The Desert Song, Kiss Me Kate*, and *The Vagabond King* (1956). In *So This Is Love* (1953), she portrayed opera singer Grace Moore, and in some of the other films she played characters attempting to audition for maestros such as José Iturbi with the intention of making a career as a classical singer. As the golden age of movie musicals drew to a close, Grayson played concert and clubs for a time, and in the 60s toured in revivals of well-known stage musicals. She emerged from retirement in 1989 to join Dorothy Lamour, June Allyson, Ann Miller, and Alice Faye and others in London for a one-night extravaganza called *The MGM Ladies And The Hollywood Great Stars*.
Selected albums: *Kathryn Grayson* (1958), *20 Golden Favourites* (1984), and film soundtracks.

Great American Broadcast, The

Even before this film was released by 20th Century-Fox in 1941, the American public's fascination with radio had already spawned several entertaining musicals - and Alice Faye had favoured more than one of them with her presence. Here she is again - this time playing a singer whose involvement with radio pioneers Jack Oakie and John Payne, along with businessman Cesar Romero, eventually leads her to stardom. Also cast were Mary Beth Hughes, William Pawley, Lucien Littlefield, Eula Morgan, and guest artists, the Ink Spots, the Nicholas Brothers, and the Wiere Brothers. Mack Gordon and Harry Warren wrote most of the songs which included 'Where You Are', 'I Take To You', 'The Great American Broadcast', 'Long Ago Last Night', 'It's All In A Lifetime', and 'I've Got A Bone To Pick With You'. They were joined by the Ink Spots' theme song 'If I Didn't Care' (Jack Lawrence), 'Give My Regards To Broadway' (George M. Cohan), and 'Alabamy Bound' (Buddy De Sylva-Bud Green-Ray Henderson). Don Ettlinger, Edwin Blum, Robert Ellis, and Helen Logan provided an entertaining and sometimes witty screenplay, and the director was Archie Mayo.

The Great Caruso

Great Caruso, The

This lavishly produced bio-pic of the celebrated Italian opera singer was released by MGM in 1951. Mario Lanza, making his third screen appearance, was the perfect choice to play the lead in a screenplay by Sonia Levian and William Ludwig which, in certain areas of Caruso's life, was somewhat economical with the truth. For instance, the existence of one of his wives was totally ignored in the haste to drastically condense his rise to fame, and get as much music up there on the screen as possible. It was all rather false, and even the hit song which emerged from the film, 'The Loveliest Night Of The Year', was not associated with Caruso, and was simply a Mexican instrumental piece, 'Over The Waves' (Juventino Rosas), adapted by Irving Aaronson and lyricist Paul Francis Webster. As for the remainder of the musical fare, it was a collection of songs and operatic excerpts which included 'Last Rose Of Summer' (Thomas Moore-Richard Alfred Milliken), 'Sextet' (Donizetti), 'La Donna E Mobile' (Verdi), 'Celeste Aida' (Verdi), 'Ave Maria' (Bach-Charles Gounod), 'Sweethearts' (Victor Herbert-Robert B. Smith), 'Vesti La Guibba' (Leoncavallo), and 'M'Appari' (Flotow). Anne Blyth played Dorothy Benjamin, Caruso's wife, and among the rest of the cast were Dorothy Kirsten, Jarmila Novotna, Richard Hageman, Eduard Franz, Carl Benton, Ludwig Donath, Ian Wolfe, and Mae Clarke. Joseph Ruttenbergs' Technicolor photography enhanced the whole spectacular affair, which was produced by Joe Pasternak and directed by Richard Thorpe. Musical directors Johnny Green and Peter Herman Adler were nominated for Oscars, and Douglas Shearer won one for sound recording. The Great Caruso grossed over $4.5 million in North America (a lot of money in those days), and proved to be the most popular of Mario Lanza's brief (seven pictures) career.

Great Ziegfeld, The

This vastly overblown, but breathtakingly opulent bio-pic of America's master showman, Florenz Ziegfeld, was produced for MGM by Hunt Stromberg in 1936. William Powell played the leading role, and William Anthony Macguire's screenplay, conveniently omitting the subject's reported excesses and philandering, concentrated on his undoubted charm, and unrivalled fervour and skill in the art of discovering a host of talented artists, before presenting them in the most lavish of settings which displayed those talents to the full. The most impressive - and extravagant - scene involves an enormous fluted spiral structure which is surrounded by an imposing staircase. Dennis Morgan (dubbed by Alan Jones) sings 'A Pretty Girl Is Like A Melody', which segues into various classical excerpts as dozens of singers, dancers, and 'musicians', dressed in a variety of costumes ranging from white tie and tails, to bewigged

Regency-style, 'perform' musical excerpts from the classics. As the sequence draws to a close, Virginia Bruce, as the Spirit of the Follies, appears high up on top of the set. Morgan resumes his song, and a circular curtain descends, shrouding everything and everybody, and somehow forms itself precisely on to the spiral surface. An extraordinary experience, and something that has to be seen to be believed. In complete contrast, the other most remarked-on sequence in the film comes when Luise Rainer, as Ziegfeld's first wife, Anna Held, makes a frenzied telephone call to her husband after discovering that he has married Billy Burke (played here by Myrna Loy). However, the film was mostly a feast of lavish spectacle and music featuring some memorable songs, including 'It's Delightful To Be Married' (Vincent Sotto-Anna Held), 'A Circus Must Be Different In A Ziegfeld Show' (Con Conrad-Herb Magidson), 'Shine On Harvest Moon' (Jack Norworth-Nora Bayes), 'Won't You Come And Play With Me' (Held), 'If You Knew Susie' (Buddy De Sylva-Joseph Meyer); and 'She's A Follies Girl', 'You Gotta Pull The Strings', 'Queen Of The Jungle', and 'You Never Looked So Beautiful' (all Walter Donaldson-Harold Adamson). Fanny Brice, the biggest star to emerge from the real-life Ziegfeld Follies, sang 'Yiddle On Your Fiddle' (Irving Berlin) and part of another of her all-time favourites, 'My Man' (Maurice Yvain-Channing Pollack) Also among the starry cast were Ray Bolger, Frank Morgan, Reginald Owen, Nat Pendleton, Herman Bing, Raymond Walburn, Ernest Cossart, Joseph Cawthorn, Virginia Grey, Buddy Doyle, Jean Chatburn, and Robert Greig. The credit for the film's splendid photography went to Oliver T. Marsh, Ray June, and George Folsey, and the dance sequences were staged by Seymour Felix. The director was Robert Z. Leonard. The Great Ziegfeld won Academy Awards for best picture and actress (Luise Rainer). William Powell played Florenz Ziegfeld again in the 1946 film Ziegfeld Follies.

Green, Adolph (see Comden, Betty)

Green, Johnny

b. 10 October 1908, New York City, New York, USA, d. 16 May 1989. Fascinated by music from childhood, Green studied piano from the age of five. By the time he entered his teens he had mastered orchestration, and throughout his years at Harvard University he greatly advanced his knowledge and understanding of all aspects of musical theory. While at Harvard he led a band which made records. During one vacation he was hired by Guy Lombardo as an arranger. Green's first song, 'Coquette', was written in collaboration with Lombardo's brother, Carmen, and Gus Kahn. After graduating from Harvard, Green worked on Wall Street but continued his musical studies, eventually making the decision in 1928 to

The Great Ziegfeld

concentrate on music for his livelihood. For the next few years he arranged music for films, working in the east coast studios of Paramount. With different lyricists he wrote several songs during the 30s, including 'I'm Yours' (lyrics by E.Y. 'Yip' Harburg), 'Hello, My Lover, Goodbye' (Edward Heyman), 'Out Of Nowhere' (Heyman), 'I Wanna Be Loved' (Heyman and Billy Rose), 'Rain, Rain, Go Away' (Heyman and Mack David), 'I Cover The Waterfront' (Heyman) and the massively successful 'Body And Soul' (Heyman and Robert Sour). 'Body And Soul' was written for Gertrude Lawrence to sing in a show; in later years Green casually dismissed his timeless composition, remarking 'I only knew I was writing for Gertie and it had to be ready for Wednesday'. Also during the 30s, Green led a dance band, appearing regularly on radio and also worked on Broadway as musical director for shows. In 1942 he moved to Hollywood where he began writing scores for motion pictures. He was nominated for an Oscar for *Fiesta* (1947), his music including passages from Aaron Copland's 'El Salón México'. He won an Oscar the following year for his score for *Easter Parade*. During the 50s Green was General Music Director at MGM, working either directly or indirectly on many of the best musicals of the period. He won a second Oscar for his arrangements for *An American In Paris* (1951) and a third for his work on *The Merry Wives Of Windsor* (1953). He continued to write songs, including 'The Song Of Raintree County' (lyrics by Paul Francis Webster). In the 60s he added two more Oscars for his work on *West Side Story* (1960) and *Oliver* (1968). Green's musical range was such that he frequently appeared as guest conductor of symphony orchestras, notably the Los Angeles Philharmonic with which he worked regularly for many years. Green was the recipient of many honours and awards, and in the late 70s was artist-in-residence at Harvard.

Greenwood, Charlotte

b. 25 June 1890, Philadelphia, Pennsylvania, USA, d. 18 January 1978, Beverly Hills, California, USA. A tall, slender and immensely likeable musical comedy and film actress who graced several musical pictures in the 40s with her spunky and eccentric style and amazingly loose-jointed high-kick. Greenwood first came to notice on Broadway in *The Passing Show Of 1913*, and in the following year made such an impression with her 'flat-footed' kicks and 'splits' in *Pretty Miss Smith*, particularly in one number, 'Long, Lean, Lanky Letty', that producer Oliver Morosco re-titled the show *Long-Legged Letty*. The 'Letty' character kept Greenwood in occasional employment during the next few years via *So Long, Letty* (1916), *Linger Longer Letty* (1919), and *Letty Pepper* (1922), and there were subsequent film versions. Greenwood also appeared in several Broadway revues in the 20s, but by then she had also established herself in silent

movies. In the 30s she easily made the transition into talkies, mostly with comedies, but also in occasional musicals such as *Flying High* (1931) and the Eddie Cantor vehicle *Palmy Days* (1932). In 1940 she co-starred with Shirley Temple and Jack Oakie in *Young People*, and during the rest of the decade made effective and highly entertaining contributions to a number of 20th Century-Fox musicals including *Down Argentine Way*, *Tall, Dark And Handsome*, *Moon Over Miami*, *Springtime In The Rockies*, *The Gang's All Here*, *Wake Up And Dream*, and *Oh, You Beautiful Doll* (1949). She also had her own US networked radio show in the 40s. In 1950 Greenwood returned to Broadway (high-kicks and all) in Cole Porter's musical *Out Of This World*, and stopped the show every night with the plaintive (but hilarious) 'Nobody's Chasing Me' ('Nobody wants to own me/And I object/Nobody wants to 'phone me/Even collect'). Three years later she showed Esther Williams a few aquatic tricks in *Dangerous When Wet*, and in 1957 made her last screen appearance as Aunt Eller in *Oklahoma!*. According to the obituary in *Variety* following her sudden death at the age of 87, the part had originally been written for her by Oscar Hammerstein II, in the historic 1943 Broadway production. For some reason she had been unable to accept it then.

Further reading: *Never Too Tall* (her autobiography).

Grusin, Dave

b. 26 June 1934, Littleton, Colorado, USA. He played piano semi-professionally while studying at the University of Colorado, and almost abandoned music to become a veterinary surgeon. Grusin stated 'I'm still not sure I made the right decision, a lot of dead cows might still be alive today if I hadn't gone to music school.' His musical associates at the time included Art Pepper, Terry Gibbs and Spike Robinson, with whom he worked extensively in the early 50s. In 1959 Grusin was hired as musical director by singer Andy Williams, a role he maintained into the mid-60s. An eclectic musician, Grusin worked with mainstream artists such as Benny Goodman and Thad Jones and also worked with hard bop players. He made many recording dates, including several in the early 70s, accompanying singers amongst whom were Sarah Vaughan and Carmen McRae. Around this same time Grusin began to concentrate more and more on electric piano and keyboards, recording with Gerry Mulligan, Lee Ritenour in the jazz world and with Paul Simon and Billy Joel in pop. He has arranged and produced for the Byrds, Peggy Lee, Grover Washington Jnr., Donna Summer, Barbra Streisand, Al Jarreau, Phoebe Snow and Patti Austin. He is also co-founder and owner, with Larry Rosen, of GRP Records, a label which they founded in 1976 and has an impressive catalogue of singers, jazz and jazz-rock artists including Diane Schuur, Lee

Ritenour, David Benoit, his brother Don Grusin, Michael Brecker, Chick Corea, Steve Gadd, Dave Valentin, Special EFX and Gary Burton. The success of GRP has much to do with Grusin's refusal to compromise on quality. With Rosen he pioneered an all digital recording policy, and using 'state of the art' technology their productions reach a pinnacle of recorded quality. In addition to his activities as a player and producer, Grusin has written extensively for films and television. His portfolio is most impressive; in addition to winning a Grammy in 1984 his film scores have received several Academy Award nominations, and include *Divorce Italian Style, The Graduate, The Heart Is A Lonely Hunter, Three Days Of The Condor, Heaven Can Wait, Reds, On Golden Pond, The Champ, Tootsie, Racing With The Moon, The Milagro Beanfield War, Clara's Heart, Tequila Sunrise, A Dry White Season, The Fabulous Baker Boys, Bonfire Of The Vanities, Havana, For The Boys*, and *The Firm* (1993). Additionally one of his most evocative songs 'Mountain Dance' was the title song to *Falling In Love*. His American television credits include *St. Elsewhere, Maude, Roots, It Takes A Thief* and *Baretta*. Grusin is a master musical chemist - able to blend many elements of pop and jazz into uplifting intelligent and accessible music. In 1993 he appeared as a performer on the international jazz circuit.

Albums: *Candy* (1961), *The Many Moods Of Dave Grusin* (1962), *Kaleidoscope* (1964), *Don't Touch* (c.1964), *Discovered Again* (1976), *One Of A Kind* (1977), *Dave Grusin And The GRP All Stars Live In Japan Featuring Sadao Watanabe* (1980), *Out Of The Shadows* (1982), *Mountain Dance* (1983), *Night Lines* (1984), with Lee Ritenour *Harlequin* (1984), *The NYLA Dream Band* (1988), with Don Grusin *Sticks And Stones* (1988), *Migration* (1989), *The Fabulous Baker Boys* (1989, film soundtrack), *Havana* (1990), *The Gershwin Collection* (1992), *Homage To Duke* (1993). Compilations: *Cinemagic* (1987), *Dave Grusin Collection* (1991).

Guys And Dolls

Producer Sam Goldwyn pulled off quite a coup when he cast Frank Sinatra and Marlon Brando in this 1955 screen version of the smash-hit Broadway show. In Joseph L. Mankiewicz's screenplay, which was based on Abe Burrows' libretto and Damon Runyan's short story *The Idyll Of Miss Sarah Brown*, Sinatra plays Nathan Detroit, the operator of the oldest established permanent floating crap game in New York. Constantly harassed by Inspector Brannigan (Robert Keith), and his fiancée of 14 years, Miss Adelaide (Vivian Blaine), Nathan bets 'the highest roller in town', Sky Masterson (Brando), that he cannot

Guys And Dolls

transport Salvation Army stalwart Sarah Brown (Jean Simmons), from the Save Our Souls Mission in New York, to Havana. Against all the odds, Sky and Sarah make the trip, but Nathan subsequently loses nothing - except his precious freedom - when he and Adelaide, along with Sky and Sarah, make it a double wedding in Times Square. Rumour has it that Sinatra wanted to play the Brando role because, in the original, Nathan does not have a solo number. In the event, composer Frank Loesser gave him a new song, 'Adelaide', and he also wrote another new one for Brando, 'A Woman In Love', because the actor reportedly could not handle the tender 'I've Never Been In Love Before'. In fact, both he and Jean Simmons were surprisingly good on 'I'll Know' and 'If I Were A Bell'. The rest of the magnificent score - arguably Loesser's masterpiece - included 'Fugue For Tinhorns' (Sinatra-Silver-Danny Dayton), 'The Oldest Established' (Sinatra-Silver-Kaye-ensemble), 'Pet Me Poppa' (which replaced 'A Bushel And A Peck') (Blaine and chorus), 'Adelaide's Lament' (Blaine), 'Guys And Dolls' (Sinatra-Silver-Kaye), 'Take Back Your Mink' (Blaine and chorus), 'Luck Be A Lady' (Brando), 'Sue Me' (Sinatra-Blaine), and 'Sit Down, You're Rockin' The Boat'. The latter number was performed by the irrepressible Stubby Kaye, recreating his Broadway role of Nicely-Nicely Johnson. Other veterans of the stage show playing two of the loveable Runyanesque rogues, were Johnny Silver (Benny Southstreet) and B.S. Pully (Big Jule), along with the marvellous Vivian Blaine and choreographer Michael Kidd. Also in the cast were Sheldon Leonard, George E. Stone, Regis Toomey, Kathryn Givney, Veda Ann Borg, and Alan Hokanson. Directed by Mankiewicz, and photographed in Eastman Color and CinemaScope for MGM, Guys And Dolls was derided by the critics, but welcomed by the cinema-going public who made it one of the top box-office favourites of the 50s.

Gypsy

This entertaining and faithful screen adaptation of the hit Broadway musical which opened in 1959, was released by Warner Brothers three years later. Rosalind Russell gave a memorable performance as the show-business mother who is determined that if she cannot become a star herself, then one of her daughters, June (Ann Jillian) or Louise (Natalie Wood), damn-well will. Louise is the one who finally makes it in the guise of classy stripper Gypsy Rose Lee, and, while Russell could not be expected to have the vocal power of Ethel Merman who created the role on Broadway, she did manage to bring to the part a mixture of spunky charm and vulnerability that was all her own. Her singing voice on some of the numbers was provided by Lisa Kirk, and Natalie Wood was dubbed by Marni Nixon. Jule Styne and Stephen Sondheim's score, which has long been

recognised as one of the finest of all-time, arrived in Hollywood intact. All the songs are classics of their kind, including 'Let Me Entertain You', 'Some People', 'Small World, 'Mr. Goldstone, I Love You', 'Little Lamb', 'You'll Never Get Away From Me', 'If Mama Was Married', 'All I Need Is The Girl', 'Everything's Coming Up Roses', 'Together Wherever We Go', 'You Gotta Have A Gimmick', and 'Rose's Turn'. Karl Malden was fine as Rose's long-suffering fiancé who just wants her to give it all up for a cottage with roses round the door, and among the rest of the strong cast were Paul Wallace, Faith Dane, Betty Bruce, Harry Shannon, Roxanne Arlen, Harvey Korman, Danny Locklin, Guy Raymond, and Parley Baer. Leonard Spigelgass's screenplay was based on Gypsy Rose Lee's memoirs, and Robert Tucker was responsible for the spirited (and sometimes hilarious) choreography. The producer-director was Mervyn LeRoy, and the film was shot in Technicolor and Technirama.

Half A Sixpence

Most of the original songs survived, but much of the charm was lost when this British screen version of the West End and Broadway hit show was released by Paramount in 1967. Beverley Cross adapted his original libretto which had been based on H.G. Wells' 1925 novel Kipps, and Tommy Steele recreated his stage role - and dominated the whole affair - as the shop assistant who wins a fortune but loses his head and his childhood sweetheart Ann (Julia Foster), before realising that money cannot buy love or happiness. There was still plenty to enjoy in David Heneker's appealing score, including the exuberant 'Flash, Bang, Wallop!' and the tender 'She's Too Far Above Me' and 'Half A Sixpence', along with 'All In The Cause Of Economy', 'If The Rain's Got To Fall', 'I'm Not Talking To You', 'I Know What I Am', 'I Don't Believe A Word Of It', and 'A Proper Gentleman'. Heneker also wrote two additional numbers especially for the film, 'The Race Is On' and 'This Is My World' (with Irvin Kostal). James Villiers, renowned in British films and television shows for his portrayal of upper-class snooty characters, was prominent among a strong supporting cast which also featured Cyril Ritchard, Penelope Horner, Grover Dale, Elaine Taylor, and Hilton Edwards. Gillian

Lynne, who came to world-wide fame in the 70s with her contribution to Andrew Lloyd Webber's *Cats*, staged the imaginative and energetic dance sequences, and George Sidney was the director. Marti Webb, the original 'Ann' in the 1963 London production, dubbed the singing voice of Julia Foster.

Hamlisch, Marvin

b. 2 June 1944, New York City, New York, USA. Hamlisch was a pianist, arranger, and composer for Broadway musical shows and films. A child prodigy, he played the piano by ear at the age of five and when he was seven became the youngest student ever to be enrolled at the Juilliard School of Music. One of the first songs he wrote as a teenager was 'Travelin' Man', which was eventually recorded by his friend, Liza Minnelli on her first album, *Liza, Liza*. Through Minnelli, he was able to obtain work as a rehearsal pianist and assistant vocal arranger for some Broadway shows. Lesley Gore gave him his first song hit, in 1965, when she took his 'Sunshine, Lollipops And Rainbows' (lyric by Howard Liebling) into the US Top 20. After majoring in music at Queen's College, Hamlisch wrote the theme music for Sam Spiegel's 1968 film, *The Swimmer*, starring Burt Lancaster. After that, he moved to Hollywood and wrote the music for two Woody Allen comedies, *Take The Money And Run* (1969) and *Bananas* (1971). He also scored two Jack Lemmon films *The April Fools* (1969) and *Save The Tiger* (1973), for which Lemmon won an Oscar. In 1971 his song 'Life Is What You Make It', with a lyric by Johnny Mercer, written for the Walter Matthau movie, *Kotch*, was nominated for an Academy Award.
Three years later, in April 1974, he collected an impressive total of three Oscars. For *The Way We Were*, he won Best Original Dramatic Score and Best Title Song in conjunction with lyricists Alan and Marilyn Bergman. His third Oscar was for his adaptation of Scott Joplin's music for *The Sting*. Hamlisch's piano recording of one of the film's main themes, 'The Entertainer', sold over a million copies. In July 1975, his first Broadway musical, *A Chorus Line*, opened at the Schubert Theatre. Conceived and directed by Michael Bennett, the songs included 'One', 'What I Did For Love', 'Nothing' and 'I Hope I Get It', with lyrics by the virtually unknown Edward Kleban, which suited perfectly the story of a group of dancers auditioning for an idiosyncratic director. The production was showered with awards: the Pullitzer Prize For Drama (1976); Tony Award for Best Musical; New York Drama Critics Circle Award for Best Musical; and several others including a Tony Award for the Hamlisch-Kleban score. The Original Cast album was estimated to have sold 1,250,000 copies by October 1983. *A Chorus Line* closed in March 1990 after an incredible run of 6,137 performances, making it Broadway's longest-running

show. It was filmed in 1985, with a somewhat controversial choice of director in Richard Attenborough.
Hamlisch was back on Broadway in 1979 with *They're Playing Our Song*, which had a book by Neil Simon, and lyrics by Carole Bayer Sager. This two-hander, starring Robert Klein and Lucie Arnaz, about the stormy relationship between two songwriters, (with three singing alter egos each), is said to have been based on Hamlisch's and Sager's own liaison. The songs included 'Fallin'', 'If He Really Knew Me', 'They're Playing Our Song', 'When You're in My Arms 'and 'I Still Believe In Love'. The show played over 1,000 performances on Broadway and did well at London's Shaftesbury Theatre, where it starred Gemma Craven and Tom Conti. Hamlisch also provided the music (with lyrics by Christopher Adler) for a production of *Jean Seberg,* which enjoyed a brief run a London's National Theatre in 1983, and, three years later, was represented on Broadway again, with *Smile* (lyrics by Howard Ashman), which closed after only 48 performances. Movie collaborations between Hamlisch and Carole Bayer Sager during the 70s included the Oscar-nominated 'Nobody Does It Better', from the James Bond feature, *The Spy Who Loved Me* (a US number 2 hit for Carly Simon), 'Better Than Ever' (from the Burt Reynolds' film, *Starting Over*), the theme from *Ice Castles*, 'Through The Eyes Of Love' (Academy Award nomination) and 'If You Remember Me' (from Franco Zeffirelli's *The Champ*). Hamlisch also wrote the scores for three Neil Simon film comedies, *Chapter Two* (1979), *Seems Like Old Times* (1980) and *I Ought To Be In Pictures* (1982); the 1981 US film version of *Pennies From Heaven,* (in collaboration with veteran bandleader Billy May); *The January Man*, a Kevin Kline thriller; and *Ordinary People*, the Academy Award-winning film for 1980. He received an ASCAP award for his score to *Three Men And A Baby*, one of 1987's top-grossing films, and gained Academy Award nominations for songs written with Alan and Marilyn Bergman, 'The Last Time I Felt Like This' from *Same Time Next Year* (1978), and 'The Girl Who Used To Be Me' from *Shirley Valentine* (1989). He was also nominated for his score for the Oscar-winning film *Sophie's Choice* (1982) and, with Edward Kleban, found himself on the short list again, with 'Surprise, Surprise', from the movie version of their Broadway show, *A Chorus Line*. Hamlisch's film scores in the early 90s included *Frankie And Johnny*, *The January Man*; and *Missing Pieces*, which contained the song 'High Energy', written with David Zippel. Hamlisch collaborated with Zippel again, on the score for Neil Simon's *The Goodbye Girl*, which, even with Bernadette Peters in the cast, could only manage a run of 188 performances in 1993. In the same year, Hamlisch conducted the London Symphony Orchestra at the Barbican Hall in the European

premiere of his 25-minute work 'The Anatomy Of Peace'.

Albums: *The Sting* (1974, film soundtrack), *The Entertainer* (1974), *The Way We Were* (1974, film soundtrack), *A Chorus Line* (1975, Broadway Cast), *The Spy Who Loved Me* (1977, film soundtrack), *Ice Castles* (1979, film soundtrack), *They're Playing Our Song* (1979, Broadway Cast), *They're Playing Our Song* (1980, London Cast).

Further reading: *The Way I Was*, Marvin Hamlisch with Gerald Gardner.

Hammerstein, Oscar, II

b. 12 July 1895, New York City, New York, USA, d. 23 August 1960. Hammerstein was born into a family with long-standing theatrical associations. His father, William Hammerstein, was manager of New York's Victoria theatre, and an uncle, Arthur Hammerstein, was a Broadway producer. Most famous of all his ancestors was his grandfather, Oscar Hammerstein I, who had made a fortune in industry before becoming one of New York's leading theatrical impresarios and founder of the Manhattan Opera. Although he studied law, the young Oscar's background inevitably affected him and, while still at school he wrote for shows. He was doubtless also influenced by some of his fellow students, who included future songwriters Lorenz Hart and Howard Dietz. Oscar's show business career began when he was employed by his uncle as assistant stage manager and soon afterwards he wrote a stage play and then a musical together with Herbert Stothart, who later became General Music Director at MGM. Hammerstein then wrote *Tickle Me* (1920) in collaboration with Otto Harbach. Subsequently, Hammerstein and Harbach teamed up again as co-lyricists and co-librettists to write a show with Vincent Youmans and Stothart, the successful *Wildflower* (1923). They followed this by working with Rudolf Friml on *Rose-Marie* (1924), which proved to be a classic of American operetta. The hit songs of the show were 'Rose-Marie' and 'Indian Love Call'. Hammerstein's next partnership was with Jerome Kern, which resulted in *Sunny* (1925), with 'Sunny' and 'Who?' as the big hits.

The following year he worked with George Gershwin on *Song Of The Flame*, and the year after that with Harbach and Sigmund Romberg on *The Desert Song*, which produced lasting successes such as 'The Desert Song' ('Blue Heaven') and 'One Alone'. Hammerstein teamed up again with Kern in 1927 for *Show Boat*, writing lyrics for 'Why Do I Love You?', 'Can't Help Lovin' Dat Man', 'Only Make Believe' and 'Ol' Man River'. In 1928 he rejoined Harbach and Friml to gain further acclaim with *The New Moon*, which featured 'Lover Come Back To Me' and 'Softly As In A Morning Sunrise'. He continued to work with Kern, and during the next few years their shows were liberally scattered with songs which became standards,

among them 'The Song Is You', 'I've Told Ev'ry Little Star', and 'All The Things You Are'.

In the early 30s Hammerstein was lured to Hollywood, where he met with only limited success. Although some of the films on which he worked were box-office failures, he nevertheless co-authored several timeless songs, including, 'When I Grow Too Old To Dream' (with Romberg) and 'I Won't Dance' (with Harbach and Kern), the latter for the 1935 Astaire-Rogers film, *Roberta*. Other songs written with Kern for films were 'Can I Forget You', 'The Folks Who Live On The Hill', 'I'll Take Romance' and 'The Last Time I Saw Paris', which won an Oscar in 1941. In the early 40s Hammerstein's career took a new direction and the ups and downs of the past were forgotten with a series of smash-hit Broadway shows, all written with a new partner. He had worked briefly with Richard Rodgers in 1928 and again in 1935, but now with Rodgers's regular collaborator, Lorenz Hart, silenced by alcoholism and despair, a new partnership was formed. The first production of Rodgers and Hammerstein was *Oklahoma!* (1943), which was followed by *Carousel* (1945), *Allegro* (1947), *South Pacific* (1949), *The King And I* (1951), *Me And Juliet* (1953), *Pipe Dream* (1955), *Flower Drum Song* (1958) and *The Sound Of Music* (1959). Collectively, these shows were among the most successful in the history of the American musical theatre, with *Oklahoma!* running for 2,212 performances and winning a Pulitzer Prize - as did *South Pacific*, which ran for 1,925 performances. In addition to their stage successes, Rodgers and Hammerstein wrote a film, *State Fair* (1945), which included the Oscar-winning song, 'It Might As Well Be Spring', and a television show, *Cinderella* (1957). A brief list of songs from their stage musicals includes such well-loved hits as 'Oh, What A Beautiful Morning', 'People Will Say We're In Love', 'The Surrey With The Fringe On Top', 'If I Loved You', 'You'll Never Walk Alone', 'Some Enchanted Evening', 'Younger Than Springtime', 'Bali Ha'i', 'Hello, Young Lovers', 'Shall We Dance?', 'No Other Love' and 'Climb Ev'ry Mountain'. In between *Oklahoma!* and *Carousel*, Hammerstein wrote a new libretto and new lyrics for Georges Bizet's opera, *Carmen*. The new show, *Carmen Jones*, opened on Broadway in 1943 and was a great success. The show was transferred to the screen in 1954 and, most recently, was revived in London's West End in 1991. One of Broadway's most successful lyricists, Hammerstein wrote with engaging simplicity, a trait which set him well apart from his predecessor, Hart. His remarkable contribution to America's theatrical tradition was profound and his irreproachable standards represented the culmination of the traditional, operetta-based style of musical comedy. In 1993, the 50th anniversary of Rodgers and Hammerstein's first collaboration on 'America's most loved musical', was celebrated by the publication of

OK! The Story Of Oklahoma!, by Max Wilk. In addition, A Grand Night For Singing, a revue which was packed with their songs, played for a brief spell on Broadway.

Further reading: Some Enchanted Evening: The Story Of Rodgers and Hammerstein, J.D. Taylor. The Rodgers And Hammerstein Story, Stanley Green. The Sound Of Their Music: The Story Of Rodgers And Hammerstein, Frederick Nolan.

Hans Christian Andersen

This extremely popular, but critically slated, musical bio-pic of the legendary Danish story-teller was produced by Samuel Goldwyn in 1952. Estimates vary as to how many prospective screenplays were rejected by the producer (and the Danish authorities) before Moss Hart came up with the final draft. Eschewing all pretensions of biographical accuracy, this 'fairy tale about a great spinner of fairy tales' set in 1830, told of a simple cobbler (Danny Kaye) who falls in love with a beautiful ballerina (Jeanmaire) after he has made some shoes for her. When his love is rejected, he returns to his home town and eventually makes a fortune from writing children's stories. Kaye, whose renowned zany style had made him a controversial choice for the leading role, toned down the histrionics and gave a brilliant performance. He was assisted in no small part by a marvellous Frank Loesser score, much of which was inspired by Andersen's original tales. It included several endearing numbers, such as 'Thumbelina', 'No Two People', 'I'm Hans Christian Andersen', 'The King's New Clothes', 'Wonderful Copenhagen', 'Anywhere I Wander', 'The Ugly Duckling', and 'The Inchworm'. The delightful ballet sequences were choreographed by Roland Petit, who made an appearance in one of them. Also in the cast were Farley Granger, Joey Walsh, John Brown, Philip Tonge, Erik Bruhn, and John Qualen. The director was Charles Vidor, and the film was beautifully photographed in Technicolor by Harry Stradling. It grossed $6 million in the USA, and went on to become one of the most celebrated film musicals of the decade. A successful stage production, entitled Hans Andersen, with a new book by Beverley Cross and additional songs by Marvin Laird, was presented in London's West End. It starred Tommy Steele, who was also in the 1977 revival.

Happy

'A Capital Comedy With New Laughs' was how the studio publicity machine described this vehicle for the broad and British comedian Stanley Lupino when it was released by British International Pictures (BIP) in 1933. Lupino played Frank, a bandleading inventor who comes up with a device that is supposed to scream 'Police!' when his car is stolen. Initial teething troubles cause it to do exactly the opposite. Meanwhile, Frank goes to Paris with his friend

George (Laddie Cliff). While there, he meets and falls in love with the beautiful blonde Lillian (Dorothy Hyson), whose father is a millionaire car insurance financier who just might be able to help Frank exploit his brilliant - if erratic idea. After the most tortured complications, things work out well for everybody. Scottish comedian Will Fyffe had some funny moments, especially in a scene where he tried to get a gander to lay eggs, and also in the strong supporting cast were Harry Tate, Renee Gadd, Gus McNaughton, Jimmy Godden, Bertha Belmore, and Hal Gordon. The screenplay, by Austin Melford, Frank Launder, Arthur Woods, and Stanley Lupino, was adapted from an original story by Jacques Bachrach, Alfred Hahm, and Karl Notl. Occasionally, there was a pause in the frenetic action in order to accommodate the following songs: 'There's So Much I'm Wanting To Tell You', 'Will You Dance Through Life With Me', 'There Was A Poor Musician', and 'Happy', which were all written by Noel Gay. The man who tried to make sense of it all was the director-producer Fred Zelnik.

Harbach, Otto

b. Otto Abels Hauerbach, 18 August 1873, Salt Lake City, Utah, USA, d. 24 January 1963, New York City, New York, USA. An important lyricist and librettist for more than 20 years, Harbach was one of the links between traditional operetta and America's indigenous musical comedy. After beginning his career as an academic, Harbach wrote for newspapers and advertising agencies in the early part of the century before collaborating with the composer Karl Hoschna on the score for the successful Broadway musical The Three Twins in 1908. One of the show's songs, 'Cuddle Up A Little Closer, Lovey Mine', became popular at the time for Ada Jones and Billy Murray. Harbach and Hoschna worked together on four more shows, Madame Sherry ('Every Little Movement'; 'The Smile She Means For Me'), Dr. Deluxe, The Girl Of My Dreams, and The Fascinating Widow. After Hoschna's death in 1911 Harbach collaborated with several notable composers including Oscar Hammerstein II, Rudolph Friml, Herbert Stothart, Louis Hirsch, Aladar Renyi, Alfred Newman, Vincent Youmans, William Daly, Sigmund Romberg, George Gershwin, and Jerome Kern. There are several all-time hits among his list of nearly 40 shows which included The Firefly ('Giannina Mia'; 'Sympathy'; 'Love Is Like A Firefly'), High Jinks ('Love's Own Kiss'; 'The Bubble'), Katinka ('My Paradise'), You're In Love ('I'm Only Dreaming'), Going Up ('Kiss Me; 'If You Look Into Her Eyes'; 'The Tickle Toe'), Mary ('The Love Nest'; 'Waiting'), Tickle Me ('If A Wish Could Make It So'), Wildflower ('Bambalina'; 'April Blossoms'), Rose Marie ('Rose Marie'; 'Indian Love Call'; 'Song Of The Mounties'), No, No, Nanette ('I've Confessed To The Breeze';

'No, No, Nanette'), *Sunny* ('Who'; 'D'Ya Love Me?'), *The Desert Song* ('The Desert Song'; 'The Riff Song'; 'One Alone'), *The Wild Rose* ('Brown Eyes'), *Lucky* ('The Same Old Moon'), *The Cat And The Fiddle* ('The Night Was Made For Love'; 'She Didn't Say 'Yes''; 'Try To Forget'), and *Roberta* (1933) ('Smoke Gets In Your Eyes'; 'The Touch Of Your Hand'; 'Yesterdays'). Over the years, several of them such as *The Desert Song, The Cat And The Fiddle, Roberta, Rose Marie,* and *No, No, Nanette,* were turned into popular films. One of Harbach's earliest shows, *Madame Sherry,* was subsequently rewritten following its original run and several popular songs by other composers were added, such as 'Put Your Arms Around Me, Honey', 'Oh! You Beautiful Doll', 'Ciribiribin', and 'Walking the Dog'. This later version was revived at the Goodspeed Opera House, Connecticut, in 1992. The acclaimed production was adapted and directed by Martin Connor who re-staged it at London's Guildhall School of Music in 1993.

Harburg, E.Y. 'Yip'

b. Edgar Harburg, 8 April 1896, New York City, New York, USA, d. 5 March 1981, Los Angeles, California, USA. An important lyricist during the 30s and 40s, Harburg was born on New York's Lower East Side, the son of Jewish immigrant parents, and given the nickname 'Yipsel' (meaning 'squirrel'). At high school, he worked on the student newspaper with fellow pupil, Ira Gershwin, before they both attended the City College of New York, where Harburg began to write light verse. After graduating in 1918, he worked for a time as a journalist in South America, before returning to New York to run his own electrical supply business. Hit by the stock market crash of 1929, he resorted to versifying, and, with composers such as Jay Gorney, Vernon Duke and Lewis Gensler, contributed songs to several Broadway revues and musicals, including *Earl Carroll's Sketch Book, Earl Carroll's Vanities, Garrick Gaieties, Shoot The Works* and *Ballyhoo Of 1932.*

In 1932, in the midst of the Depression, Harburg and Gorney wrote the socially significant 'Brother, Can You Spare A Dime', for the revue *Americana* (or *New Americana*). It became extremely successful on records for Bing Crosby and Rudy Vallee. *Americana* also contained several other Harburg lyrics, including 'Satan's Li'l Lamb', which marked the beginning of his long and fruitful collaboration with the composer Harold Arlen. Another of their early songs, 'It's Only A Paper Moon' (1933), was written in association with Billy Rose. In collaboration with Vernon Duke, Harburg wrote another future standard, 'April In Paris', for the Beatrice Lillie stage musical, *Walk A Little Faster,* and 'I Like The Likes Of You' and 'What Is There To Say?' for the *Ziegfeld Follies Of 1934.* Also in 1934, together with Arlen and Ira Gershwin, he

contributed the score to *Life Begins At 8.40*, which included 'You're A Builder-Upper', 'Fun To Be Fooled', 'What Can You Say In A Love Song' and 'Let's Take A Walk Around The Block'. After that, Harburg moved to Hollywood and worked with Arlen on three Warner Brothers movie musicals, *The Singing Kid,* starring Al Jolson ('You're The Cure For What Ails Me', 'I Love To Sing-A'), *Stage Struck* ('Fancy Meeting You', 'In Your Own Quiet Way'), and *Gold Diggers Of 1937* ('Let's Put Our Heads Together', 'Speaking Of The Weather').

Around this time, the two writers also produced one of their most memorable songs, 'When The World Was Young', which received a classic reading from Frank Sinatra nearly 20 years later on his *In The Wee Small Hours*. A brief spell in New York for Harburg resulted in the stage score (with Arlen) for *Hooray For What?* ('God's Country', 'Down With Love'), but both songwriters were back in Hollywood in 1939 to work on one of the most famous films in the history of the cinema. *The Wizard Of Oz*, starring Judy Garland and such beloved characters as the Tin Man, the Scarecrow, and the Cowardly Lion, was one of the first movies in which the songs were seamlessly integrated into the plot. Harburg is also said to have made a significant contribution to the screenplay, collecting and blending several different stories together. The film included numbers such as 'Ding Dong The Witch Is Dead', 'We're Off To See The Wizard', 'If I Only Had A Brain', 'Follow The Yellow Brick Road', and the immortal, yearning, 'Over The Rainbow', for which Harburg and Arlen won an Academy Award. It was all a far cry from their next movie project, *The Marx Brothers At The Circus*, which contained the amusing 'Lydia, The Tattooed Lady' ('When her robe is unfurled, she will show you the world/If you step up, and tell-her-where/For a dime you can see Kankakee or Paree/Or Washington crossing the Delaware'). During the 40s Harburg continued to write mostly for films. These included *Babes On Broadway* ('Chin Up, Cheerio, Carry On'), *Ship Ahoy* (with Burton Lane), in which Frank Sinatra sang 'The Last Call For Love', 'Poor You' and 'Moonlight Bay' with the Tommy Dorsey Orchestra, *Cabin In The Sky* (with Arlen) ('Happiness Is Just A Thing Called Joe'), *Thousands Cheer* (with Earl Brent) ('Let There Be Music'), *Can't Help Singing* (with Jerome Kern), starring Deanna Durbin, with songs such as 'More And More', 'Swing Your Sweetheart', 'Cal-i-for-ni-ay', and *Hollywood Canteen* (1944) (with Burton Lane) ('You Can Always Tell A Yank').

Harburg teamed up with Lane again, in 1947, for the Broadway show, *Finian's Rainbow*. This time, as well as the lyrics, Harburg, with Fred Saidy, also wrote the book - a fantasy laced with social commentary, and a score which included numbers such as 'How Are Things In Glocca Morra?', 'If This Isn't Love', 'Look To The Rainbow', 'Old Devil Moon', 'When I'm

Not Near The Girl I Love', 'Something Sort Of Grandish', 'Necessity', 'When The Idle Poor Become The Idle Rich', 'That Great Come-On-And-Get-It Day', and 'The Begat'. The show ran for over 700 performances on Broadway, but it was 1968 before Hollywood took a chance on the whimsical piece. The film version, directed by Francis Ford Coppola, starred Fred Astaire, Petula Clark, and Tommy Steele. Harburg had always been strongly political, and in the 40s and early 50s, the time of the McCarthy witch hunts, he became even more so. His work for the stage show, *Bloomer Girl*, (1944, with Arlen), which had a Civil War background, included 'The Eagle And Me', a passionate plea for racial equality and freedom; and *Flahooley* (1951) (with Sammy Fain), took as swipe at the incongruities of 'Big Business'. Its score included songs such as 'Here's To Your Ilusions', 'The Springtime Cometh', and 'He's Only Wonderful'. In *Jamaica* (which starred Lena Horne, and had another Harburg/Saidy libretto.), urban life was scrutinized. The Harburg/Arlen songs included 'Coconut Sweet', 'Take It Slow, Joe', 'Ain't It The Truth?', 'Push De Button' and 'Napoleon'. Harburg's last two Broadway shows, *The Happiest Girl The World* (1961) and *Darling Of The Day* (1968), did not survive for long.

After a period of nearly 20 years, Harburg was invited back to Hollywood in 1962 to write the songs, with Arlen, for the movie cartoon *Gay Purr-ee*. They included 'Little Drops Of Rain', 'Mewsette', and 'Paris Is A Lonely Town'. Also with Arlen, he wrote the title song for *I Could Go On Singing* (1963), Judy Garland's last film. Throughout his life Harburg received many awards and citations, including the Humanity in Arts Award from Wayne State University. He died in a car crash in Los Angeles, in March 1981. Four years later, a biographical revue, *Look To The Rainbow*, devised and directed by Canadian author and broadcaster Robert Cushman, and starring Broadway veteran Jack Gilford, played in London's West End.

Further reading: *Rhymes For The Irreverent*, E.Y. Harburg. *At This Point In Rhyme*, E.Y. Harburg. *The Making Of 'The Wizard Of Oz'*, Al Jean Harmetz. *Who Put The Rainbow In The Wizard Of Oz? Yip Harburg, Lyricist*, Harold Meyerson and Ernie Harburg.

Hard Day's Night, A

The first Beatles' feature broke many pop film taboos. Director Richard Lester, famed for his work with the madcap Goons, brought elements of that tradition to this innovative venture. Shot in black-and-white with the merest whiff of kitchen-sink realism, it captured the quartet's natural humour and left their Liverpudian accents intact. Superb support from Wilfred Brambell, as Paul's 'grandfather', and Victor Spinetti as the harassed television producer,

compliment the Beatles' performances superbly. If the plot was slight, the imagery and camera work were captivating, buoyed by a slew of superior John Lennon/Paul McCartney compositions. The sequence featuring 'I Should Have Known Better', set in a train, is particularly memorable, but the entire film is a fast-moving kaleidoscope of sound and picture. 'If I Fell', 'Tell Me Why' and 'Can't Buy Me Love' encapsulate Beatlemania at its height, while the six songs completing the *A Hard Day's Night* album, not featured in the film, show its sound and scope maturing. A landmark in British cinema and pop.

Hart, Lorenz

b. 2 May 1895, New York City, USA, d. 22 November 1943. An outstanding student, Hart was writing both poetry and prose in his mid-teens. In 1918 he met Richard Rodgers, with whom he established an immediate rapport. They wrote numerous songs together in their first year of collaboration, among them some which were used in current Broadway shows. Nevertheless their songs were not widely known, at that time. The situation changed in 1925 with 'Manhattan' and 'Sentimental Me', both written for *The Garrick Gaieties*. They followed this with their first complete Broadway show, *Dearest Enemy* (1925), which included 'Here In My Arms'. The following year brought *The Girl Friend*, with hits in the title song and 'Blue Room'. In 1926 they wrote 'Mountain Greenery' and the same year, for *Peggy-Ann*, 'A Tree In The Park'. In 1927 they wrote 'Thou Swell' for *A Connecticut Yankee*, a show which also featured 'My Heart Stood Still', a song written originally for an earlier show. In the late 20s and early 30s their shows met with only moderate success, but the songs continued to flow - 'You Took Advantage Of Me', 'With A Song In My Heart', 'A Ship Without A Sail', 'Ten Cents A Dance' and 'Dancing On The Ceiling'. Rodgers and Hart worked together in Hollywood for a while, their songs including 'Isn't It Romantic', 'Love Me Tonight', 'Lover' and 'It's Easy To Remember'. Back on Broadway in 1935, they wrote *Jumbo*, which included 'My Romance', 'Little Girl Blue' and 'The Most Beautiful Girl In The World'. They followed *Jumbo* with *On Your Toes* (1936) which included 'There's A Small Hotel', *Babes In Arms* (1937) which introduced 'Where Or When', 'My Funny Valentine' and 'The Lady Is A Tramp' and *I'd Rather Be Right* (1937) with 'Have You Met Miss Jones?'. Their two shows of 1938 were *I Married An Angel* and *The Boys From Syracuse*, featuring, respectively, 'I Married An Angel' and 'Spring Is Here' and 'Falling In Love With Love' and 'This Can't Be Love'. Later song successes for the duo were 'I Didn't Know What Time It Was', from *Too Many Girls* (1939), 'It Never Entered My Mind', from *Higher And Higher* (1940) and 'Bewitched, Bothered And Bewildered' and 'I Could Write A

Book' from *Pal Joey* (1940). Their last show together was *By Jupiter* (1942) from which came 'Careless Rhapsody' and 'Wait Till You See Her'. In addition to the stage productions, Rodgers and Hart wrote songs for a number of movies, including *The Hot Heiress* (1931), *Love Me Tonight, Hallelujah, I'm A Bum, Dancing Lady, Hollywood Party, Evergreen, Nana, Manhattan Melodrama, Mississippi, Dancing Pirate, They Met In Argentina, Fools For Scandal*, and *Stage Door Canteen* (1943). Hart was of a nervous and unstable disposition, caused mainly by a troubled personal life. He was perpetually disorganized, fulfilling popular assumptions about songwriters by scribbling ideas and sometimes complete lyrics on scraps of paper which he stuffed into pockets and forgot about until Rodgers, a thoroughly organized man, urged him into action. Worried over his small stature, his latent homosexuality and the problems of meeting theatrical deadlines, Hart turned increasingly to alcohol. He backed out of a show he and Rodgers were to have written in 1942 and drifted into despair, seeking solace in drink. He died in November 1943. Of all the many gifted lyricists to appear in the USA in the 20s and 30s, Hart was perhaps the most poetic. His early studies and deep appreciation of language gave him insight into words and their uses. Many of his best lyrics stand apart from their musical context and have a life of their own. His ear for rhymes, and his ability to create vivid word pictures, contributed towards some of the finest popular songs of all time. Despite the difficulties and unhappiness he experienced in his private life, his work is filled with lightness, enduring charm and ready wit; qualities which mark him as a true genius among songwriters.

Further reading: *The Complete Lyrics Of Lorenz Hart*, eds. Dorothy Hart and Robert Kimball. *Thou Swell, Thou Witty*, Dorothy Hart. *Rodgers And Hart*, S. Marx and J. Clayton.

Harvey Girls, The

As the railroads opened up the Wild West in America during the 1880s, in their wake came Fred Harvey's chain of restaurants complete with their immaculate facilities and prim and proper waitresses. They are the ones who are said to have 'conquered the undeveloped territory with a beefsteak and a cup of coffee'. In this story, set in Sandrock, New Mexico, one of those winsome women, Susan Bradley (Judy Garland), gets involved with the opposition - a saloon which is owned and operated by Ned Trent (John Hodiak), and populated with some girls who are really not very nice, especially a floozy named Em (Angela

The Harvey Girls

Lansbury). Actually, Hodiak turns out to be all right. It is the evil Judge Sam Purvis (Preston Foster) and his mob of villains who set fire to the Harvey House in an attempt to drive the girls out of town. Susan does board the departing train, but it has not travelled far before Hodiak catches up with it, and their subsequent embrace dissolves into a wedding picture. Ray Bolger with his marvellous eccentric dancing and Virginia O'Brien with her 'dead-pan' humour, led a first-class supporting cast which included Kenny Baker, Marjorie Main, Chill Wills, Cyd Charisse, Selena Royle, and Stephen McNally. Johnny Mercer and Harry Warren's score provided Judy Garland with another of her 'travelling' songs (following soon after 'The Trolley Song' in *Meet Me In St. Louis*). This time it was a train number, 'On The Atcheson, Topeka And The Santa Fe', which won the Oscar for best song. Garland was also involved in 'In The Valley (Where The Evening Sun Goes Down)', 'Swing Your Partner Round And Round' (with Bolger and Main), and 'It's A Great Big World' (with Charisse and O'Brien). The rest of the songs included 'Oh You Kid', 'Wait And See', and 'The Train Must Be Fed'. The screenplay, by Edmund Beloin, Nathaniel Curtis, Samson Ralphaelson, James O'Hanlon, and Harry Crane, was based on Samuel Hopkins Adams' book and a story by Eleanor Griffin and William Rankin. Robert Alton staged the dances and the musical sequences were arranged by Robert Edens, a close colleague of producer Arthur Freed. *The Harvey Girls* was photographed in Technicolor by George Folsey and released by MGM in 1946. The director was George Sidney.

Haver, June

b. June Stovenour, 10 June 1926, Rock Island, Illinois, USA. A vivacious singer and actress in several 20th Century-Fox musicals of the 40s and early 50s, who gave up her career after marrying the highly successful film actor Fred MacMurray. A talented all-round entertainer as a youngster - she is said to have played the piano with the Cincinnati Symphony Orchestra - Haver sang with dance bands before landing the part of a hat-check girl in the Alice Faye movie *The Gang's All Here* in 1943. A year later, when she co-starred with crooner Dick Haymes in *When Irish Eyes Are Smiling*, she was being tipped as the successor to Betty Grable. In the course of *Where Do We Go From Here?* (1945) she lost Fred MacMurray to Joan Leslie - but got him back (in real life) some years later. Before then, Haver decorated a series of period musicals - mostly set around the turn-of-the-century - which included *The Dolly Sisters, Three Little Girls In Blue, Wake Up And Dream, I Wonder Who's Kissing Her Now?, Look For The Silver Lining, Oh You Beautiful Doll, The Daughter Of Rosie O'Grady*, and *I'll Get By* (1950). *The Girl Next Door* (1953), in which Haver co-starred with Dan Dailey,

was her last film (and among her best), and the only one with contemporary costumes and setting. Her decision to leave the movie business while she was still at her peak and enter The Sisters of Charity Convent at Xavier, Kansas, in February 1953, was branded by many as a publicity stunt. This conclusion seemed the more credible when she emerged into the outside world after only seven and a half months. However, she claimed that she 'did not have the physical strength to withstand the strain of religious life', and after meeting up with Fred MacMurray again, and marrying him in June 1954, she has not made another motion picture (to date) since. Even that union, in view of the difference in their ages (he was 45, she 28), came in for a fair amount of criticism, but they raised their twin daughters and were still together when MacMurray died in 1991 at the age of 83.

Hayman, Richard

b. 27 March 1920, Cambridge, Massachusetts, USA. As a young man, Hayman taught himself to play the harmonica and accordion, and performed in local bands before moving to the west coast. In the late 30s he worked for three years with Borrah Minevitch's Harmonica Rascals, and later played with Leo Diamond. He also appeared in vaudeville, and had several 'bit' parts in movies. In the early 40s he arranged background music for films such as *Girl Crazy* (1943), *Meet Me In St Louis* (1944) and *State Fair* (1945). In the late 40s he was arranger for Vaughan Monroe for a long spell, and in the early 50s was musical director and arranger for Bobby Wayne, providing the accompaniment on such Wayne hits as, 'Let Me In' and 'Oh Mis'rable Lover'. In 1953 he started recording for Mercury Records with his own orchestra, featuring his own harmonica solos, and others by Jerry Murad, leader of the Harmonicats. His hits included 'Ruby' (from the film, *Ruby Gentry*), 'April In Portugal', 'Limelight (Terry's Theme)', 'Eyes Of Blue' (theme from the film, *Shane*), 'The Story Of Three Loves' (the film title theme), 'Off Shore' and 'Sadie Thompson's Song' (from the Rita Hayworth movie, *Miss Sadie Thompson*). His last chart entry, in 1956, was 'A Theme From *The Threepenny Opera* (Moriat)', featuring pianist Jan August. He also made some recordings under the name of Dick Hayman And The Harmonica Sparklers. He composed several numbers such as 'Dansero', 'No Strings Attached', 'Serenade To A Lost Love', 'Carriage Trade', 'Skipping Along' and 'Valse d'Amour'. In the 80s he was reportedly playing piano in nightclubs around the USA.

Albums: *Reminiscing* (c.50s), *My Fair Lady* (c.60s), *Great Motion Picture Themes Of Victor Young* (c.60s), *Serenade For Love* (c.60s).

Haymes, Dick

b. Richard Benjamin Haymes, 13 September 1916,

Buenos Aires, Argentina, d. 28 March 1980, Los Angeles, California, USA. One of the outstanding ballad singers to emerge from the swing era of the late 30s/early 40s, with a deep, warm baritone voice and a straighforward style similar to Bob Manning, another singer who was popular in the 50s. Son of a Scottish father, and an Irish mother who was a concert singer and vocal coach, Haymes was educated in several countries including France, Switzerland and the USA. After working as a radio announcer, film extra and stuntman, and taking small parts in vaudeville, he replaced Frank Sinatra in the Harry James Band in 1941 and worked briefly for Benny Goodman and Tommy Dorsey before going out as a solo act in 1943. Signed for US Decca, he had a string of hits through to 1951, including 'It Can't Be Wrong' (number 1), 'You'll Never Know' (number 1), 'Wait For Me Mary', 'Put Your Arms Around Me Honey', 'How Blue The Night', 'Laura', 'The More I See You', 'I Wish I Knew', 'Till The End Of Time', 'Love Letters', 'That's For Me', 'It's A Grand Night For Singing', 'It Might As Well Be Spring', 'How Are Thing In Glocca Morra?', 'Mamselle', 'I Wish I Didn't Love You So', 'Little White Lies', 'You Can't Be True Dear', 'It's Magic', 'Room Full Of Roses', 'Maybe It's Because', 'The Old Master Painter' and 'Count Every Star'. During this time he also recorded duets with Judy Garland, such as in 'For You, For Me, Forever More' (1947), as well as joining Bing Crosby and the Andrews Sisters in 'There's No Business Like Show Business' (1947), and Ethel Merman in 'You're Just In Love', (1951). He also had several hits with another ex-Harry James singer, Helen Forrest, which included 'Long Ago And Far Away', 'It Had To Be You', 'Together', 'I'll Buy That Dream', 'Some Sunday Morning', 'I'm Always Chasing Rainbows' and 'Oh! What It Seemed To Be'. Haymes was also successful on radio with his *Here's To Romance*, and the *Autolite* shows. Haymes' first starring role in films was in *Irish Eyes Are Smiling* (1944), a musical bio-pic of composer Ernest R. Ball ('When Irish Eyes Are Smiling', 'Dear Little Boy Of Mine', 'A Little Bit Of Heaven' and 'Let The Rest Of The World Go By'). His other film musicals included *Billy Rose's Diamond Horseshoe* (1945), *State Fair* (1945), *Do You Love Me?* (1946), *The Shocking Miss Pilgrim* (1947), *Up In Central Park* and *One Touch Of Venus* (both 1948). In most of the movies he featured opposite some of the most glamorous leading ladies of the day, including June Haver, Betty Grable, Jeanne Crain, Maureen O'Hara, Deanna Durbin and Ava Gardner. His career waned somewhat in the 50s, hampered by tax problems and immigration departments. He also had financial troubles over the years with some of his various wives, who included film stars Rita Hayworth and Joanne Dru, singers Edith Harper and Fran Jeffries, Errol Flynn's ex-wife Nora, and finally, model Wendy Patricia Smith. A

switch from Decca to Capitol Records in 1955 produced two albums of standard ballads, *Rain Or Shine* and *Moondreams*, with arrangements by Johnny Mandel and Ian Bernard, which are generally considered to be classics of their kind. Both are now available together on one CD in the UK. During the 60s Haymes lived and worked mostly in Europe and in 1969 made an album in the UK entitled *Now And Then*, a mixture of his old favourites and more contemporary material. In the 70s he returned to the USA and undertook television and cabaret dates. He recorded a live album, *Dick Haymes Comes Home! First Stop: The Coconut Grove*, on which he was backed by an old name from the swing era, the Les Brown Band of Renown.

Selected albums: *Rain Or Shine* (1955), *Moondreams* (1957), *Now And Then* (1969), *Dick Haymes Comes Home! First Stop: The Coconut Grove* (early 70s). Compilations: *The Special Magic Of Dick Haymes* (1979), *The V-Disc Years* (1979), *The Best Of Dick Haymes* (1982), *The Last Goodbye* (1983), *Great Song Stylists, Volume One* (1983), *Dick Haymes Sings Irving Berlin* (1984), *Golden Greats* (1985).

Hayworth, Rita

b. Margarita Carmen Cansino, 17 October 1918, Brooklyn, New York, USA, d. 14 May 1987, New York, USA. An actress and dancer; one of the most popular and glamorous film stars of the 40s. In Hollywood she was dubbed 'The Love Goddess', and the pin-up picture (from the cover of *Life* magazine) of her on a bed clad only in a sheer negligee rivalled that of another Forces' favourite, Betty Grable, and was stuck on the side of the atom bomb that was dropped on Hiroshima. Hayworth started taking dancing lessons when she was six years old, and later, after the family had moved to Mexico, she formed a dance act with her father Eduardo, a well-known Spanish dancer. From the age of 16, she appeared as a dancer in several low-budget movies until she met the Texan promoter Edward C. Judson. He obtained a contract for her with Columbia Pictures and the couple were married in 1937. After appearing in several movies, including musicals such as *Music In My Heart* and *Strawberry Blonde* (with James Cagney), she made her breakthrough in 1941 when she partnered Fred Astaire in *You'll Never Get Rich*, and they were teamed again the following year for *You Were Never Lovelier*. Around this time she also co-starred with Victor Mature in *My Gal Sal*. Having broken up with Judson, she married the actor Orsen Welles in 1943, and a year later made what was arguably her best musical, *Cover Girl*, with Gene Kelly. This was followed in 1945 by *Tonight And Every Night* which was set in London and was supposedly a tribute to the famous Windmill Theatre. After periods of dispute with Columbia during which she refused to make films, and two more marriages - to wealthy playboy

Aly Khan and singer Dick Haymes - Hayworth made her final musical film, *Pal Joey*, with Frank Sinatra and Kim Novak, in 1957. Although only a small percentage of her more than 60 movies were musicals, several of the films in which she played dramatic roles contained some memorable musical sequences, such as 'Put The Blame On Mame' from perhaps her most famous film, *Gilda*, and the incredibly erotic 'The Heat Is On' from *Miss Sadie Thompson*. According to the experts she was always dubbed by singers such as Anita Ellis, Martha Mears, Nan Wynn and Jo Ann Greer, and it will be their voices that are heard on the album *The Rita Hayworth Collection: 20 Golden Greats*. After a fifth marriage to producer James Hill from 1958-61, Hayworth continued to make films into the 70s. During that decade her behaviour led people to believe that she was a reclusive alcoholic, and it was only in later years that her daughter, Princess Yasmin Aga Kahn, revealed that her mother had been suffering from Alzheimer's disease. In 1981 she was moved from California to New York and a court placed her in the care of Yasmin until her death.
Further reading: *Rita Hayworth: The Time, The Place, And The Woman*, John Kobal.

Hear My Song

To many Britons of a certain age, that title makes them think of the 1938 song 'Hear My Song, Violetta' (Rudolph Luckesch-Othmar Klose-Harry S. Pepper), which was a big hit in the late 40s and 50s for the enormously popular Irish tenor Josef Locke. By the early 60s, after a series of disagreements with the Inland Revenue, Locke had 'retired' to Ireland where, it was revealed many years later, he started a new life as a gentleman farmer. Subsequently, a look-alike billed as Mr. X ('Is he or isn't he Josef Locke?') made a comfortable living touring the UK variety theatres singing all the familiar Locke songs. This film is set Liverpool in the early 80s. Micky O'Neill (Adrian Dunbar) books Mr. X (William Hootkins) in an effort to boost the takings of the financially troubled nightclub he manages. Although the audience are taken in by Mr. X's performance, the impostor fails to convince Locke's former lover, Cathleen Doyle (Shirley Anne Field) - especially when he tries to seduce her. Sacked from his job, Micky tracks down the real Locke (Ned Beatty) and persuades him to perform a free concert in the club. While the customers are still applauding, Locke makes his escape - Chief of Police Jim Abbott (David McCallum) captures Mr. X - and is reunited with Cathleen. Tara Fitzgerald played Nancy Doyle, Mickey's girlfriend (and Cathleen's daughter), and the remainder of a strong supporting cast included Harold Berens, James Nesbitt, John Dare, Stephen Marcus, Britta Smith, Gladys Sheehan, Gina Moxley, and comedian Norman Vaughan as himself. Ned Beatty was dubbed by operatic tenor Vernon Midgely, and Brian Hoey was the voice of Mr. X. Many of Locke's old favourites were given an airing, including 'I'll Take You Home Again Kathleen' (Thomas Westendorf), 'Come Back To Sorrento' (Ernesto De Curtis-Claude Aveling), 'Blaze Away' (Abe Holzmann), 'Goodbye' (Ralph Benatzky-Harry Graham), and, of course, 'Hear My Song, Violetta'. John Altman composed the splendid background score which was performed by his own Jazz Orchestra. Peter Chelsom directed, and co-wrote the screenplay with Adrian Dunbar. It was photographed in Fujicolor by Sue Gibson. This perfectly delightful and thoroughly enjoyable film, which became a surprise smash hit in the USA in 1991, was produced in the UK by Alison Owen-Allen.

Hefti, Neal

b. 29 October 1922, Hastings, Nebraska, USA. One of the most influential big band arrangers of the 40s and 50s, Hefti's early charts were played by the Nat Towles band in the late 30s. His material was also used by Earl Hines; however, his first real taste of the big time came when he joined Charlie Barnet in 1942 and then moved into the Woody Herman band in 1944. Both engagements were as a member of the trumpet section, but his writing became steadily more important than his playing. For Herman he arranged many of the band's most popular recordings, including 'The Good Earth' and 'Wild Root', and was co-arranger with Ralph Burns of 'Caldonia'. In 1946 Hefti's charts were among those used by the ill-fated Billy Butterfield big band and by Charlie Ventura's equally short-lived band. In the late 40s he wrote for what was one of the best of Harry James's bands; in the mid-50s, along with Ernie Wilkins and Nat Pierce, he helped to give the Count Basie band the new distinctive, tighter style which led to a wholesale re-evaluation of big band music, especially in the UK. Throughout the 50s and 60s Hefti was deeply involved in composing for films and television (including the theme for the US *Batman* television series) and, while much of his work in these quarters was geared to the demands of the medium, there were many moments when he was able to infuse his work with echoes of his jazz heritage. Throughout those years and into the 70s Hefti periodically formed big bands either for club, concert or record dates. The tradition of precise, disciplined arranging, of which Hefti was one of the more important exponents, continues to make itself heard in the work of Sam Nestico, which has proved immensely popular with college and university bands on both sides of the Atlantic.
Albums: *Coral Reef* (1951-52), *Pardon My Doo-wah* (1954), *Light And Right* (c.1954), *Hot 'N' Hearty* (1955), by Count Basie *Basie* (1957), *Basie Plays Hefti* (1958). Compilation: *The Best Of Woody Herman* (1944-48 recordings).

Hello, Dolly!

Hello, Dolly!

From it's still-frame sepia beginning on the streets of New York (c.1890) through to the triumphant finalé, in which Dolly Levi (Barbra Streisand), widow, and matchmaker supreme, finally meets her own match with wealthy merchant owner Horace Vandergelder (Walter Matthau) in a white-walled church overlooking the lake, this was a thoroughly enjoyable film. Those who are supposed to know said that, at the age of only 27, Streisand was far too young for the role, but it did not prevent the cinema-going public from making this 1969 20th Century-Fox release one of the 10 most popular musical movies of the decade in the USA. Michael Crawford, as Cornelius Hackle, Horace's head clerk, and Danny Locklin as his assistant, were among a strong supporting cast which also included Marianne McAndrew as milliner Irene Molloy (Horace's date before Dolly decided to have him for herself), E.J. Peaker, Tommy Tune, Fritz Feld, and Joyce Ames. But it was Streisand's film, and she gloried in a marvellous Jerry Herman score which gave her such numbers as 'Just Leave Everything To Me', 'Love Is Only Love', 'Put On Your Sunday Clothes', (with Crawford, Locklin and ensemble), 'So Long, Dearie', 'Before The Parade Passes By', and the title number during which she makes her triumphant entrance into the swell Harmonia Gardens restaurant where she is greeted by none other than Louis Armstrong, who had himself enjoyed a US number 1 hit with the song some years previously. Crawford and Locklin were delightful on 'Elegance' and the tender 'It Only Takes A Moment', and when they joined forces with Matthau for the philosophical 'It Takes A Woman'. Other numbers included 'Ribbons Down My Back', 'Dancing', and 'Waiter's Gavotte'. In a production as lavish and expensive (it cost $24 million) the dance sequences were always going to be spectacular and interesting, especially with director Gene Kelly and choreographer Michael Kidd around, but the finished production was well worthwhile. Adapted from the 1964 Broadway show by producer-screenwriter Ernest Lehman, *Hello, Dolly!* was shot in De Luxe Color and Todd-AO, and won Academy Awards for several of its outstanding qualities, art-set direction, sound, and music direction.

Hello, Frisco, Hello

This typically lavish 20th Century-Fox period musical reunited the popular team of Alice Faye and John Payne in 1943 for a story which was set in the gaudy, bawdy Barbary Coast area of San Francisco. Payne has a nightspot there, and Faye is his girlfriend and singer until he loses everything following his brief marriage to the high-faluting Lynn Bari. Meanwhile, Faye goes to London where she becomes a big star before returning to help Payne reopen his establishment and resume their romantic relationship. Jack Oakie and June Havoc co-starred, and the supporting cast included Laird Cregar, George Barbier, Ward Bond, John Archer, and Esther Dale. Alice Faye introduced the only new song in the film, Harry Warren and Mack Gordon's lovely ballad, 'You'll Never Know', which went on to win an Academy Award. The rest of the ample score consisted of a mixed bag of good old familiar numbers such as 'By The Light Of The Silvery Moon' (Gus Edwards-Edgar Madden), 'Why Do They Always Pick On Me?' (Harry Von Tilzer-Stanley Murphy), 'When You Wore A Tulip' (Jack Mahoney-Percy Wenrich), 'Has Anybody Here Seen Kelly?' (Charles Moore-C.W. Murphy-William McKenna), 'Ragtime Cowboy Joe' (Lewis Muir-Grant Clarke-Maurice Abrahams), and 'Hello, Frisco, Hello' (Louis Hirsch-Gene Buck). Robert Ellis, Helen Logan and Richard Macauley wrote the screenplay, and the choreographer was Val Raset. H. Bruce Humberstone directed this pleasant and undemanding picture which, with its attractive costumes and settings, was a pleasure to look at.

Help!

The Beatles' second feature film was, like *A Hard Day's Night*, directed by Richard Lester. His eccentricity was still evident, but the simple plot and location scenes resulted in a finished work closer in style to classic 60s teen movies than its predecessor. This is not to deny *Help!*'s many good qualities, particularly the Beatles' unpretentious performances, superb comedic support by Victor Spinetti and Roy Kinnear and the dazzling array of original songs providing the soundtrack. 'Ticket To Ride', which accompanies antics on an Alpine ski-slope, and 'You've Got To Hide Your Love Away', set in a communal living room, are particularly memorable. The corresponding album is completed by several more superb John Lennon/Paul McCartney compositions, notably 'Yesterday', plus a handful of cover versions, including a rousing take of Larry Williams' 'Dizzy Miss Lizzy'. *Help!*'s breathtaking scope compliments the film from which its takes its cue.

Henderson, Ray

b. Raymond Brost, 16 December 1896, Buffalo, New York, USA, d. 31 December 1970. Born into a show business family, Henderson studied music but was a self-taught pianist. In 1918 he became a song promotor New York City and spent his free time writing songs. He met with no success until 1922, when he joined lyricist Lew Brown. They had a succession of popular hits with 'Georgette',

Help!

'Humming' and 'Annabelle' (all 1922). During the early and mid-20s Henderson worked with various other lyricists, his triumphs included 'That Old Gang Of Mine' (1923, with Billy Rose and Mort Dixon), 'Bye Bye Blackbird' (1926, with Dixon), 'Five Feet Two, Eyes Of Blue' and 'I'm Sitting On Top Of The World' (both 1925, with Sam M. Lewis and Joe Young). In 1925 he began an association with Buddy De Sylva with 'Alabamy Bound'. The same year Brown joined the team, and the three men quickly became one of the most formidable songwriting teams in the USA for their work on Broadway musicals such as *Good News*, *Hold Everthing*, *Follow Through*, *Flying High*, *George White's Scandals*. They wrote 'It All Depends On You', 'Lucky Day', 'Black Bottom', 'Broken-Hearted', 'The Birth Of The Blues', 'The Best Things In Life Are Free' (which became the title of a 1956 Hollywood bio-pic about the trio), 'The Varsity Drag', 'You're The Cream In My Coffee' and 'Good News'. In the late 20s De Sylva, Brown and Henderson went to Hollywood, where they wrote 'Sonny Boy' overnight for Al Jolson to sing in a film that was approaching completion. Although written as a spoof, Jolson sang it straight and it became one of his greatest hits. The team then wrote the score for *Sunny Side Up* (1929), which included the title song, 'If I Had A Talking Picture Of You' and 'I'm A Dreamer Aren't We All'. Other film songs include 'Button Up Your Overcoat' and 'I Want To Be Bad'. In 1931 the partnership was dissolved, with De Sylva becoming a successful film producer. Henderson and Brown remained collaborators for further hit songs such as 'Life Is Just A Bowl Of Cherries', 'My Song' and 'The Thrill Is Gone'. In the late 30s Henderson's other collaborators included Ted Koehler, Irving Caesar and Jack Yellen. Henderson retired in the late 40s, and worked sporadically on a never-completed opera. He died in 1970.

Herrmann, Bernard

b. 29 June 1911, New York, USA, d. 24 December 1975, Los Angeles, USA. One of the most highly regarded composers and arrangers of background music for films, from the early 40s through to the 70s. Herrmann studied at New York University and the Juilliard School of Music, before joining CBS broadcasting in 1933. While serving as a composer conductor for radio documentaries and dramas he became associated with Orson Welles, and began his film career by scoring Welles' legendary *Citizen Kane*, for which he was nominated for an Academy Award in 1941. He did win the Oscar that year, not for *Citizen Kane*, but for his music to *All That Money Can Buy* (also known as *The Devil And Danny Webster* amongst other titles), generally thought of as among his best work. His other early scores included another Welles classic, *The Magnificent Ambersons*, *Jane Eyre*, *Hangover Square*, *Anna And The King Of Siam*, The

Ghost And Mrs Muir, *The Day The Earth Stood Still*, *Five Fingers*, *Beneath The 12 Mile Reef*, *King Of The Khyber Rifles*, *Garden Of Evil*, *The Egyptian* (with Alfred Newman), *The Man In The Grey Flannel Suit*, *Prince Of Players* and *The Kentuckian* (1955). Herrmann then proceeded to make several films with Alfred Hitchcock - he became known as the director's favourite movie composer. They included thrillers such as *The Man Who Knew Too Much*, *The Wrong Man*, *Vertigo*, *North By Northwest*, *Psycho* and *Marnie*. He was also a consultant on Hitchcock's sinister *The Birds*. Herrmann was 'gravely wounded' when Hitchcock rejected his score for *Torn Curtain* in favour of one by John Addison; this decision terminated their relationship.

His other dramatic scores included *A Hatful Of Rain*, *The Naked And The Dead*, *Journey To The Centre Of The Earth*, *The Three Worlds Of Gulliver*, *Mysterious Island*, *Cape Fear*, *Tender Is The Night*, *Joy In The Morning*, *Sisters*, *It's Alive*. Between 1965 and 1975, Herrmann spent much of his time based in Britain, and composed the background music for a good many European productions, such as *Jason And The Argonauts*, *Fahrenheit 451*, *The Bride Wore Black*, *Twisted Nerve*, *The Battle Of Nereveta*, *The Night Digger* and *Endless Night*. At the end of his career, as at the beginning, Herrmann was nominated for an Academy Award twice in the same year. This time, however, neither *Taxi Driver* nor *Obsession* won the Oscar for Original Score, and Herrmann died, the day after he completed recording the music of Martin Scorsese's *Taxi Driver*, in 1975. The many recordings of his vast output include *Classic Fantasy Film Scores*, conducted by Herrmann, and *Citizen Kane - Classic Film Scores Of Bernard Herrmann* with the National Philharmonic Orchestra. In 1992, an hour-long, analytical documentary, *Music For The Movies: Bernard Herrmann*, which included home movies, interviews, and a scene from Hitchcock's *Torn Curtain* accompanied by Herrmann's original, rejected music, was shown on US television.

Further reading: *Bernard Herrmann*, E. Johnson. *The Life And Music Of Bernard Herrmann*, Steven C. Smith. Albums: *Scarlet Ribbons* (late-50s), *Carolyn Hester* (1961), *Carolyn Hester* (1962) *This Is My Living* (1963), *That's My Song* (1964), *Carolyn Hester At The Town Hall* (1965), *The Carolyn Hester Coalition* (1969), *Thursday's Child Has Far To Go* (1971), *Carolyn Hester* (1974).

High Society

This enjoyable musical adaptation of Philip Barry's stylish play, *The Philadephia Story*, which was filmed (without songs) in 1940 with Katharine Hepburn, Cary Grant and James Stewart, was released by MGM in 1956. Apart from some changes in characterization and locales, John Patrick's screenplay, which was set in swanky Newport, Rhode Island, stayed fairly close

High Society

to the original and concerns Tracey Lord (Grace Kelly), who is set to marry an insufferable snob, George Ketteridge (John Lund), when her former husband, C.K. Dexter Haven (Bing Crosby), returns to his house next door, ostensibly to organize a jazz festival. This situation is further complicated by the arrival of Mike Connor (Frank Sinatra) and Liz Imbrie (Celeste Holm), two reporters from *Spy* Magazine which has been allowed access to the wedding because it is in possession of certain information regarding the (alleged) philandering of Tracey's father, Seth Lord (Sidney Blackmer). Louis Calhern is especially amusing as Tracey's uncle, and also in the cast were Lydia Reed, Margalo Gillmore, Richard Keene, Hugh Boswell, and jazz giant Louis Armstrong who played - who else? - but himself. By the end of the film Tracey comes to her senses, sends George off in a huff, and re-marries Dexter. It is obvious that Mike and Liz will be making their own arrangements soon. Cole Porter's score contained several pleasing numbers such as 'High Society Calypso' (Armstrong), 'Now You Has Jazz' (Crosby-Armstrong), 'Little One' (Crosby), 'Who Wants to Be A Millionaire?' (Sinatra-Holm), 'You're Sensational' (Sinatra), 'I Love You, Samantha' (Crosby), 'Now You Has Jazz' (Crosby-Armstrong), and 'Well, Did You Evah?' (Crosby-Sinatra). Bing Crosby and Grace Kelly's record of 'True Love' made the Top 5 in both UK and US charts, and Sinatra's version of the 'Mind If I Make Love To You?' remains one of his most endearing recorded performances. The director-choreographer was Charles Walters, and, in a decade that produced a feast of film musicals, *High Society* grossed nearly six million dollars. A 1986 UK stage adaptation of the movie, starring Trevor Eve, Stephen Rea, Natasha Richardson, and Angela Richards, incorporated some of Porter's other numbers into the score.

High, Wide And Handsome

This film is usually mentioned in conjunction with two of the acknowledged masterpieces of the musical theatre, *Show Boat* and *Oklahoma!*. This is partly, although not solely because Oscar Hammerstein II wrote the book (or in the case of the film, the screenplay) and lyrics for all three projects. The other common factor is that each, in its own way, succeeds in musicalizing a slice of cherished American history. In the case of *High, Wide And Handsome*, which is set in the state of Pennsylvania in the year 1859, the story concerns the efforts of a group of militants led by a crooked railway mogul (Alan Hale), to prevent a farmer (Randolph Scott) and his showgirl sweetheart (Irene Dunne) from setting up a pipeline to transport the newly discovered oil from their land to the refinery. Irene Dunne introduced two of Jerome Kern and Oscar Hammerstein II's most enduring standards, 'The Folks Who Live On The Hill' and 'Can I Forget You?', and the score also included 'Will You Marry Me Tomorrow, Maria?', 'Allegheny Al', 'The Things I Want', and the spirited title song. Dorothy Lamour - just three years before she donned her sarong and joined Bob Hope and Bing Crosby on the *Road To Singapore* - was also in the cast, along with Akim Tamiroff, William Frawley, Charles Bickford, Raymond Walburn, Elizabeth Patterson, and Ben Blue. *High, Wide And Handsome*, which was choreographed by LeRoy Prinz and directed by Rouben Mamoulian, was released by Paramount in 1937. A sobering thought: neither 'The Folks Who Live On The Hill' or 'Can I Forget You' was even nominated for an Academy Award in 1937. The Oscar for best song went to 'Sweet Leilani' from the film *Waikiki Wedding*.

Higher And Higher

Idol of the bobby-soxers Frank Sinatra made his acting debut - as himself - in this 1944 screen version of the Broadway show, which was released by RKO in 1944. The screenplay, by Jay Dratler and Ralph Spence, stayed close to Gladys Hurlbut and Joshua Logan's original stage book in which a group of servants, headed by butler Jack Haley, plan to turn one of their number, a kitchen maid (Michele Morgan), into a debutante in order to raise money for their bankrupt boss (Leon Errol), to whom they owe so much (and vice-versa). For probably the only time in his film life, Sinatra did not get the girl - Michele preferred Haley - but he did get to sing a bunch of marvellous songs by Jimmy McHugh and Harold Adamson, including 'I Couldn't Sleep A Wink Last Night', 'This Is A Lovely Way To Spend An Evening', 'The Music Stopped', 'You're On Your Own', and 'I Saw You First'. The rest of the numbers consisted of 'It's A Most Important Affair', 'Today I'm A Debutante', 'Minuet In Boogie'; and 'Disgustingly Rich', the only song retained from Richard Rogers and Lorenz Hart's original stage score. Another fine singer, Mel Tormé, made the first of his infrequent screen appearances, and also in the sprightly cast were Victor Borge, Mary Wickes, Marcy McGuire, Elizabeth Risdon, Barbara Hale, Paul and Grace Hartman, Ivy Scott, and Dooley Wilson. Additional dialogue was provided by William Bowers and Howard Harris, and the lively dance sequences were choreographed by Ernest Matray. The producer-director was Tim Whelan.

Hit The Deck

Considering the wealth of talent on board, this 1955 screen adaptation of the 1927 Broadway musical proved to be a pretty disappointing affair, mainly owing to a lack-lustre screenplay by Sonya Levien and William Ludwig. It told the by now familiar story of three off-duty sailors, (Tony Martin, Russ Tamblyn and Vic Damone) and their search for three lovely gals (Ann Miller, Debbie Reynolds and Jane Powell) with whom to embark on the voyage of life. Fortunately, there were plenty of musical highlights in composer Vincent Youmans' score, such as the lovely 'More Than You Know' (Tony Martin) (lyric: Billy Rose-Edward Eliscu), 'Sometimes I'm Happy' (Vic Damone-Jane Powell) (lyric: Clifford Grey-Irving Caesar), 'Hallelujah' (Martin-Tamblyn-Damone) (lyric: Grey-Leo Robin), 'I Know that You Know' (Damone-Powell) (lyric: Anne Caldwell), and 'Keepin' Myself For You' (Martin-Ann Miller) (lyric: Sidney Clare). The other songs included 'Join The Navy', 'Why, Oh Why', and 'Lucky Bird' (all with lyrics by Robin and Grey), and 'Lady From The Bayou' and 'A Kiss Or Two' (lyrics: Robin), and 'Ciribiribin' (Albert Pestalozza). Hermes Pan staged the dance sequences with his usual imagination and flair (especially in the sequences which involved Ann Miller) and Roy Rowland directed a cast which also included Walter Pidgeon, Kay Armen, Gene Raymond, J Carrol Naish, and Allan King. *Hit The Deck* was photographed in Eastman Color and Cinemascope, and produced for MGM by Joe Pasternak. Hubert Osborne's play *Shore Leave*, which was the basis for this film and the original Broadway musical, had been filmed before in 1930 with Jack Oakie, Polly Walker and Roger Gray.

Hold My Hand

Another in the series of comedy musicals starring the popular British funny-man Stanley Lupino. This one, which was released by the Associated British Picture Corporation in 1938, cast Lupino as Eddie Marston, a soft-hearted gentleman who secretly finances a newspaper which is run by his dependant, Paula (Polly Ward), who thinks he is after the profits. Further farcical complications ensue when Eddie's fiancée, Helen (Sally Gray), falls in love with Pop Currie (Jack Melford) the paper's editor; his friend Bob Crane (John Wood) is attracted by Polly; and his secretary, Jane (Barbara Blair) find it difficult to keep her hands off him! While all this is going on, Eddie gets involved in a bizarre cat burglary with Lord Milchester (Fred Emney), and the others joining in the fun and games included Bertha Belmore (as Lady Milchester), Syd Walker, Arthur Rigby, and Gibb McLaughlin. Polly Ward and John Wood handled most of the songs which included 'Turn On The Love-light', 'As Long As I Can Look At You', and 'Hold My Hand'. Clifford Grey, Bert Lee, William Freshman, adapted the screenplay from Stanley Lupino's original story. American Thornton Freeland, a leading exponent of this zany kind of musical entertainment in the US and UK, directed with flair.

Hit The Deck

Holiday Inn

The cinema's favourite singer and dancer of the 30s and 40s, Bing Crosby and Fred Astaire, co-starred for the first time in this Paramount release of 1942. Irving Berlin contributed a wonderful score, and he is also credited with the original idea for what turned out be a novel story, which was adapted for the screen by the distinguished playwright, Elmer Rice. Claude Binyon's screenplay concerned a couple of song and dance men, Jim Hardy (Crosby) and Ted Hanover (Astaire), who were doing all right before Jim gets tired of the nightly grind and takes up farming. That proves a little too taxing too, so he turns a large New England farmhouse into a night club that will only be open on holidays. The Holiday Inn has it's gala opening on New Year's Eve, and proves to be a tremendous success. Berlin celebrated that holiday by writing 'Let's Start The New Year Right', and each of the other seven important annual vacations, such as Lincoln's Birthday and Valentine's Day, was allocated it's own song, with the Fourth of July getting two. Two of the numbers, 'Lazy' and 'Easter Parade', had been used before in other productions, but the rest of the score was new, and included 'I'll Capture Your Heart Singing', 'You're Easy To Dance With', 'Happy Holiday', 'Holiday Inn', 'Abraham', 'Be Careful, It's My Heart', 'I Can't Tell A Lie', 'Let's Say It With Firecrackers' (an explosive Astaire solo dance), 'Song Of Freedom', 'Plenty To Be Thankful For', and 'White Christmas'. The latter song won an Academy Award, was inducted into the NARAS Hall of Fame, and went on to become an enduring Christmas favourite. Crosby's recording is reputed to have sold in excess of 30 million copies. In the film, he and Astaire were perfect together - each with his own relaxed and easygoing style, and a mutual flair for comedy. Their characters, Jim and Ted, clash for a while - over a girl, naturally - but eventually Jim finds happiness with Linda (Marjorie Reynolds), and Ted settles for Lila (Virginia Dale). Also in the cast were Bing's brother Bob and his Bobcats, and Harry Barris, a former member, with Bing and Al Rinker, of the famous Rhythm Boys. The dance director was Danny Dare, and *Holiday Inn*, which took nearly $4 million at the US box-office, was produced and directed by Mark Sandrich, who had worked so successfully with Fred Astaire at RKO.

Hollywood Hotel

A slice of Hollywood hokum starring crooner Dick Powell and directed by Busby Berkeley. The film's wan plot is centred around a small-town boy's attempt to hit the bigtime via a radio show broadcast from the hotel of the title. The film's one virtue for the fans of big band swing (and quite a big virtue at that) is the appearance of the current sensation of the era, Benny Goodman And His Orchestra. The quartet of Goodman, Teddy Wilson, Lionel Hampton and Gene Krupa is featured. Showing an integrated group like this on screen in 1937 was as much a departure for Hollywood as it was for the music business when Goodman first presented Wilson a year earlier. The quartet plays 'I've Got A Heartful Of Music' and the big band, including Harry James, Ziggy Elman, Chris Griffin, Murray McEachern, Red Ballard, Vido Musso, Hymie Schertzer and Jess Stacy, performs several numbers including the film's title song and a short, breakneck version of the Goodman-Krupa showstopper, 'Sing, Sing, Sing'.

Hope, Bob

b. Leslie Townes Hope, 26 May 1903, Eltham, England. One of the all-time great entertainers; an actor and comedian, whose singing ability has usually been sadly under-rated. Hope was taken to the USA at the age of four and grew up in Cleveland. As a teenager he tried his hand at various jobs including boxing, and toured in vaudeville as a song-and-dance-man for a time. In the late 20s and early 30s he had small parts and some chorus work in a few Broadway shows before making a big impression in *Roberta* in 1933. He had the amusing duet, 'Don't Tell Me It's Bad', with Linda Watkins in *Say When* (1934), and in 1936 introduced the lovely 'I Can't Get Started' in the *Ziegfeld Follies*, and (with Ethel Merman) Cole Porter's amusing 'It's De-lovely' in *Red, Hot And Blue*. By this time he had broken into radio, and in 1938 he was given his own show. In the same year he made his first feature film, *The Big Broadcast Of 1938*, in which he introduced (with Shirley Ross) yet another durable song, Leo Robin and Ralph Rainger's 'Thanks For The Memory', which won an Oscar and went on to become his life-long theme tune. In 1939 Hope was highly acclaimed for his performance in the comedy-thriller *The Cat And The Canary*, and he continued to appear in musicals such as *College Swing*, *Give Me A Sailor*, and *Some Like It Hot*. In 1940 he teamed up with Bing Crosby and Dorothy Lamour for *Road To Singapore*, the first of seven comedy musicals which took the trio to Zanzibar, Morocco, Utopia, Rio, Bali, and finally, in 1962, to Hong Kong. Over the years the comedy pictures far outweighed the musicals, but during the 40s and 50s Hope still appeared in a few, such as *Louisiana Purchase* (1941), *Star Spangled Rhythm* (1942), *Let's Face It* (1943), *My Favourite Spy* (1951), *Here Come The Girls* (1953), *The Seven Little Foys* (1955), and *Beau James* (1957). He also sang the occasional engaging number in other films, including two by Jay Livingston and Ray Evans: 'Buttons And Bows', another Oscar-winner, from *The Paleface* (1948), and 'Silver Bells' from *The Lemon Drop Kid* (1950). In

1958 he joined Crosby for one of their 'insulting' duets, 'Nothing In Common', which Sammy Cahn and Jimmy Van Heusen composed for the zany *Paris Holiday*. Hope's ongoing 'feud' with Crosby has been a permanent feature of his act since the 30s, and has featured prominently on the comedian's annual trips overseas to entertain US troops, events that were particularly newsworthy during the years of the Vietnam War. Hope has been with NBC radio and television since 1934, the year his first *Pepsodent* show was aired - his 1992 Christmas TV Special was his 43rd - and there was a good deal of speculation when, following the 1993 tribute *Bob Hope: The First 90 Years*, his annual contract was not immediately renewed. During his career he has been showered with awards from many organizations and countries, including Emmys, a Peabody, 50 honorary academic degrees, and five special Academy Awards for humanitarianism and contributions to the film industry. He has also hosted the Academy Awards ceremony itself on numerous occasions. In 1994 he appeared at the Royal Albert Hall in London as part of the D-Day 50th Anniversary celebrations, and called in at the American Embassy to collect a Supreme Headquarters Allied Expeditionary Forces plaque to commemorate his war-time work. He is supposed to be 'the most wealthy entertainer who has ever lived', a point which was touched on by fellow comedian Milton Berle at a Friar's Club Roast in Hope's honour in 1989. Berle noted: 'This guy owns so much property in America he should be Japanese.' Further reading: *The Amazing Careers Of Bob Hope*, Joe Morelli, Edward Epstein, Eleanor Clarke. *The Secret Life Of Bob Hope*, Arthur Marx. *Have Tux Will Travel. I Owe Russia $1,200. They Got Me Covered. I Never Left Home. The Road To Hollywood* (autobiography), all by Bob Hope.

Horne, Lena

b. 30 June 1917, Brooklyn, New York, USA. A dynamic performer, of striking appearance and elegant style. The daughter of an actress and a hotel operator, she was brought up mainly by her paternal grandmother, Cora Calhoun Horne. She made her professional debut at the age of 16 as a singer in the chorus at Harlem's Cotton Club, learning from Duke Ellington, Cab Calloway, Billie Holiday and Harold Arlen, the composer of a future big hit, 'Stormy Weather'. From 1935-36 she was featured vocalist with the all-black Noble Sissle's Society Orchestra, (the same Noble Sissle who, with Eubie Blake wrote several hit songs including 'Shuffle Along' and 'I'm Just Wild About Harry') and later toured with the top swing band of Charlie Barnet, singing numbers such as 'Good For Nothin' Joe' and 'You're My Thrill'. Sometimes, when Barnet's Band played the southern towns, Horne had to stay in the band bus. She made her Broadway debut in 1934 as 'A Quadroon Girl' in

Dance With Your Gods, and also appeared in Lew Leslie's *Blackbirds Of 1939*, in which she sang Mitchell Parish and Sammy Fain's, 'You're So Indifferent' - but only for the show's run of nine performances.

After a spell at the Café Society Downtown in New York, she moved to Hollywood's Little Troc Club and was spotted by Roger Edens, musical supervisor for MGM Pictures, and former accompanist for Ethel Merman, who introduced her to producer, Arthur Freed. In her first film for MGM, *Panama Hatti* (1942), which starred Merman, Horne sang Cole Porter's 'Just One Of Those Things', and a rhumba number called 'The Sping'. To make her skin appear lighter on film, the studio used a special make-up called 'Light Egyptian'. Horne referred to herself as 'a sepia Hedy Lamarr'. Her next two films, *Cabin In The Sky* and *Stormy Weather* both 1943, are generally regarded as her best. In the remainder of her 40s and 50s movie musicals (which included *Thousands Cheer, Swing Fever, Broadway Rhythm, Two Girls And A Sailor, Ziegfeld Follies, Till The Clouds Roll By, Words And Music, Duchess Of Idaho* and *Meet Me In Las Vegas*); she merely performed guest shots which were easily removable, without spoiling the plot, for the benefit of southern-state distributors.

Her 40s record hits included her theme song, 'Stormy Weather' and two other Arlen songs, "Deed I Do" and 'As Long As I Live'. She also recorded with several big swing era names such as Artie Shaw, Cab Calloway and Teddy Wilson. During World War II, she became the pin-up girl for many thousands of black GIs and refused to appear on US tours unless black soldiers were admitted to the audience. In 1947 she married pianist/arranger/conductor Lennie Hayton, who also became her manager and mentor until his death in 1971. For a time during the 50s Lena Horne was blacklisted, probably for her constant involvement with the Civil Rights movement, but particularly for her friendship with Communist sympathizer Paul Robeson. Ironically she was at the peak of her powers at that time, and although she was unable to appear much on television and in films, she continued to make records and appear in nightclubs which were regarded as her special forte. Evidence of that was displayed on *Lena Horne At The Waldorf Astoria*. The material ranged from the sultry 'Mood Indigo', right through to the novelty 'New Fangled Tango' and *Lena At The Sands*, with its medleys of songs by Richard Rodgers/Oscar Hammerstein II, Jule Styne and E.Y. 'Yip' Harburg. Other US Top 30 chart albums included *Give The Lady What She Wants* and *Porgy And Bess*, with Harry Belafonte. Horne also made the US Top 20 singles charts in 1955 with 'Love Me Or Leave Me', written by Gus Kahn and Walter Donaldson for Ruth Etting to sing in the 1928 Broadway Show, *Whoopee*.

In 1957 Horne had her first starring role on Broadway when she played Savannah, opposite Ricardo Montalban, in the Arlen/Harburg musical, *Jamaica*. In the 60s, besides the usual round of television shows and records, she appeared in a dramatic role, with Richard Widmark, in *Death Of A Gunfighter* (1969). After Hayton's death in 1971 she worked less, but did feature in *The Wiz*, an all-black film version of *The Wizard Of Oz*, starring Diana Ross and Michael Jackson, and in 1979 she received an honorary doctorate degree from Harvard University. In May 1981, she opened on Broadway in her own autobiographical show, *Lena Horne: The Lady And Her Music*. It ran at the Nederland Theatre to full houses for 14 months, a Broadway record for a one-woman show. Horne received several awards including a special Tony Award for 'Distinguished Achievement In The Theatre', a Drama Desk Award, New York Drama Critics' Special Award, New York City's Handel Medallion, Dance Theatre of Harlem's Emergence Award, two Grammy Awards and the NAACP Springarn Award. She took the show to London in 1984, where it was also acclaimed. In 1993, after not singing in public for several years, Lena Horne agreed to perform the songs of Billy Strayhorn at the US JVC Jazz Festival.

Selected albums: *Lena Horne At The Waldorf Astoria* (1957), *Give The Lady What She Wants* (1958), with Harry Belafonte *Porgy And Bess* (1959), *Lena At The Sands* (1961), *Lena On The Blue Side* (1962), *Lena...Lovely And Alive* (1963), *Lena Goes Latin* (1963), with Gabor Szabo *Lena And Gabor* (1970), *Lena* (1974), *Lena, A New Album* (1976), *The Twenty Golden Pieces Of Lena Horne* (1979), *Lena Horne And Pearl Bailey* (1979), *Lena Horne: The Lady And Her Music* (1981, stageshow soundtrack), *Lena Horne And Frank Sinatra* (1984), *A Song For You* (1992)

Further reading: *In Person*, Lena Horne. *Lena*, Lena Horne with Richard Schikel.

Horner, James

b. 1953, Los Angeles, California, USA. Horner was a composer; arranger and conductor for films from the late 70s through to the 90s. He studied at the Royal College Of Music in London, and at USC, Los Angeles, and UCLA. In the late 70s he worked on several films for Roger Corman's New World production company, including *Up From The Depths, The Lady In Red, Battle Beyond The Stars* and *Humanoids From The Deep* (1980); reminders of Corman's Z Grade movies of the 50s. During the 80s he scored some 35 feature films, mainly with recurring themes of grisly tales of horror, violence, science-fiction, fantasy, and sinister drama. These included *Deadly Blessing, The Hand, Wolfen, Star Trek II: 48 Hours* (Eddie Murphy's screen debut), *The Wrath Of Khan; Brainstorm; Krull, Testament; Gorky Park, Star Trek III: The Search For Spock, Cocoon, Commando, The Name Of The Rose, Project X, Batteries Not Included, Willow, Red Heat, Cocoon: The Return* and *Honey, I*

Shrunk The Kids (1989). In 1986 Horner was nominated for an Academy Award for his *Aliens* score, and for the song 'Somewhere Out There' (written with Barry Mann and Cynthia Weil), for the animated feature, *American Tail*. Both compositions gained ASCAP Awards. Horner was nominated again for an Oscar in 1989 for his music for another fantasy, *Field Of Dreams*, starring Kevin Costner, and, in the same year, won a Grammy for his score to *Glory*. Horner's 90s feature film credits included *Thunderheart, My Heroes Have Always Been Cowboys*, a tribute to the 'Wild West'; the live-action *Rocketeer*, two animated features, *An American Tail: Fievel Goes West* and *Fish Police* (1992), *Patriot Games, Unlawful Entry, Sneakers, House Of Cards, Jack The Bear, Swing Kids, A Far Off Place, Once Upon A Forest, The Man Without A Face, Innocent Moves*, and *The Pelican Brief* (1993). Horner also worked in television, composing music for such as *Angel Dusted, A Few Days In Weasel Creek, Rascals And Robbers - The Secret Adventures Of Tom Sawyer And Huck Finn, A Piano For Mrs Cimino, Between Friends* and *Surviving*.

Howard, James Newton

b. USA. Howard was a musician (keyboards, synthesizer, mellotron) and a composer of film music from the mid-80s. During the 70s Howard played on record sessions with rock artists such as Ringo Starr, Neil Diamond, Melissa Manchester, Harry Nilsson, Neil Sedaka, Yvonne Elliman and Boz Scaggs. From 1975-80, he was member of Elton John's Band (Mark II), and served as his studio arranger. Howard, and another American, bassist Joe Passarelli, were part of the new John line-up which was introduced to the 75,000 crowd at Wembley Stadium in 1975. He was on Elton John's *Rock Of The Westies, Blue Moves, 21 At 33* and *The Fox* (1980) and, in the same year, played at John's free concert in New York's Central Park to an estimated audience of 400,000. Howard was also a member of the band, China, and John produced one of their albums. In the 80s Howard began composing music for films. His first feature credit, Ken Finkleman's comedy *Head Office*, was followed by *Wildcats* (co-composed with Hawk Wolinski), *Never Too Young To Die, 8 Million Ways To Die, Nobody's Fool, Tough Guys, Campus Man, Five Corners* ('an appropriately moody score'), *Russkies, Promised Land, Off Limits, Some Girls, Everybody's All-American, Tap*, a tribute to tap dancing, starring Gregory Hines and Sammy Davis Jnr. in the latter's last feature film; *Major League* and *The Package* (1989). In the 90s, Howard became known as 'hot' in Hollywood, with his scores for movies such as *Pretty Woman, Flatliners, King Ralph, Marked For Death, Guilty By Suspicion, Dying Young, Three Men And A Little Lady, Coupe De Ville, The Man In The Moon, My Girl, American Heart, A Private Matter* (television), *Grand Canyon, Diggstown, Glengarry Glen Ross, Night*

And The City, Alive, Falling Down, The Fugitive, Dave, and *The Saint Of Fort Washington* (1993). His status was not diminished when Barbra Streisand chose him to replace John Barry on *The Prince Of Tides* (1991). Selected album: *James Newton Howard & Friends* (1988).

Hulbert, Jack

b. 24 April 1892, Ely, England, d. 25 March 1978, London, England. A popular actor, singer, dancer, director, author choreographer, and producer, whose jaunty onstage image was of the 'terribly British, "I say, old chap"' variety. Hulbert began to develop his various skills in undergraduate productions while he was studying at Cambridge University. In 1913, while appearing in the *Pearl Girl* in the West End, he met Cicely Courtneidge, the daughter of producer Robert Courtneidge, and they were married in the following year. *The Pearl Girl* was the first of 13 musicals in which they appeared together. During the next few years Hulbert established himself in a mixture of musical comedies and revues such as *The Cinema Star, The Arcadians, The Light Blues* (for which he was also co-librettist), *See-Saw, Bubbly, Bran-Pie, A Little Dutch Girl, Ring Up, Pot Luck*, and *The Little Revue Starts At 9* (1923). From 1925 onwards he co-produced and/or directed (and sometimes choreographed) a range of productions, particularly those in which he also acted. These included *By The Way* (in London and New York), *Lido Lady, Clowns In Clover, The House That Jack Built, Follow A Star* (1930), *Under Your Hat, Full Swing*, and *Something In The Air* (1943). After World War II, with *Oklahoma!* and the other American blockbusters on the horizon, Hulbert's smart and sophisticated style of musical comedy was less in demand, although he directed Cicely Courtneidge in the highly successful *Gay's The Word* in 1951. Over the years he introduced several popular songs, including 'The Flies Crawled Up The Window', 'My Hat's On The Side Of My Head', 'She's Such A Comfort To Me', and 'I Was Anything But Sentimental', a duet with his wife from their film *Take My Tip* (1937). Hulbert made several other comedy movies during the 30s, - he and Courtneidge were just as popular on the screen as on the stage - such as *Elstree Calling* (1930), *The Ghost Train, Jack's The Boy, Bulldog Jack, Paradise For Two*, and *Kate Plus Ten*. From then on there were only occasional releases which included *Under Your Hat* (1940), *Into The Blue* (1951) *Spider's Web* (1960), and *Not Now Darling* (1973). Selected album: *The Golden Age Of Cicely Courtneidge And Jack Hulbert* (1984).
Further reading: *The Little Woman's Always Right*, Jack Hulbert.

Hunter, Tab

b. Arthur Andrew Kelm, 11 July 1931, New York City, New York, USA. This blond-haired, blue-eyed

pop vocalist/actor used his mother's maiden name, Gelien, until he was spotted in 1948, working at a stable, by talent scout Dick Clayton. He introduced him to Rock Hudson's Hollywood agent Harry Wilson, who said 'We've got to tab you something' then named him Tab Hunter. He made his screen debut in the 1950 film *The Lawless* and two years later co-starred with Linda Darnell in the British film *Island Of Desire*. In late 1956 he received a phone call from Randy Wood, president of Dot Records, asking him to record a song, recently cut by US country star Sonny James, the lilting ballad, 'Young Love'. Both versions made the US charts, Hunter reached number 1 and James peaked at 2. He also topped the UK chart but James lagged behind at number 11. He continued recording for Dot and hit with the slightly uptempo '99 Ways', which narrowly missed the US Top 10 but made the UK Top 5 (1957). In the following year he appeared in the film version of the Broadway show, *Damn Yankees*, with Gwen Verdon and Ray Walston. As Warner Brothers had him under contract to make films, they resented him recording for Dot and established their own record label in 1958. He signed, with moderate success, and in 1960 starred in his own NBC US television series. He kept up his acting and appeared opposite Fabian in the 1964 'beach party' film, *Ride The Wild Surf*. He was still acting in the 80s, notably with the late Divine in *Polyester* and *Lust In The Dust* and also in the *Grease* sequel, *Grease 2*.
Selected albums: *Young Love* (1961), *R.F.D.*, (1962).

Hutton, Betty

b. 26 February 1921, Battle Creek, Michigan, USA. While still a small child, Hutton began singing in the streets to help support her impoverished family. By her early teens she was already beginning to make a name for herself when she was hired by Vincent Lopez, then leader of a popular radio band. In 1940, by now known as 'The Blonde Bombshell' in recognition of her fizzing vitality, Hutton appeared on Broadway and the following year was snapped up by Hollywood. She appeared in a string of popular musicals including *Star Spangled Rhythm* (1942), *And The Angels Sing* (1944) and *Incendiary Blonde* (1945). She also appeared in several non-musicals, among them *The Miracle Of Morgan's Creek* (1944). It was her appearance in the title role of *Annie Get Your Gun* (1950) that established her as a major star. Her energetic performance in this film gained her an international reputation, which she enhanced with roles in *The Greatest Show On Earth* and *Somebody Loves Me* (both 1952). However, contractual difficulties with the studio arose and her career came to an abrupt halt. She made a brief appearance in a 1957 film and was fleetingly on Broadway in 1965. Two years later she was financially broke and thereafter was rarely seen until a newspaper account of her poverty appeared in 1974. She was then a cook at

a rectory in Rhode Island. Thereafter, she suffered a nervous breakdown and plans for a comeback were aborted. Her sister, Marion, two years her senior, was also a singer who worked with Glenn Miller's band.

Hyman, Dick

b. 8 March 1927, New York City, New York, USA. After studying classical music, Hyman broadened his interests to encompass jazz and many other areas of music. In the late 40s he played piano in and around his home town, working with leading bop musicians, including founding fathers Charlie Parker and Dizzy Gillespie. Early in the 50s he began a long career as a studio musician, playing piano, arranging, composing and leading orchestras. His work in the studios did not keep him from actively participating in jazz dates, many of which he organized. He also became deeply interested in the history of jazz and especially the development of jazz piano. He demonstrated his interest in radio broadcasts and concert performances. His enormously eclectic taste allowed him to range from ragtime to freeform with complete confidence. Through performances and recordings with the New York Jazz Repertory Orchestra, he encouraged interest in the music of Jelly Roll Morton, Fats Waller, James P. Johnson and Louis Armstrong. He also formed a small group, the Perfect Jazz Repertory Quintet. During his freeform period he played electric piano and later added the organ to the instruments at his command, recording *Cincinnati Fats*, *New School Concert* and other duo albums with Ruby Braff. Later still, he recorded with Braff using, however improbably in a jazz context, a Wurlitzer organ. Unusual though it might be, *A Pipe Organ Recital Plus One* was a critical and popular success. As a composer Hyman has written for large and small ensembles and composed the score for the film *Scott Joplin* (1976). A master of jazz piano, his performances not only display his extraordinary virtuoso technique but also demonstrate his deep understanding and abiding love for the great traditions of the music. Through his broadcasting and lectures, and by way of his enthusiasm and example, he has helped to expand interest in and appreciation of jazz of all kinds.
Selected albums: *The Electric Eclectics* (c.1969), *The Happy Breed* (1972), *Genius At Play* (1973), with NYJRO *Satchmo Remembered* (1974), *Scott Joplin: The Complete Works For Piano* (c.1975), *A Waltz Dressed In Blue* (c.1977), *Charleston* (c.1977), *Sliding By* (1977), *Ragtime, Stomp And Stride* (c.1977), with NYJRO *The Music Of Jelly Roll Morton* (1978), *The Perfect Jazz Repertory Quintet Plays Irving Berlin* (1979), with Ruby Braff *Cincinnati Fats* (1981), with Braff *A Pipe Organ Recital Plus One* (1982), *Kitten On The Keys: The Music Of Zez Confrey* (1983), with Braff *The New School Concert 1983* (1983), *Eubie* (1984), *Manhattan Jazz* (1985), *Music Of 1937* (1990), with Braff *Younger Than Swingtime* (1990).

I Could Go On Singing

Nine years elapsed between Judy Garland's critically acclaimed performance in *A Star Is Born* and this, her next musical film, which was released in 1963 and provoked an entirely opposite response. Mayo Simon's often poignant story was about a star American singer, Jenny Bowman (Garland), who travels to England for a concert tour and, while there, engineers a meeting with Harley Street surgeon David Donne (Dirk Bogarde), in an effort to get to know their illegitimate son, Matt (Gregory Phillips). Jenny's craving for the boy's affection, and his sudden realization that she is his mother, bordered on the maudlin and was generally unconvincing. Not so the musical sequences, though, in which Garland was at the top of her form. She pulled all the stops out on E.Y. 'Yip' Harburg and Harold Arlen's highly appropriate title song, and on the other lovely numbers such as 'It Never Was You' (Kurt Weill-Maxwell Anderson), 'By Myself' (Arthur Schwartz-Howard Dietz), and 'Hello, Bluebird' (Cliff Friend). Dirk Bogarde himself provided some additional (and much-needed) extra dialogue, and gave his usually efficient performance. Also in the cast were Jack Klugman as George Kogan (Jenny's long-suffering manager), Aline MacMahon, Pauline Jameson, and Russell Waters. Ronald Neame directed what sadly proved to be Judy Garland's last film. It was produced by Stuart Millar and Laurence Turman in Eastman Color and Panavision for Barbican Films in Great Britain, and released by United Artists.

I Give My Heart

This film version of the celebrated 1931 German operetta *The Dubarry* by Paul Knepler and J.M. Welleminsky, with music by Carl Millöcker adapted by Theo Mackeben, was released by British International Pictures in 1935. The story is set in France in 1769, where the delightful Gitta Alpar, who starred in the original production, recreates her role as Jeanne, the little milliner who dispenses her favours rather freely to, amongst others, her compatriot René (Patrick Waddington), and husband Count Dubarry (Arthur Margetson), in an effort to achieve her ambition of becoming the mistress of Louis XV (Owen Nares). The Marechale de Luxembourg (Margaret Bannerman) and Choiseul (Hugh Miller) plot together to rouse the Paris mob against her, but they are overwhelmed by the majority of people who have come to love their little Jeanne. Other roles were taken by Gibb McClaughlin, Iris Ashley, and Hay

Petrie. All the famous songs were retained, and Gitta Alpar in particular excelled in a cast of all-round excellent vocal abilities. A charming and appealing film, which had a screenplay by Frank Launder, Roger Burford, Kurt Siodmak, and Paul Perez, adapted from the original play. After directing this film, director Marcel Varnel left the world of operetta and devoted all his energies to creating classic comedy films starring Will Hay, George Formby, the Crazy Gang and Arthur Askey.

I'll Be Your Sweetheart

This film was regarded at the time of its release in 1945 as Britain's answer to the highly popular 20th Century-Fox musicals. Set in London in 1900, it deals with the bitter struggle between the popular songwriters of the day and the pirates who copy their sheet music and sell it for a fraction of the true price. Screen newcomer Michael Rennie plays the young, idealistic song publisher Bob Fielding, who leads the fight for justice - that is when he is not vying with fellow songwriter Jim Knight (Peter Graves) for the hand of music-hall star Edie Storey, who is played by Margaret Lockwood (singing voice dubbed by Maudie Edwards). Vic Oliver and Moore Marriott, as songwriters Sammy Kahn and George Le Brunn, lead a strong supporting cast which includes Frederick Burtwell, Maudie Edwards, Garry Marsh, and George Merrit. Several of the songs in the film were hits of the time, such as 'I'll Be Your Sweetheart' (Harry Dacre), 'Oh! Mr. Porter' (Thomas Le Brunn-George Le Brunn), 'Honeysuckle And The Bee' (W.H. Penn-A.H. Fitz), 'I Wouldn't Leave My Little Wooden Hut For You' (Tom Mellor-Charles Collins), and 'Liza Johnson' (George Le Brunn-Edgar Bateman). These were supplemented by three compositions written by Manning Sherwin and Val Guest: 'I'm Banking Everything On You', 'Sooner Or Later', and 'Mary Anna'. The musical numbers were devised by Robert Nesbitt and choreographed by Wendy Toye. Director Val Guest, who wrote the screenplay with Val Valentine, captured the style of the period perfectly, and although not *quite* in the class of the Fox movies (Alice Faye was missing for a start), *I'll Be Your Sweetheart* was certainly an extremely diverting film. The producer for Gainsborough Pictures was Louis Levy.

I'll Get By (see *Tin Pan Alley*)

If You Feel Like Singing (see *Summer Stock*)

Invitation To The Dance

Filming began on this ambitious Gene Kelly project in 1952, but the finished product was only set before the public four years later. Produced by Arthur Freed for MGM, the picture was a gallant but unsuccessful attempt by Kelly to bring ballet to the cinema-going masses. There was no dialogue, and the film consisted of three individual ballet sequences (another, featuring several popular songs, had been cut prior to release). The first, 'Circus', in which Kelly plays a Pierrot character whose love for a ballerina (Claire Sombert) ends in tragedy, had music by Jacques Ibert. The second, 'Ring Around The Rosy', with music by André Previn, had overtones of La Ronde in its story of a bracelet which, after being presented by a husband to his wife, then passed through the hands of an artist, a nightclub singer, and whore, amongst others, before finally being returned to the husband. The final sequence, 'Sinbad The Sailor', composed by Rimsky-Korsakov, revived memories of Kelly's innovative dance with Jerry the cartoon mouse in *Anchors Aweigh* (1945). This time he was a sailor once more, involved with animated characters as well as the real-life Carol Haney and David Kasday. Other artists featured in the first two scenes were Igor Youskevitch, Claude Bessey, Tommy Rall, Tamara Toumanova, Belita, Irving Davies, Diana Adams, and David Paltenghi. Gene Kelly was also the overall director-choreographer, and the film was beautifully photographed in Technicolor by Freddie Young and Joseph Ruttenberg, and shot mostly in England. Although it was critical and financial flop, the picture became something of a cult item, especially in Europe where it was awarded the Grand Prize in the 1958 West Berlin film festival. It is invariably included in Gene Kelly retrospectives.

It Happened In Brooklyn

This pleasant MGM musical was released in 1947, and had a typically post-war story. Isobel Lennart's screenplay told of a shy ex-GI (Frank Sinatra) who returns to his beloved Brooklyn in New York, determined to make it to the top as a singer. As in the earlier *Anchors Aweigh*, he meets up with Kathryn Grayson (this time playing a music teacher) who, as usual, feels that she is destined for great things in the operatic vocal department. Jimmy Durante - the old scene stealer himself - is a kindly school caretaker who makes it his business to boost Sinatra's self confidence (!) in the film's highspot, 'The Song's Gotta Come From The Heart'. In this joyous hymn to sincerity and success, Sinatra spoofs Durante's straight-legged strut, and even manages to work in an excerpt from the traditional Russian folk song 'Orchi Chornya' ('Dark Eyes'). Apart from that piece, and the obligatory classical extracts from Grayson, the rest of the score was provided by Sammy Cahn and Jule Styne, and contained some lovely ballads for Sinatra such as 'Time After Time', 'It's The Same Old Dream', and 'The Brooklyn Bridge', as well as the livelier 'I Believe' and 'Whose Baby Are You?'. They did not do the singer much good, though, because his best friend, played by Peter Lawford, ended up with Grayson, and, when last seen, Sinatra was on the trail

of a nurse (Gloria Grahame) he left behind in the US Army. Also in the cast were Aubrey Mather, Marcy McGuire, Tamara Shayne, Bobby Long and Billy Roy. Jack Donahue staged the dance sequences, and Richard Thorpe directed this unpretentious little film which became quite a hit.

It's Always Fair Weather

As the opening titles fade in this entertaining, and somewhat satirical musical which was released by MGM in 1955, three US soldier buddies, back home in New York after serving together in World War II, have a final drink and sing the poignant 'The Time For Parting' as they pledge to meet again 10 years later. However, when the threesome, played by Gene Kelly, Dan Dailey and Michael Kidd, reunite in their favourite bar all those years later, things have changed. Dailey is conceited, continually stressed and hates his job in advertising; Kelly has turned into a tough city dweller with one eye on the fight scene and the other looking over his shoulder; and Kidd is the only one who seems reasonably content with his life as the owner of a provincial diner grandly named the Cordon Bleu. High-powered executive (and boxing fan) Cyd Charisse deviously manoeuvres them and their 'fascinating' story on to the tacky television show *The Throb Of Manhattan*, which is hosted by the gorgeously over the top Dolores Gray. When Kelly is threatened by some unsavoury colleagues in the fight racket and Dailey and Kidd jump in to defend him with all fists blazing, the years roll back and it is just like old times for the three pals again. Originally conceived by screenwriters Betty Comden and Adolph Green as a sequel to *On The Town* (1949), *It's Always Fair Weather* turned out to be quite different from that project, with a marked cynical edge, especially in regard to the burgeoning US television industry. The basic creative team remained the same though, with Arthur Freed producing and Gene Kelly and Stanley Donen sharing the director-choreographer credit. The score, by composer André Previn and Comden and Green (lyrics) had some marvellous moments, such as 'Situation-Wise', Dailey's exposé of the advertising industry; Kelly's escape from a gang of hoodlums via a song, dance and a pair of roller skates in 'I Like Myself'; Gray's magnificently syrupy and effusive 'Thanks A Lot But No Thanks'; and Charisse boxing clever in 'Baby You Knock Me Out'. The three male stars come together for a split screen rendition of 'Once Upon A Time' (the Cinemascope effect is generally destroyed when shown on television), and for an exhilarating dance routine through the streets, at one point using dustbin lids as improvised tap shoes. The other numbers included 'March, March' (Kelly-Dailey-Kidd), 'Stillman's Gym' (Charisse and boxers), and 'Music Is Better Than Words' (lyric: Comden-Green-Roger Edens) (ensemble). Also featured were Jay C. Flippen,

David Burns, Hal March, and Lou Lubin.

It's Great To Be Young

Although rock 'n' roll was gathering pace throughout the world in 1956, this engaging British musical, which was released by AB-Pathé-Marble Arch, showed no sign of any such influence. Set in a co-educational school, it concerns the charismatic Mr Dingle (John Mills), a teacher whose interest in the school orchestra leads to a clash with the newly appointed (and very square) headmaster Mr Frome (Cecil Parker). Dingle is eventually dismissed, and his infuriated pupils stage a massive sit-in in order to get him reinstated. All ends happily when the combatants realise that a bit of give and take is all that is needed to live and learn in harmony together. The most memorable song remains the pretty ballad, 'You Are My First Love' (Paddy Roberts-Lester Powell), which is sung over the opening titles by Ruby Murray, and reprised during the sit-in by Paulette (Dorothy Bromiley, dubbed by Edna Savage). She aims it straight at Nicky (Jeremy Spenser), the young man she has decided to give her adolescent heart to. Other songs include 'Rhythm Is Our Business' (Sammy Cahn-Saul Chaplin-Jimmy Lunceford), performed engagingly by a group of pupils, singing and dancing on the sidewalk (dubbed by the Coronets). John Mills was perfect in the role of the trumpet-playing music master who 'moonlights' on the piano in the local pub. Jazzman Humphrey Lyttelton helped out on the trumpet, and it was pianist Winifred Atwell's excellent version of 'The Original Dixieland One-Step' that was heard on the soundtrack. The film's musical director, Ray Martin, contributed the title song the rousing 'Marching Strings', and the film's background score. In fact he also co-wrote the big ballad, 'You Are My First Love', because 'Lester Powell' was just one of his several aliases. *It's Great To Be Young* was directed by Cyril Frankel, produced by Victor Skutezky and had a screenplay by Ted Willis. Among the cast of this immensely enjoyable, unpretentious (and rare) British musical were Eleanor Summerfield, John Salew, Bryan Forbes, Brian Smith, Carole Shelley, Derek Blomfield, and a 13-years-old Richard O'Sullivan.

It's In The Air

Another George Formby vehicle - and this time the vehicle is a motor-cycle, which George (wearing a friend's RAF uniform) borrows in order to post a letter. Mistaken for a dispatch rider, he is forced to drive the Commanding Officer (Garry Marsh) of the RAF station around, and eventually has to take an experimental aeroplane into the air and demonstrate it to a Government official, Sir Philip Bargrave (C. Denier Warren). The slapstick fun is fast and furious, with George getting involved in many complicated adventures, one of which concerns certain nocturnal experiences in an NCO's bedroom. Throughout it all, he wears that endearing toothy grin and ingenuous expression, and pauses occasionally to pull out his ukulele and slip in the odd song, such as 'They Can't Fool Me', 'It's In The Air', and 'Our Sergeant Major' (George Formby-Fred E. Cliffe-Harry Gifford). Polly Ward was his long-suffering fiancée, and among the other familiar names were Julien Mitchell, Jack Hobbs, Jack Melford, Hal Gordon, Frank Leighton, Michael Shepley, Ilena Sylva, and O.B. Clarence. Anthony Kimmins wrote the story and directed, and Basil Dean produced the film for Associated Talking Pictures in Britain in 1938.

It's Love Again

Having captivated London theatre audiences with her enchanting dancing and singing during the 20s, in the next decade Jessie Matthews established herself as one of Britain's brightest film stars. In this picture, which was released by Gaumont in 1936, she plays Elaine Bradford, an ambitious, but frustrated young performer who impersonates the alluring and mysterious Mrs. Smythe-Smythe, a dashing pilot, big-game hunter and friend of maharajahs whose exciting exploits are constantly being revealed in the *Daily Record*. Unbeknown to her, Mrs. Smythe-Smythe does not in fact exist, and has been dreamed up by gossip columnist Peter Carlton (Robert Young) in an effort to boost the paper's circulation. Even when he acquaints her with the facts, Elaine still perpetuates the masquerade, and, after performing a the sensational 'Temple Dance Of The East' at a party, she is engaged by impresario Archibald Raymond (Ernest Milton) for his new revue. Threatened with exposure by one of Peter's rival columnists (Cyril Raymond), she resigns, but is re-hired as Elaine Bradford, a name she changes soon enough to Mrs. Peter Carlton. Jessie Matthews' real-life husband, Sonnie Hale, led a supporting cast which also included lugubrious comedian Robb Wilton, Sara Allgood, Warren Jenkins, Glennis Lorimer, and Athene Seyler. Marion Dix and Lesser Samuels wrote the screenplay, and American songwriters Sam Coslow and Harry Woods came up with sòme snappy numbers, including 'Gotta Dance My Way To Heaven', 'I Nearly Let Love Go Slipping Through My Fingers', 'Tony's In Town', and 'It's Love Again'. The attractive musical score was written by Louis Levy and Bretton Byrd, and the dances were arranged by Buddy Bradley. This popular feature was directed by Victor Saville and produced by Michael Balcon.

It's Magic (see Romance On The High Seas)

Ives, Burl

b. Burl Icle Ivanhoe Ives, 14 June 1909, Hunt Township, Jasper County, Illinois, USA. One of the world's most celebrated singers of folk ballads, with a gentle, intimate style. Ives was also an actor on the stage and screen, an anthologist and editor of folk music. A son of tenant farmers in the 'Bible Belt' of Illinois, Ives was singing in public for money with his brothers and sisters when he was four years old. Many of the songs they sang originated in the British Isles, and were taught to them by their tobacco-chewing grandmother. After graduating from high school in 1927 Ives went to college intending to become a professional football coach. Instead, he left college early, in 1930, and hitch-hiked throughout the USA, Canada and Mexico, supporting himself by doing odd jobs and singing to his own banjo accompaniment, picking up songs everywhere he went. After staying for awhile in Terre Haute, Indiana, attending the State Teachers College, he moved to New York, and studied with vocal coach, Ekka Toedt, before enrolling for formal music training at New York University. Despite this classical education, he was determined to devote himself to folk songs. In 1938, he played character roles in several plays, and in the same year had a non-singing role on Broadway, in George Abbott's musical comedy, *The Boys From Syracuse*, followed by a four-month singing engagement at New York's Village Vanguard nightclub. He then toured with the Richard Rodgers/Lorenz Hart musical, *I Married An Angel*. In 1940 Ives performed on radio, singing his folk ballads to his own guitar accompaniment on programmes such as *Back Where I Come From*, and was soon given his own series entitled *Wayfaring Stranger*. The introductory, 'Poor Wayfaring Stranger', one of America's favourite folk songs, and by then already over 100 years old, became his long-time theme. Drafted into the US Army in 1942, Ives sang in Irving Berlin's military musical revue, *This Is The Army*, both on Broadway and on tour. In 1944, after medical discharge from the Forces, Ives played a long stint at New York's Cafe Society Uptown nightclub, and also appeared on Broadway with Alfred Drake in *Sing Out Sweet Land*, a 'Salute To American Folk And Popular Music'. For his performance, Ives received the Donaldson Award as Best Supporting Actor. During the following year, he made his concert bow at New York's Town Hall, and played a return engagement in 1946. Also in that year he made his first film, *Smoky*, with Fred McMurray and Anne Baxter, and appeared with Josh White in a full-length feature about folk music. Ives's other movies, in which he played characters ranging from villainous to warmly sympathetic, included *So Dear To My Heart* (1948), *East Of Eden* (1955) and *Cat On A Hot Tin Roof* (1958), in which he played Big Daddy, re-creating his highly acclaimed Broadway performance in the Tennessee Williams play; *Wind Across The Everglades* (1958), *Desire Under The Elms* (1958), *The Big Country* (1958), for which he received an Oscar as the Best Supporting Actor; and *Our Man In Havana* (1960). In 1954, Ives played the role of Cap'n Andy Hawkes in a revival of Jerome Kern and Oscar Hammerstein II's *Show Boat* at the New York City Center. In the 60s and 70s he appeared regularly on US television, sometimes in his dramatic series, such as *O K Crackerby* and *The Bold Ones*, and several music specials. In the 80s, he was still continuing to contribute character roles to feature films and television, and perform in concerts around the world. Back in 1948, his first chart record, 'Blue Tail Fly', teamed him with the Andrews Sisters. The song, written by Dan Emmett in 1846, had been in the Ives repertoire for some years. Other US Top 30 hits, through to the early 60s, included 'Lavender Blue (Dilly Dilly)', 'Riders In The Sky (Cowboy Legend)', 'On Top Of Old Smokey', 'The Wild Side Of Life', 'True Love Goes On And On', 'A Little Bitty Tear', 'Funny Way Of Laughin'' and 'Call Me Mr In-Between'. Many other songs were associated with him, such as 'Foggy Foggy Dew', 'Woolie Boogie Bee', 'Turtle Dove', 'Ten Thousand Miles', 'Big Rock Candy Mountain', 'I Know An Old Lady (Who Swallowed A Fly)', 'Aunt Rhody' and 'Ballad Of Davy Crockett'. Ives published several collections of folk ballads and tales, including *America's Musical Heritage - Song Of America*, *Burl Ives Song Book*, *Tales Of America*, *Burl Ives Book Of Irish Songs*, and for children, *Sailing On A Very Fine Day*.

Albums: *The Wayfaring Stranger* (1959), *Burl Ives Sings Irving Berlin* (1961), *The Versatile Burl Ives!* (1962), *It's Just My Funny Way Of Laughin'* (1962), *Ballads And Folk Songs* (early 60s), *Walt Disney Presents Burl Ives - Animal Folk* (1964), *Times They Are A-Changin'* (late 60s), *Chim Chim Cheree* (1974), with the Korean Children Choir *Faith And Joy* (1974), *Bright And Beautiful* (1979), *Burl Ives Live In Europe* (1979), *How Great Thou Art* (1974), *Songs I Sang At Sunday School* (1974), *I Do Believe* (1974), *Junior Choice* (1974), *Payin' My Dues Again* (mid-70s), *Little White Duck* (1977), *Shall We Gather At River* (1978), *Talented Man* (1978), *Live In Europe* (1979), *Stepping In The Light* (1984), *Love And Joy* (1984), *The Very Best Of* (1993), *A Little Bitty Tear: The Nashville Years 1961-65* (1993), and the series *Historical America In Song*, for Encyclopedia Britannica.

Further reading: *The Wayfaring Stranger*, Burl Ives.

J

Jailhouse Rock

Although hamstrung by mediocre films throughout much of his Hollywood career, Elvis Presley did complete some outstanding early features. In *Jailhouse Rock* he was aided by a superior plot in which the singer is taught to play guitar while serving in prison for manslaughter. Fame and egotism follow suit until his former cell-mate returns to haunt him and, eventually, prick his conscience. The film also provides an insight into record company practices during the 50s and has a visual impact many contemporary works lacked. The highly-choreographed scene which the title track accompanies has passed into pop cinema history. The Leiber And Stoller songwriting team, famed for their work with the Coasters, provided all of the soundtrack material which ranges from the electric 'Baby I Don't Care' to the ballad-styled 'Young And Beautiful'. Taken together, the album and film provide a high-water mark in Presley's output.

James, Harry

b. 15 March 1916, Albany, Georgia, USA, d. 5 July 1983. James father played trumpet in the band of a touring circus. At first Harry played drums but then he, too, took up the trumpet and at the age of nine was also playing in the circus band. He showed such enormous promise that his father had soon taught him everything he knew. Harry left the circus and played with various bands in Texas before joining Ben Pollack in 1935. Early in 1937 James was hired by Benny Goodman, an engagement which gave him maximum exposure to swing era audiences. Heavily featured with Goodman and, with Ziggy Elman and Chris Griffin, forming part of a powerful and exciting trumpet section, James quickly became a household name. He remained with Goodman a little under two years, leaving to form his own big band. James popularity increased and his public image, aided by his marriage to film star Betty Grable, reached remarkable heights for a musician. The band's popularity was achieved largely through James own solos, but a small part of its success may be attributed to his singers, Louise Tobin, to whom he was briefly married before Grable, Frank Sinatra, who soon left to join Tommy Dorsey, Dick Haymes and Kitty Kallen. James maintained his band throughout the 40s and into the early 50s, establishing a solid reputation thanks to distinguished sidemen such as Willie Smith, Buddy Rich, Corky Corcoran and Juan Tizol. Owing chiefly to the recorded repertoire, much of which featured James playing florid trumpet solos on tunes such as 'The Flight Of The Bumble Bee', 'The Carnival of Venice', 'I Cried For You' and 'You Made Me Love You', his band was at times less than popular with hardcore jazz fans. This view should have altered when, in the mid-50s, after a period of re-evaluation, James formed a band to play charts by Ernie Wilkins and Neal Hefti. One of the outstanding big bands, this particular group is often and very unfairly regarded as a copy of Count Basie's, a point of view which completely disregards chronology. In fact, James band can be seen to have pre-empted the slightly later but much more widely recognized middle-period band led by Basie, which also used Wilkins's and Hefti's charts. James continued leading into the 60s and 70s, dividing his time between extended residencies at major hotel and casino venues, mostly in Las Vegas, Nevada, and touring internationally. Amongst the first-rate musicians James used in these years were Willie Smith again, a succession of fine drummers (including Rich, Sonny Payne and Louie Bellson) and lead trumpeter Nick Buono, who had joined in December 1939 and showed no signs of relinquishing his chair and would, indeed, remain until the end. In his early years James was a brashly exciting player, attacking solos and abetting ensembles with a rich tone and what was at times an overwhelmingly powerful sound. With his own band he exploited his virtuoso technique, performing with great conviction the ballads and trumpet spectaculars that so disconcerted his jazz followers but which delighted the wider audience at whom they were aimed. Over the years James appeared in several movies - with his band in *Private Buckaroo* (1942), *Springtime In The Rockies, Best Foot Forward, Bathing Beauty, Two Girls And A Sailor, Do You Love Me?, If I'm Lucky, Carnegie Hall*, and *I'll Get By* (1950) - and as a solo artist in *Syncopation* (1942) and *The Benny Goodman Story* (1956). He also played trumpet on the soundtrack of *Young Man With A Horn* (1950). Later in his career, James work combined the best of both worlds - jazz and the more flashy style - and shed many of its excesses. He remained popular into the 80s and never lost his enthusiasm, despite suffering from cancer, which eventually claimed him in 1983.

Albums: with Benny Goodman *Carnegie Hall Concert* (1938), *The New James* (1958), *Harry's Choice!* (1958), *Harry James And His New Swingin' Bands* (1959), *The Spectacular Sound Of Harry James* (1961), *Harry James Plays Neal Hefti* (1961), *The Solid Trumpet Of Harry James* (1962), *Double Dixie* (1962), *On Tour In '64* (1964), *Harry James Live At The Riverboat* (1966), *Live From Clearwater, Florida Vols 1-3* (1970), *Live In London* (1971), *King James Version* (1976), *Still Happy After All These Years* (1979). Compilations: with Goodman *Jazz Concert No. 2* (1937-38), *Texas Chatter* (1938), *The Unheard Harry James* (1939), *The Young Harry James* (1939), *Flash Harry* (1942-44), *Coast To*

Jailhouse Rock

Coast (1944), *The Uncollected Harry James Vols 1-5* (c.1939-46), *Sounds Familiar* (1946), *Spotlight On Harry James* (1946), *Trumpet Blues* (1949-50), *Big John Special* (1949-50).

Jammin' The Blues

Held by many to be the finest jazz short ever filmed, and with considerable justification. The film, released in 1944, features superbly evocative photography by Gjon Mili, who also directed, and was supervised by Norman Granz. The musicians include Red Callender, Big Sid Catlett, Harry Edison, Illinois Jacquet, Jo Jones, Barney Kessel and the magnificent Lester Young. Timeless music by these assembled giants, allied to moody, smoky chiaroscuro makes this a must for any self-respecting jazz fan.

Jarre, Maurice

b. 13 September 1924, Lyons, France. An important composer for films for over 40 years. As a youngster, Jarre intended to be an electrical engineer, but changed his mind and studied music at the Paris Conservatoire in 1944. He joined the orchestra of the Jean Louise Barrault Theatre, and, in 1951, composed the music for Kleist's *Le Prince De Homburg*. Soon afterwards he moved into films, and, during the 50s, wrote the scores for such French productions as *Hotel Des Invalides*, *Le Grand Silence*, *Le Tetre Contre Les Murs* and *Les Yeux Sans Visage (Eyes Without A Face)*. During the early 60s he started to make the occasional non-gallic movie, such as *Crack In The Mirror*, starring Orson Welles, *The Big Gamble* and 'the last great epic of World War II', *The Longest Day* (1962). In the same year Jarre won his first Academy Award for his memorable score for *Lawrence Of Arabia*, and was honoured again, three years later, for his music to *Doctor Zhivago*, containing the haunting 'Lara's Theme' ('Somewhere, My Love'), which, with a lyric by Paul Francis Webster, became a Top 10 singles hit for the Ray Conniff Singers, and was the title track of one of their million-selling albums. Jarre's other 60s scores for English-speaking films included *Behold A Pale Horse*, *The Collector*, *Is Paris Burning?*, *The Professionals*, *Grand Prix*, *Gambit*, *The Night Of The Generals*, *Villa Rides!*, *Five Card Stud*, *The Fixer*, *Isadora*, *The Damned* and Alfred Hitchcock's *Topaz* (1969). He continued to write prolifically in the 70s for films such as director George Steven's swansong, *The Only Game In Town*, one of Neil Simon's funniest comedies, *Plaza Suite*, and many others, such as *The Effect Of Gamma Rays On Man-In-The-Moon Marigolds*, *The Life And Times Of Judge Roy Bean*, in which Andy Williams sang Jarre's 'Marmalade, Molasses And Honey' (lyric by Alan and Marilyn Bergman), *The Mackintosh Man*, *Great Expectations*, *Posse*, *The Man Who Would Be King*, *The Last Tycoon*, *Mohammed, Messenger Of God*, *March Or Die* and *Winter Kills*. His third Oscar came in 1984 for his 'anachronistic' score

for David Lean's *A Passage To India*, and he was nominated in the following year for his work on *Witness*, starring Harrison Ford. His other 80s scores included *Resurrection*, *Lion Of The Desert*, *Taps*, *The Year Of Living Dangerously*, *Dreamscape*, *The Bride*, *Mad Max And The Thunderdrome*, *Enemy Mine*, *The Mosquito Coast*, *No Way Out*, *Fatal Attraction*, *Distant Thunder*, *Gorillas In The Mist* (another Academy Award nomination for Jarre), *Moon Over Parador*, *Chances Are*, *Dead Poet's Society* (*BAFTA* Award (1989)), *Prancer* and *Enemies, A Love Story*. In 1991, Jarre received an ASCAP Award as the composer of the music for *Ghost*, the 'top box office film of 1990'. His other early 90s work included *After Dark, My Sweet*, *School Ties*, *Shadow Of The Wolf* (aka *Agaguk*), and the romantic comedy, *Only The Lonely*, starring veteran actress Maureen O'Hara. Apart from feature films, Jarre also wrote extensively for television. His credits included *The Silence*, *Jesus Of Nazareth* (mini-series), *Ishi, The Last Of His Tribe*, *Shogun* (mini-series), *Enola Gay*, *Coming Out Of The Ice*, *The Sky's No Limit*, *Samson And Delilah*, *Apology*, *The Murder Of Mary Phagan* (mini-series) and *Robinson Crusoe And Man Friday*. Recordings include: *Jarre By Jarre*, *Maurice Jarre At Abbey Road* and *The Collector*.

Jazz Dance

In 1954 an excellent idea took director Roger Tilton and a film crew into New York City's Central Plaza Dance Hall. Without gimmickry, they filmed the dancers and the end result is a marvellous feeling for the occasion. The band on the stand features Jimmy Archey, George 'Pops' Foster, Jimmy McPartland, Willie 'The Lion' Smith, Pee Wee Russell and George Wettling.

Jazz In Exile

American jazz musicians in Europe have been the cynosure of fascinated interest not only by audiences but also by jazz historians. Magazine articles abound and there have been several good books on the subject. There have also been a number of films but none as good or effective as this exceptional documentary directed by Chuck France released in 1978. There are many interviews with musicians such as Gary Burton, Richard Davis, Dexter Gordon, Freddie Hubbard, Ben Sidran, McCoy Tyner and Phil Woods. There is some fine music to be heard, notably from Davis and Woods.

Jazz Is Our Religion

Directed by John Jeremy, this excellent documentary released in 1972 features the idiosyncratic photography of Valerie Wilmer. There are numerous audio interviews with Art Blakey, Bill Evans, Jimmy Garrison, Dizzy Gillespie, Johnny Griffin, Jo Jones, Blue Mitchell, Sunny Murray and Dewey Redman, amongst many. Music by Griffin, Dizzy Reece, Jon

Hendricks, Lol Coxhill and the Clarke-Boland Big Band and others fills the soundtrack.

Altogether a satisfactory mixture that goes a long way to confirming the premise of the film's title and creating an understanding of its meaning.

Jazz On A Summer's Day

From its opening moments, depicting reflected sailboats while Jimmy Giuffre's 'The Train And The River' bubbles on the soundtrack, this film sets out to create an unforgettable record of the 1958 Newport Jazz Festival. Directed by Bert Stern in 1960, repeated viewing might make some of the 60s photo-gimmickry a little trying and there are certainly too many audience cutaways during performances, but, overall, the concept is very well-realized. And the music is magnificent. Amongst the assembled giants are Louis Armstrong, Bob Brookmeyer, Ben Webster, Thelonious Monk, Roy Haynes, Rex Stewart, Sonny Stitt, Dinah Washington singing superbly and also clowning very musically on vibes with Terry Gibbs, Max Roach, Gerry Mulligan, Art Farmer, Chico Hamilton seen in rehearsal, Eric Dolphy, George Shearing, Jack Teagarden, Buck Clayton and Jo Jones. Mahalia Jackson brings the show to a sacred finale but for most people the outstanding moment is the considerably less-sacred sight of Anita O'Day, in high heels, cartwheel hat, gloves, and tight dress, struggling up onto the stage where she memorably recomposes 'Sweet Georgia Brown' and 'Tea For Two' in her own image. The video of this film should be on every jazz fan's shelf.

Jazz Singer, The

Al Jolson, one of the world's all-time great entertainers, spoke a few words and sang a few songs in this, the first feature length talking picture which was released by Warner Brothers in 1927, and the screen musical was born. Alfred A. Cohen's screenplay was adapted from the short story, *The Day Of Atonement*, by Samson Raphaelson, which had been produced as a play on Broadway in 1925. It told of Jakie Rabinowitz (Jolson), a cantor's son who breaks his parents' hearts when he gives up his life in the synagogue for a career as a popular singer. Of course it was all pure schmaltz, and cinema audiences wept when, after his father has died, he returns to his beloved mother and tries to explain to her his love of music and his need to perform. Jolson, who appeared in blackface for the theatre sequences, was sensational, especially on songs which he had previously introduced in various stage productions such as 'My Mammy' and 'Toot Toot Tootsie'. The rest of the numbers included 'Dirty Hands, Dirty Face', 'Blue

The Jazz Singer

Skies', 'Mother Of Mine, I Still Have You', 'My Gal Sal', and the traditional Jewish 'Yahrzeit'. Also in the cast were Warner Oland, May McAvoy, Otto Lederer, Eugenie Besserer, Bobby Gordon, and Myrna Loy. The sound, which was only heard on the musical sequences and some short pieces of dialogue - the rest of the film was silent - was recorded on the Vitaphone sound-on-disc system, and the film was directed by Alan Crosland and produced by Darryl F. Zanuck.

The exciting and extremely complicated changeover from silents to talkies was brilliantly spoofed in one of the world's favourite musicals, *Singin' In The Rain*, which was made in 1952. In the same year, Warner released a remake of *The Jazz Singer* starring Danny Thomas, Peggy Lee, and Mildred Dunnock. This time the sentimental screenplay dealt with the return of US soldier from the Korean war. The score consisted of a bunch of well-tried musical standards. A third version, with Neil Diamond as Jess Rabinovitch and Laurence Olivier as his father, was made in 1980. The story remained fairly true to the 1927 original, and the cast included Lucie Arnaz, Catlin Adams, and Paul Nicholas as a particularly unpleasant recording artist. Diamond took three of the film's songs, 'America', 'Love On The Rocks', and 'Hello Again', all co-written by him, into the US Top 10.

Jivin' In Bebop

Forget the amateur-night quality of the storyline and concentrate instead on the musical numbers which include a dozen powerful performances by Dizzy Gillespie's big band. Given the relatively short life of this outstanding band, and the fact that it made only a handful of records, this 1946 film thus gains a value far in excess of its other shaky qualities. Milt Jackson, John Lewis and James Moody are on hand as is the inimitable Helen Humes.

Johnson, Laurie

b. 7 February 1927, England. A musical director, and composer for the stage, television and films, Johnson studied at the Royal College Of Music in London, before establishing himself on the UK entertainment scene in the late 50s and 60s. One of his first major projects, early in 1959, was to write the music, and act as musical director, for *Lock Up Your Daughters*, a musical adaptation of Henry Fielding's *Rape Upon Rape*, which opened Bernard Miles' Mermaid Theatre in the City of London. Johnson's score, in collaboration with lyricist, Lionel Bart, won an Ivor Novello Award. The show returned to the Mermaid in 1969 for a 10th anniversary season, and also played around the world including a spell at the Godspeed Opera House in Connecticut, USA. The film version omitted the songs and featured a score by Ron Grainer. His other work for the West End stage included music for the Peter Cook revue *Pieces Of*

Eight (1959), and the score, with lyrics by Herbert Kretzmer (*Les Miserables*), to *The Four Musketeers* (1967), starring singer-comedian, Harry Secombe. Despite attracting venomous reviews, *The Four Musketeers* ran for over a year. In 1961, the Laurie Johnson Orchestra had a UK Top 10 chart entry with the Latin-styled, 'Sucu Sucu', written by Tarateno Rosa, the theme from the UK television series, *Top Secret*. On the b-side, was a Johnson composition, the title theme for another television production, *Echo Four-Two*. This was one of over 50 themes or scores that he wrote for television, a list that included *No Hiding Place, When The Kissing Had To Stop, Jason King, Shirley's World, The Aventurers, Thriller, The Avengers, The New Avengers* and *The Professionals*. The latter two were produced by Johnson's company, Avengers (Film And TV) Enterprises, formed with Albert Fennell and Brian Clemens. Johnson also composed extensively for the cinema, from the late 50s. His film scores included *The Moonraker* (1958), *No Trees In The Street* (1958), *Tiger Bay* (1959), *I Aim At The Stars* (1960), *Spare The Rod* (1961), *Dr Strangelove - Or: How I Learned To Stop Worrying And Love The Bomb* (1964), *The First Men In The Moon* (1964), *The Beauty Jungle* (1966), *East Of Sudan* (1966), *Hot Millions* (1968), *And Soon The Darkness* (1970), *The Belstone Fox* (1976), *Diagnosis: Murder* (1976), *It's Alive II (It Lives Again)* (1978), *It Shouldn't Happen To A Vet* (1979), *Bitter Harvest* (1981). Johnson also composed the music for the television movie, *Jericho*, which involved many of the original *Avengers* team, including Patrick MacNee. Johnson's later album releases mostly contained television and film themes.

Albums: *A Brass Band Swinging* (late 50s), *Operation Orchestra* (1958), *Songs Of The Three Seasons* (1958), *Music From The Avengers, The New Avengers & The Professionals* (1980), *First Men In The Moon* (1981).

Joker Is Wild, The

One of the first artists that Frank Sinatra signed to his own brand-new Reprise label in the early 60s was nightclub comedian, Joe E. Lewis. Before then, the two had been close friends, so it was logical, that when Paramount decided in 1957 to make the film biography of a singer with a slick line in patter, Sinatra's name would be to the fore. Shot in black and white, presumably to heighten the dramatic effect, the film turned out to be a hard-hitting, realistic account as to what was likely to happen to a young man in the Roaring 20s if he declined to cooperate with men in dark overcoats carrying violin cases. Young Lewis is getting along fine in one particular nightspot, singing songs such as 'At Sundown' (Walter Donaldson) and 'I Cried For You' (Arthur Freed-Gus Arnheim-Abe Lyman). After ignoring warnings against moving elsewhere, he manages to impress audiences in the new venue ('where they carry the drunks out - they

The Joker Is Wild (Frank Sinatra)

don't just toss 'em out into the street') with 'If I Could Be With You One Hour Tonight' (Henry Creamer-Jimmy Johnson) and 'All The Way' (Sammy Cahn-Jimmy Van Heusen), before his vocals chords are slashed and he finds a new career as a comedian. Subsequent fractured vocalising is confined to parodies of songs such as 'Out Of Nowhere' (music-John Green), 'Swinging On A Star' (music-Van Heusen), and 'Naturally' (music-Flotow), all with new lyrics by Harry Harris. Before he finally conquers his weakness for the bottle, Lewis has become a physical wreck and ruined the lives of the two women who have loved him, played by Jeanne Crain and Mitzi Gaynor. Eddie Albert plays Lewis's (nervous) accompanist whose wife (Beverly Garland) forces him to give up on the comedian, and the cast also included Jackie Coogan, Barry Kelley, Ted de Corsia, Valerie Allen, Hank Henry, and Sophie Tucker. Oscar Saul's screenplay was adapted from a book by Art Cohn, and the film, which was photographed in VistaVision, was directed by Charles Vidor. The song 'All The Way' won an Academy Award, and gave Frank Sinatra a number 2 hit in the USA.

Jolson Sings Again (see *Jolson Story, The*)

Jolson Story, The

This enormously successful, sanitised film biography of 'The World's Greatest Entertainer', who was actually in at the birth of screen musicals with *The Jazz Singer*, was released by Columbia in 1946. In fact, Stephen Longstreet's screenplay for *The Jolson Story* was very much along the lines of that earlier pioneering film: a cantor's son, Asa Yoelson (Al Jolson), breaks his father's heart by leaving home to make a successful career in show business as the black-faced entertainer who had an extraordinary effect on audiences all over the world. After countless actors had been tested for the leading role (Jolson put forward himself [aged 60] and James Cagney), Larry Parks got the part, with Evelyn Keyes as his wife Julie Benson (Ruby Keeler would not allow her name to be used). So it was Parks who strutted and gestured in that electrifying manner, but, at his insistence, it was Jolson's own voice that was heard on the carefully selected favourites that he had, over the years, made his own - songs such as 'My Mammy' (Joe Young-Sam Lewis-Walter Donaldson), 'California, Here I Come' (Joseph Meyer-Buddy De Sylva), 'Let Me Sing And I'm Happy' (Irving Berlin), 'Swanee' (George Gershwin-Irving Caesar), 'I'm Sitting On Top Of The World' (Ray Henderson-Lewis-Young), 'April Showers' (Louis Silvers-De Sylva), 'Toot Toot Tootsie' (Robert King-Ted Fiorito-Gus Kahn), 'Avalon' (Jolson-Vincent Rose), 'The Spaniard That Blighted My Life' (Billy Merson), 'Rock-A-Bye Your Baby With A Dixie Melody' (Lewis-Jean Schwartz-Young), 'Liza' George Gershwin-Ira Gershwin-

Kahn), and the rest. There was also a new number, 'Anniversary Song', which was based on 'Danube Waves' and credited to Jolson, Saul Chaplin and Ion Ivanovici. William Demarest played the part of Jolson's mentor, Steve Martin, and the rest of the cast included Tamara Shayne, Ludwig Donath, Bill Goodwin, and Scotty Beckett as the boy Jolson. Jolson himself managed to make a brief appearance, albeit in long shot. Jack Cole staged the dances, and director Alfred E. Green skilfully blended all the various elements into a Technicolor film of blockbuster proportions. It grossed in excess of $7.5 million and was the seventh most popular film of the decade in the USA (after *This Is The Army, The Bells Of St. Mary's* and four Walt Disney animated features).

The inevitable sequel, *Jolson Sings Again*, which was almost, but not quite as successful as the original, came along in 1949 complete with a screenplay by Sidney Buchman in which Jolson (again played by Larry Parks) is seen entertaining US troops during World War II before retiring, initially because of ill-health. Permanently bored with his inactivity, it does not take a lot of persuading for him to agree to appear at a benefit show - which leads to a comeback, which leads to negotiations for a film of his life . . . *The Jolson Story*. Ludwig Donath and Tamara Shayne, who played his parents in that film were in this one too, and so was William Demarest. Barbara Hale was the nurse who helped Jolson to recover after his illness, and then married him, and also featured were Myron McCormick and Bill Goodwin. As before, the score provided a welcome opportunity to wallow in the Jolson songbook. The songs included 'When The Red, Red Robin Comes Bob, Bob Bobbin' Along' (Harry Woods), 'Carolina In The Morning' (Gus Kahn-Walter Donaldson), 'I'm Looking Over A Four Leaf Clover' (Woods-Mort Dixon), 'Sonny Boy' (De Sylva, Brown And Henderson), 'Back In Your Own Back Yard' (Billy Rose-Dave Dreyer), and many more. Henry Levin directed, and the film, which would have been known in more contemporary times as *The Jolson Story II*, grossed over $5 million in the US and was another worldwide hit.

Jolson, Al

b. Asa Yoelson, c.1885, Snrednicke, Lithuania, d. 23 October 1950. Shortly before the turn of the century, Jolson's father, Moses Yoelson, emigrated to the USA. In a few years he was able to send for his wife and four children, who joined him in Washington DC. Moses Yoelson was cantor at a synagogue and had hopes that his youngest son, Asa, would adopt this profession. After the death of their mother, the two sons, Asa and Hirsch, occasionally sang on street corners for pennies. Following the example of his brother, who had changed his name to Harry, Asa became Al. When family disagreements arose after his father remarried, Al went to New York where his brother had gone to try his luck in show business. For food-money, he sang at McGirk's, a saloon/restaurant in New York's Bowery and later sang with military bands during the time of the Spanish-American War. Back in Washington, he attracted attention when, as a member of the audience at the city's Bijou Theater, he joined in the singing with entertainer Eddie Leonard. The vaudevillian was so impressed he offered the boy a job, singing from the balcony as part of the act. Al refused but ran away to join a theatrical troupe. This venture was short-lived and a week or so later he was back home but had again altered the spelling of his name, this time to Al Joelson. In the audience, again at the Bijou, he sang during the stage act of burlesque queen Aggie Beeler. Once more he was made an offer and this time he did not refuse. This job was also brief, because he was not content to merely sing from the balcony and Beller would not allow him to join her on the stage.

Joelson moved to New York and found work as a singing waiter. He also appeared in the crowd scenes of a play which survived for only three performances. Calling himself Harry Joelson, he formed a double act with Fred E. Moore but abandoned this when his voice broke. Reverting to the name Al he now joined his brother Harry and formed an act during which he whistled songs until his voice matured. The brothers teamed up with Joe Palmer to form the act Joelson, Palmer and Joelson, but again changed the spelling to shorten the space taken on playbills. In 1905 Harry dropped out of the act and the following year Al Jolson was on his own. In San Francisco he established a reputation as an exciting entertainer and coined the phrase which later became an integral part of his performance: 'All right, all right, folks - you ain't heard nothin' yet!' In 1908 Jolson was hired by Lew Dockstader, leader of one of the country's two most famous minstrel shows, and quickly became the top attraction. Around this time he also formed a lifelong association with Harry Akst, a song plugger who later wrote songs including 'Dinah', 'Baby Face' and 'Am I Blue?'. Akst was especially useful to Jolson in finding songs suitable for his extrovert style. In 1911 Jolson opened at the Winter Garden in New York City, where he was a huge success. That same year he made his first records, reputedly having to be strapped to a chair as his involuntary movements were too much for the primitive recording equipment. Also in 1911 he suggested that the Winter Garden show be taken on tour, sets and full cast, orchestra and all, something that had never been done before. In 1912 he again did something new, putting on Sunday shows at the Garden so that other show business people could come and see him. Although he sang in blackface for the regular shows, local bylaws on religious observance meant that the Sunday shows had to be put on without sets and make-up. He devised an extended platform so that he could come out in front of the proscenium arch, thus allowing him to be closer to his audience with whom he was already having a remarkable love affair.

Among his song successes at this time were 'The Spaniard That Blighted My Life' and 'You Made Me Love You'. One night, when the show at the Garden was overrunning, he sent the rest of the cast off stage and simply sang to the audience who loved it. From then on, whenever he felt inclined, which was often, he would ask the audience to choose if they wanted to see the rest of the show or just listen to him. Invariably, they chose him. Significantly enough, on such occasions, the dismissed cast rarely went home, happily sitting in the wings to watch him perform. By 1915 Jolson was being billed as 'America's Greatest Entertainer' and even great rivals such as Eddie Cantor and George Jessel had to agree with this title. In 1916 Jolson made a silent film but found the experiment an unsatisfactory experience. Jolson's 1918 Broadway show was *Sinbad* and his song successes included 'Rockabye Your Baby With A Dixie Melody', 'Swanee' and 'My Mammy'. In 1919 he again tried something unprecedented for a popular entertainer, a concert at the Boston Opera House where he was accompanied by the city's symphony orchestra. Jolson's 1921 show was *Bombo* which opened at a new theatre which bore his name, Jolson's 59th Street Theater. The songs in the show included 'My Mammy', 'April Showers', 'California Here I Come' and 'Toot, Toot, Tootsie (Goo' Bye)'.

During the mid-20s Jolson tried some more new departures; in 1925 he opened in *Big Boy*, which had a real live horse in the cast, and in 1927 he performed on the radio. Of even more lasting significance, in 1926 he returned to the film studios to participate in an experimental film, a one-reel short entitled *April Showers* in which he sang three songs, his voice recorded on new equipment being tested by Vitaphone, a company which had been acquired by Warner Brothers. Although this brief film remained only a curio, and was seen by few people, the system stirred the imagination of Sam Warner, who believed that this might be what the company needed if it was to stave off imminent bankruptcy. They decided to incorporate sound into a film currently in pre-production. This was *The Jazz Singer* which, as a stage show, had run for three years with George Jessel in the lead. Jessel wanted more money than the Warners could afford and Eddie Cantor turned them down flat. They approached Jolson, cannily inviting him to put money into the project in return for a piece of the profits. *The Jazz Singer* (1927) was a silent film into which it was planned to interpolate a song or two but Jolson, being Jolson, did it his way, calling out to the orchestra leader, 'Wait a minute, wait a minute. You ain't heard nothin' yet!' before launching into 'Toot, Toot, Tootsie'. The results were sensational and the motion picture industry was revolutionized overnight. The Warner brothers were saved from bankruptcy and Jolson's piece of the action made him even richer than he already was. His follow-up film, *The Singing Fool*, (1928) included a song especially written for him by the team of De Sylva, Brown And Henderson. Although they treated the exercise as a joke, the results were a massive hit and Jolson's recording of 'Sonny Boy' became one of the first million sellers.

Although Jolson's films were popular and he was one of the highest paid performers in Hollywood, the cinema proved detrimental to his career. The cameras never fully captured the magic that had made him so successful on Broadway. Additionally, Jolson's love for working with a live audience was not satisfied by the film medium. His need to sing before a live audience was so overpowering that when his third wife, the dancer Ruby Keeler, opened on Broadway in *Show Girl*, he stood up in his seat and joined in with her big number, 'Liza'. He completely upstaged Keeler, who would later state that this was one of the things about him that she grew to hate the most. Jolson continued to make films, among them *Mammy* (1930) which included 'Let Me Sing And I'm Happy', and *Big Boy* (1930), generally cited as the film which came closest to capturing the essence of his live performances. Back on Broadway in 1931 with *The Wonder Bar*, Jolson was still popular and was certainly an extremely rich man, but he was no longer the massive success that he had been in the 20s. For a man who sang for many reasons, of which money was perhaps the least important, this was a very bad time. Fuelling his dissatisfaction was the fact that Keeler, whose film career he had actively encouraged and helped, was a bigger box-office attraction. Despite spreading a thin talent very wide, Keeler rose while Jolson fell. In 1932 he stopped making records and that year there were no shows or films, even though there were still offers. He made a film with Keeler, *Go Into Your Dance* (1935) in which he sang 'About A Quarter To Nine', and participated in an early television pilot. Not surprisingly for a man who had tried many new ventures in show business, Jolson was impressed by the medium and confidently predicted its success, but his enthusiasm was not followed up by producers. He made more films in the late 30s, sometimes cameos, occasionally rating third billing but the great days appeared to be over. Even his return to Broadway, in 1940 in *Hold Onto Your Hats*, was fated to close when he was struck down with pneumonia. The same year Jolson's marriage to Keeler ended acrimoniously.

On 7 December 1941, within hours of learning of the Japanese attack on Pearl Harbor, Jolson volunteered to travel overseas to entertain troops. Appearing before audiences of young men, to whom he was at best only a name, Jolson found and captured a new audience. All the old magic worked and during the next few years he toured endlessly, putting on shows to audiences of thousands or singing songs to a couple of GIs on street corners. With Harry Akst as his accompanist, he visited Europe and the UK, Africa and the Near and Far East theatres of war. Eventually, tired and sick, he returned to the USA where doctors advised him not to resume his overseas travels. Jolson agreed but instead began a punishing round of hospital visits on the mainland. Taken ill again, he was operated on and a part of one lung was removed. The hospital visits had a happier ending when he met Erle Galbraith, a civilian X-ray technician on one of the army bases he visited, who became his fourth wife. The war over, Jolson made a cameo appearance in a film and also performed on a couple of records, but it appeared as though his career, temporarily buoyed by the war, was ended. However, a man named Sidney Skolsky had long wanted to make a film about Jolson's life and, although turned down flat by all the major studios, eventually was given the go-ahead by Harry Cohn, boss of the ailing independent Columbia Pictures, who happened to be a Jolson fan. After surmounting many difficulties, not least that Jolson, despite being over 60 years old, wanted to play himself on the screen, the film was made. Starring Larry Parks as Jolson and with a superb soundtrack on which Jolson sang all his old favourites in exciting new arrangements by Morris Stoloff, *The Jolson Story* (1946) was a hit. Apart from making a great deal of money for Columbia, who thus became the second film company Jolson had saved, it put the singer back in the public eye with a bang. He signed a deal with Decca for a series of records using the same Stoloff arrangements and orchestral accompaniment. All the old songs became hugely popular as did 'The Anniversary Song' which was written especially for a scene in the film in which his father and mother dance on their wedding anniversary (Hollywood having conveniently overlooked the fact that his real mother had died when he was a boy). The film and the records, particularly 'The Anniversary Song', were especially popular in the UK.

In the USA Jolson's star continued to rise and after a string of performances on radio, where he became a regular guest on Bing Crosby's show, he was given his own series, which ran for four years and helped encourage Columbia to create another Jolson precedent. This was to make a sequel to a bio-pic. *Jolson Sings Again* (1949) recaptured the spirit and energy of the first film and was another huge success. In 1950 Jolson was again talking to television executives and this time it appeared that something would come from the discussions. Before anything could be settled, however, the US Army became involved in the so-called 'police action' in Korea and Jolson immediately volunteered to entertain the troops. With Harry Akst again accompanying him, he visited front-line soldiers during a punishing tour. Exhausted, he returned to the USA where he was booked to appear on Crosby's radio show which was scheduled to be aired from San Francisco. On 23 October 1950, while playing cards with Akst and other long-time friends at the St. Francis hotel, he complained of chest pains and died shortly afterwards. Throughout the 20s and into the mid-30s, Jolson was the USA's outstanding entertainer and in 1925 his already hyperbolic billing was changed to 'The World's Greatest Entertainer'. Unfortunately, latterday audiences have only his films and records to go on. None of the films can be regarded as offering substantial evidence of his greatness. His best records are those made with Stoloff for the soundtrack of the biographical films, by which time his voice was deeper and, anyway, recordings cannot recapture the stage presence which allowed him to hold audiences in their seats for hours on end. Although it is easy to be carried away by the enthusiasm of others, it would appear to be entirely justified in Jolson's case. Unlike many other instances of fan worship clouding reality, even Jolson's rivals acknowledged that he was the best. In addition, most of those who knew him disliked him as a man, but this never diminished their adulation of him as an entertainer. On the night he died they turned out the lights on Broadway, and traffic in Times Square was halted. It is hard to think of any subsequent superstar who would be granted, or who has earned, such testimonials. There has been only a small handful of entertainers, in any medium, of which it can be truly said, we shall never see their like again. Al Jolson was one of that number.

Selected albums: *The Best Of Jolson* (1963), *Say It With Songs* (1965), *Immortal Al Jolson* (1975), *Jolson Sings Again* (1974), *You Ain't Heard Nothin' Yet* (1975), *20 Golden Greats* (1981), *20 More Golden Greats* (1981), *The Man And The Legend Vols 1 & 2* (1982), *The Man And The Legend Vol 3* (1983), *Al Jolson Collection Vols. 1 & 2* (1983), *The World's Greatest Entertainer* (1983).

Further reading: *Jolie: The Story Of Al Jolson*, Michael Freedland.

Jones, Allan

b. 14 October 1908, Scranton, Pennsylvania, USA. d. 27 June 1992, New York, USA. A popular, romantic tenor star in movies in the late 30s and early 40s. After studying singing in Paris, Jones returned to the USA and worked in provincial operettas. He appeared on Broadway in *Roberta* (1933) and the 1934 revival of *Bitter Sweet* before gaining a part in the film *Reckless* (1935). In the same year he made a big impression singing 'Alone' in the Marx Brothers film *A Night At The Opera*. This was followed by leading screen roles in *Rose-Marie*, *Show Boat* (1936), *A Day At The Races*, *The Firefly* (in which he introduced his signature tune 'The Donkey Serenade), *Everybody Sing*, *The Great Victor Herbert*, *The Boys From Syracuse*, *One Night In The Tropics*, *There's Magic In Music*, *True To The Army*, *Moonlight In Havana*, *When Johnny Comes Marching Home*, *Larceny With Music*, *Rhythm Of The Islands*, *Crazy House*, *You're A Lucky Fellow Mr. Smith*, *The Singing Sheriff*, *Honeymoon Ahead*, and *Senorita From The West* (1945). Jones married actress Irene Hervey and their son, Jack Jones, went on to become a popular singer with big hits in the 60s. Allan Jones quit Hollywood in 1945 following a dispute with MGM boss Louis B. Mayer, and took to the nightclub circuit. In the 50s he starred in a major US tour of *Guys And Dolls*, and in the 70s he toured with *Man Of La Mancha*. He had recently returned from tour of Australia when he died of lung cancer in June 1992.

Jones, Quincy

b. 14 March 1933, Chicago, Illinois, USA. Jones began playing trumpet as a child and also developed an early interest in arranging, studying at the Berklee College Of Music. When he joined Lionel Hampton in 1951 it was as both performer and writer. With Hampton he visited Europe in a remarkable group which included rising stars Clifford Brown, Art Farmer, Gigi Gryce and Alan Dawson. Leaving Hampton in 1953, Jones wrote arrangements for many musicians, including some of his former colleagues and Ray Anthony, Count Basie and Tommy Dorsey. Mostly, he worked as a freelance but had a stint in the mid-50s as musical director for Dizzy Gillespie, one result of which was the 1956 album *World Statesman*. Later in the 50s and into the 60s Jones wrote charts and directed the orchestras for concerts and record sessions by several singers, including Frank Sinatra, Billy Eckstine, Brook Benton, Dinah Washington (an association which included the 1956 album *The Swingin' Miss 'D'*), Johnny Mathis and Ray Charles, whom he had known since childhood. He continued to write big band charts, composing and arranging albums for Basie, *One More Time* (1958-59) and *Li'l Ol' Groovemaker...Basie* (1963). By this time, Jones was fast becoming a major force in American popular music. In addition to playing he was busy writing, arranging and was increasingly active as a record producer. In the late 60s and 70s he composed scores for about 40 feature films and hundreds of television shows. Among the former were *The Pawnbroker* (1965), *In Cold Blood* (1967) and *In The Heat Of The Night* (1967) while the latter included the long-running *Ironside* series and *Roots*. He continued to produce records featuring his own music played by specially assembled orchestras. As a record producer Jones had originally worked for Mercury's Paris-based subsidiary Barclay but later became the first black vice-president of the company's New York division. Later, he spent a dozen years with A&M before starting up his own label, Qwest. Despite suffering two brain aneurysms in 1974 he showed no signs of letting up his high level of activity. In the 70s and 80s he produced successful albums for Aretha Franklin, George Benson, Michael

Jackson, the Brothers Johnston and other popular artists. With Benson he produced *Give Me The Night*, while for Jackson he helped to create *Off The Wall* and *Thriller*, the latter proving to be the best-selling album of all time. He was also producer of the 1985 number 1 charity single 'We Are The World'. Latterly, Jones has been involved in film and television production, not necessarily in a musical context. As a player, Jones was an unexceptional soloist; as an arranger, his attributes are sometimes overlooked by the jazz audience, perhaps because of the manner in which he has consistently sought to create a smooth and wholly sophisticated entity, even at the expense of eliminating the essential characteristics of the artists concerned (as some of his work for Basie exemplifies). Nevertheless, with considerable subtlety he has fused elements of the blues and its many offshoots into mainstream jazz, and has found ways to bring soul to latterday pop in a manner which adds to the latter without diminishing the former. His example has been followed by many although few have achieved such a level of success. A major film documentary, *Listen Up: The Lives Of Quincy Jones*, was released in 1990.

Selected albums: *Clifford Brown Memorial Album* (1953), *This Is How I Feel About Jazz* (1956), *The Birth Of A Band* (1959), *The Great Wide World Of Quincy Jones* (1959), *Quincy Jones Live At Newport* (1961), *Quintessence* (1961), *Walking In Space* (1969), *Gula Matari* (1970), *Smackwater Jack* (1971), *Mellow Madness* (1972), *The Hot Rock* (1972), *I Heard That!* (1973), *Body Heat* (1973), *Roots* (1977), *Sounds...And Stuff Like That* (1977-78), *The Dude* (1980), with Miles Davis *Live At Montreux* (1993, rec. 1991).

Video: *Miles Davis And Quincy Jones: Live At Montreux* (1993).

Jones, Shirley

b. 31 March 1934, Smithton, Pennsylvania, USA. An actress and singer whose film portrayals of sweet and wholesome ingenues in the 50s contrasted sharply with her Academy Award-winning performance as Burt Lancaster's prostitute girlfriend in *Elmer Gantry* (1960). After taking singing lessons from an early age, Jones performed in stage productions before making her film debut opposite Gordon MacRae in the excellent film version of Richard Rodgers and Oscar Hammerstein's *Oklahoma!* (1955). So successful was the collaboration, that the two stars came together again a year later for another Rodgers and Hammerstein project, *Carousel*. After appearing with Pat Boone in *April Love* (1957), Jones turned in an impressive acting performance alongside James Cagney in the musical comedy-drama *Never Steal Anything Small*, joined a host of other stars in *Pepe*, and made one or two lack-lustre features before partnering Robert Preston in another fine adaptation of a Broadway show, *The Music Man* (1962). From

then on, Shirley Jones eschewed musical films for dramatic roles in big-screen features and on television. She was married for a time to the actor and singer Jack Cassidy, and she co-starred with her step-son, David Cassidy, in the top-rated television series *The Partridge Family* in the early 70s. Later in the decade she had her own show entitled *Shirley*. She continued to sing in nightclubs and concerts, and in the late 80s undertook a 14-week tour of the US in *The King And I* with David Carradine. In the summer of 1994 she appeared with Marty Ingels in a provincial production of A.R. Gurney's two-hander *Love Letters*, and also starred in a Detroit revival of *The King And I*.

Jumbo (see **Billy Rose's Jumbo**)

Jungle Book, The (see **Disney, Walt**)

K

Kahn, Gus

b. 6 November 1886, Koblenz, Germany, d. 8 October 1941. Kahn was a prolific lyricist during the 20s and 30s, for Tin Pan Alley, stage and films. He was not particularly well-known by the public, but was highly regarded in the music business for his vivacious, colloquial lyrics. He was once voted by a 'trade' poll as the second most popular US songwriter after Irving Berlin. In 1891, he was brought by his immigrant parents to Chicago where the family settled. He started writing songs while at high school, but it was not until after he collaborated with his future wife, composer Grace LeBoy, that he had some success with 'I Wish I Had A Girl', in 1908. His first big hit came in 1915 with 'Memories', written with composer Egbert van Alstyne. In the following year, Kahn collaborated with him again, and Tony Jackson, for 'Pretty Baby', which became one of Kahn's biggest hits, and was featured in the bio-pics *Jolson Sings Again* (1949) and *The Eddie Cantor Story* (1953); two artists who benefited substantially from Kahn's output. 'Pretty Baby' was just one of a series of Kahn 'baby' songs which evoke the 'jazz age' of the 20s. These included 'Yes Sir, That's My Baby', 'There Ain't No Maybe In My Baby's Eyes', 'My Baby Just Cares for Me', 'I Wonder Where My Baby Is Tonight' and 'Sing Me A Baby Song', all written with composer Walter Donaldson, Khan's major collaborator. Donaldson, with his playboy image, was the antithesis of Kahn with his sober, family background. Other songs by the team included 'That Certain Party', 'Carolina In The Morning', 'My Buddy' and 'Beside A Babbling Brook'. Some of their best work was contained in the 1928 Broadway show *Whoopee!*. Starring Ruth Etting and Eddie Cantor, it introduced 'I'm Bringing A Red Red Rose', 'Love Me Or Leave Me', 'My Baby Just Cares for Me' and 'Makin' Whoopee', the lyric of which is considered to be one of Kahn's best. The show later became an early sound movie in 1930.

In 1929, Kahn contributed to another Broadway musical, *Show Girl*. This time his collaborators were George and Ira Gershwin. The trio produced 'Liza', for the show's star, Ruby Keeler. It is said that, during at least one performance, Keeler's husband, Al Jolson, stood up in the audience and sang the song *to her*. In 1933, Kahn went to Hollywood to work on various movies ranging from the Marx Brothers' *A Day At The Races* ('All God's Chillun Got Rhythm'), to *Spring Parade*, starring Deanna Durbin, singing 'Waltzing In The Clouds'. In 1933, his first Hollywood project, with composer Vincent Youmans, was *Flying Down To Rio*, which featured the title song, and 'The Carioca'. It was also the first film to bring together Fred Astaire and Ginger Rogers. Unfortunately it was Youmans' last original film score before he died in 1946. For the next eight years Kahn's output for films was prolific. They included *Bottoms Up* ('Waiting At The Gate For Katy'), *Caravan* ('Ha-Cha-Cha' and 'Wine Song'), *Hollywood Party* ('I've Had My Moments'), *Kid Millions* ('Okay Toots', 'When My Ship Comes In' and 'Your Head On My Shoulder'), *One Night Of Love*, *The Girl Friend*, *Love Me Forever*, *Thanks A Million* (with Dick Powell singing the title song), *San Francisco* (the title song sung by Jeanette MacDonald), *Rose Marie* ('Just For You' and 'Pardon Me, Madame'), *Three Smart Girls* (Deanna Durbin singing 'Someone To Care For Me'), *Everybody Sing* ('The One I Love'), *Girl Of The Golden West* ('Shadows On the Moon' and 'Who Are We To Say'), *Lillian Russell* (a bio-pic of the famous 1890s entertainer) and *Ziegfeld Girl* ('You Stepped Out Of A Dream', written with composer Nacio Herb Brown, and sung by Tony Martin). Kahn's last song, in 1941, realised a life-long ambition to write with Jerome Kern; their song was called 'Day Dreaming'.

Throughout his career Kahn had many different collaborators, including bandleader Isham Jones ('I'll See You In My Dreams', 'The One I Love Belongs To Somebody Else', 'Swingin' Down The Lane', and 'It Had To Be You'), Richard Whiting ('Ukulele Lady'), Whiting and Ray Egan ('Ain't We Got Fun'), Whiting and Harry Akst ('Guilty'), Ted Fio Rito ('I Never Knew', 'Charley My Boy' and 'Sometime'), Ernie Erdman, Elmer Schoebel and Billy Meyers ('Nobody's Sweetheart Now'), Erdman and Dan Russo ('Toot Toot Tootsie, Goodbye'), Wilbur Schwandt and Fabian Andre ('Dream A Little Dream Of Me' - a later hit for 'Mama' Cass Elliott), Charlie Rossoff ('When You And I Were Seventeen'), Carmen Lombardo and John Green ('Coquette'), Neil Moret ('Chloe'), Wayne King ('Goofus'), Matty Malneck and Fud Livingston ('I'm Through With Love'), Malneck and Frank Signorelli ('I'll Never Be The Same') and Victor Schertzinger ('One Night Of Love'). In the 1951 movie, *I'll See You In My Dreams*, based on his life, Kahn was portrayed by Danny Thomas, and his wife, Grace LeBoy by Doris Day. Gus Kahn had died 10 years earlier in October 1941, in Beverley Hills, California, USA.

Kalmar, Bert

b. 10 February 1884, New York City, New York, USA, d. 18 September 1947. Ill-educated and a runaway before he was in his teens, Kalmar's life was completely immersed in showbusiness. In the years before World War I he wrote lyrics for a number of songs with various composers, among them Harry Ruby. For the next few years each wrote with other collaborators, but by the beginning of the 20s they recognized the special qualities of their work together. Throughout the 20s they wrote for Broadway musicals such as *Ladies First*, *Broadway Brevities Of 1920*, *Ziegfeld Follies Of 1920*, *Midnight Rounders Of 1921*, *Greenwich Village Follies Of 1922*, *Helen Of Troy-New York*, *Puzzles Of 1925*, *The Ramblers*, *Five O'Clock Girl*, *Lucky*, *Good Boy*, and *Animal Crackers*. The latter score was written for the Marx Brothers, and contained songs such as 'Who's Been Listening To My Heart?', 'Watching The Clouds Roll By', and 'Hooray For Captain Spaulding'. Other songs from those shows included 'Oh! What A Pal Was Mary', 'So Long, Oo-long', 'Who's Sorry Now?', 'Thinking Of You', 'The Same Old Moon', 'Dancing The Devil Away', 'Some Sweet Someone', and 'I Wanna Be Loved By You'. By the 30s Kalmar and Ruby were writing songs for films and one of their first, and the song by which they are best remembered, was 'Three Little Words' (from *Check And Double Check*). It became the title of the songwriters' 1950 film biography when they were played by Fred Astaire and Red Skelton. Their other film work included *The Cuckoos*, *Horse Feathers*, *The Kid From Spain*, *Hips Hips Hooray*, *Kentucky Kernels*, *Thanks A Million*, aand *The Story Of Vernon And Irene Castle*. They contained numbers such as 'I Love You So Much', 'What A Perfect Combination', 'Only When You're In My Arms', and 'Keep Romance Alive'. Most of their songs were written for either stage or screen but among their great successes were 'Nevertheless' and 'A Kiss To Build A Dream On' - written for neither medium. (This last song did not become popular until the 50s after some rewriting by Oscar Hammerstein II.)

Kamen, Michael

b. 1948, New York, USA. A Composer, conductor, and arranger for films, from the 70s through to the 90s. After studying at the Juilliard School Of Music, Kamen contributed some music to the off-beat rock Western film, *Zachariah* in 1971. Later in the 70s, he wrote the complete scores for *The Next Man*, *Between The Lines*, and *Stunts* (1977). During the 80s he scored co-composed the music for several films with some of contemporary pop music's most illustrious names, such as Eric Clapton (*Lethal Weapon*, *Homeboy*, and *Lethal Weapon II* (also with David Sanborn), George Harrison (*Shanghai Surprise*), David A. Stewart (*Rooftops*), and Herbie Hancock (*Action Jackson*). Subsequently, Kamen scored some of the period's most entertaining and diverting UK and US movies, which included *Venom*, *Pink Floyd-The Wall*, *Angleo, My Love*, *The Dead Zone*, *Brazil*, *Mona Lisa*, *Riot*, *Sue And Bob, Too*, *Someone To Watch Over Me*, *Suspect*, *Die Hard* and *Die Hard II*, *Raggedy Rawney*, *Crusoe*, *For Queen And Country*, *The Adventures Of Baron Munchausen*, *Dead-Bang* (with Gary Chang), *Road House*, *Renegades*, and *Licence To Kill* (1989), Timothy Dalton's second attempt to replace Connery and Moore as James Bond. In the early 90s Kamen composed the music for *The Krays* and *Let Him Have It*, two films which reflected infamous criminal incidents in the UK, and others such as *Nothing But Trouble*, *Hudson Hawk*, *The Last Boy Scout*, *Company Business*, *Blue Ice*, *Lethal Weapon 3*, *Shining Through* (1992), *Blue Ice*, *Splitting Heirs*, *Last Action Hero*, and *The Three Musketeers* (1993). In several instances, besides scoring the films, Kamen served as musical director, music editor, and played keyboards and other instruments. In 1991, he provided the music for the smash hit Kevin Kostner movie, *Robin Hood: Prince Of Thieves*, and, with lyricists Bryan Adams and Robert John Lange, composed the closing number, '(Everything I Do) I Do For You'. Adams' recording of the song enjoyed phenomenal success, staying at the top of the UK chart for an unprecedented 16 weeks. The song was nominated for an Academy Award, and Kamen received two Grammys and a special Ivor Novello Award. Besides his work for feature films, Kamen also wrote for television. His credits included tele-films such as *Liza's Pioneer Diary*, *S*H*E*, *Shoot For The Sun*, and two mini-series, *The Duty Men* (theme: 'Watching You' (with Sashazoe)), and *Edge Of Darkness*. The theme from the latter, written with Eric Clapton, gained another Ivor Novello Award (1985). Kamen also wrote several scores for the Joffrey Ballet and the La Scala Opera Company.

Kane, Helen

b. Helen Schroder, 4 August 1904, New York, USA, d. 26 September 1966. Kane is remembered these days as the singer portrayed by Debbie Reynolds in *Three Little Words*, the 1950 film biography of songwriters Bert Kalmar and Harry Ruby. Kane, (who dubbed the Reynolds vocal), was the baby-voiced singer who rose to fame on Broadway in the late 20s. She began her career in vaudeville and night clubs but was much-acclaimed for an appearance with Paul Ash And His Orchestra at New York's Paramount Theatre. She was then featured in such Broadway shows as *A Night In Spain* (1927) and *Good Boy* (1928) in which she sang 'I Wanna Be Loved By You', the 'Boop-Boop-A-Doop' hit that was re-created by Reynolds. After her Broadway success she moved to Hollywood in the late 20s, appearing in several films, including *Nothing But The Truth* (1929), featuring one of her biggest hits, 'Do Something', plus *Sweetie* (1929), *Pointed Heels* (1930), *Dangerous Nan McGrew* (1930), *Heads Up* (1930), and the all-star spectacular, *Paramount On Parade* (1930). Meanwhile, she continued to make hit records such as 'That's My Weakness Now', 'Get Out And Get Under The Moon', 'Me And The Man In The Moon' and 'Button Up Your Overcoat'. Often acknowledged to have been a major influence in the creation of Grim Natwick's cartoon character Betty Boop, Kane continued her career throughout the 30s playing mainly nightclubs. Kane was, for the most part, largely forgotten until the arrival of *Three Little Words*, at which point she became a minor celebrity amid a new generation.

Kaper, Bronislaw (Bronislau)

b. 5 February 1902, Warsaw, Poland, d. 26 April 1983, Beverly Hills, California, USA. A composer, arranger and conductor for films, from the mid-30s through to the late 60s. Kaper studied at the Warsaw Conservatory of Music and in Berlin before working as a composer in several European countries, including London and Paris. In 1935, after moving to the USA, he began a collaboration with Walter Jurmann, and sometimes with Gus Kahn and Ned Washington, on songs for movies such as *A Night At The Opera* ('Cosi Cosa'), *Mutiny On The Bounty* ('Love Song Of Tahiti'), *Escapade* ('You're All I Need'), *San Francisco* (the title song and 'Happy New Year'), *A Day At The Races* ('All God's Chillun Got Rhythm'), 'A Message From The Man In The Moon', 'Tomorrow Is Another Day', *Three Smart Girls* ('Someone To Care For Me' and 'My Heart Is Singing'), and *Everybody Sing* ('The One I Love' and 'Swing, Mr. Mendelssohn'). With Kahn, Kaper also wrote 'Blue Lovebird' for the bio-pic, *Lillian Russell* (1940). During the 40s, Kaper composed complete scores for films such as *Johnny Eager*, *The Chocolate Soldier*, *Two Faced Woman*, *Keeper Of The Flame*, *Somewhere I'll Find You*, *Gaslight*, *Mrs. Parkinson*, *Without Love*, *Green Dolphin Street* (the song, 'One Green Dolphin Street', became a jazz standard), and contributed 'I Know, I Know I Know', to Mario Lanza's debut movie, *That Midnight Kiss*. In 1953,

172

Kaper won an Academy Award for his score to *Lili*, which also contained the song 'Hi-Lili, Hi-Lo' (lyric by Helen Deutsch). Sung by Leslie Caron and Mel Ferrer in the movie, the song later became a hit for both Richard Chamberlain and Alan Price. In the following year, Kaper, Caron and Deutsch were together again for the film musical *The Glass Slipper*, which included 'Take My Love'. Kaper's other movie music in the 50s and 60s included *A Life Of Her Own*, *The Red Badge Of Courage*, *The Wild North*, *The Naked Spur*, *Them*, *Somebody Up There Likes Me*, *The Swan*, *Don't Go Near The Water*, *Auntie Mame*, *The Brothers Karamazov*, *Butterfield 8*, *Green Mansions*, *The Angel Wore Red*, *Two Loves*, *Mutiny On The Bounty* (the 1962 version, containing 'Follow Me', with a lyric by Paul Francis Webster, which was nominated for an Oscar), *Kisses For My President*, *Lord Jim*, *The Way West*, *Tobruk*, *Counterpoint* and *A Flea In Her Ear* (1968). Kaper also composed for television programmes such as *The F.B.I.*, and, in 1945, adapted music by Chopin for the score of the Broadway show, *Polonaise*. His collaborators included Herbert Stothart, Bob Russell and Hector Villa-Lobos.

Karas, Anton
b. 7 July 1906, Vienna, Austria, d. 9 January 1985. The man who arguably did more to popularize the zither than anyone before or after, is best remembered as the sound behind the famous 'Third Man Theme' (Harry Lime). The Carol Reed film classic, *The Third Man* (1949), utilized Karas's music throughout, and it was no surprise that film-goers went out and made the song and its accompanying album a number 1 hit in 1950. Although Karas was a virtuoso, he remains one of the more famous one-hit-wonders of our time.
Albums: *World Of Anton Karas* (1971), *Folk Songs Of Austria* (1974), *Bons Bons De Vienne* (1977), *Harry Lime Theme (The Third Man)* (1974).

Kaye, Danny
b. David Daniel Kominsky, 18 January 1913, Brooklyn, New York, USA, d. 3 March 1987, Los Angeles, California, USA. Kaye was an extraordinary entertainer and an apparently inexhaustible comedian, mimic and dancer who seemed to be able to twist his face and body into any shape he wanted. As a singer, he specialized in very fast double talk and tongue-twisters, but could present a gentle ballad equally well. He was also an indefatigable ambassador for numerous charities, especially the United Nations International Children's Emergency Fund (now UNICEF), for which he travelled and worked for many years. A son of Jewish immigrant parents from Russia, Kominsky originally wanted to join the medical profession, but dropped out of high school when he was 14 years old, and hitch-hiked to Florida with his friend, Louis Eilson, where they sang for money. On their return to New York, they formed an act called Red And

Blackie, and performed at private functions. During the day, Kominski worked as a soda-jerk, and then as an automobile appraiser with an insurance company. The latter job was terminated after he made a mistake which is said to have cost the company some $40,000. Kominski and Eilson then obtained summer work as 'toomlers', creators of tumult or all-round entertainers, in the Borscht Circuit summer hotels and camps in the Catskill Mountains. After five years, Kominski was earning $1,000 per season.
In 1933, he joined David Harvey and Kathleen Young on the vaudeville circuit in their dancing act, the Three Terpsichoreans, and was billed for the first time as Danny Kaye. An early on-stage accident in which he split his trousers, elicited much laughter from the audience and was incorporated into the act. Signed by producer A.B. Marcus, the group toured the USA for five months in the revue, *La Vie Paree*, before sailing for the Orient in February 1934. It is often said that during this period of playing to non-English speaking audiences in Japan, China and Malaya, was when Kaye developed his face-making and pantomiming techniques, and his 'gibberish' singing with the occasional recognized word. Back in the USA in 1936, Kaye worked with comedian Nick Long Jnr. and toured with Abe Lyman's Band, before being booked by impresario Henry Sherek, to appear in cabaret at London's Dorchester Hotel. The engagement, in 1938, was not a success. Kaye commented: 'I was too loud for the joint'. (Ten years later in London, it would be an entirely different story.) While appearing in Max Liebman's *Sunday Night Varieties* in New York, Kaye met pianist-songwriter Sylvia Fine, who had been raised in the same Brooklyn neighbourhood, and majored in music at Brooklyn College. She became a powerful influence throughout his career, as his director, coach and critic. Working with Liebman's Saturday night revues at Camp Taimiment in the Pennsylvania Hills, during the summer of 1939, they started their collaboration, with Fine accompanying Kaye on the piano, and writing special material which included three of his most famous numbers, 'Stanislavsky', 'Pavlova' and the story of the unstable château designer, 'Anatole Of Paris'. The best of the material was assembled in *The Straw Hat Revue* in which Kaye appeared with Imogene Coca, and opened on Broadway in September 1939. The show also featured a young dancer named Jerome Robbins. After Fine and Kaye were married in January 1940, Kaye appeared in a smash hit engagement at La Martinique nightclub in New York, which led to a part in *Lady In The Dark*, starring Gertrude Lawrence. On the first night, Kaye stopped the show with the Kurt Weill and Ira Gershwin tongue-twister 'Tchaikovsky', in which he reeled off the names of 50 real, or imagined, Russian composers in 38 seconds. After playing a return engagement at La Martinique, and a five-week

Danny Kaye with Corinne Calvet (*On The Riviera*)

stint at the Paramount Theatre, Kaye appeared again on Broadway, starring in the Cole Porter musical, *Let's Face It*, which opened in October 1941. Porter allowed Sylvia Fine and Max Liebman to interpolate some special material for Kaye, which included a 'jabberwocky of song, dance, illustration and double-talk' called 'Melody In 4F'. Kaye had to leave the show early in 1942, suffering from nervous exhaustion, but having recovered, he toured on behalf of the war effort and is said to have sold a million dollars worth of government bonds in six months. Rejected by the US Army because of a back ailment, he entertained troops with his two-hour shows in many theatres of operations including the South Pacific.

In 1944, Kaye made his feature film debut in *Up In Arms*, the first of a series of five pictures for Sam Goldwyn at MGM. His performance as a hypochondriac elevator boy, involving yet another memorable Fine-Liebman piece, 'Manic Depressive Pictures Presents: Lobby Number', moved one critic to hail his introduction as 'the most exciting since Garbo's'. Goldwyn was criticized, however for having Kaye's red hair dyed blonde. His remaining films for the studio included *Wonder Man*, in which he gave his impression of a sneezing Russian baritone with 'Orchi Tchornya'. This was the first of several films in which

he played more than one character; *The Kid From Brooklyn* (1946), which featured 'Pavlova', *The Secret Life Of Walter Mitty* (1947), one of his best-remembered roles (six of them), and *A Song Is Born* (1948), one of his least remembered. In 1945, Kaye appeared for a year on his own CBS radio show with Harry James and Eve Arden, and during the following year the Kayes' daughter, Dena was born. When Kaye recorded the old standard, 'Dinah', he changed some of the 'i' sounds to 'e', so that the song ran: 'Denah, is there anyone fener? In the State of Carolena . . .' etc. His other hit songs included 'Tubby The Tuba', 'Minnie The Moocher', 'Ballin' The Jack', 'Bloop Bleep', 'Civilization' and 'The Woody Woodpecker Song', both with the Andrews Sisters; 'C'est Si Bon'; and 'Blackstrap Molasses', recorded with Jimmy Durante, Jane Wyman and Groucho Marx. In 1948, Kaye returned to England, to appear at the London Palladium. His enormously successful record-breaking performances began an affectionate and enduring relationship with the British public. He is said to have received over 100,000 letters in a week. His shows were attended by the Royal Family; he met both Winston Churchill and George Bernard Shaw, and was cast in wax for London's Madame Tussauds Museum. He returned in 1949 for the first of several Royal Command Performances, and also toured provincial music halls throughout 1952. He endeared himself to the British by singing some of their parochial songs such as the novelty 'I've Got A Lovely Bunch Of Coconuts' and 'Maybe It's Because I'm A Londoner'. During one performance at the Palladium, when a member of the audience enquired after the state of Kaye's ribs, following a car accident, he ordered the lights to be lowered while he displayed the actual X-ray plates! Kaye went to Canada in 1950 and became the first solo performer to star at the Canadian National Exhibition, where he sold out the 24,000-seater stadium for each of his 14 performances. He returned to his multiple roles in films such as *The Inspector General* (1949) and *On The Riviera* (1951), before embarking on the somewhat controversial, *Hans Christian Andersen* (1952). After 16 different screenplays over a period of 15 years, and protests in the Danish press about the choice of Kaye to play their national hero, the film, with a final screenplay by Moss Hart, was the third biggest money-spinner in MGM's history. Frank Loesser's score produced several appealing songs, including 'No Two People', 'Anywhere I Wander', 'Inchworm', 'Thumbelina', 'The Ugly Duckling' and 'Wonderful Copenhagen', the latter reaching the UK Top 5. Kaye's other films during the 50s and early 60s included *Knock On Wood* (1954), said to be his favourite, in which he sang two more Fine numbers, the title song, and 'All About Me', *White Christmas* (1954), co-starring with Bing Crosby, Rosemary Clooney and Vera-Ellen, *The Court Jester* (1956), *Me And The Colonel* (1958), *Merry Andrew* (1958), *The Five Pennies* (1959), a bio-pic of 20s cornet player Red Nichols (including a rousing version of 'When The Saints Go Marching In', with Louis Armstrong), *On The Double* (1961) and *The Man From The Diners' Club* (1963). After a break, he came back for *The Madwoman Of Challiot* (1969), and the following year, returned to Broadway in the role of Noah, in the Richard Rodgers and Martin Charnin musical, *Two By Two*. Shortly after the show opened, Kaye tore a ligament in his leg during a performance, and subsequently appeared on crutches or in a wheel chair, in which he tried to run down the other actors, adapting the show to his injury, much to the distaste of producer and composer, Richard Rodgers. During the 70s and 80s, Kaye conducted classical orchestras and appeared on several television shows including *Peter Pan*, *Pinocchio* and *Danny Kaye's Look At The Metropolitan Opera*. He also played dramatic roles on television in *Skokie* and *The Twilight Zone*, but concentrated mainly on his charity work. He had started his association with UNICEF in the early 50s, and in 1955 made a 20-minute documentary, *Assignment Children*. He eventually became the organization's ambassador-at-large for 34 years, travelling worldwide on their behalf, and entering the *Guinness Book Of Records* by visiting 65 US and Canadian cities in five days, piloting himself in his own jet plane. During his career he received many awards including the French Legion d'Honneur, the Jean Hersholt Humanitarian Award, the Knight's Cross of the First Class of the Order of Danneborg, given by the Danish Government. Other awards included a special Academy Award in 1954, along with Tonys for his stage performances, plus Emmys for his successful 60s television series. He died in March 1987, following a heart attack.

Albums: *Hans Christian Andersen* (1953, film soundtrack), *Mommy, Gimme A Drink Of Water* (1958), with Louis Armstrong *The Five Pennies* (1959, film soundtrack), *For Children* (1974), with Ivor Moreton *Happy Fingers* (1977). Compilations: *The Best Of Danny Kaye* (1982), *The Very Best Of Danny Kaye - 20 Golden Greats* (1987).

Further reading: *The Danny Kaye Saga*, Kurt Singer.

Kaye, Stubby

b. 18 November 1918, New York City, New York, USA. An actor and singer who carved himself an instant slice of musical history by stopping the show as Nicely-Nicely Johnson in the original Broadway production of *Guys And Dolls* - and then doing it all over again three years later in London. Kaye got his first break when he came first on the Major Bowes Amateur Hour on US radio in 1939. During the late 30s and early 40s he toured as a comedian in vaudeville, and made his London debut in USO shows during World War II. His role in *Guys And Dolls* (1950) was not a leading one, but he was outstanding in numbers such as 'Fugue For Tinhorns', 'The Oldest Established', 'Guys And Dolls', and the rousing 'Sit Down You're Rockin' The Boat'. He had one more big success on Broadway in 1956 as Marryin' Sam in *Li'l Abner*, and subsequently toured in revivals, played nightclubs as a comedian, and appeared on the television series *Love And Marriage* and *My Sister Eileen*. Unlike many stage performers he moved easily into films, and appeared in a variety features including *Guys And Dolls*, *Li'l Abner*, *40 Pounds Of Trouble*, *Cat Ballou* (with Nat King Cole), *Sweet Charity*, *The Cockeyed Cowboys Of Calico County*, *The Dirtiest Girl I Ever Met*, *Six Pack Annie*, and *Who Framed Roger Rabbit?*. The ample figure and sunny disposition he displayed as Nicely-Nicely in 1953 endeared him to London audiences and he made frequent appearances in the UK, including one in the musical *Man Of Magic* in 1956. Eventually he settled in Britain and married Angela Bracewell who came to fame in the 50s in her role as the hostess of the audience participation game 'Beat The Clock' in the television variety show *Sunday Night At The London Palladium*. After appearing in the West End in 1983 in the short-lived musical *Dear Anyone*, Kaye returned to Broadway two years later and won the only good notices in the musical *Grind*, a real disaster which was described by one critic as 'art slaughter'. He continued

to work in the UK and in 1986 starred as Ring Lardner in the radio play *Some Like Them Cold*.
Selected album: *Music For Chubby Lovers* (1962), and Original Cast and film sountrack recordings.

Keel, Howard

b. Harold C. Leek, 13 April 1917, Gillespie, Illinois, USA. After starting his career as a singing waiter in Los Angeles, Keel became an 'in-house entertainer' for the huge Douglas aircraft manufacturing company. In 1945, he appeared in *Carousel* on the west coast and then travelled to the UK to appear in the London production of *Oklahoma!*. At this time he was known as Harold Keel, having reversed the spelling of his last name. Now, he changed his first name and after making a non-singing appearance in the film, *The Small Voice* (1948), he returned to the USA where he landed the role of Frank Butler in the film *Annie Get Your Gun* (1950). He continued to make films, mostly musicals, including *Show Boat* (1951), *Kiss Me Kate* and *Calamity Jane* (both 1953), *Rose Marie* and *Seven Brides For Seven Brothers* (both 1954) and *Kismet* (1955). By the 60s he was touring the US in revivals of popular shows, and appearing in non-musical low-budget western movies. In 1981 his acting career received a boost when he started to appear in the long-running television soap, *Dallas*. This revived interest in his singing, particularly in the UK, and in 1984 he recorded his first solo album. Although untrained, Keel's rich and powerful baritone voice and commanding stage and screen presence made him a good leading actor for musical comedies. In 1993, with his tongue firmly in his cheek, he announced his Farewell Tour of the UK.
Selected albums: *And I Love You So* (1984), *Reminiscing* (1985), *The Collection* (1989), *The Great MGM Stars* (1991), *Close To My Heart* (1991), and the soundtrack albums from the above musicals.

Keeler, Ruby

b. Ethel Keeler, 25 August 1909, Halifax, Nova Scotia, Canada, d. 28 February 1993, Rancho Mirage, California, USA. A charming and petite actress and singer renowned for the Busby Berkeley 'Depression-era' musicals she made with Dick Powell in the 30s, particularly for *42nd Street* in which Warner Baxter barked at her: 'You're going out a youngster but you've got to come back a star.' That is exactly what she did do, some time after taking dance lessons as a child and tap-dancing in the speakeasies of New York while she was still a teenager. In 1927 she danced her way into three Broadway musicals *Bye, Bye Bonnie*, *Lucky*, and *The Sidewalks Of New York*, and Florenz Ziegfeld offered her an important role with Eddie Cantor and Ruth Etting in *Whoopee!*. While the show was being cast she travelled to Hollywood to make a short film, and there met Al Jolson. He followed her back to New York, and they were married in September 1928. At her husband's request, Keeler left *Whoopee!* before it reached Broadway, and for the same reason she only spent a few weeks in *Show Girl* (in which she was billed as Ruby Keeler Jolson). While she was performing in the latter show, Jolson rose from his seat in the stalls and serenaded his wife with a song. For the next few years she stepped out of the spotlight and concentrated on being just Mrs. Jolson. That is, until 1933, when Darryl F. Zanuck at Warner Brothers saw a film test she had made some years before, and signed her for the ingenue role *42nd Street*. All her years of training paid off as she and Dick Powell and those marvellous Busby Berkeley dance routines (coupled with a tremendous Harry Warren and Al Dubin score) made the film a smash hit. Keeler's most memorable moment came with a soft shoe number, 'Shuffle Off To Buffalo', but her demure, sincere personality and fancy footwork delighted audiences throughout the picture. *42nd Street* was followed by more of the same in the form of *Gold Diggers Of 1933*, *Footlight Parade*, *Flirtation Walk*, *Shipmates Forever*, and *Colleen*. In 1934 she and Jolson starred in their only film together, *Go Into Your Dance*. Keeler made her last film for Warners, *Ready Willing And Able* in 1937. It contained what is supposed to be one of her favourite sequences in which she dances with co-star Lee Dixon on the keys of a giant typewriter. After playing a straight dramatic role in *Mother Carey's Chickens* (1938) and appearing in one more musical, *Sweetheart Of The Campus* (1941), she retired from the screen. In between making those two films, she had divorced Jolson in 1940, and, a year later, married John Homer Lowe, a wealthy broker from California, and they raised four children. Apart from making some guest appearances on television during the 50s and 60s, and playing in a brief revival tour of the play *Bell, Book And Candle*, Keeler stayed well away from the public eye until 1970, a year after Lowe died. She was tempted back to Broadway for a revival of the 1925 musical *No, No Nanette*, partly because she was assured that it would not ridicule the old musicals, and also because Busby Berkeley was to be the production supervisor. The show was a triumph, running for 871 performances and winning several Tony Awards. Even after being divorced for 30 years, she still could not shake off the Jolson tag. During the run of *No, No Nanette* she stuck a notice on her dressing room door saying: 'Will Miss Reynolds (her co-star Debbie Reynolds) please note that my name is not Mrs. Al Jolson. My name is Miss Keeler, and I am a Broadway dancer of some note.' US television viewers were reminded of her prowess in 1986 when Ruby Keeler made her last major public appearance in the ABC special *Happy Birthday Hollywood*.

Kelly, Gene

b. Eugene Curran Kelly, 23 August 1912, Pittsburgh,

Pennsylvania, USA. An actor, dancer, singer, choreographer, director, producer, and one of the most innovative and respected figures in the history of the screen musical. Kelly was taking dance lessons at the age of eight - albeit against his will - and excelled at sports when he was at high school. During the Depression he had a variety of jobs, including gymnastics instructor, and, with his brother Fred, performed a song-and-dance act at local nightclubs. In the early 30s, he spent a few months at law school before opening the Gene Kelly Studios of the Dance, and discovering that he had a real aptitude for teaching., which would manifest itself throughout his career in some of the most creative choreography ever seen on the big screen. In 1937 Kelly moved to New York, and gained a small part as a dancer in the musical comedy, *Leave It To Me*, in which Mary Martin also made her Broadway debut. A larger role followed in the revue, *One For The Money*, and he also played Harry, the 'good natured hoofer', in the Pulitzer prize-winning comedy, *The Time Of Your Life*. In 1940, after working in summer stock, and serving as a dance director at Billy Rose's Diamond Horseshoe club, Kelly won the title role in the new Richard Rodgers and Lorenz Hart musical, *Pal Joey*. His portrayal of the devious, unscrupulous nightclub entertainer made him a star overnight in New York, but, after choreographing another Broadway hit show, *Best Foot Forward*, he moved to Hollywood in 1942, and made his screen debut, with Judy Garland, in *For Me And My Gal*. He appeared in two more musicals for MGM, *DuBarry Was A Lady* and *Thousands Cheer*, before the company loaned him to Columbia for *Cover Girl* (1944). Co-starred with Rita Hayworh and Phil Silvers, the film was a major landmark in Kelly's career, and an indication of the heights he would achieve during the next 10 years. It was memorable in many respects, particularly for Kelly's sensitive rendering of Jerome Kern and Ira Gershwin's 'Long Ago And Far Away'; and the 'Alter Ego' dance, during which Kelly danced with his own reflection in a shop window. Back at MGM, he was called upon to play several dramatic roles as well as appearing in *Anchors Aweigh* (1944), for which he received an Oscar nomination for best actor. In the film, as a couple of sailors on leave, Kelly and Frank Sinatra were accompanied by Kathryn Grayson, a Sammy Cahn and Julé Styne score - and Jerry - an animated mouse, who joined Kelly in a live-action/cartoon sequence that is still regarded as a classic of its kind. After spending two years in the real US Navy during World War II, supervising training films, Kelly resumed at MGM with *Ziegfeld Follies* (1946), in which he sang and danced with Fred Astaire for the first time on screen, in 'The Babbitt And The Bromide'. Two years later he was reunited with Judy Garland for *The Pirate*, an somewhat underrated film, with a score by Cole Porter which included 'Be A

Clown'. He then choreographed the 'Slaughter On Tenth Avenue' sequence in the Rodgers And Hart bio-pic, *Words And Music*, in which he danced with Vera-Ellen, before joining Sinatra and Jules Munshin, first for the lively *Take Me Out To The Ball Game* (1949), and again, in the following year, for *On The Town*, 'the most inventive and effervescent movie musical Hollywood had thus far produced'. Although criticized for its truncation of the original Broadway score, *On The Town*, with its integrated music and plot, and the filming of the athletic dance sequences on the streets of New York, was acclaimed from all sides. After his triumph in *On The Town*, Kelly went on to *Summer Stock*, with Judy Garland again, before turning to what many consider to be the jewel in MGM's musical crown - *An American In Paris* (1951). Directed by Vincente Minnelli, and set in an idealised version of Paris, Kelly and his partner, Leslie Caron, dance exquisitely to a Gershwin score which included 'I've Got Rhythm', 'Our Love Is Here To Stay', "S'Wonderful, and 'I'll Build A Stairway To Paradise'. The film ended with a 17 minute ballet sequence, a 'summation of Gene Kelly's work as a film dancer and choreographer, allowing him his full range of style - classical ballet, modern ballet, Cohanesque hoofing, tapping, jitterbugging, and sheer athletic expressionism'. It won eight Academy Awards, including one for best picture. Kelly received a special Oscar 'in appreciation of his versatility as an actor, singer, director, and dancer, and sepecifically for his brilliant achievements in the art of choreography on film'. If *An American In Paris* was MGM's jewel, then *Singin' In The Rain* (1952), was probably its financial plum - arguably the most popular Hollywood musical of them all. Produced by Arthur Freed, who also wrote the songs with Nacio Herb Brown, the film's witty screenplay, by Betty Comden and Adolph Green, dealt with the Hollywood silent movie industry trying to come to terms with talking pictures. Debbie Reynolds and Donald O'Connor joined Kelly in the joyous spoof, and sang and danced to a score which included 'You Were Meant For Me', 'Make 'Em Laugh', 'Good Mornin'', and 'Moses Supposes'. The scene in which Kelly sings the title song, while getting completely drenched, is probably the most requested film clip in the history of the musical cinema.

For *Deep In My Heart* (1955), the Sigmund Romberg bio-pic, Kelly went back to his roots and danced with his younger brother, Fred, in one of the film's highspots, 'I Love To Go Swimmin' With Wimmen'. Kelly's final major musical projects for MGM were *Brigadoon* (1954) and *It's Always Fair Weather* (1955). In the former, 'the magical story of a Scottish village long lost to history and coming to life once every hundred years for a single day', Kelly co-starred with Cyd Charisse and Van Johnson in a production that was criticized for being shot in Cinemascope, and in the studio, rather than on location. For the latter film, Kelly co-starred with Dan Dailey and Phil Silvers for what was essentially a satirical swipe at the cynical commercialism of the US television industry - with music. His next project, *Invitation To The Dance* (1956), with script, choreography, and direction by Kelly, consisted of three unrelated episodes, all entirely danced, with Kelly accompanied by a classically trained troupe. A commercial failure in the USA, it was acclaimed in some parts of Europe, and awarded the grand prize at the West Berlin film festival in 1958. Following its success there, Kelly choreographed a new ballet for the Paris Opera's resident company, and was made a Chevalier of the Legion of Honor by the French government. *Les Girls* (1956) was Kelly's final MGM musical, and Cole Porter's last Hollywood score - the golden era of screen musicals was over. Subsequently, Kelly played several straight roles in films such as *Marjorie Morningstar* and *Inherit The Wind*, but spent much of his time as a director on projects such as Rodgers and Oscar Hammerstein's Broadway musical, *Flower Drum Song*, and 20th Century-Fox's $20,000,000 extravaganza, *Hello Dolly* (1969), which starred Barbra Streisand, Walter Matthau and a young Michael Crawford. In 1974, *That's Entertainment*, 'a nostalgia bash, featuring scenes from nearly 100 MGM musicals', became a surprise hit, and two years later, in *That's Entertainment Part Two*, Kelly and Fred Astaire hosted the inevitable sequel. After viewing all that vintage footage, it would be interesting to know what Kelly really thought about a more modern musical film, such as *Xanadu* (1980), in which he appeared with Olivia Newton-John. By then, together with director Stanley Donen, the complete Arthur Freed Unit , and the rest of the talented personnel who produced mo st of his musicals at MGM, Kelly, with his athletic performance, choreography and direction, had completed a body of work that was only equalled by the other master of dance on film, Fred Astaire - but in a very different style. Whereas Astaire purveyed the smooth, top hat, white tie and tails image, Kelly's 'concept of a cinema dancer was an 'ordinary Joe' in sports shirt, slacks and white socks (to draw attention to the feet)'. As he said himself: 'Astaire represents the aristocracy when he dances - I represent the proletariat!'

Selected albums: *Song And Dance Man* (1954), *Singin' In The Rain Again* (1978), and film soundtracks.

Further reading: *Gene Kelly: A Biography*, Clive Hirschhorn. *The Films Of Gene Kelly*, Tony Thomas. *Gene Kelly*, J. Basinger.

Kern, Jerome

b. 27 January 1885, New York City, New York, USA, d. 11 November 1945. Taught piano by his mother, Kern proved to be a gifted musician with a remarkable ear. While still at junior school he was dabbling with composition and by his mid-teens was simultaneously studying classical music and writing songs in the popular vein. He became a song plugger in New York's Tin Pan Alley and occasionally accompanied leading entertainers of the day. Some of his early songs were picked up by producers of Broadway shows and were also used in London, a city Kern visited first in 1902-3 and thereafter held in great affection. During the next few years Kern became a familiar figure at theatres in London and New York, working on scores and acting as a rehearsal pianist. Throughout this period, Kern was learning his craft as a songwriter and in the 1914 Broadway show, *The Girl From Utah*, originally staged in London, his ability flowered with the song 'They Didn't Believe Me'. A string of musical shows followed, most enjoying only modest success but Kern's talent was growing and theatrical impresarios were fully aware of his potential. In 1917, *Oh, Boy!* opened. The score was by Kern with lyrics by P.G. Wodehouse, with whom Kern had already collaborated. The hit of this show was 'Till The Clouds Roll By'. The following year he wrote 'Bill' for *Oh, Lady! Lady!!*, but the song was dropped in deference to the wishes of the leading lady. During the early 20s Kern was perhaps the most prolific composer on Broadway, with numerous shows to his credit. Among the songs and shows were 'Look For The Silver Lining' from *Sally* (1920) and 'Who?' from *Sunny* (1925). The highlight of Kern's 20s musicals was *Show Boat* (1927), with lyrics by Oscar Hammerstein II. Apart from the earlier song, 'Bill', which he had written with Wodehouse, and which was revived for the new show, the Kern-Hammerstein partnership produced a succession of show-stopping songs: 'Ol' Man River', 'Make Believe', 'Why Do I Love You?', 'Can't Help Lovin' Dat Man' and 'It Still Suits Me'. Subsequent shows for Broadway did not match the enormous success of *Show Boat*, but fine songs were invariably found in every score, among them 'Smoke Gets In Your Eyes' from *Roberta* (1933). When this became a film in 1935, two new songs were added, 'Lovely To Look At' and 'I Won't Dance'. Even one of Kern's most unsuccessful shows, *Very Warm For May* (1939) contained the classic 'All The Things You Are'. From the late 30s Kern had begun to spend more time working on films than on stage productions and by the early 40s this was where most of his energies were spent. Among his film songs were 'The Way You Look Tonight' (lyrics by Dorothy Fields), which won the Oscar for Best Song in 1936, 'A Fine Romance' (again, with Fields), 'Dearly Beloved' (Johnny Mercer), 'Long Ago And Far Away' (Ira Gershwin - an especially beautiful if rarely performed song), 'In Love In Vain' (Leo Robin) and 'The Last Time I Saw Paris' (Hammerstein), the latter won Kern another Oscar in 1940. Having conquered Broadway and Hollywood, Kern now turned to writing music for the concert platform, writing a classical suite based upon his music for *Show Boat* and a suite entitled 'Mark Twain: A Portrait For Orchestra'. He was discussing the possibility of a new Broadway show, *Annie Get Your Gun*, when he collapsed and died in November 1945. An outstanding songwriter with an ability to find beautiful lilting melodies with deceptive ease, Kern's work has remained popular with singers and jazz musicians. Half a century after his last great songs were written, his music remains fresh and undated. There are several compilations of Kern's music, performed by various artists currently available.

Kid From Spain, The

One of the most lavish and successful musicals of the early 30s, and 'the kid' in question was, of course, the irrepressible Eddie Cantor. On this hilarious occasion, while on the run from the US Federal authorities, he winds up in Spain where, through no fault of his own, he is somehow mistaken for a famous bullfighter. His efforts to justify this exalted position - actually in the bullring - are delightful to see. Robert Young and Lyda Roberti gave him all the support they could, and the rest of the cast included Ruth Hall, John Miljan, Noah Beery, and J. Carrol Naish. Soon-to-be-familiar faces in the chorus were those of Betty Grable and Paulette Goddard. Cantor's most engaging vocal

moment came with 'What a Perfect Combination' (Bert Kalmar-Irving Caesar [lyric]; Harry Ruby-Harry Askst [music]), and Ruby and Kalmar also contributed 'The College Song', 'Look What You've Done', and 'In The Moonlight'. The two songwriters also wrote the screenplay in collaboration with William Anthony McGuire. Busby Berkeley was the choreographer so the dance sequences were imaginative and high-class, and Samuel Goldwyn produced the film so the Goldwyn Girls were present - and pretty. Leon McCarey was responsible for directing a kind of musical and comedy masterpiece.

Kid Millions

In fact, all of $77 millions - that is the sum the naive kid from Brooklyn (Eddie Cantor) inherits from his archaeologist father early on in this 1934 Samuel Goldwyn picture (released by United Artists). Naturally, as soon as the word gets around regarding his windfall, several unsavoury individuals come crawling out of the woodwork - or rather, the stonework, as in this case the loot is hidden somewhere in Egypt. Arthur Sheekman, Nat Perrin, and Nunnally Johnson wrote the screenplay, but it was all academic anyway, because, as usual with a Cantor vehicle, its Eddie's infectious humour and a batch of peppy numbers that propel the film along. A talented

Kid Millions

supporting cast helps as well, and in this case, Ann Sothern, Ethel Merman, George Murphy, Jesse Block, Warren Hymer, the Nicholas Brothers and Eve Sully, along with Goldwyn girls Lucille Ball and Paulette Goddard, more than filled the bill. Cantor managed to don his traditional blackface for some of the time, and he had four splendid songs, 'When My Ship Comes In' and 'Okay Toots' (both Walter Donaldson-Gus Kahn), 'I Want To Be A Minstrel Man' (Burton Lane-Harold Adamson) featuring the marvellous dancing Nicholas Brothers, and 'Mandy' (Irving Berlin). Merman was thrilling on 'An Earful Of Music' (Donaldson-Kahn), and Murphy and Sothern tender on 'Your Head On My Shoulder' (Lane-Adamson). Cantor, Merman, Hymer, and the Goldwyn Girls were all involved in the spectacular 'Ice Cream Fantasy' finale which was filmed in Technicolor. Seymour Felix was the choreographer, and *Kid Millions* was directed by Roy Del Ruth.

Kidd, Michael

b. Milton Greenwald, 12 August 1919, New York City, New York, USA. An important choreographer and director who pioneered a joyful and energetic style of dancing. Kidd was a soloist with the Ballet Theatre (later called the American Ballet Theatre) before making his Broadway debut as choreographer with *Finian's Rainbow* in 1947. He won a Tony Award for his work on that show, and earned four more during the 50s for *Guys And Dolls* (1950), *Can-Can* (1953), *Li'l Abner* (1956), and *Destry Rides Again* (1959). His other shows around that time were *Hold It*, *Love Life*, and *Arms And The Girl*. From *Li'l Abner* onwards he also directed, and sometimes produced, most of the shows on which he worked, but it was as a choreographer of apparently limitless invention that he dominated the Broadway musical during the 50s. In the 60s and early 70s he worked on productions such as *Wildcat*, *Subways Are For Sleeping*, *Here's Love*, *Ben Franklin In Paris*, *Skyscraper*, *Breakfast At Tiffany's* (which closed during previews), *The Rothschilds* (1970), *Cyrano*, and a revival of *Good News* (1974). Kidd also filled the big screen with his brilliant and exuberant dance sequences in classic Hollywood musicals such as *The Band Wagon*, *Seven Brides For Seven Brothers*, *It's Always Fair Weather*, and *Hello, Dolly!*. He also co-starred with Gene Kelly and Dan Dailey in *It's Always Fair Weather*, and appeared in several other films including *Movie Movie*, an affectionate parody of a typical 30s double-feature which went largely unappreciated in 1979.

Kids From *Fame*

In 1980, British film director Alan Parker made his Hollywood debut with a movie about the New York City High School for Performing Arts called *Fame*. The movie did not make that much of an impression at the box office, but American television network NBC bought the rights and developed the original idea into a weekly serial. The series was originally dropped in the USA, but subsequently hit the top of the ratings in the UK and further episodes were produced. In the UK, the success crossed over to the record industry where a soundtrack album of songs from the first series was compiled. Written by top writers such as Rick Springfield, Gary Portnoy and Carole Bayer Sager, the series produced five top-selling albums, and three Top 20 singles, including the US number 4/UK number 1 hit, 'Fame' for Irene Cara. Each song was sung by a different cast member and backed by top session musicians. The series ran for a couple of years before UK interest declined. The series turned out to be a showcase for many aspiring young actors.
Albums: *Kids From Fame* (1982), *Kids From Fame, Again* (1982), *Kids From Fame, Live* (1983), *Kids From Fame, Songs* (1983), *Kids From Fame, Sing For You* (1983). Compilation: *Best Of Fame* (1984).

King And I, The

Yul Brynner became a legend in the 1951 Broadway show, and no other actor could have even been considered for the leading role in this 1956 screen version. Brynner's stage partner, Gertrude Lawrence, died during the Broadway run, and his co-star for this film, the British actress Deborah Kerr, proved to be an ideal replacement. She plays Anna, the widowed English governess, who is engaged by King Mongkut of Siam (Brynner) to educate his many children. In spite of their fundamental differences and principles, they fall in love, but are parted by the King's death. The film's other love story is that between one of the King's daughter's, Tuptim (Rita Moreno) and Lun Tha (Carlos Rivas), but that romance, too, is destined to end unhappily. Other parts were taken by Martin Balsam, Rex Thompson, Terry Saunders, Alan Mowbray, Patrick Adiarte, Yuriko, Michiko, Geoffrey Toone, and Charles Irwin. The highly emotional story was complemented by Richard Rodgers and Oscar Hammerstein II's magnificent score, which included 'I Whistle A Happy Tune' (Kerr), 'March Of The Siamese Children' (instrumental), 'Hello, Young Lovers' (Kerr), 'A Puzzlement' (Brynner), 'Getting To Know You' (Kerr with the children), 'We Kiss In A Shadow' (Moreno-Rivas), 'Something Wonderful' (Saunders), 'The Small House Of Uncle Thomas' (ballet), and 'Song Of The King' (Brynner). Perhaps the film's most memorable moment came when Anna tried to teach the King how to dance, and they - awkwardly at first - and then exuberantly whirled around the floor to the sublime 'Shall We Dance?'. Deborah Kerr's singing voice was dubbed by Marni Nixon. Ernest Lehman's screenplay was based on Hammerstein's original libretto and Margaret Landon's novel *Anna And The King Of Siam*. Jerome

Robbins was the choreographer and the film, which was directed by Walter Land, was superbly photographed by Leon Shamroy in DeLuxe Color and CinemaScope. It won Oscars for best actor (Brynner), its sumptuous costumes (Irene Shariff), sound recording, art-set decoration, and scoring of a musical picture (Alfred Newman and Ken Darby), and went on to gross well over $8 million in the USA, ranking high in the Top 10 musical films of the 50s.

King Creole

This 1958 film is, for many, the best of Elvis Presley's Hollywood career. Based on the Harold Robbins' novel, *A Stone For Danny Fisher*, it afforded him a first-rate plot - that of a singer performing in a New Orleans club owned by mobsters - providing Elvis with a dramatic role equal to the memorable soundtrack. 'Trouble', 'Crawfish' and the title track itself rank among the finest tracks he recorded and the content ranged from compulsive rock 'n' roll numbers to melodic ballads. Presley's singing is self-assured yet unmannered and only his induction into the US Army derailed the direction both his acting and musical were taking.

King Of Jazz

The title of this lavish and spectacular musical revue which was released by Universal in 1930 refers, of course, to Paul Whiteman, who led the most popular orchestra of his time. Although not a jazzman himself, he did promote that brand of music by employing many fine jazz musicians over the years, such as Joe Venuti, Eddie Lang, and Frankie Trumbauer. That trio are all featured prominently in this film along with Whiteman's most famous vocalist, Bing Crosby and his fellow Rhythm Boys Harry Barris and Al Rinker, plus a host of other artists including John Boles, Jeannie Lang, the Brox Sisters, William Kent, Grace Hayes, Stanley Smith, Jeanette Loff, Walter Brennan, Laura La Plante, and Slim Summerville. Inevitably the spotlight is very firmly on Paul Whiteman And His Orchestra throughout, from the opening 'Rhapsody In Blue' (George Gershwin), during which the entire orchestra seated inside - and at the keyboard - of a gigantic grand piano, through to the breathtaking finalé when, beginning with 'D'Ye Ken John Peel' and 'Santa Lucia', the music from various countries around the world is symbolically blended together in 'The Melting Pot Of Music'. In between those two amazing sequences, and introduced every time by a caption card giving song title and performer details, were well over 50 musical items ranging from folk and classical pieces to popular songs such as 'Mississippi Mud' (Harry Barris-James Cavanaugh), 'It Happened In Monterey' (Mabel Wayne-Billy Rose), 'So The Bluebirds And The Blackbirds Got Together' (Barris-Billy Moll), 'Ragamuffin Romeo' (Wayne-Harry DeCosta); and

'A Bench In The Park', 'Happy Feet', 'Music Hath Charms', and 'Song Of The Dawn' (all by Milton Ager and Jack Yellen). As well as conducting the orchestra, Whiteman appeared at other times in a variety of costumes (including baby clothes, complete with feeding bottle), mugging to the camera and looking not unlike Oliver Hardy *sans* Stan Laurel. Russell Markert staged the dances, and the sketches were written by John Murray Anderson who had enjoyed a great deal of success on Broadway with several editions of the *Greenwich Village Follies*, and his own *John Murray Anderson's Almanac*. He was also the director, the man responsible for assembling this whole marvellously original concept, parts of which eventually influenced many a future screen musical. Hal Mohr, Jerome Ash and Ray Rennahan photographed the film in two-colour Technicolor which gave the film a charm of its own, and contributed to the desire to watch it over again, if only to catch some of the details and bits of business missed the first time around.

Kirkwood, Pat

b. 24 February 1921, Manchester, England. An actress and singer; one of the premier leading ladies of 40s and 50s West End musicals, British films, and Christmas pantomimes. Her frequent appearances in the latter medium earned her the title of 'the greatest principal boy of the Century', and the critic Kenneth Tynan called her legs 'the eighth wonder of the world'. She started her career at the age of 14 at the Salford Hippodrome, and a year later appeared in pantomime in Cardiff. When she was 16 she made her West End debut as Dandini in *Cinderella* at London's Princes' Theatre. In 1939 at the age of only 18, Pat Kirkwood headlined the revue *Black Velvet* at the London Hippodrome and sang a sizzling version of 'My Heart Belongs To Daddy', a song that is forever identified with her. Further West End successes followed, including *Top Of The World* (1940), *Lady Behave* (1941), *Let's Face It!* (1942), *Starlight Roof* (1947), *Ace Of Clubs* (1950) (in which she introduced Noël Coward's witty song 'Chase Me Charlie'), *Fancy Free* (1951), *Wonderful Town* (1955), and *Chrysanthemum* (1956). It was while she was appearing in *Starlight Roof* (in which the 12-years-old Julie Andrews made her West End debut) that Kirkwood was introduced to Prince Philip, consort of Queen Elizabeth, by her boyfriend, the fashion photographer Baron. Rumours that they had an affair - always strenuously denied by the actress - continue to surface even in the 90s. Her film career began in 1938 with *Save A Little Sunshine*, and continued with *Me And My Pal* (1939), *Band Waggon* (with Arthur Askey and Richard Murdoch) (1939), *Come On George* (with George Formby) (1939), *Flight From Folly* (1944), *No Leave, No Love* (made in America with Van Johnson) (1946), *Once A Sinner* (1950), *Stars In Your Eyes*

(1956), and *After The Ball* (1957). Miss Kirkwood also appeared in several Royal Command Performances, in cabaret, and on radio and television. On the small screen during the 50s she portrayed the renowned musical hall performers Marie Loyd in *All Our Yesterdays* and *Our Marie*; and Vesta Tilley in *The Great Little Tilley*. Two years after her second husband wealthy Greek-Russian ship-owner Spiro de Spero died in 1954, she married the actor-broadcaster-songwriter ('Maybe It's Because I'm A Londoner', 'I'm Going To Get Lit Up') Hubert Gregg. They were divorced in 1976, and Kirkwood went to live in Portugal for four years where she met the solicitor Peter Knight who subsequently became her fourth husband. They retired to Yorkshire, where Pat Kirkwood consistently turned down offers to return to the stage. Even Cameron Mackintosh was unable to tempt her with the prime role of Carlotta Campion in the 1987 London production of *Follies*. Eventually, however, she did emerge into the spotlight again with her own show, *Glamorous Nights Of Music*, which opened to excellent reviews at the Wimbledon Theatre in the outskirts of London in April 1993.

Kismet

This opulent but unsatisfying adaptation of the hit Broadway musical reached the screen in 1955, courtesy of Arthur Freed's renowned MGM production unit. Although the show's librettists, Charles Lederer and Luther Davis, were entrusted with the screenplay, much of the magic in this Arabian Nights saga somehow got lost in the transfer. For some strange reason, Alfred Drake, who had enjoyed such a triumph in the stage production, was replaced by Howard Keel. He plays the public poet-turned beggar Hajj who lives on the streets of old Baghdad, and embarks on a hectic day-long adventure during which his daughter (Ann Blyth) gets married to the young Caliph (Vic Damone), while he runs off with the lovely Lalume (Dolores Gray) after getting rid of her husband, the evil Wazir (Sebastian Cabot). Robert Wright and George Forrest's majestic score was based on themes by Alexander Borodin, and there were several memorable songs in the score which included 'Baubles, Bangles, And Beads', 'The Olive Tree', 'Stranger In Paradise', 'And This Is My Beloved', 'Not Since Ninevah', 'Fate', 'Bored', 'Sands Of Time', 'Night Of My Nights', 'Rhymes Have I', and 'Gesticulate'. While perhaps regretting the absence of Drake (he only ever made one film), there is no doubt that Keel was in fine voice and he made an adequate substitute. Also taking part were Jay C. Flippen, Monty Woolley, Jack Elam, Ted De Corsia, and Aaron Spelling. Jack Cole was the choreographer,

Kiss Me Kate

and the film was directed by Vincente Minnelli. Whatever its faults, the film did at least look beautiful, owing in no small part to the Eastman Color and Cinemascope photography of Joseph Ruttenberg. The source of *Kismet* - the 1911 play by Edward Knoblock - has also been adapted into three other, non-musical films, in 1920, 1930 and 1944.

Kiss Me Kate

This film had most of the elements of a great screen musical - an outstanding score, a witty screenplay, and a fine cast. The original Broadway show from which it was adapted is generally considered to be Cole Porter's masterpiece, and this 1953 version only served to emphasise and reaffirm that view. The story of thespians Fred Graham (Howard Keel) and his ex-spouse, Lilli Vanessi (Kathryn Grayson), who allow their on-stage conflict in an out-of-town production of *The Taming Of The Shrew* to spill over into their own tempestuous private lives, was both hilarious and musically thrilling. The dance sequences, which were choreographed by Hermes Pan and his assistant Bob Fosse, were stunning, involving as they did, high class hoofers such as Ann Miller, Bobby Van, Tommy Rall, and Carol Haney. Most observers cite Miller's scintillating 'Too Darn Hot' as the film's highspot, but all the songs were performed memorably, including 'I Hate Men' (Grayson), 'So In Love', 'Wunderbar', and 'Kiss Me Kate' (Grayson-Keel), 'I've Come To Wive It Wealthily Ir Padua', 'Were Thine That Special Face', and 'Where Is The Life That Late I Led?' (Keel), 'Always True To You In My Fashion' and 'Why Can't You Behave? (Miller-Rall), 'We Open In Venice' (Keel-Grayson-Miller-Rall), and 'From This Moment On' (Miller-Rall-Haney-Van-Fosse-Jeannie Coyne). One other item, which would have stopped the show every night if it had been performed in a similar fashion on stage, was 'Brush Up Your Shakespeare', in which James Whitmore and Keenan Wynn, as a couple of affable debt-collecting gangsters, mangle the Bard courtesy of Porter in such as 'If your blonde won't respond when you flatter 'er/Tell her what Tony told Cleopaterer'. George Sidney directed, and the film was photographed in Ansco Color. Dorothy Kingsley's screenplay was based on Bella and Sam Spewack's original libretto. Some sequences appeared slightly puzzling and unnerving - even unnatural - until it was realised that certain effects, such as characters throwing articles towards the camera, were inserted to take advantage of the 3D process in which the film was originally shot.

Kiss The Boys Goodbye

Screen adaptations of Broadway plays and musicals generally make alterations to the story which are considered to be desirable. In this case one of the changes at least was essential, because the central topic of Clare Booth's 1938 play *Kiss The Boys Goodbye* was

the all-consuming question of who was going to play the role of Scarlett in the film of *Gone With The Wind*. So, three years later, that had to go, and along with it went a lot of the play's bite and satire. What was left turned out to be a more or less conventional backstage story in which Broadway producer Don Ameche falls for chorus girl Mary Martin. She introduced most of Frank Loesser and Victor Schertzinger's songs, including 'I'll Never Let A Day Pass By', 'That's How I Got My Start', and the lively title song, but Connee Boswell provided the film's musical highlight with her sultry rendering of 'Sand In My Shoes'. Oscar Levant, who invariably raised the laughter (and musical) quota of any film in which he appeared, was in the supporting cast, along with Eddie (Rochester) Anderson, Raymond Walburn, Virginia Dale, Barbara Jo Allen, and Elizabeth Patterson. Harry Tugend and Dwight Taylor wrote the amusing screenplay, and the film was directed by Victor Schertzinger.

Kissing Bandit, The

Frank Sinatra himself is among the many (including his friend Dean Martin) who have been known to mock this 1948 MGM release in which he co-starred (yet again) with Kathryn Grayson. At least on this occasion Grayson was not trying to make it to the top as an operatic singer - that would have been rather difficult anyway because the setting for Isobel Lennart and John Briard Harding's screenplay was way out west in old California. Sinatra, with long hair and even longer sideburns, was in the middle of his early 'shy' period (*Anchors Aweigh*, *Step Lively*, *It Happened In Brooklyn*, *On The Town*). He played the young and retiring son of an infamous womanizing bandit who is reluctantly forced to follow in his father's footsteps. Two of the screen's favourite dancing ladies, Ann Miller and Cyd Charisse, were also in the cast, along with Ricardo Montalban, J. Carrol Naish, Mildred Natwick, Billy Gilbert, Mikhail Rasumny, and Clinton Sundberg. Most of the songs, by Nacio Herb Brown, Earl K. Brent and Edward Heyman were romantic ballads tailored for Sinatra, such as 'Siesta', 'If I Steal A Kiss', 'Senorita', 'What's Wrong With Me?', but things livened up a lot when Charisse, Miller and Montalban got together for the scintillating 'Dance Of Fury'. Grayson had the best song, 'Love Is Where You Find It' (Brown-Brent). Laszlo Benedek directed this Technicolor flop which gave no indication whatsoever that Sinatra was just a few years away from the sophisticated comedy of *The Tender Trap*, and an Oscar-winning performance in *From Here To Eternity*.

Korngold, Erich Wolfgang

b. 29 May 1897, Brno (Brunn), Czechoslovakia, d. 29 November 1957, Hollywood, California, USA. An important composer, conductor and arranger for films, from the mid-30s into the 50s. Korngold was a child prodigy, and, in his teens, wrote short operas, such as

The Ring Of Polycrates and Violant. He performed as a pianist in concerts, and was the resident conductor at the Hamburg Opera House for several years. He also re-scored vintage operetta classics, giving them a new lease of life. During the 20s, his own operatic compositions, including Die Tote Stadt (The Dead City), and The Miracle Of Heliane, played European opera houses, and his enormous popularity on that continent led him to move to the USA in 1934, where he subsequently became an American citizen in 1943. In 1935, he worked on the first of a series of films for Warner Brothers Studio, when he adapted Mendelssohn's music for the highly regarded film A Midsummer Night's Dream, starring Dick Powell and James Cagney. In the same year, he composed the score for Captain Blood, the movie that made Errol Flynn a star. Such was his prestige, Korngold was able to pick and choose which movies he cared to work on. During the 30s, his film scores included Give Us This Night, Anthony Adverse, for which Korngold won his first Academy Award (1936), The Green Pastures, The Prince And The Pauper, Another Dawn, Of Human Bondage, The Adventure Of Robin Hood, (another Oscar for Korngold), Juarez and The Private Lives Of Elizabeth And Essex. In 1940, Korngold composed some of his most stirring music for Sea Hawk, his last for an historical adventure, and was nominated for another Academy Award. His other scores during the 40s included Sea Wolf, King's Row, The Constant Nymph, Between Two Worlds, Devotion, Deception and Escape Me Never (1947). In 1944, he conducted and adapted Offenbach's music for the Broadway show, Helen Goes To Troy, and added a few things of his own. In the late 40s, Korngold became disenamoured with movies, and turned again to classical composing. These included 'Piano Sonata In E', 'Violin Concerto In D', 'Piano Trio', and 'Piano Concerto For The Left Hand', and the opera, Die Kathrin, which flopped in Vienna in 1950. He returned to films in 1955 with his score for the 'uninspired' Richard Wagner bio-pic, The Magic Fire, but died two years later in 1957. In spite of his relatively small output, he is still regarded as the leader of his craft. Recordings include: Elizabeth And Essex and The Sea Hawk, both played by the National Philharmonic Orchestra, and Music Of Erich Wolfgang Korngold, conducted by Lionel Newman. Further reading: Erich Wolfgang Korngold by R.S. Hoffman, and Erich Wolfgang Korngold: Ein Lebensbild by L. Korngold.

Kristofferson, Kris

b. 22 June 1936, Brownsville, Texas USA. Kristofferson, a key figure in the 'New Nashville' of the 70s, began his singing career in Europe. While studying at Oxford University in 1958 he briefly performed for impresario Larry Parnes as Kris Carson while for five years he sang and played at US Army bases in Germany. As Captain Kristofferson, he left the army in 1965 to concentrate on songwriting. He worked as a cleaner at the CBS studios in Nashville, until Jerry Lee Lewis became the first to record one of his songs, 'Once More With Feeling'. Johnny Cash soon became a champion of Kristofferson's work and it was he who persuaded Roger Miller to record 'Me And Bobby McGee' (co-written with Fred Foster) in 1969. With its atmospheric opening, 'Busted flat in Baton Rouge, waiting for a train/feeling nearly faded as my jeans', the bluesy song was a country hit and became a rock standard in the melodramatic style by Janis Joplin and the Grateful Dead. Another classic among Kristofferson's early songs was 'Sunday Morning Coming Down', which Cash recorded. In 1970, Kristofferson appeared at the Isle of Wight pop festival while Sammi Smith was charting with the second of his major compositions, the passionate 'Help Me Make It Through The Night', which later crossed over to the pop and R&B audiences in Gladys Knight's version. Knight was also among the numerous artists who covered the tender 'For The Good Times', a huge country hit for Ray Price, while 'One Day At A Time' was a UK number 1 for Lena Martell in 1979. Kristofferson's own hits began with 'Loving Her Was Easier (Than Anything I'll Ever Do Again)' and 'Why Me', a ballad which was frequently performed in concert by Elvis Presley. In 1973, Kristofferson married singer Rita Coolidge and recorded three albums with her before their divorce six years later.

Kristofferson had made his film debut in Cisco Pike (1971) and also appeared with Bob Dylan in Pat Garrett And Billy The Kid, but he achieved movie stardom when he acted opposite Barbra Streisand in a 1976 re-make of the 1937 picture A Star Is Born. For the next few years he concentrated on his film career but returned to country music with The Winning Hand, which featured duets with Brenda Lee, Dolly Parton and Willie Nelson. A further collaboration, Highwaymen, (with Nelson, Cash and Waylon Jennings) headed the country chart in 1985. The four musicians subsequently toured as the Highwaymen and issued a second collaborative album in 1991. A campaigner for radical causes, Kristofferson starred in the post-nuclear television drama Amerika (1987) and came up with hard-hitting political commentaries on Third World Warrior. Kristofferson compared and performed at the Bob Dylan Tribute Concert in 1992, during which he gave Sinead O'Conner a sympathetic shoulder to cry on after she was booed off stage.

Albums: Kristofferson (1970), The Silver-Tongued Devil And I (1971), Me And Bobby McGee (1971), Border Lord (1972), Jesus Was A Capricorn (1972), with Rita Coolidge Full Moon (1973), Spooky Lady's Sideshow (1974), with Coolidge Breakaway (1974), Who's To Bless...And Who's To Blame (1975), Surreal Thing (1976), five tracks on A Star Is Born (1976, film soundtrack), Easter Island (1977), with Coolidge

Natural Act (1979), *The Winning Hand* (1983), with Willie Nelson *Music From Songwriter* (1984, film soundtrack), with Nelson, Johnny Cash, Waylon Jennings *Highwaymen* (1985), *Repossessed* (1986), *Third World Warrior* (1990), with Nelson, Cash, Jennings *Highwaymen II* (1991). Compilations: *Songs Of Kristofferson* (1977), *Country Store* (1988).

Kyser, Kay

b. James King Kern Kyser, 18 June 1906, Rocky Mount, North Carolina, USA, d. 23 July 1985, Chapel Hill, North Carolina, USA. A popular bandleader in the USA during the 30s and 40s, Kyser was born into an academically excellent family, and he too became a 'professor', though hardly in the conventional sense. Whilst at high school he developed a flair for showmanship, and entered the University of North Carolina in 1924 with the intention of studying law. The subject was soon discarded in favour of music, and Kyser took over the leadership of the campus band from Hal Kemp when Kemp departed to form one of the most popular 'sweet' bands of the 30s. Kyser was soon on the road himself, and in 1927 he recruited George Duning, a graduate of the Cincinnati Conservatory of Music, as the chief arranger of what was originally a jazz unit. This turned out to be a smart move, because Kyser could not read or write a note of music. Duning stayed with the Kyser band for most of its life, before going on to write films scores as diverse as *Jolson Sings Again* and *Picnic*. By 1933, when Kyser played the Miramar Hotel in Santa Monica, California, the band had developed a 'sweeter' style, and had become a major attraction. Kyser, the showman, also injected several gimmicks. For example, instead of a having a spoken introduction to a song, the vocalist would *sing* the title at the beginning of each number; and later, just before the vocal chorus, the band would play a few bars of its theme, Walter Donaldson's 'Thinking Of You', while Kyser announced the singer's name. It was simple, but highly effective. In the following year, Kyser took over from Hal Kemp yet again, this time at the Blackhawk Restaurant in Chicago. The band's sell-out performances at the venue were supplemented by regular radio broadcasts, and so the renowned *Kay Kyser's Kollege Of Musical Knowledge* was born. It was a zany, comedy quiz programme in which the Blackhawk's patrons' skill in identifying song titles was rewarded with prizes (there were rarely any losers). NBC's networked airings brought Kyser (by then known as the 'old perfesser'), national recognition, and in the late 30s he and the band had several hit records, including 'Did You Mean It?', 'Cry, Baby, Cry', 'Music, Maestro, Please!', 'Ya Got Me', 'Two Sleepy People', 'I Promise You', 'Cuckoo In The Clock', 'The Tinkle Song', 'The Little Red Fox', 'The Umbrella Man', 'Three Little Fishies', and 'Stairway To The Stars'. Throughout its life, Kyser's

band had a string of popular vocalists, including Harry Babbitt, Ginny Simms, Sully Mason, Gloria Wood, Julie Conway, Trudy Erwin, Dorothy Dunn, Lucy Ann Polk, and Ish Kabibble. The latter name was a pseudonym for trumpeter Merwyn Bogue (d. 5 June 1994, Joshua Tree, California, USA), and he featured on most of the band's many novelty numbers, and in their series of comedy films which included *That's Right, You're Wrong* (1939), *You'll Find Out*, *Playmates*, *My Favorite Spy*, *Around The World*, *Swing Fever*, and *Carolina Blues* (1944). Mike Douglas, who later became a popular television talk show host, also sang with the band in the 40s, and for a few months in the 50s. In the early 40s, the recruitment of Van Alexander, who had arranged the Chick Webb-Ella Fitzgerald recording of 'A-Tisket A-Tasket', coincided with a critical reappraisal of Kyser's musical output. As well as winning polls in the 'corn' category, the band came to be regarded as a genuine swing unit that also had a way with a ballad. During World War II, Kyser toured extensively for the USO, entertaining troops in over 500 service camps and hospitals over a wide area. In 1944, he married the blonde Hollywood model, Georgia Carroll, who had decorated such movies as *Ziegfeld Girl* and *Du Barry Was A Lady*. She was a singer, too, and provided the vocals on one of the band's 1945 hits, 'There Goes That Song Again'. Throughout the decade Kyser band was almost permanently in the US Top 20 with a variety of titles such as 'You, You, Darlin'', 'Playmates', 'With The Wind And The Rain In Your Hair', 'Friendship', 'Blue Love Bird', 'Tennessee Fish Fry', 'Who's Yehoodi?', 'Blueberry Hill', 'Ferryboat Serenade', 'You Got Me This Way'. 'Alexander The Swoose (Half Swan, Half Goose)', '(Lights Out) 'Til Reveille', 'Why Don't We Do This More Often?', '(There'll Be Bluebirds Over) The White Cliffs Of Dover', 'A Zoot Suit (For My Sunday Girl)', 'Who Wouldn't Love You', 'Johnny Doughboy Found A Rose In Ireland', 'Got The Moon In My Pocket', 'Jingle, Jangle, Jingle', 'He Wears A Pair Of Silver Wings', 'Strip Polka', 'Ev'ry Night About This Time', 'Praise The Lord And Pass The Ammunition' (the band's biggest hit), 'Can't Get Of This Mood', 'Let's Get Lost', 'Bell Bottom Trousers', 'One-Zy, Two-Zy (I Love You-Zy)', 'Ole Buttermilk Sky', 'The Old Lamp-Lighter', 'Huggin' And Chalkin'', 'Managua, Nicaragua', 'Woody Woodpecker', and 'Slow Boat To China' (1948). During that period *The Kollege Of Musical Knowledge* continued to delight and amuse American radio audiences who knew that when Kyser welcomed them with: 'Evenin' Folks. How y'all?', in that strong southern accent, he was dressed in his professor's white gown and mortarboard, 'jumping, cavorting, mugging, and waving his arms like a dervish', just for the benefit of the few in the studio. In 1949, while the show was still high in the ratings, it was unexpectedly cancelled by the sponsors, and

Kyser switched the concept to television, but it made little impact. By 1951 he had lost interest, and retired to North Carolina a wealthy man. He devoted the rest of his life to Christian Science, a subject in which he was an authorised practitioner, and died in July 1985. Selected albums: *Greatest Hits* (c.50s), *Dance Date* (c.80s).

L

L'Aventure Du Jazz

An outstanding documentary produced and directed by Louis and Claudine Panassie, this film features numerous leading mainstream musicians. Amongst the artists on view are Eddie Barefield, Buck Clayton, William 'Cozy' Cole, Jimmy Crawford, Vic Dickenson, Sister Rosetta Tharpe, Milt Hinton, Pat Jenkins, Budd Johnson, Jo Jones, Eli Robinson, Zutty Singleton, Willie 'The Lion' Smith, Tiny Grimes, Buddy Tate and Dick Vance. Also on hand are blues singers John Lee Hooker and Memphis Slim and the exciting dance team, Lou Parks' Lindy Hoppers. Rarely seen, this film is a major achievement and worth a place on the shelf of any collector lucky enough to come across a copy. Soundtrack excerpts were issued as a double album on the Jazz Odyssey label. (80 mins) (1969/70)

Lady And The Tramp (see Disney, Walt)

Lady Is A Square, The

This was Britain's high-kicking 50s heart-throb Frankie Vaughan's third picture - and his first musical. He played Johnny Burns, a pop singer who poses as a butler in the service of a hard-up society lady Frances Baring (Anna Neagle), and secretly helps her to prolong the life of her husband's symphony orchestra. Janette Scott plays the dutiful daughter, and other roles went to Anthony Newley, Wilfred Hyde White, Ted Lune, Christopher Rhodes, Kenneth Cope, and Josephine Fitzgerald. Vaughan sang the lovely Ray Noble ballad, 'Love Is The Sweetest Thing', as well as the more contemporary 'The Lady Is A Square' (Raymond Dutch-Johnny Franz), 'That's My Doll' (Dick Glasser-Ann Hall), and 'Honey Bunny Baby'. The last number is credited to 'Frank Able', which sounds suspiciously like an abridged version of Vaughan's real name of Frank Abelson. Harold Purcell, Pamela Bower and Nicholas Phipps adapted the screenplay from a story by Purcell, and the director was Herbert Wilcox. He and his wife, Anna Neagle, produced the picture in 1959 for Everest Films in the UK.

Lady Sings The Blues

Roundly criticized at the time of its release in 1972 (in some instances before it was even seen), this bio-pic purports to tell the life story of Billie Holiday. Loosely based upon Lady Day's autobiography, which was itself only linked tenuously with reality, the film misses the essential tragedy while simultaneously failing to establish the young Holiday's often over-exuberant love of life. Instead, the film settles for gloomy melodrama. One of the men in Holiday's later life was on hand in an advisory capacity and, predictably, the plot line suffered as axes were ground and excuses made. Most of the initial critical flak came from the casting of Diana Ross in the lead (the production originated with Motown to whom Ross was contracted). In fact, Ross's performance was very good and she was nominated for an Oscar in this, her first acting role. Ross also drastically altered her singing style to leave behind her Tamla/Motown origins and move towards jazz. Of course, she did not sound at all like Holiday but, wisely, that was never her intention.

Lai, Francis

b. 1932, Nice, France. A composer and conductor for films from the early 60s. After scoring *Circle Of Love*, Roger Vadim's re-make of Ophuls' classic *La Ronde*, starring Jane Fonda, Lai won an Academy Award for his music to director Claud Lelouch's classic love story *A Man And A Woman* (1966). He also scored Lelouch's follow-up, *Live For Life*, before going on to something lighter with the comedy-drama, *I'll Never Forget What's 'Is Name*; followed by others in the late 60s such as *Three Into Two Won't Go*, *Mayerling* and *Hannibal Brooks*. In 1970, Lai won his second Oscar for *Love Story*, one of the most popular movies of the decade. The soundtrack album stayed at number 2 in the US album chart for six weeks, and the film's theme, 'Where Do I Begin?' (lyric by Carl Sigman), was a singles hit in the USA for Andy Williams, Henry Mancini and Lai himself; and in the UK for Williams and Shirley Bassey. In the same year, Lai, with his Orchestra, had a big hit in Japan with the title music for the film *Le Passager De La Pluie (Rider Of The Rain)*. During the 70s, Lai's cosmopolitan career included several more films for Lelouch, such as *The Crook, Money, Money, Money, Happy New Year, Cat And Mouse, Child Under A Leaf, Emannuelle II* and *Another Man, Another Chance*; and others, such as . . . *And Hope To Die, Visit To A Chief's Son, And Now My Love, International Velvet* and the sequel to *Love Story, Oliver's Story* (1979) (music written with Lee Holdridge). In the 80s and early 90s the majority of

Lady Sings The Blues (Diana Ross)

Lai's music continued to be for French productions, and the Lelouch connection was maintained through films such as *Bolero* (in conjunction with Michel LeGrand), *Edith And Marcel, Bandits, La Belle Histoire (The Beautiful Story)* (co-composer Philippe Servain) and *Les Cles Du Paradis (The Keys To Paradise)* (1992). His work for other directors included *Beyond The Reef, Marie; A Man And A Woman: 20 Years Later* and *My New Partner II*. Besides his scores for feature films, Lai also contributed music to television programmes such as *Berlin Affair* and *Sins* (mini-series).
Recordings include: *Great Film Themes; A Man, A Woman And A Love Story*; and the soundtracks, *Bilitis* and *Dark Eyes*.

Lamour, Dorothy

b. Dorothy Stanton, 10 December 1914, New Orleans, Louisiana, USA. An actress and singer particularly remembered for the series of 'Road' films with Bing Crosby and Bob Hope in which she invariably wore her trademark sarong. Crowned Miss Orleans at the age of 14, she moved to Chicago in the early 30s and worked in clubs and on radio, becoming known as the 'Sultry Songstress of the Airwaves' even though the listeners were unaware that she had 'a stunning statuesque figure'. She married bandleader Herbie Kay in 1934 and they were divorced in 1939. A subsequent marriage lasted for 35 years until 1979. She made her breakthrough into films in 1936 with *The Jungle Princess*, the first of what she calls 'those silly, but wonderful jungle pictures', which included *Her Jungle Love* and *Moon Over Burma*. In the late 30s she appeared in several musical films, including *Swing High Swing Low, College Holiday, High Wide And Handsome, Thrill Of A Lifetime, The Big Broadcast Of 1938*, and *Tropic Holiday*. One of her best roles came in *St. Louis Blues* (1939), in which she played an ex-Broadway star and sang several appealing numbers such as 'Blue Nightfall', 'I Go For That', 'Let's Dream In The Moonlight', and the title song. She joined Crosby and Hope on *The Road To Singapore* in 1940, and continued to travel with them along other 'Roads', to Zanzibar (1941), Morocco (1942), Utopia (1946), Rio (1947), and Bali (1953). Rumour has it that she nearly did not make the trip to Hong Kong in 1962, but Hope is said to have insisted on her presence in the picture, although Joan Collins played the main female role. Over the years, in between the 'Roads', she made several other mostly entertaining musicals including *The Fleet's In, Star Spangled Rhythm, Dixie, Riding High, And The Angels Sing, Rainbow Island, Duffy's Tavern, Variety Girl, Lulu Belle, Slightly French*, and *The Greatest Show On Earth* (1952). This was in addition to films in which she played straight roles - a total of more than 60 in all. She was still making the occasional feature film and television appearance into the 80s. In her one-woman show she pokes fun at her image - the sarongs and all that - and tells of the occasion when she received a standing ovation from 5,000 people while heading a touring company of *Hello, Dolly!* in the late 60s. All the sarongs have been auctioned off for charity, and there is a rumour that one resides in the Smithsonian Museum.
Selected album: *Favourite Hawaiian Songs*.
Further reading: *My Side Of The Road*, Dorothy Lamour and D. McInnes.

Lane, Burton

b. 2 February 1912, New York City, New York, USA. A distinguished composer for films and the stage. After studying piano as a child, Lane later played stringed instruments in school orchestras. Some early compositions written for the school band attracted attention, and while still in his early teens he was commissioned to write songs for a projected off-Broadway revue, which never came to fruition. In his mid-teens Lane joined the staff of the Remick Music Company where he was encouraged in his songwriting career by George Gershwin. In 1929 he worked with Howard Dietz on some songs for the Broadway revue *Three's A Crowd*, and with Harold Adamson on *Earl Carroll's Vanities Of 1931*. When the effects of the Depression hit Broadway, Lane went to Hollywood and wrote for numerous musical films, often with Adamson. During the 30s his screen songs included 'Heigh Ho, The Gang's All Here', 'You're My Thrill', 'Stop, You're Breaking My Heart', 'Says My Heart' and his first major hit, 'Everything I Have Is Yours'. Perhaps the most popular of his songs of this period were 'The Lady's In Love With You' (Frank Loesser), from the film *Some Like It Hot*, 'I Hear Music' (Loesser) and 'How About You?' (Ralph Freed). The latter was sung by Judy Garland and Mickey Rooney in *Babes On Broadway* (1940). Lane also contributed scores or single songs to other movies such as *Dancing Lady, Bottoms Up, Her Husband Lies, Love On Toast, Artists And Models, Champagne Waltz, College Holiday, Swing High, Swing Low, Cocoanut Grove, College Swing, St. Louis Blues, Spawn Of The North, She Married A Cop, Dancing On A Dime, Ship Ahoy, Dubarry Was A Lady, Hollywood Canteen, Royal Wedding*, and *Give A Girl A Break* (1952). *Royal Wedding* contained one of the longest song titles ever - 'How Could You Believe Me When I Said I Love You When You Know I've Been A Liar All My Life?', as well as the lovely 'Too Late Now' and 'Open Your Eyes' (all Alan Jay Lerner). Among the other songs in those aforementioned pictures were 'I Hear Music', 'Poor You', 'Last Call For Love', 'I'll Take Tallulah', 'Tampico', 'Moonlight Bay', 'Madame, I Love Your Crepe Suzettes', 'You Can Always Tell A Yank', 'What Are You Doing The Rest Of Your Life?', and 'I Dig A Witch In Witchita'. In the 40s Lane wrote the score for the Broadway musicals *Hold On To Your Hats* (with E.Y. 'Yip'

Harburg), *Laffing Room Only* (with Al Dubin), and the whimsical *Finian's Rainbow* (Harburg). The latter show, which opened in 1947 and ran for more than 700 performances, contained a fine set of songs including 'That Great Come-And-Get-It Day', 'Old Devil Moon', 'How Are Things In Glocca Morra?', 'When I'm Not Near The Girl I Love', 'If This Isn't Love', and 'Look To The Rainbow'. It was 18 years before Lane was back on Broadway with *On A Clear Day You Can See Forever* (Lerner) from which came 'Come Back To Me', 'Hurry! It's Lovely Up Here!', 'Melinda', and several other fine numbers. Lane and Lerner were teamed again in 1978 for *Carmelina*, which, despite the engaging 'One More Walk Around The Garden', 'Someone In April', 'I'm A Woman', and 'It's Time for A Love Song', was a resounding flop. Throughout his long career Lane has worked with many partners. As well as the men already mentioned, these have included Ted Koehler, Sam Coslow, Ira Gershwin, and Sammy Cahn with whom he collaborated on songs such as 'Can You Imagine?' and 'That's What Friends Are For' for the Hanna-Barbera animated film *Heidi's Song* in 1982. Ten years after that, at the age of 80, Burton Lane was inducted into the US Theatre Hall Of Fame and was presented with the Berkshire Festival Theatre's fourth American Theatre Award at a benefit performance appropriately entitled *Hold On To Your Hats*. One of the stars of the show, singer and music archivist Michael Feinstein, released two CDs of Lane's songs in the early 90s. On each one he was accompanied by the composer himself on the piano.

Langford, Frances

b. 4 April 1913, Lakeland, Florida, USA. Langford began singing as a child and after some stage work, mostly in vaudeville, she established a reputation as a nightclub singer. By the mid-30s her light, sweet singing voice had made her a popular recording and broadcasting star and she was invited to Hollywood. Some of her films were merely vehicles in which she played supporting roles and sang a couple of songs, such as in *Hollywood Hotel* (1937) and *Follow The Band* (1943), the latter an early Robert Mitchum film. Occasionally, she was the female lead as in *Palm Springs* (1936), where she played opposite David Niven in his first leading role in Hollywood, and *Girl Rush* (1944), a Wally Brown-Alan Carney comedy, in which she worked again with Mitchum. By the end of the 40s Langford's film career was virtually over but she continued to broadcast on the radio and make records, often teaming up with major stars such as Louis Armstrong. For several years she was a regular on Bob Hope's popular radio show. In 1954, she played herself in *The Glenn Miller Story*. Subsequently, her career has drifted quietly away.
Compilation: *Gettin' Sentimental* (1988).

Lansbury, Angela

b. Angela Brigid Lansbury, 16 October 1925, London, England. An actress and singer who enjoyed a prolific career in Hollywood before blossoming into a star of Broadway musicals in the 60s. Angela Lansbury's grandfather was George Lansbury, the legendary social reformer, and leader of the British Labour Party for a time during the 30s. She was taken to America in 1942 by her widowed mother, a popular actress named Moyna MacGill. After attending drama school in New York, Lansbury received an Oscar nomination for her first film performance in *Gaslight* (1944). It was the beginning of a long career in Hollywood during which she appeared in several musicals including *The Harvey Girls* (1946), *Till The Clouds Roll By* (1947), *The Court Jester* (1956), *Blue Hawaii* (1961, as Elvis Presley's mother), and *Bedknobs And Broomsticks* (1971). For much of the time she played characters a good deal older than herself. From 1957 onwards, Lansbury played several straight roles on Broadway, but it was not until 1964 that she appeared in her first musical, *Anyone Can Whistle*, which had a score by Stephen Sondheim. It only ran for nine performances, but Lansbury's subsequent excursions into the musical theatre proved far more successful. She won wide acclaim, and Tony Awards, for her roles in *Mame* (1966), *Dear World* (1969), *Gypsy* (1974 revival), and *Sweeney Todd* (1979). She also took *Gypsy* to London in 1973. In the 80s, Lansbury began to work more in television and created the part of the writer-come-supersleuth, Jessica Fletcher, in the US series *Murder, She Wrote*. The programmes's long-term success resulted in her being rated as one of the highest-paid actresses in the world by the early 90s. In 1991 she received a Lifetime Achievement Award from the British Academy of Film and Television Arts (BAFTA), and, in the same, year, she lent her voice to Mrs Potts, the character that sang the Academy Award-winning title song in the highly acclaimed Walt Disney animated feature, *Beauty And The Beast*. In 1992, Angel Lansbury was back to her Cockney roots playing a charlady in the film *Mrs 'Arris Goes To Paris*.
Further reading: *Angela Lansbury - A Biography*, Margaret Wander Bonanno.

Lanza, Mario

b. Alfredo Cocozza, 31 January 1921, Philadelphia, Pennsylvania, USA, d. 7 October 1959. Lanza was an enormously popular star of film musicals and on records during the 50s, with a magnificent operatic tenor voice. The son of Italian immigrants, he took his stage name from his mother's maiden name, Maria Lanza. From the age of 15, Lanza studied singing with several teachers, and was introduced into society circles with the object of gaining a patron. He was signed to Columbia Artistes Management as a concert singer, but their plans to send him on an introductory

Mario Lanza

tour were quashed when Lanza was drafted into the US Army in 1943. He appeared in shows, billed as 'the Service Caruso', and sang in the chorus of the celebratory Forces show *Winged Victory*. After release, he lived in New York, gave concerts and worked on radio shows. One of the audition recordings that he made for RCA found its way to the MGM Film Studios, and when he deputized for another tenor at the Hollywood Bowl, MGM chief Louis B. Mayer was in the audience. Soon afterwards Lanza was signed to a seven-year MGM contract by Hungarian producer, Joe Pasternak, who was quoted as saying: 'it was the most beautiful voice I had ever heard - but his bushy hair made him look like a caveman!'

Lanza's contract allowed him to continue with his concert career, and in April 1948 he made his first, and last, appearance on the professional operatic stage, in two performances of *Madame Butterfly*, with the New Orleans Opera. Lanza's first film in 1949 for MGM, *That Midnight Kiss*, co-starred Kathryn Grayson and pianist Jose Iturbi, and contained a mixture of popular standards as diverse as 'They Didn't Believe Me' and 'Down Among The Sheltering Palms', and classical pieces, including 'Celeste Aida', (from Verdi's *Aida*), which gave Lanza one his first record hits. The film was a big box-office success, and was followed by *The Toast Of New Orleans*, also with Grayson, which, along with the operatic excerpts, contained some songs by Sammy Cahn and Nicholas Brodszky, including one of Lanza's all-time smash hits, the million-seller, 'Be My Love'. Lanza starred in the bio-pic *The Great Caruso* (1951), performing several arias associated with his idol. He also introduced 'The Loveliest Night Of The Year', a song adapted by Irving Aaronson from 'Over the Waves', by Juventino Rosas, with a new lyric by Paul Francis Webster; it gave Lanza his second million-selling record.

By now, he was one of Hollywood's hottest properties, and as his career blossomed, so did his waistline. There were rumours of breakfasts consisting of four steaks and six eggs, washed down with a gallon of milk, which caused his weight to soar to 20 stone. He claimed that 'nervousness' made him eat. In 1951, Lanza embarked on a country-wide tour of 22 cities, and also appeared on his own CBS radio series. Back in Hollywood, he initially turned down MGM's next project, *Because You're Mine*, because of its 'singer-becomes-a-GI' storyline. After some difficulties, the film was eventually completed, and was chosen for the 1952 Royal Film Premiere in the UK. The title song, by Cahn and Brodszky, was nominated for an Academy award in 1952, and became Lanza's third, and last, million-selling single.

He had already recorded the songs for his next MGM project, *The Student Prince*, when he walked out on the studio following a disagreement with the director. He avoided damaging breach of contract lawsuits by allowing MGM to retain the rights to his recordings for the film. British actor, Edmund Purdom took his place, miming to Lanza's singing voice. Ironically, Lanza's vocal performances for the film were considered to be among his best, and *Songs From The Student Prince And Other Great Musical Comedies* (containing 'The Drinking Song'), was number 1 in the USA for several weeks. Beset by problems with alcohol, food, tranquillizers and the US tax authorities, Lanza became a virtual recluse, not performing for over a year, before appearing on CBS Television with Betty Grable and Harry James. He was criticized in the press for miming to his old recordings on the show, but proved the voice was still intact by resuming his recording career soon afterwards. In 1956, Lanza returned to filming, this time for Warner Brothers. *Serenade*, adapted from the novel by James M. Cain, in which Lanza co-starred with Joan Fontaine, was considered by the critics to be one of his best movies. Once again, the operatic excerpts were interspersed with some romantic songs by Cahn and Brodszky, including 'Serenade' and 'My Destiny'. In 1957, tired of all the crash diets, and disillusioned by life in the USA, Lanza moved to Italy, and settled in Rome. He made one film there, *The Seven Hills Of Rome* (1958). Apart from the sight of Lanza playing an American entertainer doing impersonations of Dean Martin, Frankie Laine and Louis Armstrong, the film is probably best remembered for the inclusion of the 1955 hit song, 'Arrivederci, Roma', written by Renato Rascel (Ranucci) and Carl Sigman, impressively sung in the film by Lanza, and which became the accompaniment to many a backward glance by tourists ever since. In 1958, Lanza visited the UK, making his first stage appearances for six years, in concert at London's Royal Albert Hall and on the Royal Variety Show. From there, he embarked on a European tour. While on the Continent, he made *For The First Time* (1959), which was the last time he was seen on film. He appeared relatively slim, and was still in excellent voice. In the autumn of 1959 he went into a Rome clinic; a week later, he died of a heart attack. Much later it was alleged that he was murdered by the Mafia because he refused to appear at a concert organized by mobster, Lucky Luciano. The city of Philadelphia officially proclaimed 7 October as 'Mario Lanza Day'. His wife, Betty, died five months later. Opinions of his voice, and its potential, vary. José Carreras is quoted as saying that he was 'turned on' to opera at the age of 16 by seeing Lanza in *The Great Caruso*. Arturo Toscannini is supposed to have called it the greatest voice of the 20th century. On the other hand, one critic, perhaps representing the majority, said: 'He just concentrated on the big 'lollipops' of the opera repertoire, he had a poor musical memory, and would never have been an opera star.'

Selected albums: *Songs From The Student Prince And*

Other Great Musical Comedies, Serenade (1956, film soundtrack), *Seven Hills Of Rome* (1958, film soundtrack), *Songs From The Student Prince/The Great Caruso* (1958), *For The First Time* (1959, film soundtrack), *Lanza Sings Christmas Carols* (1959), *Mario Lanza Sings Caruso Favourites/The Great Caruso* (1960), *You Do Something To Me* (1969). Compilations: *I'll Walk With God* (1962), *His Greatest Hits, Volume 1* (1971), *His Greatest Hits From Operettas And Musicals, Volumes One, Two & Three* (all 1981), *20 Golden Favourites* (1981), *The Legendary Mario Lanza* (1981), *A Portrait Of Mario Lanza* (1987), *Diamond Series: Mario Lanza* (1988).

Further reading: *Mario Lanza*, Matt Bernard. *Mario Lanza*, Michael Burrows. *Lanza - His Tragic Life*, Raymond Strait.

Last Of The Blue Devils, The

A superior documentary, worth its place in any collection, this film celebrates the remarkable contribution to jazz provided by Kansas City-based musicians. Extensive interviews and live performances filmed especially for the documentary mingle effectively with archive film clips. Amongst the artists displaying their considerable talents are Count Basie, Jimmy Forrest, Dizzy Gillespie, Budd Johnson, Gus Johnson, Jo Jones, Jay McShann, Charlie Parker, Jesse Price, Buster Smith, Joe Turner and Lester Young.

Laye, Evelyn

b. Elsie Evelyn Lay, 10 July 1900, London, England. An actress and singer - one of the most celebrated leading ladies of the English musical stage. Her father was the actor and composer Gilbert Laye (he added the 'e' on to the family name for stage appearances) and her mother the actress Evelyn Stewart. Known as 'Boo' from when she was a baby, Evelyn Laye was constantly performing as a child, and made her professional stage debut at the age of 15 as a Chinese servant in a production entitled *Mr. Wu*. After appearing in *The Beauty Spot, Going Up*, and *The Kiss Call*, she had her first West End success in 1920 with *The Shop Girl*, in which she was backed by a chorus of real guardsmen as she sang 'The Guards' Parade'. In the early 20s she delighted London audiences in shows such as *Phi-Phi*, and *The Merry Widow. Madame Pompadour* (1923), her first show for C.B. Cochran, was a significant landmark in her career, and was followed by more good roles in stylish productions such as *Cleopatra, Betty In Mayfair, Merely Molly*, and *Blue Eyes*. By 1929, when Evelyn Laye introduced Drury Lane audiences to 'Lover, Come Back To Me' in Sigmund Romberg's musical *The New Moon*, she had become the brightest star on the London theatre scene; Cochran called her 'the fairest prima donna this side of heaven'. Around this time she was separated from her husband, the comedian Sonny Hale, and he later married one of her main 'rivals', the enchanting

Jessie Matthews. She turned down the leading role in the London production of Noël Coward's *Bitter Sweet*, but triumphed in the 1929 Broadway production, and later succeeded Peggy Wood in the West End version. Her success on Broadway resulted in a trip to Hollywood and appearances in *One Heavenly Night* with John Boles, and *The Night Is Young*, in which she co-starred with Ramon Novarra and sang Sigmund Romberg and Oscar Hammerstein II's enduring 'When I Grow Too Old To Dream'. While in America she married the British actor, Frank Lawton, and they were together until he died in 1969. On her return to England she made more film musicals, including *Princess Charming, Waltz Time*, and *Evensong* (1934). The latter is regarded as perhaps the most accomplished of her relatively few screen appearances. Even in the 90s it continues to be re-shown in cinema retrospective seasons, and on television, providing a tantalising glimpse of an artist who lit up the screen whenever she chose to neglect her beloved stage for a while. During the remainder of the 30s, Evelyn Laye was a 'ravishing' Helen of Troy in *Helen!*, appeared with the embryonic John Mills in *Give Me A Ring*, co-starred with the far more mature Viennese tenor Richard Tauber in *Paganini*, and returned to Broadway in 1937 with Jack Buchanan and Adele Dixon for *Between The Devil*. The show made history when it was presented for one night at the National Theatre in New York on the occasion of President Roosevelt's birthday, thereby becoming the first American Command Performance. In 1940 she sang 'You've Done Something To My Heart', 'Only A Glass Of Champagne', and 'Let The People Sing' in Ronald Jean's revue, *Lights Up*. During the remainder of World War II she appeared in the 1942 revival of *The Belle Of New York* and another Romberg/Hammerstein show, *Sunny River*. She also served as Entertainments Director for the Royal Navy, and led the first-ever concert party for the troops based in the remote Scapa Flow in the Orkneys. In 1945 Evelyn Laye returned to the London stage in *Three Waltzes*. Immediately after the war, when suitable parts in the musical theatre were few and far between, she played straight roles in plays throughout the UK and on a 1951 tour of Australia, but made a triumphant comeback to the London musical stage in *Wedding In Paris* in 1954. More straight plays followed before she starred in the musical, *Strike A Light* (1966), and replaced Anna Neagle for a time in the long-running *Charley Girl*. In her last musical (to date), *Phil The Fluter* (1969), she reflected on a better, more civilised age, in the memorable 'They Don't Make Them Like That Any More', a number that was so perfectly suited to her. In 1971 she appeared with Michael Crawford in the comedy, *No Sex, Please - We're British*, and two years later was awarded the CBE. During the rest of the 70s and 80s she made several more films, including *Say*

Hello To Yesterday, with Jean Simmons and *Never Never Land* with Petula Clark, and did a good deal of television work. In 1992, at the age of 92, she toured parts of the UK with the nostalgia show, *Glamorous Nights At Drury Lane*, and received standing ovations. In July of that year, in *A Glamorous Night With Evelyn Laye At The London Palladium*, the elite of British show-business gathered to pay tribute and nod in assent as she sang 'They Don't Make Them Like That Any More'.

Selected albums: *Golden Age Of Evelyn Laye* (1985), *When I Grow Too Old To Dream* (1991).

Further reading: *Boo To My Friends*, Evelyn Laye.

Legrand, Michel

b. 24 February 1932, Paris, France. Legrand grew up in a musical environment - his father was an orchestra leader and film composer - and studied formally at the Paris Conservatoire. In the 50s he was an active pianist but was most successful as an arranger. Later in the decade he moved to New York and continued to arrange, but now with a strong orientation towards the contemporary jazz scene, for leading artists such as Miles Davis and John Coltrane. In France he had occasionally led his own bands and did so again in the USA. In these years he was also a prolific composer, writing material performed by Stan Getz, Phil Woods and others, and occasionally playing with jazzmen such as Shelly Manne. He had begun to compose music for French films in 1953, and, in the 60s, developed this area of his work on productions such as *Lola*; *Cleo From 5 To 7*, which he also appeared in, and *My Life To Live*. In 1964 he received the first of his many Academy Award nominations, for the score to *The Umbrellas Of Cherbourg*, which contained 'I Will Wait For You' and 'Watch What Happens' (English lyrics by Norman Gimbel). His second Oscar came for his work on the follow-up, *The Young Ladies Of Rochefort* (1968). In the late 60s he began to compose for US and British films. His score for one of the first of these, *The Thomas Crown Affair*, included 'The Windmills Of Your Mind' (lyric by Alan and Marilyn Bergman), which became popular for Noel Harrison (son of actor Rex) and Dusty Springfield, and won an Academy Award in 1968. Another collaboration with Alan and Marilyn Bergman produced 'What Are You Doing The Rest Of Your Life?', from *The Happy Ending* (1969). Throughout the 70s, Legrand continued to write prolifically for films such as *The Go-Between*, *Wuthering Heights*, *Summer Of 42* (another Oscar), *Lady Sings The Blues*, *One Is A Lonely Number* and *The Three Musketeers*. He teamed with the Bergmans yet again for Barbra Streisand's film *Yentl* (1983). Two of their 12 songs, 'Papa, Can You Hear Me?' and 'The Way He Makes Me Feel' were nominated, and the complete score won an Academy Award. Legrand's other film music included *Never Say Never Again*, Sean Connery's eagerly awaited return to the role of James Bond; *Secret Places* (title song written with Alan Jay Lerner); the amusing *Switching Channels* (theme written with Neil Diamond), starring Kathleen Turner, Burt Reynolds and Christopher Reve; *Fate* and *The Burning Shore*. In 1991 Legrand was back to his jazz roots for the score to *Dingo*, which he wrote with Miles Davis. Davis also gave an impressive performance in the movie. At his best with lyrical and sometimes sentimental themes, Legrand's writing for films remains his major contribution to popular music. Besides his feature film credits, Legrand also worked extensively in television, contributing music to *Brian's Song*, *The Adventures Of Don Quixote*, *It's Good To Be Alive*, *Cage Without A Key*, *A Woman Called Golda*, *The Jesse Owens Story*, *Promises To Keep*, *Sins* (mini-series), *Crossings*, *Casanova* and *Not A Penny More, Not A Penny Less* (1990).

Selected albums: *Legrand Jazz* (1958), *At Shelly's Manne Hole* (1968), *Michel Legrand Recorded Live At Jimmy's* (1973), *After The Rain* (1982).

Lerner, Alan Jay

b. 31 August 1918, New York, USA, d. 14 February 1988, Florida, USA. A lyricist and librettist; one of the most eminent and literate personalities in the history of the Broadway musical theater. Lerner played the piano as a child, and studied at the Juilliard School of Music, the Bedales public school in England, and Harvard University where he took a Bachelor of Science degree in the late 30s. After working as a journalist and radio scriptwriter, he met composer Frederick Loewe at the Lamb's Club in 1942. Loewe was educated at the Military Academy and at Stern's Conservatory in Berlin. He made his concert debut as a pianist at the age of 13, and, two years later, composed 'Katrina', a song which became popular throughout Europe. After moving to the USA in 1924, he did ranch work in the west, played the piano in beer halls and silent movie houses, and was a bantam-weight boxer for a time. Before he met Lerner, Loewe had also been involved in some unsuccessful musical shows. The new team's first efforts, *What's Up?* and *The Day Before Spring* (1945) ('A Jug Of Wine', 'I Love You This Morning'), did not exactly set Broadway on fire, but, two years later, they had their first hit with *Brigadoon*. Lerner's whimsical fantasy about a Scottish village which only comes to life every 100 years, contained numbers such as 'Waitin' For My Dearie', 'I'll Go Home To Bonnie Jean', 'The Heather On The Hill', 'Come To Me, Bend To Me', 'From This Day On', and the future standard, 'Almost Like Being In Love'. A film version was made in 1954, starring Gene Kelly, Cyd Charisse and Van Johnson.

After *Brigadoon*, Lerner collaborated with Kurt Weill on the vaudeville-style *Love Life* (1948), and then spent some time in Hollywood writing the songs, with Burton Lane, for *Royal Wedding* (1951). Among them was one of the longest-ever titles: 'How Could You Believe Me When I Said I Loved You (When You Know I've Been A Liar All My Life?)', expertly manipulated by Fred Astaire. Another of the numbers, 'Too Late Now', sung by Jane Powell, was nominated for an Academy Award. In the same year, Lerner picked up an Oscar for his story and screenplay for George and Ira Gershwins' musical film, *An American In Paris* (1951). Also in 1951, Lerner re-united with Loewe for the 'Gold Rush' Musical, *Paint Your Wagon*. The colourful score included 'They Call The Wind Maria', 'I Talk To The Trees', 'I Still See Elisa', 'I'm On My Way' and 'Wand'rin' Star', which, in the 1969 movie, received a lugubrious reading from Lee Marvin. Precisely the opposite sentiments prevailed in *My Fair Lady* (1956), Lerner's adaptation of *Pygmalion*, by Bernard Shaw, which starred Rex Harrison as the irascible Higgins, and Julie Andrews as Eliza ('I'm a good girl, I am'). Sometimes called 'the most perfect musical', Lerner and Loewe's memorable score included 'Why Can't The English?', 'Wouldn't It Be Loverly?', 'The Rain In Spain', 'I Could Have Danced All Night', 'On The Street Where You Live', 'Show Me', 'Get Me To The Church On Time', 'A Hymn To Him', 'Without You' and 'I've Grown Accustomed To Her Face'. 'Come To The Ball', originally written for the show, but discarded before the opening, was, subsequently, often performed, particularly by Lerner himself. After a run of 2,717 performances on Broadway, and 2,281 in London, the show was filmed in 1964, when Andrews was replaced by Audrey Hepburn (dubbed by Marni Nixon). The Broadway Cast album went to number 1 in the US charts, sold over five million copies, and stayed in the Top 40 for 311 weeks, still a record in the late 80s. In 1958 Lerner was back in Hollywood, with a somewhat reluctant Loewe, for one of the last original screen Musicals, the charming *Gigi*. Lerner's stylish treatment of Colette's turn-of-the-century novellae, directed by Vincente Minnelli, starred Maurice Chevalier, Leslie Caron, Louis Jordan and Hermione Gingold, and a delightful score which included 'The Night They Invented Champagne', 'Say A Prayer For Me Tonight', 'I'm Glad I'm Not Young Anymore', 'Thank Heaven For Little Girls', 'Waltz At Maxim's', 'She Is Not Thinking Of Me' and the touching, 'I Remember It Well', memorably performed by Chevalier and Gingold. Lerner won one of the film's nine Oscars for his screenplay, and another, with Loewe, for the title song.

Two years later Lerner and Loewe returned to Broadway with *Camelot*, a musical version of the Arthurian legend, based on T.H. White's *The Once And Future King*. With Julie Andrews, Richard Burton and Robert Goulet, plus a fine score which included 'C'Est Moi', 'The Lusty Month Of May', 'If Ever I Would Leave You', 'Follow Me', 'How To Handle A Woman' and the title song; the show was on Broadway for two years. During that time it became indelibly connected with the Kennedy presidency . . . 'for one brief shining moment, that was known as Camelot' . . . The 1967 movie version was poorly received. In the early 60s, partly because of the composer's ill health, Lerner and Loewe ended their partnership, coming together again briefly in 1973 to write some new songs for a stage presentation of *Gigi*, and, a year later, for the score to the film *The Little Prince*. Lerner's subsequent collaborators included Burton Lane for *On A Clear Day You Can See Forever* (1965) ('Come Back To Me', 'On The S.S. Bernard Cohn', and others). Lerner won a Grammy Award for the title song, and maintained that it was his most oft-recorded number. He wrote with Lane again in 1979 for *Carmelina*. In the interim teamed-up with André Previn for *Coco* (1969), which had a respectable run of 332 performances, mainly due to its star, Katherine Hepburn; and Leonard Bernstein for *1600 Pennsylvania Avenue* (1976). Lerner's last Musical, *Dance A Little Closer* (1983), which starred his eighth wife, English actress Liz Robertson, closed after one performance. They had met in 1979 when he directed her, as Eliza, in a major London revival of *My Fair Lady*.

Just before he died of lung cancer on 14 June 1986, he was still working on various projects including a musical treatment of the 30s film comedy *My Man Godfrey*, in collaboration with pianist-singer Gerard Kenny, and *Yerma*, based on the play by Federico Garcia Lorca. Frederick Loewe, who shared in Lerner's triumphs, and had been semi-retired since the 60s, died in February 1988, in Palm Springs, Florida, USA. In 1993, New Yorkers celebrated the 75th anniversary of Lerner's birth, and a remarkable and fruitful partnership, with *The Night They Invented Champagne: The Lerner And Loewe Revue*, which played a season at the Rainbow and Stars.

Further reading: *The Musical Theatre: A Celebration*, Alan Jay Lerner. *The Street Where I Live: The Story Of My Fair Lady, Gigi And Camelot*, Alan Jay Lerner. *A Hymn To Him: The Lyrics Of Alan Jay Lerner*.

Les Girls

To many it must have seemed like the end of an era when Gene Kelly completed his very last MGM musical. The string of hits he left behind are firmly registered in the vaults of movie musical history. His last project, *Les Girls*, released in October 1957, and adapted by John Patrick from a Vera Caspery story, does not quite live up to Kelly's own high standard, but there are enough entertaining sequences to keep the momentum flowing. Directed by George Cukor and produced by Sol C Siegel, the film is based in Paris 1949. It follows the adventures of Kelly, a musical performer, and his female trio, Les Girls, played by Mitzi Gaynor, Kay Kendall and Taina Elg.

The unusual story is revealed in a series of flashbacks. The first of them concerns the courtroom battle between two of the girls which opens the film. Lady Wren (Kay Kendall) has included an account of her experiences with Les Girls in her memoirs, and stands in the dock defending her words, while furious Taina Elg refuses to accept any of the book as the truth. As the film continues the viewer begins to wonder who is really telling the truth, and which one of the girls Kelly is in love with. Or did he have flings with all of them? It is only towards the movie's conclusion that it is revealed that Mitzi Gaynor is the girl he truly desires. Indeed during one of the flashbacks he reveals a whole wall of Gaynor's photos, and pretends he is terribly ill in order to win his way into her affections. In the aftermath of the court case she needs Kelly's assurance that his flings with the other girls have been purely fictional. With all these complications it is hardly surprising that the film becomes rather weighed down, but one or two individual performances, and the words and music of Cole Porter save the day (*Les Girls* was his original score for the big screen). The musical highlights included Kelly and Gaynor's tongue-in-cheek send-up of Marlon Brando in 'Why Am I So Gone About That Gal?' and Kendall's almost music hall routine with Kelly, 'You're Just Too, Too'. Other songs were 'Ladies In Waiting' and 'Ca, C'est L'Amour'. Among the supporting cast, which had a definite European flavour, were Leslie Phillips, Jacques Bergerac, Henry Daniell, and Patrick MacNee. Jack Cole was the choreographer, and it was photographed in Metrocolor and CinemaScope. Not an MGM classic for Kelly and Porter to end on, but amusing and enjoyable all the same.

Let George Do It

In the early years of World War II, George Formby's comedy-musical films raised the spirits of millions of people in the Britain. This one was typical of the genre: George is about to join his fellow members of the Dinkie Doo Concert Party when he is whisked off to Bergen in Norway to replace a ukulele player (a member of British Intelligence) who has died in mysterious circumstances while playing in a hotel band. George discovers that its leader, Mark Mendez (Garry Marsh), is a German spy who is transmitting shipping information by code in his band's broadcasts. With the help of Mary Wilson (Phyllis Calvert), George breaks the code, warns the Admiralty, and as a result five U-Boats are sunk. Not surprisingly, he flees the country - in a German submarine! In the midst of all that derring-doo, he found the time to introduce two of his best-known novelty numbers, 'Grandad's Flannelette Nightshirt' and 'Mr Wu's A Window Cleaner Now', as well as the cheery 'Count Your Blessings And Smile' and 'Oh, Don't The Wind Blow Cold' (Formby-Fred E. Cliffe-Harry Gifford). Ronald Shiner, a leading star of the famous Whitehall farces

after the war, had a minor role as a clarinettist in this picture, and other parts went to Romney Brent, Bernard Lee (he played 'M' in the James Bond films), Ian Fleming (an Australian character, not the Bond author), Coral Browne, Percy Walsh, Diana Beaumont, Donald Calthrop, Torin Thatcher, Hal Gordon, Jack Hobbs, and Alec Clunes. The screenplay was written by John Dighton, Austin Melford, Angus Macphail, and Basil Dearden. The latter was also the Associated Producer for Ealing-Associated Talking Pictures. The director was Marcel Varnel, and this invaluable little morale booster was released in 1940.

Let's Make Love

The story worked well in *On The Avenue* (1937), so screenwriter Norman Krasna adapted it slightly for this 20th Century-Fox release some 23 years later. A seriously wealthy businessman (Yves Montand) discovers that he is going to be lampooned in a satirical Off Broadway revue, so, after honing his almost non-existent performing skills with the help of Gene Kelly (dancing), Bing Crosby (singing), and Milton Berle (comedy), he joins the show as a lookalike of himself and immediately falls for the leading lady (Marilyn Monroe). Her boyfriend-in-residence is British singer Frankie Vaughan, but after Montand turns on the Gallic charm he does not stand a chance and might as well go home. (In fact that is what Vaughan did shortly after filming was finished and Mrs Vaughan had explained that when Monroe offered to help him with his lines that was not really what she meant). Sammy Cahn and Jimmy Van Heusen's were pleasant but uninspired, and included 'Let's Make Love', 'Incurably Romantic' (which Monroe sang with both Vaughan and Montand), 'Latin One', 'Specialization', 'Hey You With The Crazy Eyes', and 'Strip City'. However, the film's musical highlight was Monroe's sizzling version of Cole Porter's 'My Heart Belongs To Daddy'. Tony Randall was his usual amusing self as Montand's long-suffering personal assistant, and other parts went to Wilfred Hyde White, David Burns, Michael David, and Mara Lynn. Jack Cole staged the smart and contemporary dances, and the director was George Cukor. This good-looking picture was photographed in De Luxe Color and CinemaScope by Daniel L. Fapp.

Levant, Oscar

b. 27 December 1906, Pittsburg, Pennsylvania, USA, d. 14 August 1972, Beverly Hills, California, USA. Hypochondriacal, witty, neurotic, grouchy, melancholic, acidic, and eccentric, are just a few of the adjectives that have been used over the years in a desperate attempt to accurately describe one of the most original characters in films, radio, and popular and light classical music. All the above definitions

Let's Make Love

apparently apply to his personal as well as his public image. After graduating from high school, Levant struggled to make a living as pianist before moving to New York where he studied with Sigismund Stojovkskis and Arnold Schoenberg. He also played in clubs, and appeared on Broadway in the play, Burlesque (1927), and in the movie version entitled The Dance Of Life, two years later. In 1930 Levant worked with Irving Caesar, Graham John and Albert Sirmay on the score for another Broadway show, the Charles B. Dillingham production of Ripples, which starred Fred and Dorothy Stone and included songs such as 'Is It Love?', 'There's Nothing Wrong With A Kiss', and 'I'm A Little Bit Fonder Of You'. In the same year Levant collaborated with Irving Caesar again on 'Lady, Play Your Mandolin' which was successful for Nick Lucas and the Havana Novelty Orchestra, amongst others. He wrote his best-known song, 'Blame It On My Youth', with Edward Heyman in 1934, and it is still being played and sung 60 years later. Levant spent much of the late 20s and 30s in Hollywood writing songs and scores for movies such as My Man (Fanny Brice's film debut in 1928), Street Girl, Tanned Legs, Leathernecking, In Person, Music Is Magic, and The Goldwyn Follies (1938). Out of those came several appealing songs, including 'If You Want A Rainbow (You Must Have Rain)', 'Lovable And Sweet', 'Don't Mention Love To Me', 'Honey Chile', and 'Out Of Sight Out Of Mind'. His collaborators included Ray Heindorf, Mort Dixon, Billy Rose, Sam M. Lewis, Vernon Duke, Sidney Clare, Dorothy Fields, Stanley Adams, and Joe Young. Beginning in the late 30s, Levant also demonstrated his quick wit on the long-running radio series Information Please, and brought his grumpy irascible self to the screen in films such as In Person (1935), Rhythm On The River, Kiss the Boys Goodbye, Rhapsody In Blue (in which he played himself), Humoresque, Romance On The High Seas, You Were Meant For Me, The Barkleys Of Broadway, An American In Paris, and The Band Wagon (1953). In the last two pictures, both directed by Vincente Minnelli, he seemed to be at the peak of his powers, especially in the former which has a famous dream sequence in which Levant imagines he is conducting part of Gershwin's Concert In F and every member of the orchestra is himself. His final musical, The 'I Don't Care Girl', was a fairly dull affair, and his last picture of all, The Cobweb (1955), was set in a mental hospital. That was both sad and ironic, because for the last 20 years of his life Levant suffered from failing mental and physical health, emerging only occasionally to appear on television talk shows. In 1989 a one-man play based on the works of Oscar Levant entitled At Wit's End ('An Irreverent Evening'), opened to critical acclaim in Los Angeles.

Selected album: Plays Gershwin (recorded in the 40s).

Further reading: all by Oscar Levant A Smattering Of Ignorance. Memoirs Of An Amnesiac. The Unimportance Of Being Oscar.

Li'l Abner

Probably because most of the original cast of the 1956 hit Broadway show recreated their roles, this 1959 screen version was a satisfying and entertaining affair. Norman Panama and Melvin Frank adapted their libretto, which was based on Al Capp's popular cartoon character, and the community of Dogpatch - one of the most underrated areas in the whole of the USA - was up there on the screen in Technicolor and VistaVision. When they learn that their town has been earmarked as a testing sight for atom bombs, the residents, Daisy Mae (Leslie Parrish), Abner Yokum (Peter Palmer), Pappy and Mammy Yokum (Joe E. Marks and Billie Hayes), Marryin' Sam (Stubby Kaye), Earthquake McGoon (Bernie Hoffman), Stupifyin' Jones (Julie Newmar) and the rest, discover that, many years ago, their beloved Dogpatch was designated a national shrine. Johnny Mercer and Gene De Paul's witty score sounded as good as ever and included 'If I Had My Druthers', 'Jubilation T. Cornpone', 'The Country's In The Very Best Of Hands', 'Put 'Em Back', 'Namely You', 'Room Enuff For Us', 'A Typical Day', 'Don't Take That Rag Off'n The Bush', 'I'm Past My Prime', 'Unnecessary Town', and 'I Wish It Could Be Otherwise'. Dee Dee Wood and Michael Kidd's exuberant and exhilarating choreography, coupled with Panama and Frank's skilful and sympathetic direction, made this a film to savour and remember. Another, non-musical, version of Al Capp's tale was released in 1940.

Lili

Just two years after she made her Hollywood debut in Vincente Minnelli's An American In Paris (1951), Leslie Caron delighted cinema audiences once again with this enchanting film which was also released by MGM. She plays a 16-year-old French orphan who joins a carnival and falls madly in love with a handsome magician (Jean-Pierre Aumont). After she is fired for devoting too much her time to him and his illusions, she finds consolation in talking to a group of puppets operated by a disillusioned cripple (Mel Ferrer), and their subsequent, touching relationship makes this a rather special film. One of the highlights came when Caron danced a dream ballet with the puppets to the lovely, haunting music of Bronislau Kaper for which he won an Oscar. He and lyricist Helen Deutsch also wrote the song 'Hi-Lili, Hi-Lo', which was performed in captivating fashion by the puppets, and later became quite a hit. Helen Deutsch was also responsible for the screenplay which she adapted from a novel by Paul Gallico. Charles Walters and Dorothy Jarnac were responsible for the imaginative choreography, and Walters also directed. Zsa Zsa Gabor led a strong supporting cast which also

HER DADDY HOCKED HER FOR 20 BUCKS
TO THE TOUGHEST MUGS ON BROADWAY

DAMON
RUNYON

author of "Lady for a
Day" writes another
great human heart story

Paramount
Pictures

"*Little* MISS
MARKER"

A Paramount Picture with

Little Miss Marker

included Kurt Kasznar, Alex Gerry, Amanda Blake, and Wilton Graff. The film was produced by Edwin H. Knopf and photographed in Technicolor. In 1961 the magic of *Lili* was transferred to the stage in *Carnival*, the first Broadway musical show to be adapted from a screen musical. With a score by Bob Merrill, and starring Anna Maria Alberghetti, it became a popular hit and ran for 719 performances.

Lisbon Story, The

Released by British National in 1946, this war-time story of intrigue set in Lisbon and Paris in 1940, was adapted by Jack Whittingham from Harold Purcell's long-running musical which opened in London in 1943. The delightful Patricia Burke recreated her stage role as Gabrielle Girard, a French actress and singer, who risks accusations of collaborating with the invading Germans to assist a member of British Intelligence, David Warren (David Farrar), in his successful efforts to smuggle atom scientist Pierre Sargon (John Ruddock) back to England. David returns to Gabrielle after Paris has been liberated by the Allies, and they are married. The celebrated tenor, Richard Tauber, played Andre Joubert, Gabrielle's singing partner, and Walter Rilla was suitably evil as Karl von Schriner, Director of German Propaganda in Paris. Other roles went to Lawrence O'Madden, Austin Trevor, Harry Welchman, Paul Bonifas, Esme Percy, Noele Gordon, John Ruddock, and Joan Seton. Violin virtuoso Stéphane Grappelli was in it too, and so were two of the original show's hit songs, 'Pedro the Fisherman', 'Never Say Goodbye' (music Harry Parr-Davies, lyrics Harold Purcell). The former song was enormously popular during and after the war, especially in a recording by Gracie Fields. The picture itself, which was directed by Paul Stein, was pretty popular as well.

Little Miss Marker

That old show-biz maxim about not working with animals or children must have crossed Adolphe Menjou's mind more than once during the filming of this Paramount musical which was released in 1934. He was top-billed, but, although she was only six years old, Shirley Temple dominated the Damon Runyon story in which she is adopted by bookmaker Sorrowful Jones (Menjou), after being used as security for a losing bet. Shirley then proceeds to look after Jones while having a far more beneficial effect on the New York gambling fraternity than any government commission could hope for. Shell-shocked as he must have been, Menjou gave a creditable performance under heavy fire. Also suffering from the tremendous impact of this little blonde bombshell were Charles Bickford, Dorothy Dell, Lynne Overman, Willie Best, and Frank McGlynn Snr. Leo Robin and Ralph Rainger wrote the songs which included 'Low Down Lullaby', 'I'm A Black Sheep Who Is Blue', and

'Laugh, You Son-Of-A-Gun'. William R. Lipman, Sam Hellman and Gladys Lehman were responsible for the neat screenplay, and the director was Alexander Hall. The 'marker' of the title being an indigenous American term for IOU, the name of the film was changed to *The Girl In Pawn* for UK distribution. *Little Miss Marker* was remade in 1949 as *Sorrowful Jones*, in 1963 as *40 Pounds Of Trouble*, and again in 1980 under its original title, but none of them made anything like the impact of the 1934 version.

Little Shop Of Horrors

As a film to put audiences off gardening for life, *Little Shop Of Horrors*, released in December 1986, is top of the heap. It tells the story of Seymour (Rick Moranis), a rather sweet but accident-prone character - a sort of Norman Wisdom of the 80s - whose working life at Mushnik's Skid Row flower shop just is not going to plan. On to the scene comes Audrey II, named after the girl Seymour adores, who changes from a tiny shrub to a sinister blood sucking flytrap. When Seymour has bled his fingers dry in an attempt to feed it, the plant forces him to find some human meat to satisfy its hunger. In return Seymour is to have as much success in love and life as he can handle. Eventually, realising that the man-eating plant really wants to take over the world, Seymour faces up to its menace and, with the help of a few volts of electricity, blows Audrey II into oblivion. *Little Shop Of Horrors* was first seen Off Broadway in 1982, and that production itself was based on Roger Corman's 60s low budget horror movie. Directed by Frank Oz, and produced by David Geffen for the Geffen Company, the show's author and lyricist, Howard Ashman, also wrote the movie's screenplay. It is interesting to note that the film's ending is distinctly different in tone from its stage predecessor, when Seymour and Audrey are both eaten and Audrey II succeeds. It appears the preview audiences preferred a happy ending and so it was changed. Ashman was joined by Alan Menken to write the quirky, clever and often extremely funny score. Highlights included 'Skid Row', the film's only real production number of any sorts, involving most of the cast, and 'Suddenly Seymour', by no means an average love song. A host of guest stars joined in the fun, among them Steve Martin, James Belushi, John Candy, and Bill Murray. Ellen Greene recreated her stage role as Audrey. Martin plays Audrey's sadistic dentist boyfriend (in 'Somewhere's That Green', she sings 'I know Seymour's the greatest, but I'm dating a semi-sadist'). Consequently it is not surprising that Martin becomes Audrey II's first human victim. The plant's big number is 'Mean Green Mother From Outer Space' (the voice is that of the Four Tops' Levi Stubbs). The song was written especially for the film, and is quite a treat, especially its flower bud chorus. The rest of the score included 'Little Shop Of Horrors', 'Grow For Me', 'Dentist', 'Feed Me', and

'Suppertime'. Pat Garrett was the choreographer, and the film was photographed in Technicolor and Panavision by Robert Paynter.

Living It Up

One of the best films that Dean Martin and Jerry Lewis made together in the early-middle 50s, this 1954 Paramount release was twice blessed - with an amusing story and a set of good songs. Jack Rose and Melville Shavelson's screenplay was based on James Street's story *Letter To The Editor* and the 1937 movie *Nothing Sacred* which starred Fredric March and Carole Lombard. Proving that nothing really is sacred in Hollywood, Lombard's role was played this time by Jerry Lewis who gave a typically zany performance as a man who thinks he has a hefty dose of radiation poisoning. Encouraged by his doctor (Martin), who knows very well it is only a sinus condition, and a newspaper reporter (Janet Leigh), who believes he is going to die and knows a good story when she sees one, Lewis takes a press-sponsored trip to New York for one final all-out binge. It was all very entertaining, but much of the original film's bite and satire seemed to get lost on the journey. Two of Jule Styne and Bob Hilliard's songs, 'How Do You Speak To An Angel?' and 'Money Burns A Hole In My Pocket' became popular record hits, and Martin's relaxed and easy manner was ideal for the engaging 'That's What I Like' and a duet with Lewis, 'Ev'ry Street's A Boulevard (In Old New York)'. The other songs were 'Champagne And Wedding Cake' and 'You're Gonna Dance With Me, Baby'. Also featured were Edward Arnold, Fred Clark, Sheree North, Sig Ruman, and Sammy White. Norman Taurog was the director and the film was shot in Technicolor. Jule Styne and Bob Hilliard also wrote the score for a 1953 Broadway musical based on this story. It was called *Hazel Flagg*, and ran for just 190 performances.

Livingston, Jay

b. 28 March 1915, Pittsburgh, Pennsylvania, USA. After studying music at school, Livingstone attended the University of Pennsylvania. While there, he met and formed a lasting friendship with Ray Evans, with whom he worked in shipboard bands on transatlantic and cruise liners. Their joint careers as songwriters were barely under way when they were interrupted by World War II. In the post-war years Livingston and Evans worked in Hollywood, writing songs for films. Their major success in this period was the title song from *To Each His Own* (1946). Other films they contributed to included *The Cat And The Canary, On Stage Everybody, The Stork Club, My Favourite Brunette, Dream Girl, Whispering Smith, Samson And Delilah, Bitter Victory, The Great Lover, Sorrowful Jones, My Friend Irma, Fancy Pants, The Lemon Drop Kid, Here Comes The Groom, Aaron Slick From Punkin Crick, Thunder In The East, Here Come The Girls*, and *Red Garters*. While continuing their partnership, in which Livingston usually wrote the music and Evans the words, both men occasionally worked with other composers. Their joint successes included the Oscar-winning songs 'Buttons And Bows' (*The Paleface* 1948) and 'Mona Lisa' (*Capt. Carey, USA* 1950). Among their other film songs were 'Golden Earrings' (music by Victor Young), 'My Love Loves Me', 'Silver Bells', 'I'll Always Love You', 'Home Cookin'', 'A Place In The Sun' (music by Franz Waxman), 'Never Let Me Go' and another Oscar winner and Doris Day hit, 'Whatever Will Be, Will Be (Que Sera, Sera)'. Throughout the 50s Livingston and Evans continued to write songs for films, among them 'Tammy' and 'Almost In Your Arms'. In 1958, they wrote the score for a Broadway show, *Oh, Captain!*, which included 'Femininity'. Their film songs of the 60s included 'In The Arms Of Love' and 'Wait Until Dark' and the duo also wrote the themes for the television series, *Bonanza* and *Mr. Ed*. In the 70s, Livingston and Evans continued to write occasional material for films and television and for such Broadway-based nostalgia as *Sugar Babies* (1979).

Loesser, Frank

b. Henry Frank Loesser, 29 June 1910, New York City, New York, USA, 28 July 1969. Loesser was a leading songwriter for the stage and films, from the 30s until the 60s. Initially, he wrote only lyrics, but later provided the music and lyrics, and sometimes co-produced through his Frank Productions. Born into a musical family, (his father was a music teacher, and his brother a music critic and pianist), Loesser declined a formal musical education, and trained himself. During the Depression years of the early 30s, following a brief spell at City College, New York, Loesser worked in a variety of jobs including city editor for a local newspaper, a jewellery salesman, and a waiter. His first published song, written with William Schuman in 1931, was 'In Love With a Memory Of You'. Loesser also wrote for vaudeville performers and played piano in nightclubs around New York's 52nd Street. In 1936, he contributed some lyrics to *The Illustrators Show*, with music by Irving Actman, including 'Bang-The Bell Rang!' and 'If You Didn't Love Me'; but the show closed after only five Broadway performances.

In 1937, Loesser went to Hollywood and spent the next few years writing lyrics for movies such as *Cocoanut Grove* ('Says My Heart'), *College Swing* ('Moments Like This' and 'How'dja Like To Make Love To Me?'), *Sing You Sinners* (Bing Crosby singing 'Small Fry'), *Thanks For The Memory* (Bob Hope and Shirley Ross singing 'Two Sleepy People'), *Hurricane* (Dorothy Lamour singing 'Moon Over Manakoora'), *Man About Town* ('Fidgity Joe' and 'Strange Enchantment'), *Some Like It Hot* (1939 film starring Bob Hope and Shirley Ross singing 'The Lady's In

Love With You'), *Destry Rides Again* (Marlene Dietrich with a memorable version of 'See What The Boys In The Backroom Will Have'), *Dancing On A Dime* ('I Hear Music'), *Las Vegas Nights* ('Dolores'), *Kiss The Boys Goodbye* ('I'll Never Let A Day Pass By', 'Sand In My Shoes' and the title song), *Sweater Girl* ('I Don't Want To Walk Without You' and 'I Said No'), *Forest Rangers* ('Jingle Jangle Jingle'), *Happy-Go-Lucky* ('Let's Get Lost' and "Murder' She Says'), *Seven Days Leave* ('Can't Get Out Of This Mood') and *Thank Your Lucky Stars* (Bette Davis singing one of Loesser's most amusing lyrics, which included the couplet: 'I either get a fossil, or an adolescent pup/I either have to hold him off, or have to hold him up!'). These songs were written in collaboration with composers: Burton Lane, Hoagy Carmichael, Alfred Newman, Matty Malneck, Frederick Hollander, Louis Alter, Victor Schertzinger, Jule Styne, Joseph Lilley, Jimmy McHugh and Arthur Schwartz.

The first song for which Loesser wrote both music and lyrics is said to be 'Praise The Lord And Pass The Ammunition', and when he left Hollywood for military service during World War II he added some more service songs to his catalogue, including 'First Class Private Mary Brown', 'The Ballad Of Rodger Young', 'What Do You Do In The Infantry?' and 'Salute To The Army Service Forces'. He also continued to write for films such as *Christmas Holiday* (1944), 'Spring Will Be A Little Late This Year') and *The Perils Of Pauline* (1947), the bio-pic of silent movie-queen Pearl White, with Loesser's songs, 'Poppa Don't Preach To Me' and 'I Wish I Didn't Love You So', which was nominated for an Academy Award. Loesser finally received his Oscar in 1949 for 'Baby It's Cold Outside', from the Esther Williams/Red Skelton movie, *Neptune's Daughter*. In 1948, Loesser wrote 'On A Slow Boat To China', which became a hit for several US artists including Kay Kyser, Freddy Martin, Eddy Howard and Benny Goodman. In the same year he again turned his attention to the Broadway stage, writing the score for a musical adaptation of Brandon Thomas's classic English farce, *Charley's Aunt*. *Where's Charley?*, starring Ray Bolger, included the songs, 'My Darling, My Darling', 'Once In Love With Amy', 'The New Ashmoleon Marching Society And Student Conservatory Band' and 'Make A Miracle'. The show ran for a creditable 792 performances.

Far more successful, two years later, was *Guys And Dolls*, a musical setting of a Damon Runyan fable, starring Robert Alda, Vivian Blaine, Sam Levene, Isabel Bigley and Stubby Kaye. It ran for 1,200 performances, and is considered to be Loesser's masterpiece. As with *Where's Charley?*, he was now writing both music and lyrics, and the show is such a legend that it is worth listing all the principal songs; they were 'Fugue For Tinhorns', 'The Oldest Established', 'I'll Know', 'A Bushel And A Peck', 'Adelaide's Lament', 'Guys And Dolls', 'If I Were A Bell', 'My Time Of Day', 'I've Never Been In Love Before', 'Take Back Your Mink', 'More I Cannot Wish You', 'Luck Be A Lady', 'Sue Me', 'Sit Down, You're Rockin' The Boat' and 'Marry The Man Today'. The original cast album is still available in the 90s, and among the other associated issues were an all-black cast album, released on the Motown label, and *Guys And Dolls: The Kirby Stone Four*. A film adaptation of *Guys And Dolls* was released in 1955, starring Frank Sinatra, Marlon Brando, Jean Simmons, and Vivian Blaine. The movie version left out some of the original songs, and replaced them with 'A Woman In Love' and 'Adelaide'. In 1952, *Where's Charley?* was released on film, and the same year saw a movie of the *Hans Christian Andersen* fairy tale, starring Danny Kaye in the title role, and a Loesser score which included 'Wonderful Copenhagen', 'No Two People', 'Anywhere I Wander', 'Inchworm' and 'Thumbelina'. The latter song was nominated for an Oscar, but was beaten by Dmitri Tiomkin and Ned Washington's 'High Noon'.

Loesser's next Broadway project was *The Most Happy Fella*, for which he also wrote the libretto. The show was adapted from the original story, *They Knew What They Wanted*, by Sidney Howard, which told the tale of an elderly Italian winegrower living in California, who falls in love at first sight with a waitress. Loesser created what has been called 'one of the most ambitiously operatic works ever written for the Broadway musical theatre'. Arias such as 'Rosabella' and 'My Heart Is So Full Of You' are contrasted with more familiar Broadway fare such as 'Standing On the Corner', 'Big D' and 'Happy To Make Your Acquaintance'. The show ran for 676 performances, far more than Loesser's 1960 production of the folksy *Greenwillow*, which closed after 95. It starred Anthony Perkins in his first musical, and contained a religious hymn, the baptism of a cow, and wistful ballads such as 'Faraway Boy' and 'Walking Away Whistling', along with 'Never Will I Marry' and 'Summertime Love', both sung by Perkins. A 3-album set, was issued, containing the complete score. In terms of the number of performances, (1,417), Loesser's last Broadway show, which opened in 1961, was his most successful. *How To Succeed In Business Without Really Trying* was a satire on big business which starred Robert Morse as the aspiring executive, J. Pierpont Finch, and Rudy Vallée as his stuffy boss, J.B. Biggley. The songs which, most critics agreed, fitted the plot completely, included 'The Company Way', 'A Secretary Is Not A Toy', 'Grand Old Ivy', 'Been A Long Day', 'I Believe In You' and 'Brotherhood Of Man'. The show became one of the select band of American musicals to be awarded a Pulitzer Prize; a film version was released in 1967. Loesser died of lung cancer on 28 July 1969, with cigarettes by his side. A life-long smoker, with a contentious, volatile temperament, he is regarded as one of the most original, innovative men of the musical theatre. In 1992, a major revival of *Guys And Dolls* was mounted on Broadway.

Further reading: *A Most Remarkable Fella*, Susan Loesser.

Loewe, Frederick

b. 10 June 1901, Vienna, Austria, d. 14 February 1988. Born into a musical family, (his father was a professional singer), Loewe studied piano as a child, appearing with the Berlin Symphony Orchestra in 1917. In 1924, he visited the USA, but failed to make an impact upon the local classical music scene. Instead, he eked out a living playing piano in restaurants and bars, then roamed throughout the USA, tackling a variety of jobs, including prospecting and cowpunching. As a young teenager he had written songs and he resumed this activity in New York in the early 30s. His style was closely related to that popular in his birthplace and proved generally unsuccessful in his new homeland. In 1942, he formed a musical partnership with Alan Jay Lerner with whom he wrote songs for a succession of shows with results which varied between flops and modest successes. In 1947, the collaborators had their first major hit with *Brigadoon*, from which came 'The Heather On The Hill', 'From This Day On' and 'Almost Like Being In Love'. The association was renewed in 1951 with *Paint Your Wagon* with such songs as 'They Call The Wind Maria', 'I Talk To The Trees' and 'Wand'rin' Star'. In 1956, the team had their major success with *My Fair Lady*, which ran on Broadway for 2,717 performances. The score included such lasting favourites as 'On The Street Where You Live', 'Get Me To The Church On Time', 'With A Little Bit Of Luck', 'Wouldn't It Be Loverly?', 'The Rain In Spain', 'Why Can't The English?', 'I'm An Ordinary Man' and 'I Could Have Danced All Night'. After the huge success of *My Fair Lady* the team was invited to write a musical film and while Lerner was keen, Loewe was reluctant. In the end he agreed and the result, *Gigi* (1958) was one of the final flourishes of the old-style Hollywood musical. Among the songs from the film were 'Thank Heaven For Little Girls', 'I'm Glad I'm Not Young Anymore', 'I Remember It Well' and the title song. After being hospitalized with heart trouble, Loewe returned to his collaboration with Lerner in a new Broadway show, *Camelot*, which opened in 1960. Although the show's preproduction was marred with problems, the result was another success with such outstanding songs as 'If Ever I Would Leave You' and 'How To Handle A Woman'. This show proved to be the last important collaboration for Loewe and Lerner. They teamed up again in 1973 with a stage production of *Gigi* and the following year made their swan song with *The Little Prince*. Loewe died in February 1988.

London Town

This 1946 release, the first picture be made at 'Sound City Studios', Shepperton, England, after World War II, was an attempt to mount a lavish Technicolor British musical to rival the legendary Hollywood productions. It failed dismally, even though the American producer-director Wesley Ruggles was joined by several of his fellow countrymen including highly experienced songwriters Johnny Burke and Jimmy Van Heusen, and musical director-arranger Salvador 'Tutti' Camarata. The dreary and overly sentimental screenplay by Elliot Paul and Siegfried Herzig concerns ambitious comedian Jerry Ruggles (Sid Field), who is merely the understudy for star Charlie DeHaven (Sonnie Hale) in the West End production of *London Town*, until his fawning daughter, Peggy (14-years-old Petula Clark), gets to work. She persuades Charlie's dresser, Belgrave (Claude Hulbert), to feed him a potion which makes his face go green. Naturally, he cannot go on stage like that, so, step forward Jerry, the world of show business is at your feet. The delectable Kay Kendall rose above it all, and also trying their best were Greta Gynt, Tessie O'Shea, and Mary Clare. Jerry Desmonde, Sid Fields' regular straight man, was also on hand to assist him in several of the celebrated comedian's classic routines, including his famous golfing sketch. 'My Heart Goes Crazy' was the big number, and it was reprised several times. Burke and Van Heusen's other songs consisted of an appealing ballad, 'So Would I' (introduced by Beryl Davis) 'You Can't Keep A Good Dreamer Down', and 'Any Way The Wind Blows'. Drummer-singer Jack Parnell turned up in 'The 'Amstead Way' production number which topped and tailed a knees-up medley of Cockney favourites such as 'Don't Dilly Dally On The Way' (Fred W. Leigh-Charles Collins), 'Any Old Iron' (Collins-Fred Terry-E.A. Sheppard), and 'Wot Cher' ('Knock 'Em In The Old Kent Road') (Albert Chevalier-Charles Ingle). The finalé, which featured an enormous grand piano with 10 men seated at the keyboard, reminded many of previous films in which the instrument was featured in a visually effective fashion, such as *King Of Jazz* and *Gold Diggers Of 1935*. Unfortunately, *London Town* was just not in the same class as either of those pictures. In America it was re-titled *My Heart Goes Crazy*.

Love In Las Vegas (see *Viva Las Vegas*)

Love Me Or Leave Me

This realistic bio-pic of the popular 20 and 30s torch singer Ruth Etting was produced by Joe Pasternak for MGM in 1955. Daniel Fuchs won an Oscar for his original story which he and Isobel Lennart adapted for the absorbing screenplay. Doris Day shrugged off her 'goody-goody' image and gave a fine performance as the singer whose dramatic rise from dancehall hostess

Love Me Or Leave Me

to nightclub and Ziegfeld star was masterminded by her gangster husband Martin 'Moe the Gimp' Snyder. James Cagney was outstanding as the domineering Snyder whose response to his wife's relationship with her pianist (Cameron Mitchell) was to shoot him. Although cinematic convention (and box office returns) required a happy ending, there was enough reality left to make this an unusual film. Most of the songs were authentic Etting favourites, too, and included 'Ten Cents A Dance' (Richard Rodgers-Lorenz Hart), 'Shaking The Blues Away' (Irving Berlin), 'It All Depends On You' (De Sylva, Brown And Henderson), 'You Made Me Love You' (Jimmy Monaco-Joseph McCarthy), 'Everybody Loves My Baby' (Jack Palmer-Spencer Williams), 'Mean To Me' (Roy Turk-Fred Ahlert), 'Sam The Old Accordion Man' (Walter Donaldson), 'My Blue Heaven' (Donaldson-George Whiting), 'At Sundown' (Donaldson), and the singer's theme song 'Love Me Or Leave Me' (Donaldson-Gus Kahn). One of the new songs, 'I'll Never Stop Loving You', which was written by Nicholas Brodszky and Sammy Cahn, became a US Top 20 record hit for Doris Day. The strong supporting cast featured Robert Keith, Tom Tully, Harry Bellaver, Claude Stroud, Richard Gaines, Peter Leeds, and Audrey Young. Alex Romero was the choreographer and Charles Vidor directed this popular, and sometimes intriguing film which grossed over $4 million in the US alone.

Love Me Tonight

This stylishly adventurous musical which was released by Paramount in 1932, bore many of the hallmarks of Ernst Lubitsch. However, it was, in fact, superbly directed by Rouben Mamoulian whose innovative work on dramatic films such as *Applause*, *City Streets* and *Dr. Jekyll And Mr. Hyde*, had already marked him out as a master of the medium. The sometimes risqué and satirical screenplay, by Samuel Hoffenstein, Waldemar Young, and George Marion Jnr., was set in France where a simple tailor (Maurice Chevalier) is passed off as a baron by the Vicomte de Vareze (Charlie Ruggles) who owes him a great deal of money. Chevalier is eventually paid in full and also wins the hand of Princess Jeanette (Jeanette MacDonald). The film is brimful of memorable scenes, such as in the early moments when the city of Paris rouses itself from sleep, and especially the sequence in which one song, 'Isn't It Romantic?', is used to transport the action from place to place - a technique which was, at the time, entirely original. The lyric for that song was inextricably linked to the film's story, referring as it did to Chevalier's occupation as a 'tailor', and its composers, Richard

Rodgers and Lorenz Hart, wrote a new set of words for the number's wider publication. Their score also contained another enduring standard, 'Lover', which was introduced by Jeanette MacDonald, and she had 'The Son Of A Gun Is Nothing But A Tailor', as well as duetting with Chevalier and others on 'A Woman Needs Something Like That', 'Love Me Tonight', and 'Song Of Paree'. Chevalier was his charming self on 'The Poor Apache', and, especially, 'Mimi'. Also among the cast were Charles Butterworth, Myrna Loy, C. Aubrey Smith, Elizabeth Patterson, and George 'Gabby' Hayes, who would eventually become a respected character actor in Western movies. *Love Me Tonight*, which is regarded by film buffs all over the world as one of the most perfect and important films in the history of the cinema, was photographed by Victor Milner and produced, as well as directed, by Rouben Mamoulian.

Love Parade, The

Sometimes called 'the first truly cinematic screen musical in America', *The Love Parade* was released by Paramount in 1929. Jeanette MacDonald, who was making her screen debut, co-starred with Maurice Chevalier in Ernest Vajda and Guy Bolton's adaptation of the French play, *Le Prince Consort*. The somewhat bawdy story concerned the Queen of Sylvania (Macdonald), who, having heard on the royal grapevine that her emissary-at-large, Count Alfred (Chevalier), is engaging in the wrong kind of foreign affairs, recalls him so that he can devote more of his energies to her. After he has measured up to her exacting standards, they marry, although her domination extends to the marriage certificate which reads 'wife and man'. Among the rest of the cast were British comedian Lupino Lane, Lillian Roth, Edgar Norton, Lionel Belmore, Virginia Bruce, and Jean Harlow. The score was written by Victor Schertzinger (music) and Clifford Grey (lyrics), and included 'Paris, Stay The Same', 'Dream Lover', 'Nobody's Using It Now', 'The Queen Is Always Right', 'March Of The Grenadiers', and 'Let's Be Common'. Chevalier and MacDonald excelled on 'Anything To Please The Queen' and 'My Love Parade', and the combination of the jaunty boulevardier and the unsophisticated, shrill soprano helped *The Love Parade* to become an enormous box-office winner. Much of the film's success was due to the innovative direction of Ernst Lubitsch, whose lavish settings, and consummate skill in the seamless blending of music, dialogue and action is constantly admired.

Lubitsch, Ernst

b. 28 January 1892, Berlin, Germany, d. 30 November 1947, Bel Air, Los Angeles, California, USA. A celebrated film director who took Hollywood

The Love Parade

by storm after moving to America in 1923. His reputation was based mainly on a series of sophisticated comedies, first with silents, and then with talkies such as *Trouble In Paradise* (1932). However, in the early 30s, he did grace several immensely successful Paramount musicals - all of which starred Maurice Chevalier - with his highly individual, innovative and delightfully risqué 'Lusbitsch touch'. These were *The Love Parade*, *Paramount On Parade* (co-directed), *Monte Carlo*, *The Smiling Lieutenant*, *One Hour With You*, and *The Merry Widow* (1934). For a time during the 30s Lubitsch was the director of production at Paramount, and he continued work as a director on a variety of films into the 40s. The sole musical among them was 20th Century-Fox's *That Lady In Ermine*, starring Betty Grable, Douglas Fairbanks Jnr., and Cesar Romero. Sadly, it had to be completed by Otto Preminger after Lubitsch's death from a heart attack in 1947. A year earlier he had received a special Academy Award for 'his distinguished contributions to the art of the motion picture'.

M

Mad About Music

Deanna Durbin was only 17 years old when she made this film in 1938, but her 'significant contribution in bringing to the screen the spirit and personification of youth', gained her a special Academy Award in the same year. In *Mad About Music* she once again plays a character bursting with imagination and energy, who, after being deposited in a swanky Swiss finishing school by her narcissistic actress mother (Gail Patrick), comes up with a father who is simply the product of that same fertile imagination. Invited to produce him for inspection, the youngster offers a rather puzzled visitor (Herbert Marshall) as her partner in the collusion. It was all good fun, and also taking part were Jackie Moran, Arthur Treacher, William Frawley, Helen Parrish, Marcia Mae Jones. The musical highlight was Miss Durbin's spirited rendering of 'I Love To Whistle' with Cappy Barra's Harmonica Band. Harold Adamson and Jimmy McHugh wrote that tune, along with 'Serenade To The Stars', 'Chapel Bells', and 'There Isn't A Day Goes By'. Durbin also joined the Vienna Boys' Choir in a beautiful version of 'Ave Maria' (Charles Gounod). Norman Taurog directed this highly popular feature

which attracted several Oscar nominations, two of which went to Marcella Burke and Frederick Kohner, the writers of the story on which Bruce Manning and Felix Jackson's screenplay was based. It received another airing in 1956 when *Mad About Music* was remade as *Toy Tiger* starring Jeff Chandler and Laraine Day, with Tim Hovey in the Deanna Durbin part.

Magidson, Herb

b. 7 January 1906, Braddock, Pennsylvania, USA, d. 5 January 1986, Beverly Hills, California, USA. A leading composer and lyricist in the 30s and 40s, particularly remembered for 'The Continental', which he wrote the lyric to Con Conrad's tune for the Fred Astaire-Ginger Rogers picture *The Gay Divorcée*. It became the first winner of the 'Best Song' Academy Award in 1934. The team also wrote another good song for Astaire to sing in the film - 'Needle In A Haystack'. Magidson studied journalism at the University of Pittsburg before moving to New York and writing special material for Sophie Tucker. In the late 20s and early 30s he contributed a few numbers to Broadway shows such as *Earl Carroll's Vanities Of 1928* and *George White's Musical Hall Varieties*, but the majority of his output was for movies. Through to 1939 he wrote single songs or complete scores for *The Time, The Place And The Girl* (1929), *Show Of Shows*, *Little Johnny Jones*, *No, No, Nanette*, *I Like It That Way*, *The Gift Of Gab*, *George White's 1935 Scandals*, *Here's To Romance*, *The Great Ziegfeld*, *Hats Off*, *Music For Madame*, *Life Of The Party*, *Radio City Revels*, and *George White's Scandals Of 1939*. From these films came songs such as 'The Racoon', 'Somebody To Love', 'Dance Of The Wooden Shoes', 'Singin' In The Bathtub', 'Talkin' To Myself', 'Oh, I Didn't Know', 'According To The Moonlight', 'Here's To Romance', 'Midnight In Paris', 'Twinkle, Twinkle, Little Star' (not the nursery rhyme), 'Where Have You Been All My Life?', 'Let's Have Another Cigarette', 'Roses In December', 'Goodnight Angel', 'When The Cat's Away', and 'Something I Dreamed Last Night'. In the 40s, two of Magidson's wartime songs, 'Say A Prayer For The Boys Over There' (written with Jimmy McHugh for *Hers To Hold*) and 'I'll Buy That Dream' (with Allie Wrubel for *Sing Your Way Home*) were nominated for Oscars, and he also had numbers in *Sleepy Time Gal*, *Music In Manhatten*, *Do You Love Me?*, and *Make Mine Laughs*, amongst others. Throughout his career Magidson did not neglect Tin Pan Alley, and several of his best songs, unassociated with either films or shows, have been sung and played by the finest vocalists and bands. Among them are 'Gone With The Wind', 'Music, Maestro Please', '(I'm Afraid) The Masquerade Is Over', 'How Long Has This Been Going On?', 'I Can't Love You Anymore', 'A Pink Cocktail For A Blue Lady', 'I'm Stepping Out With A Memory Tonight', 'I'll Dance At Your Wedding', 'Enjoy

Yourself (It's Later Than You Think)', and one of his earliest successes, 'Black-Eyed Susan Brown'. Besides the ones already mention, his many collaborators included Carl Sigman, Michael Cleary, Sammy Fain, Ben Oakland, Sam Stept, and Jule Styne. Like so many of the Old Guard, he seems to have been a casualty of rock 'n' roll, and there is no apparent record of him composing songs after the early 50s.

Mambo Kings, The

Adapted by Cynthia Cidre from Oscar Hijuelos' Pulitzer Prize-winning novel *The Mambo Kings Play Songs Of Love*, this 1992 Warner Brothers production tells of two Cuban brothers, trumpet player Nestor and mambo singer and percussionist Cesar Castillo (Antonio Banderas and Armand Assante). In 1952 they leave Cuba for New York where Cesar demonstrates his skills at the swish Palladium club with the renowned Tito Puente Orchestra. After forming their own group The Mambo Kings, fellow Cuban Desi Arnaz - who is played by his real-life son Desi Arnaz Jnr. - hears them singing Nestor's composition 'Beautiful Maria Of My Soul' (Robert Kraft-Arne Glimcher) and invites them to appear on the top-rated *I Love Lucy* television show. Their subsequent rise to fame and fortune is shattered when Nestor dies in a car crash. Cesar buys a bar of his own, the Club Havana, and on the opening night, at the request of his late brother's girl, Delores Fuentes (Maruschka Detmers), he sings Nestor's lovely bolero 'Beautiful Maria Of My Soul'. The song had been dedicated to Maria Rivera (Talisa Soto) Nestor's former lover in Cuba. Other roles in the large cast went to Cathy Moriarty, Pablo Calogero, Scott Cohen, Mario Grillo, Ralph Irizzary, Pete MacNamara, and Jimmy Medina. The mostly South American songs included 'Mambo Caliente' (Arturo Sandoval), 'Tanga, Rumba-Afro-Cubana' (Mario Bauza), 'Guantanamera' (Fernandez Diaz), 'Perfidia' (Alberto Dominguez), 'Quiereme Mucho' (Gonzalo Roig-Augustin Rodriguez), and 'Cuban Pete' (José Norman). The exotic background score was written by Robert Kraft and Carlos Franzetti. Michael Peters was the choreographer, and the film was photographed in Technicolor by Michael Ballhouse. The director was Arne Glimcher. 'Beautiful Maria Of My Soul' was nominated for the best song Oscar, but, unlike the original book, no other prizes came the way of this brash and colourful film.

Mamoulian, Rouben

b. 8 October 1898, Tbilisi, Georgia, Russia, d. 4 December 1987, Los Angeles, California, USA. A distinguished stage and film director whose name is particularly associated with two masterpieces of the American musical theatre - *Porgy And Bess* and *Oklahoma!*- and a legendary Hollywood movie, *Love Me Tonight*. Mamoulian spent part of his childhood in Paris before studying at Moscow University, and running his own drama school in Tbilisi. In 1920 he toured Britain with a Russian theatre group and subsequently studied drama at London University. He moved to the USA in 1923 and operettas at the George Eastman Theatre in Rochester, New Jersey, before going to New York where he became a leading light with the prestigious Theatre Guild. His reputation as a theatre director led him to Hollywood at the beginning of the talkie era, and he immediately impressed with his innovative and audacious approach to the medium. His first film, *Applause* (1929) starring Helen Morgan, was followed by a series of highly acclaimed pictures - sophisticated comedies, dramas, gangster movies - featuring the biggest stars of the day, including Fredric March, Marlene Dietrich, Tyrone Power, and Greta Garbo. Among them were several musicals, such as the charming *Love Me Tonight* (1932) with Jeanette MacDonald and Maurice Chevalier (which Mamoulian also produced), *The Gay Desperado* (1936), *High, Wide And Handsome* (1937), *Summer Holiday* (1947), and the elegant *Silk Stockings* (1957) starring Fred Astaire and Cyd Charisse. His relatively small cinema output is said to be due to persistent disagreements and confrontations with producers. He was hired and quickly fired from movies such as *Laura*, *Porgy And Bess*, and the Elizabeth Taylor-Richard Burton epic *Cleopatra* (1963). In parallel with his Hollywood career, Mamoulian directed major works on Broadway, including *Porgy And Bess* (1935), *Oklahoma!* (1943), *Sadie Thompson* (1944), *Carousel* (1945), *St. Louis Woman* (1946), *Lost In The Stars* (1949), and *Arms And The Girl* (1950). On the latter show, and on *Sadie Thompson*, he also served as co-librettist, and in later years wrote and adapted several plays and children's stories.

Mancini, Henry

b. Enrico Mancini, 16 April 1924, Cleveland, Ohio, USA, d. 14 June 1994, Los Angeles, California, USA. Prompted by his father, a steelworker who loved music, Mancini learned to play several musical instruments while still a small child. As a teenager he developed an interest in jazz and especially music of the big bands. He wrote some arrangements and sent them to Benny Goodman, from whom he received some encouragement. In 1942, he became a student at the Juilliard School of Music, but his career was interrupted by military service during World War II. Immediately following the war he was hired as pianist and arranger by Tex Beneke, who was then leading the Glenn Miller orchestra. Later in the 40s Mancini began writing arrangements for studios, prompted initially by a contract to score for a recording date secured by his wife, singer Ginny O'Connor. He was also hired to work on films, and it was here that his interest in big band music paid off. He wrote the scores for two Hollywood bio-pics, *The Glenn Miller*

Henry Mancini (left) and Andy Williams

Story (1954) and *The Benny Goodman Story* (1956). Mancini also contributed jazz-influenced scores for television, including those for the innovative *Peter Gunn* series and *Mr Lucky*. His film work continued with scores and songs for such films as *Breakfast At Tiffany's* (1961), from which came 'Moon River', (the Oscar winner that year), and the title songs for *Days Of Wine And Roses* (1962), which again won an Oscar, and *Charade* (1963). His other film work includes 'Baby Elephant Walk' from *Hatari!* (1962), the theme from *The Pink Panther* (1964), 'Sweetheart Tree' from *The Great Race* (1965), and scores for *Wait Until Dark*, *Darling Lili*, *Mommie Dearest*, *Victor/Victoria* (1982), for which he won an Oscar for 'Original Song Score' with Leslie Bricusse, *That's Dancing*, *Without A Clue*, *Physical Evidence*, *Blind Date*, *That's Life*, *The Glass Menagerie*, *Sunset*, *Fear*, *Switch*, and *Tom And Jerry: The Movie*, for which he again teamed with Leslie Bricusse. One of the most respected film and television composer - and the winner of 20 Grammy Awards - Mancini also regularly conducted orchestras in the USA and UK in concerts of his music, most of which stood comfortably on its own merits outside the context for which it was originally conceived. In the months prior to his death from cancer, Mancini was working with Leslie Bricusse on the score for the stage adaption of Victor/Victoria.

Selected albums: *The Music From Peter Gunn* (1959), *Breakfast At Tiffany's* (1961), *Hatari* (1962), *The Concert Sound Of Henry Mancini* (1964), *The Latin Sound Of Henry Mancini* (1965), *Mancini '67* (1967), *A Warm Shade Of Ivory* (1969), *Mancini Country* (1970), *Mancini Plays Theme From Love Story* (1971), with Doc Severinsen *Brass, Ivory & Strings* (1973), *Mancini's Angels* (1977).

Further reading: *Henry Mancini*, Gene Lees.

Mandel, Johnny

b. 23 November 1935, New York City, New York, USA. After playing trumpet and trombone while still in his pre-teenage years (a period in which he began to write music), Mandel played with various bands in and around New York, including those led by Boyd Raeburn and Jimmy Dorsey. In the mid- to late 40s Mandel played in the bands of Buddy Rich, Alvino Rey and others, and in the early 50s, he worked with Elliott Lawrence and Count Basie. He began to establish himself both as an arranger, contributing charts to the Basie and Artie Shaw bands, and also as a songwriter. By the mid-50s he was writing music for films and was working less in the jazz field, although his film music often contained echoes of his background. Much respected by singers and jazz instrumentalists, Mandel has a particular facility for ballads. He also orchestrated scores for Broadway and for television specials. His film work, from the 50s through to the 80s, includes music for *I Want To Live*, *The Third Voice*, *The Americanization Of Emily*, *The Sandpiper*, *The Russians Are Coming*, *Point Blank*, *MASH*, *The Last Detail*, *Escape To Witch Mountain*, *Freaky Friday*, *Agatha*, *Being There*, *The Baltimore Bullet*, *Caddyshack*, *Deathtrap*, *The Verdict*, *Staying Alive*, and *Brenda Starr* (1987). He also scored for television movies such as *The Trackers*, *The Turning Point Of Jim Molloy*, *A Letter To Three Wives*, *Christmas Eve*, *LBJ - The Early Years*, *Assault And Matrimony*, *Foxfire*, *Agatha*, *The Great Escape II - The Untold Story*, and *Single Men - Married Women* (1989). Among his songs are 'Emily', 'A Time For Love' and, perhaps his best-known, 'The Shadow Of Your Smile' (lyrics by Paul Francis Webster), written for *The Sandpiper* (1965). This song won a Grammy and the Oscar for Best Song.

Martin, Dean

b. Dino Paul Crocetti, 7 June 1917, Steubenville, Ohio, USA. Martin was always widely admired as a ballad singer with a relaxed style, and also showed talent as a light comedian and dramatic actor. After leaving school in the 10th grade, he worked as a shoe-shine boy and a gas station attendant before becoming an 'amateur' welterweight boxer, 'Kid Crochet', earning 10 dollars a fight. When he retired from the boxing arena, he became a croupier at a local casino. His first singing job is said to have been with the Sammy Watkins band in 1941, in which he was initially billed as Dino Martini, but the name was soon changed to Dean Martin. His earliest recordings were for the Diamond label, and they included 'Which Way Did My Heart Go'/'All Of Me' and 'I Got the Sun In The Morning'/'Sweetheart Of Sigma Chi'. He also recorded some tracks for the Apollo label, well known for its impressive roster of black talent. The Martin recordings included, 'Walkin' My Baby Back Home', 'Oh Marie', 'Santa Lucia', 'Hold Me', 'Memory Lane' and 'Louise'. In 1946, Martin first worked with comedian Jerry Lewis at the 500 Club in Atlantic City. Together they developed an ad-libbing, song and comedy act which became very popular on US television and radio in the late 40s. In 1949, they appeared in supporting roles in the film *My Friend Irma*, and in the sequel, *My Friend Irma Goes West*, the following year. The team then starred in another 14 popular comedies, with Martin providing the songs and romantic interest, and Lewis contributing the zany fun. These films included *At War With The Army* (1950), *Jumping Jacks* (1952), *Sailor, Beware!*, *The Stooge*, *Scared Stiff* (1953), *The Caddy* (1953), *Living It Up* (1954), *Pardners* (1956) and *Hollywood Or Bust* (1956). Their parting was somewhat acrimonious, and it was widely felt that Martin would be the one to suffer most from the split. In fact, they both did well. Martin, after a shaky start in the comedy movie, *Ten Thousand Bedrooms* (1957), blossomed as a dramatic actor in *The Young Lions* (1958), *Some Came Running* (1958), *Rio Bravo* (1959), *Ada* (1961), *Toys In The*

Attic (1963), *The Sons Of Katie Elder* (1965) and *Airport* (1970). He still retained his comedy touch in *Who Was That Lady?* (1960) and *What A Way To Go* (1964) but made surprisingly few musicals. The most notable were *Bells Are Ringing* (1960), with Judy Holliday, and *Robin And The Seven Hoods* (1964). Meanwhile, Martin had signed to Capitol Records in 1948, and for the next 10 years had a series of US Top 30 chart entries, including 'That Certain Party' (duet with Jerry Lewis), 'Powder Your Face With Sunshine', 'I'll Always Love You', 'If', 'You Belong To Me', 'Love Me, Love Me', 'That's Amore', 'I'd Cry Like A Baby', 'Sway', 'Money Burns A Hole In My Pocket, 'Memories Are Made Of This' (number 1), 'Innamorata', 'Standing On The Corner', 'Return To Me', 'Angel Baby' and 'Volare' ('Nel Blu Dipinto Di Blu'). Martin's version of 'That's Amore' surfaced again when it was featured in the 1987 hit movie, *Moonstruck*.

Although Martin was still a big attraction on film and in nightclubs, his records found difficulty in making the singles charts during the early part of the 60s. In 1961, Frank Sinatra, who had also been with Capitol Records, started his own Reprise Records. Martin, who was a member of Sinatra's 'Clan', or 'Ratpack', was one of the first recruits to the new label. In 1964, Martin was back in the US singles charts with a bang. His recording of 'Everybody Loves Somebody', produced by Jimmy Bowen, had a commercial country 'feel' about it, and knocked the Beatles' 'A Hard Day's Night' off the top of the chart. Martin's subsequent Top 30 entries were all in the same vein - records such as 'The Door Is Still Open To My Heart', 'You're Nobody Till Somebody Loves You', 'Send Me The Pillow You Dream On', 'Houston', 'In The Chapel In The Moonlight' and 'Little Ole Wine Drinker, Me'. The latter number was a fitting selection for an artist whose stage persona was that of a man more than slightly inebriated. 'Everybody Loves Somebody' became the theme song for *The Dean Martin Show* on NBC TV which started in 1964, ran for nine seasons and was syndicated world-wide. As well as being a showcase for Martin's singing talents, the show gave him the opportunity to display his improvisation skills in comedy. He continued to be a big draw in clubs, especially in Las Vegas, and played the London Palladium in the summer of 1987, to favourable reviews. Later that year, he joined ex-Rat Pack colleagues, Sinatra and Sammy Davis Jnr., in the 'Together Again' tour, involving 40 performances in 29 cities, but had to withdraw at an early stage because of a kidney ailment.

Albums: *The Stooge* (1956, film soundtrack), *Swingin' Down Yonder* (mid-50s), *Pretty Baby* (mid-50s), *This Is Martin* (late 50s), *Sleep Warm* (1959), *Winter Romance* (1959), *The Bells Are Ringing* (1960, film soundtrack), *This Time I'm Swingin'* (1961), *Dean Martin* (1961), *Dino - Italian Love Songs* (1962), *French Style* (1962),

Dino Latino (1963), *Country Style* (1963), *Dean 'Tex' Martin Rides Again* (1963), *Everybody Loves Somebody* (1964), *Hey Brother, Pour The Wine* (1964), *Dream With Dean* (1964), *The Door Is Still Open To My Heart* (1964), *Dean Martin Hits Again* (1965), *Dean Martin Sings, Sinatra Conducts* (1965), *Southern Style* (1965), *Holiday Cheer* (1965), *Lush Years* (1965), *(Remember Me) I'm The One Who Loves You* (1965), *Houston* (1965), *Somewhere There's A Someone* (1966), *Relaxin'* (1966), *Happy In Love* (1966), *The Silencers* (1966, film soundtrack), *The Hit Sound Of Dean Martin* (1966), *The Dean Martin TV Show* (1966), *The Dean Martin Christmas Album* (1966), *At Ease With Dean* (1967), *Happiness Is Dean Martin* (1967), *Welcome To My World* (1967), *Gentle On My Mind* (1968), *I Take A Lot Of Pride In What I Am* (1969), *My Woman, My Woman, My Wife* (1970), *For The Good Times* (1971), *Dino* (1972). Compilations: *The Best Of Dean Martin* (1966), *Dean Martin's Greatest Hits! Volume 1* (1968), *Dean Martin's Greatest Hits! Volume 2* (1968), *The Best Of Dean Martin, Volume 2* (1969), *20 Original Dean Martin Hits* (1976), *The Collection* (1989).

Further reading: *Everybody Loves Somebody*, Arthur Marx. *Dino: Living High In The Dirty Business Of Dreams*, Nick Tosches.

Martin, Mary

b. Mary Virginia Martin, 1 December 1913, Weatherford, Texas, USA, d. 3 November 1990, Rancho Mirage, California, USA. A legendary star of the Broadway musical theatre during the 40s and 50s, and one of its most charming, vivacious and best-loved performers. Her father was a lawyer, and her mother a violin teacher. She took dancing and singing lessons from an early age, married at 16, and eventually ran a dancing school herself before moving to Hollywood where she auditioned constantly at the film studios, and worked in nightclubs and on radio. After being spotted by the producer Lawrence Schwab, her first big break came on Broadway in 1938 when she won a secondary role in the Cole Porter musical *Leave It To Me*. Almost every night she stopped the show with her 'sensational' rendering of 'My Heart Belongs To Daddy' while performing a mock striptease perched on top of a large cabin trunk at a 'Siberian' railway station. On the strength of her performance in that show she was signed to Paramount, and made 10 films over a period of four years, beginning with *The Great Victor Herbert* in 1939. Although her delightfuly warm personality and theatrical star quality, were not so effective on film, she did have her moments, particularly in *Rhythm On The River* (with Bing Crosby and Oscar Levant) and *Birth Of The Blues*, in which she joined Crosby and Jack Teagarden for 'The Waiter, And The Porter And The Upstairs Maid'. She also sang the title song in *Kiss The Boys Goodbye*, which became a big hit for Tommy Dorsey, and duetted with Dick Powell on

'Hit The Road To Dreamland' in *Star Spangled Rhythm*. Other film appearances included *Love Thy Neighbour*, *New York Town*, *Happy-Go-Lucky*, *True To Life*, *Night And Day*, and *Main Street To Boradway* (1953). While on the west coast, she married for the second time, to a Paramount executive Richard Halliday, who became her manager. In 1943 she returned to the stage, and, after failing to reach Broadway with *Dancing In The Streets*, scored a great success with *One Touch Of Venus* which ran for 567 performances. The role of a glamorous statue that comes to life and falls in love with a human had originally been intended for Marlene Dietrich, but it fell to Martin to introduce the haunting 'Speak Low,' and the show established her as a true star. She followed it with *Lute Song*, the show which introduced Yul Brynner to Broadway, before returning to Hollywood to reprise 'My Heart Belongs To Daddy' for the Cole Porter bio-pic *Night And Day*. A trip to London in 1947 for an appearance in Noël Coward's *Pacific 1860*, proved an unsatisfactory experience, and Martin returned to the USA to play the lead in a touring version of *Annie Get Your Gun*. Richard Rodgers and Oscar Hammerstein's smash hit *South Pacific* was next, and Martin's memorable performance, funny and poignant in turns, won her a Tony Award. Starred with opera singer Ezio Pinza, she introduced several of the composers' most endearing numbers, including 'I'm Gonna Wash That Man Right Out Of My Hair' (sung while she shampooed her hair on stage), 'A Wonderful Guy', 'A Cockeyed Optimist', and the hilarious 'Honeybun'. *South Pacific* ran for 1,925 performances in New York, and Martin recreated her role for the 1951 London production at Drury Lane where she was equally well received. During the rest of the 50s Mary Martin appeared in several straight plays, two highly regarded television spectaculars - one with Ethel Merman (which included a 35-song medley), and the other with Noël Coward - as well as starring on Broadway with Cyril Ritchard in a musical version of *Peter Pan* (1954) which was taped and shown repeatedly on US television. In November 1959 Martin opened at the Lunt-Fontanne Theatre in New York in what was to prove yet another blockbuster hit. Rodgers and Hammerstein's musical about the Trapp family of Austrian folk singers, *The Sound Of Music*, immediately produced reactions ranging for raves to revulsion, but it gave Martin another Tony Award and the chance to display her homespun charm with songs such as 'My Favourite Things' and 'Do-Re-Mi'. From the 'hills that were alive with music', Mary Martin plummeted to the depths in *Jennie* (1963), her first real flop. Thereafter, she and her husband spent more time at their home in Brazil, but in 1965 she was persuaded to embark on a world tour in *Hello, Dolly!* which included a visit to Vietnam, and a five-month stay in London. Her final appearance in a Broadway musical was in 1966 with Robert Preston in the two-hander *I Do! I Do!* which ran for 560 performances. In the 70s she did more straight theatre and won a Peabody Award for the television film *Valentine*. After her husband's death in 1973, Martin moved to Palm Springs to be near her friend Janet Gaynor, but returned to New York in 1977 to star with Ethel Merman in a benefit performance of *Together Again*. In the early 80s, Martin and Janet Gaynor were severely injured in an horrific taxicab crash in San Franciso which took the life of her longtime aide Ben Washer. Martin recovered to receive the applause of her peers in *Our Heart Belongs To Mary*, and to make her final US stage appearance in 1986 with Carol Channing in a national tour of James Kirkwood's comedy *Legends*. For much of the time she had to wear a shortwave radio device to prompt her when she forgot her lines. Mary Martin made her final appearance on the London stage in the 1980 Royal Variety Performance when she performed a delightful version of 'Honeybun', and then had to suffer the embarrasment of watching her son from her first marriage, Larry Hagman (the notorious J.R Ewing from the television soap *Dallas*), forget his lines in front of a celebrity audience.

Selected albums: *Mary Martin Sings-Richard Rodgers Plays* (1958), *Sings For You* (c.50s), with Ethel Merman *Duet From Ford 50th Anniversary Telecast* (c.50s), and Broadway Cast recordings.

Further reading: *My Heart Belongs*, Mary Martin.

Martin, Ray

b. Raymond Stuart Martin, 11 October 1918, Vienna, Austria, d. February 1988, South Africa. Martin was a composer, arranger, musical director and author. After studying violin, composition and orchestration at the State Academy for Music and Fine Arts, Vienna, he moved to Britain in 1937. Martin joined the *Carroll Levis Discoveries* show as a solo violin act, and toured the UK Variety circuit. He was then chosen as the 'New Voice' in the popular BBC radio series, *Bandwaggon*, which starred Arthur Askey and Richard Murdoch. After appearing in several editions of *Sidney Torch's Half Hour*, he joined the British Army in 1940, and worked in the Intelligence Corps, aided by his fluency in German, French and English. Later, he became musical director of the Variety Department for the British Forces Network in Hamburg, Germany. He started broadcasting his *Melody From The Sky* programme from there, with a German string orchestra culled from the Hamburg Philharmonic Orchestra, and transferred the show to the BBC in December 1946, where it ran for over 500 broadcasts. Martin was also instrumental in founding the BBC Northern Variety Orchestra, and, from 1949-51, conducted at least six shows a week. He started recording for Columbia Records in 1949 with his own Concert Orchestra accompanying other artists including Julie Andrews, Steve Conway and Jimmy Young. Eventually he became the company's recording manager. His 50s instrumental hits included Leroy Anderson's 'Blue Tango', 'Swedish Rhapsody' and 'Carousel Waltz'. He also released *Lehar, Strauss And Novello, High Barbaree - 12 Famous Sea Shanties, Olives, Almonds And Raisins, Million Dollar Melodies, I Could Have Danced All Night, Boots And Saddles* and *Melodies d'Amour*. Some of his many compositions and film scores are difficult to locate because, besides his own name, he wrote under several pseudonyms, such as Tony Simmonds, Buddy Cadbury, Lester Powell and Marshall Ross. In 1956, he wrote the background score, and served as musical director, for a British musical film called *It's Great To Be Young*, starring John Mills. In addition to the title track, written under his own name, the film contained Martin's (Marshall Ross's), 1952 composition, 'Marching Strings'; and his (Lester Powell's) romantic ballad, 'You Are My First Love', written with Paddy Roberts. It also featured a very early Sammy Cahn-Saul Kaplan-Jimmie Lunceford song, 'Rhythm Is Our Business'. Martin's other compositions included 'Melody From The Sky', 'Once Upon A Winter Time', 'Muriella', 'Begorra', 'Parlour Game', 'Blue Violins' (a US hit for Hugo Winterhalter's Orchestra), 'Any Old Time', 'Waltzing Bugle Boy', 'Airborne', 'Ballet Of The Bells', 'Tango Of The Bells', 'Big Ben Blues', 'Never Too Young' and 'Sounds Out Of Sight'. He composed the incidental music for over 20 BBC Sound cartoons, and wrote the scores for several films, including *Yield To The Night*, a prison melodrama in which ex-'glamour girl', Diana Dors, gave a highly acclaimed dramatic performance; and the 1956 version of *My Wife's Father*. In 1957, Martin moved to America to work in New York and Hollywood. His US film scores included *The Young Graduates* and *The Hoax*. In 1972, he returned to work in the UK and, in 1980, appeared as himself in *The Baltimore Bullit*. During the 80s he settled in South Africa, and died there in 1988. Selected albums: *Piccadilly 2am* (1956), *Dynamica* (1961), *Favourite TV Themes* (1973), *Favourite TV Themes, Volume 2* (1975), *Viva Mariachi* (1975), *Welcome Home* (1975).

Martin, Tony

b. Alvin Morris, 25 December 1913, Oakland, California, USA. Martin was an extremely popular singer from the 30s until the late 50s, with a powerful voice and an easy, romantic style. As a teenager, Martin became proficient on the saxophone and formed his own band, the Clarion Four. For some years he worked in the San Francisco area at the Palace Hotel, playing saxophone and singing with bands such as Anson Weeks, Tom Coakley, and Tom Guran, whose outfit included Woody Herman. Morris drove across country with Herman and other members of the band to the 1933 Chicago World

Fair, and afterwards played the city's Chez Paree Club. In 1934, he changed his name to Tony Martin, and tried to break into films, without success. Two years later, he landed a 'bit' part in the Fred Astaire-Ginger Rogers hit movie, *Follow The Fleet*, along with two other young hopefuls, Lucille Ball and Betty Grable. Later in 1936, he signed for 20th Century-Fox, and sang 'When I'm With You' in *Poor Little Rich Girl*, and 'When Did You Leave Heaven?' in *Sing, Baby, Sing*. The following year he married one of the film's stars, Alice Faye.

During the late 30s, he achieved star status thanks to film musicals such as *Pigskin Parade*, with Judy Garland and Betty Grable; *Banjo On My Knee*, with Barbara Stanwyck and Joel McCrea; *The Holy Terror* and *Sing And Be Happy*, with Leah Ray; *You Can't Have Everything* and *Sally, Irene And Mary* with Alice Faye; *Ali Baba Goes To Town*, starring Eddie Cantor; *Kentucky Moonshine* and *Thanks For Everything*. When Martin left Fox, he appeared with Rita Hayworth in *Music In My Heart*, and sang Robert Wright and Chester Forest's 'It's A Blue World', which was nominated for an Academy Award in 1940. In 1941, Martin appeared with the Marx Brothers in *the Big Store*, and sang what was to become one of his 'identity songs', 'The Tenement Symphony', described in some quarters, somewhat unkindly, as the comedy highlight of the film. Martin's other movie that year was *Ziegfeld Girl*, with some spectacular Busby Berkeley production numbers, and starring, amongst others, Judy Garland, Hedy Lamarr and Lana Turner. After the attack on Pearl Harbor in December 1941, Martin enlisted in the US Armed Forces, serving first in the Navy, and then with the Army in the Far East. He also sang for a time with the Army Air Forces Training Command Orchestra, directed by Glenn Miller. While in the Services, Martin received several awards, including the Bronze Star and several citations. At the end of World War II, he returned to showbusiness and starred in the Jerome Kern bio-pic, *Till The Clouds Roll By* (1946), which was followed by *Casbah* (1948), thought by many to have been his best role. The songs were by Harold Arlen and Leo Robin, and included another Martin all-time favourite, 'For Every Man There's A Woman'. In the same year, Martin, having divorced Alice Faye, married dancer-actress Cyd Charisse, and later starred with her in *Easy To Love* (1953). Martin's other films during the 50s included *Two Tickets To Broadway* (with Janet Leigh), *Here Come The Girls* (with Bob Hope and Rosemary Clooney), the all-star Sigmund Romberg bio-pic, *Deep In My Heart*, the 1955 MGM re-make of *Hit The Deck,* and a guest appearance in *Meet Me In Las Vegas* (which starred Cyd Charisse and Dan Dailey). In 1957, Martin starred with Vera Ellen in *Let's Be Happy*, an unsuccessful British attempt to recreate the Hollywood musical. Besides his films, Martin had a very successful recording career. His first hits, 'Now It Can Be Told' and 'South Of The Border', came in the late 30s, and continued through to the mid-50s, with songs such as 'It's A Blue World', 'Tonight We Love', 'To Each His Own', 'Rumours Are Flying', 'It's Magic', 'There's No Tomorrow', 'Circus', 'Marta (Rambling Rose Of The Wildwood)', 'I Said My Pyjamas (And Put On My Prayers)' and 'Take A Letter, Miss Smith' (both duets with Fran Warren), 'La Vie En Rose', 'Would I Love You (Love You Love You)', 'I Get Ideas' (adapted from the Argentine tango 'Adios Muchachos' and thought to be quite racy at the time), 'Over A Bottle Of Wine', 'Domino', 'Kiss Of Fire', 'Stranger In Paradise', 'Here', 'Do I Love You (Because You're Beautiful)' and 'Walk Hand In Hand'. His albums included *Dream Music*, *A Night At The Copacabana* (a fair example of his club act, containing favourites such as 'Begin the Beguine', 'September Song' and 'Manhattan'), *Tenement Symphony*, *At Carnegie Hall*, *Fly Me To The Moon*, *Mr Song Man*, *Our Love Affair*, *At The Desert Inn*, *In the Spotlight* and *Tonight*. As well as having a very successful cabaret act, which he played around the world, Martin was also very active on radio in the 30s, 40s, and into the 50s, on shows such as Walter Winchell's *Lucky Strike Hour*, and others, featuring Burns And Allen, Andre Kostelanetz and David Rose. Martin appeared in his own programmes. He turned to television in the 50s and 60s, and in 1964 formed a night club act with his wife, Cyd Charisse, touring the cabaret circuit in the USA and abroad. In 1976, they published an autobiography, *The Two Of Us*. In 1986, at the age of 63, Charisse re-created the role first played by Anna Neagle over 20 years earlier in the David Heneker-John Taylor stage musical, *Charlie Girl*, at London's Victoria Palace. Martin and Charisse had first been in London in 1948, on their honeymoon, when he was playing the first of several London Palladium seasons. He has come a long way since then. Martin is still regarded as one of the most accomplished and stylish vocalists of his era.

Selected albums: *A Night At Copacabana* (1956), *Our Love Affair* (1957), *In The Spotlight* (1958), *Dream Music* (1959), *Mr. Song Man* (1960), *At The Desert Inn* (1960), *Tonight* (1960), *Fly Me To The Moon* (1962), *At Carnegie Hall* (1967). Selected compilations: *Greatest Hits* (1961), *Golden Hits* (1962), *Best Of* (1984), *Tenement Symphony* (1984), *Something In The Air* (1989).

Mary Poppins

There have been many occasions when performers who have triumphed in Broadway shows have been overlooked when the movie adaptations came along. While Julie Andrews would have no doubt dazzled as Eliza Doolittle in the film version of *My Fair Lady*, it was not to be. Instead, Andrews made up for the disappointment in a big way by making her first screen appearance in this 1964 Walt Disney classic. With supreme irony, Andrews won the best actress Oscar for her debut performance, while Audrey Hepburn, who 'took her place' in the film of Alan Jay Lerner and Frederick Loewe's masterpiece, was not even nominated. With a screenplay by Bill Walsh and Donald Da Gradi, adapted from the children's story by Pamela Travers, the action of *Mary Poppins* evolves around the Banks family, residents of 17 Cherry Tree Lane, London. Mr George Banks (David Tomlinson) is a banker by name, nature and occupation. He rules his house with a rod of iron, while Winifred, his wife (Glynis Johns), spends most of the time fighting for the Suffragettes' cause (the year is 1910). Both spend little time with their children Michael (Matthew Garber) and Jane (Karen Dotrice). Many nannies have come and gone (six in four months), and as the film begins, the time has come to employ another one. The children draw up their own advertisement, outlining what they want most in the new employee. In disgust Mr Banks throws the piece of paper into the fireplace, and unbeknown to him, it travels up the chimney, and, before you can say 'Mary Poppins', she floats down to earth, carrying her trusty umbrella, and appoints herself as the new nanny, giving the family a week's trial! Before long Mary has won the hearts of the children, tidying up by magic, and taking them on many an adventure. During one such trip she bumps into an old friend, Bert (Dick Van Dyke) who plays a number of different roles in the film), entertaining with his one-man band and drawing pictures on the pavement. As if by magic, Mary, Bert and the children escape from reality and step into the street painting. Here the movie really comes into its own as humans mix with all kinds of animated characters and animals. It is great fun to watch, as we see the group being waited on by penguins, and wooden horses galloping with freedom. Only when the pavement picture is washed away by rain, do the happy foursome have to return home. However, fun is frivolous to Mr Banks, and he decides to take the children along to his workplace to see what the real world is all about. Here Michael and Jane meet the bank president, Mr Dawes, (Dick Van Dyke again), but the trip turns into a disaster, and as a result their father is sacked. By the time he eventually gets his job back, the family have become much happier and tolerant of each other. Mary Poppins sees that her job has been accomplished and flies back to her cloud. Also among the cast were Hermione Baddeley, Ed Wynn, Arthur Treacher, Elsa Lanchester, Reginald Owen, and Reta Shaw. Directed by Robert Stevenson, this is an enchanting fairy tale, never losing its musical and comic pace for a moment. Richard M. and Robert B Sherman's outstanding score included 'A Spoonful Of Sugar', 'Feed the Birds', the infamous 'Supercalifragilisticexpialidocious', 'The Perfect Nanny', 'Sister Suffragette', 'The Life I Lead',

'Fidelity Feduciary Bank', 'Lets' Go Fly A Kite', and 'Chim Chim Cheree' which won the Oscar for best song. One of the film's highlights comes when the energetic Dick Van Dyke (complete with an amusingly artificial Cockney accent) leads a band of chimney sweeps in a dance to 'Step In Time' over the rooftops of London. The scene is a joy, and a credit to choreographers Marc Breaux and DeeDee Wood. *Mary Poppins* won Academy Awards for its music score and (predictably) for special effects and film editing. Photographed in Technicolor by Edward Colman, it went on to become the third-highest grossing musical of the 60s. In 1994 the British Oscar-winning actress Emma Thompson was being tipped to play the leading role in a future stage version.

Matthews, Jessie

b. 11 March 1907, London, England, d. 19 August 1981, Pinner, Middlesex, England. A member of a large and poor family, Matthews became a professional dancer at the age of 10. After a few years in the chorus of several shows in London's West End, she achieved recognition with a series of ingenue roles and some bit parts in films. After appearing in stage production such as *André Charlot's Revue Of 1926*, *Earl Carrol's Vanities Of 1926*, *Jordan*, *This Year Of Grace*, *Wake Up And Dream* (London and New York), *Hold My Hand*, and *Sally Who?*, by the early 30s she had become one of London's most popular stars. At the height of her career, in such shows as the 1930 London production of *Ever Green*, with a score by Richard Rodgers and Lorenz Hart, Matthews was the epitome of the English musical comedy star: her delicate build and translucent beauty fully matched songs such as that show's ethereal 'Dancing On The Ceiling'. Her film work also grew and she made several movies in the UK and in Hollywood, in which she shone effortlessly. Despite an appearance in the 1934 film version of her stage hit, slightly retitled as *Evergreen* - in which she introduced 'Over My Shoulder', one of 'identity songs - few of Matthews' film musicals were worthy of her talent. They included *Out Of The Blue*, *Waltzes From Vienna*, *First A Girl*, *It's Love Again*, *Head Over Heels*, *Gangway*, and *Sailing Along* (1938). An outstanding dancer, the variable quality of her films militated against her continuing for long and by the 40s, her career was all but over. Her last appearance on a London stage in this part of her career was in the 1942 production of *Wild Rose*. After many years away from the public eye, spent mostly in Australia, she returned to the screen in 1958 as the mother in *Tom Thumb*, and in 1963 took over the title role in the daily BBC radio serial *Mrs Dale's Diary*. In the 70s she was seen on the London stage in *The Water Babies* and *Lady Windemere's Fan*, and also appeared on television in the series *Edward And Mrs. Simpson*. Her one-woman show *Miss Jessie Matthews In Concert* won the US Drama Critics Award.
Further reading: *Over My Shoulder: An Autobiography*, Jessie Matthews and Muriel Byers. *Jessie Matthews*, Michael Thornton.

Maytime

Although this 1937 screen version retained hardly anything from the 1917 stage operetta other than the title and one of the songs, it remains one of the most accomplished and enjoyable films of its kind. Noel Langley's story, which is told in flashback, concerns the famous opera star Marcia Mornay (Jeanette MacDonald), who puts her career before her true love, Paul Allison (Nelson Eddy), and marries Nicolai Nazaroff (John Barrymore), the dominant figure in her life. The somewhat melodramatic climax comes when Allison, having been killed by Nazaroff while in a jealous rage, materialises in spiritual form and is serenaded by a remorseful Marcia. Among a strong supporting cast were Herman Bing, Lynne Carver, Tom Brown, Sig Ruman, Billy Gilbert, Harry Davenport, Walter Kingsford, Ivan Lebedeff, and Leonid Kinskey. The lovely 'Will You Remember (Sweetheart)?' (Rida Johnson Young-Sigmund Romberg), the song that survived from the original stage show, was sung with a glorious passion by Eddy and MacDonald, a feeling they also brought to bear on 'Czaritza', which consisted of excerpts from Tchaikowsky's Fifth Symphony, arranged by Robert Wright and George Forrest. The latter duo also wrote new lyrics to the folk song, 'Vive L'Opera', and the rest of the score - a mixture of songs and operatic excerpts, included 'Carry Me Back to Old Virginny' (James Bland), 'Love's Old Sweet Song' (James L. Molloy-G. Clifton Bingham), 'Le Regiment De Sambre Et Meuse' (Robert Planquette), and 'Ham And Eggs' (Herbert Stothart-Wright-Forrest). This lavish production, which is considered to be one of the best of Jeanette MacDonald and Nelson Eddy's eight films together, was produced by Hunt Stromberg for MGM and directed by Robert Z. Leonard. *Variety* reported that it grossed three and a half million dollars in US domestic theatre rentals, putting it among the most successful films of the decade.

McCarthy, Joseph

b. 27 September 1885, Somerville, Massachusetts, USA, d. 18 December 1943, New York, USA. McCarthy sang in cafes and worked for music publishers before writing songs such as 'That Dreamy Italian Waltz', 'That's How I Need You' and 'I Miss You Most Of All'. In 1913, with Jimmy Monaco, he produced one of popular music's all-time standards, 'You Made Me Love You', memorably sung and recorded by hundreds of artists, including Al Jolson, Harry James, Judy Garland and Grace La Rue. Three years later, again with Monaco, and Howard Johnson,

McCarthy wrote 'What Do You Want To Make Those Eyes At Me For?', which Betty Hutton sang in the 1945 movie *Incendiary Blonde*, the bio-pic of nightclub queen Texas Guinan. The song resurfaced in the UK in 1959, as a number 1 for Emile Ford And The Checkmates, and again in 1987, when it was a hit for rock 'n' roll revivalist, Shakin' Stevens.

McCarthy collaborated largely with Harry Tierney contributing to *The Ziegfeld Follies Of 1919*. In the same year, Tierney and McCarthy wrote the songs for the hugely successful *Irene*, which was later filmed in 1940, starring Anna Neagle and Ray Milland, and was successfully revived at the Minskoff Theatre in 1973, with Debbie Reynolds as Irene. In 1920, Tierney and McCarthy added several songs to the European score of Charles Cuvillier's *Afgar* when it was staged on Broadway, starring the toast of London and Paris, Alice Delysia. After contributing to the revues - *The Broadway Whirl*, *Up She Goes* and *Glory* - the team wrote the score for Ziegfeld's 1923 hit, *Kid Boots*. After a brief break, McCarthy was back with Tierney in 1927 for the double event of the theatrical year. The show was the operetta, *Rio Rita*, the season's biggest musical hit. The score included 'The Rangers' Song', 'If You're In Love, You'll Waltz', 'You're Always In My Arms', 'Following The Sun Around', 'The Kinkajou' and the main duet, 'Rio Rita', sung by the show's stars, Ethelind Terry and J. Harold Murray. It ran for nearly 500 performances and was twice filmed: in 1929 and again in 1942. Tierney and McCarthy's last Broadway show together was *Cross My Heart* in 1928, which ran for only eight weeks.

McCarthy's 1918 song, 'I'm Always Chasing Rainbows', written with composer Harry Carroll, was successful then for Charles Harrison, Harry Fox and Sam Ash, and was popular again in the 40s, after Judy Garland sang it so well in MGM's *Ziegfeld Girl* in 1941 - at the time McCarthy was winding up his career. His other songs included 'They Go Wild, Simply Wild, Over Me' (a hit for Marion Harris), 'Through', 'Ireland Must Be Heaven For My Mother Came From There', 'Night Time In Italy', 'I'm In The Market For You', 'Underneath The Arches' and 'Ten Pins In The Sky' (from the Judy Garland film, *Listen Darling*). In 1940, he wrote the songs for *Billy Rose's Aquacade* water carnival, including 'You Think Of Everything' and 'When The Spirit Moves Me'. McCarthy died three years later in 1943.

MacDonald, Jeanette (see Eddy, Nelson, And Jeanette MacDonald)

McHugh, Jimmy

b. James Francis McHugh, 10 July 1894, Boston, Massachusetts, USA, d. 23 May 1969, Beverly Hills, California, USA. McHugh was a prolific composer for films and the Broadway stage. He was educated at St. John's Preparatory School and Holy Cross College, where he received an honours degree in music. After receiving professional tuition he worked as a rehearsal pianist at the Boston Opera House, and later as a song-plugger for the Boston office of Irving Berlin Music. After moving to New York, he wrote for Harlem's Cotton Club revues, and had hits with 'When My Sugar Walks Down The Street' (with lyrics by Irving Mills and Gene Austin, which was a record hit for Austin and popular 20s vocalist Aileen Stanley), and 'I Can't Believe That You're In Love With Me' (with lyrics by Clarence Gaskill).

His first Broadway success was the score for the all-black revue, *Blackbirds Of 1928*, in collaboration with Dorothy Fields, who became his first main lyricist. The show's songs included 'I Can't Give You Anything But Love', 'Diga Diga Doo', 'I Must Have That Man', 'Doin' The New Low-Down' and 'Porgy'. The original stars, Adelaide Hall and Bill 'Bojangles' Robinson were joined by the Mills Brothers, Ethel Waters, and the orchestras of Cab Calloway, Duke Ellington, and Don Redman on a rare reissue album. The McHugh/Fields team wrote the songs for two more Broadway shows, *Hello Daddy* (1929) featuring 'In A Great Big Way' and 'Let's Sit And Talk About You', and *International Revue* (1930), starring Gertrude Lawrence and Harry Richman, and featuring two important McHugh songs, 'On The Sunny Side Of The Street' and 'Exactly Like You'. McHugh and Fields also wrote songs for the Chicago revue, *Clowns In Clover*, which introduced 'Don't Blame Me'. During the 30s and 40s McHugh is reputed to have written songs for over 50 films, initially with Fields, and including the title song from *Cuban Love Song*; the title song from *Dinner At Eight*, starring Fred Astaire, Joan Crawford, and Clark Gable; the title song and 'You Say The Darndest Thing', from *Singin' The Blues*; 'Lost In A Fog' from *Have A Heart*; 'I'm In The Mood For Love' and 'I Feel A Song Coming On', from *Every Night At Eight*, starring Alice Faye; The title song from *Dancing Lady*; and two songs, 'Lovely To Look At' and 'I Won't Dance', for the film of the Broadway hit, *Roberta*, on which McHugh and Fields collaborated with Jerome Kern. After Fields, McHugh's other main collaborator was Harold Adamson. Together they wrote 'There's Something In The Air', from *Banjo On My Knee*; the title song and 'My Fine Feathered Friend', from *You're A Sweetheart*, starring Alice Faye and George Murphy; 'My Own', from *That Certain Age*; 'A Serenade To The Stars' and 'I Love To Whistle', from *Mad About Music*, starring Deanna Durbin; 'How Blue The Night', from *Four Jills In A Jeep*, starring Dick Haymes, Alice Faye, and Betty Grable; and eight songs for an early Frank Sinatra film, *Higher And Higher*, including 'The Music Stopped', 'I Couldn't Sleep A Wink Last Night', 'A Lovely Way To Spend An Evening' and 'I Saw You First'; 'Have I Told You Lately That I Love You' and 'A Lovely Night To Go

Dreaming', from *Calendar Girl*; Red Hot And Beautiful' and 'Hushabye Island', from *Smash Up*; and 'In The Middle Of Nowhere' and 'I Get The Neck Of The Chicken', from *Something For The Boys*. Two other well-known McHugh/Adamson songs were 'Coming In On A Wing And A Prayer', and 'Love Me As Though There Were No Tomorrow'. In 1939, McHugh collaborated with Al Dubin for the song, 'South American Way'. It featured in the Broadway show, *Streets Of Paris*, and the movie, *Down Argentine Way*. In both show and film, it was given the full treatment by Carmen Miranda. In 1940, McHugh again wrote with Dubin, and Howard Dietz, for the show *Keep Off the Grass*, which included the songs 'Clear Out Of This World' and 'A Latin Tune, A Manhattan Moon, And You'. Other popular McHugh songs include 'I'm Shooting High', 'Let's Get Lost', I'd Know You Anywhere', 'You've Got Me This Way', 'Sing A Tropical Song', '"Murder" She Says', 'Say A Prayer For The Boys Over There', 'Can't Get Out Of This Mood', 'In A Moment Of Madness', 'Blue Again', 'Goodbye Blues', 'I've Just Found Out About Love And I Like It', 'Warm and Willing', 'The Star You Wished Upon Last Night', 'Where The Hot Wind Blows' and 'Massachusetts'. McHugh's collaborators during his long career included Ted Koehler, Frank Loesser, Johnny Mercer, Herb Magidson, Ralph Freed, Ned Washington and Arnold Johnson.

During World War II, McHugh wrote several US government commissioned 'War Savings Bond' songs such as 'Buy, Buy, Buy A Bond' and 'We've Got Another Bond to Buy'. For his work during the war he was awarded the Presidential Certificate Of Merit. He continued writing well into the 50s, and in 1955 had a hit with 'Too Young To Go Steady', recorded by Patti Page and Nat 'King' Cole. Jimmy McHugh died in May 1969.

MacRae, Gordon

b. 12 March 1921, East Orange, New Jersey, USA, d. 24 January 1986, Lincoln, Nebraska, USA. MacRae was the son of local radio celebrity, Wee Willie MacRae, and often worked on radio as a child actor before joining the Millpond Playhouse, New York. There he met actress Sheila Stephens who became his first wife in 1941. After winning an amateur singing contest at the 1939/40 New York World's Fair, he sang for two weeks with the Harry James and Les Brown bands. While working as a pageboy at NBC Radio, he was heard by bandleader Horace Heidt who signed him for two years, during which time he appeared with Heidt, James Stewart and Paulette Goddard in a movie about Heidt's radio giveaway show, *Pot O' Gold*. After serving in the US Army Air Force Corps in World War II, MacRae returned to New York to take a singing role in the 1946 Broadway revue, *Three To Make Ready*, starring Ray

Bolger. In 1947, he signed to Capitol Records and had a string of hits up until 1954, including 'I Still Get Jealous', 'At The Candlelight Cafe', 'It's Magic', 'Hair Of Gold, Eyes Of Blue', 'So In Love', 'Mule Train'/'Dear Hearts And Gentle People' and 'Rambling Rose'. After a four-year gap, he entered the US charts again in 1958 with 'The Secret'. MacRae also made a series of successful singles with ex-Tommy Dorsey singer, Jo Stafford. These included 'Say Something Sweet To Your Sweetheart', 'Bluebird Of Happiness', 'My Darling, My Darling' (a US number 1), 'A-You're Adorable', 'Need You', 'Whispering Hope', 'Bibbidi-Bobbidi-Boo' and 'Dearie'. MacRae's film career, mostly for Warner Brothers, started in 1948 with a non-singing role in *The Big Punch*. This was followed by a series of musical films such as *Look For The Silver Lining* (1949) and *The Daughter Of Rosie O'Grady* (1950), both co-starring June Haver. He made four films with Doris Day: *Tea For Two* (1950), *West Point Story* (1950), *On Moonlight Bay* (1951) and *By The Light Of The Silvery Moon* (1953). Other films included *The Desert Song*, (1953) co-starring Kathryn Grayson, and *Three Sailors And A Girl* (1953), with Jane Powell. MacRae also appeared in several dramatic roles. In 1955, he hit the movie big time when he played Curly, opposite Shirley Jones, in the successful film of the Broadway show, *Oklahoma!*, complete with Richard Rodgers and Oscar Hammerstein's Oscar award-winning score. He repeated this enormous success, again with Shirley Jones, when he replaced the first choice, Frank Sinatra, as Billy Bigelow in the movie of another Rodgers and Hammerstein stage hit, *Carousel* (1956). That same year, MacRae appeared in his last musical film role as Buddy DeSylva, in *The Best Things In Life Are Free*, the bio-pic of the 20s/30s songwriting team of DeSylva, Brown And Henderson. He made one final film appearance, in a dramatic role in *The Pilot*, in 1979. In the mid-50s, MacRae was also popular on US television, as the singing host of *The Railroad Hour*, *The Colgate Comedy Hour*, and his own *Gordon MacRae Show*. After MacRae divorced his first wife, he was remarried in 1967 to Elizabeth Lambert Schrafft. In the same year he made his first Broadway musical appearance since 1946, when he replaced Robert Preston in *I Do! I Do!*. In the 70s he struggled with alcoholism and, in the early 80s, claimed that he had won the battle. He died from cancer of the mouth and jaw in January 1986.

Albums: with Lucille Norman *New Moon/Vagabond King* (1950), with Jo Stafford *Sunday Evening Songs* (1953), with various artists *The Desert Song* (1953), with Stafford *Memory Songs* (mid-50s), *Romantic Ballads* (1956), *Oklahoma!* (1956, film soundtrack), *Carousel* (1956, film soundtrack), *Operetta Favourites* (1956), *The Best Things In Life Are Free* (1956), *Motion Picture Soundstage* (1957), *Gordon MacRae In Concert* (1958), *Cowboy's Lament* (1958), *Seasons Of Love*

(1959), *This Is Gordon MacRae* (1960), with Stafford *Whispering Hope* (1962), with Stafford *Peace In The Valley* (1963), with Stafford *Old Rugged Cross* (1978). Further reading: *Hollywood Mother Of The Year: Sheila MacRae's Own Story*, Sheila MacRae with Paul Jeffers.

Meet Me In St. Louis

Released by MGM in 1944, this enchanting film traces the adventures of the Smith family - all eight of them - as the seasons change from summer through to spring in the US city of St. Louis during 1903/4. Based on *The Kensington Stories* by Sally Benson, Irving Brecher and Fred Finklehoffe's screenplay focuses mainly on one of the Smiths' teenage daughter, Esther (Judy Garland), and her romance with the boy who lives next door to her in Kensington Avenue, John Truitt (Tom Drake). The rest of the cast was particularly fine: Esther's three sisters, Rose, Tootie and Agnes, were played by Lucille Bremer, Margaret O'Brien, and Joan Carroll; and the family group was completed by brother Lon Jnr. (Henry H. Daniels Jnr.), father and mother (Leon Ames and Mary Astor), grandpa (Harry Davenport) - and their long-time maid Katie, (Marjorie Main). Also featured were June Lockhart, Hugh Marlowe, Robert Sully, and Chill Wills. The seemingly ordinary day-to-day happenings involving collusion between Rose, her mother and Katie to advance the time of the evening meal by an hour so that it will not coincide with a long-distance telephone call from Rose's boyfriend, Tootie's Halloween night escapades, Esther and Tom's mutual joy at the Christmas dance, and the possibility of the whole family moving to New York, resulted in a most extraordinary film. To the relief of the majority, the move away from their beloved home does not materialize, and the whole family celebrate at the opening of 1904 St. Louis World Fair, singing 'Meet Me In St. Louis, Louis' (Andrew Sterling-Kerry Mills). Hugh Martin and Ralph Blane contributed three memorable songs for Judy Garland to sing: 'The Boy Next Door', 'Have Yourself A Merry Little Christmas', and the immortal 'The Trolley Song' which accompanied one of the most endearing sequences in any film musical. Garland also joined O'Brien for the charming 'Under The Bamboo Tree' (Bob Cole-J. Rosamond Johnson), and she and the rest of young people (and audiences all over the world) brushed a tear from their eyes as Leon Ames (dubbed by Arthur Freed) and Mary Astor rendered the poignant 'You And I' (Freed-Nacio Herb Brown). The dances were staged by Charles Walters, and the film, which was directed with his usual style and flair by Vincente Minnelli, was photographed in Technicolor by George Folsey. *Meet Me In St. Louis*

Meet Me In St. Louis

was an enormous commercial success, grossing over $5 million in US domestic theatre rentals alone - a fitting return for what is generally considered to be a masterpiece. Unfortunately, the magic did not extend to the 1989 Broadway stage adaptation which one critic called 'a lumbering and graceless project'. It ran for only 253 performances.

Melachrino, George

b. George Militiades, 1 May 1909, London, England, d. 18 June 1965, London, England. Melachrino was an orchestra leader, composer, arranger, multi-instrumentalist and singer. The son of Greek parents, he learned to play a miniature violin, and wrote his first composition when he was five years old. Melachrino was already an accomplished musician at 14, when he enrolled at the Trinity College Of Music; there, he specialized in chamber music and the use of strings. At the age of 16, he wrote a string sextette which was performed in London. He resolved to learn every instrument in the orchestra, and succeeded, with the exception of the harp and piano. In 1927, he began his broadcasting career, playing and singing from the BBC studio at Savoy Hill. He strayed further and further away from his initial ambition to be a classical musician, playing jazz instead, and working in dance bands for leaders such as Bert Firman, Harry Hudson, Ambrose and Carroll Gibbons' Savoy Hotel Orchestra. In 1939, Melachrino formed his own dance band to play at the prestigious London venue, the Cafe de Paris, until 1940. During the period of the 'Battle of Britain', he joined the British Army as a military policeman, eventually becoming a Regimental Sergeant-Major. He later toured in the *Stars Of Battledress* and was musical director of the Army Radio Unit, as well as the leader of British Band of the Allied Expeditionary Forces. He also led the 50-piece 'Orchestra in Khaki', recruited from professional musicians serving in the ranks, who were much amused when he was introduced on broadcasts as 'the Sentimental Sergeant-Major'. The unit held its own against the American band led by Glenn Miller and the Canadian combination led by Robert Farnon, with both of whom Melachrino guested as vocalist on occasions during the war years. While in the Forces, he experimented with large string sounds, and after the war he ran two outfits, the Melachrino Strings and the George Melachrino Orchestra, both purveying the sentimental mood music so popular in the 50s, especially in the USA. The full orchestra consisted of 30 strings, 10 reeds, seven brass, two percussion, a harp and a piano. He formed the Melachrino Music Organization, creating work in concerts, broadcasting, recordings and film music. His film scores included *Woman To Woman* (1946), *Code Of Scotland Yard* (1948), *No Orchids For Miss Blandish* (1948), *Story Of Shirley Yorke* (1948), *Dark Secret* (1949), *The Gamma People* (1956) and

Odongo (1956). In 1947, he contributed the music, with book and lyrics by Eric Maschwitz and Matt Brooks, to the revue, *Starlight Roof*, which starred Fred Emney, Pat Kirkwood and Vic Oliver, and introduced Julie Andrews to London audiences. He also wrote the music for the ill-fated *Lucky Boy*, with lyrics by Ian Douglas. His other compositions included 'First Rhapsody' (his theme tune), 'Winter Sunshine', 'Vision D'Amour', 'Woodland Revel' and 'Portrait Of A Lady'. He had a UK chart entry in 1956 with the Italian melody, 'Autumn Concerto' but, like Mantovani, who also specialized in lush string arrangements, his albums sold more in the USA than in the UK. His US hits included *Christmas In High Fidelity*, *Under Western Skies* and *Immortal Ladies*, a set of standards with girls' names as their titles such as 'Laura', 'Dolores', 'Chloe' and 'Dinah'. Also popular was his series of mood records designed for various times of the day, such as *Music For Daydreaming*, *Music For Relaxation*, *Music For Two People Alone*, *Music For Dining*, *Music for Reading*, *Music To Help You Sleep*, and others. He died in 1965 in an accident at his home in Kensington, London. The Melachrino Strings and Orchestra continued to record into the 80s, conducted by Robert Mandell.
Selected albums: *Soft Lights And Sweet Music* (1954), *Christmas In High Fidelity* (1954), *Music For The Nostalgic Traveller* (1956), *Famous Themes For Piano And Orchestra* (1957), *Moonlight Concerto* (1958), *Great Show Tunes - Medleys* (1958), *Under Western Skies* (1959), *The World's Greatest Melodies* (1962), *The World Of George Melachrino* (1969), *The World Of George Melachrino, Volume Two* (1972), *Strauss Waltzes* (1973), *The Immortal Melodies Of Victor Herbert And Sigmund Romberg* (1974).

Menken, Alan (see Ashman, Howard)

Mercer, Johnny

b. John Herndon Mercer, 18 November 1909, Savannah, Georgia, USA, d. 25 June 1976, Los Angeles, California, USA. A lyricist, composer and singer, Mercer was an important link with the first generation of composers of indigenous American popular music such as Jerome Kern and Harry Warren, through to post-World War II writers like Henry Mancini. Along the way, he collaborated with several others, including Harold Arlen, Hoagy Carmichael, Gene DePaul, Rube Bloom, Richard Whiting, Victor Schertzinger, Gordon Jenkins, Jimmy Van Heusen, Duke Ellington, Billy Strayhorn, Matty Malneck, Arthur Schwartz and more. Most of the time, Mercer wrote the most literate and witty lyrics, but occasionally the melody as well.
He moved to New York in the late 20s and worked in a variety of jobs before placing one of his first songs, 'Out Of Breath And Scared To Death Of You', (written with Everett Miller), in the *Garrick*

Gaieties Of 1930. During the 30s, Mercer contributed the lyrics to several movie songs, including 'If You Were Mine' from *To Beat The Band*, a record hit for Billie Holiday with Teddy Wilson, 'I'm An Old Cowhand' (words and music) (*Rhythm On The Range*), 'Too Marvellous For Words' (co-written with Richard Whiting for *Ready, Willing And Able*), 'Have You Got Any Castles, Baby?' (*Varsity Show*), 'Hooray For Hollywood' (*Hollywood Hotel*), 'Jeepers Creepers' (*Going Places*) and 'Love Is Where You Find It' (*Garden Of The Moon*).

Mercer's other songs during the decade included 'Fare-Thee-Well To Harlem', 'Moon Country', 'When A Woman Loves A Man' (with Gordon Jenkins and Bernard Hanighan), 'P.S. I Love You', 'Goody Goody', 'You Must Have Been A Beautiful Baby', 'And The Angels Sing', 'Cuckoo In The Clock', 'Day In - Day Out' and 'I Thought About You'. In the latter part of the decade, he appeared frequently on radio, as MC and singer with Paul Whiteman, with Benny Goodman and Bob Crosby. With his southern drawl and warm, good-natured style, he was a natural for the medium, and, in the early 40s, had his own show, *Johnny Mercer's Music Shop*. During this period, Mercer became a director of the songwriter's copyright organization, ASCAP. Also, in 1942, he combined with songwriter-turned-film-producer, Buddy DeSylva, and businessman, Glen Wallich, to form Capitol Records, which was, in its original form, dedicated to musical excellence, a policy which reflected Mercer's approach to all his work.

He had previously had record hits with other writers' songs, such as 'Mr Gallagher And Mr Sheen' and 'Small Fry', along with his own 'Mr. Meadowlark' (a duet with Bing Crosby), and 'Strip Polka'. For Capitol, he continued to register in the US Hit Parade with popular favourites such as 'Personality', 'Candy'; and some of his own numbers such as 'G.I. Jive', 'Ac-Cent-Tchu-Ate The Positive', 'Glow Worm'; and 'On The Atchison, Topeka, And The Santa Fe', which was also sung by Judy Garland in the film, *The Harvey Girls* (1946), and gained Mercer his first Academy Award.

His other 40s song successes, many of them from movies, included 'The Waiter And The Porter And The Upstairs Maid' (from *Birth Of The Blues*); 'Blues In The Night' and 'This Time's The Dream's On Me' (*Blues In The Night*); 'Tangerine', 'I Remember You' and 'Arthur Murray Taught Me Dancing In A Hurry' (*The Fleet's In*), 'Dearly Beloved' and 'I'm Old Fashioned' (*You Were Never Lovelier*) (Kern); 'Hit The Road To Dreamland' and 'That Old Black Magic', Billy Daniels' 'Identity Song' (*Star Spangled Rhythm*), 'My Shining Hour' (*The Sky's The Limit*) and 'Come Rain Or Come Shine', 'Legalize My Name' and 'Any Place I Hang My Hat Is Home', from the stage show *St. Louis Woman* (Arlen).

Two particularly attractive compositions were 'Fools Rush In' (with Rube Bloom), which was a big hit for Glenn Miller and the movie title song 'Laura', with Mercer's lyric complementing a haunting tune by David Raksin. Mercer's collaboration with Hoagy Carmichael produced some of his most memorable songs, such as 'Lazybones', 'The Old Music Master', 'Skylark', 'How Little We Know' and the Oscar-winning 'In The Cool, Cool, Cool Of The Evening', sung by Bing Crosby and Jane Wyman in the film *Here Comes The Groom* (1951). In the same year, Mercer provided both the music and lyrics for the Broadway show, *Top Banana*, a 'burlesque musical' starring Phil Silvers and a host of mature funnymen. The entertaining score included the witty 'A Word A Day'.

The 50s were extremely productive years for Mercer, with songs such as 'Here's To My Lady', 'I Wanna Be Around' (later successful for Tony Bennett), and yet more movie songs, including 'I Want To Be A Dancing Man', 'The Bachelor Dinner Song' and 'Seeing's Believing', sung by Fred Astaire in *The Belle Of New York*; 'I Like Men' (covered by Peggy Lee), 'I Got Out Of Bed On The Right Side' and 'Ain't Nature Grand' from *Dangerous When Wet;* and 'Something's Gotta Give' and 'Sluefoot' (words and music by Mercer) from another Fred Astaire film, *Daddy Long Legs*. Mercer also provided additional lyrics to 'When The World Was Young' ('Ah, The Apple Trees'), 'Midnight Sun', 'Early Autumn' and 'Autumn Leaves'. The highlight of the decade was, perhaps, *Seven Brides For Seven Brothers* (1954). Starring Howard Keel and Jane Powell, Mercer and Gene DePaul's 'pip of a score' included 'Spring, Spring, Spring', 'Bless Your Beautiful Hide', 'Sobbin' Women', 'When You're In Love', and 'Goin' Courtin', amongst others. Two years later Mercer and DePaul got together again for the stage show, *Li'l Abner*, starring Stubby Kaye, and including such songs as 'Namely You', 'Jubilation T. Cornpone' and 'The Country's In The Very Best Of Hands'. It ran on Broadway for nearly 700 performances and was filmed in 1959.

The early 60s brought Mercer two further Academy Awards; one for 'Moon River' from *Breakfast At Tiffany's* (1961), and the other, the title song to *The Days Of Wine And Roses* (1962). 'Moon River' was the song in which Mercer first coined the now-famous phrase, 'my huckleberry friend'. Danny Williams took the former song to the UK number slot in 1961, while namesake Andy Williams and Mercer's co-composer Henry Mancini both scored US Top 40 hits with the latter in 1963. Mancini also wrote other movie songs with Mercer, such as 'Charade', 'The Sweetheart Tree' (from *The Great Race*) and 'Whistling Away The Dark' (*Darling Lili*). In the early 70s, Mercer spent a good deal of time in Britain, and, in 1974, wrote the score, with André Previn, for the

West End musical, *The Good Companions*. He died, two years later, on 25 June 1976, in Los Angeles, California, USA.

Several of his 1,000-plus songs became an integral part of many a singer's repertoire. In 1992, Frank Sinatra was still using 'One For My Baby' (music by Harold Arlen), 'the greatest saloon song ever written', as a moving set-piece in his concert performances. 'Dream' (words and music by Mercer), closed Sinatra's radio and television shows for many years, and the singer also made impressive recordings of lesser-known Mercer items, such as 'Talk To Me, Baby' and 'The Summer Wind'. Memories of his rapport with Bing Crosby in their early days were revived in 1961, when Mercer recorded *Two Of A Kind* with Bobby Darin, full of spontaneous asides, and featuring Mercer numbers such as 'Bob White' and 'If I Had My Druthers', plus other humorous oldies, like 'Who Takes Care Of The Caretaker's Daughter' and 'My Cutie's Due At Two-To-Two Today'. Further recordings include: *Audio Scrap Book* (1964-74), *Johnny Mercer Sings Johnny Mercer, Ac-Cent-Tchu-Ate The Positive, Johnny Mercer's Music Shop* and *My Huckleberry Friend*. Several artists, such as Marlene VerPlanck and Susannah McCorkle, have devoted complete albums to his work. In 1992 Capitol Records celebrated its 50th anniversary by issuing *Two Marvellous For Words: Capitol Sings Johnny Mercer*, which included some of the label's most eminent artists singing their co-founder's popular song lyrics.

Further reading: *Our Huckleberry Friend: The Life, Times And Song Lyrics Of Johnny Mercer*, B. Back and G. Mercer. *Johnny Mercer In Song By Song*, C. Brahms and N. Sherrin.

Merman, Ethel

b. Ethel Agnes Zimmermann, 16 January 1909, Astoria, New York, USA, d. 15 February 1984, New York, USA. Merman was one of the most celebrated ladies of the Broadway musical stage. A dynamic entertainer, with a loud, brash, theatrical singing style, flawless diction, and extravagant manner she usually played a gutsy lady with a heart of gold. Merman worked as a secretary, then sang in nightclubs, gradually working up to the best spots. Noticed by producer Vinton Freedly while singing at the Brooklyn Paramount, she was signed for George and Ira Gershwin's Broadway show, *Girl Crazy* (1930), and was a great success, stopping the show with her version of 'I Got Rhythm', a song which became one of her life-long themes. She was equally successful in George White's *Scandals* (1931), in which she co-starred with Rudy Vallee, and sang 'My Song' and 'Life Is Just A Bowl Of Cherries', and *Take A Chance* (1932), when her two big numbers were 'Eadie Was A Lady' and 'Rise 'N' Shine'. In 1934, Merman starred in *Anything Goes*, the first of five Cole Porter musical shows. It was one of his best, full of song hits such as 'I Get A Kick Out Of You', 'All through The Night', 'You're The Top' (one of Porter's accomplished 'list' songs), 'Anything Goes' and 'Blow, Gabriel, Blow'. Merman also appeared in the 1936 film version of the show with Bing Crosby. The other Porter shows in which she appeared were *Red Hot And Blue!* (1936), co-starring Jimmy Durante and Bob Hope, with the songs, 'Down In The Depths (On The Ninetieth Floor)', 'It's De-Lovely' and 'Ridin' High'; *DuBarry Was A Lady* (1939), with 'But In The Morning, No!', 'Do I Love You?', 'Give Him The Oo-La-La', 'Katie Went To Haiti' and 'Friendship'; *Panama Hattie* (1940), featuring 'I've Still Got My Health', 'Let's Be Buddies', 'Make It Another Old-Fashioned, Please' and 'I'm Throwing A Ball Tonight'; *Something For The Boys* (1943) featuring 'Hey, Good Lookin', 'He's A Right Guy', 'Could It Be You' and 'The Leader Of A Big Time Band'. Merman's longest-running musical was Irving Berlin's *Annie Get Your Gun* (1946), which ran for 1,147 performances. As the sharp-shooting Annie Oakley, she introduced such Berlin classics as 'They Say It's Wonderful', 'Doin' What Comes Naturally', 'I Got The Sun In The Morning', 'You Can't Get A Man With A Gun', and the song which was to become another of her anthems, 'There's No Business Like Show Business'. Merman's next Broadway show, *Call Me Madam* again had an Irving Berlin score. This time, as Sally Adams, ambassador to the mythical country of Lichtenburg, she triumphed again with numbers such as 'Marrying For Love', 'You're Just In Love', 'The Best Thing For You', 'Can You Use Any Money Today?', and as 'The Hostess With The Mostest': 'On The Ball'.

She also starred in the 1953 film version of the show, with George Sanders, Donald O'Connor, and Vera-Ellen. Often called the climax to Merman's career, *Gypsy* (1959), with a score by Jule Styne and Stephen Sondheim, saw her cast as the domineering mother of stripper, Gypsy Rose Lee, and Merman gave the kind of performance for which she had never before been asked. Her songs included 'Some People', 'Small World', 'You'll Never Get Away From Me', 'Together', 'Rose's Turn', and her triumphant hymn, 'Everthing's Coming Up Roses'. Such was her command of this role that the choice of Rosalind Russell for the film version was greeted with incredility in some circles. Apart from a brief revival of *Annie Get Your Gun* (1966), and a spell as a replacement in *Hello, Dolly!*, (she had turned down the role when the show was originally cast), *Gypsy* was Merman's last Broadway appearance. Although the stage was her *metier*, she made several Hollywood films including *We're Not Dressing* (1934), *Kid Millions* and *Strike Me Pink* (both 1935 with Eddie Cantor) *Alexander's Ragtime Band* (1938), with Tyrone Power, Alice Faye, and Don Ameche; and *There's No Business Like Show Business* (1954), in which she starred with

Dan Dailey, Donald O'Connor and Marilyn Monroe. There were also non-singing roles in comedy films such as *It's A Mad, Mad, Mad, Mad World* (1963), *The Art Of Love* (1965) and *Airplane!* (1980). Merman appeared regularly on television from the 50s through to the 70s in specials and guest spots, and in cabaret. In 1953 she teamed up with another Broadway legend, Mary Martin, for the historic Ford 50th Anniversary Show, highlights of which were issued on a Decca album. On the same label was her *Musical Autobiography* (2-album set). Besides the many hits from her shows, her record successes included, 'How Deep Is The Ocean', 'Move It Over', 'Dearie'/'I Said My Pajamas (And Put On My Prayers)' and 'If I Knew You Were Coming I'd've Baked A Cake', all three duets with Ray Bolger. After a distinguished career, lasting over 50 years, Merman's final major appearance was at a Carnegie Hall benefit concert in 1982. She died in 1984. The following year a biographical tribute show, *Call Me Miss Birdseye*, starring Libby Morris, was mounted at the Donmar Warehouse Theatre in London.

Selected albums: *Merman Sings Merman* (1973), *Annie Get Your Gun* (1974), *Ethel's Ridin' High* (1975). Compilations: *Ethel Was A Lady* (1984), *The World Is Your Ballon* (1987), *Ethel Merman* (1988).

Further reading: *Who Could Ask For Anything More?* (US) *Don't Call Me Madam* (UK), Ethel Merman. *Merman*, Ethel Merman.

Midler, Bette

b. 1 December 1945, Paterson, New Jersey, USA. As a singer, comedienne and actress, Midler rose to fame with an outrageous, raunchy stage act, and became known as 'The Divine Miss M', 'Trash With Flash' and 'Sleaze With Ease'. Her mother, a fan of the movies, named her after Bette Davis. Raised in Hawaii, at school, as one of the few white students, and the only Jew, she 'toughened up fast, and won an award in the first grade for singing 'Silent Night'. Encouraged by her mother, she studied theatre at the University of Hawaii, and worked in a pineapple factory and as a secretary in a radio station before gaining her first professional acting job in 1965, in the movie, *Hawaii*, playing the bit part of a missionary wife who is constantly sick. Moving to New York, she held jobs as a glove saleswoman in Stern's Department Store, a hat-check girl and a go-go dancer before joining the chorus of the hit Broadway Musical, *Fiddler On The Roof*, in 1966. In February 1967, Midler took over one of the leading roles, as Tzeitel, the eldest daughter, and played the part for the next three years. While singing late-night after the show at the Improvisation Club, a showcase for young performers, she was noticed by an executive from the David Frost television show, and subsequently appeared several times with Frost, and on the *Merv Griffin Show*. After leaving *Fiddler On The Roof*, she appeared briefly in the Off-Broadway Musical, *Salvation*, and worked again as a go-go dancer in a Broadway bar, before taking a $50-a-night job at the Continental Baths, New York, singing to male homosexuals dressed in bath towels. Clad in toreador pants, or sequin gowns, strapless tops and platform shoes, uniforms of a bygone age, she strutted her extravagant stuff, singing songs from the 40s, 50s, and 60s - rock, blues, novelties - even reaching back to 1929 for the Harry Akst/Grant Clarke ballad, 'Am I Blue?', a hit then for Ethel Waters. News of these somewhat bizarre happenings soon got round, and outside audiences of both sexes, including show people, were allowed to view the show. Offers of other work flooded in, including the opportunity to appear regularly on Johnny Carson's *Tonight* show.

In May 1971, she played the dual roles of the Acid Queen and Mrs Walker in the Seattle Opera Company's production of the rock opera, *Tommy* and, later in the year, made her official New York nightclub debut at the Downstairs At The Upstairs, the original two-week engagement being extended to 10, to accommodate the crowds. During the following year, she appeared with Carson at the Sahara in Las Vegas, and in June played to standing room only at Carnegie Hall in New York. In November, her first album, *The Divine Miss M*, was released by Atlantic Records, and is said to have sold 100,000 copies in the first month. It contained several of the cover versions which she featured in her stage act such as the Andrew Sisters' 'Boogie Woogie Bugle Boy', the Dixie Cups' 'The Chapel Of Love', the Shangri-Las' 'The Leader Of The Pack' and Bobby Freeman's 'Do You Want To Dance?'. The pianist on most of the tracks was Barry Manilow, who was Midler's accompanist and musical director for three years in the early 70s. The album bears the dedication: 'This is for Judith'. Judith was Midler's sister who was killed in a road accident on her way to meet Bette when she was appearing in *Fiddler On The Roof*. Midler's second album, *Bette Midler*, also made the US Top 10. In 1973, Midler received the After Dark Award for Performer Of The Year and, during the 70s, attained superstar status, able to fill concert halls throughout the USA. In 1979, she had her first starring role in the movie *The Rose*, roughly based on the life of rock singer Janis Joplin. Midler was nominated for an Academy Award as 'Best Actress', and won two Golden Globe Awards for her performance. Two songs from the film, the title track (a million-seller), and 'When A Man Loves A Woman', and the soundtrack album, entered the US charts, as did the album from Midler's next film, *Divine Madness*, a celluloid version of her concert performance in Pasadena, California. After all the success of the past decade, things started to go wrong in the early 80s. In 1982, the aptly-named black comedy, *Jinxed!*, was a disaster at the box office, amid rumours of violent disagreements between Midler and her co-star Ken Wahl and director Don Siegel. Midler became persona non-grata in Hollywood, and suffered a nervous breakdown. She married Martin Von Haselberg, a former commodities broker, in 1984, and signed to a long-term contract to the Walt Disney Studios, making her come-back in the comedy, *Down And Out In Beverly Hills* (1985), with Nick Nolte and Richard Dreyfuss.

During the rest of the decade she eschewed touring, and concentrated on her acting career in a series of raucous comedy movies such as *Ruthless People* (1986) co-starring Danny De Vito; *Outrageous Fortune* (1987) and *Big Business* (1988). In 1988, *Beaches*, the first film to be made by her own company, All Girls Productions (their motto is, 'We hold a grudge'), gave her one of her best roles, and the opportunity to sing songs within the context of the story. These included standards such as 'Ballin' The Jack', Cole Porter's 'I've Still Got My Health', 'The Glory Of Love', 'Under The Boardwalk', and a deliberately tasteless tale about the invention of the brassiere, 'Otto Titsling'. Also included was 'Wind Beneath My Wings', by Larry Henley and Jeff Silbar, which reached number 1 in the US charts. Midler's recording won Grammys in 1990 for 'Record Of The Year' and 'Song Of The Year'. In 1990, Midler appeared in *Stella*, a remake of the classic weepie, *Stella Dallas*, in which she performed an hilarious mock striptease among the bottles and glasses on top of a bar; and *Scenes From A Mall*, a comedy co-staring Woody Allen. Her appearance as a USO entertainer in World War II, alongside actor James Caan, in *For The Boys* (1991), which she also co-produced, earned her a Golden Globe award for Best Actress. The movie showed her at her best, and featured her very individual readings of 'Stuff Like That' and 'P.S. I Love You'. In the same year, she released *Some People's Lives*, her first non-soundtrack album since the 1983 flop, *No Frills*. It entered the US Top 10, and one of the tracks, 'From A Distance', had an extended chart life in the USA and UK. By 1991, she was planning to revive her musical career and start touring again, although, on the evidence of 'From A Distance', with its references to the Almighty, the days of the brassy, loud-mouthed cabaret star would seem to be a thing of the past.

Albums: *The Divine Miss M* (1972), *Bette Midler* (1973), *Songs For The New Depression* (1976), *Live At Last* (1977), *Broken Blossom* (1977), *Thighs And Whispers* (1979), *The Rose* (1979, film soundtrack), *Divine Madness* (1980, film soundtrack), *No Frills* (1983), *Beaches* (1989, film soundtrack), *Some People's Lives* (1990), *Best Of* (1993).

Further reading: *Bette Midler*, R. Baker. *A View From A Broad*, Bette Midler. *The Saga Of Baby Divine*, Bette Midler.

Miller, Ann

b. Lucille Ann Collier, 12 April 1919 or 1923, Chireno, Texas, USA. A vivacious, long-legged tap dancer (500 taps per minute) who achieved stardom rather late in her career via several classic film musicals of the late 40s and early 50s. After her parents were divorced when she was about 10 years old, Miller, who is of Irish, French and Cherokee descent, moved with her mother to California and supplemented the family's finances by dancing in clubs. An RKO talent scout spotted her there, and in the late 30s she made a few films for the studio, including *New Faces Of 1937*, The *Life Of The Party*, *Stage Door*, *Having A Wonderful Time*, *Tarnished Angel*, *Room Service*, and *Radio City Revels*. In 1938 she was loaned out to Columbia for the Frank Capra comedy *You Can't Take It With You* which won the Oscar for best picture. A year later she thrilled Broadway audiences by dancing 'The Mexiconga', accompanied by the Loo Sisters and Ella Logan in *George White's Scandals*. During the early 40s she was often one of the few artists worth watching in a series of mostly low-budget features which included *Melody Ranch*, *Time Out For Rhythm*, *Go West Young Lady*, *Reveille With Beverley*, *What's Buzzin' Cousin?*, *Jam Session*, *Carolina Blues*, and *Eadie Was A Lady* (1945). In 1948 she had good role in *Easter Parade* with Fred Astaire, Judy Garland, and Peter Lawford, and provided one of the film's highspots with her scintillating solo dance number 'Shaking The Blues Away'. Her performance in that film merited a seven year MGM contract, and after performing a frenetic 'Dance Of Fury' with Ricardo Montalban and Cyd Charisse in *The Kissing Bandit*, joined Frank Sinatra, Gene Kelly, Vera-Ellen, Betty Garrett and Jules Munshin in one of the all-time great movie musicals, *On The Town* (1949). She led them all a fine dance around the anthropology museum with the clever and amusing 'Prehistoric Man'. Although she was by now around 30 years of age, Miller continued to shine during the early 50s in movies such as *Texas Carnival*, *Two Tickets To Broadway*, *Lovely To Look At* (which included her highly individual interpretation of 'I'll Be Hard To Handle'), and *Small Town Girl* in which she excelled again, this time with 'I Gotta Hear That Beat'. In *Kiss Me Kate* (1953) she played what is said to be her favourite role of Bianca, and this film was arguably the highlight of her whole career. Her memorable performances of Cole Porter's marvellous 'Too Darn Hot', 'From This Moment On', 'Tom, Dick And Harry', 'Why Can't You Behave?', 'Always True To You Darling In My Fashion', and 'We Open In Venice' were a joy to behold. By now, the golden era of MGM musicals was almost over, and after guesting in the Sigmund Romberg bio-pic *Deep In My Heart*, and emphasising just how good she still was with a top-class routine to 'The Lady From The Bayou' in *Hit The Deck*, Miller signed off in 1956 with the ordinary *The Opposite Sex* and the non-musical *The Great American Pastime* (about baseball, of course). Like so many others, in the 60s she turned to television and nightclubs and toured in stage revivals of shows such as *Hello, Dolly!*, *Panama Hattie*, and *Can-Can*. She also made a television commercial for soup in which she danced on the top of an enormous can, surrounded by water fountains, a large orchestra, and a bevy of chorus girls. In 1969 she returned to Broadway after an absence of 30 years and took over the leading role in the hit musical *Mame* to wide critical acclaim. In the early 70s her extensive tours in *Anything Goes* were interrupted for more than a year while Miller recovered from an accident in which she was struck by a sliding steel curtain. In 1979 she joined Mickey Rooney in *Sugar Babies*, a celebration of the golden era of American vaudeville which ran on Broadway for 1,208 performances before touring the US for several years, and spending a brief time in London's West End in 1988. Miller's colourful private life which includes admirers such as Conrad Hilton and Louis B. Mayer and failed marriages to three American oil millionaires, is documented in her autobiography. She is also interested in the paranormal and believes implicitly that she is a reincarnation of the first female Pharoah of Egypt.

Further reading: *Miller's High Life*, Ann Miller.

Mingus

Like its subject, this documentary made in 1968 is unflinching and at times uncomfortably honest. Mingus was being evicted from his home during the making of the film and these events are depicted as is the artist at work composing, rehearsing and performing. Amongst other musicians involved are Charles McPherson and Dannie Richmond.

Minnelli, Liza

b. Liza May Minnelli, 12 March 1946, Los Angeles, California, USA. An extremely vivacious and animated actress, singer and dancer, in films, concerts, musical shows and television. She was named Liza after the Gershwin song, and May after the mother of her film-director father, Vincente Minnelli. Liza's mother was show-business legend Judy Garland. On the subject of her first name, Miss Minnelli is musically quite precise: 'It's Liza with an 'z', not Lisa with a 's'/'Cos Liza with a 'z' goes zzz, not sss'. She spent a good deal of her childhood in Hollywood, where her playmates included Mia Farrow. At the age of two-and-a-half, she made her screen premiere in the closing sequence of *In The Good Old Summer Time*, as the daughter of the musical film's stars, Garland and Van Johnson. When she was seven, she danced on the stage of the Palace Theatre, New York, while her mother sang 'Swanee'. In 1962, after initially showing no interest in a show-business career, Minnelli served as an apprentice in revivals of the musicals, *Take Me Along* and *The Flower Drum Song*,

and later played Anne Frank in a stock production. By the following year she was accomplished enough to win a Promising Personality Award for her third lead performance in an Off-Broadway revival of the 1941 Blane/Martin Musical, *Best Foot Forward*, and later toured in road productions of *Carnival*, *The Pajama Game*, and *The Fantasticks*. She also made her first album, *Liza! Liza!* which sold over 500,000 copies after it was released in 1964. In November of that year, Minnelli appeared with Judy Garland at the London Palladium. Comparatively unknown in the UK, she startled the audience with dynamic performances of songs such as 'The Travellin' Life' and 'Gypsy In My Soul'; - almost 'stealing' the show from the more experienced artist. Her first Broadway show, and an early association with songwriters John Kander and Fred Ebb, came with *Flora And The Red Menace* (1965), for which she was given a Tony Award, though the show closed after only 87 performances. In 1966, she made her New York cabaret debut at the Plaza Hotel to enthusiastic reviews and, in 1967, married Australian singer/songwriter, Peter Allen. Her film career started in 1968, with a supporting role in Albert Finney's first directorial effort, *Charlie Bubbles*, and in 1969, she was nominated for an Academy Award for her performance as Pookie Adams in the film of John Nichols' novel, *The Sterile Cuckoo*. She took time off from making her third film, *Tell Me That You Love Me, Junie Moon*, to attend the funeral of her mother, who died in 1969. In the following year she and Peter Allen announced their separation.

In 1972, Liza Minnelli became a superstar. The film of Kander and Ebb's Broadway hit, *Cabaret*, won nine Oscars, including Best Film and, for her role as Sally Bowles, Minnelli was named Best Actress and appeared on the front covers of *Newsweek* and *Time* magazines in the same week. She also won an Emmy for her television Special, *Liza With A Z*, directed by Bob Fosse. Her concerts were sell-outs; when she played the Olympia, Paris, they dubbed her 'la petite Piaf Americano'. In 1973, she met producer/director Jack Haley Jnr. while contributing to his film project, *That's Entertainment*. Haley's father had played the Tin Man in Judy Garland's most famous picture, *The Wizard Of Oz*. Haley Jnr and Minnelli married in 1974, and in the same year she broke Broadway records and won a special Tony Award for a three-week series of one-woman shows at the Winter Garden. Her next two movies, *Lucky Lady* and *A Matter Of Time* received lukewarm reviews, but she made up for these in 1977, with her next film project, *New York, New York*. Co-starring with Robert DeNiro, and directed by Martin Scorsese, Minnelli's dramatic performance as a young band singer in the period after World War II was a personal triumph. This was the last film she made until *Arthur* (1981), in which she played a supporting role to Dudley Moore.

The musical theme for *Arthur*, 'Best You Can Do', was co-written by her ex-husband, Peter Allen. A renewed association with Kander and Ebb for the Broadway musical, *The Act* (1977), was dismissed by some critics as being little more than a series of production numbers displaying the talents of Liza Minnelli. She won another Tony Award, but collapsed from exhaustion during the show's run. In 1979, she was divorced from Jack Haley Jnr., and married Italian sculptor, Mark Gero. Rumours were appearing in the press which speculated about her drug and alcohol problems, and for a couple of years she was virtually retired. In 1984, she was nominated for yet another Tony for her performance on Broadway in *The Rink*, with Chita Rivera, but dropped out of the show to seek treatment for drug and alcohol abuse at the Betty Ford Clinic in California. She started her comeback in 1985, and the following year, on her 40th birthday, opened to a sold-out London Palladium, the first time she had played the theatre since that memorable occasion in 1964; she received the same kind of reception that her mother did then. In the same year, back in the USA, Minnelli won the Golden Globe Award as Best Actress in *A Time To Live*, a television adaptation of the true story, *Intensive Care*, by Mary-Lou Weisman.

During the late 80s, she joined Frank Sinatra and Sammy Davis Jnr. for a world tour, dubbed *The Ultimate Event!*, and in 1989 collaborated with the UK pop group, the Pet Shop Boys, on the album, *Results*. A single from the album, Stephen Sondheim's composition, 'Losing My Mind', gave Liza Minnelli her first chart entry, reaching the UK Top 10. She also appeared with Dudley Moore in *Arthur 2: On The Rocks*, and co-starred with Julie Walters in the film version of the successful British comedy musical, *Stepping Out* (1990). Minnelli's career in film and music has enabled her to transcend the title, 'Judy Garland's daughter'.

Albums: *Best Foot Forward* (1963, stageshow soundtrack), *Liza! Liza!* (1964), *It Amazes Me* (1965), *The Dangerous Christmas Of Red Riding Hood* (1965, film soundtrack), with Judy Garland *'Live' At The London Palladium* (1965), *Flora The Red Menace* (1965, film soundtrack), *There Is A Time* (1966), *New Feelin'* (1970), *Cabaret* (1972, film soundtrack), *Liza With A 'Z'* (1972, television soundtrack), *Liza Minnelli The Singer* (1973), *Live At The Winter Garden* (1974), *Lucky Lady* (1976), *Tropical Nights* (1977), *Live! - At Carnegie Hall* (1988), *Results* (1989), *Live From Radio City Music Hall* (1992).

Further reading: *Liza*, James Robert Parish.

Vincente Minnelli with daughter Liza

Minnelli, Vincente

b. 28 February 1903, Chicago, Illinois, USA, d. 25 July 1986, Los Angeles, California, USA. A distinguished film director with a sophisticated style and flair, particularly in the use of colour and the innovative filming of the most exquisite dance sequences. Minnelli is credited, in collaboration with Gene Kelly, with being the main influence on the classic MGM musicals of the 50s. As a young child Minnelli appeared in plays produced by the family Minnelli Bros. Tent Theatre which toured the American Mid-West. After leaving school at 16 he studied at the Art Institute of Chicago and worked as a window and costume designer before moving to New York and designing the settings and costumes for two 1932 Broadway shows, the *Earl Carroll Vanities* and *The Dubarry*. From 1933-35 Minnelli was art director at the Radio City Music Hall where he staged a series of ballets and musicals. In 1935 he directed as well as designed the Beatrice Lillie musical *At Home Abroad*, and throughout the 30s worked successfully on productions such as *Ziegfeld Follies*, *The Show Is On*, *Hooray For What!*, and *Very Warm For May* (1939). From 1940-42, under the aegis of MGM producer Arthur Freed, Minnelli trained in different aspects of Hollywood film techniques and supervised speciality numbers in a number of films including *Strike Up The Band*, *Babes On Broadway*, and *Panama Hattie*. He made his debut as a director in 1943 with the all-black musical *Cabin In Sky*, which was followed by *I Dood It* a year later. Then came *Meet Me In St. Louis* (1944) a delightful piece of nostalgic Americana which became one of the most beloved musicals of all time. Minnelli married its star, Judy Garland, in 1945 (divorced 1951), and in the following year their daughter, Liza Minnelli, was born. Over the next 25 years Minnelli directed a number of musicals which were generally enthusiastically (some ecstatically) received. *Yolande And The Thief* (1945), which starred Fred Astaire, was followed by the all-star spectacular *Ziegfeld Follies* (1946), and two films with Gene Kelly, the underrated *The Pirate* (1948), and *An American In Paris* (1951), which is often considered to be Minnelli's masterpiece. However, many would argue that another of the director's collaborations with Fred Astaire, *The Band Wagon* (1953), or the delightful *Gigi* (1958), were the highlights of the director's illustrious career. Certainly, whatever their merits - and they were not inconsiderable - few would submit *Brigadoon* (1954), *Kismet* (1955), *Bells Are Ringing* (1960), or *On A Clear Day You Can See Forever* (1970) as being prime examples of Vincente Minnelli's art. The latter film was made for Paramount after he had ended his association with MGM which had lasted for more than 25 years. Of course, the majority of Minnelli's films were not musicals. Over the years he made many other pictures in a wide variety of styles and moods, including *The Clock*, *Father Of The Bride*, *The Bad And The Beautiful*, *Lust For Life*, *Tea And Sympathy*, *The Cobweb*, *The Reluctant Debutante*, and *Some Came Running*. He finally achieved his ambition to work with his daughter, Liza Minnelli, on his last film *A Matter Of Time* in 1976. By then Minnelli's kind of films - particularly the musicals - were a thing of the past, and he lived quietly in retirement until his death at his home in Beverly Hills in 1986. The year of his birth has always been the subject of speculation. The one given above is that which was printed in the excellent obituary notice in *Variety*. In 1993 the young cabaret entertainer Jeff Harnar presented his solo revue *Dancing In The Dark - Vincente Minnelli's Hollywood* in New York.

Further reading: *I Remember It Well* (his autobiography).

Miranda, Carmen

b. Maria do Carmo Miranda da Cunha, 9 February 1909, near Lisbon, Portugal, d. 5 August 1955, California, USA. A flamboyant singer, dancer and actress with an animated style and a penchant for exotic, colourful costumes, 10 inch-heeled shoes, and turbans decorated with significant amounts of artificial fruit. She was raised in Rio de Janeiro and began her career there on local radio. Later she made several films and appeared in nightclubs and theatres throughout South America. Lee Shubert, the oldest of the famous trio of producer brothers, took Miranda to the USA in 1939 where she introduced Al Dubin and Jimmy McHugh's catchy 'South American Way' in the Broadway musical *The Streets Of Paris*. She sang it again (her peculiar accent turned it into 'Souse American Way') when she made her spectacular film debut with Betty Grable and Don Ameche in *Down Argentine Way* (1940). A year later she joined the comedy team of Olsen and Jolsen in another Broadway show, *Sons O' Fun*. However, her real impact was made in a series of film musicals in the 40s when she became known as the 'Brazilian Bombshell'. These included *That Night In Rio*, *Weekend In Havana*, *Springtime In The Rockies*, *The Gang's All Here*, *Four Jills In A Jeep*, *Greenwich Village*, *Doll Face*, *If I'm Lucky*, *Copacabana*, and *A Date With Judy*. By then her star had faded, and she made only two more pictures, *Nancy Goes To Rio* (1950) and *Scared Stiff* (1953), although in the late 40s and early 50s she continued to perform in theatres and nightclubs. She died suddenly of a heart attack in 1955 shortly after appearing with Jimmy Durante on his television show. A dynamic, much impersonated entertainer - Mickey Rooney's wickedly accurate takeoff in *Babes On Broadway* immediately comes to mind - Carmen Miranda was indelibly associated with several lively and diverting songs, including 'The Lady With The Tutti Frutti Hat', 'I Yi Yi Yi Yi (I Like You Very Much)', 'Chica Boom Chic', 'When I Love, I Love', 'Cuanto La

Carmen Miranda

Gusta', 'Mama, Eu Quero (I Want My Mama)', and 'The Wedding Samba' (the last two with the Andrews Sisters).

Selected album: *South American Way* (c.50s, re-released 1982).

Further reading: *Brazilian Bombshell: The Biography Of Carmen Miranda*, M. Gil-Montero.

Miss London Ltd.

Released by Gainsborough Pictures in 1943, this comedy-musical is a typical example of the cheery, tuneful fare British cinema audiences flocked to see during the dark war years. It starred Arthur 'Hallo Playmates!' Askey, one of the country's most popular funny-men. He played Arthur Bowman, the manager of the Miss London Ltd. escort agency which is visited by its attractive American owner, Terry Arden (Evelyn Dall). The business needs a shake-up, and Arthur goes on a recruitment drive and comes up with railway station announcer Gail Martin (Anne Shelton). The ensuing complications involve some of Britain's top comedy talent, such as Jack Train as Arthur's right-hand man, Max Bacon as an hilariously coy head waiter, and Richard Hearne, who plays a jitterbugging commodore in the Navy, the service into which Arthur himself is being co-opted (by another fine comic actor, Ronald Shiner) when the closing titles roll. Other parts were taken by Peter Graves and Jean Kent. Manning Sherwin and Val Guest, wrote the songs, and Evelyn Dall had one of the film's best musical moments with the punchy 'Keep Cool, Calm - And Collect!'. She also joined Askey for the lively 'It's A Fine How-Do-You-Do'. Anne Shelton, who had the distinction of singing with the Glenn Miller Orchestra during the war, was splendid on 'If You Could Only Cook', 'You Too (Can Have a Lovely Romance)', and 'The Eight Fifty Choo Choo'. Val Guest and Marriott Edgar wrote the screenplay, and Guest also directed. The producer was Edward Black.

Monaco, Jimmy

b. 13 January 1885, Genoa, Italy, d. 16 October 1945, Beverly Hills, California, USA. Coming to the USA with his family when he was six years old, Monaco taught himself to play piano. He began earning his living as a pianist in Chicago clubs while still in his teens. By 1910 he was resident in New York, playing in saloons. The following year, he began writing songs, some of which were recorded and others used in Broadway shows. In 1912, he had his first hits with 'Row, Row, Row' (lyrics by William Jerome) and 'You Made Me Love You' (Joseph McCarthy). The latter was taken up by Al Jolson, a fact which ensured its enduring popularity. Monaco continued to compose, and his songs of the next few years included 'I Miss You Most Of All', (McCarthy) 'What Do You Want To Make Those Eyes At Me For?' (McCarthy),

'Caresses' and 'Dirty Hands, Dirty Face' (Edgar Leslie and Grant Clarke), which Jolson sang in the 1927 film *The Jazz Singer*. Among Monaco's songs of the late 20s were 'Me And My Boyfriend' (Sidney Clare), 'Me And The Man In The Moon' (Leslie) and 'Through' (McCarthy). In the 30s, Monaco was active in Hollywood, where he began a fruitful collaboration with Johnny Burke. Among the results were a string of hits sung in films and recorded by Bing Crosby, including 'On The Sentimental Side', 'I've Got A Pocketful Of Dreams', 'An Apple For The Teacher', 'Too Romantic', 'That's For Me' and 'Only Forever'. He contributed to films such as *The Golden Calf*, *Doctor Rhythm*, *Sing You Sinners*, *East Side Of Heaven*, *The Star Maker*, *If I Had My Way*, *Road To Singapore*, *Rhythm On The River*, *Stage Door Canteen*, *Pin-Up Girl*, and *The Dolly Sisters* (1945). In the early 40s, Monaco had more popular successes with 'Six Lessons From Madame La Zonga' (Charles Newman), 'I Can't Begin To Tell You' (Mack Gordon), 'Ev'ry Night About This Time' (Ted Koehler), 'We Musn't Say Goodbye' (Al Dubin), and 'Time Will Tell' (Gordon). Monaco died suddenly from a heart attack in 1945.

Monroe, Marilyn

b. Norma Jean Mortenson, 1 June 1926, Los Angeles, California, USA, d. 5 August 1962, Brentwood, California, USA. As well as being a talented comedienne and the number 1 sex symbol in movies during the 50s, Monroe proved to be an appealing interpreter of flirtacious ballads in several of her most popular films. As one of the *Ladies Of The Chorus* (1949), she made a promising start with Lester Lee and Allan Roberts's 'Every Baby Needs A Da-Da-Daddy', which, with its reference to 'Tiffany's', was a precursor to one of her most celebrated performances a few years later, when the same New York store cropped up 'Diamonds Are A Girl's Best Friend', from Jule Styne and Leo Robin's score for *Gentlemen Prefer Blondes* (1953). In that film Monroe duetted with another of Hollywood's top glamour girls, Jane Russell, on 'Two Little Girls From Little Rock', 'Bye Bye Baby' and a Hoagy Carmichael/Harold Adamson number, 'When Loves Goes Wrong'. Co-starred with Robert Mitchum in *River Of No Return* (1954), Monroe's role as a saloon singer conveniently gave her the opportunity to put over the title song and 'I'm Gonna File My Claim', amongst others, and, in the same year, she registered strongly with a bundle of Irving Berlin numbers in *There's No Business Like Show Business*. These included 'A Man Chases A Girl' (with Donald O'Connor), 'After You Get What You Want You Don't Want It', 'Heatwave', 'Lazy' and 'You'd Be Surprised'. In 1959 she made what was to become her most commercially successful film - arguably the highlight of her career. The classic *Some Like It Hot*, with Tony Curtis, Jack Lemmon and Joe E. (nobody's perfect) Brown, contained some of

Monroe's most effective vocal peformances, such as 'I'm Through With Love', 'I Wanna Be Loved By You' and 'Running Wild'. She sang for the last time on screen in *Let's Make Love* (1960). Apart from contributing the film's highspot, a compelling version of 'My Heart Belongs To Daddy', Monroe duetted with a couple of European heart-throbs, Yves Montand and Frankie Vaughan, on Sammy Cahn and Jimmy Van Heusen's 'Specialization', 'Incurably Romantic' and the title song. Her final performance, a sultry rendering of 'Happy Birthday Mr. President' and 'Thanks For The Memory', was given in May 1962 for President Kennedy's birthday celebrations in Madison Square Garden. Just over two months later she died, in mysterious circumstances, at the age of 36. One of the musical selections chosen for her funeral service was a recording of 'Over The Rainbow', sung by Judy Garland, another show business legend who met a tragic end. Since her death, it has been estimated that over 100 Monroe biographies have been published. She was also the subject of several songs, the most famous being Elton John's 'Crying In the Wind'. Others included James Cunningham's 'Norma Jean Wants To Be A Movie Star' and 'Elvis And Marilyn' by Leon Russell.
Album: *Marilyn Monroe - The Complete Recordings* (1988, 2-CD set).

Monte Carlo

Slightly less risqué than *The Love Parade* (1929), *Monte Carlo*, which was released by Paramount a year later, was nevertheless a hot-bed of romance and intrigue in the hands of director-producer Ernst Lubitsch. Jeanette Macdonald, who had raised temperatures and blood pressures with her sizzling scenes in *The Love Parade*, exchanged her European co-star in that film for another - Britain's premiere suave and sophisticated song-and-dance man Jack Buchanan. In Ernest Vajda and Vincent Lawrence's screenplay, which was adapted from the play *The Blue Coast* by Ernest Mueller, MacDonald plays a countess who leaves her intended (titled) husband waiting at the church while she boards the Blue Express which takes her to Monte Carlo. After falling for a barber (Buchanan), her penchant for gambling pays off when he turns out to be a wealthy count. By this stage in his career, director Lubitsch was well into his stride as the leader in intelligent and integrated musicals. Acclaimed highlights of this particularly example of his outstanding work include his setting of the song 'Beyond The Blue Horizon', which MacDonald sings aboard the famous train accompanied by familiar sounds and movements of the train itself; and a novel operatic sequence which was based on Booth Tarkington's story *Monsieur Beaucaire*. The film's engaging score was written by Richard Whiting and W. Franke Harling (music) and Leo Robin (lyrics), and included a variety of numbers such as 'Trimmin'

With Women', 'Give Me A Moment Please', 'Whatever It Is, It's Grand', 'Always In All Ways', and 'She'll Love Me And Like It'. Also in the cast were Claud Allister, ZaSu Pitts, Tyler Brooke, and Lionel Belmore.

Moon Over Miami

This typically lavish 20th Century-Fox Technicolor extravaganza was a remake of the same studio's somewhat less opulent *Three Blind Mice* which was produced three years earlier in 1938. The slight story concerns sisters Kay and Barbara Latimer (Betty Grable and Carole Landis) and their Aunt Charlotte (Charlotte Greenwood), who anxiously anticipate a substantial legacy. When the original $55,000 is whittled down to $4,287 and 96 cents (to be split three ways), the trio give up their jobs at a roadside diner and set off for Miami with the intention of finding Kay a rich husband. After going through the usual charades and complications, Kay lands the young well-heeled smoothie (Robert Cummings) - and then turns him down for the equally smooth but less well-off Don Ameche. In the sparkling supporting cast were funny-man Jack Haley, Cobina Wright Jnr., Robert Conway, Lynne Roberts, George Lessey, and dancers Jack Cole, the Condos Brothers and Hermes Pan (who also staged the dances). Leo Robin and Ralph Rainger came up with a bright and lively score which included 'You Started Something', 'Kindergarten Conga', 'I've Got You All To Myself', 'What Can I Do For You?', 'Oh Me, Oh Mi-ami', 'Is That Good?', 'Loveliness And Love', and 'Hurrah For Today'. The screenplay was written by Vincent Lawrence and Brown Holmes, and adapted by George Seaton and Lynn Starling from a 1938 English play by Stephen Powys. The director for this entertaining and colourful film was Walter Lang. Another remake appeared in 1946 entitled *Three Little Girls In Blue* and starring June Haver, George Montgomery and Celeste Holm.

Moore, Grace

b. 5 December 1901, Slabtown, Tennessee, USA, d. 26 January 1947. Gifted with a remarkable singing voice, Moore first made her name on Broadway in musical comedies. The quality of her singing brought her to the attention of New York's Metropolitan Opera Company and from there she went to Hollywood where her physical beauty enhanced a number of 30s musicals. Moore's lyrical soprano voice was far better than anything offered by most singing actresses in Hollywood. Among her Hollywood films were *New Moon* (1931), *One Night Of Love* (1934), for which she was nominated as Best Actress, and *Love Me Forever* (1935). While on a concert tour of Europe, Moore was killed when the aircraft in which she was travelling crashed near Copenhagen. The 1953, *So This Is Love*, told an approximate version of her life.

Further reading: *You're Only Human Once*, Grace Moore.

Morgan, Helen

b. Helen Riggins, 2 August 1900, Danville, Illinois, USA, d. 8 October 1941. After working at a number of unskilled jobs, Morgan began singing in small Chicago clubs. She graduated to revue, appearing in New York in *Americana* where she was spotted by Florenz Ziegfeld, who signed her to play the role of Julie in the original production of of Jerome Kern's *Show Boat* (1927). Her performance of 'Bill' was a show-stopper. In fact, the composer had written the song some years before but had refrained from including it in earlier shows until he found someone capable of the right interpretation. When he heard Morgan sing it he knew that, at last, the song could be used. Morgan also staked a claim to a song by George and Ira Gershwin; her interpretation of 'The Man I Love' helped her gain the accolade of being not merely one of the first but also the best of the 'torch singers'. Morgan appeared on Broadway in *Sweet Adeline* (1929), the *Ziegfeld Follies* of 1931, and the 1932 revival of *Show Boat*. She was also in the 1929 and 1936 screen versions of *Show Boat*. Here other film appearances included *Applause, Roadhouse Nights, Glorifying The American Girl, Marie Galante, You Belong To Me, Sweet Music, Go Into Your Dance*, and *Frankie And Johnnie* (1936). By the late 30s her career was in disarray and she was heavily dependent upon alcohol. As owner of a number of Prohibition-era speakeasies she had ready access to liquor and her health rapidly deteriorated until she died of cirrhosis of the liver. Her life story was traced in a 1957 screen biography, *The Helen Morgan Story*.
Further reading: *Helen Morgan, Her Life And Legend*, G. Maxwell.

Morricone, Ennio

b. 11 October 1928, Rome, Italy. Morricone's revolutionary scores for 'spaghetti Westerns' have made him an influential film music composer. He studied trumpet and composition before becoming a professional composer of music for radio, television and the stage as well as the concert hall. During the 50s he wrote songs and arrangements for popular vocalist Gianni Morandi and he later arranged Paul Anka's Italian hit 'Ogni Volta' (1964). Morricone's first film score was for the comedy *Il Federale* in 1961. Three years later he was hired by Sergio Leone to compose music for *A Fistful Of Dollars*. Using the pseudonym Dan Savio, Morricone created a score out of shouts, cries and a haunting whistled phrase, in direct contrast to the use of pseudo-folk melodies in Hollywood Westerns. His work on Leone's trilogy of Italian Westerns led to collaboration with such leading European directors as Pontecorvo (*Battle Of Algiers* 1966), Pasolini (*Big Birds, Little Birds*, 1966) and Bertolucci (*1900*, 1976). In the 70s he began to compose for US films, such as *Exorcist II* (1977), *Days Of Heaven* (1978), *The Untouchables* (1987) and *Frantic* (1988). Morricone won an Oscar for Roland Joffe's *The Mission* (1986), where he used motifs from sacred music and native Indian melodies to create what he called 'contemporary music written in an ancient language'. In 1992 Morricone's score for *Bugsy* received an Oscar nomination. The composer's other scores in the early 90s included *Husbands And Lovers, City Of Joy, Tie Me Up! Tie Me Down!, Everybody's Fine, Hamlet, State Of Grace, Octopus 6 - The Force Of The Mafia, Jonah Who Lived In A Whale, In The Line Of Fire*, and *Cinema Paradiso - The Special Edition* (1993). The Spaghetti western sound has been a source of inspiration and samples for a number of rock artists including BAD, Cameo and John Zorn (*Big Gundown*, 1987). Morricone has recorded several albums of his own music and in 1981 he had a hit with 'Chi Mai', a tune he composed for a BBC television series. A double album for Virgin Records in 1988 included Morricone's own selection from the over 100 films which he has scored, while in the same year Virgin Venture issued a recording of his classical compositions.
Selected albums: *Moses* (1977), *Film Hits* (1981), *Chi Mai* (1981), *The Mission* (1986), *Chamber Music* (1988), *Frantic* (1988, film soundtrack), *The Endless Game* (1989), *Live In Concert* (1989), *Casualties Of War* (1990), *Morricone '93 Movie Sounds* (1993). Compilations: *Film Music 1966-87* (1988), *The Very Best Of* (1992).

Mother Wore Tights

20th Century-Fox teamed their top pin-up girl, Betty Grable, with one of their most popular and likeable song-and-dance-men, Dan Dailey, in this 1947 release which was produced by Lamar Trotti. He was also responsible for the screenplay which was based on a book by Miriam Young. Set in the early part of the century and told in flashback, it was a warm-hearted tale about a married vaudeville couple, Burt and McKinley (Grable and Dailey) whose hoity-toity elder daughter (Mona Freeman) derides her parents' performing lifestyle ('my friends go to the opera and things') until the entire class of her swanky music school go to see the 'old folks'' show - and enjoy it. She realises what a fool she has been, and at her graduation ceremony sings one of her father and mother's big hit songs, 'You Do'. Josef Myrow and Mack Gordon wrote that one, and several others including 'There's Nothing Like A Song', 'This Is My Favourite City', 'Kokomo, Indiana', 'Rolling Down To Bowling Green', and 'On A Little Two-Seat Tandem'. Gordon also collaborated with Harry Warren on 'Tra-la-la', and there were several other nostalgic numbers by various composers, such as 'Burlington Bertie From Bow' (William Hargreaves).

Mother Wore Tights

Musical director Alfred Newman won an Oscar for his work on the score. Connie Marshall played the younger (but more mature) daughter, and there were excellent performances from Vanessa Brown, Robert Arthur, Sara Allgood, William Frawley, Ruth Nelson, Anabel Shaw, Michael Dunne, George Cleveland, Veda Ann Borg, Sig Ruman, Lee Patrick, and especially the highly amusing Señor Wences. Seymour Felix and Kenny Williams handled the olde worlde dance sequences and the director was Walter Lang. *Mother Wore Tights* was one of the Top 20 musicals of the 40s, and Betty Grable's most financially successful picture.

Moustaki, Georges

b. 1934, Alexandria, Egypt. Moustaki was a singer, songwriter, actor and film music composer. Of Greek ancestry, he studied French which enabled him to work in Paris as a journalist. He began to write songs, and played the piano and guitar in the College Inn in Montparnasse. He also met the gypsy musician Henri Crolla, a cousin of Django Reinhardt. Crolla introduced him to the legendary performer, Edith Piaf, and in 1958, he became her guitarist and lover. With Marguerite Monnet, who was involved with many of Piaf's songs, he wrote 'Milord', which became Piaf's last big hit before she died three years later. Her record spent 15 weeks in the UK chart in 1960, easily beating a version by Frankie Vaughan, which had an English lyric by Decca recording manager Bunny Lewis. Moustaki was driving the car late in 1959 when Piaf had her third serious car accident. He escaped unscathed, and accompanied the singer on her ninth tour of the USA, where their relationship was terminated following her collapse onstage at the Waldorf Astoria, and subsequent four-hour operation. In the 60s, long haired, with a grey beard, Moustaki toured the music festivals, writing and performing his own songs. These included the dramatic 'Le Gitan Et La Fille', 'Un Etranger', 'Les Orgues De Barbarie', 'Les Gestes', which was memorably sung by Serge Reggiani and 'Le Meteque' (the outcast), perhaps the song most identified with Moustaki, which ran: 'Look at me, a bloody foreigner/A wandering Jew, a Greek peasant/Hair all over the place, eyes washed out . . .' In the 70s Moustaki worked with Jacques Potrenaud on the film of Albert Cosseri's book, *Mendiants Et Orgueilleux*, and played the central character, Hadjis. He also wrote the music for movies such as *The Man With Connections*, *Solo*, *The Five Leaf Clover* and *At The Brink Of The Bench*. Although little known outside the French-speaking world, Moustaki is enormously popular. Selected albums: *Troubador*, *Le Meteque*, *Georges Moustaki*.

Music Man, The

Despite studio chief Jack Warner's efforts to get a male superstar such as Cary Grant to play the lead, Robert Preston was eventually invited to recreate his magnificent Broadway performance for this enjoyable screen version which was released in 1962. So, film-goers the world over were able to enjoy the sight of Professor Harold Hill (Preston), a con-man of the highest order, who descends on the town Iowa with the intention of selling (non-existent) musical instruments to the parents of the parish in order that their children can form a brass band - which he will lead. Such is his charm, that, after overcoming the initial resistance of Marion Paroo (Shirley Jones), the Balzac-loving librarian, they not only fall in love, but he is absolved of all charges of deception after deciding not to make a run for it. There were some lovely performances in the supporting roles, such as the Professor's assistant and look-out man (Buddy Hackett), the always-blustering mayor (Paul Ford) and his lady wife (Hermione Gingold), and Marion's mother-with-the-blarney (Pert Kelton). Other parts were played by Ronny Howard, Timmy Everett, Susan Luckey, Mary Wickes, and the harmonising Buffalo Bills. Meredith Willson's songs were all gems in their way, and included 'Rock Island', 'Iowa Stubborn', 'Piano Lesson', 'If You Don't Mind Me Saying So', 'Goodnight My Someone', 'Sincere', 'The Sadder But Wiser Girl', 'Pick-A-Little, Talk-A-Little', 'Marion The Librarian', 'Being In Love', 'Gary, Indiana', 'The Wells Fargo Wagon', 'Lida Rose', 'Will I Ever Tell You?', 'Shipoopi', and 'Till There Was You'. Preston's musical highspot came with 'Ya Got Trouble', in which he warned the population about the perils of having a pool table in their midst, and, in the film's exuberant finalé, he was at the head of the procession during the rousing 'Seventy Six Trombones'. Onna White was the choreographer, and musical director Ray Heindorf won an Oscar for his scoring. Marion Hargrove's screenplay was adapted from Meredith Willson's stage libretto. The producer-director was Morton DaCosta, and the film was shot in Technicolor and Technirama. There was some dismay at the time that Barbara Cook, who created the role of Marion was not asked to repeat her role on the screen. As it transpired, Shirley Jones was fine - and Robert Preston sensational.

My Fair Lady

Alan Jay Lerner and Frederick Loewe's Broadway masterpiece came to the screen in 1964 complete with a controversial choice of leading lady. Julie Andrews, who created the part of Eliza Doolittle on stage, had only just made her film debut in *Mary Poppins*, and Audrey Hepburn (whose singing was dubbed by Marni Nixon) won the coveted role. Thankfully, after some bizarre alternative casting suggestions, Rex Harrison was once again the irascible confirmed bachelor, Professor Henry Higgins, who bets his companion, Colonel Pickering (Wilfred Hyde-

My Fair Lady

White), that he can take an ordinary cockney flower girl and pass her off in high society just by teaching her to 'speak like a lady'. This he does in triumphant fashion, but only after much hard work and frustration, and some delicate negotiations with the girl's philosophical dustman father, Alfred P. Doolittle, who is superbly played by Stanley Holloway reprising his stage performance. Gladys Cooper as Higgin's mother (who sides with Eliza in all disputes) and Jeremy Brett as the toff who worships the pavements that Eliza walks on, were among the supporting cast which also included Mona Washbourne, Theodore Bikel, Isobel Elsom, Charles Fredericks, and John Holland. Not surprising with Lerner writing the screenplay, all the songs from the stage production were retained. The by-now classic overture preceded this extraordinary score: 'Why Can't The English?', 'Wouldn't it be Loverly?', 'With A Little Bit Of Luck', 'I'm An Ordinary Man', 'Just You Wait', 'The Rain In Spain', 'I Could Have Danced All Night', 'Ascot Gavotte', 'On the Street Where You Live', 'Embassy Waltz', 'You Did It', 'Show Me', 'Get Me To The Church On Time', 'A Hymn To Him', 'Without You', and the sublime 'I've Grown Accustomed To Her Face'. That last number was part of an ending to the story contrary to the one in Bernard Shaw's *Pygmalion* on which the stage and film musicals were based. Shaw refused to have a happy resolution to Higgins's relationship with Eliza, but in *My Fair Lady*, the famous curtain line, 'Where the devil are my slippers?,' does seem to indicate that the teacher and his prize pupil are destined to stay together. Jack L. Warner produced the film for Warner Brothers and the choreographer was Hermes Pan. It was photographed in Technicolor and Super Panavision 70 and won nine Academy Awards including best picture, actor (Harrison), actress (Andrews), director (George Cukor), and costumes and sets (Cecil Beaton). The latter's work, especially in such scenes as the marvellous 'Ascot Gavotte', was a major factor in the film's success - even without Julie Andrews.

My Gal Sal

Another screen biography that played fast and loose with the true facts about its subject - in this case the late 19th century songwriter Paul Dresser. The screenplay, by Seton I. Miller, Darrell Ware and Karl Tunberg, was loosely based on Theodore Dreiser's book *My Brother Paul*, and purported to trace the rise of Dresser (he changed his name from Dreiser early in his career) from his time as a performer in medicine shows and as a blackface comedian in vaudeville, to fame and fortune as a great songwriter. In fact, Dresser was never a commercial success and he wrote his best-known song 'My Gal Sal' in 1905 just a year before he died of heart failure. Victor Mature, an actor guaranteed to make the hearts of female members of

the audiences go all-a-flutter, played the composer, and Rita Hayworth was the musical comedy star he fell for in a big way. No wonder, because Hayworth (whose vocals were dubbed by Nan Wynn), looked beautiful and gave one of the best and most joyful performances of her illustrious career. Other roles were played by Carole Landis, John Sutton, James Gleason, Phil Silvers, Walter Catlett, Andrew Tombes, Curt Bois, and Mona Maris. Hermes Pan also made an appearance, and he and Val Raset staged the delightful dance sequences. Several of Dresser's own numbers were featured, including 'On The Banks Of The Wabash', 'Come Tell Me What's Your Answer', 'Liza Jane', 'The Convict And The Bird', 'Mr. Volunteer', 'If You Want Me', and, of course, 'My Gal Sal'. These were supplemented by others, by Ralph Rainger and Leo Robin, such as 'Me And My Fella', 'On The Gay White Way', 'Oh! The Pity Of It All', and 'Midnight At The Masquerade'. It all added up to a colourful and entertaining period piece, which was photographed in Technicolor by Ernest Palmer and produced by Robert Bassler for 20th Century-Fox in 1942. The director was Irving Cummings.

My Heart Goes Crazy (see *London Town*)

Myers, Stanley

b. 6 October 1930, London, England, d. 9 November 1993, London, England. A composer, arranger and musical director for films and television from 1966. In the 50s Myers worked in the theatre, and contributed music to several London West End shows including *A Girl Called Jo* and served as musical director for the Julian More-James Gilbert hit musical, *Grab Me A Gondola* (1956-58). In 1966 he scored his first film, the comedy, *Kaleidoscope*, which teamed Warren Beatty with English actress Susannah York. Two other early projects included *Ulysses* and *Tropic Of Cancer* for the US director, John Strick. Throughout a career spanning over 60 feature films, Myers worked in several countries besides the UK, including the USA, Canada, Australia, and in Europe, particularly France and Germany. In the 70s his credits included *The Walking Stick*, *Age Of Consent*, *A Severed Head*, *Long Ago Tomorrow (The Raging Moon)*, *Summer Lightning*, *X, Y And Z*, *Little Malcolm And His Struggle Against The Eunuchs*, *The Apprenticeship Of Dudley Kravitz*, *The Wilby Conspiracy*, *Absolution* and *Yesterday's Hero* (1979). In 1978 Myers won his first Ivor Novello Award for his theme for the five times Oscar-winner, *The Deer Hunter*. It was a UK Top 20 entry for classical guitarist John Williams; and, under the title, 'He Was Beautiful', with a lyric by Cleo Laine, for Welsh singer Iris Williams as well. In the 80s, Myers collaborated on the music for several films with Hans Zimmer. Together they scored Jerzy Skolimowski's highly-acclaimed *Moonlighting*, starring Jeremy Irons, *Success Is The Best Revenge*, *Eureka*,

Insignificance, *Taffin*, *The Nature Of The Beast* and *Paperhouse*, amongst others. Myers' solo scores during the 80s included *The Watcher In The Woods*, *Blind Date* (Bruce Willis's big screen success), *The Chain*, *The Lightship*, *Conduct Unbecoming*, *Dreamchild*, *Castaway*, *Sammy And Rosie Get Laid*, *Wish You Were Here*, *The Boost* and *Scenes From The Class Struggle In Beverly Hills* (1989). In 1987 Myers received an award for 'the best artistic contribution' at Cannes for his music to *Prick Up Your Ears*, Steven Frear's 'realistic and evocative look' at the life of playwright Joe Orton, which included the song 'Dancing Hearts' (written with Richard Myhill).

Two years later, Myers won his second Ivor Novello Award for his score for *The Witches*, director Nicholas Roeg's treatment of a story by Roald Dahl. In the early 90s Myers' credits included *Rosencrantz And Guildenstern Are Dead*, *Iron Maze*, *Claude*, *Sarafina!*, and the French-German production *Voyager*. Myers also worked extensively in television on UK programmes such as *All Gas And Gaiters*, *Never A Cross Word*, *Robin Hood*, *Dirty Money*, *Widows I And II*, *Diana*, *Nancy Astor*, *Wreath Of Roses*, *Scoop*, *Here To Stay*, *The Russian Soldier*, *The Most Dangerous Man In The World*, *My Beautiful Laundrette*, *Christabel* and many more. For US network television he composed music for *Summer Of My German Soldier*, *The Gentleman Bandit*, *The Martian Chronicles*, *Florence Nightingale*, *Monte Carlo*, *Tidy Endings* and more.

In the early 90s Myers' was working with the saxophonist John Harle. They had just finished recording Myers' specially written piece, 'Concerto For Soprano Saxophone', before he died of cancer in November 1993.

Myrow, Joseph

b. 28 February 1910, Russia, d. 24 December 1987, Los Angeles, California, USA. Myrow was a popular composer from the 40s to the late 50s, mostly for movies. He was educated at the University of Pennsylvania, Philadelphia Conservatory of Music and the Curtis Institute of Music. He graduated as an accomplished pianist, and served as a guest soloist with several symphony orchestras, including those of Cleveland and Philadelphia. After working as musical director for some Philadelphia radio stations, Myrow started composing for nightclub revues in cities on the east coast. His early songs in the late 30s, included 'Haunting Me', 'Overheard In A Cocktail Lounge', 'The Fable Of The Rose' and 'I Love To Watch The Moonlight'. In the early 40s he wrote 'Autumn Nocturne' (a big hit for Claude Thornhill) and 'Velvet Moon'. In 1946, he and Eddie De Lange contributed several songs to the movie, *If I'm Lucky*. In the same year, Myrow began what was to be a 10-year association with lyricist Mack Gordon. Together they wrote eight songs for *Three Little Girls In Blue*, including 'Somewhere In The Night', 'Always A

Lady', 'On The Boardwalk In Atlantic City' and 'You Make Me Feel So Young', which later became linked with Frank Sinatra. From 1947-50, the team provided the songs for four movies starring Betty Grable, including *Mother Wore Tights* ('Kokomo, Indiana', 'There's Nothing Like A Song' and 'You Do', which was nominated for an Academy Award, and became a hit for Dinah Shore and Vaughn Monroe), *When My Baby Smiles At Me* ('By The Way' and 'What Did I Do?'), *The Beautiful Blonde From Bashville Bend* ('Every Time I Meet You') and *Wabash Avenue* ('Baby Won't You Say You Love Me' and 'Wilhelmina', which was also nominated for an Oscar). Myrow and Gordon continued into the 50s with *The I-Don't-Care Girl* ('This Is My Favorite City'); *I Love Melvin* starring Donald O'Connor and Debbie Reynolds ('A Lady Loves', 'Where Did You Learn To Dance?' and 'There You Are'); and *Bundle Of Joy*, in which Reynolds appeared with husband Eddie Fisher. Myrow also contributed several numbers to *The French Line*, with Ralph Blane ('Comment Allez-Vous?', 'What Is This I Feel?', 'Well, I'll Be Switched' and 'Wait Till You See Paris'). His other compositions included 'Five O'Clock Whistle' (a hit for Glenn Miller, Erskine Hawkins and Ella Fitzgerald); 'It Happens Every Spring' (movie title song), 'Endless Love', 'Love Is Eternal', 'Five Four Blues', 'Soft And Warm', 'Three Quarter Blues' and 'Someday Soon'. His other collaborators included Kim Gannon, Jean Stone and Bickley Reichner. Josef Myrow died of Parkinson's disease in 1987.

N

Naughty Marietta

Jeanette MacDonald, who had enjoyed much success with Maurice Chevalier in early musicals such as *The Love Parade*, *One Hour With You*, and *Love Me Tonight*, co-starred in this film with a new partner with whom she would always be indelibly associated . . . Nelson Eddy. In the screenplay, by John Lee Mahin, Frances Goodrich, and Albert Hackett, which was based on the 1910 stage operetta of the same name, Jeanette Macdonald plays a French princess who avoids an arranged marriage by boarding a ship bound for the Colonies. The brave Capt. Warrington (Nelson Eddy) saves her from a fate worse than death, and the couple find sanctuary in New Orleans before eventually settling down together 'Neath The Southern Moon'.

That was just one of the numbers in Victor Herbert's sumptuous score which included such delights as 'Ah! Sweet Mystery Of Life', 'Italian Street Song', 'I'm Falling In Love With Someone', and 'Tramp! Tramp! Tramp!' (all with lyrics by Rida Johnson Young), and 'Chansonette' (lyric by Gus Kahn). Veteran character actor Frank Morgan lead the supporting cast, which also included Elsa Lanchester, Joseph Cawthorn, Akim Tamiroff, Douglas Dumbrille, Edward Brophy, and Walter Kingsford. This first episode in the Macdonald-Eddy series, during which they became the screen's favourite romantic singing duo, was produced by Hunt Stromberg for MGM and directed by W.S. Van Dyke. The MGM studios were awarded an Oscar for the sound recording.

Neagle, Anna

b. Marjorie Robertson, 20 October 1904, Forest Gate, London, England, d. 3 June 1986, Surrey, England. One of the most durable and popular artists in the history of British showbusiness: an actress, dancer and singer in West End musicals and British films with a career stretching for almost 62 years. She took dancing lessons as a child, and appeared in the chorus of *Charlot's Revue* and a similar production, *Tricks*, in 1925. In the late 20s she undertook more chorus work in *Rose Marie*, *The Charlot Show Of 1926*, *The Desert Song*, and two London Pavilion revues as one of 'Mr Cochran's Young Ladies'. Up to then she had been primarily a dancer, but she developed further in 1931 when she took the ingenue lead opposite Jack Buchanan in the hit musical comedy *Stand Up And Sing*, duetting with him on the lovely song 'It's Always Tomorrow'. Herbert Wilcox produced and directed her first film, *Goodnight Vienna* in 1932. They worked together on most of her subsequent pictures, and were married in 1943. As well as making a number of acclaimed dramatic films during the 30s, Anna Neagle continued to appear in screen musicals such as *The Little Damozel*, *Bitter Sweet*, *The Queen's Affair*, *Limelight*, and *London Melody* (1939). From 1940-41 she and Wilcox were in America to make three films, *Irene* (in which she sang and danced to the delightful 'Alice Blue Gown'), *No, No, Nanette*, and *Sunny*. They returned to England to make a series of light and frothy romantic comedies, with the occasional musical number, which included *Spring In Park Lane*, *The Courtneys Of Curzon Street*, and *Maytime In Mayfair* (1949). Anna Neagle's leading man was Michael Wilding, and this magical partnership ensured that the films were among the British cinema's top box office attractions of the time. In the 50s Anna Neagle returned to the stage for *The Glorious Days* (1953), co-starred with Errol Flynn (of all people) in film versions of *Lilacs In The Spring* and *King's Rhapsody*, and then kicked up her heels with popular singer Frankie Vaughan in *The Lady Is A Square* (1958). That was her last appearance on screen, although she did produce three more of Vaughan's films, *These Dangerous Years*, *Wonderful Things!*, and *Heart Of A Man*. In the early 60s Wilcox went bankrupt when his film company and one or two of the couple's other business ventures failed. Part of their salvation came in the form of David Heneker's smash hit musical *Charlie Girl* (1965). Neagle stayed with the show - apart from the occasional holiday - for the duration of its run of over 2,000 performances and subsequent tours. On the day it was announced that she was to be made a Dame of the British Empire, the cast of *Charlie Girl* surprised her by singing 'There Is Nothing Like A Dame' at the end of the evening's performance. In 1973 the new Broadway production of *No, No, Nanette* arrived in London, and Anna Neagle played the role which had been taken by Ruby Keeler in New York. Four years later Herbert Wilcox died, but Anna Neagle continued to work. In 1978 she toured as Henry Higgins's mother in a revival of *My Fair Lady*, and in 1982 played in the pantomime *Cinderella* at the Richmond Theatre. It was as the Fairy Godmother in *Cinderella* that she made her final stage bow at the London Palladium at Christmas 1986. A few weeks after it closed she went into a Surrey nursing home to rest, and died there in June.

Further reading: both by Anna Neagle *It's Been Fun*. *There's Always Tomorrow*.

Nelson, Gene

b. Gene Berg, 24 March 1920, Seattle, Washington, USA. An actor, director, and athletic dancer in the Gene Kelly-style who was in several popular musicals of the 50s. Nelson grew up in Los Angeles and attended the renowned Fanchon and Marco dancing school there. After graduating from high school when he was 18, he took up ice skating and joined Sonja Henie's touring company and appeared in two of her films, *Second Fiddle* and *Everything Happens At Night*. After enlisting in the US Signals Corps early in World War II, he became a member of the cast of Irving Berlin's celebrated wartime musical, *This Is The Army*, which opened on Broadway in 1942 and was then filmed before touring the UK and US military bases throughout the world. Following his discharge, Nelson went to Hollywood in 1947 and made the musical, *I Wonder Who's Kissing Her Now*, with June Haver. Ironically, it was while he was starring in the hit Broadway revue *Lend An Ear* (1949), that Nelson was noticed by a representative of Warner Brothers Pictures. After playing a minor role in *The Daughter Of Rosie O'Grady*, he was signed to a long-term contract and given the third-lead to Doris Day and Gordon MacRae in *Tea For Two* (1950). From then on, he appeared in a string of musicals for the studio, including *The West Point Story*, *Lullaby Of Broadway* (his first starring role, opposite Doris Day), *Painting The Clouds With Sunshine*, *She's Working Her Way*

New Orleans

Through College, She's Back On Broadway, Three Sailors And A Girl, So This Is Paris, and *Oklahoma!* (1955). In the latter film he had the best role of his career - and two great numbers, 'Kansas City' and 'All Er Nothin'' (with Gloria Grahame as Ado Annie). In the late 50s Nelson worked in television until he suffered a horse riding action which put an end to his dancing - at least for a while. He turned to directing, and in the 60s worked on some melodramas, and two musical films starring Elvis Presley, *Kissin' Cousins* (which he also co-wrote) and *Harum Scarum*. He also directed *Your Cheatin' Heart*, a film biography of country singer Hank Williams. In 1971 he was back on Broadway with other veteran entertainers such as Yvonne De Carlo and Alexis Smith in Stephen Sondheim's *Follies*. Nelson played Buddy Plummer and had one of the show's outstanding numbers, the rapid-fire 'Buddy's Blues'. He continued to direct in the 70s and 80s, mostly for television, and worked on the top-rated series *Washington Behind Closed Doors*. In 1993 his projects included staging a US provincial production of Richard Harris's popular comedy *Stepping Out*.

Neptune's Daughter

Following their successful portrayal of a pair of twins in the bullfighting musical *Fiesta* (1947), MGM re-united Esther Williams and Ricardo Montalban two years later for this Jack Cummings Technicolor production which proved to be one of the top screen musicals of the decade, grossing $3.5 million in North America alone. Williams plays an up-market swim-suit designer who falls for millionaire Montalban, a member of a visiting South American polo team. The two stars nearly had the film stolen away from them via an hilarious sub-plot which involved Betty Garrett and comedian Red Skelton. He is a simple polo club masseur, but she is convinced that he is the wealthy Montalban, and wants to play her own kind of games with him. Joining in the fun were Keenan Wynn, Mel Blanc, Ted De Corsia, Mike Mazurki, and Xavier Cugat And His Orchestra. Jack Donahue staged the dance sequences and the obligatory underwater ballet. Frank Loesser's songs included 'My Heart Beats Faster', 'I Love Those Men', and the enduring 'Baby, It's Cold Outside', which was introduced by Williams and Montalban, and went on to win an Oscar. Dorothy Kingsley, who wrote the witty screenplay, later worked on major musicals such as *Kiss Me Kate, Seven Brides For Seven Brothers*, and *Pal Joey*. This bright and entertaining film was directed by Edward Buzzell.

New Orleans

Jazz fans watching this feature film made in 1947 are torn between embarrassment (at the corny jazz vs. classics storyline) and frustration at the waste of the talent available to the film's makers. Billie Holiday and Louis Armstrong have acting roles (as servants - what else?) and also perform on screen. Alongside them are musicians such as Barney Bigard, Meade 'Lux' Lewis, Kid Ory, Zutty Singleton, Lucky Thompson and Woody Herman And His Orchestra. Holiday longed to act in films and when she was cast for this part asserted her disappointment: 'I fought my whole life to keep from being somebody's damn maid. It was a real drag . . . to end up as a make-believe maid'.

New York, New York

Although greeted with mixed reviews at the time of its release in 1977, Martin Scorcese's vibrantly-directed film has two major virtues: Robert De Niro is extremely convincing as a big band tenor saxophonist who wants to play bop, and the simulation of the musical ethos of the era (the late 40s) which is remarkably accurate. Otherwise, much of the criticism might be thought fair, the film is too long and the leading roles (the other is Liza Minnelli as a band singer-turned-superstar) are rather unsympathetic. Georgie Auld dubbed for De Niro and the film's musical director was Ralph Burns.

Newley, Anthony

b. 24 September 1931, London, England. After attending the Italia Conti Stage School Newley worked as a child actor in several films, including *The Little Ballerina*, *Vice Versa*, and in 1948 played the Artful Dodger in David Lean's successful version of *Oliver Twist*. He made his London theatrical debut in John Cranko's revue, *Cranks* in 1955, and had character parts in well over 20 films before he was cast as rock 'n' roll star Jeep Jackson in *Idle On Parade* in 1959. Newley's four-track vocal EP, and his version of the film's hit ballad, Jerry Lordan's 'I've Waited So Long', started a three-year UK chart run which included 'Personality', 'If She Should Come To You', 'And The Heavens Cried', the novelty numbers 'Pop Goes The Weasel' and 'Strawberry Fair' and two UK number 1 hits, 'Why' and Lionel Bart's, 'Do You Mind'. Newley also made the album charts in 1960 with his set of old standards, *Love Is A Now And Then Thing*. He made later appearances in the charts with *Tony* (1961), and the comedy album *Fool Britannia* (1963), on which he was joined by his wife, Joan Collins and Peter Sellers. In 1961 Newley collaborated with Leslie Bricusse (b. 29 January 1931, London) on the off-beat stage musical, *Stop The World - I Want To Get Off*. Newley also directed, and played Littlechap, the small man who fights the system. The show, which stayed in the West End for 16 months, ran for over 500 performances on Broadway, and was filmed in 1966. It produced several hit songs, including 'What Kind Of Fool Am I?', 'Once In A Lifetime' and 'Gonna Build A Mountain'.

In 1964 Bricusse and Newley wrote the lyric to John Barry's music for Shirley Bassey to sing over the titles of the James Bond movie, *Goldfinger*. The team's next

musical show in 1965, *The Roar Of The Greasepaint - The Smell Of The Crowd*, with comedian Norman Wisdom in the lead, toured the north of England but did not make the West End. When it went to Broadway Newley took over (co-starring with Cyril Ritchard), but was not able to match the success of *Stop The World*, despite a score containing such numbers as 'Who Can I Turn To?', 'A Wonderful Day Like Today', 'The Joker', 'Look At That Face' and 'This Dream'. In 1967 Newley appeared with Rex Harrison and Richard Attenborough in the film musical *Doctor Dolittle*, with script and songs by Bricusse. Despite winning an Oscar for 'Talk To The Animals', the film was considered an expensive flop, as was Newley's own movie project in 1969, a pseudo-autobiographical sex-fantasy entitled *Can Heironymus Merkin Ever Forget Mercy Humppe And Find True Happiness?* Far more successful, in 1971, was *Willy Wonka And The Chocolate Factory*, a Roald Dahl story with music and lyrics by Bricusse and Newley. Sammy Davis Jnr. had a million-selling record with one of the songs, 'The Candy Man'. They also wrote several songs for the 1971 NBC television musical adaptation of *Peter Pan*, starring Mia Farrow and Danny Kaye. Bricusse and Newley's last authentic stage musical, *The Good Old Bad Old Days*, opened in London in 1972 and had a decent run of 309 performances. Newley sang some of the songs, including 'The People Tree', on his own *Ain't It Funny*. In his cabaret act he continually bemoans the fact that he has not had a hit with one of his own songs. A major 1989 London revival of *Stop The World - I Want To Get Off*, directed by Newley, and in which he also appeared, closed after five weeks, and, in the same year, he was inducted into the Songwriters' Hall Of Fame, along with Leslie Bricusse. In 1991, Newley appeared on UK television with his ex-wife, Joan Collins, in Noël Coward's *Private Lives*, which included the famous 'Red Peppers' segment. In the following year, having lived in California for some years, Newley announced that he was returning to Britain, and bought a house there to share with his 90-year-old mother. In the same year, he also appeared in England, at the Alexandra Theatre, Birmingham, in a successful limited run of the musical, *Scrooge*, which Bricusse adapted for the stage from the 1970 film.
Albums: *Love Is A Now And Then Thing* (1960), *Tony* (1961), *Stop The World - I Want To Get Off* (1962, London Cast), with Peter Sellers and Joan Collins *Fool Britannia* (1963), *The Roar Of The Greasepaint - The Smell Of The Crowd* (1965, Broadway Cast). Compilations: *The Romantic World Of Anthony Newley* (1970), *The Lonely World Of Anthony Newley* (1972), *The Singer And His Songs* (1978), *Anthony Newley: Mr. Personality* (1985), *Greatest Hits* (1991).

Newman, Alfred

b. 17 March 1901, New Haven, Connecticut, USA, d. 17 February 1970, Hollywood, California, USA. An important figure in the history of film music, Newman was a composer, conductor, arranger and musical director. A child prodigy on the piano, he went to New York before he was 10 years old, to study piano and harmony. At the age of 13 he was playing in several vaudeville shows a day, while also fitting in appearances as a soloist with various classical orchestras. In the 20s he conducted for the Broadway Theatre, and contributed the occasional song to shows such as *Jack And Jill* ('Voodoo Man') (1923). In 1930 he moved to Hollywood, shortly after the movies had started to talk and worked as an arranger, then as a composer for United Artists, on films such as *The Devil To Pay*, *Indiscreet*, *The Unholy Garden* and *Arrowsmith*. His 'immortal' melancholy title theme for *Street Scene* (1931), echoed through the years in many a later film depicting urban decay. His scores for other 30s films included *I Cover The Waterfront* (1933), *Nana* (1934), *The Count Of Monte Cristo* (1934), *Clive Of India* (1935), *Les Miserables* (1935), *Dodsworth* (1936), *The Prisoner Of Zenda* (1937), *The Goldwyn Follies* (1938), *The Cowbay And The Lady* (1938), *Trade Winds* (1938), *Gunga Din* (1939), *Wuthering Heights* (1939), *Young Mr. Lincoln* (1939) and *Beau Geste* (1939). He also served as musical director for Sam Goldwyn (1933-39), and won Academy Awards for *Alexander's Ragtime Band* (1938), *Tin Pan Alley* (1940), *Mother Wore Tights* (1947), *With A Song In My Heart* (1952), *Call Me Madam* (1953), *The King And I* (1956, with co-writer Ken Darby), *Camelot* (1967, again with Darby) and *Hello, Dolly!* (1969, with Lennie Hayton). He gained further Oscars, for his complete background scores, for *The Song Of Bernadette* (1943) and *Love Is A Many Splendored Thing* (1955). His film credits during the 40s included *The Grapes Of Wrath* (1940), *The Blue Bird* (1940), *Lillian Russell* (1940), *How Green Was My Valley* (1941), *Charley's Aunt* (1941), *Life Begins At Eight Thirty* (1942), *The Black Swan* (1942), *Heaven Can Wait* (1943), *Claudia* (1943), *The Keys Of The Kingdom* (1944), *Wilson* (1944), *Leave Her To Heaven* (1945), *A Tree Grows In Brooklyn* (1945), *The Razor's Edge* (1946), *Captain From Castille* (1947), *Centennial Summer* (1946), *Unfaithfully Yours* (1948), *The Snake Pit* (1948), *A Letter To Three Wives* (1949), *Yellow Sky* (1948), *Twelve O'Clock High* and *Pinky* (1949). During the 40s Newman spent several years as musical director for 20th Century-Fox with his brothers, Lionel and Emil, working for him. In 1950 while still at Fox, Newman wrote the score for 'the wittiest, most devastating, adult and literate motion picture ever made', *All About Eve*, starring Bette Davis and George Sanders. The remainder of his 50s music was of a superb standard, too, for films such as *Panic In The Streets* (1950), *David And Bathsheba* (1951), *What Price Glory?* (1952), *The Snows Of*

Kilimanjaro (1952), The Robe (1953), The Seven Year Itch (1955), Anastasia (1956), Bus Stop (1956, with Cyril Mockridge), A Certain Smile (1958), The Diary Of Anne Frank (1959) and The Best Of Everything (1959). The last film's title song (lyric by Sammy Cahn) became popular for Johnny Mathis, and several other earlier pieces of Newman's film music had lives of their own apart from the soundtrack, such as 'Moon From Manakoora' (lyric by Frank Loesser), sung by Dorothy Lamour in Hurricane and popularized by her 'Road' buddy, Bing Crosby; 'Through A Long And Sleepless Night' (words by Mack Gordon), from Come To The Stable; and the title songs from How Green Was My Valley, Anastasia and The Best Of Everything. In the 60s his rousing scores for How The West Was Won and The Greatest Story Ever Told spawned best-selling albums. His music for the melodramatic Airport (1970), which included the popular theme, was the last of Newman's works for the big screen. He died in February 1970, in Hollywood. Recordings include: Captain From Castile-Classical Film Scores. His son, David Newman (b. 1954), composed a number of television and feature film scores in the 80s and 90s, including Throw Momma From The Train, Bill And Ted's Excellent Adventure, The War Of The Roses, Madhouse, The Freshman and Marrying Man.

Newman, Lionel

b. 4 January 1916, New Haven, Connecticut, USA, d. 3 February 1989. Newman was a talented pianist as a child, and while in his teens started out as a rehearsal pianist for the Earl Carroll Vanities show, ending up as the musical director. He toured with other shows, played piano for Mae West for a while, and performed the same function at 20th Century-Fox when he joined them in 1943. Earlier in 1938, he had composed the title song (lyric by Arthur Quenzer) for the movie The Cowboy And The Lady, which had a score by his elder brother, Alfred Newman. In the late 40s Lionel's songs included 'As If I Didn't Have Enough On My Mind' (with Harry James), sung by Dick Haymes in Do You Love Me?, as well as 'The Morning Glory Road', 'Ramblin' Around' and 'Sentimental Souvenirs'. He had a smash hit in 1948 with the romantic ballad 'Again' (lyric by Dorcas Cochrane), from the film Road House. It was successful at the time for, among others, Doris Day, Gordon Jenkins and Vic Damone. Another of his numbers, Never (lyric by Eliot Daniel), sung by Dennis Day in Golden Girl (1951), was nominated for an Oscar. In his career as a musical director, Newman worked on such films as Cheaper By The Dozen (1950), The Jackpot (1950), Mother Didn't Tell Me (1950), I'll Get By (1950), Dangerous Crossing (1953), Love Me Tender (1956, Elvis Presley's first film), The Best Things In Life Are Free (1956), Mardi Gras (1958), Doctor Doolittle (1967), The Great White Hope (1970) and The Saltzburg

Connection (1972). He supervised all Marilyn Monroe's productions for Fox, such as Gentlemen Prefer Blondes (1953), River Of No Return (1954) and There's No Business Like Show Business (1954). As the Studio's general music director, and senior vice-president in 1982, he was a powerful influence on the Fox output. His original music scores included Don't Bother To Knock (1952), The Proud Ones (1956), A Kiss Before Dying (1956), Compulsion (1959), North To Alaska (1960), Move Over Darling (1963), The Pleasure Seekers (1964, with Alexander Courage) and Do Not Disturb (1965). He was nominated for 11 Academy Awards, and won the Oscar, with Lennie Hayton, in 1969 for his adaptation of Jerry Herman's score for the film version of Hello, Dolly!. During the early 80s he conducted the Boston Pops Orchestra in the USA, and performed at London's Royal Albert Hall. He retired in 1985, but was persuaded by MGM to return to the business in 1987. He died two years later in California.

Newman, Randy

b. 28 November 1943, Los Angeles, California, USA. One of the great middle America songwriters, Newman is William Faulkner, Garrison Keillor, Edward Hopper and Norman Rockwell, all set to music. Newman's songs are uncompromising and humorous but are often misconceived as being cruel and trite. His early compositions were recorded by other people, as Newman was paid $50 a month as a staff songwriter for Liberty Records housed in the famous Brill Building, New York. Early hit songs included 'Nobody Needs Your Love' and 'Just One Smile' by Gene Pitney, 'I Don't Want To Hear It Anymore' recorded by Dusty Springfield and P.J. Proby, 'I Think It's Going To Rain Today', by Judy Collins, UB40 and again by Dusty, as was the superb 'I've Been Wrong Before' which was also a hit for Cilla Black. Alan Price found favour with 'Simon Smith And His Amazing Dancing Bear' and 'Tickle Me', Peggy Lee succeeded with 'Love Story', and Three Dog Night and Eric Burdon did well with 'Mama Told Me Not To Come'. In addition, Newman's songs have been recorded by Manfred Mann, Harpers Bizarre, Frankie Laine, the Walker Brothers, the Nashville Teens, Jackie DeShannon, Nina Simone, Ringo Starr and Ray Charles. Newman's debut album came as late as 1968 and was the subject of bizarre advertising from Reprise Records. In February 1969 they announced through a hefty campaign that the record was not selling; they changed the cover and added a lyric sheet. This bold but defeatist ploy failed to increase the meagre sales. In 1970 he contributed to the Performance soundtrack and that same year his work was celebrated by having Harry Nilsson record an album of his songs. His introspective lyrics are never self-indulgent; he writes in a morose way but it all merely reflects the human condition. Songs like 'Old Kentucky Home' and 'Baltimore' have hidden warmth. 'Rednecks' and 'Short People' are genuine observations, but on these songs Newman's humour was too subtle for the general public and he received indignant protests and threats. In 1979's 'Story Of A Rock 'N' Roll Band' he castigated both Kiss and ELO. One of the first examples of his film music came in 1971, with *Cold Turkey*, and he was nominated for an Oscar in 1982 for his soundtrack to *Ragtime*, and again, in 1984, for *The Natural*. In 1983, his 'I Love Love L.A.' was used to promote the Los Angeles Olympic Games of the following year. In 1986, he wrote 'Blue Shadows', the theme for *The Three Amigos!*, which was performed in the hit movie by Steve Martin and Chevy Chase. More film soundtracks followed, such as *Awakenings*, *Parenthood* (including the song, 'I Love To See You Smile'), and *Avalon* (1990). His music for the last two films attracted more Academy Award nominations. His most recent studio work was *Land Of Dreams*, ironically co-produced by one of the victims of his acerbic wit, Jeff Lynne. Newman continues to observe, infuriate and mock as his croaky voice turns out more masterpieces commenting on American society.

Albums: *Randy Newman* (1968), *12 Songs* (1970), *Performance* (1970), *Randy Newman/Live* (1971), *Sail Away* (1972), *Good Old Boys* (1974), *Little Criminals* (1977), *Born Again* (1979), *Ragtime* (1982, film soundtrack), *Trouble In Paradise* (1983), *The Natural* (1984, film soundtrack), *Land Of Dreams* (1988), *Parenthood* (1990, film soundtrack), *Awakenings* (1991, film soundtrack). Compilation: *Lonely At The Top - The Best Of Randy Newman* (1987).

Newton-John, Olivia

b. 26 September 1948, Cambridge, England. Her showbusiness career began when she won a local contest to find 'the girl who looked most like Hayley Mills' in 1960 after the Newton-Johns had emigrated to Australia. Later she formed the Sol Four with schoolfriends. Though this vocal group disbanded, the encouragement of customers who heard her sing solo in a cafe led her to enter - and win - a television talent show. The prize was a 1966 holiday in London during which she recorded her debut single, Jackie De Shannon's 'Till You Say You'll Be Mine' after a stint in a duo with Pat Carroll. Staying on in England, Olivia became part of Toomorrow, a group created by bubblegum-pop potentate Don Kirshner, to fill the gap in the market left by the disbanded Monkees (not to be confused with Tomorrow). As well as a science-fiction movie and its soundtrack, Toomorrow was also responsible for 'I Could Never Live Without Your Love,' a 1970 single, produced by the Shadows' Bruce Welch - with whom Olivia was romantically linked. Although Toomorrow petered out, Newton-John's link with Cliff Richard and the Shadows was a source

of enduring professional benefit. A role in a Richard movie, tours as special guest in *The Cliff Richard Show*, and a residency - as an comedienne as well as a singer - on BBC television's *It's Cliff!* guaranteed steady sales of her first album, and the start of a patchy British chart career with a Top 10 arrangement of Bob Dylan's 'If Not For You' in 1971. More typical of her output were singles such as 'Take Me Home Country Roads', penned by John Denver, 'Banks Of The Ohio' and, from the late John Rostill of the Shadows, 1973's 'Let Me Be There'. This last release sparked off by an appearance on the USA's *The Dean Martin Show* and crossed from the US country charts to the Hot 100, winning her a controversial Grammy for Best Female Country Vocal. After an uneasy performance in 1974's Eurovision Song Contest, Newton-John became omnipresent in North America, first as its most popular country artist, though her standing in pop improved considerably after a chart-topper with 'I Honestly Love You,' produced by John Farrar, another latter-day Shadow (and husband of the earlier mentioned Pat Carroll), who had assumed the task after the estrangement of Olivia and Bruce.

Newton-John also became renowned for her duets with other artists, notably in the movie of the musical Grease in which she and co-star John Travolta featured 'You're The One That I Want'. This irresistibly effervescent song became one of the most successful UK hit singles in pop history, topping the charts for a stupendous nine weeks. The follow-up, 'Summer Nights' was also a UK number 1 in 1978. Her 'Xanadu', the film's title opus with the Electric Light Orchestra, was another global number 1. However, not such a money-spinner was a further cinema venture with Travolta (1983's 'Two Of A Kind'). Neither was 'After Dark,' a single with the late Andy Gibb in 1980 nor *Now Voyager* a 1984 album with his brother Barry. With singles like 'Physical' (1981) and the 1986 album *Soul Kiss* on Mercury Records she adopted a more raunchy image in place of her original perky wholesomeness.

During the late 80s/early 90s much of her time was spent, along with Pat (Carroll) Farrar, running her Australian-styled clothing business, Blue Koala. Following *The Rumour*, Olivia signed to Geffen for the release of a collection of children's songs and rhymes, *Warm And Tender*. The award of an OBE preceded her marriage to actor and dancer Matt Lattanzi; she remains a showbusiness evergreen although this was clouded in July 1992, when it was announced that she is undergoing treatment for cancer.

Albums: *If Not For You* (1971), *Let Me Be There* (1973), *Olivia Newton-John* (1973), *If You Love Me Let Me Know* (1974), *Music Makes My Day* (1974), *Long Live Love* (1974), *Have You Never Been Mellow?* (1975), *Clearly Love* (1975), *Come On Over* (1976), *Don't Stop Believin'* (1976), *Making A Good Thing Better* (1977), with various artists *Grease* (1978, film soundtrack), *Totally Hot* (1978), with the Electric Light Orchestra *Xanadu* (1980, film soundtrack), *Physical* (1981), with various artists *Two Of A Kind* (1983, film soundtrack), *Soul Kiss* (1986), *The Rumour* (1988), *Warm And Tender* (1990). Compilations: *Olivia Newton-John's Greatest Hits* (1977, US MCA issue), *Greatest Hits* i (1978, UK EMI issue), *Olivia's Greatest Hits, Volume 2* (1982, US MCA issue), *Greatest Hits* ii (1982, UK EMI issue).

Nicholas Brothers

Fayard Nicholas (b. c.1918) and Harold Nicholas (b. c.1924), constituted what was, without a doubt, the most talented and spectacular power tap-dancing duo in the history of show business. They grew up in Philadelphia where their parents played in the orchestra at the Standard Theatre, a vaudeville house for blacks. The brothers were soon in vaudeville themselves, billed initially as the Nicholas Kids. By 1932 they had graduated to the renowned Cotton Club in Harlem, where, for the next two years they delighted the all-white audiences and rubbed shoulders with great black entertainers such as Ethel Waters, Duke Ellington, and Cab Calloway. In 1936 the Nicholas Brothers made their Broadway debut with Bob Hope and Fanny Brice in *Ziegfeld Follies*, and also appeared in London in Lew Leslie's revue *Blackbirds Of 1936*. A year later they were back on Broadway in the Richard Rodgers and Lorenz Hart hit musical, *Babes In Arms*. Their film career had begun in 1932 with two short films, *Black Network* and *Pie Pie Blackbird* (featuring Eubie Blake And His Band), and it continued via *Calling All Stars* (1936), and the Don Ameche-Betty Grable film *Down Argentine Way* (1940), in which the brothers did a breathtaking dance to the lively number 'Down Argentina Way'. The sequence was choreographed by Nick Castle who worked with the duo on most of their subsequent pictures, and gained them a five year contract with 20th Century-Fox. During the rest of the 40s the Nicholas Brothers contributed some electrifying and superbly acrobatic dances to films such as *Tin Pan Alley*, *The Great American Broadcast*, *Sun Valley Serenade*, *Orchestra Wives*, *Stormy Weather*, and *The Pirate* (1948). In 1946 they both starred in the Broadway musical *St. Louis Woman* in which Harold introduced Harold Arlen and Johnny Mercer's appealing 'Ridin' On The Moon' and (with Ruby Hill) the all-time standard, 'Come Rain Or Come Shine'. Of course, as blacks, in films they were only allowed to be a speciality act and were never considered for leading roles. This is apparently one of the main reasons why, in the 50s, they worked in Europe for several years where audiences and managements were more racially tolerant. When Fayard decided to return to the USA, Harold stayed in France and carved out a solo career for himself there.

After seven years they were reunited in America and played in nightclubs and on television until Fayard contracted arthritis and underwent two hip-replacement operations. Harold continued as a solo performer and was top-cast in the musical, *Back In The Big Time* (1986). Fayard was still active in non-performing areas of the business and won a Tony Award when he co-choreographed the 1989 Broadway musical, *Black And Blue*, with Cholly Atkins, Henry LeTang and Frank Manning. In 1991 the Nicholas Brothers received Kennedy Center Honours for their outstanding work over a period of more than 60 years. A year later, a documentary film *We Sing & We Dance*, celebrated their wonderful careers and included tributes from Mikhail Baryshnikov, Gregory Hines, M.C. Hammer, and Clarke Peters. In 1994 members of the cast of *Hot Shoe Shuffle*, London's 'New Tap Musical', also paid tribute to their 'inspiration' - the Nicholas Brothers.

Night And Day

Benny Green, the British author and critic, has often commented that if only the screenwriters of these lavish Hollywood film biographies had told the subject's real life story instead of writing the usual insipid puff, some fascinating pictures would have resulted. This theory could have been especially true in the case of *Night And Day* which was released by Warner Brothers in 1946. It was supposed to be a celebration of the smart and sophisticated songwriter Cole Porter, but hardly any of the important incidents in his life - apart from his tragic accident - were touched upon. The inclusion of a good many of his magnificent songs more than made up for the omissions, though, and these included 'I've Got You Under My Skin', 'Night And Day', 'Miss Otis Regrets', 'In The Still Of The Night', 'Begin The Beguine', 'What Is This Thing Called Love?', 'Just One Of Those Things', 'I Get A Kick Out Of You', 'Easy To Love', 'You Do Something To Me', 'Let's Do It', 'Old Fashioned Garden', 'Love For Sale', 'You've Got That Thing', and 'Anything Goes'. Mary Martin reprised 'My Heart Belongs To Daddy' which she originally introduced to rapturous acclaim in *Leave It To Me!* back in 1938, and several of the other numbers were sung by Ginny Simms and Jane Wyman. Cary Grant played Porter, and it was interesting, if unsatisfying, to hear his version of 'You're The Top', one of the composer's all-time great 'list' songs. Alexis Smith was Mrs. Porter, and also cast were Monty Woolley (as himself), Eve Arden, Alan Hale, Victor Francen, Dorothy Malone, Selena Royle, Donald Woods, Henry Stephenson, Sig Rumann, and Carlos Ramirez. Charles Hoffman, Leo Townsend and William Bowers were responsible for the screenplay, and the dances were staged by Leroy Prinz. Arthur Schwartz, a legendary songwriter himself, was the producer and Michael Curtiz provided the lack-lustre direction. It was photographed in Technicolor by J. Peverell Marley and William Skall. In spite of their obvious drawbacks, these kind of films were always crowd-pullers, and *Night And Day* proved to be no exception, grossing $4 million in North America alone.

North, Alex

b. 4 December 1910, Chester, Pennsylvania, USA, d. 8 September 1991, Pacific Palisades, California, USA. An important composer for films, theatre, television, ballet and classical music, his career ranged from the late 30s through to the 80s. After studying at Juilliard with the distinguished composer Aaron Copland, as well as at the Moscow Conservatory (1933-35), North composed for the Federal Theatre Project in the late 30s. During those years, through to 1950, he wrote the scores for government documentary and information films, and served in the US Army in World War II. In 1948 he composed the incidental score for Arthur Miller's landmark play, *Death Of A Salesman* on Broadway, and repeated the role for the film version in 1951. For that, and for his innovative jazz-tinged score to *A Streetcar Named Desire* (1951), he gained the first two of his 15 Academy Award nominations. Other early 50s film music included *The 13th Letter*, *Viva Zapata!* (considered an early milestone in his career), *Les Miserables*, the ballet music for Fred Astaire and Leslie Caron in *Daddy Long Legs*, and *Unchained*. The last film contained 'Unchained Melody' (lyric by Hy Zaret), a ballad of yearning which became popular at the time for Les Baxter (US number 1), Al Hibbler, and Jimmy Young (UK number 1), amongst others, and through the years was constantly remembered and revived. The Righteous Brothers' 1965 smash-hit version accompanied an erotic scene in the movie *Ghost*, some 25 years later. North's other 50s scores included *The Man With The Gun* (1955), *I'll Cry Tomorrow* (1955), *The Rose Tattoo* (1955), *The Bad Seed* (1956), *The Rainmaker* (1956), *Four Girls In Town* (1956), *The King And Four Queens* (1956), *The Bachelor Party* (1957), *The Long Hot Summer* (1958), *Stage Struck* (1958), *Hot Spell* (1958), *The Sound And The Fury* (1959) and *The Wonderful Country* (1959).

Early in the 60s North began an association with director John Huston which lasted until Huston's death in 1987. Together they worked on such films as *The Misfits* (1961), *Wise Blood* (1979), *Under The Volcano* (1984), *Prizzi's Honor* (1985) and *The Dead* (1987), Huston's Swan-song. North's 60s film work began with the epic *Spartacus* ('magnificent score, staggering battle scenes'), followed, in complete contrast, by *The Children's Hour*. His other scores of the decade included another epic, *Cleopatra*, John Ford's *Cheyenne Autumn*, *The Agony And The Ecstasy*, *Who's Afraid Of Virginia Woolf?*, *The Shoes Of The Fisherman*, *Hard Contract*, and *A Dream Of Kings*. In the 70s, as his kind of spectacular, dramatic scores went out of style, North worked less for the big screen. However, in the later years he composed the music for movies such as *Pocket Money*, *Once Upon A Scoundrel*, *Bite The Bullet*, and *Somebody Killed Her Husband*. In the 80s, besides his collaborations with Huston, North was still being critically acclaimed for scores such as *Carny*, *Dragonslayer*, *Under The Volcano*, *Good Morning Vietnam*, and his final film, *The Penitent* (1988). In 1986 he became the first composer to receive an honorary Academy Award 'in recognition of his brilliant artistry in the creation of memorable music for a host of distinguished motion pictures'. He died, five years later, in 1991. As well as films, his occasional television work included the feature documentary, *Africa* (1967), music for the mini-series *The Word* which was nominated for an Emmy, and *Rich Man, Poor Man*, which won two; the telefeature, *Death Of A Salesman* (again), and music for other programmes, such as *Your Show Of Shows*, *77 Sunset Strip*, *Playhouse 90* and *The F.D.R. Story*. Many of his scores were made available on albums, and several individual items such as the title themes from *I'll Cry Tomorrow* and *The Long Hot Summer*, and 'Unchained Melody', of course, endure.

O'Connor, Donald

b. Donald David Dixon Ronald O'Connor, 30 August 1925, Chicago, Illinois, USA. One of the most likeable and nimble of all Hollywood's song-and-dance-men, who seems to have retained his youthful looks and casual charm throughout a career stretching for well over 50 years. O'Connor was the seventh child of parents who were circus and vaudeville performers. After his father died, Donald (aged three) joined his mother and two of his brothers in the family act until he made his film debut in the minor musical *Melody For Two* in 1937. A year later, at the age of only 13, he made a big impact in *Sing You Sinners* in which he completely captivated cinema audiences in his role as the younger brother of Fred MacMurray and Bing Crosby. The trio's version of 'Small Fry' was the highlight of the picture. After a few straight parts and one other musical, *On Your Toes*, O'Connor went back to vaudeville until 1941 when he signed a contract with Universal which resulted in supporting roles in musicals such as *What's Cookin?*, *Private Buckaroo*, *Get Hep To Love*, and *Give Out Sisters*. These led to better parts in *It Comes Up Love*, *When Johnny Comes Marching Home*, *Strictly In The Groove*, and especially *Mister Big*. He was top-billed for the first time in *Top Man* (1943) with soprano Susanna Foster. Funny-girl Peggy Ryan was also in the latter, and several other of O'Connor's films around this time, including *Chip Off The Old Block*, *This Is The Life*, *Follow The Boys*, *Bowery To Broadway*, *The Merry Monahans* (all 1944) and *Patrick The Great* (1945). After service in the US Army, O'Connor 'stole' *Something In The Wind* from Universal's premiere female star, Deanna Durbin, and further re-established himself in *Are You With It?*, *Feudin' Fussin' And A-Fightin'*, and *Yes Sir, That's My Baby* for which he was teamed with Gloria De Haven. He was paired with a rather more unusual partner next - a 'talking mule' named Francis. The popular series, which began with *Francis* (1950), continued until O'Connor called a halt, saying: 'When you've made six pictures and the mule still gets more mail than you do . . .' In 1950 O'Connor starred at the London Palladium, and, on his return to the US, joined Gene Kelly and Debbie Reynolds for what is probably his best-remembered film - *Singin' In The Rain*. All the routines are classics, but O'Connor's marvellous solo moment, 'Make 'Em Laugh', a series of pratfalls and back-flips performed in the company of a headless dummy, was improvised by O'Connor himself and remains one of the all-time great sequences from any movie musical. Ironically, he revealed that the first take was ruined by 'foggy film' in the camera and he had to do the whole thing over again three days later. The early 50s were good times for O'Connor. He featured on television's *The Colgate Comedy Hour* for three years, and continued to sing, dance and clown his way through *Call Me Madam*, *I Love Melvin*, *Walking My Baby Back Home*, *There's No Business Like Show Business*, and *Anything Goes* (1956). After that, with the glossy big screen musical in a state of terminal decline, he returned to television and played the big cabaret rooms and clubs throughout the USA. He continued to appear in the occasional straight roles in films such as *The Buster Keaton Story* (1957) and *Ragtime* (with James Cagney in 1981), and *Toys* (1992). In the 80s he toured in revivals of immortal stage musicals such as *Show Boat*, and, late in the decade, was attracting enthusiastic reviews in Las Vegas for his shows with fellow movie legends Debbie Reynolds and Mickey Rooney. In June 1994 he brought his classy cabaret act to London for the opening of the capital's latest cabaret space, the Connaught Room.

Oklahoma!

The show that opened on Broadway in 1943, and is credited with being a significant turning point in the history of the musical theatre, was transferred to the screen in the not-so-glorious Todd-AO wide-screen process in 1955. The skilful integration of Richard Rodgers and Oscar Hammerstein II's wonderful songs into the sentimental but sincere story for which the stage production is so rightly admired, was equally impressive in this celluloid version. The action takes place just after the turn of the century on and around a ranch in the Oklahoma Territory, where Laurey (Shirley Jones) lives with her Aunt Eller (Charlotte Greenwood). The handsome and decent Curly (Gordon MacRae) and the evil-looking and devious Judd (Rod Steiger) both want to take Laurey to the 'box social'. Her decision to spite Curly (who she really wants to go with) by accepting Jud's invitation, sets off a train of events which culminate in Jud's death, for which Curly is immediately charged, but just as swiftly exonerated. Jones and MacRae were perfect together, and the supporting cast was exceptionally fine, with Gene Nelson as Will Parker and Gloria Grahame as his girlfriend Ado Annie, who 'just cain't say no'. Eddie Albert plays a travelling pedlar-man, Ali Akim, whose indiscriminate use of a kissing technique known in his native country as 'A Persian Goodbye' results in a shotgun wedding. Other parts were taken by James Whitmore, Marc Platt, Barbara Lawrence, Roy Barcroft. Dancers James Mitchell and Bambi Lynn were stunning in the ballet sequence to the music of 'Out Of My Dreams'. Most of the rest of Rodgers and Hammerstein's rich and varied score was retained, and included all the favourites such as 'Oh, What A Beautiful Mornin'', 'The Surrey With The Fringe On Top', 'Kansas City', 'I Cain't Say No', 'Many A New Day', 'People Will Say We're In Love', 'Poor Jud Is Dead', 'The Farmer And The Cowman', 'All Er Nothin'', and the rousing 'Oklahoma'. Choreographer Agnes de Mille and musical arranger Robert Russell Bennett adapted their original stage work for the film, and Russell Bennett, together with Jay Blackton and Adolph Deutsch, won an Oscar for 'scoring of a musical picture'. It was photographed in Eastman color and produced for Magna by Arthur Hornblow Jnr. The director was Fred Zinnemann. Sonya Levian and William Ludwig's screenplay was adapted from the original libretto by Oscar Hammerstein II which was based on Lynn Riggs's play *Green Grow The Lilacs*.

Oliver!

'Please sir, can I have some more' was not just the tragic cry of the young orphan in Charles Dickens' famous story, but the plea of theatregoers both in Britain and on Broadway when they witnessed the tremendous success of Lionel Bart's stage musical *Oliver!* in the early 60s. So it is not surprising that the film adaptation of the stage hit, released in December 1968, with just two songs missing from the original score, did so well and became such a favourite with adults and children alike. Adapted for the screen by Vernon Harris, this musical version of the Dickens story follows young Oliver (Mark Lester) as he runs away from his desperately unhappy existence in a poor house and his job as an undertaker's assistant, only to find himself lost in the big city. Here he meets the worldly-wise Artful Dodger (Jack Wild), and falls in with a group of young pickpockets. At the head of this gang is Fagin (Ron Moody in the part he orginally played on stage), a scoundrel who always keeps one eye on his 'bank' balance and the other on the boys in his charge. It is in Fagin's hideout that Oliver has his first stealing lessons, but the innocent boy gets caught on one of his first attempts. His subsequent arrest leads to the discovery of a loving and wealthy relative, and, eventually a happy ending to the story. Oliver Reed gives a truly villainous performance as Bill Sikes, and Shani Wallis is more than adequate in the role of Nancy, the girl who loves him no matter how evil he becomes. Directed by Carol Reed, and produced by John Woolf, Oliver! is an enchanting film full of great musical sequences and emotional drama. Mark Lester is perfectly innocent in the leading role. His rendition of the plaintive 'Where is Love?' tugs at the audience's heartstrings, and the scene in Fagin's den when he joins Nancy for 'I'd Do Anything' is gentle and touching. Other highspots included Nancy's powerful reaffirmation of her love for Bill in 'As Long As He Needs Me', and Fagin's 'You've Got To Pick A Pocket Or Two' which is a quirky and irresistible celebration of villainy, while his indecision and frustration are perfectly captured in the witty lyrics of 'Reviewing The Situation'. However, it is not just the individual performances which make the film so successful. The ensemble musical numbers are often breathtaking, ranging from the fantasising of 'Food Glorious Food' to the brotherhood of 'Consider Yourself.' The rest of the fine score included 'Boy For Sale', 'Who Will Buy?', and the joyous 'Oom-Pah-Pah'. Among the excellent supporting cast were Harry Secombe, Leonard Rossiter, Hugh Griffith, Fred Emney and James Hayter. The film was beautifully photographed in Technicolor and Panavision by Oswald Morris. Oliver! won five Oscars, including best picture, director, choreographer (Onna White), and remains one of the all-time great British movies.

On A Clear Day You Can See Forever

Alan Jay Lerner's long-time partnership with Frederick Loewe had lapsed by the early 60s partly owing to the composer's ill health, when he decided to write a Broadway show based on his absorbing interest in the subject of extrasensory perception (ESP). Lerner's first choice for a project which was originally entitled I Picked A Daisy, was Richard Rodgers, who had been searching for a new partner since the death of Oscar Hammerstein in 1960.

According to reports, the collaboration resulted in the irrisistable force meeting the immovable object, so Lerner turned instead to Burton Lane. The new show, now called On A Clear Day You Can See Forever, made its debut at the Mark Hellinger theatre on 17 October 1965. In Lerner's book, Dr. Mark Bruckner (John Cullum) discovers that one of his patients, Daisy Gamble (Barbara Harris), can not only foresee the future, and persuade her plants to grow by just talking to them, but is prepared to go into details about her life as Melinda, an early feminist, who lived in 18th century London. They fall in love, but when Daisy begins to believe (mistakenly) that Mark is more interested in Melinda than in her, she walks out. Although miles away, she hears and responds when he gives out with 'Come Back To Me' ('Leave behind all you own/Tell your flowers you'll telephone/Let your dog walk alone/Come back to me!'). McCallum also had two lovely ballads, the title song, 'On A Clear Day (You Can See Forever)', and 'Melinda'. The remainder of a fine score included the delightful 'Hurray! It's Lovely Up Here', 'She Wasn't You', 'Wait Till We're Sixty-Five', 'When I'm Being Born Again', 'What Did I Have That I Don't Have?', 'Don't Tamper With My Sister', and 'Tosy And Cosh'. The show ran for an unsatisfactory 280 performances, and, as usual, while Lerner's lyrics were admired, his book came in for a deal of criticism. Barbara Harris was particularly applauded for her work, but, in the 1970 film, her role was taken by Barbra Streisand, who starred with Yves Montand.

On The Avenue

After enjoying tremendous success in partnership with several American leading ladies in movie musicals such as 42nd Street, Dames and the Gold Diggers series, Dick Powell teamed with English actress Madeleine Carroll for this picture which was released by 20th Century-Fox in 1937. Carroll plays wealthy socialite Mimi Caraway who objects violently to being lampooned in a satirical revue by Gary Blake (Dick Powell). Naturally, they eventually resolve their differences and fall in love. This leaves Blake's previous girlfriend, Mona Merrick (Alice Faye), out in the cold, but she consoles herself by singing the lion's share of Irving Berlin's wonderful score, including the enduring 'This Year's Kisses', 'He Ain't Got Rhythm' and 'Slumming On Park Avenue' (the last two with the Ritz Brothers); and 'I've Got My Love To Keep Me Warm' and 'The Girl On The Police Gazette' (both with Dick Powell). Powell himself had the superior 'You're Laughing At Me', which later became popular for Fats Waller. Also among the cast of On The Avenue were Alan Mowbray, George Barbier, Cora Witherspoon, Walter Catlett, Billy Gilbert, and Stepin Fetchit. Gene Markey and William Conselman wrote the amusing screenplay, the stylish dances were staged by Seymour Felix, and the film was directed by

On The Avenue

Roy Del Routh. The basic plot of this film was used again in *Let's Make Love* (1960) starring Marilyn Monroe, Yves Montand and Frankie Vaughan.

On The Riviera

Post-war cinema audiences got a double ration of Danny Kaye in this Sol C. Siegel Technicolor production when it was released by 20th Century-Fox in 1951. Henry and Phoebe Ephron's screenplay concerned a well-known nightclub entertainer who is the spitting image of a philandering businessman. If that plot sounds familiar, it is because it cropped up on the screen in *Folies Bergère De Paris* (1934) and *That Night In Rio* (1941), and, with a slight twist and another change in location, formed the basis of *On The Double* (1961). Kaye played both roles, of course, and had a great time with all the complications that naturally spring from this kind of situation. Gene Tierney was the businessman's wife who could not tell the difference between her real husband and his stand-in, and also taking part in the hilarious shenanigans were Corinne Calvert, Marcel Dalio, Clinton Sundberg, Henri Letondal, Sig Ruman, and Joyce McKenzie. Future dancing star Gwen Verdon was in the chorus. Sylvia Fine, Kaye's wife, tailored four songs especially for him: 'Popo The Puppet', 'Rhythm Of Romance', 'Happy Ending', and 'On

The Riviera', and he also sang one of his much-loved favourites, the 1913 number 'Ballin' The Jack' (James Henry Burris-Chris Smith). Jack Cole staged the imaginative dance sequences, and the film was directed by Walter Lang.

On The Road With Duke Ellington

A remarkable film record, made originally in 1967 and updated after Duke Ellington's death in 1974. In addition to Ellington talking about his life there are sequences showing him receiving honorary doctorates, rehearsing and recording his orchestra, playing the piano and, most intriguing of all, composing and arranging. If anything, the casual manner in which he does this simply adds to the mystique. Sprawled out on a couch, feet up, he and Billy Strayhorn put together a piece of music with such deceptive ease as to make even a Hollywood songwriter bio-pic seem forced. Apart from the Maestro, musicians such as Harry Carney, Jimmy Hamilton, Johnny Hodges, Paul Gonsalves and Louis Armstrong also make appearances.

On The Town

Remembered particularly for its innovative staging of some of the musical sequences on the streets of New York, *On The Town* was released by MGM in 1949.

One Hour With You

Betty Comden and Adolph Green's screenplay (they also wrote all the lyrics) was based on their book for the 1944 stage musical, which itself was inspired by choreographer-director Jerome Robbins' ballet *Fancy Free*. From the moment that the three sailors, played by Gene Kelly, Frank Sinatra, and Jules Munshin come dashing from their ship to the strains of the rousing 'New York, New York' (music-Leonard Bernstein), eager to enjoy the delights of New York on their 24-hours leave, the film sings and dances along in an exhilarating fashion. Naturally, they each find their ideal partner: Kelly first sees the girl of his dreams, Vera-Ellen, on a poster in the subway, and their delightful *pas-de-deux* 'Main Street' (music-Roger Edens) is one of the film's many highspots; Munshin is pursued through the Museum of Natural History by the anthropological Ann Miller who considers him to be a perfect example of a 'Prehistoric Man' (music-Edens); while the ingenuous Sinatra is invited to 'Come Up to My Place' (music-Bernstein) by the amusingly man-hungry taxi driver Betty Garrett. Stage musical buffs were offended by the way Bernstein's original Broadway score was 'decimated', with only five numbers surviving - the two already mentioned, plus 'I Feel Like I'm Not Out Of Bed Yet' and two ballets, 'Miss Turnstiles' and 'A Day In New York'. The substitutes, with music by Roger Edens, included 'You're Awful' and 'On The Town'. Edens was also co-musical director with Lennie Hayton, and both men won Oscars for music scoring. Alice Pearce recreated her original stage role as Betty Garrett's flatmate, a girl with a permanent cold, and also in the cast were Florence Bates, Carol Haney, Hans Conried, and George Meader. Gene Kelly and Stanley Donen's first film together was photographed in Technicolor and produced by Arthur Freed.

One Hour With You

This highly acclaimed musical, a delightful and sophisticated picture which was released by Paramount in 1932, reunited Maurice Chevalier and Jeanette MacDonald following their joint triumph two years earlier in *The Love Parade*. As with that film *One Hour With You* bore the unmistakeable touch of director Ernst Lubitsch, and was, in fact, a remake of his 1924 silent, *The Marriage Circle*. Samson Raphaelson's screenplay told of a happily married couple, played by Chevalier and MacDonald, whose domestic bliss is shattered when he becomes far too friendly with her flirtatious best friend (Genevieve Tobin). Also in the cast were Roland Young, Charlie Ruggles, Josephine Dunn, Donald Novis, and George Barbier. The songs, with music by Oscar Straus and Richard Whiting and lyrics by Leo Robin, included

'Three Times A Day', 'One Hour With You', 'We Will Always Be Sweethearts', 'What Would You Do?', 'It Was Only a Dream Kiss', 'Oh, That Mitzi', and 'What A Little Thing Like A Wedding Ring Can Do'. For various complicated reasons, Lubitsch shared directorial credit with George Cukor for a film that is considered a classic of its kind.

One Hundred Men And A Girl

'Anything can be achieved if you just try hard enough', was the message that came through loud and clear in this charming and delightful Deanna Durbin film which was produced by Charles Rogers and Joe Pasternak for Universal in 1937. In the wonderfully optimistic screenplay, by Bruce Manning, Charles Kenyon, and Hans Kraly, the 16-year-old female star uses all her unbounded energy and enthusiasm to persuade the celebrated maestro Leopold Stokowski to conduct an orchestra consisting of her father (Adolphe Menjou) and a number of other out-of-work musicians. Given that scenario, the songs such as 'It's Raining Sunbeams' (Sam Coslow-Frederick Hollander) and 'A Heart That's Free' (Alfred Robyn-Thomas T. Reilly), were joined by several classical pieces including '2nd Hungarian Rhapsody' (Liszt), '*Lohengrin* Prelude' (Wagner), 'Alleluja' (Mozart), and

'La Traviata' (Verdi). Charles Previn, head of Universal Studio's music department, won an Oscar for the film's score. In the strong supporting cast were Alice Brady, Eugene Pallette, Mischa Auer, and Billy Gilbert. Henry Koster directed the film which immediately proved to have enormous box-office appeal and touched the hearts of all who saw it.

One In A Million

Forty years before John Curry, and then others such as Robin Cousins and Torvill And Dean, caused television ratings to soar with their graceful and imaginative ice dancing, Norwegian champion Sonja Henie was delighting cinema audiences with her own individual brand of ice skating. She made he screen debut in this 1936 film, playing the daughter of a Swiss innkeeper who trains her for the Winter Olympic Games. Naturally, after some hitches along the way, she wins a medal - and the heart of press reporter Don Ameche. He headed an impressive cast along with Adolph Menjou as a band-leading impresario, the always hilarious Ritz Brothers, Jean Hersholt, Arline Judge, Dixie Dunbar, Ned Sparks, Montagu Love, Leah Ray, and Borrah Minevitch and his Harmonica Rascals. Sidney Mitchell and Lew Pollack's songs, which cropped up occasionally

Orchestra Wives

throughout an amusing and entertaining picture, included 'We're Back In Circulation Again', 'The Moonlight Waltz', 'Who's Afraid Of Love?', 'Lovely Lady In White', and 'One In A Million'. Producer Darryl F. Zanuck, who produced the film for 20th Century-Fox, is credited with the inspiration for bringing Sonja Henie to Hollywood - an idea that paid off handsomely at the box-office. Leonard Praskins and Mark Kelly wrote the screenplay, the choreographers were Jack Haskell and Nick Castle, and *One In A Million* was directed by Sidney Lanfield.

One Night Of Love

Grace Moore brought her wonderful world of opera to the screen for the first time proper in this classic musical which was released by Columbia in 1934. In the uncomplicated story, by S.K. Lauren, James Gow, and Edmund North, she plays a young American soprano whose eventual worldwide fame is mainly due to the efforts of her music mentor and guru played impressively by Tullio Carminati. Also in the cast were Lyle Talbot, Mona Barrie, Jessie Ralph, and Jane Darwell. The score was a mixed bag of extracts from popular operettas and arias, along with some classical songs such as 'Ciribiribin' (Rudolph Thaler-Alberto Pestalozza) and 'None But The Lonely Heart' (Peter I. Tchaikowsky). The title number, by the film's director Victor Schertzinger (music) and Gus Kahn (lyric), won an Academy Award for Thematic Music although the award went to Louis Silvers, head of Columbia's music department - that was the custom in those days. *One Night Of Love* won another Oscar for sound recording, and was nominated best film, actress (Moore), and director.

Orchestra Wives

The marvellous music more than made up for a dull plot in this, the second of only two films in which the enormously popular Glenn Miller Orchestra appeared. The story concerns the glitz and the grind of a band on the road in the heyday of the Swing Era. Glamour-boy trumpeter George Montgomery cannot bear to leave his young sweetheart Ann Rutherford behind so he marries her and brings her aboard the bus - much to the chagrin of the hard-bitten wives of the other orchestra members who give the poor girl a hard time. After providing the Miller band with several hits in their previous movie, *Sun Valley Serenade*, Harry Warren and Mack Gordon came up trumps this time with 'At Last', 'Serenade In Blue', 'People Like You And Me', and 'I Got A Gal In Kalamazoo'. The latter number was a speciality for Tex Beneke And The Modernaires, and they were joined by most of Miller's regular sidemen, including Hal McIntyre, Ray Anthony, Billy May, and singers Marion Hutton and Ray Eberle. Also in the cast were Cesar Romero, Lynn Bari, Carole Landis, Mary Beth Hughes, Jackie Gleason, Virginia Gilmore, Tamara

Geva, Harry Morgan, and the marvellously athletic dancing team, the Nicholas Brothers. Karl Tunberg and Darrell Ware wrote the screenplay, and Nick Castle choreographed the dances. The director was Archie Mayo. A film to watch again and again - just for those historic musical sequences.

Paint Your Wagon

Opinions vary widely as to the quality of this film, but, in general, the 'noes' seem to have it. *Paint Your Wagon* started its musical journey on Broadway in 1951, with music by Frederick Loewe and a book and lyrics by Alan Jay Lerner. Lerner's screenplay for this 1969 version was based on a fresh adaptation of the story by Paddy Chayevsky. The action still takes place during the California gold rush of the late 1800s, but the sometimes droll story now concerns the relationship between the lovely young Elizabeth (Jean Seberg) and the two men in her life, Ben Rumson (Lee Marvin) and 'Pardner' (Clint Eastwood). She wants to live in No Name City with both of them, which does not please Ben because he used part of his stake to buy her from a Mormon, and then made her his wife. Also up to their knees in the mud of the goldfields were Harve Presnell ('Rotten Luck Willie), Ray Walston ('Mad Jack' Duncan), Tom Ligon, Alan Dexter, William O'Connell, Ben Baker, Alan Baxter, Paul Truman, and a whole heap of others. Several of Lerner and Loewe's songs survived from the stage score, including the rousing 'Main Title (I'm On My Way)', and the contrasting 'They Call The Wind Maria' and 'There's A Coach Comin' In', both of which were sung admirably by Presnell. Eastwood surprised and delighted with his handling of 'I Still See Elisa' and 'I Talk To The Trees', and Marvin brought his very own individual treatment to 'Hand Me Down That Can O' Beans', and 'Wand'rin Star'. The latter number gave him a number 1 hit in the UK, but did not make the Top 40 in the USA. The rest of the numbers, with Lerner's lyrics and music by André Previn, consisted of 'The First Thing You Know', 'A Million Miles Away Behind The Door', 'The Gospel Of No Name City', 'Best Things', and 'Gold Fever'. Nelson Riddle and his impressive musical arrangements were nominated for an Oscar. Jack Baker staged the energetic dance sequences and the director was Joshua Logan. Alan Jay Lerner produced for Paramount, and the film was photographed in Technicolor and Panavision by William Fraker. In spite of the critics' reservations, *Paint Your Wagon* grossed well over $14 million in the USA, and was just outside the Top 10 musicals of the decade.

Pajama Game, The

Hardly any screen version of a hit Broadway musical is considered to better than the original, but this one was. Perhaps it was because several members of the original stage team made the trip to Hollywood to recreate their originals roles. Two of them, George Abbot and Richard Bissell, adapted their libretto (which had been based on Bissell's novel *Seven And A Half Cents*) for the screenplay. Based in and around the Sleep Tite Pajama Factory in Iowa, it concerns the efforts of union leader Babe Williams (Doris Day) and her Grievance Committee, to extract a rise in pay for their members of seven and a half cents from the new (and extremely dishy) new superintendent, Sid Sorokin (John Raitt). Naturally, Babe falls for Sid, in spite of her protests ('I'm Not At All In Love'), and the negotiations are satisfactorily concluded. This was one of only two scores that Richard Adler and Jerry Ross wrote together (the other was *Damn Yankees*) before the latter's tragic death, and it was a complete joy. Not only did the principals, Day and Raitt, share 'Hey, There', 'Small Talk', and 'There Once Was A Man', but the gifted singer and dancer, Carol Haney, dazzled with 'Steam Heat' and 'Hernando's Hideaway', while Eddie Foy Jnr. was delightfully unconvincing as he assured Reta Shaw: 'I'll Never Be Jealous Again'. In addition there were pleasing ensemble pieces such as 'Once-A-Year-Day' and 'Racing With The Clock'. Also in the cast were Buzz Miller, Peter Gennaro, Barbara Nicholls, Thelma Pelish, and Kenneth LeRoy. Bob Fosse, a veteran of the stage show, was responsible for the lively and imaginative choreography (much of it alfresco), and the producer-directors were George Abbott and Stanley Donen. The film was shot in WarnerColor.

Pal Joey

This somewhat sanitized version of the 1940 Broadway show and John O'Hara's witty essays on which it was based, came to the screen in 1957. Frank Sinatra proved to be the ideal choice for the role of 'the heel of all-time', Joey Evans, the nightclub singer and compere, whose apparent mission in life is to seduce each 'mouse' in the chorus with the offer of 'shrimp cocktail, a steak, french fries, a little wine - the whole mish-mosh,' so that he can 'help her with her arrangements'. The ingenuous Linda English (Kim Novak) accepts his offer, and, after the usual complications and to the surprise of many who had read O'Hara's original short stories, goes off with him into the sunset. The musical highspot came when Joey sang an electrifying version of 'The Lady Is A Tramp'

straight to the wealthy widow, Vera Simpson (Rita Hayworth), who had been known as 'Vanessa The Undresser' in her former life as a stripper. London film critics at the time thought it slightly ridiculous when some of their number applauded a piece of celluloid, but it was that kind of performance. Hank Henry, as the grumpy owner of the Barbary Coast nightspot where Joey 'operates', and Bobby Sherwood the leader of its orchestra, headed a supporting cast which also included Barbara Nicholls and Elizabeth Patterson. The majority of Richard Rodgers and Lorenz Hart's fine stage score was retained, with four additional songs from their other shows. Sinatra was in great voice on 'I Could Write A Book', 'There's a Small Hotel' and 'What Do I Care For A Dame?', while Hayworth shimmied her way through 'Zip' and 'Bewitched' (vocals dubbed by Jo Ann Greer). Trudy Erwin's voice was behind Novak's sultry rendering of 'My Funny Valentine' and 'That Terrific Rainbow'. Hermes Pan was the choreographer, and Dorothy Kingsley's screenplay was adequate - O'Hara's version of events would never have been acceptable even in the late 50s - and this entertaining film grossed nearly $5 million in US rentals alone. It was produced in Technicolor for Columbia by Fred Kohlmar. The director was George Sidney.

Pan, Hermes

b. Hermes Panagiotopulos, between 1905 and 1910, Memphis, Tennessee, USA, d. 19 September 1990, Beverly Hills, California, USA. A dancer and legendary choreographer who worked closely with Fred Astaire on most of his film musicals and television specials. Pan danced in clubs and in the singing chorus of the Broadway musical *Top Speed*, which featured Ginger Rogers, before moving to Hollywood in the early 30s. After serving as assistant to dance director Dave Gould on *Flying Down To Rio*, Astaire and Rogers' first picture together, and the follow-up, *The Gay Divorcee*, Pan choreographed all of Astaire's films at RKO, including *Roberta*, *Top Hat*, *Follow The Fleet*, *Swing Time*, *Shall We Dance*, *Carefree*, and *The Story Of Vernon And Irene Castle*. He won an Oscar for his imaginative staging of the 'Fun House' sequence in another RKO feature, *A Damsel In Distress* (1937), in which Astaire appeared with George Burns and Gracie Allen. Pan also worked with Astaire on *Second Chorus*, *Blue Skies*, *The Barkleys Of Broadway* (with Ginger Rogers again), *Three Little Words*, *Let's Dance*, *Silk Stockings*, and *Finian's Rainbow* (1968) which was their last movie together. Pan also made one of his rare on-screen appearances in that one. Over the years, he had occasionally danced in films such as *My Gal Sal*, *Sweet Rosie O'Grady*, *Moon Over Miami*, *Kiss Me Kate*, and *Pin-Up Girl*. However, for most of his career, he was content to make major stars - Betty Grable, Rita Hayworth, Don Ameche, Howard Keel, Juliet Prowse, Alice Faye, Carmen

Miranda, Ann Miller, Kathryn Grayson and many others - look good in a variety of mostly entertaining musical pictures such as *Billy Rose's Diamond Horseshoe*, *Song Of The Islands*, *That Night In Rio*, *Footlight Serenade*, *Springtime In The Rockies*, *Coney Island*, *Lovely To Look At*, *That Lady In Ermine*, *Hit The Deck*, *The Student Prince*, *Meet Me In Las Vegas*, *Pal Joey*, *Can-Can*, *Flower Drum Song*, *My Fair Lady*, *Darling Lili*, and *Lost Horizon*. He also staged Cleopatra's spectacular entry into Rome for the Elizabeth Taylor-Richard Burton epic *Cleopatra* in 1963. Pan won Emmy Awards for his work on the highly acclaimed television specials *An Evening With Fred Astaire* (1959) and *Astaire Time* (1961). In 1981 he received the National Film Award for achievement in cinema, and six years later was presented with the prestigious Joffrey Ballet Award. A true innovator, many of the films in which he mixed ballet, jazz and tap, are now rightly regarded as classics.

Paramor, Norrie

b. 1913, London, England, d. 9 September 1979. The most prolific producer of UK pop chart-toppers was a mild, bespectacled gentleman who had studied piano, and worked as an accompanist, prior to playing and arranging with a number of London dance bands, among them Maurice Winnick's Orchestra. During his time in the RAF during World War II, Paramor entertained servicemen in the company of artists such as Sydney Torch and Max Wall, served as a musical director for Ralph Reader's Gang Shows, and scored music Noël Coward, Mantovani and Jack Buchanan. After the war he was the featured pianist with Harry Gold And His Pieces Of Eight, and toured with the lively dixieland unit for five years. In 1950 he cut some sides for the Oriole label with Australian singer, Marie Benson, and, two years later, joined Columbia Records, an EMI subsidiary, as arranger and A&R manager. In 1954, he produced the first of two UK number 1 hits for Eddie Calvert, and another for Ruby Murray the following year. Although quoted as believing that rock 'n' roll was 'an American phenomenon - and they do it best', he still provided Columbia with such an act in Tony Crombie's Rockets but had better luck with the mainstream efforts of Michael Holliday and the Mudlarks - both backed by the Ken Jones Orchestra. Then, in 1958, a demo tape by Cliff Richard And The Drifters arrived on his desk. With no rock 'n' roller currently on his books, he contracted Cliff intending to play it safe with a US cover with the Jones band until persuaded to stick with the Drifters (soon renamed the Shadows) and push a group original ('Move It') as the a-side. Partly through newspaper publicity engineered by Paramor, 'Move It' was a smash, and a consequent policy was instigated of Richard recording singles of untried numbers - among them, at Paramor's insistence, Lionel Bart's 'Living Doll'. Columbia was

successful too with the Shadows - even if Paramor wished initially to issue 'Apache' - their first smash - as a b-side. Later, he offended Shadows purists by augmenting the quartet on disc with horn sections and his trademark lush string arrangements.

Other Paramor signings were not allowed to develop to the same idiosyncratic extent as Richard and his associates. Ricky Valance scored his sole chart-topper with a cover of Ray Peterson's US hit, 'Tell Laura I Love Her', while Helen Shapiro was visualized as a vague 'answer' to Brenda Lee; Paramor even booking and supervising some Shapiro sessions in Nashville in 1963. His greatest success during this period, however, was with Frank Ifield, who dominated the early 60s UK pop scene with three formidable number 1 hits. Even as late as 1968, Paramor racked up another number 1 with Scaffold's 'Lily The Pink'. Throughout his career, Paramor wrote, and co-wrote, many hit songs, several of them for films, such as *Expresso Bongo* ('A Voice In The Wilderness', Cliff Richard), *The Young Ones* ('The Savage') and *The Frightened City* (title song), both performed by the Shadows; *Play It Cool* ('Once Upon A Dream', Billy Fury), *It's Trad, Dad!* ('Let's Talk About Love', Helen Shapiro) and *Band Of Thieves* ('Lonely', Acker Bilk). He also composed several complete movie scores, and some light orchestral works such as 'The Zodiac' and 'Emotions', which he recorded with his Concert Orchestra, and released several 'mood' albums in the USA, including *London After Dark*, *Amore, Amore!*, *Autumn*, and *In London, In Love*, which made the US Top 20. In complete contrast, the Big Ben Banjo, and Big Ben Hawaiian Bands, along with similar 'happy-go-lucky' 'trad jazz' line-up, were originally formed in 1955 purely as recording units, utilising the cream of UK session musicians. Paramor was in charge of them all, and their popularity was such, that 'live' performances had to be organized. The Big Ben Banjo Band appeared in the Royal Variety Performance in 1958, and was resident on BBC Radio's *Everybody Step* programme, as well as having its own Radio Luxembourg series. Two of the band's 'Let's Get Together' singles, and *More Minstrel Melodies*, reached the UK Top 20. One of the highlights of Paramor's career came in 1960 when he arranged and conducted for Judy Garland's British recording sessions, and was her musical director at the London Palladium and subsequent dates in Europe. In the same year, with his Orchestra, he made the UK singles chart with 'Theme From A Summer Place' and in 1962, registered again with 'Theme From Z Cars'. From 1972-78 Paramor was the Director of the BBC Midland Radio Orchestra, but he continued to dabble in independent production for such as the Excaliburs, and his publishing company was still finding material for Cliff in the 70s. Paramor remains one of the most underrated figures in the history of UK pop and a posthumous reappraisal of his work is overdue.

Selected albums: *In London, In Love ...* (1956), *The Zodiac* (1957), *New York Impressions* (1957), *Emotions* (1958), *Dreams And Desires* (1958), *The Wonderful Waltz* (1958), *My Fair Lady* (1959), *Paramor In Paris* (1959), *Jet Flight* (1959), *Lovers In Latin* (1959), *Staged For Stereo* (1961), *Autumn* (1961), *The Golden Waltz* (1961), *Lovers In London* (1964), with Patricia Clark *Lovers In Tokio* (1964), *Warm And Willing* (1965), *Shadows In Latin* (1966), *Norrie Paramor Plays The Hits Of Cliff Richard* (1967), *Soul Coaxing* (1968), *BBC Top Tunes* (1974), *Radio 2 Top Tunes, Volume 1* (1974), *Radio 2 Top Tunes, Volume 2 and 3* (both 1975), *Love* (1975), *My Personal Choice* (1976), *Silver Serenade* (1977), *Norrie Paramor Remembers ... 40 Years Of TV Themes* (1976), *Temptation* (1978), *Rags And Tatters* aka *Ragtime* (1978), *Classical Rhythm* (1979). Compilations: *Paramagic Pianos* (1977), *The Best Of Norrie Paramor* (1984), *Ragtime* (1985).

Paris Blues

For a few moments at the beginning hopes are raised that this is a film to take seriously the problems of racial intolerance. Soon, however, jazz musicians Paul Newman and Sidney Poitier drift into stereotypes and there is little left for the audience to do except enjoy the scenes of Paris and the music. Fortunately, much of the latter, including the film's score, is in the hands of Duke Ellington which almost makes up for the disappointment in the dramatics. Apart from Ellington And His Orchestra, which includes Cat Anderson, Willie Cook, Johnny Hodges, Ray Nance, Clark Terry and Sam Woodyard, other musicians include Max Roach, Philly Joe Jones and local boys Joseph Reinhardt and Guy Lafitte. Louis Armstrong puts in an appearance and locks horns with Ellington ensemble in a rowdy nightclub sequence. The playing of Newman and Poitier was dubbed respectively by Murray McEachern and Paul Gonsalves. Directed by Martin Ritt, ths 1961 film was based upon the novel by Harold Flender which did not dodge the issues and in which the black musician was the sole protagonist, his white sidekick being very much a minor character.

Pete Kelly's Blues

A marvellous opening sequence, depicting the funeral of a New Orleans jazz musician, is the best moment in what is otherwise a fairly predictable tale of jazzmen and gangsters in the 20s. Other bright spots are of singers Peggy Lee and Ella Fitzgerald. Teddy Buckner plays in the opening scene and elsewhere can be heard the likes of Nick Fatool, Matty Matlock, Eddie Miller, George Van Eps and Joe Venuti. The

Pete Kelly's Blues

role of Pete Kelly is played by Jack Webb, who also directed, and his trumpet playing was dubbed by Dick Cathcart. Lee Marvin made the most unlikely-looking clarinettist in jazz history, with the possible exception of Pee Wee Russell. Four years later, in 1959, a television spin-off lasted 13 episodes.

Pinocchio (see Disney, Walt)

Pirate, The

Released by MGM in 1948, *The Pirate* is set on a Caribbean island in the early part of the 19th century, and tells the colourful story of Manuela (Judy Garland) who is betrothed to the fat and arrogant mayor, Don Pedro (Walter Slezak). Serafin (Gene Kelly), the leader of a group of wandering actors, discovers that Manuela dreams of being with the famous pirate Macoco - Mack the Knife to his friends - and so he claims to be the renegade himself. At first Manuela is taken in by his ruse, but when Don Pedro is hypnotised by Serafin at one of the troupe's performances, he admits he is the real Mack the Knife. Not surprisingly, Manuela then loses her overwhelming passion for pirates and realises that she really loves Serafin. Although not a commercial success by any means, the film is impressive, not only for its exuberant music and dance sequences, but for its attempt to do something different. Both Garland and Kelly gave appropriately stylised performances (Garland's furious antics when Serafin's disguise is revealed are hilarious - probably one of the best tantrums ever to be seen in a Hollywood musical). Cole Porter's sophisticated score contained several good numbers including 'Nina', which accompanied a scintillating dance sequence during which Kelly makes his way through the town serenading every pretty young woman he meets; 'Mack The Black', a dream sequence in which Kelly imagines he is the awesome Macoco (somewhat reminiscent of Kelly's vision of serenading Kathryn Grayson in *Anchors Aweigh*); 'You Can Do No Wrong' and 'Love Of My Life', two ballads which are handled beautifully by Garland; and 'Be A Clown', performed early in the film by Kelly and the amazing Nicholas Brothers, and later given the full circus treatment by Kelly and Garland. Also featured were Reginald Owen, Gladys Cooper, George Zucco, Lola Albright, Lester Allen, and Cully Richards. The spirited and innovative choreography was designed by Robert Alton and Gene Kelly, and Frances Goodrich and Albert Hackett's screenplay was adapted from a play by S.N. Behrman. Vincente Minnelli was the director, and the film, which was brilliantly photographed in Technicolor by Harry Stradling, was produced by the Arthur Freed MGM unit. All in all it proved to be an interesting and frenetic experience for all concerned - almost experimental in parts - and was certainly different from other musicals of that era.

Poor Little Rich Girl

By the time she made this film in 1936, Shirley Temple was an eight-year-old superstar with nearly 20 pictures to her credit. Cinema audiences all over the world had taken her to their hearts, and she did not disappoint them in this latest outing which continued along the familiar well-trodden path. In the screenplay, by Sam Hellman, Gladys Lehman, and Harry Tugend, Shirley runs away from her wealthy workaholic father (Michael Whalen) and is co-opted into a vaudeville act (Alice Faye and Jack Haley). Family reconciliation is eventually accomplished, but only after the loveable youngster has wowed the crowds with numbers such as 'You Gotta Eat Your Spinach, Baby', 'Military Man', 'But Definitely', and 'When I'm With You'. Harry Revel and Mack Gordon wrote those, and some others including 'Oh, My Goodness' and 'Wash Your Necks With A Cake Of Beck's' (Shirley did a lot of work on sponsored radio shows). Gloria Stuart, Sara Haden, Claude Gillingwater, Jane Darwell, and Henry Armetta were in the cast, and future singing heart-throb Tony Martin also made a brief appearance. The dance directors were Jack Haskell and Ralph Cooper, and the film, which was directed by Irving Cummings, was produced for 20th Century-Fox by Darryl F. Zanuck and Buddy De Sylva.

Porgy And Bess

The last film of producer Sam Goldwyn's illustrious career, which was released by Columbia in 1959, proved to be an expensive and troubled affair. After various disputes with his first choice director, Rouben Mamoulian (who had staged the original 1935 Broadway production), Goldwyn replaced him with Otto Preminger whose work on this occasion was considered to be somewhat laboured and uninspired. For some reason the well-known story of the crippled beggar Porgy (Sidney Poitier), who lives in the Catfish Row slum area and loves the tempestuous Bess (Dorothy Dandridge) did not transfer at all well to the big screen. The supporting cast was excellent, with Sammy Davis Jnr. (Sportin' Life), Pearl Bailey (Maria), Brock Peters (Crown), Diahann Carroll (Clara), and Ruth Attaway (Serena), all turning in outstanding performances. Other roles were taken by Leslie Scott, Clarence Muse, and Joel Fluellen. Because of the extremely demanding operatic score by composer George Gershwin and lyricists DuBose Heyward and Ira Gershwin, several of the principals were dubbed, including Poitier (Robert McFerrin), Dandridge (Adele Addison), Carroll (Loulie Jean Norman), and Attaway (Inez Matthews). Even so, there were some reservations regarding the vocal quality of the production, but these were swept aside by the sheer magnificence of the songs, which included 'Summertime', 'Bess, You Is My Woman', 'There's A Boat Dat's Leavin' Soon For New York',

Porgy And Bess

'I Loves You Porgy', 'A Woman Is A Sometimes Thing', 'I Got Plenty O' Nuttin'', 'It Ain't Necessarily So', 'My Man's Gone Now', and 'Oh Bess, Oh Where's My Bess'. André Previn and Ken Darby both won Oscars for 'scoring a dramatic picture', and Leo Shamroy was nominated for his superb photography in Technicolor and Panavision. Hermes Pan, who had been associated with many top musical films in his long career including the Fred Astaire and Ginger Rogers RKO series, staged the dances. The screenplay, by N. Richard Nash, was based on the original Broadway libretto and novel by Heyward, and his and Dorothy Heyward's play *Porgy*. In the early 90s, this film remained one of the few big musicals not to have been released on video. Cinema distribution has also been curtailed, the Gershwin estate has had the film firmly under lock and key for some years now.

Porter, Cole

b. 9 June 1891, Peru, Indiana, USA, d. 15 October 1964, Santa Monica, California, USA. Born into a rich family, Porter was taught privately, with music prominent amongst his studies. He composed his first songs before reaching his teens. At the age of 15 he attended school, where he excelled in many academic subjects and continued to write songs and play piano for his own amusement – activities he later pursued at Yale University. Later he attended Harvard where he

reluctantly studied law. Fortunately, his other talents had been noted and on faculty advice he switched to the study of music. While still at college some of his songs were used in Broadway productions and in 1916 his first full score, for *See America First*, opened and closed almost at once. The Porter family's wealth allowed him to travel extensively and he visited Europe both before and after World War I. In 1920 another Broadway show, the revue *Hitchy-Koo*, opened and was almost as disastrously received as his first effort. He persevered, however, and some of the songs from these earlier shows survived in their own right. It was a song written for the 1928 show, *Paris*, that gave him his first major song success with 'Let's Do It' and the following year his persistence paid off with two moderately successful Broadway shows, *Fifty Million Frenchmen* and *Wake Up And Dream*, which included, respectively, 'You Do Something To Me' and 'What Is This Thing Called Love?'. During the early 30s Porter wrote for several shows and among the songs which became standards were 'Love For Sale' and 'Night And Day'. In 1932 he had his first major Broadway hit with *Anything Goes*, which included 'Blow, Gabriel, Blow', 'I Get A Kick Out Of You', 'You're The Top' and the title song. Other 30s shows, while less popular than *Anything Goes*, had their own hit songs: 'My Heart Belongs To Daddy', 'Get Out Of Town', 'Friendship', 'Do I Love You?', 'Begin The Beguine', 'Just One Of Those Things' (these last two from the unsuccessful *Jubilee*), 'It's De-Lovely' and 'At Long Last Love'.

Not surprisingly, Porter was lured to Hollywood, where he began his screen musical career with 'I've Got You Under My Skin' and 'Easy To Love', written for the 1936 film *Born To Dance*. His second film, *Rosalie* (1937), had hits with 'Rosalie' and 'In The Still Of The Night'. In 1937 Porter was seriously injured in a riding accident. Astonishingly, a series of more than two dozen operations, several years in a wheelchair and almost constant pain (his right leg would be amputated in 1958), seemed to have little effect on his creative ability. Among his songs of the early 40s were 'I Concentrate On You', 'I've Got My Eyes On You', 'Let's Be Buddies', 'Ace In The Hole', 'Everything I Love' and 'I Love You'. During this time Porter was dividing his time and talent between stage and films and his song successes came in both mediums: 'You'd Be So Nice To Come Home To' from the film *You'll Never Get Rich* (1941) and 'Ev'ry Time We Say Goodbye', from the 1944 show *Seven Lively Arts*. Although written some years before for an aborted film project, another song, 'Don't Fence Me In', was used in *Hollywood Canteen* (1944). Two unsuccessful Porter scores followed in the late 40s, one a show, the other a film, but in 1948 he had his biggest Broadway hit with *Kiss Me, Kate*, for which he wrote 'So In Love', 'Always True To You In My Fashion', 'Wunderbar', 'I Hate Men', 'Too Darn Hot' and 'Brush Up Your Shakespeare'. In 1950, Porter followed *Kiss Me, Kate* with another unsuccessful show, *Out Of This World*, but even this had its hit song, 'From This Moment On'.

The mid-50s found Porter still capable of bringing Broadway to its feet with two more smash hits: *Can-Can* (1953) from which came 'I Love Paris', 'C'est Magnifique' and 'It's All Right With Me'; and *Silk Stockings* (1955) with 'Paris Loves Lovers' and 'Without Love'. Porter then returned to Hollywood with two film scores: *High Society* (1956) and *Les Girls* (1957). From the former came 'True Love', 'Samantha' and 'Did You Ever', while the latter included 'Ça C'est Amour'. Marked by wit and sophistication often far ahead of the times in which he lived, Porter's music and lyrics set standards which were the envy of most of his contemporaries and even so distinguished a composer as Irving Berlin was fulsome in his praise. Although Porter stopped writing in the late 50s, his music continued to be used in films and on television and he was the subject of television specials and numerous honours and awards. In 1991, the centenary of his birth, there were tributes galore. In a gala concert at Carnegie Hall, artists such as Julie Wilson, Kathryn Grayson, and Patricia Morison paid tribute to him, as did songwriters Jule Styne, Sammy Cahn, and Burton Lane. Among the other special events were an Off Broadway revue *Anything Cole*, the West End production *A Swell Party*, and a London concert entitled *Let's Do It*, starring Elaine Delmar and Paul Jones. The special occasion was also marked by the release of complete recordings of his scores for *Nymph Errant* and *Kiss Me, Kate*.

Further reading: *The Cole Porter Story*, David Ewen. *Cole: A Biographical Essay*, Brendan Gill and Richard Kimball. *The Cole Porter Story*, Cole Porter and Richard Hubler. *Cole Porter: The Life That Late He Led*, George Eells. *Travels With Cole Porter*, Jean Howard.

Powell, Dick

b. Richard Ewing Powell, 14 November 1904, Mountain View, Arkansas, USA, d. 3 January 1963, Hollywood, California, USA. Powell was an extremely popular singing star of major 30s film musicals, with an appealing tenor voice, and 'matinee-idol' looks. He sang firstly as a boy soprano, and later, tenor, in school and church choirs. He learnt to play several musical instruments including the cornet, saxophone and banjo. In his late teens he was a member of the Royal Peacock Orchestra in Kentucky, and in the late 20s sang and played for Charlie Davis, with whom he made some early recordings, and other mid-west bands. In the early 30s he worked as a Master of Ceremonies and singer at the Circle Theatre, Indianapolis, and the Stanley Theatre in Pittsburg, where he was discovered by a Warner Brothers talent scout, and signed to a film contract. He made his film debut in *Blessed Event* (1932), followed by *Too Busy To Work* and *The King's Vacation* (1933), before making an enormous impact, along with another young newcomer, Ruby Keeler, in the spectacular Busby Berkeley back-stage musical, *42nd Street* (1933). The film's score, by Harry Warren and Al Dubin, included the title song; 'Shuffle Off To Buffalo', 'You're Getting To Be A Habit With Me' and 'Young And Healthy'. Co-starring with Keeler, his wife Joan Blondell, and several more glamorous leading ladies, Powell embarked on a series of, mostly lavish, movie musicals for Warners, 20th Century-Fox, and other studios, through to the mid-40s.

Containing some of the classic popular songs of the time, the films included *Gold Diggers Of 1933* (1933), ('We're In The Money', 'Shadow Waltz', 'I've Got To Sing A Torch Song' and 'Pettin' In The Park'); *Footlight Parade* (1933), ('By A Waterfall'); *Twenty Million Sweethearts* (1934), ('I'll String Along With You'); *Dames* (1934), (the title song and 'I Only Have Eyes For You'); *Gold Diggers Of 1935* (1935), ('Lullaby Of Broadway' and 'The Words Are In My Heart'); *Broadway Gondolier* (1935), ('Lulu's Back In Town' and 'The Rose In Her Hair'); *Gold Diggers Of 1937* (1936), ('With Plenty Of Money And You' and 'All's Fair In Love And War'); *On The Avenue* (1937), ('The Girl On The Police Gazette', This Year's Kisses', 'I've Got My Love To Keep Me Warm', Slumming On Park Avenue' and 'You're Laughing At

Me'); *Varsity Show* (1937), ('Have You Got Any Castles Baby?') and *Going Places* (1938), ('Jeepers Creepers'). During this period, Powell was also very active on US radio, with programmes such as the *Old Gold* show with the Ted Fio Rito Band (1934), *Hollywood Hotel* (1934-37, with Frances Langford), *Your Hollywood Party* (1938, the show that gave Bob Hope's career a big boost), *Tuesday Night Party* (1939), *American Cruise* (1941) and *Dick Powell Serenade* (1942-43). He also had several hit records, mostly with songs from his films. During the early 40s, Powell concentrated more and more on comedy and dramatic film roles. In 1944, he confirmed his change of direction when he appeared as private-eye Philip Marlowe in the highly-acclaimed movie, *Farewell My Lovely* (aka *Murder My Sweet*). From then on, singing was abandoned, as he undertook a series of 'tough guy' roles in crime and detective movies, becoming just as popular as he had been in the musicals of the 30s. He was also a pioneer of early US television drama in the 50s, directing and producing, as well as performing. From 1959-61, he presented the popular television series, *Dick Powell Theatre*. Despite some pressure, he never went back to singing, but was still working up to his death, from cancer, in January 1963.
Compilations: *In Hollywood* (1974), *Lullaby Of Broadway* (1986, London label double set), *Lullaby Of Broadway* (1986, Living Era label), *On The Avenue* (1988), *Rare Recordings 1934-1951* (1989).

Powell, Eleanor

b. 21 November 1912, Springfield, Massachusetts, USA, d. 11 February 1982, Beverly Hills, California, USA. Often billed as 'the world's greatest female tap dancer', Powell is regarded by many as the most accomplished of Fred Astaire's screen partners, but without, of course, the indefinable magic of Ginger Rogers. She studied ballet at an early age and later took up tap dancing. After only a few lessons she is said to have achieved 'machine-gun rapidity' - up to five taps per second. Powell moved to New York in 1928 and appeared in *The Optimists* revue at the Casino de Paris Theatre, and a year later made her Broadway debut in the musical *Follow Through*. This was followed by other stage shows, *Fine And Dandy*, *Hot-Cha*, and *George White's Scandals (1932)*. A small, but highly impressive role in the film of that same revue, *George White's Scandals* (1935), led to Powell being elevated to star status immediately after the release of *Broadway Melody Of 1936*. Signed to a seven year contract with MGM, her exhilarating tap dancing was on display in musicals such as *Born To Dance*, *Broadway Melody Of 1938*, *Rosalie*, *Honolulu*, *Broadway Melody Of 1940*, *Lady Be Good*, *Ship Ahoy*, *Thousands Cheer*, *I Dood It*, and *Sensations Of 1945*. By that stage, Powell, who married the actor Glenn Ford in 1943, had retired from show business to devote more time

to her family. She made just one more film, *Duchess Of Idaho*, in 1950. A devout Presbyterian, she became a Sunday school teacher in the 50s and starred in her own religious television programme, *Faith Of Our Children*, which won five Emmy Awards. After she and Ford were divorced in 1959, Powell made a brief comeback playing large clubs and showrooms in Las Vegas and New York with a classy cabaret act. Reminders of her remarkable terpsichorean skills flooded back in 1974 when the marvellous 'Begin the Beguine' routine she did with Fred Astaire in *Broadway Melody Of 1940* was included in MGM's *That's Entertainment!*. As Frank Sinatra said when he introduced it in that film: 'You know, you can wait around and hope, but I'll tell you - you'll never see the likes of this again.'

Powell, Jane

b. Suzanne Burce, 1 April 1929, Portland, Oregon, USA. An petite, vivacious, actress and singer with a thrilling soprano voice who excelled in several popular MGM musicals of the 50s. After singing a mixture of classical and popular songs on local radio, she won a film contract with MGM when she was just 15 years old. Her debut in *Song Of The Open Road* was followed in the 40s and early 50s by *Delightfully Dangerous*, *Holiday In Mexico*, *Three Daring Daughters*, *A Date With Judy*, *Luxury Liner*, *Nancy Goes To Rio*, *Two Weeks With Love*, *Rich, Young And Pretty*, *Small Town Girl*, and *Three Sailors And A Girl* (1953). In 1951 she co-starred with Fred Astaire in *Royal Wedding*, and they duetted on one of the longest song titles ever - 'How Could You Believe Me When I Said I Love You When You Know I've Been A Liar All My Life?'. Their recording became a million-seller. In 1956 she made the US Top 20 on her own with 'True Love' from *High Society*. Her best film role came in 1954 when he joined Howard Keel in the marvellous *Seven Brides For Seven Brothers*, and continued to appear on the screen into the late 50s in musicals such as *Athena*, *Deep In My Heart*, *Hit The Deck*, and *The Girl Most Likely* (1957). The golden era of movie musicals was drawing to close by then, and Powell turned to provincial theatre and nightclubs. In the 70s she was active on US television in programmes such as *Murdoch*, *The Letters*, and *Mayday At 40,000 Feet*. She also succeeded Debbie Reynolds in the leading role of the 1973 Broadway revival of *Irene*. In 1988 Powell married her fifth husband, Dick Moore, who was a child star himself and is an authority on the genre having written a book entitled *Twinkle, Twinkle Little Star (But Don't Have Sex Or Take The Car)*. In the same year she appeared in concert at Carnegie Hall with Skitch Henderson and the New York Pops.
Albums: *Two Weeks For Love* (1950, film soundtrack), *Rich, Young And Pretty* (1951, film soundtrack), *Three Sailors And A Girl* (1953, film soundtrack), *Romance*

(50s), *A Date With Jane Powell* (50s), *Athena* (1954, film soundtrack), *Alice In Wonderland* (50s), *Can't We Be Friends?* (50s). Compilations: *Songs From Her Films* (1989).

Presley, Elvis

b. Elvis Aaron Presley, 8 January 1935, Tupelo, Mississippi, USA, d. 16 August 1977, Memphis, Tennessee. The most celebrated popular music phenomenon of his era and, for many, the purest embodiment of rock 'n' roll, Elvis's life and career have become part of rock legend. The elder of twins, his younger brother, Jesse Garon, was stillborn, a tragedy which partly contributed to the maternal solicitude that affected his childhood and teenage years. Presley's first significant step towards a musical career took place at the age of eight when he won $5.00 in a local song contest performing the lachrymose Red Foley ballad, 'Old Shep'. His earliest musical influence came from attending the Pentecostal Church and listening to the psalms and gospel songs. He also had a strong grounding in country and blues and it was the combination of these different styles that was to provide his unique musical identity.

By the age of 13, Presley had moved with his family to Memphis and during his later school years began cultivating an outsider image with long hair, spidery sideburns and ostentatious clothes. After leaving school he took a job as a truck driver, a role in keeping with his unconventional appearance. In spite of his rebel posturing, Elvis remained studiously polite to his elders and was devoted to his mother. Indeed, it was his filial affection that first prompted him to visit Sun Records, whose studios offered the sophisticated equivalent of a fairground recording booth service. As a birthday present to his mother, Gladys, Elvis cut a version of the Ink Spots' 'My Happiness', backed with the Raskin/Brown/Fisher standard 'That's When Your Heartaches Begin'. The studio manager, Marion Keisker, noted Presley's unusual but distinctive vocal style and informed Sun's owner/producer Sam Phillips of his potential. Phillips nurtured the boy for almost a year before putting him together with country guitarist Scotty Moore and bassist Bill Black. Their early sessions showed considerable promise, especially when Presley began alternating his unorthodox low-key delivery with a high-pitched whine. The amplified guitars of Moore and Black contributed strongly to the effect and convinced Phillips that the singer was startlingly original. In Presley, Sam saw something that he had long dreamed of discovering: a white boy who sang like a negro.

Presley's debut disc on Sun was the extraordinary 'That's All Right (Mama)', a showcase for his rich, multi-textured vocal dexterity, with sharp, solid backing from his compatriots. The b-side, 'Blue Moon Of Kentucky', was a country song but the arrangement showed that Presley was threatening to slip into an entirely different genre, closer to R&B. Local response to these strange-sounding performances was encouraging and Phillips eventually shifted 20,000 copies of the disc. For his second single, Presley cut Roy Brown's 'Good Rockin' Tonight' backed by the zingy 'I Don't Care If The Sun Don't Shine'. The more roots-influenced 'Milkcow Blues Boogie' followed, while the b-side 'You're A Heartbreaker' had some strong tempo changes which neatly complemented Presley's quirky vocal. 'Baby Let's Play House'/'I'm Left, You're Right, She's Gone' continued the momentum and led to Presley performing on the *Grand Old Opry* and *Louisiana Hayride* radio programmes. A series of live dates commenced in 1955 with drummer D.J. Fontana added to the ranks. Presley toured clubs in Arkansas, Louisiana and Texas billed as 'The King Of Western Bop' and 'The Hillbilly Cat'. Audience reaction verged on the fanatical, which was hardly surprising given Presley's semi-erotic performances. His hip-swivelling routine, in which he cascaded across the stage and plunged to his knees at dramatic moments in a song, was remarkable for the period and prompted near-riotous fan mania. The final Sun single, a cover of Junior Parker's 'Mystery Train', was later acclaimed by many as the definitive rock 'n' roll single with its chugging rhythm, soaring vocal and enticing lead guitar breaks. It established Presley as an artist worthy of national attention and ushered in the next phase of his career, which was dominated by the imposing figure of Colonel Tom Parker.

The Colonel was a former fairground huckster who managed several country artists including Hank Snow and Eddy Arnold. After relieving disc jockey Bob Neal of Presley's managership, Parker persuaded Sam Phillips that his financial interests would be better served by releasing the boy to a major label. RCA Records had already noted the commercial potential of the phenomenon under offer and agreed to pay Sun Records a release fee of $35,000, an incredible sum for the period. The sheer diversity of Presley's musical heritage and his remarkable ability as a vocalist and interpreter of material enabled him to escape the cultural parochialism of his R&B-influenced predecessors. The attendant rock 'n' roll explosion, in which Presley was both a creator and participant, ensured that he could reach a mass audience, many of them newly-affluent teenagers.

It was on 10 January 1956, a mere two days after his 21st birthday, that Elvis entered RCA's studios in Nashville to record his first tracks for a major label. His debut session produced the epochal 'Heartbreak Hotel', one of the most striking pop records ever released. Co-composed by Hoyt Axton's mother Mae, the song evoked nothing less than a vision of absolute funereal despair. There was nothing in the pop charts of the period that even hinted at the degree of desolation described in the song. Presley's reading was extraordinarily mature and moving, with a determined avoidance of any histrionics in favour of a pained and resigned acceptance of loneliness as death. The economical yet acutely emphatic piano work of Floyd Cramer enhanced the stark mood of the piece, which was frozen in a suitably minimalist production. The startling originality and intensity of 'Heartbreak Hotel' entranced the American public and pushed the single to number 1 for an astonishing eight weeks. Whatever else he achieved, Presley was already assured a place in pop history for one of the greatest major label debut records ever released. During the same month that 'Heartbreak Hotel' was recorded, Presley made his national television debut displaying his sexually-enticing gyrations before a bewildered adult audience whose alleged outrage subsequently persuaded producers to film the star exclusively from the waist upwards. Having outsold his former Sun colleague Carl Perkins with 'Blue Suede Shoes', Presley released a debut album which contained several of the songs he had previously cut with Sam Phillips, including Little Richard's 'Tutti Fruitti', the R&B classic 'I Got A Woman' and an eerie, wailing version of Richard Rodgers/Lorenz Hart's 'Blue Moon', which emphasized his remarkable vocal range.

Since hitting number 2 in the UK lists with 'Heartbreak Hotel', Presley had been virtually guaranteed European success and his profile was increased via a regular series of releases as RCA took full advantage of their bulging back catalogue. Although there was a danger of overkill, Presley's talent, reputation and immensely strong fan base vindicated the intense release schedule and the quality of the material ensured that the public was not disappointed. After hitting number 1 for the second time with the slight ballad 'I Want You, I Need You, I Love You', Presley released what was to become the most commercially successful double-sided single in pop history, 'Hound Dog'/'Don't Be Cruel'. The former was composed by the immortal rock 'n' roll songwriting team of Leiber And Stoller, and presented Presley at his upbeat best with a novel lyric, complete with a striking guitar solo and spirited handclapping from his backing group the Jordanaires. Otis Blackwell's 'Don't Be Cruel' was equally effective with a striking melody line and some clever and amusing vocal gymnastics from the hiccupping King of Western Bop, who also received a co-writing credit. The single remained at number 1 in the USA for a staggering 11 weeks and both sides of the record were massive hits in the UK.

Celluloid fame for Presley next beckoned with *Love Me Tender*, produced by David Weisbert, who had previously worked on James Dean's *Rebel Without A Cause*. Elvis's movie debut received mixed reviews but was a box office smash, while the smouldering, perfectly-enunciated title track topped the US charts for five weeks. The spate of Presley singles continued in earnest through 1957 and one of the biggest was another Otis Blackwell composition, 'All Shook Up' which the singer used as a cheekily oblique comment on his by now legendary dance movements. By late 1956 it was rumoured that Presley would be drafted into the US Army and, as if to compensate for that irksome eventuality, RCA, 20th Century-Fox and the Colonel stepped up the work-rate and release schedules. Incredibly, three major films were completed in the next two-and-a-half years. *Loving You* boasted a quasi-autobiographical script with Presley playing a truck driver who becomes a pop star. The title track became the b-side of '(Let Me Be Your) Teddy Bear' which reigned at number 1 for seven weeks. The third movie, *Jailhouse Rock*, was Elvis's most successful to date with an excellent soundtrack and some inspired choreography. The Leiber and Stoller title track was an instant classic which again topped the US charts for seven weeks and made pop history by entering the UK listings at number 1. The fourth celluloid outing, *King Creole* (adapted from the Harold Robbins' novel, *A Stone For Danny Fisher*) is regarded by many as Presley's finest film of all and a firm indicator of his sadly unfulfilled potential as a serious actor. Once more the soundtrack album featured some surprisingly strong material such as the haunting 'Crawfish' and the vibrant 'Dixieland Rock'.

By the time *King Creole* was released in 1958, Elvis had already been inducted into the US Forces. A publicity photograph of the singer having his hair shorn symbolically commented on his approaching musical emasculation. Although rock 'n' roll purists mourned the passing of the old Elvis, it seemed inevitable in the context of the 50s that he would move towards a broader base appeal and tone down his rebellious image. From 1958-60, Presley served in the US Armed Forces, spending much of his time in Germany where he was regarded as a model soldier. It was during this period that he first met 14-year-old Priscilla Beaulieu, whom he would later marry in 1967. Back in America, the Colonel kept his absent star's reputation intact via a series of films, record releases and extensive merchandising. Hits such as 'Wear My Ring Around Your Neck', 'Hard Headed Woman', 'One Night', 'I Got Stung', 'A Fool Such As I' and 'A Big Hunk O' Love' filled the long two-year gap and by the time Elvis reappeared, he was ready to assume the mantle of an all-round entertainer. The change was immediately evident in the series of number 1 hits that he enjoyed in the early 60s. The enormously successful 'It's Now Or Never', based on the Italian melody 'O Sole Mio', revealed the King as an operatic crooner, far removed from his earlier raucous recordings. 'Are You Lonesome Tonight?', originally recorded by Al Jolson as early as 1927, allowed Presley to quote some Shakespeare in the spoken-word middle section as well as showing his ham-acting ability with an overwrought vocal. The new clean-cut Presley was presented on celluloid in *GI Blues*. The movie played upon his recent Army exploits and saw him serenading a puppet on the charming chart-topper 'Wooden Heart', which also allowed Elvis to show off his knowledge of German. The grandiose 'Surrender' completed this phase of big ballads in the old-fashioned style. For the next few years Presley concentrated on an undemanding spree of films including *Flaming Star, Wild In The Country, Blue Hawaii, Kid Galahad, Girls! Girls! Girls!, Follow That Dream, Fun In Acapulco, It Happened At The World's Fair, Kissin' Cousins, Viva Las Vegas, Roustabout, Girl Happy, Tickle Me, Harem Scarem, Frankie And Johnny, Paradise Hawaiian Style* and *Spinout*. Not surprisingly, most of his album recordings were hastily completed soundtracks with unadventurous commissioned songs. For his singles he relied increasingly on the formidable Doc Pomus/Mort Shuman team who composed such hits as 'Mess Of Blues', 'Little Sister' and 'His Latest Flame'. More and more, however, the hits were adapted from films and their chart positions suffered accordingly. After the 1963 number 1 'Devil In Disguise', a bleak period followed in which such minor songs as 'Bossa Nova Baby', 'Kiss Me Quick', 'Ain't That Lovin' You Baby' and 'Blue Christmas' became the rule rather than the exception. Significantly, his biggest success of the mid-60s, 'Crying In The Chapel', had been recorded five years before, and part of its appeal came from the realization that it represented something ineffably lost.

In the wake of the Beatles' rise to fame and the beat boom explosion Presley seemed a figure out of time. Yet, in spite of the dated nature of many of his recordings, he could still invest power and emotion into classic songs. The sassy 'Frankie And Johnny' was expertly sung by Elvis as was his moving reading of Ketty Lester's 'Love Letters'. His other significant 1966 release, 'If Everyday Was Like Christmas', was a beautiful festive song unlike anything else in the charts of the period. By 1967, however, it was clear to critics and even a large proportion of his devoted following that Presley had seriously lost his way. He continued to grind out pointless movies such as *Double Trouble, Speedway, Clambake* and *Live A Little, Love A Little*, even though the box office returns were increasingly poor. His capacity to register instant hits, irrespective of the material was also wearing thin as such lowly-placed singles as 'You Gotta Stop' and 'Long Legged Woman' demonstrated all too alarmingly. However, just as Elvis's career had reached its all-time nadir he seemed to wake up, take stock, and break free from the artistic malaise in which he found himself.

Two songs written by country guitarist Jerry Reed, 'Guitar Man' and 'US Male', proved a spectacular return to form for Elvis in 1968, such was Presley's conviction that the compositions almost seemed to be written specifically for him. During the same year Colonel Tom Parker had approached NBC-TV about the possibility of recording a Presley Christmas special in which the singer would perform a selection of religious songs similar in feel to his early 60s album *His Hand In Mine*. However, the executive producers of the show vetoed that concept in favour of a one-hour spectacular designed to capture Elvis at his rock 'n' rollin' best. It was a remarkable challenge for the singer, seemingly in the autumn of his career, and he responded to the idea with unexpected enthusiasm. The *Elvis TV Special* was broadcast in America on 3 December 1968 and has since gone down as one of the most celebrated moments in pop broadcasting history. The show was not merely good but an absolute revelation, with the King emerging as if he had been frozen in time for 10 years. His determination to recapture past glories oozed from every movement and was discernible in every aside. With his leather jacket and acoustic guitar strung casually round his neck, he resembled nothing less than the consummate pop idol of the 50s who had entranced a generation. To add authenticity to the proceedings he was accompanied by his old sidekicks Scotty Moore and D.J. Fontana. There was no sense of self-parody in the show as Presley joked about his famous surly curled-lip movement and even heaped passing ridicule on his endless stream of bad movies. The music concentrated heavily on his 50s classics but, significantly, there was a startling finale courtesy of the passionate 'If I Can Dream' in which he seemed to sum up the frustration of a decade in a few short lines.

The critical plaudits heaped upon Elvis in the wake of his television special prompted the singer to undertake his most significant recordings in years. With producer Chips Moman overseeing the sessions in January 1969, Presley recorded enough material to cover two highly-praised albums, *From Elvis In Memphis* and *From Memphis To Vegas/From Vegas To Memphis*. The former was particularly strong with such distinctive tracks as the eerie 'Long Black Limousine' and the engagingly melodic 'Any Day Now'. On the singles front, Presley was back in top form and finally coming to terms with contemporary issues, most notably on the socially aware 'In The Ghetto' which hit number 2 in the UK and number 3 in the USA. The glorious 'Suspicious Minds', a wonderful song of marital jealously with cascading tempo changes and an exceptional vocal arrangement, gave him his first US chart-topper since 'Good Luck Charm' back in 1962. Subsequent hits such as the maudlin 'Don't Cry Daddy', which dealt with the death of a marriage, ably demonstrated Elvis's ability to read a song. Even his final few films seemed less disastrous than expected. In 1969's *Charro*, he grew a beard for the first time in his portrayal of a moody cowboy, while *A Change Of Habit* dealt with more serious matter than usual. More importantly, Presley returned as a live performer at Las Vegas with a strong backing group including guitarist James Burton and pianist Glen D. Hardin. In common with John Lennon, who also returned to the stage that same year with the Plastic Ono Band, Presley opened his set with Carl Perkins' 'Blue Suede Shoes'. His comeback was well-received and one of the live songs, 'The Wonder Of You', stayed at number 1 in Britain for six weeks during the summer of 1970. There was also a revealing documentary film of the tour Elvis - *That's The Way It Is* and a companion album which included contemporary cover songs such as Tony Joe White's 'Polk Salad Annie', Creedence Clearwater Revival's 'Proud Mary' and Neil Diamond's 'Sweet Caroline'.

During the early 70s Presley continued his live performances, but soon fell victim to the same artistic atrophy that had bedevilled his celluloid career. Rather than re-entering the studio to record fresh material he relied on a slew of patchy live albums which saturated the marketplace. What had been innovative and exciting in 1969 swiftly became a tedious routine and an exercise in misdirected potential. The backdrop to Presley's final years was a sordid slump into drug dependency, reinforced by the pervasive unreality of a pampered lifestyle in his fantasy home, Gracelands. The dissolution of his marriage in 1973 coincided with a further decline and an alarming tendency to put on weight. Remarkably, he continued to undertake live appearances, covering up his bloated frame with brightly coloured jump suits and an enormous, ostentatiously-jewelled belt. He collapsed onstage on a couple of occasions and finally on 16 August 1977 his tired, burnt-out body expired. The official cause of death was a heart attack, no doubt brought on by barbiturate usage over a long period. In the weeks following his demise, his record sales predictably rocketed and 'Way Down' proved a fittingly final UK number 1.

The importance of Presley in the history of rock 'n' roll and popular music remains incalculable. In spite of his iconographic status, the Elvis image was never captured in a single moment of time like that of Bill Haley, Buddy Holly or even Chuck Berry. Presley, in spite of his apparent creative inertia, was not a one-dimensional artist clinging to history but a multi-faceted performer whose career spanned several decades and phases. For purists and rockabilly enthusiasts it is the early Elvis who remains of greatest importance and there is no doubting that his personal fusion of black and white musical influences, incorporating R&B and country, produced some of the finest and most durable recordings of the century. Beyond Elvis 'The Hillbilly Cat', however, there was the face that launched a thousand imitators, that black-haired, smiling or smouldering presence who stared from the front covers of numerous EPs, albums and film posters of the late 50s and early 60s. It was

that well-groomed, immaculate pop star who inspired a generation of performers and second-rate imitators in the 60s. There was also Elvis the Las Vegas performer, vibrant and vulgar, yet still distant and increasingly appealing to a later generation brought up on the excesses of 70s rock and glam ephemera. Finally, there was the bloated Presley who bestrode the stage in the last months of his career. For many, he has come to symbolize the decadence and loss of dignity that is all too often heir to pop idolatry. It is no wonder that Presley's remarkable career so sharply divides those who testify to his ultimate greatness and those who bemoan the gifts that he seemingly squandered along the way. In a sense, the contrasting images of Elvis have come to represent everything positive and everything destructive about the music industry.

Albums: *Rock 'N' Roll* (1956), *Rock 'N' Roll No. 2* (1957), *Loving You* (1957), *Elvis' Christmas Album* (1957), *King Creole* (1958), *Elvis' Golden Records, Volume 1* (1958), *Elvis* (1959), *A Date With Elvis* (1959), *Elvis' Golden Records, Volume 2* (1960), *Elvis Is Back!* (1960), *G.I. Blues* (1960), *His Hand In Mine* (1961), *Something For Everybody* (1961), *Blue Hawaii* (1961), *Pot Luck* (1962), *Girls! Girls! Girls!* (1963), *It Happened At The World's Fair* (1963), *Fun In Acapulco* (1963), *Elvis' Golden Records, Volume 3* (1964), *Kissin' Cousins* (1964), *Roustabout* (1964), *Girl Happy* (1965), *Flaming Star And Summer Kisses* (1965), *Elvis For Everyone* (1965), *Harem Holiday* (1965), *Frankie And Johnny* (1966), *Paradise, Hawaiian Style* (1966), *California Holiday* (1966), *How Great Thou Art* (1967), *Double Trouble* (1967), *Clambake* (1968), *Elvis' Golden Records, Volume 4* (1968), *Speedway* (1968), *Elvis - TV Special* (1968), *From Elvis In Memphis* (1970), *On Stage February 1970* (1970), *That's The Way It Is* (1971), *I'm 10,000 Years Old - Elvis Country* (1971), *Love Letters From Elvis* (1971), *Elvis Sings The Wonderful World Of Christmas* (1971), *Elvis Now* (1972), *He Touched Me* (1972), *Elvis As Recorded At Madison Square Garden* (1972), *Aloha From Hawaii Via Satellite* (1973), *Elvis* (1973), *Raised On Rock* (1973), *A Legendary Performer, Volume 1* (1974), *Good Times* (1974), *Elvis Recorded On Stage In Memphis* (1974), *Hits Of The 70s* (1974), *Promised Land* (1975), *Having Fun With Elvis On Stage* (1975), *Today* (1975), *The Elvis Presley Sun Collection* (1975), *From Elvis Presley Boulevard, Memphis, Tennessee* (1976), *Welcome To My World* (1977), *A Legendary Performer* (1977), *He Walks Beside Me* (1978), *The '56 Sessions, Vol. 1* (1978), *Elvis's 40 Greatest* (1978), *Elvis - A Legendary Performer, Volume 3* (1979), *Our Memories Of Elvis* (1979), *The '56 Sessions, Vol. 2* (1979), *Elvis Presley Sings Leiber And Stoller* (1980), *Elvis Aaron Presley* (1979), *Elvis Sings The Wonderful World Of Christmas* (1979), *The First Year* (1979), *The King . . . Elvis* (1980), *This Is Elvis* (1981), *Guitar Man* (1981), *Elvis Answers Back* (1981), *The Ultimate Performance* (1981), *Personally Elvis* (1982), *The Sound*

Of Your Cry (1982), Jailhouse Rock/Love In Las Vegas (1983), The First Live Recordings (1984), A Golden Celebration (1984), Rare Elvis (1985), Essential Elvis (1986), Elvis From Nashville To Memphis: The Essential '60s Masters I (1993, five CD boxed-set).
Further reading: Elvis: A Biography, Jerry Hopkins. Elvis: The Final Years, Jerry Hopkins. Elvis '56: In The Beginning, Alfred Wertheimer And Gregory Martinelli. Elvis, Albert Goldman. Up And Down With Elvis Presley, Marge Crumbaker. Elvis, Dave Marsh. Elvis: The Complete Illustrated Record, Roy Carr And Mick Farren. Elvis And Gladys: The Genesis Of The King, Elaine Dundy.

Preston, Robert

b. Robert Preston Meservey, 8 June 1918, Newton Highlands, Massachussetts, USA, d. 21 March 1987, Santa Barbara, California, USA. An actor and singer, Preston had already had a busy, but undistinguished career in Hollywood for nearly 20 years when he landed the role of a lifetime on Broadway in The Music Man (1957). He grew up in Hollywood, and spent several of his teenage years in the theatre before signing for Paramount and making his first movie, King Of Alcatraz, in 1938. From then, until 1942, he made some 15 films, including Union Pacific, Beau Geste, Typhoon, Moon Over Burma, Northwest Mounted Police, and This Gun For Hire (1942). After serving in the US Army Air Force during World War II, Preston resumed his film career in features such as The Macomber Affair, Tulsa, and When I Grow Up, until 1951 when he moved to New York. He appeared on Broadway in number of straight plays including Twentieth Century, The Tender Trap, and Janus, and was out of town in Philadelphia with Boy Meets Girl when he was asked to audition for The Music Man. His portrayal of the likeable con-man, Harold Hill, who travels to small US towns such as Iowa, selling band instruments (which never materialise) to parents for their children to play, made Preston a gilt-edged Broadway star. Meredith Willson's fine score contained numbers such as 'Seventy-Six Trombones', ''Til There Was You', and Preston's tour de force 'Ya Got Trouble'. He won the Tony Award for best actor in a musical, and stayed with the show for over two years. After being virtually ignored during initial casting, he recreated the part in the 1962 film version. Cary Grant, who was one of the actors to whom the role was offered, reportedly said: 'Not only won't I play it, but unless Robert Preston plays it, I won't even go see it.' After appearing in several more straight parts, Preston returned to the musical stage in 1964 with Ben Franklin In Paris, but, unlike the large on-stage floating balloon in which Preston rode, the show did not really take off. Much more satisfying was I Do! I Do!, a two-hander with Mary Martin for which Preston won another Tony Award. His final Broadway musical appearance came in 1974 with Mack And Mabel, which, despite a splendid Jerry Herman score, only lasted for six weeks. During the 50s and 60s he had continued to make films, and in the 70s and early 80s he appeared in several more, including the musical Mame (1973), with Lucille Ball, and S.O.B. and Victor/Victoria (1982), both with Julie Andrews. He also starred in several television movies, including the highly regarded Finnegan Begin Again, a poignant story of the love of an older man for a young woman played by Mary Tyler Moore. Preston died of lung cancer in 1987, and in the same year was awarded a special posthumous Tony, the Lawrence Langner Memorial Award for Distinguished Lifetime Achievement in the American Theatre.

Previn, André

b. 6 April 1929, Berlin, Germany. After studying music in Berlin and Paris, Previn came to the USA in 1938 when his family emigrated. Resident in Los Angeles, he continued his studies and while still at school worked as a jazz pianist and as an arranger in the film studios. From the mid-40s he made records with some measure of success, but it was in the middle of the following decade that he achieved his greatest renown. The breakthrough came with a series of jazz albums with Shelly Manne, the first of which featured music from the popular show My Fair Lady. Previn recorded with lyricist Dory Langdon, who he later married. The marriage broke-up in 1965 and was controversially chronicled in Dory Previn's later solo recordings. In the 60s Previn continued to divide his time between jazz and studio work but gradually his interest in classical music overtook these other fields. By the 70s he was established as one of the world's leading classical conductors. His term as conductor for the London Symphony Orchestra saw him emerge as a popular personality, which involved him television advertising and making celebrated cameo appearances for light-entertainers such as Morecambe And Wise. He became conductor of the Pittsburg Symphony Orchestra in 1976 and later the London Philharmonic, the Los Angeles Philharmonica. He continues to involve himself in many facets of music throughout the 80s and into the 90s - his most recent project, in 1992, was a jazz album with opera singer Dame Kiri Te Kanawa and jazz bass player Ray Brown.
Selected albums: Previn At Sunset (1945), André Previn All-Stars (1946), André Previn Plays Fats Waller (1953), Let's Get Away From It All (1955), But Beautiful (1956), with Shelly Manne My Fair Lady i (1956), André Previn And His Friends: Li'l Abner (1957), André And Dory Previn (1957), Double Play (1957), Pal Joey (1957), Gigi (1958), Sessions, Live (1958), André Previn Plays Songs By Vernon Duke (1958), King Size (1958), André Previn Plays Songs By Jerome Kern (1959), West Side Story (1959), with the David Rose Orchestra Secret Songs For Young Lovers (1959), The Previn Scene (c.1959), Composer, Arranger, Conductor, Pianist (60s),

The Magic Moods Of André Previn (60s), *Like Love* (1960), *André Previn Plays Harold Arlen* (1961), *André Previn* (1960), *Give My Regards To Broadway* (1960), *Thinking Of You* (1960), *Music From Camelot* (1960), *A Touch Of Elegance* (1961), *André Previn And J.J. Johnson Play Mack The Knife And Bilbao Song* (1961), *André Previn And J.J. Johnson* (c.1962), *Two For The See-saw* (c.1962), *Sittin' On A Rainbow* (1962), *The Light Fantastic: A Tribute To Fred Astaire* (c.1963), *4 To Go!* (1963), *André Previn In Hollywood* (1963), *Soft And Swinging* (1964), *Sound Stage* (1964), *My Fair Lady* ii (1964), *Previn At Sunset* (1975), with Itzhak Perlman *A Different Kind Of Blues* (1981), with Perlman *It's A Breeze* (c.1981).

Further reading: *André Previn*, Michael Freedland. *Music Face To Face*, André Previn. *Orchestra*, André Previn. *André Previn's Guide To The Orchestra*, André Previn. *No Minor Chords: My Days In Hollywood*, André Previn.

Q

Queen Of Hearts

After the successful teaming of handsome Old Etonian John Loder with the far more down-to-earth Gracie Fields in *Love Life And Laughter* (1933) and *Sing As We Go* (1934), producer Basil Dean brought them together again for this Associated Talking Pictures release which eager British audiences enjoyed in 1936. Early in the film there is a famous scene in which seamstress Grace Perkins (Fields) pursues the famous (inebriated) actor Derek Cooper (Loder) for his autograph, and gets involved in a hair-raising car drive through London streets, during which she is thrown 'from the running board into the dicky seat'. Next day, at the theatre where Cooper is appearing in *Queen Of Hearts*, Grace is mistaken for the wealthy Mrs. Vandeleur who has promised to invest money in the show if she can have a small part in it. The ensuing events are even more complicated than usual, with Grace appearing as La Perkinosa (she has to do an apachè dance), and the whole thing ending with a wild police chase through the theatre, after which Derek takes Grace into his own personal custody. At intervals amid the chaos, Fields managed to sing three appealing ballads, 'My First Love Song', 'Why Did I Have To Meet You?', 'Queen Of Hearts', and the amusing 'One Of The Little Orphans Of The Storm'. A strong supporting cast included Enid Stamp-Taylor,

Fred Duprez, Jean Lister, Edward Rigby, Julie Suedo, Jean Lister, Hal Gordon, Madelaine Seymour, Syd Crossley, Tom Payne, and Vera Hilliard. Monty Banks, who subsequently married Gracie Fields, had a small role, and he also directed the picture. The screenplay was written by Anthony Kimmins, Douglas Furber and Gordon Wellesley. It was another box-office success for Our Gracie, the most popular British entertainer of her time.

R

Rainger, Ralph

b. 7 October 1901, New York City, New York, USA, d. 23 October 1942. After studying classical music as a child Rainger won a scholarship to New York's Institute of Musical Art. Despite his academic success and enthusiasm, his family disapproved and persuaded him to study law. By the mid-20s, however, he had become a professional pianist, playing in dance and jazz bands. He was also in several pit orchestras in Broadway theatres and worked briefly with Paul Whiteman. While playing in a revue, *Little Show*, in 1929, Rainger wrote 'Moanin' Low' (lyrics by Howard Dietz), which was sung in the show by Libby Holman. After the success of this song, Rainger and Dietz continued their collaboration with 'Got A Man On My Mind' and 'I'll Take An Option On You', and Rainger also wrote 'Breakfast Dance' (lyrics by Edward Eliscu). In the early 30s Rainger was drawn to Hollywood, where he wrote 'When A Woman Loves A Man' (lyrics by Billy Rose) and began a fruitful collaboration with Leo Robin. Many of their joint efforts were sung by Bing Crosby, among them 'Please', 'Love In Bloom', 'June In January', 'With Every Breath I Take' and 'Blue Hawaii'. The team's 'Thanks For The Memory' won the Oscar after it was sung by Bob Hope and Shirley Ross in *Big Broadcast Of 1938*. Robin and Rainger's film work included *The Big Broadcast* (1932), *Little Miss Marker, She Loves Me Not, Here Is My Heart, The Big Broadcast Of 1937, Palm Springs, Three Cheers For Love, Rhythm On The Range, College Holiday, Waikiki Wedding, Ebb Tide, Artists And Models, Give Me A Sailor, Paris Honeymoon, Moon Over Miami, Tall, Dark And Handsome, My Gal Sal, Footlight Serenade, Coney Island*, and *Riding High* (1943). Rainger was killed in a flying accident in October 1942 shortly before the last film waas released.

Raise The Roof

This is reputed to be the first British musical comedy film - as opposed to the revue-style *Elstree Calling* which was simply a collection of songs and sketches not linked by a story; both features were released in 1930 by British International Pictures. Walter Summers and Philip MacDonald's simple screenplay concerns Rodney Langford (Maurice Evans) whose ambitions to enter show business are realised when he becomes the owner of an unsuccessful touring company. One of its members, Maisie Gray (Betty Balfour), is on his side from the start, but his parents (played by Sam Livesey and Ellis Jeffreys) are totally opposed to this new venture. Their efforts to ruin the show with the assistance of the company's corrupt leading man, Atherley Armitage (Jack Raine), fail miserably and inspire the company to even greater success. On the opening night, Rodney is reconciled with his father, and he and Maisie embark on their own (personal) long-running partnership. The attractive and tuneful score was complemented by a supporting cast which included Arthur Hardy, Louie Emery, the Plaza Tiller Girls, and specialities Dorothy Minto and Malandrinos, and Josephine Earle. Betty Balfour, who enjoyed a successful career as a comedienne in 20s silent films, proved to be a pleasing singer and dancer, and had one of the best numbers, 'I'm Trembling On The Brink Of Love'. The director, Walter Summers, also worked on silents, and he went on to write and direct the unconventional and highly acclaimed *The Return Of Bulldog Drummond*, starring Ralph Richardson.

Raksin, David

b. 4 August 1912, Philadelphia, Pennsylvania, USA. A composer, lyricist, and arranger for film background music, whose career lasted for over 50 years. Raksin was originally taught to play the clarinet by his father, and, after further studying at Pennsylvania University, where he was a soloist with the band, he performed and arranged for society outfits, and on the radio station WCAU. After further stints as a sideman-arranger with New York bands, and a spell with Harms Publishing House in the early 30s, he broke into the movie business in 1936 when he arranged Charlie Chaplin's music for *Modern Times*. In the late 30s and early 40s, he worked on several films as co-composer, including *San Quentin*, *Suez*, *Hollywood Cavalcade*, *Stanley And Livingstone*, *The Magnificent Dope* and *The Undying Monster*, and had a few solo credits such as *The Man In Her L:ife* and *Tampico*. In 1944, Raksin's score for Otto Preminger's highly acclaimed murder mystery *Laura* included the haunting title theme, which, complete with a later lyric by Johnny Mercer, became popular for Dick Haymes, Johnnie Johnston and Freddie Martin, among others, and endured as an all-time standard. Raksin's other 40s film music included another

Preminger project *Fallen Angel* (1945) (which included 'Slowly', a hit for Kay Kyser), and *Where Do We Go From Here?*, *Smoky*, *The Shocking Miss Pilgrim*, *The Secret Life Of Walter Mitty*, *Apartment For Peggy*, *Force Of Evil* and *Forever Amber* (1947), for which Raksin was nominated for an Academy Award. Johnny Mercer again added words to Raksin's title theme. In the 50s and 60s Raksin scored movies with a wide variety of themes, such as courtroom dramas (*The Magnificent Yankee* and *Until They Sail*), boxing (*Right Cross*), Sinatra as an assassin (*Suddenly*), gangsters galore (*Al Capone* and *Pay Or Die*), Westerns (*Invitation To A Gunfighter*), a Jerry Lewis comedy (*The Patsy*), and others such as *The Girl In White*, *Carrie*, *Seven Wonders Of The World* (Cinerama), *Love Has Many Faces*, including some of the most highly acclaimed productions of their time, such as *The Bad And The Beautiful*, (containing 'Love Is For The Very Young' with Dory Previn), *Two Weeks In Another Town*, *Sylvia*, *A Big Hand For The Little Lady*, *Will Penny* and *Separate Tables* for which Raksin won another Oscar nomination. In 1962 Raksin contributed a jazz-oriented score to *Too Late Blues*, in which John Cassavetes made his Hollywood debut. It featured musicians such as Benny Carter, Shelly Manne and Red Mitchell, and numbers like 'Sax Raises Its Ugly Head' and 'Benny Splits, While Jimmy Rowles'. In the 70s and 80s, apart from occasional feature films such as *What's The Matter With Helen?* and *Glass Houses*, Raksin worked more and more in television on such as *The Over-The Hill Gang Rides Again*, *The Ghost Of Flight 401*, *The Day After* and *Lady In A Corner*. His earlier work for the small screen had included music for *Ben Casey* and *The Breaking Point*. He also scored several movie cartoons including *Sloppy Jaloppy*, *Madeline*, *Giddyap* and *The Unicorn In The Garden*, and wrote several serious works.

Rat Race, The

Better than its original reception suggests, this downbeat tale of a jazz musician and his dancehall girl has a quirky charm. Directed by Robert Mulligan and staring Tony Curtis and Debbie Reynolds, this 1960 film was based upon the stage play by Garson Kanin who also wrote the screenplay. In the forefront of the jazz musicians taking part is Gerry Mulligan.

Raye, Don

b. Donald McRae Wilhoite Jnr., 16 March 1909, Washington, D.C., USA, d. January 1985. Raye was an accomplished dancer as a boy, and won the Virginia State Dancing Championship. From the mid-20s he worked as a singer and dancer in Vaudeville and, later, toured theatres and nightclubs in France and England, while also writing songs for himself and other performers. In 1935 he collaborated with Sammy Cahn, Saul Chaplin and band leader Jimmie Lunceford on 'Rhythm In My Nursery Rhymes' and, in the late 30s, worked for a New York music publishing house. After moving to Hollywood in 1940, Raye was commissioned to write the songs for *Argentine Nights*, in which the Andrews Sisters made their screen debut. Together with Hughie Prince and the Sisters' arranger Vic Schoen, Raye wrote 'Hit The Road' and 'Oh! How He Loves Me'. With Prince, he produced 'Rhumboogie', the first of a series of 'boogie woogie' numbers, several of which became hits for the Andrews Sisters, pianist Freddie Slack, and Will Bradley And His Orchestra. Raye and Prince's next assignment was *Buck Privates*, which also featured the Andrews Sisters, and rocketed the comedy duo, Abbott And Costello to movie stardom. The songs included 'You're A Lucky Fellow, Mr Smith', 'Bounce Me Brother With A Solid Four' and 'Boogie Woogie Bugle Boy From Company B', which was nominated for an Academy Award, and revived successfully in 1973 by Bette Midler. Raye's other boogie ballads included 'Beat Me Daddy (Eight To The Bar)', 'Rock-A-Bye The Boogie', 'Down The Road A Piece' and 'Scrub Me, Mamma, With A Boogie Beat'. His long partnership with Gene De Paul followed, in which they collaborated on songs for the 1941 films *In The Navy*, *San Antonio Rose*, *Moonlight In Hawaii* and *Keep 'Em Flying*; in 1942, *Hellzapoppin'*, *What's Cookin'*, *Ride 'Em Cowboy*, *Almost Married*, *Pardon My Sarong* and *Behind The Eight Ball*; in 1943, *When Johnny Comes Marching Home* and *Hi Buddy*, *Reveille With Beverly*, *What's Buzzin' Cousin?*, *Larceny With Music*, *Crazy House* and *I Dood It*; in 1944, *Hi Good Lookin'* and *Stars On Parade*. They also enjoyed success with 'Who's That In Your Love Life?', 'Irresistible You' and 'Solid Potato Salad'. 'Milkman, Keep Those Bottles Quiet' (from *Broadway Rhythm*). Towards the end of World War II, De Paul spent two years in the Armed Forces. He and Don Raye resumed writing their movie songs in 1947 with 'Who Knows?' for *Wake Up And Dream* and 'Judaline' for *A Date With Judy*. In 1948 they contributed to *A Song Is Born* and also wrote 'It's Whatcha Do With Whatcha Got' for the Walt Disney live-action feature, *So Dear To My Heart*. De Paul and Raye's last film work together was in 1949, for another Disney project, the highly acclaimed cartoon, *The Adventures Of Ichabod And Mr Toad*. During the period working with De Paul, Raye also collaborated with others writers on 'Yodelin' Jive', 'Why Begin Again?', 'This Is My Country', 'I Love You Too Much', 'Music Makers', 'The House Of Blue Lights', 'Your Home Is In My Arms', 'Domino', 'They Were Doin' The Mambo' (a US hit for Vaughn Monroe), 'Roses And Revolvers', 'I'm Looking Out The Window' and 'Too Little Time'. After the mid-50s, Raye only wrote occasionally, although his 'Well, All Right', written with Frances Faye and Dan Howell, and a hit in 1959 for the Andrews Sisters, was interpolated into the 1978 bio-pic, *The Buddy Holly Story*.

Red Shoes, The

One of the most outstanding films in the history of the British cinema. *The Red Shoes*, which was produced and directed by Michael Powell and Emeric Pressburger, was released in 1948 to worldwide acclaim. Pressburger also wrote the screenplay which was based on a story by Hans Christian Andersen. It told the tragic and romantic tale of Vicky Page (Moira Shearer in her film debut), a gifted young dancer who is forced by the Svengali-like impresario, Boris Lermontov (Anton Walbrook), to choose between a glittering career in the ballet and her love for the brilliant composer Julian Craster (Marius Goring). After enjoying spectacular success in *The Red Shoes* ballet, Vicky assures Lermontov that dancing will be the sole purpose of her life. However, her conceptions change as soon as she falls in love with the ballet's composer. When Lermontov discovers their liaison, Julian is immediately dismissed from the company, and, despite the impresario's protestations, Vicky goes with him. Some time later, still intoxicated by glamour of the theatre, she returns to dance *The Red Shoes* ballet once more. She is still torn between going on stage or re-joining Julian, but the shoes themselves seem to take control and they whisk her out of the theatre where she falls to her death under the wheels of a passing train. Opinions in the film world are divided as to whether she committed suicide. Robert Helpmann plays Boleslawsy, the company's leading dancer, and he was also responsible for the film's outstanding choreography which was so skilfully integrated into the story. The part of the shoemaker was created and danced by Leonide Massine, and the remainder of the fine supporting cast included Albert Basserman, Ludmilla Tcherina, Esmond Knight, Irene Browne, Austin Trevor, Jerry Verno, Marcel Poncin, and Hay Petrie. Brian Easdale, who first came to prominence for his work on GPO film shorts, composed, arranged and conducted the music, which was played by the Royal Philharmonic Orchestra. Sir Thomas Beecham conducted the orchestra for *The Red Shoes* ballet. Easdale won an Academy Award for his memorable score, and other Oscars went to Hein Heckroth and Arthur Lawson for colour art direction-set direction. The film was also nominated for best picture, story, and film editing, although not, strangely, for Jack Cardiff's stunning Technicolor photography. This exquisite and thrilling picture, which has inspired so many young people over the years with its revealing glimpse of the backstage world of ballet, is still viewed with a mixture of awe and admiration to this day. Not so the Broadway musical which was based on the film and Hans Christian Andersen's original story. It opened on 16 December 1993, and closed three days later, losing a reported $8 million.

Reveille With Beverley

Reveille With Beverley

Fluffy but engaging war-time musical, made in 1943, about a radio station DJ, Ann Miller, who plays swing music for the boys in local army camps. Several leading musicians of the era appear including the orchestras of Count Basie, Bob Crosby and Duke Ellington. Amongst the singers on hand are the Mills Brothers, Ella Mae Morse, Betty Roché and Frank Sinatra.

Revel, Harry

b. 21 December 1905, London, England, d. 3 November 1958, New York City, New York, USA. An important composer, mostly remembered for the series of appealing songs that he and his chief collaborator Mack Gordon contributed to movie musicals of the 30s. After demonstrating a remarkable ability on the piano as a young child, Revel studied at the Guildhall School of Music and seemed destined for a career as a classical musician. Instead, he went to Europe at the age of 15 and toured with dance orchestras, later composing light and operatic music. In 1929 he moved to America where he met vaudevillian Mack Gordon, and in the early 30s they contributed some songs to mostly unsuccessful Broadway shows such as *Fast And Furious* (with Harold Adamson), the 1931 *Ziegfeld Follies* (with Harry Richman), *Everybody's Welcome*, *Marching By*, and *Smiling Faces*. In 1932 Joe Rines, Don Redman, Chick Bullock and Fletcher Henderson all had hits with Revel and Gordon's 'Underneath The Harlem Moon', and in the following year they wrote the score for their first movie, *Broadway Thru A Keyhole*. This was followed during the remainder of the 30s by scores or single songs for a string of mostly entertaining features which included *Sitting Pretty*, *We're Not Dressing*, *Shoot The Works*, *She Loves Me Not*, *The Gay Divorcee*, *College Rhythm*, *Love In Bloom*, *Paris In The Spring*, *Two For Tonight*, *Stowaway*, *Collegiate*, *Poor Little Rich Girl*, *You Can't Have Everything*, *Head Over Heels In Love*, *Wake Up And Live*, *Thin Ice*, *Ali Baba Goes To Town*, *My Lucky Star*, *Rebecca Of Sunnybrook Farm*, *Sally, Irene And Mary*, *In Old Chicago*, *Thanks For Everything*, *Josette*, *Tailspin*, *Love Finds Andy Hardy*, *Love And Hisses*, and *Rose Of Washington Square* (1939). From out of those pictures came popular numbers such as 'Did You Ever See A Dream Walking?', 'Good Morning Glory', 'You're Such A Comfort To Me', 'It Was A Night In June', 'May I?', 'Love Thy Neighbour', 'She Reminds Me Of You', 'With My Eyes Wide Open, I'm Dreaming', 'Don't Let It Bother You', 'Stay As Sweet As You Are', 'My Heart Is An Open Book', 'Here Comes Cookie', 'Without A Word Of Warning', 'I Feel Like A Feather In The Breeze', 'When I'm With You', 'Oh, My Goodness', 'Goodnight, My Love',

'One Never Knows, Does One?', 'Never In A Million Years', 'There's A Lull In My Life', 'You Can't Have Ev'rything', 'An Old Straw Hat', 'I've Got A Date With A Dream', 'Meet The Beat Of My Heart', 'It Never Rains But It Pours', and 'I Never Knew Heaven Could Speak'. After working on *The Rains Came* in 1939, the team split up and Gordon went off to write with Harry Warren. Revel worked in an administrative capacity for US Forces entertainment units during World War II and continued to write film songs in the 40s, mostly with lyricist Mort Greene, although he was unable to match his previous success. He provided several numbers, including 'You Go Your Way (And I'll Go Crazy)' and 'I'm In Good Shape (For The Shape I'm In)', for the Ray Bolger picture *Four Jills And A Jeep*, and also worked on *Call Out The Marines, Joan Of Arzak, Midnight Masquerade, Hit The Ice, The Dolly Sisters, I'll Tell The World, It Happened On Fifth Avenue*, and *The Stork Club*. Two of Revel and Greene's songs, 'There's A Breeze On Lake Louise' (from *The Mayor Of Forty-Fourth Street*) and 'Remember Me To Carolina' (from *Minstrel Man*) were nominated for Oscars. There were no awards for Revel and Arnold B. Horwitt's score for the 1945 Broadway show *Are You With It?*, but it enjoyed a reasonable run. Revel's other collaborators included Paul Francis Webster, and Bennie Benjamin and George Weiss with whom he wrote one of his last songs, 'Jet', in 1951. It became a modest hit for Nat 'King' Cole.

Further reading: *Meet The Musikids-They Wrote Your Songs*, Harry Revel.

Reynolds, Debbie

b. Mary Frances Reynolds, 1 April 1932, El Paso, Texas, USA. After moving to California in 1940 she became a majorette and played French horn with the Burbank Youth Orchestra. It was here she was spotted by talent scouts at a Miss Burbank competition in 1948. She quickly became a leading light in film musicals such as *The Daughter Of Rosie O'Grady* (1950), *Three Little Words, Singing In The Rain* (one of her most memorable roles), *Skirts Ahoy, Give A Girl A Break, Hit The Deck, The Tender Trap, Bundle Of Joy, Meet Me In Las Vegas, Say One For Me*, and *The Unsinkable Molly Brown* (1964 Oscar nomination). In 1951 she recorded her first million-selling single 'Aba Daba Honeymoon' (from the film *Two Weeks With Love*) on which she duetted with Carleton Carpenter. She also went to the top of the US charts in 1957 with million-selling 'Tammy' (from *Tammy And The Bachelor*). She married the singer and actor Eddie Fisher in September 1955, and their daughter Carrie became an established actor and writer. They divorced in 1959 when Fisher married Elizabeth Taylor. In

Rhapsody In Blue

1966 Reynolds returned to play *The Singing Nun* (a fictionalized story about Soeur Sourire) on film, before appearing in her own television series *Debbie* in 1969. She later became a successful comedienne and produced her own keep fit videos.

Albums: *The Singing Nun* (1966), *Debbie* (1985).

Further reading: *Debbie - My Life*, Debbie Reynolds with David Patrick Columba.

Rhapsody In Blue

Yet another film biography which bears little resemblance to reality. Fortunately, in this case the subject is composer George Gershwin and so the music more than makes up for the inadequacies and fantasies of the screenplay. Robert Alda, the well-known Broadway and radio actor, made his film debut as Gershwin, and Joan Leslie and Alexis Smith played two of the important women in his life. Leslie, whose singing voice was dubbed by Louanne Hogan, handled several songs in the predictably glorious score which included 'Fascinating Rhythm', 'I Got Rhythm', 'Love Walked In', 'Embraceable You', 'An American In Paris', 'Someone To Watch Over Me', 'Mine', 'The Man I Love', 'Oh, Lady, Be Good', 'Bidin' My Time', and 'Clap Yo' Hands' (all with lyrics by Ira Gershwin); and 'Summertime' (Du Bose Heyward), 'Swanee' (Irving Caesar), 'Somebody Loves Me' (Buddy De Sylva-Ballard Macdonald), 'Do It Again' (DeSylva), and 'I'll Build A Stairway To Paradise' (DeSylva-Ira Gershwin). Oscar Levant played the celebrated 'Concerto In F' and 'The Rhapsody In Blue' (conducted by Paul Whiteman), and among the other artists who appeared as themselves were Al Jolson, Hazel Scott, George White and Anne Brown. Rosemary DeCamp and Morris Carnovsky played Gershwin's mother and father, and other roles were taken by Charles Coburn (as music publisher Max Dreyfuss), Albert Basserman, Julie Bishop, Herbert Rudley, Mickey Roth, Darryl Hickman, Johnny Downs, Tom Patricola, Stephen Richard, Martin Noble, and Will Wright. Howard Koch and Elliot Paul dreamed up the screenplay, and LeRoy Prinz was responsible for the choreography which, like the rest of the picture, benefited from some fine black and white photography by Sol Polito. Irving Rapper was the director, and *Rhapsody In Blue*, which was produced for Warner Brothers in 1945 by Jesse L. Lasky, still retains its appeal to this day.

Richard, Cliff

b. Harry Roger Webb, 14 October 1940, Lucklow, India. One of the most popular and enduring talents in the history of UK showbusiness, Richard began his career as a rock 'n' roll performer in 1957. His fascination for Elvis Presley encouraged him to join a skiffle group and several months later he teamed up with drummer Terry Smart and guitarist Ken Payne to form the Drifters. They played at various clubs in the Cheshunt/Hoddesdon area of Hertfordshire before descending on the famous 2Is coffee bar in London's Old Compton Street. There they were approached by lead guitarist Ian Samwell and developed their act as a quartet. In 1958, they secured their big break in the unlikely setting of a Saturday morning talent show at the Gaumont cinema in Shepherd's Bush. It was there that the senatorial theatrical agent George Ganyou recognized Cliff's sexual appeal and singing abilities and duly financed the recording of a demonstration tape of 'Breathless' and 'Lawdy Miss Clawdy'. A copy reached the hands of EMI producer Norrie Paramor who was impressed enough to grant the ensemble an audition. Initially, he intended to record Richard as a solo artist backed by an orchestra, but the persuasive performer insisted upon retaining his own backing group. With the assistance of a couple of session musicians, the unit recorded the American teen ballad 'Schoolboy Crush' as a projected first single. An acetate of the recording was paraded around Tin Pan Alley and came to the attention of the influential television producer Jack Good. It was not the juvenile 'Schoolboy Crush' which captured his attention, however, but the Ian Samwell b-side 'Move It'. Good reacted with characteristically manic enthusiasm when he heard the disc, rightly recognizing that it sounded like nothing else in the history of UK pop. The distinctive riff and unaffected vocal seemed authentically American, completely at odds with the mannered material that usually emanated from British recording studios. With Good's ceaseless promotion, which included a full-page review in the music paper *Disc*, Cliff's debut was eagerly anticipated and swiftly rose to number 2 in the UK charts. Meanwhile, the star made his debut on Good's television showcase *Oh Boy!*, and rapidly replaced Marty Wilde as Britain's premier rock 'n' roll talent. The low-key role offered to the Drifters persuaded Samwell to leave the group to become a professional songwriter, and by the end of 1958 a new line-up emerged featuring Hank B. Marvin and Bruce Welch. Before long, they changed their name to the Shadows, in order to avoid confusion with the black American R&B group, the Drifters.

Meanwhile, Richard consolidated his position in the rock 'n' roll pantheon, even outraging critics in true Elvis Presley fashion. The *New Musical Express* denounced his 'violent, hip-swinging' and 'crude exhibitionism' and pontificated: 'Tommy Steele became Britain's teenage idol without resorting to this form of indecent, short-sighted vulgarity'. Critical mortification had little effect on the screaming female fans who responded to the singer's boyish sexuality with increasing intensity.

1959 was a decisive year for Richard and a firm indicator of his longevity as a performer. With management shake-ups, shifts in national musical taste and some distinctly average singles his career could easily have been curtailed, but instead he matured and transcended his Presley-like beginnings. A recording of Lionel Bart's 'Living Doll' provided him with a massive UK number 1 and three months later he returned to the top with the plaintive 'Travellin' Light'. He also starred in two films, within 12 months. *Serious Charge*, a non-musical drama, was banned in some areas as it dealt with the controversial subject of homosexual blackmail. The Wolf Mankowitz directed *Expresso Bongo*, in which Richard played the delightfully named Bongo Herbert, was a cinematic pop landmark, brilliantly evoking the rapacious world of Tin Pan Alley. It remains one of the most revealing and humorous films ever made on the music business and proved an interesting vehicle for Richard's varied talents.

From 1960 onwards Richard's career progressed along more traditional lines leading to acceptance as a middle-of-the-road entertainer. Varied hits such as the breezy, chart-topping 'Please Don't Tease', the rock 'n' rolling 'Nine Times Out Of Ten' and reflective 'Theme For A Dream' demonstrated his range, and in 1962 he hit a new peak with 'The Young Ones'. A glorious pop anthem to youth, with some striking guitar work from Hank Marvin, the song proved one of his most memorable number 1 hits. The film of the same name was a charming period piece, with a strong cast and fine score. It broke box office records and spawned a series of similar movies from its star, who was clearly following Elvis Presley's cinematic excursions as a means of extending his audience. Unlike the King, however, Richard supplemented his frequent movie commitments with tours, summer seasons, regular television slots and even pantomime appearances. The run of UK Top 10 hits continued uninterrupted until as late as mid-1965. Although the showbiz glitz had brought a certain aural homogeneity to the material, the catchiness of songs like 'Bachelor Boy', 'Summer Holiday', 'On The Beach' and 'I Could Easily Fall' was undeniable. These were neatly, if predictably, complemented by ballad releases such as 'Constantly', 'The Twelfth Of Never' and 'The Minute You're Gone'.

The formula looked likely to be rendered redundant by the British beat boom, but Richard expertly rode that wave, even improving his selection of material along the way. He bravely, though relatively unsuccessfully, covered a Rolling Stones song, 'Blue Turns To Grey', before again hitting top form with the beautifully melodic 'Visions'. During 1966, he had almost retired after converting to fundamentalist Christianity, but elected to use his singing career as a positive expression of his faith. The sparkling 'In The Country' and gorgeously evocative 'The Day I Met Marie' displayed the old strengths to the full, but in the swiftly changing cultural climate of the late 60s, Richard's hold on the pop charts could no longer be guaranteed. The 1968 Eurovision Song Contest offered him a chance of further glory, but the jury placed him a close second with the 'oom-pah-pah'-sounding 'Congratulations'. The song was nevertheless a consummate Eurovision performance and proved one of the biggest UK number 1s of the year. Immediately thereafter, Cliff's chart progress declined and his choice of material proved at best desultory. Although there were a couple of solid entries, Raymond Froggatt's 'Big Ship' and a superb duet with Hank Marvin 'Throw Down A Line', Richard seemed a likely contender for Variety as the decade closed.

The first half of the 70s saw him in a musical rut. The chirpy but insubstantial 'Goodbye Sam, Hello Samantha' was a Top 10 hit in 1970 and heralded a notable decline. A second shot at the Eurovision Song Contest with 'Power To All Our Friends' brought his only other Top 10 success of the period and it was widely assumed that his chart career was spent. However, in 1976 there was a surprise resurgence in his career when Bruce Welch of the Shadows was assigned to produce his colleague. The sessions resulted in the best-selling album *I'm Nearly Famous*, which included two major hits 'Miss You Nights' and 'Devil Woman'. The latter was notable for its decidedly un-Christian imagery and the fact that it gave Richard a rare US chart success. Although Welch remained at the controls for two more albums, time again looked as though it would kill off Richard's perennial chart success. A string of meagre singles culminated in the dull 'Green Light' which stalled at number 57, his lowest chart placing since he started singing. Coincidentally, his backing musicians, Terry Britten and Alan Tarney, had moved into songwriting and production at this point and encouraged him to adopt a more contemporary sound on the album *Rock 'N' Roll Juvenile*. The most startling breakthrough however was the attendant single 'We Don't Talk Anymore', written by Tarney and produced by Welch. An exceptional pop record, which gave the singer his first UK number 1 hit in over a decade and also reached the Top 10 in the US. The 'new' Richard sound, so refreshing after some of his staid offerings in the late 70s, brought further well arranged hits, such as 'Carrie' and 'Wired For Sound', and ensured that he was a chart regular throughout the 80s.

Although he resisted the temptation to try anything radical, there were subtle changes in his musical approach. One feature of his talent that emerged during the 80s was a remarkable facility as a duettist. Collaborations with Olivia Newton-John, Phil Everly, Sarah Brightman, Sheila Walsh, Elton John and Van Morrison added a completely new dimension to his career. It was something of a belated shock to realize that Richard may be one of the finest harmony singers working in the field of popular music. His perfectly enunciated vocals and the smooth texture of his voice have the power to complement work that he might not usually tackle alone.

The possibility of his collaborating with an artist even further from his sphere than Van Morrison remains a tantalizing challenge. Throughout his three decades in the pop charts, Cliff has displayed a valiant longevity. He parodied one of his earliest hits with comedy quartet the Young Ones and registered yet another number 1; he appeared in the stage musical *Time*; he sang religious songs on gospel tours; he sued the *New Musical Express* for an appallingly libellous review far more vicious than their acerbic comments back in 1958; he was decorated by the Queen; and he celebrated his 50th birthday with a move into social commentary with the anti-war hit 'From A Distance'. And so he goes on. Richard has outlasted every musical trend of the past four decades with a sincerity and commitment that may well be unmatched in his field. He is British pop's most celebrated survivor.

Selected albums: *Cliff* (1959), *Cliff Sings* (1959), *Me And My Shadows* (1960), *Listen To Cliff* (1961), *21 Today* (1961), *The Young Ones* (1961), *32 Minutes And 17 Seconds With Cliff Richard* (1962), *Summer Holiday* (1963), *Cliff's Hit Album* (1963), *When In Spain* (1963), *Wonderful Life* (1964), *Aladdin And His Wonderful Lamp* (1964), *Cliff Richard* (1965), *More Hits By Cliff* (1965), *When In Rome* (1965), *Love Is Forever* (1965), *Kinda Latin* (1966), *Finders Keepers* (1966), *Cinderella* (1967), *Don't Stop Me Now* (1967), *Good News* (1967), *Cliff In Japan* (1968), *Two A Penny* (1968), *Established 1958* (1968), *The Best Of Cliff* (1969), *Sincerely Cliff* (1969), *It'll Be Me* (1969), *Cliff 'Live' At The Talk Of The Town* (1970), *All My Love* (1970), *About That Man* (1970), *Tracks 'N' Grooves* (1970), *His Land* (1970), *Cliff's Hit Album* (1971), *The Cliff Richard Story* (1972), *The Best Of Cliff Volume 2* (1972), *Take Me High* (1973), *Help It Along* (1974), *The 31st Of February Street* (1974), *Everybody Needs Somebody* (1975), *I'm Nearly Famous* (1976), *Cliff Live* (1976), *Every Face Tells A Story* (1977), *Small Corners* (1977), *Green Light* (1978), *Thank You Very Much* (1979), *Rock 'N' Roll Juvenile* (1979), *40 Golden Greats* (1979), *Rock On With Cliff* (1980), *The Cliff Richard Songbook* (1980), *Listen To Cliff* (1980), *I'm No Hero* (1980), *Love Songs* (1981), *Wired For Sound* (1981), *Now You See Me, Now You Don't* (1982), *Dressed For The Occasion* (1983), *Silver* (1983), *Cliff In The 60s* (1984), *Cliff And The Shadows* (1984), *Walking In The Light* (1984), *The Rock Connection* (1984), *Time* (1986), *Hymns And Inspirational Songs* (1986), *Always Guaranteed* (1987), *Private Collection* (1988), *The Album* (1993).

Further reading: *Cliff Richard: The Autobiography*, Steve Turner.

Riddle, Nelson

b. Nelson Smock Riddle, 1 June 1921, Oradell, New Jersey, USA, d. 6 October 1985. After studying piano, Riddle took up the trombone when in his early teens and in the late 30s played in a number of big bands, including those led by Jerry Wald, Charlie Spivak, Tommy Dorsey and Bob Crosby. After a stint in the army, he settled in California and studied arranging with Mario Castelnuovo-Tedesco and conducting with Victor Bay. In the late 40s Riddle joined NBC, but was lured to Capitol Records and registered immediately with a driving arrangement of 'Blacksmith Blues' for Ella Mae Morse. He confirmed his outstanding ability when he began work on records by Nat 'King' Cole, and Frank Sinatra. Among these were some of Cole's most engaging and memorable sides, such as 'Unforgettable', 'Somewhere Along The Way' and 'Ballerina', along with a good many of his best-selling albums. In addition, Riddle usually conducted the orchestra, and his backings can be heard on Sinatra's important early Capitol albums, such as *Songs For Young Lovers*, *Swing Easy*, *Songs For Swingin' Lovers*, *In the Wee Small Hours*, and many other later ones. He also served as musical director on most of the singer's popular television specials To a considerable extent, Riddle's easy swinging charts, with their echoes of the big band music of an earlier era (and the distinctive solos of George Roberts (trombone) and Harry Edison (trumpet)), were of considerable importance in re-establishing Sinatra as a major star of popular music. Riddle also worked extensively with Ella Fitzgerald on such as *Ella Swings Brightly With Nelson*, and the highly acclaimed *Songbook* series. Other artists to benefit from the distinctive Riddle touch were Judy Garland (*Judy*), Rosemary Clooney (*Rosie Solves The Swinging Riddle*), Sammy Davis Jnr., (*That's Entertainment*), Eddie Fisher (*Games That Lovers Play*), Jack Jones (*There's Love*), Peggy Lee (*Jump For Joy*), Dean Martin (*This Time I'm Swinging*), Johnny Mathis, (*I'll Buy You A Star*), Antonio Carlos Jobim (*The Brazilian Mood*), Shirley Bassey (*Let's Face The Music*), Dinah Shore (*Yes Indeed*) and many more. In 1954, Riddle had some success with 'Brother John', adapted from the French song, 'Frere Jacques', and, in the following year his instrumental version of 'Lisbon Antigua' topped the US chart, and he made some fine, non vocal albums too, which contrasted the lush ballads of *The Tender Touch* and *The Joy Of Living* with the up-tempo exuberance of *Hey...Let Yourself Go* and *C'mon...Get Happy*. Although under contract to Capitol at the time, he is usually credited with conducting and arranging another label's *Phil Silvers Swings Bugle Calls For Big Band*, which contained Riddle compositions (with US Army/Sgt. Bilko connotations) such as 'Chow, A Can Of Cow And Thou' and 'The Eagle Screams'. Another unusual record item was *Sing A Song With Riddle*, a set of genuine Riddle arrangements, complete with sheet music and an invitation to the listener to become the featured vocalist. From the mid-50s Riddle was also active in television and feature films; he wrote the theme for the long-running series *Route 66*, and received Oscar nominations for his background scores for movies such as *Li'l Abner, Can-Can, Robin And The Seven Hoods*, and *Paint Your Wagon*, and won an Academy Award in 1974 for his music for *The Great Gatsby*. Some of his other film credits included *The Pajama Game, St. Louis Blues, Merry Andrew* and several Sinatra movies such as *The Joker Is Wild* and *Pal Joey*. After attempting retirement, Riddle made an unexpected and hugely successful comeback in the early 80s, when he recorded three albums with Linda Ronstadt: *What's New, Lush Life*, and *For Sentimental Reasons*. A gentle, self-effacing man, he was in poor heath in his later years, and died in October 1985.

Selected albums: *Oklahoma!* (1955), *Moonglow* (1955), *Lisbon Antigua,* (1956), *Hey...Let Yourself Go!* (1957), *The Tender Touch* (1957), *C'mon...Get Happy!* (1958), *Sea Of Dreams* (1958), *Sing A Song With Riddle* (1959), *The Joy Of Living* (1959), *Love Tide* (1961), *Tenderloin* (1961), *Magic Moments* (1962), *Route 66 And Other Great TV Themes* (1962), *Love Is Just A Game Of Poker* (1962), *British Columbia Suite* (1963), *Bright And The Beautiful* (1967), *Music For Wives & Lovers* (1967), *Riddle Of Today* (1968), *The Today Sound Of Nelson Riddle* (1969), *Nat - An Orchestral Portait* (1969), *Nelson Riddle Conducts The 101 Strings* (1970), *Vivé Legrand!* (1973), *The Look Of Love* (1982), *Romance Fire And Fancy* (1983). Selected compilations: *The Silver Collection* (1985), *The Capitol Years* (1993).

Road To Singapore

The first in the enormously successful Paramount series starring Bing Crosby, Bob Hope and Dorothy Lamour was released in 1940. Frank Butler and Don Hartman's screenplay concerns Josh Mallon (Crosby), the easy-going heir to a shipping fortune, and his buddy, Ace Lannigan (Hope), who decide to get away from it all. After ending up in Singapore, they rescue the lovely Mima (Lamour) from a seedy nightspot in which she has a lighted cigarette removed from her mouth every night by Caesar (Anthony Quinn), her swarthy South American partner. After the usual complications, Lamour chooses Crosby for her romantic partner as she did in all the 'Road' trips, although Hope was in there pitching right up to the final episode in 1962. The main reason for Crosby's continued success with the lady in the sarong may well be that he always had the big love ballad – in this case, 'Too Romantic'. Johnny Burke and Jimmy Monaco wrote that one, along with 'Sweet Potato Piper' and 'Kaigoon', while Burke and the film's director, Victor Schertzinger, contributed 'Captain Custard' and 'The Moon And The Willow Tree'.

The Road To Utopia

LeRoy Prinz handled the choreography, and the producer was Harlan Thompson. The general critical opinion at the time was that this film was nothing special, although it rated highly at the box-office. However, subsequent journeys to *Zanzibar* 1941, *Morocco* 1942, *Utopia* 1945, *Rio* 1947, and *Bali* 1952, were acclaimed for the outrageous laid-back humour and zany antics of the two male stars. Generally cast as a couple of likeable swindlers, with Crosby as the 'brains' and Hope in the role of the incredibly gullible fall guy, they were able to extricate themselves from any scrape simply by facing each other and going into their 'Patta-cake' routine which always ended with one of their captors, or similar adversaries, being knocked to the ground. As well as the fun and games, each of the above films in the series had some good songs by Jimmy Van Heusen and Johnny Burke, an engaging mixture of ballads and lively comedy numbers. Over the years these included 'You Lucky People You', 'It's Always You', 'Birds Of A Feather', 'Road To Morocco', 'Ain't Got A Dime To My Name (Ho-Hum)', 'Constantly', 'Moonlight Becomes You', 'Personality', 'Put It There, Pal', 'But Beautiful', 'You Don't Have To Know The Language', 'Experience', 'The Merry Go Runaround', 'Chicago Style', 'Hoot-Mon', and 'To See You'. After *Road To Bali* there was a gap of 10 years before the trio were reunited for *The Road To Hong Kong* (1962) which was made in England by Melnor Pictures (producer Melvin Frank and director Norman Panama). At the time, Hope and Crosby were both 59, and, in spite of the inclusion of the young and attractive Joan Collins (Lamour still came along for the ride - as herself) and a starry list of guest artists such as Frank Sinatra, Dean Martin, Peter Sellers, David Niven, and Jerry Colonna, it was too much to ask that things would be the same. The magic just was not there any more, and it was obviously the end of the 'Road' - and of an era - although the film did well at the box-office. Even the songs, by Van Heusen and Sammy Cahn, were not in the previous class, but the two veterans did their best with 'Let's Not Be Sensible', 'Teamwork', 'It's The Only Way To Travel', 'We're On The Road To Hong Kong', and 'Warmer Than A Whisper.' No matter, the memories of that historic, much-loved series remain, and bring a smile to the lips even in the 90s.

Roberta

The Fred Astaire and Ginger Rogers bandwagon gathered pace with this 1935 adaptation of another successful Broadway musical. Naturally, the original libretto, which itself was based on Alice Duer Miller's book *Gowns By Roberta*, was tinkered with by screenwriters Jane Murfin, Sam Mintz, Glen Tryon and Allan Scott, but the basic plot remained. This concerned all-American fooballer John Kent (played by Randolph Scott without a horse), who inherits his aunt's Parisian dress salon and falls in love with her assistant, a Russian princess (Irene Dunne). The latter lady was top-billed, but, as usual, Astaire and Rodgers dominated proceedings - in the nicest possible way. Four of Jerome Kern and Otto Harbach's songs from the show were retained: 'Smoke Gets In Your Eyes', 'Let's Begin', 'Yesterdays', and 'I'll Be Hard To Handle' - the latter number being given a new lyric by Bernard Dougall. Three other songs were added: 'Indiana' (written by Ballard MacDonald and James F. Hanley in 1917); the delightful ballad 'Lovely To Look At' (Kern-Dorothy Fields) which was introduced by Irene Dunne and decorated the film's gigantic fashion parade finale; and 'I Won't Dance' (Kern-Fields-Oscar Hammerstein II) - an Astaire *tour de force*. He also served as the film's (uncredited) dance director with Hermes Pan, and this RKO production was directed by Willam A. Seiter. Another version of *Roberta* entitled *Lovely To Look At*, starring Howard Keel and Kathryn Grayson, was released in 1952.

Robin, Leo

b. 6 April 1895, Pittsburgh, Pennsylvania, USA, d. 29 December 1984. After studying law, Robin turned to writing lyrics for songs. In the mid-20s, in collaboration with various composers, he had a number of minor successes including 'Looking Around' (music by Richard Myers) and one major hit with 'Hallelujah' (Vincent Youmans), written for the 1927 show, *Hit The Deck*. After a few uncertain years on Broadway, Robin went to Hollywood where he came into his own. Amongst his songs written for films during the next few years were 'Louise', 'Beyond The Blue Horizon' (both with Richard Whiting), 'My Ideal' (Newell Chase), 'True Blue Lou' (Sam Coslow), 'If I Were King' (Chase and Coslow), 'Prisoner Of Love' (Clarence Gaskill and Russ Columbo), 'Whispers In The Dark' (Frederick Hollander), 'Zing A Little Zong', 'No Love, No Nothin'' (both Harry Warren) and an often-overlooked little gem, written with Jerome Kern, 'In Love In Vain'. Many of Robin's best Hollywood songs were written with composer Ralph Rainger. This collaboration produced 'Please', 'Here Lies Love', 'Give Me Liberty Or Give Me Love', 'June In January', 'With Every Breath I Take', 'Here's Love In Your Eye', 'Blue Hawaii', 'Here You Are' and two songs which became theme songs for two of America's best-known comedians, Jack Benny and Bob Hope, 'Love In Bloom' and 'Thanks For The Memory'. They were featured in pictures such as *The Big Broadcast* (1932), *International House*, *Little Miss Marker*, *Shoot The Works*, *She Loves Me Not*, *Here Is My Heart*, *The Big Broadcast Of 1936*, *The Big Broadcast Of 1937*, *Palm Springs*, *Three Cheers For Love*, *Rhythm On The Range*, *Artists And Models*, *College Holiday*, *St. Louis Blues*, *The Big Broadcast Of 1938*, *Give Me A*

Sailor, Paris Honeymoon, Moon Over Miami, My Gal Sal, Footlight Serenade, and *Coney Island* (1943). After Rainger's death in 1943, Robin collaborated with other composers including Jule Styne, Harry Warren, Arthur Schwartz and Sigmund Romberg. With Styne he wrote the score for the memorable stage musical *Gentlemen Prefer Blondes,* which included songs such as 'Bye Bye, Baby', 'A Little Girl From Little Rock' and 'Diamonds Are A Girl's Best Friend'. He also worked on several films including *The Gang's All Here, Centennial Summer, The Time, The Place And The Girl, Casbah, Meet Me After The Show, Just For You, Latin Lovers,* and *Small Town Girl.* Out of these came notables songs such as 'Paducah', 'The Lady In The Tutti-Frutti Hat', 'Oh, But I Do', 'A Gal In Calico', A Rainy Night In Rio', 'What's Good About Goodbye?', 'It Was Written In The Stars', 'My Flaming Heart', 'Lost In Loveliness', and Love Is The Funniest Thing'.The last two numbers were the result of a partnership with Sigmund Romberg on the stage show *The Girl In Pink Tights* (1954), although the score had to be completed by Don Walker after Romberg's death. In 1982, in sprightly disregard of his age, Robin appeared in New York in a presentation of many of his songs.

Robinson, Bill 'Bojangles'

b. 25 May 1878, Richmond, Virginia, USA, d. 25 November 1949. As a child Robinson worked in racing stables, nursing a desire to become a jockey. He danced for fun and for the entertainment of others, first appearing on stage at the age of eight. Three years later he decided that dancing was likely to prove a more lucrative career than horseback riding. He became popular on the black vaudeville circuit and also appeared in white vaudeville as a 'pick', from pickaninny, where his dancing skills gave a patina of quality to sometimes second-rate white acts. As his reputation grew so did his prominence in showbusiness. In 1921 while working at the Palace in New York, he danced up and down the stairs leading from the stage to the orchestra pit and out of this developed his famous 'stair dance'. Although Robinson was not the first to dance on stairs, he refined the routine until it was one of the most spectacular events in the world of vernacular dance. Towards the end of the decade, though he was now 60-years-old, he was a huge success in the smash-hit production of Lew Leslie's *Blackbirds Of 1928.* In the mid-30s he appeared at nightclubs in revues, musical comedies and other stage shows, amongst which was *The Hot Mikado.* He was so active in these years that he sometimes played different shows in different theatres on the same night. Robinson had no doubts that he was the best at what he did, a self-confidence that some took to be arrogance and which was mixed with a sometimes brooding depression at the fact that, because he was black, he had to wait until he was in

his 60s before he could enjoy the fame and fortune given to less talented white dancers. In fact, he appears to have been a remarkably generous man and in addition to his massive work-load, he never refused to appear at a benefit for those artists who were less successful or ailing. It has been estimated that in one year he appeared in a staggering 400 benefits. In 1930 Robinson had made a film, *Dixiana,* but it was not until he went to Hollywood in the middle of the decade that he made a breakthrough in this medium. He danced in a string of popular films, including some with Shirley Temple. By 1937 Robinson was earning $6,600 a week for his films, a strikingly high sum for a black entertainer in Hollywood at the time. In 1943 he played his first leading role in *Stormy Weather,* an all-black musical in which he starred opposite Lena Horne. Despite being in his early 70s when he made the film he performed his stair dance and even if he was outglossed by the Nicholas Brothers, his was a remarkable performance. In addition to dancing, Robinson also sang in a light, ingratiating manner, memorably recording 'Doing The New Low Down' in 1932 with Don Redman And His orchestra. Although his high salary meant that he was estimated to have earned more than $2 million during his career, Robinson's generosity was such that when he died in November 1949 he was broke. Half a million people lined the funeral route of the man who was known with some justification as the Mayor of Harlem. In 1993, a potential Broadway show entitled *Bojangles,* with a book by Douglas Jones and a score by Charles Strouse and the late Sammy Cahn, was being workshopped in various provincial theatres.

Rodgers, Richard

b. 28 June 1902, Hammells Station, Arverne, Long Island, USA, d. 30 December 1979. Raised in a comfortable middle-class family, Rodgers developed an early love for the musical theatre. He first attempted songwriting at the age of 14 and within two years he had composed several dozen songs. In 1918, a family friend, aware of Rodgers's potential but realizing that he needed a collaborator, introduced him to Lorenz Hart. Together, Rodgers and Hart wrote many songs in their first year as partners, some of which were taken up for current Broadway shows. However, it was not until 1925 and the appearance of 'Manhattan' and 'Sentimental Me', both written for *The Garrick Gaieties,* that the public became aware of this new songwriting team. That same year their first complete Broadway show, *Dearest Enemy,* was staged. Included in this show was 'Here In My Arms'. The following year they brought *The Girl Friend* to Broadway, with hits in the title song and 'Blue Room' and wrote 'Mountain Greenery' and for *Peggy-Ann,* 'A Tree In The Park'. In 1927 came 'Thou Swell' for *A Connecticut Yankee,* a show which also featured 'My Heart Stood Still', a song written originally for an earlier show. In the late 20s and early 30s, although their shows met with only moderate success, the songs from them were exceptional and became independently successful. Among these hit songs were 'You Took Advantage Of Me', 'With A Song In My Heart', 'A Ship Without A Sail', 'Ten Cents A Dance' and 'Dancing On The Ceiling'.

In the early 30s Rodgers and Hart worked together in Hollywood, their songs including 'Isn't It Romantic', 'Love Me Tonight', 'Lover' and 'It's Easy To Remember'. Back on Broadway, in 1935 they wrote *Jumbo*, which included 'My Romance', 'Little Girl Blue' and 'The Most Beautiful Girl In The World'. *On Your Toes* (1936) followed, which included 'There's A Small Hotel', then *Babes In Arms* (1937) with 'Where Or When', 'My Funny Valentine' and 'The Lady Is A Tramp' and *I'd Rather Be Right* (1937), which had 'Have You Met Miss Jones?'. Their two shows of 1938 were *I Married An Angel*, with hits in the title song and 'Spring Is Here', and *The Boys From Syracuse*, which featured 'Falling In Love With Love' and 'This Can't Be Love'. The partnership's song successes continued with 'I Didn't Know What Time It Was', from *Too Many Girls* (1939), 'It Never Entered My Mind', from *Higher And Higher* (1940) and 'Bewitched, Bothered And Bewildered' and 'I Could Write A Book' from *Pal Joey* (1940). Their last show together was *By Jupiter* (1942), from which came 'Careless Rhapsody'. The seamless nature of their work together belied the fact that Rodgers and Hart were very different characters. Unlike Hart, who was undisciplined, casual, unpunctual, unreliable and irresponsible, Rodgers was a dedicated individual who set for himself and maintained strict working habits. Despite the problems he experienced in working with the mercurial Hart, Rodgers was fully aware how much they needed one another and was distressed when, in 1942, Hart indicated that he no longer wished to continue writing.

Fortunately, Rodgers's practical nature took over and he set about finding a new collaborator. He found a kindred spirit in Oscar Hammerstein II. Utterly different, both musically and in his personal characteristics, from Hart, Hammerstein brought to the new partnership an appreciation of an earlier kind of musical show (he was seven years older than Rodgers). Structurally, the shows Rodgers and Hammerstein created owed much to the formalities of operetta, while maintaining a sprightly contemporary approach to music and lyrics. Significantly for the development of the American musical, the songs were integral to the libretto, furthering plot and character development. Their first show together was *Oklahoma!*, which opened on Broadway on 31 March 1943 and ran for 2,248 performances. The songs from the show included 'Oh, What A Beautiful Mornin'', 'The Surrey With A Fringe On Top' and 'People Will Say We're In Love'. Rodgers and Hammerstein

followed the success of *Oklahoma!* by collaborating on a musical film. This was *State Fair* (1945), which featured 'It Might As Well Be Spring', 'That's For Me' and 'It's A Grand Night For Singing'. Before the film was released the pair were already working on a new Broadway show, *Carousel*, which opened in April 1945. The show's 890 performances made it a huge hit helped by such songs as 'If I Loved You', 'June Is Bustin' Out All Over' and 'You'll Never Walk Alone'. The partnership's next Broadway show was strikingly less successful but *Allegro* included some fine songs, among them 'A Fellow Needs A Girl' and 'The Gentleman Is A Dope'. The comparative failure of *Allegro* was probably due to the abstract sets and the unusual staging. If that was the case, then Rodgers and Hammerstein clearly learned from their mistakes, returning to more orthodox ways with their next production. This was *South Pacific* (1949), which ran for almost 2,000 performances and followed the example of *Oklahoma!* by becoming a hugely successful film. The songs from the show included several hits: 'Some Enchanted Evening', 'Younger Than Springtime', 'A Wonderful Guy', 'Bali Ha'i', 'I'm Gonna Wash That Man Right Out Of My Hair' and 'There Is Nothing Like A Dame'. Rodgers and Hammerstein began the 50s with *The King And I*, another major success both on stage and as a film and, like its predecessors, the subject of numerous revivals. Songs included 'Shall We Dance', 'Hello, Young Lovers' and 'We Kiss In The Shadow'.

Other 50s' shows were less successful but there were still good songs to be heard, among them 'No Other Love', from *Me And Juliet*. During this same period Rodgers developed a long-suppressed interest in writing music of a quasi-symphonic kind. Most successful of these ventures were his scores for the television series *Victory At Sea* (1952) and *The Valiant Years* (1960). Another collaboration of Rodgers and Hammerstein, the musical, *Cinderella* (1957), was also for television. In 1958 the pair returned to Broadway with *The Flower Drum Song*, from which came the hit 'I Enjoy Being A Girl'. The following year the partners ended their Broadway career with the opening of one of their greatest successes, *The Sound Of Music*. In addition to the title song the score included 'Do Re Mi', 'Edelweiss', 'My Favourite Things' and 'Climb Ev'ry Mountain'. Hammerstein's death in 1960 was a serious blow to Rodgers and thereafter his work lost some of its sparkle. Nevertheless, he continued to write, creating the score and writing the lyrics for *No Strings* (1962), from which came 'The Sweetest Sounds'. He followed this with collaborations with Stephen Sondheim on *Do I Hear A Waltz ?* (1965) and Martin Charnin on *Two By Two* (1970). Although he continued working into the 70s, Rodgers was by now a sick man. His last shows, *Rex* (1976) and *I Remember Mama* (1979), were box office failures. Rodgers was a marvellously adaptable composer. In his collaboration with Hart, he wrote the music first, to which his partner fitted his sophisticated and witty lyrics. Contrastingly, with Hammerstein, Rodgers wrote the music to suit the completed lyrics, which were necessarily structured to forward the tale being unfolded on stage. Much honoured during the closing years of his life, including a special Tony Award, Rodgers died in December 1979. In 1993, on the 50th anniversary of the birth of his second momentous partnership, a celebratory revue, *A Grand Night For Singing*, which was crammed with Rodgers and Hammerstein's songs, played on Broadway.

Selected album: *Mary Martin Sings Richard Rodgers Plays* (1958).

Further reading: *Musical Stages: His Autobiography*, Richard Rodgers. *Some Enchanted Evening: The Story Of Rodgers And Hammerstein*, J.D. Taylor. *With A Song In His Heart*, David Ewen. *The Rodgers And Hammerstein Story*, Stanley Green. *Rodgers And Hart: Bewitched, Bothered And Bedevilled*, S. Marx and J. Clayton. *The Sound Of Their Music: The Story Of Rodgers And Hammerstein*, Frederick Nolan.

Rogers, Ginger

b. Virginia Katherine McMath, 16 July 1911, Independence, Missouri, USA. A charming and vivacious actress, dancer and singer, best-known for her partnership with Fred Astaire in a series of memorable movie musicals between 1933 and 1949. She grew up in Fort Worth, Texas, and, after winning a Charleston contest at the age of 15, worked in vaudeville for a time before making a big impression in the 1929 Guy Bolton-Bert Kalmar-Harry Ruby Broadway musical *Top Speed*. A year later she played the lovelorn postmistress Molly Gray, introducing George and Ira Gershwin's lovely song 'But Not For Me', in the show *Girl Crazy*. Also in 1930, Rogers made her first feature film, *Young Man Of Manhattan*, which was followed by several others, in which she generally played streetwise blondes (after dying her hair), including *42nd Street* (as Anytime Annie) and *Gold Diggers Of 1933*. That was also the year in which she was teamed with Astaire for the first time in RKO's *Flying Down To Rio*, the first of 10 light-hearted and tuneful musicals which made them the most beloved dance duo in movie history. The films were *The Gay Divorcee*, *Roberta*, *Top Hat*, *Follow The Fleet*, *Swing Time*, *Shall We Dance*, *Carefree*, *The Story Of Vernon And Irene Castle*, and - after a break of 10 years - *The Barkleys Of Broadway* (1949). Even before the two stars went their separate ways in 1939, Ginger Rogers had been playing critically acclaimed dramatic roles in films such as *Stage Door*, and, during the rest of her film career, she continued to excel in both serious and comedy parts, winning the best actress Oscar for her outstanding performance in *Kitty Foyle* (1940). After making her last picture, *Harlow*, in 1964,

she returned to the stage in the following year, taking over the leading role from Carol Channing on Broadway in *Hello, Dolly!*, and subsequently toured with the show. In 1969 she opened at London's Theatre Royal Drury Lane in another Jerry Herman musical, *Mame*, the first time British audiences had been given the opportunity to see the show. On her return to the USA she formed the *Rogue River Revues*, out of which came the *Ginger Rogers Show* which toured major cities in the USA in the late 70s and played two weeks at the London Palladium. In later years she became a fashion and beauty consultant and also spent a good deal of time pursuing her hobby of painting. In 1986 Rogers attempted to block the distribution of Federico Fellini's film *Ginger And Fred*, which told of two small-time entertainers who do an impression of Astaire and Rogers, because 'it depicted the film's dance team as having been lovers'. In real life Ginger Rogers was married five times, first to Jack Pepper with whom she danced for a time in the early days; and then to actor Lew Ayres, US marine Jack Briggs, actor Jacques Bergerac, and finally actor-director-producer William Marshall. In 1993, more than 60 years after she came to prominence when playing Molly in *Girl Crazy*, Ginger Rogers attended a performance of the hit Broadway show, *Crazy For You*, which was adapted from that very same Gershwin show.

Selected albums: *Miss Ginger Rogers* (1978), *20 Golden Greats* (1986), *Curtain Calls* (1988), *Rare Recordings 1930-1972* (1989) *Fred Astaire And Ginger Rogers Story* (1989).

Further reading: *The Fred Astaire And Ginger Rogers Book*, Arlene Croce. *Ginger: My Story* (her autobiography).

Roman Scandals

This Eddie Cantor vehicle, which was produced by Samuel Goldwyn and released by United Artists in 1933, proved to be one the most entertaining of all the comedian's 15 or so films. The screenplay, which was the work of William Anthony McGuire, George Oppenheimer, Nat Perrin, and Arthur Sheekman, cast Cantor as a law-abiding resident of a small town in Oklahoma. Concerned at the level of bribery and corruption all around him, he joins in the political process to try and change things for the better. Most of the film is concerned with a dream in which he is transported back in time to ancient Rome where he discovers what *real* corruption is all about! Cantor ran the full gamut of his energetic, eye-rolling shtick, and director Frank Tuttle managed to manoeuvre his star into blackface (even in ancient Rome), a chariot race, and a scene in which the modesty of a gaggle of gorgeous girls (including the 23-year-old Lucille Ball) is only maintained by their fashionably long tresses. Broadway torch singer Ruth Etting, making her movie debut, introduced the lovely ballad, 'No More

Roman Scandals

Love', and Cantor's high-pitched voice was heard to great effect on Harry Warren and Al Dubin's other songs, 'Keep Young And Beautiful', 'Build A Little Home', and 'Put A Tax On Love' (lyric also with L. Gilbert Wolfe). Also among the cast were Gloria Stuart, David Manners, Edward Arnold, Veree Teasdale, and Alan Mowbray.

Romance On The High Seas

Songwriter Sammy Cahn used to claim much of the credit for bringing band singer Doris Day to the attention of the Warner Brothers studio which led to her feature film debut in this movie released in 1948. Whatever the facts of the case, Day just about stole the film from under the noses of top-billed stars Janis Paige, Jack Carson and Don DeFore. Her light comedy touch was evident right from the start of this slight and corny story about mistaken identities on a luxurious Caribbean cruise. Oscar Levant was in the supporting cast - which is always an encouraging sign - along with S.Z Sakall, Eric Blore, Fortunio Bonanova, William Bakewell, Franklin Pangborn, and guest artists the Page Cavanaugh Trio, Sir Lancelot, the Samba Kings and Avon Long. Jule Styne and that same Sammy Cahn produced an enjoyable score which gave Day two big record hits, 'It's Magic' and 'Put 'Em In A Box, Tie 'Em With A Ribbon', as well

as 'I'm In Love' and 'It's You Or No One'. The rest of the songs were 'Run, Run, Run', 'The Tourist Trade', and 'Cuban Rhapsody' (Levant-Ray Heindorf). The musical numbers were created and directed by Busby Berkeley and the screenplay was written by Philip G. Epstein (with additional dialogue by I.A.L. Diamond) from a story by S. Pondal Rios and Carlos A. Olivari. Michael Curtiz directed this bright, entertaining Technicolor film which was re-titled *It's Magic* for UK distribution.

Romberg, Sigmund

b. 29 July 1887, Nagykanizsa, Hungary, d. 9 November 1951. After formal training as a violinist, Romberg began writing music while in his late teens. Despite these early interests, Romberg's main studies were in engineering and it was not until 1909, after completing a period of service in the Hungarian army, most of which was spent in Vienna, that he decided to make his career in music. Romberg showed a practical streak by recognizing that he would do better away from the Viennese 'hot house', which already contained numerous important composers. He emigrated to the USA, taking up residence in New York City where he found work in a factory, supplementing his income playing piano in restaurants and bars. He graduated to leading an orchestra, which proved very popular but his heart was set on composing for the musical stage. His first show, written in collaboration with lyricist Harold Atteridge, was *The Whirl Of The World*, which opened in 1914, the year in which Romberg became an American citizen. Romberg and Atteridge continued their partnership for several years, creating numerous shows, few of which were especially successful despite starring such leading theatrical personalities as Marilyn Miller, Nora Bayes and Al Jolson. The shows that fared best were *The Blue Paradise* (1915) and *Maytime* (1917); in both Romberg drew upon his musical heritage, writing waltzes in the Viennese manner. This was a practice he revived in 1921 with *Blossom Time*, which told a fanciful version of the life of classical composer Franz Schubert. The score included 'Song Of Love', by far Romberg's most popular song up to this time. Convinced that the operetta was where he was most at ease, Romberg turned increasingly to this form even though he was obliged to write in other contexts to make a living. It was not until 1924 and the opening of *The Student Prince*, that he was able to prove conclusively that he was right in his belief. *The Student Prince*, in which Romberg was joined by lyricist Dorothy Donnelly, included such major song successes as 'Deep In My Heart', 'Serenade', 'Golden Days' and the 'Drinking Song'. With the evidence of this show as his guide, he concentrated on operettas and, despite some failures, soon became America's leading exponent of this type of musical theatre. In 1926 he wrote *The Desert Song* (lyrics by Otto Harbach and Oscar Hammerstein II), from which came 'Blue Heaven', 'One Alone' and the rousing 'Riff Song'. Romberg followed this with *The New Moon* (1928), for which his collaborator was Hammerstein. Both on stage and as a film, in 1930, *The New Moon* was hugely popular, with hit songs in 'Lover, Come Back To Me', 'One Kiss', 'Stouthearted Men' and 'Softly, As In A Morning Sunrise'. Inevitably, Romberg's inclination towards operetta endangered his continuing popularity through the 30s. Changing musical tastes conspired against him, although he still wrote many engaging songs, among them 'When I Grow Too Old To Dream', written with Hammerstein for the 1934 film *The Night Is Young*. In 1935 he adapted to the vogue for musical comedy with *May Wine*, before settling in California to write for films. In the early 40s he was relatively inactive but he made a comeback on Broadway in 1945 with *Up In Central Park*. With lyrics by Dorothy Fields, the show included such songs as 'Close As Pages In A Book' and 'Carousel In The Park'. Despite this show's success, Romberg's subsequent work drifted between operetta and musical comedy and met with little interest from audiences. He died in 1951.

Rooney, Mickey

b. Joe Yule Jnr., 23 September 1920, Brooklyn, New York, USA. A five feet three-high bundle of dynamite - an actor, singer, comedian, dancer, songwriter - and much else. The son of vaudevillian parents, Rooney made his stage debut when he was 18 months old, and was taken to Hollywood by his mother soon afterwards. He got his big break at the age of six when he made the first of over 50 two-reel comedies featuring the comic-strip character Mickey McGuire. For most of the 30s he was cast in mainly minor roles, but received critical acclaim for his performances in *Ah Wilderness!* and as Puck in *A Midsummer Night's Dream* (both 1935). The year 1937 marked the beginning of two important associations for Rooney. In *Thoroughbreds Don't Cry* (1937) he was teamed for the first time with Judy Garland, and he also made *A Family Affair*, the first in a highly successful series of 'Andy Hardy' pictures which continued until 1946. In 1938 he created 'cinema's first punk kid' in *Boys' Town*, with Spencer Tracy. In the same year Garland joined him in one of the Hardy pictures, *Love Finds Andy Hardy*, but their real impact together came in the enormously popular musicals *Babes In Arms* (1939), *Strike Up the Band* (1940), *Babes On Broadway* (1941), and *Girl Crazy* (1943). By then, Rooney was at the peak of his career, topping box-office charts in the US and all over the world. However, after an appearance in *Thousands Cheer*, MGM's tribute to the US Armed Forces - and then a stint in the real thing during World War II - he made only two more musicals, *Summer Holiday* and *Words and Music* (both 1948). After that, for many different reasons, his career declined rapidly, although he turned in fine dramatic performances in several films during the 50s. After filing for bankruptcy in 1962 his life hit rock bottom, but he continued to work in movies, nightclubs, dinner-theatres and on television, and in 1979, after being nominated for an Oscar for his role in the adventure movie *Black Stallion*, made a sensational comeback on Broadway with *Sugar Babies*. This celebration of the golden age of American burlesque with its old song favourites and many examples of classic schtick, was perfect for Rooney, and, with co-star Ann Miller, he toured with the show for several years following its New York run of nearly 1,500 performances, and took it to London in 1988. In 1981 he won an Emmy for the television film *Bill*, and a year later received an Honorary Oscar 'in recognition of his 60 years of versatility in a variety of memorable film performances'. He had received a special Academy Award 44 years earlier, when he and Deanna Durbin had been cited for 'their significant contribution in bringing to the screen the spirit and personification of youth, and as juvenile players setting a high standard of ability and achievement'. He continues to film in the 90s, and is estimated to have made in excess of 200 pictures. In 1990 he returned to

The Rose (Bette Midler)

Broadway and played the role of Will Rogers' father Clem during the final weeks of the musical *The Will Rogers Follies*. He remains an immensely likeable character who has continually bounced back at every stage of adversity. A good deal of the money he earned from his films up until 1965 (estimated box-office taking $3, 000 million - Rooney's share $12 million) went on alimony to ex-wives. He has (to date) been married eight times: ranging from Ava Gardner ('We were both under contract to MGM and I was dressed as Carmen Miranda at the time, so she could hardly refuse'), through Barbara Thomason (she was murdered by her lover), to his present wife for more than 15 years, C&W singer Jan Chamberlain. At the time of writing he is only 73 so much else can be expected of Mickey Rooney, especially if he abides by the US Mickey Rooney Old People's Association's principal motto which is 'Never Retire But Inspire'.
Further reading: *The Nine Lives Of Mickey Rooney*, Arthur Marx. *I.E.* and *Life Is Too Short* (his autobiographies).

Rose, The

Bette Midler's brassy singing style brought her an immediate cult following, but it was several years before she gained a wider audience. Rather than her recordings, this was largely achieved through film roles, although this early venture deftly combines elements of both. Its plot revolves around a singer doomed by self-destructive tendencies, one many compare to rock/blues vocalist Janis Joplin. The melodramatic material is ideally suited to Midler's show-business inclinations, resulting in a set which is as effective in its own right as its is a soundtrack. *The Rose* was Midler's first step towards international acclaim, and the tribute it paid to another artist was highly effective.

Rose Marie

Previously filmed in 1928 as a silent, this MGM adaptation of the highly successful Broadway operetta was released in 1936. Starring Jeanette MacDonald and Nelson Eddy, it came to the screen with a radically revised plot and minus most of the original songs. In the new story, by Frances Goodrich, Albert Hackett, and Alice Duer Miller, MacDonald is a famous Canadian opera star whose brother (James Stewart) is on the run from the law. Nelson Eddy plays the Mountie intent on bringing him to justice which interrupts his romance with MacDonald for a time, but the inevitable happy ending is always just around the bend. As for the score, there were four survivors from the stage show, 'Indian Love Call' and 'Rose Marie' (Rudolph Friml-Oscar Hammerstein II-Otto Harbach), and 'The Mounties' and 'Totem Tom-Tom' (Herbert Stothart-Hammerstein-Harbach). They were joined by several others including 'Just for You' (Friml-Gus Kahn), 'Pardon

Me, Madame' (Stothart-Kahn), 'Some Of These Days' (Shelton Brooks), and 'Dinah' (Sam M. Lewis-Joe Young-Harry Akst). The names of two future film idols also appeared in the credits, Allan Jones, whose marvellous voice was heard in many a screen musical, and the young David Niven who went on to become the epitome of the dashing and debonair Englishman abroad. Other members of the large cast included Reginald Owen, Alan Mowbray, Una O'Connor, Robert Greig, George Regas, and Herman Bing. Chester Hale was the choreographer, and the film was directed by MGM stalwart W.S. Van Dyke. *Rose Marie* was re-made again in 1954 with Howard Keel, Ann Blyth, Fernando Lamas, Bert Lahr, and Marjorie Main. This version was choreographed by Busby Berkeley and directed by Mervyn LeRoy.

Rose Of Washington Square

More than 30 years before Barbra Streisand shot to screen stardom in *Funny Girl* (1968), this unauthorised version of the Fanny Brice story starred Alice Faye and Tyrone Power - and attracted a successful writ for invasion of privacy from the subject herself. As Power goes steadily downhill, eventually ending up in prison, Faye's career goes from strength to strength supported by a great bunch of songs which included 'I Never Knew Heaven Could Speak' (Mack Gordon-Harry Revel), 'The Curse Of An Aching Heart' (Al Piantadosi-Henry Fink), 'I'm Just Wild About Harry' (Noble Sissle-Eubie Blake), 'Rose Of Washington Square' (Ballard MacDonald-James F. Hanley) and 'My Man' (Channing Pollock-Maurice Yvain) - the last two especially associated with Fanny Brice. Although Faye and Power were top-billed, their star status was threatened by Al Jolson, who gave typically dynamic performances of favourites such as 'Toot Toot Tootsie' (Gus Kahn-Ernie Erdman-Ted Fio Rito-Robert A. King), 'California, Here I Come' (Buddy De Sylva-Jolson-Joseph Meyer), and 'Pretty Baby' (Kahn-Egbert Van Alstyne-Tony Jackson). Also in the cast were William Frawley, Hobart Cavanaugh, Joyce Compton, and Louis Prima with his band. The screenplay that caused all the legal problems was by Nunnally Johnson, and Gregory Ratoff directed this thoroughly entertaining film which was released by 20th Century-Fox in 1936.

Rose, David

b. 15 June 1910, London, England, d. 23 August, 1990. Rose was taken to the USA when he was just four-years-old. After leaving the Chicago College of Music at the age of 16, he joined Ted Fio Rito's dance band, and three years later became a pianist/arranger/conductor for NBC Radio. In 1936 he provided the arrangement for Benny Goodman's big hit 'It's Been So Long'. He moved to Hollywood, and in 1938 formed his own orchestra for the Mutual Broadcasting System, and featured on the programme

California Melodies. In the same year Rose married comedienne/singer Martha Raye and backed her on her hit record 'Melancholy Mood'. The marriage was later dissolved, and, after meeting Judy Garland when she was appearing on Bob Hope's radio show, he became the first of her five husbands from 1941 until 1945. During military service in World War II Rose was composer/conductor for the Army/Air Force morale-boosting stage musical *Winged Victory*, which was filmed in 1944. In 1943 he had a big hit with his own composition 'Holiday For Strings' and, a year later, with 'Poinciana (Song Of The Tree)', By the late 40s he was a regular on Red Skelton's radio show, moving with him into television. He later wrote scores and themes for over 20 television series and won Emmy awards for his 14 year stint on *Bonanza*, 10 years with *Little House On The Prairie* and his work on three much-acclaimed Fred Astaire specials, starting with *An Evening With Fred Astaire* in 1959.

Rose began working in movies in 1941 and is credited with scoring 36 films through to the 60s including *Texas Carnival* (1951), *Rich, Young And Pretty* (1951), *Everything I Have Is Yours* (1952), *Operation Petticoat* (1959), *Please Don't Eat The Daisies* (1960) and *Never Too Late* (1965). He received an Oscar nomination for his song 'So In Love', with a lyric by Leo Robin, which was featured in the 1944 Danny Kaye movie *Wonder Man*. His other compositions included 'Our Waltz' and 'Dance Of The Spanish Onion', and a collection of 32 piano solos entitled *Music For Moderns*. After chart success with 'Calypso Melody' in 1957 and his accompaniment for the Connie Francis 1959 hit 'My Happiness', Rose had a worldwide smash hit in 1962 with another of his own tunes, a humorous, satirical and sleazy piece called 'The Stripper', which was naturally included on *The Stripper And Other Fun Songs For The Family*, one of the 50 or so albums he recorded, including the best-selling *Like Young* and *Like Blue*, made with André Previn. Apart from his record, film and television work, Rose was guest conductor with several symphony orchestras. His 'Concerto For Flute And Orchestra' was first played by the Los Angeles Philharmonic Orchestra and later by the Boston Pops. David Rose died in Burbank, California in 1990.

Selected albums: *The Stripper And Other Fun Songs For The Family* (1962), *Like Young, Like Blue* (1974), *In The Still Of The Night* (1976), *Melody Fair* (1977), *Great Orchestras Of The World* (1978), *Very Thought Of You* (1984). Compilation: *16 Original Hits* (1984).

Rosenman, Leonard

b. 7 September 1924, Brooklyn, New York, USA. A composer and arranger for films and television, who only studied music seriously after serving in the US Air Force during World War II. His first film score, *East Of Eden* (1955), was followed in the same year by another James Dean vehicle, *Rebel Without A Cause*. Rosenman's other 50s scores included dramas like *Bombers B-52*, *Edge Of The City*, *The Young Stranger*, *Lafayett Escadrille*, *Pork Chop Hill* and *The Savage Eye*. After providing music for more of the same genre in the 60s, such as *The Rise And Fall Of Legs Diamond*, *The Bramble Bush*, *The Chapman Report*, *A Covenant With Death* and *Hellfighters*, plus essays into science-fiction with *Countdown* and *Fantastic Voyage*, Rosenman received much critical acclaim for his score to *A Man Called Horse* and *Beneath The Planet Of The Apes* (1970). He also scored two 'Apes' sequels. During the 70s Rosenman received two Academy Awards for his adaptation of the scores to *Barry Lyndon* (1975) and *Bound For Glory* (1976). Rosenman's original background scores around that time included *Birch Interval*, *The Car*, *Race With The Devil*, *Prophecy*, *Promises In The Dark* and the animated feature *The Lord Of The Rings*. In the 80s and early 90s, apart from the occasional feature film such as *Hide In Plain Sight*, *Making Love*, *Cross Creek* (Oscar nomination), *The Voyage Home - Star Trek IV*, *Robocop 2*, *Heart Of The Stag* and *Ambition* (1992), Rosenman wrote more and more for television, although he still managed to score the occasional big one, such as *The Jazz Singer* and *Star Trek IV: The Voyage Home*. Rosenman's music for television included *Stranger On The Run*, *Shadow Over Elveron*, *Any Second Now*, *Banyon*, *Vanished*, *In Broad Daylight*, *The Bravos*, *The Cat Creature*, *The Phantom Of Hollywood*, *Nakia*, *Lanigan's Rabbi*, *Kingston: The Power Play*, *The Possessed*, *Friendly Fire*, *City In Fear*, *The Wall*, *Murder In Texas*, *Celebrity* (mini-series), *Heartsounds*, *First Steps*, *Promised A Miracle*, *Where Pigeons Go To Die*, the popular series, *The Defenders*, *Marcus Welby MD*, its sequel, *The Return Of Marcus Welby MD* and the telefilm *Keeper Of The City* (1991). He also composed several classical works.

Rota, Nino

b. 3 December 1911, Milan, Italy, d. 10 April 1979, Rome, Italy. A prolific composer for films, from the early 30s to the late 70s. A child prodigy, Rota wrote an oratorio and an opera before he was aged 15. He studied at the Curtis Institute in Philadelphia, and, later, at the Liceo Musicale in Bari, eventually becoming its director from 1950-78. He began composing for Italian movies in 1933, but had enormous success in Britain in 1949 with his score for *The Glass Mountain* starring the husband and wife team, Michael Denison and Dulcie Gray. By 1950, when he started collaborating with Federico Fellini, he had composed the scores to some 30 films. His association with the influential Italian director lasted nearly 30 years and included movies such as *Lo Sceicco Bianco*, *I Vitelloni*, *La Strada* (including the 'Love Theme'), *Il Bidone*, *La Dolce Vita* (including 'The Sweet Life'), *Boccaccio*, *Eight And A Half* (with its popular 'Love Theme'), *Juliet Of The Spirits*, *Fellini-Satyricon*, *The Clowns*, *Casanova*, *The Orchestra Rehearsal* and more. Meanwhile, for other directors, Nino provided the music for *The Hidden Room* ('Obsession'), *Anna*, *The White Sheik*, *Star Of India*, *War And Peace*, *Rocco And His Brothers*, *Shoot Louder, Louder ... I Don't Understand*, Franco Zefferelli's *Romeo And Juliet* (1968), and *Waterloo* (1970). In 1972 Rota composed the scores for Francis Ford Coppola's *The Godfather*, 'the 70s' answer to *Gone With The Wind*'. Oscar-laden as it was, Rota had to wait for the sequel, *The Godfather, Part Two* (1974), for his Academy Award. Andy Williams had a minor hit in the USA and UK with the 'Love Theme' from the original movie, entitled 'Speak Softly Love' (lyric by Larry Kusik). Rota's other 70s film music included *The Abdication*, *Boys From The Suburbs*, *Casanova*, *Hurricane* and *Death On The Nile* (1978), with Peter Ustinov as Agatha Christie's Poirot. Rota's last, of an impressive number of scores, was for Fellini's *Orchestra Rehearsal* (1979), which was originally made for television.

Round Midnight

A long step (if not exactly a leap) forward in the treatment of jazz and jazz musicians in feature films, this film released in 1986, loosely traces the life and times of Bud Powell in Paris. Centring upon the characters of an alcoholic American jazzman and his Parisian fan-cum-mentor, the film contains an excellent performance from Dexter Gordon as the saxophonist for which he was unsuccessfully nominated for an Oscar. The music, an approximation of late 50s bop, is generally well-realized by Gordon and musicians such as Ron Carter, Billy Higgins, Bobby Hutcherson, Freddie Hubbard, John McLaughlin, Pierre Michelot, Wayne Shorter, Cedar Walton, Tony Williams and Herbie Hancock (who was also responsible for the score). The mostly restrained, unmelodramatic development of an essentially tragic storyline is the responsibility of director Bernard Tavernier yet there is rather too much reliance upon stereotype and cliché to warrant the accolades heaped upon the film. Undoubtedly, it is an important improvement upon many jazz-based films but, as so often before, film-makers seem unwilling, or unable, to either leave historical context undamaged or acknowledge the fact that most musicians do what they do because they are musicians. They play to hear the music; film-makers apparently feel obliged to give them non-musical motivation which, as often or not, diminishes them when, presumably, the intention is to uplift.

Royal Wedding

Inspired by the wedding of Princess Elizabeth to Philip Mountbatten in 1947, this film, which was released by MGM four years later in 1951, was also loosely based on the experiences of one of its stars,

Fred Astaire. In 1928, he and his sister Adele appeared in the London production of the stage musical *Funny Face*. They were feted by the city's fashionable high society, and, eventually, Adele broke up their double act and married Lord Charles Cavendish in 1932. Alan Jay Lerner's screenplay for *Royal Wedding* also concerns a brother and sister dance team, Tom and Ellen Bowen (Astaire and Jane Powell), who take their Broadway hit show, *Every Night At Seven*, to the British capital where Ellen marries her Lord John Brindale (Peter Lawford) and gives up her show business career. Tom also finds happiness in London with a music hall performer (played by Sarah Churchill, daughter of Britain's new Prime Minister in 1951), and all three couples (including Elizabeth and Philip) get married on the same November day. Burton Lane (music) and Alan Jay Lerner (lyrics) wrote the score which contained one of the longest song titles ever: 'How Could You Believe Me When I Said I Loved You When You Know I've Been A Liar All My Life.' That number provided a humorous no-punches-pulled knockabout duet for Astaire and Powell, a young and up and coming singer-actress who surprised a lot of people with her all-round versatility in this film. She also had the tender 'Too Late Now' and 'Open Your Eyes', while Fred, amazingly innovative as usual, danced with a hat stand in 'Sunday Jumps', and appeared to dance on the floor, walls and ceiling of a room filled with furniture, accompanied by 'You're All The World To Me'. Illustrated lectures have since been given as to how that last feat was accomplished. Nick Castle (with an uncredited assist from Astaire, was responsible for the choreography). The rest of the score included 'I Left My Hat In Haiti', 'Open Your Eyes', 'Ev'ry Night At Seven', 'The Happiest Day Of My Life', and 'What A Lovely Day For A Wedding'. Stanley Donen directed the film, which was photographed in Technicolor and re-titled *Wedding Bells* when it was released in the UK.

Rozsa, Miklos

b. 18 April 1907, Budapest, Hungary. An important composer for films from the early late 30s until the early 80s, who had an equally distinguished career in the world of classical music. Rozsa began to play the piano at the age of five and soon added the violin to his studies. He gave his first public performance when he was seven, playing a movement from a Mozart violin concerto and conducting a children's orchestra in Haydn's 'Toy Symphony'. In his teens Rozsa attended Leipzig University and, during his four years there, completed his first serious compositions. His big breakthrough came in 1934 with his 'Theme, Variations, And Finale (Opus 13)'. A year later he moved to London to write a ballet, and was invited to compose the music for Alexandra Korda's film, *Knight Without Armour*, starring Robert Donat and Marlene

Dietrich. The successful outcome marked the beginning of Rozsa's five-year association with Korda which, in the late 30s, produced *The Squeaker*, *The Divorce Of Lady X*, *The Spy In Black* and *The Four Feathers*. In 1940, Rozsa went to Hollywood to finish work on *The Thief Of Baghdad* and then scored *Sundown* and *The Jungle Book*. All three films gained him Oscar nominations, and together with *The Four Feathers*, were designated as his 'Oriental' period. Rozsa was nominated again, for *Lydia*, before Korda shut down London Films for the duration of World War II. Rozsa moved to Paramount where he provided the 'stark, powerful, dissonant score' for 'the archetypal film noir of the 40s', Billy Wilder's *Double Indemnity* (1944), followed by other Wilder movies such as *Five Graves To Caioro* and *The Lost Weekend* (1945). In the latter, Rozsa introduced a new instrument, the theremin, 'an ideal accompaniment to torture'. It was one of around 10 'psychological' movies with which Rozsa was involved during his career. Another, in the same year, was Alfred Hitchcock's *Spellbound*, for which Rozsa won his first Academy Award for a 'bleak and exciting' score.

In the late 40s, besides Paramount, Rozsa worked mostly for United Artists and Universal on films such as *Because Of Him*, *The Strange Love Of Martha Ivers*, *The Killers* (Burt Lancaster's first movie), *The Red House*, *The Macomber Affair*, *Brute Force*, *The Naked City* (with Frank Skinner) and *A Double Life* (1947), for which he won another Oscar. At the end of the decade Rozsa began to work for MGM and, embarked on his 'religious and historical epic' period, with 'majestic' scores for *Quo Vadis*, *Ivanhoe*, *Julius Caesar*, *Knights Of The Round Table*, *Valley Of The Kings*, *Ben Hur* (1959) (his third Academy Award, and his last major assignment for MGM). Rozsa pursued the epic into the 60s with blockbusters *King Of Kings* and *El Cid* (1961), both of which were made in Spain. By no means all of Rozsa scores in the 50s and 60s were of such gigantic proportions. He also provided the music for movies with a wide variety of subjects, including: *The Asphalt Jungle*, *Crisis*, *The Story Of Three Loves*, *Moonfleet*, *Tribute To A Bad Man*, *Bhowani Junction*, *Lust For Life*, *Something Of Value*, *The World, The Flesh And The Devil*, *The V.I.P's*, *The Power*, *The Green Berets*, and many more.

In 1970 Rozsa made his last film with Billy Wilder, *The Private Life Of Sherlock Holmes*, and played a cameo role as a ballet conductor. His other 70s film music included *The Golden Voyage Of Sinbad*, *The Secret Fifles Of J. Edgar Hoover*, *Fedora*, *The Last Embrace*, *Time After Time* and *Providence*, his 'most inspiring project for years'. Somewhat ironically, during the 70s and 80s, when the demand for elaborate orchestra movie scores had declined, to be replaced by a montage of pop records, renewed interest in Rozsa's earlier classic film works caused record companies to make new recordings of his scores. In 1981, Rozsa's music for *Eye Of The Needle*, was, for some, shades of Korda's *The Spy In Black* over 40 years earlier and, *Dead Men Don't Wear Plaid* (1982), a parody of 40s film noir which included footage from classics of the genre, found Rozsa writing music for scenes that he had originally scored many years ago. Even though he was partly paralysed by a stroke in 1982, he continued to compose classical works and, on his 80th birthday, was presented with a Golden Soundtrack Award by ASCAP. The anniversary was declared 'Miklos Rozsa Day' in Los Angeles, and the composer was presented with greetings from President Reagan, Queen Elizabeth, and other luminaries such as Margaret Thatcher and Pope John Paul II. Later in 1987 Rozsa was the guest of honour at a gala charity concert of his music given by the Royal Philharmonic Orchestra at London's Royal Festival Hall.

Further reading: *Miklos Rozsa: A Sketch Of His Life And Work*, C. Palmer. *Double Life: The Autobiography Miklos Rozsa*, Miklos Rozsa.

Ruby, Harry

b. Harry Rubinstein, 27 January 1895, New York, USA, d. 23 February 1974, Woodland Hills, California, USA. Ruby was a successful composer for stage and film over a long career, mostly in collaboration with lyricist Bert Kalmar (b. 16 February 1884, New York, USA, d. 18 September 1947, Los Angeles, California, USA). Ruby played piano in music publishing houses, and accompanied vaudeville acts such as the Messenger Boys, before starting to write songs. He had an early hit in 1919 with 'And He'd Say Oo-La-La, Wee-Wee', written with comedian George Jessel, and a hit for the specialist novelty singer Billy Murray. From 1918-28 Kalmar and Ruby wrote songs for Broadway shows, with Ruby sometimes contributing to the libretto. These included *Helen Of Troy, New York* ('I Like A Big Town', 'Happy Ending'); *The Ramblers* ('All Alone Monday', 'Just One Kiss', 'Any Little Tune'); *Five O'Clock Girl* ('Thinking Of You', 'Up In The Clouds'); *Good Boy* ('Some Sweet Someone', 'I Wanna Be Loved By You', the latter memorably revived by Marilyn Monroe in the 1959 Billy Wilder movie, *Some Like It Hot*); and *Animal Crackers* ('Watching The Clouds Roll By, 'Who's Been Listening To My Heart?', 'Hooray For Captain Spaulding'). While working on *Animal Crackers*, Kalmar and Ruby formed a friendship with the Marx Brothers, and, after moving to Hollywood in 1928, supplied songs for some of the Marx Brothers' early movies, including *Horse Feathers* (1932) and *Duck Soup* (1933), and the film version of *Animal Crackers*. Groucho Marx later used their 'Hooray For Captain Spaulding' as a theme for his radio and television shows. While in Hollywood, Kalmar and Ruby wrote what was probably their most popular song, 'Three

Little Words', for the comedy film *Check And Double Check* (1930), featuring radio's famous double-act, Amos 'N Andy. The songwriting team continued to write consistently for films through the 30s, including: *The Cuckoos* (1931) ('I Love You So Much', 'Dancing The Devil Away'); *The Kid From Spain* (1932) ('Look What You've Done', 'What A Perfect Combination'); *Hips, Hips, Hooray* (1934) ('Keep On Doin' What You're Doin''); and *Kentucky Kernels* (1934) ('One Little Kiss'). Their last film together, in 1939, was *The Story Of Vernon And Irene Castle* ('Only When You're In My Arms', 'Ain'tcha Comin' Out?'), starring Fred Astaire and Ginger Rogers, although their 1947 song, 'A Kiss To Build A Dream On', written with Oscar Hammerstein II, featured in the 1951 movie, *The Strip*, and was nominated for an Academy Award. In 1941, they also contributed to another Broadway show, *The High Kickers* ('You're On My Mind', 'A Panic In Panama', 'Time To Sing'). In the 1950 bio-pic, *Three Little Words*, Red Skelton played Ruby, and Fred Astaire was cast as Kalmar. The film featured most of their big hits including 'Who's Sorry Now', 'Nevertheless', and the novelty, 'So Long, Oo-Long (How Long You Gonna Be Gone?'). During the 40s, Ruby also wrote songs with other lyricists, including Rube Bloom, ('Give Me The Simple Life'), and provided both music and lyrics for the title song to the Dick Haymes-Maureen O'Hara film, *Do You Love Me?* (1946). After the early 50s Ruby was semi-retired, emerging occasionally to appear on television programmes to celebrate songwriters and associated artists.

S

Sailing Along

This was the last of the three films, made in 1938, that Jessie Matthews appeared under the direction of her husband Sonnie Hale. She plays 'water gypsy' Kay Martin, the ambitious step-daughter of bargemaster Skipper Barnes (Frank Pettingell). She is in love with Skipper's studious son, Steve (Barry Mackay), and, in an effort to attract his attention, she breaks into show business and is rapidly propelled to stardom by eccentric millionaire Victor Gulliver (Roland Young) and producer and song-and-dance-man Dick Randall (Jack Whiting). Meanwhile, Steve is also taking Victor's advice, and makes a killing on the Stock Exchange. It all ends with Kay fending off the advances of the pushy American press agent, Windy (Noel Madison), and sailing off to foreign climes with Steve in his new yacht. The frothy story, which was adapted by Lesser Samuels from a story by Selwyn Jepson, gave Jessie Matthews and Jack Whiting ample opportunity for some slick dance routines which were staged by Buddy Bradley. There were also several appealing songs by Arthur Johnston and Maurice Sigler, including 'My River', 'Souvenir Of Love', 'Trusting My Luck', 'Your Heart Skips A Beat', and the delightful 'Sailing Along'. Athene Seyler and Alastair Sim (the future star of Ealing comedies and St. Trinian's films), provided the comic relief, and also in the cast were Margaret Vyner, Peggy Novak, and William Dewhurst. The screenplay was adapted by Lesser Samuels from a story by Selwyn Jepson.

Sally In Our Alley

Gracie Fields was already the 'talk of the North' - of England, that is - when she made her film debut in this 1931 Basil Dean production for Associated Talking Pictures. The screenplay, by Miles Malleson, Archie Pitt, and Alma Reville, was based on the play *The Likes Of 'Er* by Charles McEvoy. Gracie Fields plays Sally Winch, a lively young lady who has left Rochdale in Lancashire for a job in a coffee shop in London's Mile End Road which is run by Sam Bilson (Ben Field). After many years of waiting she has given up all hope of seeing her true love, George Miles (Ian Hunter), again, fearing him lost in action during World War I. However, George's terrible wounds have healed, and, in spite of the efforts of jealous Florrie Small (Florence Desmond), 'a child of the gutter - cunning suspicious and pretty' - to keep them apart, he and Sally are eventually reunited. Renee Macready and Helen Ferrers play Lady Daphne and the Duchess of Wexford, a couple of toffs who try, without success, to turn Sally's head, and also among a strong supporting cast were Fred Groves, Gibb McLaughlin, Ivor Barnard, Barbara Gott, and Florence Harwood. Rising above the action was Gracie Fields' thrilling voice on songs such as 'Following The Sun Around' (Joseph McCarthy-Harry Tierney), 'Moonlight On The Alster' (Osacar Fetras), 'Lancashire Blues', 'Fred Fernackerpan', and the immortal 'Sally' (Will Haines-Harry Leon-Leo Towers), the number which became her life-long theme. This film, which was directed by Maurice Elvy, helped Gracie on her way to becoming one of the best-loved British entertainers of all time.

San Francisco

Jeanette MacDonald arranged a temporary 'divorce' from her celebrated singing partner Nelson Eddy, and co-starred with Clark Gable in what must have one of the very first 'disaster' movies (at least with sound), when it was released by MGM in 1936. In Anita Loo's superb screenplay (based on a story by Robert

San Francisco

Hopkins) Macdonald plays singer Mary Blake, whose association with Blackie Norton (Gable), a cabaret club owner in the rough, tough Barbary Coast area of San Francisco, leads to a career in opera and a temporary suspension of their romantic affair. They get back together again after the earth moves for them - and all the other residents of the city - in a spectacular 'quake sequence towards the end of the picture. Spencer Tracy gave an excellent performance as Gable's best buddy, and also in the cast were Jessie Ralph, Jack Holt, Shirley Ross, Ted Healy, Edgar Kennedy, Al Shean, and Richard Carle. The songs were a mixed bag of operatic excerpts and popular numbers and included 'Would You? (Nacio Herb Brown-Arthur Freed), 'Sempre Libera' (from Verdi's *La Traviata*), 'A Heart That's Free' (Alfred J. Robyn-T. Railey), 'The Holy City' (Stephen Adams-F.E. Weatherley), and the title song which was mercilessly lampooned by Judy Garland on her celebrated Carnegie Hall concert recording in 1961. *San Francisco*, which was produced by John Emerson and Bernard Hyman, and skilfully directed by W.S. Van Dyke, is considered to be a classic of its kind and a fine example of the film makers' art.

Satchmo The Great

Made for television by Ed Murrow, this 1956 film follows Louis Armstrong on a tour of Europe and Africa. Intercut with scenes of live performance by Armstrong And His All Stars, and their welcome, often by tens of thousands of well-wishers, at airports, are interviews with Armstrong. Although one of the finest and most respected journalists of his, or any other era, Murrow's questions are sometimes a shade naïve but Armstrong takes it all in his stride. The film ends with a New York concert performance of 'St Louis Blues' in which Armstrong and his men are joined by Leonard Bernstein and the New York Philharmonic to play to a capacity audience which includes W.C. Handy. One moving moment shows Handy, then turned 80, removing his hat to take his handkerchief from his head to mop a tear from his blind eyes. The All Stars featured are Trummy Young, Edmond Hall, Billy Kyle, Jack Lesburg and Barrett Deems with singer Velma Middleton.

Schertzinger, Victor

b. 8 April 1880, Mahanoy City, Pennsylvania, USA, d. 26 October 1941, Hollywood, California, USA. A leading composer, conductor and director for movies, from the early days of silents, through the 30s and 40s. A gifted violinist as a child, Schertzinger toured as a concert soloist and studied music in Europe before returning and becoming a well-known conductor by the time he was 30. A few years later he began to compose the music for popular songs such as 'Marchetta' and 'My Wonderful Dream', and in 1916 moved to Hollywood to write scores for a series of silent movies, including Thomas Ince's revolutionary *Civilization*. Almost immediately he began to direct as well, and from then, throughout his career, he successfully combined the two occupations. With the advent of sound in the late 20s, Schertzinger contributed complete scores or individual songs to musicals such as *The Love Parade*, *Heads Up*, *One Night Of Love*, *Love Me Forever*, *Follow Your Heart*, *The Music Goes 'Round*, *Something To Sing About*, *Road To Singapore*, *Rhythm On The River*, *Kiss The Boys Goodbye*, and *The Fleet's In*. Several of his most appealing songs, with lyrics by Johnny Mercer, came from that last movie which was released in 1942, shortly after his death. These included 'I Remember You', 'Tangerine', 'If You Build A Better Mousetrap', 'Arthur Murray Taught Me Dancing In A Hurry', 'When You Hear The Time Signal', and 'The Fleet's In'. Among his other songs from that period were 'Magnolias In The Moonlight', 'Life Begins When You're In Love', 'Captain Custard', 'The Moon And The Willow Tree', 'I Don't Want To Cry Anymore', 'Kiss The Boys Goodbye', 'Sand In My Shoes', and 'I'll Never Let A Day Pass By'. Schertzinger also directed several of the above musicals, as well as numerous dramatic features. After directing Bing Crosby, Bob Hope and Dorothy Lamour, in *Road To Singapore*, the first of the popular 'Road' pictures, Schertzinger worked again with the 'Old Groaner' on *Road To Zanzibar* - arguably the best of the series - *Rhythm On The River*, and *Birth Of The Blues*. As well as Mercer, Schertzinger's songwriting collaborators included Clifford Grey, Johnny Burke, Gus Kahn, and Frank Loesser. They all shared his ability to write lively, optimistic and amusing numbers, with the occasional memorable ballad as well.

Schifrin, Lalo

b. 21 June 1932, Buenos Aires, Argentina. Schifrin was taught classical piano from the age of six but later studied sociology and law at university. He won a scholarship to the Paris Conservatoire where he studied with Olivier Messiaen. In 1955 he represented Argentina in the Third International Jazz Festival in Paris. He met Dizzy Gillespie first in 1956 when the trumpeter was touring South America. Schifrin had founded the first Argentine big band in the Count Basie tradition and in 1957 wrote his first film music. He moved to New York in 1958 and toured Europe in 1960 with a Jazz At The Philharmonic ensemble which included Dizzy with whom he played between 1960 and 1962. He had become increasingly interested in large-scale compositions and wrote two suites for Gillespie - *Gillespiana* and *New Continent*. He worked with Quincy Jones when he left Gillespie, but became more and more involved in scoring for television and feature films including *The Cincinatti Kid* (1965), *Bullitt* (1968) and *Dirty Harry* (1971). His more than 150 scores over a period of nearly 30 years also have included *The Liquidator, Cool Hand Luke, The Fox, Coogan's Bluff, Kelly's Heros, Hit!, Magnum Force, Voyage Of The Damned, The Eagle Has Landed, Rollercoaster, The Amityville Horror, The Competition, The Sting II, Hollywood Wives* (television mini-series), *The Fourth Protocol, F/X2 - The Deadly Art Of Illusion, The Dead Pool, Return From The River Kwai,* and *A Woman Called Jackie* (1992 television series). He taught composition at the University of California, Los Angeles (1968-71).

Selected albums: *Bossa Nova - New Brazilian Jazz* (1962), *New Fantasy* (1966), *Music From 'Mission: Impossible'* (1967), *Towering Toccata* (1977), *Black Widow* (1976), *Free Ride* (1979), *Guitar Concerto* (1985), *Anno Domini* (1986), with Jimmy Smith *The Cat Strikes Again* (1986).

Schwartz, Arthur

b. 25 November 1900, New York City, New York, USA, d. 3 September 1984. Prohibited by his family from learning music, Schwartz began composing while still a teenager at high school. He studied law and continued to write as a hobby but in 1924 he met Lorenz Hart, with whom he immediately began to collaborate on songs. They enjoyed some modest success but not enough to turn Schwartz from his path as a lawyer. In the late 20s he practised law in New York City, continuing to write songs in his spare time with a string of lyricists as collaborators until Hart convinced him that he could make a career in music. He took time off from his practice and was advised to seek a permanent collaborator. He was introduced to Howard Dietz, with whom he established immediate rapport. Among their first joint efforts were some contributions to the music for *The Little Show* (1929). For this revue, one of the songs Schwartz had written with Hart, 'I Love To Lie Awake In Bed', was given a new lyric by Dietz. This now became 'I Guess I'll Have To Change My Plan'. Later songs for revues included 'Something To Remember You By' and 'The Moment I Saw You'. In 1931, Schwartz and Dietz had a major success with *The Band Wagon*, which starred Fred Astaire and his sister Adele. The partners' score included their most important song success, 'Dancing In The Dark'. Other shows of the 30s were less successful but there were always excellent songs: 'Louisiana Hayride', 'Alone Together', 'A Shine On Your Shoes', 'What A Wonderful World', 'Love Is A Dancing Thing' and 'You And The Night And The Music'. The pair also wrote for radio and interspersed their collaborations with songs written with other partners. Schwartz wrote songs for shows such as *Virginia* (1937) and *Stars In Your Eyes* (1939). During the 40s and 50s he wrote songs with various collaborators for several film musicals, including *Navy Blues, Thank Your Lucky Stars* ('They're Either Too Young Or Too Old' with Frank Loesser), *The Time, The Place And The Girl* ('Gal In Calico', 'A Rainy Night In Rio' with Leo Robin), and *Excuse My Dust* (1951). He also served as producer on pictures such as *Cover Girl, Night And Day,* and *The Band Wagon.* Schwartz was reunited with Dietz in 1948 on a revue, *Inside USA,* and in 1953 they wrote a new song, 'That's Entertainment', for the screen version of *The Band Wagon.* In 1951, Schwartz collaborated with Dorothy Fields on *A Tree Grows In Brooklyn,* from which came 'Love Is The Reason' and 'I'll Buy You A Star'. Schwartz and Fields also wrote *By The Beautiful Sea* (1954), which included 'Alone Too Long'. Later Broadway shows by Schwartz and Dietz proved unsuccessful and although their songs, such as 'Something You Never Had Before' and 'Before I Kiss The World Goodbye', were pleasant and lyrically deft, they were not of the high standard they had previously set themselves. In the late 60s Schwartz settled in London, England, for a while where he wrote *Nicholas Nickleby* and *Look Who's Dancing* (a revised version of *A Tree Grows In Brooklyn* with several new songs). He also recorded an album of his own songs, *From The Pen Of Arthur Schwartz,* before returning to live in the USA.

Album: *From The Pen Of Arthur Schwartz* (1976).

Scrooge

By all accounts, Albert Finney was by no means the first choice to play the lead in this musical version of Charles Dickens's celebrated novel *A Christmas Carol* which was released in 1970. As it turns out, he makes a wonderfully crotchety Ebenezer Scrooge, the miserable miser who becomes a totally reformed character following eerie visitations by his late partner, Jacob Marley (Alec Guinness), and the ghosts of Christmases Past, Present and Yet To Come (Edith Evans, Kenneth More and Paddy Stone). The main beneficiaries of this new-found munificence are Scrooge's clerk, Bob Cratchit (David Collings) and his son Tiny Tim (Richard Beaumont). Also taking part in this extremely good looking production which was designed by Terry Marsh and photographed in Technicolor and Panavision by Oswald Morris, were Michael Medwin, Laurence Naismith, Anton Rodgers, Suzanne Neve, Frances Cuka, Roy Kinnear and Gordon Jackson. Leslie Bricusse, who co-produced the film with Robert Solo in the UK for Cinema Center, also wrote the screenplay and the songs. His uninspired score included the lively 'Thank You Very Much', 'Father Christmas', 'I'll Begin Again', 'A Christmas Carol', 'December The 25th', 'Happiness', 'I Like Life', and 'The Beautiful Day'. Paddy Stone staged the dances and the director was Ronald Neame. British reference books record another seven screen versions of *Scrooge* from 1901 onwards, starring such distinguished actors as Seymour Hicks, Bransby Williams, and Alastair Sim. There was also a more contemporary interpretation of *A Christmas Carol* entitled *Scrooged,* which was made in the USA in 1988 and starred Bill Murray and Karen Allen. Four years after that, Bricusse adapted his screen musical for the stage. It had its world premiere in November 1992 in Birmingham, England, with Bricusse's old writing partner Anthony Newley in the leading role.

Second Chorus

This 1940 film is an enjoyable hokum about two swing band trumpeters, Fred Astaire and Burgess Meredith, vying for the affections of Paulette Goddard. The musicians play with Artie Shaw's band and there are some excellent musical sequences featuring the leader's clarinet, backed in a performance of 'Concerto For Clarinet' by Nick Fatool's drums, and the trumpets of Bobby Hackett and Billy Butterfield ghosting for Astaire and Meredith.

Seven Brides For Seven Brothers

Adapted from Stephen Vincent Benet's short story *The Sobbin' Women*, which was 'inspired' by Plutach's *Rape Of The Sabine Women*, this film was released by MGM in 1954 and, somewhat surprisingly, became one of the hit screen musicals of the decade. Frances Goodrich, Albert Hackett, and Dorothy Kingsley wrote the screenplay which told of Adam Pontipee (Howard Keel), who leaves his six scruffy brothers to the squalor of their farmhouse in Oregon (c.1850s) to go into town in search of a hard-working wife. He finds her in the shape of Milly (Jane Powell), and their subsequent life together, during which Milly successfully advises the slovenly sextet on how to live and love, makes for an endearing and entertaining film. Her first 'lesson' is 'Goin' Co'tin', just one of the many musical highlights in Gene De Paul and Johnny Mercer's spirited and exuberant score. Others included the optimistic 'Bless Your Beautiful Hide' (Keel), 'Wonderful, Wonderful Day' (Powell), 'When You're In Love' (Powell-Keel), 'Sobbin' Women' (Keel-brothers), 'June Bride' (Powell-brides), and 'Spring, Spring, Spring' (Powell-brothers-brides). The six virile brothers, named by their god-fearing mother as Benjamin, Caleb, Ephram, Daniel, Frankincense, and Gideon, were played by Russ Tamblyn, Tommy Rall, Jeff Richards, Marc Platt, Matt Mattox, and Jacques d'Amboise. In the end, they all got their brides (Virginia Gibson, Julie Newmeyer, Betty Carr, Nancy Kilgas, Norma Doggett, and Rita Kilmonis) by somewhat unconventional methods, after displaying exceptionally brilliant dancing skills in the contrasting languorous 'Lonesome Polecat' and spectacular 'barn-raising' scenes. The choreography for those, and rest of the innovative dance numbers was designed by Michael Kidd. Saul Chaplin and Adolph Deutsch won Academy Awards for 'scoring of a musical picture'. Stanley Donen directed with style and vigour. George Folsey was responsible for the breathtakingly beautiful photography in Amsco and CinemaScope. This film is considered by many to be among the all-time great musicals, but a 1982 stage version was not welcomed in New York and folded after five performances. Four years later a West End version fared a little better.

Shall We Dance?

Screenwriter Allan Scott, whose name was a familiar feature on the credits of Fred Astaire and Ginger Rogers movies, excelled himself with the plot for this 1937 vehicle for the popular duo's delightful dance routines. Together with Ernest Pagano, Scott fashioned a story in which ballet dancer Pete Rogers (Astaire) falls for Broadway musical star Linda Keen (Rogers) in Paris - serenades her on the liner back to New York - and later, with her help, fulfills his lifetime ambition by mixing his beloved ballet with modern tap-dancing. Before that happens - and this is where Scott and Pagano really score - the couple dispel constant rumours that they are married by *getting* married - so that that they can divorce! There was nothing as complicated as that about the sublime songs by George and Ira Gershwin. They were all simply terrific, and included three of the composers' all-time standards, 'They All Laughed', 'Let's Call The Whole Thing Off' (Fred and Ginger on roller-skates!), and 'They Can't Take That Away From Me', along with the lively '(I've Got) Beginner's Luck' and 'Slap That Bass', the rhythmic title song, and a catchy little instrumental piece, set on the deck of the liner, 'Walking The Dog'. Directed by Mark Sandrich, with dance sequences choreographed by Hermes Pan and Harry Losee, *Shall We Dance?* was the seventh Fred Astaire-Ginger Rogers film, and, while they were as great as ever, and the supporting cast which included Edward Everett Horton and Eric Blore were always amusing, somehow things were beginning to pall. In fact, to some, this picture marked the beginning of their decline.

She Done Him Wrong

Mae West's second - and some say her best - film was adapted by screenwriters Harvey Thew, John White, and West herself from her own play, *Diamond Lil*, which was set in the late 19th century. The trio toned down the erotic element somewhat, but with West's laconic delivery and skin-tight gowns, wholesomeness was just not possible - and not even desirable. Ironically, as saloon hostess Lady Lou, she directed her first invitation to 'Come up and see me . . . ?' to Cary Grant ('Mr. Clean'), who played a federal agent, masquerading as a church mission man, intent on terminating her various nefarious activities. Among the accomplished cast were Noah Beery, Owen Moore, Gilbert Roland, Fuzzy Knight, Grace LaRue, and Rochelle Hudson. The songs came from various composers and included 'I Like A Guy What Takes His Time', 'Maisie', and 'Haven't Got No Peace Of Mind' (all with words and music by Ralph Rainger); 'Silver Threads Among The Gold' (Eben E. Rexford-

Hart Pease Danks), 'I Wonder Where My Easy Rider's Gone' (Shelton Brooks), and 'Frankie And Johnny' (traditional). Directed by Lowell Sherman, *She Done Him Wrong* shocked and disgusted some sections of the public in 1933, but took a remarkable $3 million at the box-office.

Sherman, Richard M., And Robert B.

Richard M. Sherman (b. 12 June 1928, New York, USA) and Robert B. Sherman (b. 19 December 1925, New York, USA) followed in their father, Al Sherman's footsteps as songwriters who collaborated on complete scores, mainly for Walt Disney movies of the 60s and 70s. They contributed to several films in the early 60s, including *The Parent Trap*, *In Search Of The Castaways*, *Summer Magic* and *The Sword In The Stone*. Massive success came in 1964 with the music and lyrics for *Mary Poppins*. The Oscar-winning score included 'A Spoonful Of Sugar', 'Feed The Birds', 'Jolly Holiday', 'Let's Go Fly A Kite' and 'Chim Chim Cher-ee' (which won the Academy Award for 'Best Song'). When the brothers accepted their award they commented: 'There are no words. All we can say is: "Supercalafragelisticexpialidocious"' - which was the title of another famous song from the film. *Mary Poppins* was dubbed the 'best and most original musical of the decade', and 'the best live-action film in Disney's history'. The soundtrack album went to number 1 in the US and remained in the charts for 18 months. Julie Andrews, appearing in her first feature film, was voted 'Best Actress' for her performance in the title role. Another British performer, Tommy Steele, was not so fortunate in *The Happiest Millionaire*. It was called 'miserable and depressing' despite a lively score by the Shermans, which included 'Fortuosity'. The film was the last to be personally supervised by Walt Disney before he died in 1966. Much more to the critics' liking was the delightful animated feature, *The Jungle Book*, which was inspired by the Rudyard Kipling *Mowgli* stories. The Shermans' songs, including 'I Wan'na Be Like You' and 'That's What Friends Are For', were amusingly delivered by the voices of Phil Harris, Sebastian Cabot, Louis Prima, George Sanders and Sterling Holloway. The songs and much of the dialogue were released on a lavishly illustrated album.
The late 60s were extremely fertile years for the Sherman brothers. Among the films to which they contributed music and lyrics were *The One And Only Genuine Original Family Band* (another highly acclaimed animal animation); *The Aristocats*; *Bedknobs And Broomsticks* and *Chitty Chitty Bang Bang*. In 1974 the Sherman brothers' score for the Broadway musical, *Over Here*, starred the two survivors from the Andrews Sisters, Maxene and Patti. The show, which echoed the styles and sounds of World War II and the swing era, ran for a year. Throughout the 70s, and beyond, the Shermans continued to write songs and scores for films, including *Charlotte's Webb*, *Tom Sawyer*, *Huckleberry Finn*, *The Slipper And The Rose* and *The Magic Of Lassie*. Lassie's voice was dubbed by Pat Boone's daughter, Debbie Boone. Several songs from those films were nominated for Academy Awards, and the Sherman brothers were also involved in writing some of the screenplays. They were set to return to Broadway in 1992 with *Busker Alley*, a musical adaptation of the 1938 British movie, *St. Martin's Lane'*, which starred Charles Laughton and Viven Leigh.

Shilkret, Nat

b. Nathaniel Shilkret, 25 December 1895, New York, USA, d. 1982. A clarinettist, composer, arranger, conductor and an executive with Victor Records for many years. Shilkret was also an accomplished classical violinist. Early in his career, he played with the New York Symphony, the New York Philharmonic, and the Metropolitan Opera House Orchestra. He also worked in the concert bands of John Philip Sousa and Arthur Pryor, before joining Victor, eventually becoming their Director of Light Music. From 1924-32 he conducted his Victor Orchestra on over 50 US chart hits, including 'Tell Me You'll Forgive Me', 'June Brought The Roses', 'Rio Rita', 'On The Riviera', 'All Alone Monday', 'One Alone', 'The Riff Song', 'I Know That You Know', 'Flapperette', 'When Day Is Done', 'What Does It Matter Now?', 'The Doll Dance', 'Hallelujah!', 'Me And My Shadow', 'It's A Million To One You're In Love', 'Paree (Ca C'est Paris)', 'Diane', 'Thinking Of You', 'Did You Mean It?', 'Why Do I Love You?', 'The Sidewalks Of New York', 'Out Of The Dawn', 'One Kiss', 'Marie', 'You Were Meant For Me', 'Pagan Love Song', 'Love Me', 'Chant Of The Jungle', 'Get Happy' and 'Delishious'. 'Dancing With Tears In My Eyes' was his most successful record, reaching number 1 in the US chart. Vocalists on some of those tracks included Vernon Dalhart, Lewis James, Carl Mattieu, Johnny Marvin, the Revellers, Elliott Shaw, Franklyn Baur, and Paul Small. Shilkret also provided the orchestral accompaniment for many other Victor artists, such as Allan Jones, who had a big hit with 'The Donkey Serenade', from the film *The Firefly* (1937). He was the conductor on 'Indian Love Call', a hit for Jeanette MacDonald with Nelson Eddy, *Nelson Eddy Favorites* and Jane Froman's *Gems From Gershwin*. Some of his own compositions, too, were recorded successfully, by Buddy Berigan and Jimmie Lunceford ('The First Time I Saw You'), the Hilo Hawaiian Orchestra ('Down The River Of Broken Dreams'), and Ben Selvin and Gene Austin ('Jeannie, I Dream Of Lilac Time'). With Austin, Shilkret wrote his best remembered song, 'The Lonesome Road', which was included in the Jerome Kern/Oscar Hammerstein II score for the part-talking movie version of *Show Boat* (1927). Thirty years later Frank Sinatra remembered it on his Capitol release, *A Swingin' Affair*. Shilkret also composed several classical pieces, such as 'New York Ballet' and 'Southern Humoresque'. Throughout the 30s he worked extensively on radio in such shows as *Hall Of Fame*, *Camel Caravan*, *Relaxation Time*, *Palmolive Beauty Box Theatre* and his own programmes. In 1935 he moved to Hollywood and, for the next 20 or so years as an arranger, conductor and musical director, contributed to a great many movies, including *The Plough And The Stars* (starring Barbara Stanwyck); 'Mary Of Scotland' (an historical drama, staring Katharine Hepburn, John Ford and Frederic March); *The Toast Of New York* (with Cary Grant), *She Went To The Races*, *The Hoodlum Saint*, *Kentucky Derby Story* and *Airline Glamour Girls*. One of the last films he worked on, in 1953, was a short about fishing entitled *Flying Tarpons*. He also contributed the occasional film song, such as 'Heart Of A Gypsy' (with Robert Shayon), for *The Bohemian Girl*, and 'King Of The Road' (with Eddie Cherkose), for *Music For Madame*.

Shocking Miss Pilgrim, The

Difficult to believe in these more enlightened times, that the lady was shocking because she had the temerity to work in an office. After Mr. Remington came up with his new-fangled invention in 1874, the thoroughly modern Miss Cynthia Pilgrim (Betty Grable) comes top of her class at a New York business school and takes a position as a typewriter (typist) with the Pritchard Shipping Company in Boston. After overcoming initial opposition from her boss, John Pritchard (Dick Haymes), and the office manager (Gene Lockhart), Miss Pilgrim then compounds the felony by becoming leader of the local suffragette movement, but this only postpones the inevitable romantic union between worker and management. Somewhat unusually, audiences were accorded only a very brief glimpse of the famous Grable legs when she lifted her skirt to check a run in her stockings. The charming score had lyrics by Ira Gershwin to what he called 'posthumous' music. He and the composer-musician Kay Swift spent several weeks going through his late brother George Gershwin's manuscripts, and the result was several delightful songs which included two outstanding duets for Grable and Haymes, 'For You, For Me, For Evermore' and 'Aren't You Kind Of Glad We Did?', along with several other appropriate items such as 'The Back Bay Polka', 'One Two Three', 'Waltz Me No Waltzes', Demon Rum', 'Changing My Tune', 'But Not In Boston', 'Waltzing Is Better Than Sitting Down', 'Sweet Packard', and 'Stand Up And Fight'. Hermes Pan staged the dances, and the screenplay, which was adapted from a story by Ernest and Frederica Maas, was written by George Seaton who also directed. The splendid supporting cast included Ann Revere, Allyn Joslyn, Elizabeth Patterson, Elizabeth Risdon, Arthur Shields, Charles Kemper, and Roy Roberts. *The Shocking Miss Pilgrim* was photographed in Technicolor by Leon Shamroy and produced for 20th Century-Fox by William Perlberg.

Shore, Dinah

b. Frances Rose Shore, 1 March 1917, Winchester, Tennessee, USA, d. 24 February 1994, Los Angeles, California, USA. One of her country's most enduring all-round entertainers, Shore staked her first claim to fame, while still at school, on Nashville radio. Further broadcasting and theatre engagements in New York soon followed, and she recorded with Xaviar Cugat and Ben Bernie; she sang on some of Cugat's early 40s hits, such as 'The Breeze And I', 'Whatever Happened To You?', 'The Rhumba-Cardi', and 'Quierme Mucho (Yours)', initially under the name Dinah Shaw. Shore was one of the first vocalists to break free from the big bands (she had ben rejected at auditions for Benny Goodman and Tommy Dorsey) and become a star in her own right. She became extremely popular on both radio and disc, making her solo recording debut in 1939. Her smoky, low-pitched voice was especially attractive on slow ballads and from 1940-57, she had a string of 80 US chart hits, including 'Yes, My Darling Daughter', 'Jim', 'Blues In The Night', 'Skylark', 'You'd Be So Nice To Come Home To', 'Murder, He Says', 'Candy', 'Laughing On The Outside (Crying On The Inside)', 'All That Glitters Is Not Gold', 'Doin' What Comes Natur'lly', 'You Keep Coming Back Like A Song', 'I Wish I Didn't Love You So', 'You Do', 'Baby, It's Cold Outside' (with Buddy Clark), 'Dear Hearts And Gentle People', 'My Heart Cries For You', 'A Penny A Kiss', 'Sweet Violets'; and number 1's, 'I'll Walk Alone', 'The Gypsy', 'Anniversary Song', and 'Buttons And Bows'. She made a number of film appearances, including *Thank Your Lucky Stars* (1943), *Up In Arms* (1944), *Follow The Boys* (1944), *Belle Of The Yukon* (1945), *Till The Clouds Roll By* (1946), *Aaron Slick From Punkin Crick* (1952). She also lent her voice to two Walt Disney animated features, *Make Mine Music* (1946) and *Fun And Fancy Free* (1957), and was last seen on the big screen in the George Burns comedy *Oh God!* (1977), and Robert Altman's quirky political satire *H.E.A.L.T.H.* (1979). In 1951 Shore began appearing regularly on television, making several spectaculars. Later, it was her continuing success on the small screen that brought about a career change when she became host on a highly rated daytime talk show, a role she maintained into the 80s. Her popularity on television barely declined throughout this period, and she won no less than 10 Emmys in all. The late 80s saw her performing on stage once more, though she returned to the television format for *Conversation With Dinah*, which ran from 1989-91.

Selected albums: *Blues In The Night* (1952), with

Buddy Clark 'SWonderful (c.50s), *Holding Hands At Midnight* (1955), *Moments Like These* (c.50s), *Buttons And Bows* (1959), *Dinah, Yes Indeed!* (1959), with André Previn *Dinah Sings, Previn Plays* (1960), *Lavender Blue* (1960), with the Red Norvo Quintet *Some Blues With Red* (1962), *Dinah, Down Home!* (1962), *Lower Basin St. Revisted* (1965), *Make The World Go Away* (1987), *Oh Lonesome Me* (c.80s).

Show Boat

The first screen adaptation of Jerome Kern and Oscar Hammerstein II's Broadway show was a part-talkie released in 1929. Seven years later, Hammerstein himself wrote the screenplay which retold the familiar story of life on the Mississippi showboat operated by Captain Andy Hawks. This version starred several of the artists who had, at one time or another, appeared on stage in this beloved American classic. Irene Dunne and Allan Jones plays the young ingenue Magnolia Hawks, and Gaylord Ravenal, her no-good gambler of a husband; Helen Morgan is the mulatto Julie (she also took the role in the 1929 film), with Donald Cook as her husband Steve; Charles Winniger plays the jovial and understanding Captain Hawks, and Paul Robeson, as Joe, sang the immortal 'Ol' Man River'. Most of the songs from the original score were retained, including 'Make Believe' (Dunne and Jones), 'Can't Help Lovin' Dat Man' (Morgan), 'Bill' (lyric also with P.G. Wodehouse) (Morgan), and 'You Are Love' (Dunne and Jones). In addition, Kern and Hammerstein wrote three new ones, 'Ah Still Suits Me' (Robeson), 'Gallivantin' Around' (Dunne), and the lovely 'I Have The Room Above Her' (Dunne and Jones). LeRoy Prinz choreographed the spirited and imaginative dance sequences, and the film was produced for Universal by Carl Laemmle Jnr. and directed by James Whale. From the opening titles with their cardboard cut-out figures and models on a carousel, through to the film's final moments when Ravenal, reduced to working as theatre doorman, is reunited with Magnolia and their daughter Kim, this picture was a total delight.

Show Boat was remade in 1951 by the renowned Arthur Freed Unit at MGM. This extremely satisfying version starred Kathryn Grayson (Magnolia), Howard Keel (Ravenal), Ava Gardner (Julie, singing dubbed by Annette Warren), and Joe E. Brown (Captain Hawks). William Warfield sang 'Ol' Man Man River', and Marge and Gower Champion's song-and-dance routines based around 'I Might Fall Back On You' and 'Life Upon The Wicked Stage' were utterly charming. Those two songs were from the 1927 stage show, and another of the original numbers, 'Why Do I Love You?', which not used in the 1936 film, was sung here by Grayson and Keel. John Lee Mahin's screenplay differed in some respects from Hammerstein's earlier effort, but remained generally faithful to the spirit of the piece. The choreography was the work of Robert Alton, the film was directed by George Sidney.

Shuman, Mort

b. 12 November 1936, Brooklyn, New York, USA, d. 2 November 1991, London, England. After studying music, Shuman began writing songs with blues singer, Doc Pomus, in 1958. Early in 1959 two of their songs were Top 40 hits: 'Plain Jane' for Bobby Darin, and Fabian's 'I'm A Man'. During the next six years, their catalogue was estimated at over 500 songs, in a mixture of styles for a variety of artists. They included 'Surrender', 'Viva Las Vegas', 'Little Sister' and 'Kiss Me Quick' (Elvis Presley), 'Save The Last Dance For Me', 'Sweets For My Sweet' and 'This Magic Moment' (the Drifters), 'Teenager In Love' (Dion And The Belmonts), 'Can't Get Used To Losing You' (Andy Williams), 'Suspicion' (Terry Stafford); 'Seven Day Weekend' (Gary 'U.S.' Bonds) and 'Spanish Lace' (Gene McDaniels). Around the time of the team's break-up in 1965, Shuman collaborated with several other writers. These included John McFarland for Billy J. Kramer's UK number 1, 'Little Children', Clive Westlake for 'Here I Go Again' (the Hollies), ex-pop star, Kenny Lynch, for 'Sha-La-La-La-Lee' (Small Faces), 'Loves Just A Broken Heart' (Cilla Black), producer Jerry Ragavoy for 'Get It While You Can' and 'Look At Granny Run, Run' (Howard Tate). Subsequently, Shuman moved to Paris, where he occasionally performed his own one-man show, and issued solo albums such as *Amerika* and *Imagine...*, as well as writing several songs for one of France's few rock 'n' roll stars, Johnny Halliday. In 1968 Shuman translated the lyrics of French composer Jacques Brel; these were recorded by many artists including Dusty Springfield, Scott Walker and Rod McKuen. Together with Eric Blau, he devised, adapted and wrote lyrics for the revue, *Jacques Brel Is Alive And Well And Living In Paris*. Shuman also starred in the piece, which became a world-wide success. In October 1989, *Budgie*, a musical set in London's Soho district, with Schuman's music and Don Black's lyrics, opened in the West End. It starred former pop star, turned actor and entrepreneur, Adam Faith, and UK soap opera actress, Anita Dobson. The show closed after only three months, losing more than £1,000,000. Shuman wrote several other shows, including *Amadeo, Or How To Get Rid Of It*, based on an Ionesco play, a Hong Kong portrayal of *Madame Butterfly* and a re-working of Bertolt Brecht and Kurt Weill's opera, *Aufstieg Und Fall Der Stadt Mahogonny*. None has yet reached the commercial theatre. After undergoing a liver operation in the spring of 1991, he died in London.

Silk Stockings

Two years after *Silk Stockings* began its successful run on Broadway, MGM released this screen version which reunited Fred Astaire with one of his most thrilling dancing partners, Cyd Charisse. Leonard Gershe and Leonard Spigelgass's screenplay was adapted from the show's libretto, which itself was based on the 1939 Greta Garbo movie *Ninotchka* and a story by Melchior Lengyel. The plot concerns a beautiful Russian emissary, Nina (Ninotchka), played by Charisse, who eventually falls for an American businessman (Astaire) after being sent to the US in an effort to discover why three previous 'comrades' have failed to retrieve a Russian composer who is believed to be contemplating defection to the West. However, by then, the trio of messengers, Jules Munshin, Peter Lorre and Joseph Buloff, are themselves well on the way to capitulating to the capitalist way of life. Most of Cole Porter's songs from the stage show were retained and two new ones, 'Fated To Be Mated' and 'The Ritz Roll And Rock', added. The dancing, predictably, was 'out of this world', and Astaire was his usual charming vocal self on numbers such as 'All Of You', 'Paris Loves Lovers' and 'It's A Chemical Reaction, That's All' (with Charisse, dubbed by Carol Richards), and 'Stereophonic Sound' (with Janis Paige). Other numbers included 'Too Bad', 'Silk Stockings', 'Satin And Silk', 'Without Love', 'Josephine', and 'The Red Blues'. After helping themselves to generous portions of Western liquid hospitality, the three reluctant Reds, Munshin, Lorre and Buloff, were hilarious as they muse - musically - on the subject of 'Siberia'. *Silk Stockings*, which turned out to be Fred Astaire's last musical film (apart from the generally unsatisfactory *Finian's Rainbow*, made when he was nearly 70), was a fine affair. The choreographers were Hermes Pan and Eugene Loring (with Fred Astaire, as usual, uncredited) and the director was Rouben Mamoulian. The musical director was André Previn, and the film was photographed in Metrocolor and Cinemascope.

Silvestri, Alan

b. New York, USA. A composer of film music, from the 70s through to the 90s. Silvestri studied at the Berklee College Of Music in Boston, Massachusetts, before scoring some low-budget movies and working on the US television series, *Chips* In the late 70s and early 80s he composed the music for *Las Vegas Lady*, *The Amazing Dobermans* (starring Fred Astaire in an off-beat role), and *Par Ou Tes Rentre?* (1984). Subsequently he scored blockbuster productions such as *Romancing The Stone*, *Back To The Future*, and the remarkable live-action *Who Framed Roger Rabbit* (1988). His other credits during the 80s included *Fandang*, *Summer Rental*, *Delta Force*, *Flight Of The Navigator*, *No Mercy*, *Outrageous Fortune*, *Predator*, *Overboard*, *My Stepmother Is An Alien*, *She's Out Of Control*, *The Abyss*, and *Back To The Future Part II* (1989). In the following year Silvestri also scored the third and final episode of director Robert Zemeckis'

time-travel series, *Back To The Future Part III*, starring Michael J. Fox. During the early 90s Silvestri continued to compose for highly commercial movies such as *Young Guns II*, *Predator 2*, *Dutch*, *Soapdish*, *Ricochet*, *Shattered*, *Driving Me Crazy*, *Father Of The Bride* (a re-make of the 1950 classic starring Steve Martin), *Stop! Or My Mom Will Shoot*, *Death Becomes Her*, *The Bodyguard*, *Cop And A Half*, *Super Mario Brothers*, *The Abyss: Special Edition*, and *Grumpy Old Men* (1993). In 1992, following Ashman and Menken's recent success with *The Little Mermaid* and *Beauty And The Beast*, Silvestri scored the animated feature, *Ferngully...The Last Rainforest*, based on Diana Young's stories, *Ferngully*.

Sinatra, Frank

b. Francis Albert Sinatra, 12 December 1915, Hoboken, New Jersey, USA. After working for a while in the office of a local newspaper, *The Jersey Observer*, Sinatra decided to pursue a career as a singer. Already an admirer of Bing Crosby, Sinatra was impelled to pursue this course after attending a 1933 Crosby concert. Sinatra sang whenever and wherever he could, working locally in clubs and bars. Then, in 1935 he entered a popular US radio talent show, *Major Bowes Amateur Hour*. Also on the show was a singing trio and the four young men found themselves teamed together by the no-nonsense promoter. The ad-hoc teaming worked and the group, renamed 'The Hoboken Four', won first prize. Resulting from this came a succession of concert dates with the Major Bowes travelling show along with club and occasional radio dates. By 1938 Sinatra was singing on several shows on each of a half-dozen radio stations, sometimes for expenses often for nothing. The experience and especially the exposure were vital if he was to be recognised. Among the bands with which he performed was one led by songwriter Harold Arlen but in 1939, shortly after he married his childhood sweetheart, Nancy Barbato, he was heard and hired by Harry James who had only recently formed his own big band. James recognised Sinatra's talent from the start and also identified the source of his determination to succeed, his massive self-confidence and powerful ego. During their brief association, James remarked to an interviewer, 'His name is Sinatra, and he considers himself the greatest vocalist in the business. Get that! No one's even heard of him! He's never had a hit record, and he looks like a wet rag, but he says he's the greatest.' In 1939 and early 1940 Sinatra made a number of records with James and began to develop a small following. His records with James included 'My Buddy' and 'All Or Nothing At All'.

In 1940 Sinatra was approached with an offer by Tommy Dorsey, then leading one of the most popular swing era bands. Only some six months had expired on Sinatra's two-year contract with James, who must have realised he was parting with a potential goldmine but he was a generous-spirited man and let the singer go. Sinatra had many successful records with Dorsey including 'Polka Dots And Moonbeams', 'Imagination', 'Fools Rush In', 'I'll Never Smile Again', 'The One I Love', 'Violets For Your Furs', 'How About You?' and 'In The Blue Of The Evening', some of which became fixtures in his repertoire. One record from this period became a major hit a few years later when the USA entered World War II. This song, recorded at Sinatra's second session with Dorsey in February 1940, was 'I'll Be Seeing You' and its lyric gained a special significance for servicemen and the women they had left behind. Sinatra's popularity with those females, achieved despite or perhaps because of his gangling unheroic and rather vulnerable appearance, prompted him to leave Dorsey and begin a solo career. Despite a tough line taken by Dorsey over the remaining half of his five-year contract (Dorsey allegedly settled for 43% of the singer's gross over the next 10 years), Sinatra quit. Within months his decision was proved to be right. He had become the idol of hordes of teenage girls, his public appearances were sell-outs and his records jostled with one another for hit status. In the early 40s he had appeared in a handful of films as Dorsey's vocalist but by the middle of the decade was appearing in feature films as actor-singer. These included lightweight if enjoyable fare such as *Higher And Higher* (1944), *Anchors Aweigh* (1945), *It Happened In Brooklyn* (1947), *The Kissing Bandit* (1948) and *Double Dynamite* (1951). By the 50s, however, Sinatra's career was in trouble; both as singer and actor he appeared to have reached the end of the road. His acting career had suffered in part from the quality of material he was offered, and accepted. Nevertheless, it was his film career that was the first to revive when he landed the role of Angelo Maggio in *From Here To Eternity* (1953) for which he won an Academy Award as Best Supporting Actor. Thereafter, he was taken seriously as an actor even if he rarely was given the same standard of role or achieved the same quality of performance.

He continued to make films, usually in straight acting roles but occasionally in musicals. Among the former were *The Man With The Golden Arm* (1955), one of the roles which matched his breakthrough performance as Maggio, *Johnny Concho* (1956), *Kings Go Forth* (1958), *A Hole In The Head* (1959), *The Manchurian Candidate* (1962), *Robin And The 7 Hoods* (1964), *Von Ryan's Express* (1965), *Assault On A Queen* (1966), *Tony Rome* (1967) and *The Detective* (1968). His musicals included *Guys And Dolls* (1955), *High Society* (1956) and *Can-Can* (1960). Later, he appeared in an above average television movie, *Contract On Cherry Street* (1977) and *The First Deadly Sin* (1980).

Soon after his Oscar-winning appearance in *From Here To Eternity*, Sinatra made a comeback as a recording artist. He had been recording for Columbia where he fell out of step when changes were made to the company's musical policy and in 1953 he was signed by Capitol Records. Sinatra's first session at Capitol was arranged and conducted by Axel Stordahl whom Sinatra had known on the Dorsey band. For the next session, however, he was teamed with Nelson Riddle. Sinatra had heard the results of earlier recording sessions made by Nat 'King' Cole at Capitol on which Riddle had collaborated. Sinatra was deeply impressed by the results and some sources suggest that on joining Capitol he had asked for Riddle. The results of this partnership set Sinatra's singing career firmly in the spotlight. Over the next few years classic albums such as *Songs For Young Lovers*, *This Is Sinatra*, *A Swingin' Affair*, *Come Fly With Me*, *Swing Easy*, *In The Wee Small Hours* and the exceptional *Songs For Swingin' Lovers* set standards for popular singers which have been rarely equalled and almost never surpassed. The two men were intensely aware of one another's talents and although critics were unanimous in their praise of Riddle, the arranger was unassumingly diffident, declaring that it was the singer's 'great talent that put him back on top.' For all Riddle's diffidence, there can be little doubt that the arranger encouraged Sinatra's latent feeling for jazz which helped create the relaxed yet superbly swinging atmosphere which epitomised their work together. On his albums for Capitol, his own label Reprise, and other labels, sometimes with Riddle, other times with Robert Farnon, Neal Hefti, Gordon Jenkins, Quincy Jones, Billy May or Stordahl, Sinatra built upon his penchant for the best in American popular song, displaying a deep understanding of the wishes of composer and lyricist.

Fans old and new bought his albums in their tens of thousands and several reached the top in the *Billboard* charts. The 1955 album, *In The Wee Small Hours*, was in for 29 weeks reaching number 2; the following year's *Songs For Swingin' Lovers* charted for 66 weeks, also reaching the second spot. *Come Fly With Me*, from 1958, spent 71 weeks in the charts reaching number 1 and other top positions were attained by 1958's *Only The Lonely*, 120 weeks, 1960's *Nice 'N' Easy*, 86 weeks, and in 1966, *Strangers In The Night*, 73 weeks. The title song from this last album also made number 1 in *Billboard*'s singles charts as did the following year's 'Something Stupid' on which he duetted with his daughter, Nancy Sinatra. At a time in popular music's history when ballads were not the most appealing form, and singers were usually in groups and getting younger by the minute, these were no mean achievements for a middle-aged solo singer making a comeback. The secret of this late success lay in Sinatra's superior technical ability, his wealth of experience, his abiding love for the material with which he worked and the invariably high standards of professionalism he brought to his recordings and public performances. During his stint with Dorsey, the singer had taken a marked professional interest in the band leader's trombone playing. He consciously learned breath control, in particular circular breathing, and the use of dynamics from Dorsey. Additionally, he employed Dorsey's legato style which aided the smooth phrasing of his best ballad work. Complementing this, Sinatra's enjoyment of jazz and the company of jazz musicians prompted him to adopt jazz phrasing which greatly enhanced his rhythmic style. More than any other popular singer of his or previous generations, Sinatra learned the value of delayed phrasing and singing behind the beat, and he and his arrangers invariably found exactly the right tempo. His relaxed rhythmic style contrasted strikingly with the stiffer-sounding singers who preceded him. Even Crosby, whose popularity Sinatra eventually surpassed, later accommodated some of Sinatra's stylistic devices. (Crosby's habitual lazy-sounding style was of a different order from Sinatra's and until late in his career he never fully shook off his 2/4 style while Sinatra, almost from the start, was completely at home with the 4/4 beat of swing.)

Sinatra's revived career brought him more attention even than in his heyday as the bobby-soxers' idol. Much of the interest was intrusive and led to frequently acrimonious and sometimes violent clashes with reporters. With much of what is written about him stemming from a decidedly ambivalent view, the picture of the man behind the voice is often confused. Undoubtedly, his private persona is multi-faceted. He has been described by acquaintances as quick-tempered, pugnacious, sometimes vicious and capable of extreme verbal cruelty and he has often displayed serious misjudgement in the company he keeps. In marked contrast, others have categorically declared him to be enormously generous to friends in need and to individuals and organizations he believes can benefit from his personal or financial support. His political stance has changed dramatically over the years and here again his judgement seems to be flawed. At first a Democrat, he supported Roosevelt and later Kennedy with enormous enthusiasm. His ties with the Kennedy clan were close, and not always for the best of reasons. Sinatra was unceremoniously dropped by the Kennedys following revelations that he had introduced to John Kennedy a woman who became simultaneously the mistress of the President of the United States and a leading figure in the Mafia. Sinatra then became a Republican and lent his support as fund-raiser and campaigner to Richard Nixon and Ronald Reagan, apparently oblivious to their serious flaws.

An immensely rich man, with interests in industry, real estate, recording companies, film and television production, Sinatra has chosen to continue working, making frequent comebacks and presenting a never-ending succession of 'farewell' concerts which, as time passed, became less like concerts and more like major events in contemporary popular culture. He continued to attract adoring audiences and in the late 80s and early 90s, despite being in his mid- to late seventies, could command staggering fees for personal appearances. Ultimately, however, when an assessment has to be made of his life, it is not the money or the worship of his fans that matters; neither is it the mixed quality of his film career and the uncertainties surrounding his personal characteristics and shortcomings. What really matters is that in his treatment of the classics from the Great American Songbook, Sinatra has made a unique contribution to 20th-century popular music. Despite an occasional lapse, when he replaces carefully-crafted lyrics with his own inimitable (yet all-too-often badly imitated) phrases, over several decades he fashioned countless timeless performances. There are some songs which, however many singers may have recorded them before or since Sinatra, or will record them in the future, have become inextricably linked with his name: 'I'll Walk Alone', 'It Could Happen To You', 'I'll Never Smile Again', 'Violets For Your Furs', 'How About You?', 'Jeepers Creepers', 'All Of Me', 'Taking A Chance On Love', 'Just One Of Those Things', 'My Funny Valentine', 'They Can't Take That Away From Me', 'I Get A Kick Out Of You', 'You Make Me Feel So Young', 'Old Devil Moon', 'The Girl Next Door', 'My One And Only Love', 'Three Coins In The Fountain', 'Love And Marriage', 'Swingin' Down The Lane', 'Come Fly With Me', 'Fly Me To The Moon', 'The Tender Trap', 'Chicago', 'New York, New York', 'Let Me Try Again', 'Night And Day', 'Here's That Rainy Day', 'You Make Me Feel So Young', 'Strangers In The Night', 'I Thought About You', 'Lady Is A Tramp', 'Anything Goes', 'Night And Day', 'All The Way', 'One For My Baby', 'I've Got You Under My Skin'.

Not all these songs are major examples of the songwriters' art yet even on lesser material, of which 'My Way' is a notable example, he provides a patina of quality the songs and their writers may not deserve and which no one else could have supplied. Since the 70s Sinatra's voice has shown serious signs of decay. The pleasing baritone had given way to a worn and slightly rusting replica of what it once had been. Nevertheless, he sang on, adjusting to the changes in his voice and as often as not still creating exemplary performances of many of his favourite songs. In these twilight years he was especially effective in the easy swinging mid-tempo he had always preferred and which concealed the inevitable vocal deterioration wrought by time. He made records into the 80s, *LA Is My Lady* being the last although with so many farewell concerts and television spectaculars who can say if the last record has yet been released. In assessing Sinatra's place in popular music it is very easy to slip into hyperbole. After all, through dedication to his craft and his indisputable love for the songs he sang, Sinatra became the greatest exponent of a form of music which he helped turn into an art form. In so doing he became an icon of popular culture which is no mean achievement for a skinny kid from Hoboken. Writing in the *Observer*, when Sinatra's retirement was thought, mistakenly, to be imminent, music critic Benny Green observed: 'What few people, apart from musicians, have never seemed to grasp is that he is not simply the best popular singer of his generation . . . but the culminating point in an evolutionary process which has refined the art of interpreting words set to music. Nor is there even the remotest possibility that he will have a successor. Sinatra was the result of a fusing of a set of historical circumstances which can never be repeated.' Sinatra himself has never publicly spoken of his work in such glowing terms, choosing instead to describe himself simply as a 'saloon singer'. Deep in his heart, however, Sinatra must know that Green's judgement is the more accurate and it is one which will long be echoed by countless millions of fans all around the world. Musically at least, it is a world better for the care which Frank Sinatra has lavished upon its popular songs. In 1992, a two-part television biography, *Sinatra*, was transmitted in the US, produced by Tina Sinatra, and starring Philip Casnoff in the leading role. Almost inevitably, it topped the weekly ratings. Capitol Records re-signed Sinatra after 30 years with Reprise Records and announced a new album as 'the recording event of the decade'. The title *Duets* was a brilliant piece of marketing, it had Sinatra temed up with a varied all-star cast including Aretha Franklin, Carly Simon, Barbra Streisand, Tony Bennett, Natalie Cole, Kenny G and U2's Bono.

Selected albums: *Sing And Dance With Frank Sinatra* (1950), *Songs For Young Lovers* (1955), *Swing Easy* (1955), *In The Wee Small Hours* (1955), *Songs For Swingin' Lovers* (1956), *High Society* (1956, film soundtrack), *Close To You* (1957), *A Swingin' Affair!* (1957), *Where Are You?* (1957), *Pal Joey* (1957, film soundtrack), *A Jolly Christmas From Frank Sinatra* (1957), *Come Fly With Me* (1958), *Frank Sinatra Sings For Only The Lonely* (1958), *Come Dance With Me!* (1959), *No One Cares* (1959), *Can-Can* (1960, film soundtrack), *Nice 'N' Easy* (1960), *Sinatra's Swinging Session!!!* (1961), *Ring-A-Ding Ding!* (1961), *Sinatra Swings* (1961), *Come Swing With Me!* (1961), *I Remember Tommy...*(1961), *Sinatra And Strings* (1961), *Point Of No Return* (1961), *Sinatra And Swingin' Brass* (1962), *All Alone* (1962), with Count Basie *Sinatra-Basie* (1962), *The Concert Sinatra* (1963), *The Select Johnny Mercer* (1963), *Sinatra's Sinatra* (1963), *Come Blow Your Horn* (1963, film soundtrack), *Days Of Wine And Roses, Moon River, And Other Academy Award Winners* (1964), with Bing Crosby and Fred Waring *America I Hear You Singing* (1964), with Basie *It Might As Well Be Swing* (1964), *Softly As I Leave You* (1964),

Sinatra '65 (1965), *September Of My Years* (1965), *My Kind Of Broadway* (1965), *Moonlight Sinatra* (1965), *A Man And His Music* (1965), *Strangers In The Night* (1966), *Sinatra At The Sands* (1966), *That's Life* (1966), *Francis Albert Sinatra And Antonio Carlos Jobim* (1967), *Frank Sinatra (The World We Knew)* (1967), with Nancy Sinatra *Frank And Nancy* (1967), with Duke Ellington *Francis A. And Edward K.* (1968), *Cycles* (1968), *The Sinatra Family Wish You A Merry Christmas* (1968), *My Way* (1969), *A Man Alone And Other Songs By Rod McKuen* (1969), *Watertown* (1970), with Antonio Carlos Jobim *Sinatra And Company* (1971), *Ol' Blue Eyes Is Back* (1973), *Some Nice Things I've Missed* (1974), *Sinatra - The Main Event Live* (1974), *Trilogy: Past, Present, Future* (1980), *She Shot Me Down* (1981), *LA Is My Lady* (1984), *Sings The Songs Of Cahn And Styne* (1993), *Duets* (1993). Compilations: *This Is Sinatra!* (1956), *That Old Feeling* (1956) *Frankie* (1957), *Adventures Of The Heart* (1957), *This Is Sinatra, Volume 2* (1958), *The Frank Sinatra Story* (1958), *Look To Your Heart* (1959), *All The Way* (1961), *Sinatra Sings...Of Love And Things* (1962), *Tell Her You Love Her* (1963), *Sinatra: A Man And His Music (1960-65)* (1965), *The Movie Songs (1954-60)* (1967), *Frank Sinatra's Greatest Hits!* (1968), *Frank Sinatra's Greatest Hits, Vol. 2* (1972), *Round # 1* (1974), *Portrait Of Sinatra* (1977), *Radio Years* (1987), *Rare Recordings 1935-70* (1989), *Gold Collection* (1993).

Further reading: *Sinatra*, Robin Douglas Home. *Sinatra: A Biography*, Arnold Shaw. *The Frank Sinatra Scrapbook*, Richard Peters. *Sinatra: The Man And His Music - The Recording Artistry Of Francis Albert Sinatra 1939-1992*, Ed O'Brien and Scott P. Sayers. *His Way: The Unauthorized Biography Of Frank Sinatra*, Kitty Kelly. *Frank Sinatra: My Father*, Nancy Sinatra.

Sing As We Go

Regarded by many as the best of the films that the popular Lancashire entertainer Gracie Fields appeared in, *Sing As We Go* was presented to highly appreciative audiences in 1934 courtesy of producer-director Basil Dean and Associated Talking Pictures. Not just an amusing and tuneful musical, this picture was also something of a social document as well, touching as it did on the difficulties of unemployment in the north of England. Grace Platt (Fields) leads her fellow workers out in style when the Greybeck Mill is forced to close. Not one to sit around and wait for something to happen, Grace 'gets on her bike' and cycles to Blackpool where she (briefly) works as a waitress in a boarding house, a palmist's assistant and 'The Human Spider' in a magician's show at the Pleasure Beach. She is delighted when her new-found friend, Phyllis (Dorothy Hyson), wins first prize in the Bathing Belles competition, but less than pleased when Phyllis becomes attracted to her friend from the mill, assistant manager Hugh Phillips (John Loder), who is also in Blackpool trying to drum up business.

Sing As We Go

Not one to hold a grudge, Grace helps Hugh in his efforts to re-open the mill, and, as the new Welfare Officer, is at the head of the exultant march back to work, singing (not unexpectedly) 'Sing As We Go'. That song, and 'Just A Catchy Little Tune', were the work of the Welsh songwriter Harry Parr-Davies who wrote several other numbers for Gracie Fields, and was her accompanist for a time. The other songs in *Sing As We Go* were 'Thora' (Stephen Adams-Frederick E. Weatherly) and 'Little Bottom Drawer' (Will Haines-Jimmy Harper). As usual with these small but significant British films, the supporting parts were beautifully cast. In this instance the players included Frank Pettingell as Grace's fun-loving Uncle Murgatroyd, Stanley Holloway as a policeman, Lawrence Grossmith, Arthur Sinclair, Morris Harvey, Maire O'Neill, Ben Field, Norman Walker, Margaret Yarde, and Olive Sloane. Gordon Wellesley and the distinguished English author, J.B. Priestley, adapted the screenplay from an original story by Priestley.

Sing You Sinners

One of the screen's all-time favourite song-and-dance men, Donald O'Connor, made his debut - at the age of 13 - in this Paramount release of 1938. In Claude Binyon's heart-warming story, he plays the kid brother of Bing Crosby and Fred MacMurray, two guys who never see eye-to-eye - except for music. MacMurray is a thrifty 'small town Galahad, the breakfast-eating, four button type' (as Sky Masterson says in *Guys And Dolls*), while Crosby is a gambler who continually wastes the family's money until one day he manages to buy a horse, which, with O'Connor aboard, romps home first in the big race. Ellen Drew provided the love interest, and Elizabeth Patterson was amusing (and patient) as the trio's mother. Also in the cast were William Haade, Irving Bacon, and Harry Barris. Johnny Burke and Jimmy Monaco contributed several agreeable songs including 'Laugh And Call It Love', 'Where Is Central Park?', 'I've Got A Pocketful Of Dreams', and 'Don't Let That Moon Get Away', the last two of which became hits for Crosby, and endured. However, the film's musical highspot was probably Hoagy Carmichael and Frank Loesser's 'Small Fry', which the three brothers (who gig together in the evenings) turned into an easy-going, charming routine. Bing Crosby and his friend, lyricist Johnny Mercer, also made a popular recording of the number. *Sing You Sinners*, which was directed by Wesley Ruggles, went on to make beautiful music at the box-office.

Singin' In The Rain

Generally regarded as the most entertaining film musical of all time, this MGM classic was released in 1952. Betty Comden and Adolph Green's witty screenplay parodies that momentous and painful period in Hollywood movie history when talkies took over from silent pictures. Don Lockwood (Gene Kelly) and Lina Lamont (Jean Hagen) are Monumental Studio's brightest silent stars. Lockwood, encouraged by his ex-dancing partner Cosmo Brown (Donald O'Connor), has no problem making the transition, while Lina's voice is so squeaky and sharp it could break glass. Luckily, aspiring actress Kathy Selden (Debbie Reynolds) pops out of a giant cake and provides a dubbing service and Kelly's love interest. The team's first attempt at a sound film is a total disaster, but Kelly and O'Connor turn it into a musical, and, at the triumphant premiere, Reynolds is revealed as the hidden starlet, while Hagen is hilariously disgraced. Singin' In The Rain is indeed one of the greatest film musicals of all time, and its comedy exists apart from, and within the musical numbers. The scenes poking fun at the changeover to sound are very effective, particularly when irate director Roscoe Dexter (Douglas Fowley) is attempting to place Hagen's microphone in a strategic position - desperate to find a place on the set ('It's in the bush!') or on her person where a consistent level of sound can be obtained. Most of the score consisted of a collection of songs written by Arthur Freed and Nacio Herb Brown for early MGM musicals, and every one of them is performed brilliantly. O'Connor is marvellously athletic and funny on 'Make 'Em Laugh' (all critics noted the similarities with Cole Porter's 'Be A Clown'), and on two duets with Kelly, 'Fit As A Fiddle' (Al Goodhart-Al Hoffman) and 'Moses Supposes' (Roger Edens-Comden-Green). Reynolds joins both of them for the uplifting 'Good Morning', and then, just with Kelly, milks the lovely 'You Were Meant For Me' for all its worth. Other highlights include the spectacular 'Broadway Ballet' which is presented as part of the film within a film featuring Cyd Charisse and Kelly, and 'All I Do Is Dream Of You', 'Beautiful Girl', 'I've Got A Feelin' You're Foolin'', 'Should I', and 'Would You?'. Yet the moment from the film people always remember, and the clip that most frequently crops up in nostalgia programmes, is the one in which Kelly splashes around in the teeming rain, viewed by a rather bemused and soaking-wet policeman. Truly a memorable moment from a memorable film, which was photographed in Technicolor by Harold Rosson

Singin' In The Rain

and produced by Arthur Freed's MGM unit. The director-choreographers were Gene Kelly and Stanley Donen.

In 1983 Comden and Green adapted the film into a stage musical which ran at the London Palladium for over three years, breaking all theatre records. It starred Tommy Steele (who also directed), Roy Castle, Sarah Payne and Danielle Carson, and featured several additional songs. A 1985 Broadway production failed to recover its costs.

Singing Fool, The

According to the American trade paper *Variety*, this part-talkie film - Al Jolson and Warner Brothers' follow-up to *The Jazz Singer* - grossed nearly $4 million in the US and Canada alone following its release in 1928. C. Graham Baker's screenplay was even more schmaltz-laden than Jolson's previous trail-blazing effort, with that film's tear-jerking 'My Mammy' being more than matched on the maudlin scale by 'Sonny Boy', which Jolson croons to his three-year-old screen son (Davey Lee) when he knows the boy is dying. Songwriters De Sylva, Brown And Henderson are said to have written the cliché-ridden number for a laugh, but there was nothing funny about the character who sang it. Even before his son's illness, the successful singer's wife (Josephine Dunn) had walked out on him, and he was going rapidly downhill before a nightclub cigarette girl (Betty Bronson) gave him some loving and self respect. Once again Jolson was tremendous, his magnetic personality overwhelming every other aspect of the production as he punched out song after song. These included 'It All Depends On You' and 'I'm Sitting On Top Of The World' (De Sylva, Brown And Henderson), 'There's a Rainbow 'Round My Shoulder' (Dave Dreyer-Billy Rose-Al Jolson), 'Golden Gate' (Dreyer-Joseph Meyer-Rose-Jolson), 'Keep Smiling At Trouble' (Jolson-De Sylva-Lewis Gensler), and 'The Spaniard That Blighted My Life' (Billy Merson). The dance director for *The Singing Fool* was Larry Ceballos, and the film was directed by Lloyd Bacon and produced by Darryl F. Zanuck.

Sleeping Beauty (see Disney, Walt)

Slipper And The Rose, The

Generally regarded as a disappointing attempt to musicalize the traditional Cinderella fairy tale, this film was made in the UK by Paradine Co-Productions (Executive producer David Frost; producer Stuart Lyons). Director Bryan Forbes's screenplay (written with Robert and Richard Sherman) had some delightful and endearing moments, but there were more than a few dull periods too in the running time of nearly two and a half hours. Richard Chamberlain was a suitably regal Prince Edward, and Gemma Craven gave a charming performance as the young girl who did - eventually - go to the ball. The list of supporting players contained some of the best and most distinguished actors in British films, theatre and television, including Annette Crosbie (Fairy Godmother), Edith Evans (Dowager Queen), Michael Hordern (King of Euphrania), Margaret Lockwood (Stepmother), Kenneth More (Chamberlain), and Christopher Gable, Julian Orchard, John Turner, Roy Barraclough, Valentine Dyall, and André Morell. The talented and prolific Sherman Brothers provided the score, which consisted of: 'Why Can't I Be Two People?', 'What Has Love Got To Do With Getting Married?', 'Once I Was Loved', 'What A Comforting Thing To Know', 'Protocoligorically Correct', 'A Bride-Finding Ball', 'Suddenly It Happens', 'Secret Kingdom', 'He/She Danced With Me', 'Position And Positioning', 'Tell Me Anything (But Not That I Love Him)', and 'I Can't Forget The Melody'. It all looked beautiful, due in no small part to production designer Ray Simm and the Technicolor and Panavision photography by Toni Imi. It was reissued in 1980 with 20 minutes cut.

Soldiers Of The King

Although the popular British actress, singer and comedienne Cicely Courtneidge was not accompanied on the screen in this 1933 Gainsborough release by her husband, Jack Hulbert, he did co-write the screenplay with W.P. Lipscomb and John Horton, and is said to have assisted Maurice Elvey with the direction. It all came about from an original story by Douglas Furber in which Courtneidge plays the dual roles of retired music hall artist Jenny Marvello and her daughter Maisie, the reigning queen of a variety troupe. In the latter part she runs through her impressive range of male impersonations and comic business, while as the older woman she demonstrates an hitherto unseen dramatic acting ability. There were several well-known names such as Edward Everett Horton, Anthony Bushell, Bransby Williams, Dorothy Hyson, Frank Cellier, and Leslie Sarony in a the supporting cast which also included Rebla, Herschel Henlere, Arty Ash, Ivor McLaren, David Deveen, and Olive Sloan. The two most memorable songs were 'The Moment I Saw You' (Noel Gay-Clifford Grey) and the rousing 'There's Something About A Soldier' (Gay). This solo outing for Courtneidge enjoyed considerable success, but, even so, the old team were back together again later in the same year with *Falling For You*.

Song Is Born, A

A lame remake, seven years later, by director Howard Hawks of his own 1941 film, *Ball Of Fire*, this tells broadly the same story. A group of bookish professors, locked away for years writing an encyclopedia, discover that the world of music has moved on and send one of their number out into the streets to discover what has been going on. Unfortunately for the dramatics, Danny Kaye and Virginia Mayo are no match for the original's Gary Cooper and Barbara Stanwyck. Fortunately for jazz lovers, there is rather a lot of talent on display. As might be expected, who you see on the screen is not always who you hear on the soundtrack but, amongst others, there are the considerable presence's of Louis Armstrong, Lionel Hampton, Tommy Dorsey, Charlie Barnet, Mel Powell and Louie Bellson. Benny Goodman has an acting role as one of the professors who is also a dab hand on the clarinet.

Sound Of Jazz, The

An outstanding achievement in the presentation of jazz on US television, this 1957 film was conceived and produced by Robert Herridge with the advice of jazz writers Nat Hentoff and Whitney Balliett. Directed by Jack Smight, the film shows the musicians playing in an atmosphere of complete relaxation and achieving an exceptionally high standard of performance. Regardless of who the musicians might have been, the concept and format would have been commendable. The fact that the musicians on display are some of the greatest figures in the history of jazz make this an hour of continuous joy. The all-star bands led by Count Basie and Red Allen feature Doc Cheatham, Freddie Green, Coleman Hawkins, Jo Jones, Roy Eldridge, Joe Newman, Gerry Mulligan, Rex Stewart, Earle Warren, Dicky Wells, Ben Webster, Lester Young, singer Jimmy Rushing, Vic Dickenson, Danny Barker, Milt Hinton, Nat Pierce (who also contributed the arrangements played by the Basie-led band) and Pee Wee Russell. Also on hand is the Jimmy Giuffre trio with Jim Hall and Jim Atlas playing 'The Train And The River', and Thelonious Monk plays 'Blue Monk' accompanied by Ahmed Abdul-Malik and Osie Johnson. If all this were not enough there is Billie Holiday accompanied by Mal Waldron. She sings her own composition, 'Fine And Mellow', in what must be this song's definitive performance, backed by many of the listed musicians with Lester Young contributing a poignant solo. Four decades after its making, this film remains a highwater mark in jazz and its standards remain those to which all other film-makers must aspire.

Sound Of Miles Davis, The

Produced and directed by the same team responsible for *The Sound Of Jazz* (Robert Herridge and Jack Smight), this 1959 film was originally entitled *Theater For A Song*. Davis is presented with his quintet (John Coltrane, Wynton Kelly, Paul Chambers and Jimmy Cobb) and also with Gil Evans And His Orchestra. The performance captures Davis in eloquent form and the contribution from the other musicians on hand help make this an important filmed record of one of the music's most important figures.

Sound Of Music, The

Dubbed 'The Sound Of Mucus' by some for its almost overwhelming sentimentality and sweetness, this film is nevertheless still, in the early 90s, hovering around the Top 40 highest-earning movies of all-time in the USA, and that level of success has been reiterated around the world. Ernest Lehman' screenplay, which was based on the 1959 Broadway musical and the real-life story of the Austrian Von Trapp family of folk singers. Maria (Julie Andrews), a postulant nun in a Saltzburg convent, whose unconventional ways drive her fellow nuns to despair, is engaged by widower Captain Von Trapp (Christopher Plummer) as governess to his seven children. After one or two domestic disagreements (such as when she cuts up the curtains to make clothes for the children), they eventually fall in love and marry. Their happiness is disturbed by the imminence of World War II and the presence of the Nazi army in Austria. When Von Trapp is required to report for military service, the whole family escape from the soldiers' clutches at the end of a concert performance, just as the real Von Trapp family did. Some of the film's most charming moments came when Maria is teaching the children music, and also when they are operating a marionette theatre together. Julie Andrews gave a tender, most appealing performance as the young girl maturing into a woman, and Plummer was bombastic and tender in turns. Eleanor Parker (as the Captain-hungry Baroness) and Richard Haydn (in the role of Max Detweiler, a man who would go anywhere in the world for a free bed and breakfast), led a supporting cast which included Peggy Wood, Charmian Carr, Anna Lee, Portia Nelson, and Marni Nixon. Most of Richard Rodgers and Oscar Hammerstein's songs from the stage show were retained, along with two new ones ('Something Good' and 'I Have Confidence In Me') in a score that consisted of 'The Sound Of Music', 'Maria', 'Sixteen Going On Seventeen', 'My Favourite Things', 'Climb Ev'ry Mountain', 'The Lonely Goatherd', 'Do-Re-Mi', 'Edelweiss', and 'So Long, Farewell'. Bill Lee dubbed Plummer's vocals. Marc Breaux and DeeDee Wood choreographed the delightful dance sequences, and the producer-director for 20th Century-Fox was Robert Wise. The memorable opening alpine aerial shot was credited to Ted McCord who photographed the film superbly in DeLuxe Color and Todd-AO. *The Sound Of Music* won Academy Awards for best film, director, and music scoring (Irwin Kostal), and became the highest-grossing film in the USA during the 60s. Its soundtrack album spent a total of 70 weeks at number 1 in the UK, and was over a year in the US chart.

South Pacific

This enormously successful screen version of the Richard Rodgers and Oscar Hammerstein's 1949

The Sound Of Music

Broadway hit musical was released by 20th Century-Fox in 1958. Paul Osborn's screenplay, which was adapted from the stage production and James A. Michener's *Tales Of The South Pacific*, told the by now familiar story of life on a South Sea island which is temporarily occupied by American troops during World War II. Two love stories run in parallel: that between the mature, sophisticated French planter, Emile de Becque (Rossano Brazzi), and a young nurse, Nellie Forbush (Mitzi Gaynor); and the other, which involves Lt. Joe Cable (John Kerr) and Liat (France Nuyen), the Polynesian daughter of Bloody Mary (Juanita Hall). Some felt that Oscar Hammerstein and Joshua Logan, who wrote the original libretto, fudged the 'racial issue' by allowing Cable to be killed in action so that he could not marry Liat. On the other hand, Nellie, after much personal torment and heart-searching, found herself able to accept de Becque's ethnic children from a previous marriage. The supporting cast was excellent, with Ray Walston outstanding as Luther Billis. Early on in the film he led a group of fellow marines in the rousing, but poignant 'There Is Nothing Like A Dame', one of the songs in Rogers and Hammerstein's marvellous score that came from Broadway intact - with the addition of one other number, 'My Girl Back Home', which had been written, but not used, for the 1949 show. The remainder of the film's much-loved songs

were 'Dites-moi', 'A Cockeyed Optimist', 'Twin Soliloquies', 'Some Echanted Evening', 'Bloody Mary', 'Bali Ha'i', 'I'm Gonna Wash That Man Right Outa My Hair', 'A Wonderful Guy', 'Younger Than Springtime', 'Happy Talk', 'Honey Bun', 'Carefully Taught', and 'This Nearly Was Mine'. The singing voices of Rossano Brazzi, John Kerr, and Juanita Hall were dubbed by Giorgio Tozzi, Bill Lee, and Muriel Smith respectively. The choreographer was LeRoy Prinz, and Joshua Logan directed, as he had done on Broadway. *South Pacific* was photographed by Leon Shamroy in Technicolor and the Todd-AO wide-screen process. There was a good deal of adverse criticism regarding the use of colour filters in the various musical sequences. The sountrack album proved to be one of the best-sellers of all time, spending an unprecedented (to date) total of 115 weeks at the top of the UK chart, and 31 weeks at number 1 in the USA.

Spring Parade

Remembered particularly for the joyous 'Waltzing In The Clouds' (Robert Stolz and Gus Kahn), this Deanna Durbin vehicle was released by Universal in 1940. This 'veteran' of eight films in the space of four years - and still only 19 years old - was cast as a baker's assistant in old Vienna. She falls for a handsome would-be composer (Robert Cummings), who plays the drums in the army while waiting for his music to be appreciated. S.K. Sakall, as the baker, and Henry Stephenson, in the role of Emperor Franz Joseph, turned Bruce Manning and Felix Jackson's light-hearted (and lightweight) screenplay into an amusing and entertaining movie. Also contributing to the pleasure were Mischa Auer, Henry Stephenson, Anne Gwynne, and the lively duo, Butch And Buddy. The music helped a lot, too. As well as 'Waltzing In the Clouds', which was nominated but beaten for the Oscar that year by 'When You Wish Upon A Star' (from *Pinocchio*), Stolz and Kahn wrote 'When April Sings' and another catchy bit of nonsense, 'It's Foolish But It's Fun'. The other numbers were 'In A Spring Parade' (Charles Previn-Kahn), 'The Dawn Of Love' (Previn-Ralph Freed), and 'Blue Danube Dream' (Johann Strauss II-Kahn). Henry Koster directed yet another in the long line of Durbin hits which would continue for a few years yet.

St Louis Blues

One of the first talkies, and one of few early films to feature jazz or blues artists, this offers the only screen appearance of Bessie Smith, the Empress of the Blues. Directed by Dudley Murphy (who in the same year made *Black And Tan*), this 1929 film features an extended performance of the title song built around a thin story which fully exploits elements of pathos in the lyrics. There is an excellent accompanying band, including Joe Smith and Kaiser Marshall, mostly drawn from the ranks of Fletcher Henderson's band but led on this occasion by James P. Johnson. For all such attractions, however, this film's value lies in this solitary opportunity to see Smith, one of the greatest figures in the history of American popular music and through it to glean some fleeting understanding of the manner in which she commanded attention and dignified the blues.

NB: the same title was used for a 1939 feature film, which includes performances by Maxine Sullivan, and for the 1958 bio-pic based upon the life of W.C. Handy and starring Nat 'King' Cole.

Stage Door Canteen

Released in 1943, this film was a paper-thin excuse for Hollywood to bring onto the screen a stream of mostly front-rank entertainers to brighten war-time gloom. Alongside screen stars are leading figures from Broadway, vaudeville, popular music and jazz. Benny Goodman And His Orchestra, including Jack Jenney, Conrad Gozzo, Jess Stacy, Louie Bellson and Peggy Lee, perform two numbers. Count Basie And His Orchestra, including Buck Clayton, Freddie Green, Walter Page, Harry Edison, Dicky Wells, Buddy Tate, Don Byas, Earle Warren and Jo Jones, perform one number backing Ethel Waters.

Star!

While this 1968 movie biography of London-born actress Gertrude Lawrence failed to even nearly recoup its massive $12 million investment and was generally considered to be far too long, it is by no means a poor picture mainly because the central role is played by Julie Andrews. Wisely, she does not attempt an impersonation, but rather gives an impression of what this darling of London and Broadway musical shows and revues, from the 20s through to the 50s, must have been like. William Fairchild's screenplay begins with Lawrence's childhood days in Clapham when she was part of the family music hall act along with her father (Bruce Forsyth) and his 'lady friend' (Beryl Reid). Director Robert Wise places the adult Lawrence in a projection room watching (and commenting on) the rushes of a biography being compiled about her career and the men in her life, including Richard Crenna as her second husband Richard Aldrich. Noël Coward was probably her greatest influence, and Daniel Massey's portrayal of 'The Master' as an amiable and sophisticated character is one of the movie's most appealing features. His elegant version of 'Forbidden Fruit' which Coward often used as his 'audition song', is a delight. The two stars combine for the 'Red Peppers' sequence from Coward's play *Tonight At 8.30*, and Andrews handles most of the remaining songs with great flair and panache. They included 'Someone to Watch Over Me', 'Do Do Do', and 'Dear Little Boy' (all George Gershwin-Ira Gershwin), "N' Everything' (Buddy De Sylva-Gus Kahn-Al Jolson), 'Limehouse Blues' (Douglas Furber-Philip Braham), 'Burlington Bertie From Bow' (William Hargreaves), 'Jenny' and 'My Ship' (both Kurt Weill-Ira Gershwin), 'The Physician' (Cole Porter), and 'Parisian Pierrot', 'Someday I'll Find You' and 'Has Anybody Seen Our Ship?' (all Coward). The brand new title number was by James Van Heusen and Sammy Cahn. Also among the cast were Michael Craig, Robert Reed, Garrett Lewis, Don Knoll, John Collin, and Alan Oppenheimer, Richard Anthony, and J. Pat O'Malley. Michael Kidd was the choreographer and the film was superbly photographed by Ernest Laszlo in Deluxe Color and Todd-AO. It was directed by Robert Wise and produced for 20th Century-Fox by Saul Chaplin. *Star!* was eventually cut from nearly three hours to just over two, and re-released under the title of *Those Were The Happy Times*. That version lost money too.

Star Is Born, A

Over the years, several films have attempted to strip the veneer of glamour from Hollywood, the film capital of the world, and expose the sadness and bitterness that sometimes lies beneath. *Sunset Boulevard* (1950) is, perhaps, the prime example of the genre, and, more recently, *The Player* (1992) dwelt on the greed and double-dealing inherent in the movie

Star! (Julie Andrews)

business. Adela Rogers St. John's original story, which eventually evolved into the 1954 Warner Brothers musical picture, A Star Is Born, first came to the screen in 1932 under the title of What Price Hollywood? Then, five years later, it was adapted for an Academy Award winning dramatic film entitled A Star Is Born, which had a story by William A. Wellman, a screenplay by Dorothy Parker, Alan Campbell and Robert Carson, and starred Janet Gaynor and Fredric March. Moss Hart's superbly crafted screenplay for the 1954 musical version, which stayed fairly closely to the plot of the previous film, tells of Norman Maine (James Mason), a has-been movie actor, whose temperamental and brutish behaviour result in him being ostracised from Hollywood studios and society. While taking solace in the bottle, he is forced to become dependent on his wife, Esther Blodgett (professional name Vicki Lester), played by Judy Garland. Mainly through his influence (and her talent) she has become a big star herself. Eventually, unable to cope with life at the bottom of the barrel, he drowns himself. Garland was outstanding throughout - this was probably her greatest film role - and Mason, who is said to have been about fifth choice for the part, was wonderful, too. Charles Bickford as the studio head who is reluctant to let Maine go, and Jack Carson in the role of the studio's publicity chief who is only too glad to get rid of him, were in a fine supporting cast along with Lucy Marlow, Grady Sutton, Tommy Noonan, Amanda Blake, Irving Bacon, and James Brown. Harold Arlen and Ira Gershwin wrote most of the songs, including the compelling 'The Man That Got Away', 'Gotta Have Me Go With You', 'Someone At Last', 'It's A New World' and two that were cut because of the film's excessive length, 'Lose That Long Face' and 'Here's What I'm Here For'. The remainder were 'Swanee' (George Gershwin-Irving Caesar) and 'Born In A Trunk' (Leonard Gershe-Roger Edens) which topped and tailed a medley of old songs. The choreographer was Richard Barstow, and the film was produced by Sidney Luft (Garland's then husband), directed by George Cukor, and photographed in Technicolor and CinemaScope. One of the all-time great film musicals, A Star Is Born was rereleased in the 80s with the two songs that were cut from the original print and some other scenes restored.

In the 1976 remake of A Star Is Born, starring Barbra Streisand and Kris Kristofferson, screenwriters John Gregory Dunne, Frank Pierson and Joan Didion set their new plot in the world of rock music, with an appropriate score which included such numbers as 'Lost Inside Of You' (Streisand-Leon Russell), 'I Believe In Love' (Kenny Loggins-Alan And Marilyn Bergman), 'Queen Bee' (Rupert Holmes), and 'The Woman In The Moon' (Paul Williams-Kenny Ascher). Barbra Streisand and Paul Williams also collaborated on 'Love Theme (Evergreen)', which won an Academy Award and topped the US chart. The film was released by Warner Brothers and photographed in Metrocolor and Panavision. The director was Frank Pierson, and A Star Is Born (Mark III) was a smash hit, grossing nearly $40 million in the USA and Canada alone.

Star Spangled Rhythm

Just the thing for the troops - a rousing, star-studded spectacle that must have raised the spirits of war-weary forces and civilians alike when it was released by Paramount in December 1942. For what it was worth, Harry Tugend's screenplay had the Paramount gatekeeper (Victor Moore) pretending to be an important studio executive in order to impress the buddies of his sailor son (Eddie Bracken). The latter's efforts to organize a massive show is the perfect hook on which to hang a bundle of songs and sketches performed by many of Paramount's principal players. Joining in the fun and games were Betty Hutton, Bing Crosby, Bob Hope, Dorothy Lamour, Franchot Tone, Vera Zorina, Fred MacMurray, Jerry Colonna, Veronica Lake, Alan Ladd, Marjorie Reynolds, Eddie 'Rochester' Anderson, Paulette Goddard, Arthur Treacher, Cass Daley, Susan Hayward, Macdonald Carey, William Bendix, Sterling Holloway, Marjorie Reynolds, Gil Lamb, Edward Fielding, Walter Abel, and many more. Harold Arlen and Johnny Mercer's appealing score contained two of their all time standards, 'That Old Black Magic', introduced by Johnny Johnston, and 'Hit The Road To Dreamland' which was given a fine treatment by Mary Martin, Dick Powell and the Golden Gate Quartet. The rest of the songs were 'I'm Doing It For Defence', 'On The Swing Shift', 'A Sweater, A Sarong And A Peek-A-Boo Bang', 'He Loved Me Till The All-Clear Came', 'Sharp As A Tack', and 'Old Glory'. Danny Dare and George Ballanchine staged the dances, and the director of this lively and entertaining affair was George Marshall. Joesph Sistrom produced, and it was photographed in black and white by Leo Tover.

State Fair

This warm-hearted, idealistic slice of Americana came to the screen in 1945 courtesy of producer William Perlberg and 20th Century-Fox. It contained the only score that Richard Rodgers and Oscar Hammerstein II wrote especially for a film, and Hammerstein also contributed the screenplay (adapted from Phil Stong's novel) which was short on narrative and seemed to consist simply of a series of relationships. Abel Frake (Charles Winninger) and his wife Melissa (Fay Bainter) of Brunswick, Iowa, spend a few days at the state fair with their children, Margie (Jeanne Crain), Wayne (Dick Haymes), and Abel's temperamental boar, Blue Boy. By the time they return to their farm, Blue Boy has won the prestigious blue ribbon; Melissa's sour pickle and mincemeat have both gained first prize; Margie has fallen for a small-time (soon to be Chicago columnist) newspaper reporter Pat Gilbert (Dana Andrews); and Wayne is serenading band singer Emily Edwards (Vivian Blaine) with 'It's A Grand Night For Singing' in the middle of the day. Blaine had two nice songs, 'That's For Me' and 'Isn't It Kinda Fun?', (with Haymes), but the best number in the score was the lovely 'It Might As Well Be Spring' which was introduced by Jeanne Crain (dubbed by Louanne Hogan) and went on to win the Oscar for best song. Other numbers were the celebratory 'Our State Fair' and 'All I Owe Ioway'. The film's charming and affectionate style extended to the supporting cast which contained many familiar faces including Donald Meek, Frank McHugh, Percy Kilbride, William Marshall, and Harry Morgan. Leon Shamroy photographed beautifully in Technicolor and the director, Walter Lang, captured the mood of the times perfectly. There had been a previous (non-musical) film of *State Fair* in 1933 starring Will Rogers and Janet Gaynor, and there was a further musical version in 1962. This featured Tom Ewell, Alice Faye, Pamela Tiffin, Bobby Darin, Pat Boone, Ann-Margret and some additional songs with both music and lyrics by Richard Rodgers.

Steele, Tommy

b. Thomas Hicks, 17 December 1936, Bermondsey, London, England. After serving as a merchant seaman Hicks formed the skiffle trio, the Cavemen with Lionel Bart and Mike Pratt, before being discovered by entrepreneur John Kennedy in the 2I's coffee bar in Soho, London. A name change to Tommy Steele followed and after an appearance at London's Condor Club the boy was introduced to manager Larry Parnes. From thereon, his rise to stardom was meteoric. Using the old 'working-class boy makes good' angle, Kennedy launched the chirpy cockney in the unlikely setting of a debutante's ball. Class conscious Fleet Street lapped up the idea of Tommy as the 'Deb's delight' and took him to their hearts. His debut single, 'Rock With The Caveman' was an immediate Top 20 hit and although the follow-up 'Doomsday Rock'/'Elevator Rock' failed to chart, the management was unfazed. Their confidence was rewarded when Steele hit number 1 in the UK charts with a cover of Guy Mitchell's 'Singing The Blues' in January 1957. By this point, he was Britain's first and premier rock 'n' roll singer and, without resorting to sexual suggestiveness, provoked mass teenage hysteria unseen since the days of Johnnie Ray. At one stage, he had four songs in the Top 30, although he never

Tommy Steele

restricted himself to pure rock 'n' roll. A bit part in the film *Kill Me Tomorrow* led to an autobiographical musical *The Tommy Steele Story*, which also spawned a book of the same title. For a time Steele performed the twin role of rock 'n' roller and family entertainer but his original persona faded towards the end of the 50s. Further movie success in *The Duke Wore Jeans* (1958) and *Tommy The Toreador* (1959) effectively redefined his image. His rocking days closed with covers of Ritchie Valens' 'Come On Let's Go' and Freddy Cannon's 'Tallahassee Lassie'. The decade ended with the novelty 'Little White Bull', after which it was goodbye to rock 'n' roll.

After appearing on several variety bills during the late 50s, Steele sampled the 'legit' side of show business in 1960 when he played Tony Lumpkin in *She Stoops To Conquer* at the Old Vic, and he was back in the straight theatre again in 1969, in the role of Truffaldino in *The Servant Of Two Masters* at the Queen's Theatre. In years between those two plays, he experienced some of the highlights of his career. In 1963, he starred as Arthur Kipps in the stage musical, *Half A Sixpence*, which ran for 18 months in the West End before transferring to Broadway in 1965; Steele re-created the role in the film version in 1967. A year later, he appeared in another major musical movie, *Finan's Rainbow*, with Fred Astaire and Petula Clark. His other films included *Touch It Light*, *It's All Happening*, *The Happiest Millionaire* and *Where's Jack?* In 1974, Steele made one of his rare television appearances, in the autobiographical, *My Life, My Song*, and, in the same year, appeared at the London Palladium in *Hans Anderson*, the first of three stage adaptations of famous Hollywood films. He also starred in the revival three years later. In 1979/80 his one-man musical show was resident at London's Prince of Wales Theatre for a record 60 weeks - the Variety Club Of Great Britain made him their Entertainer Of The Year. He was also awarded the OBE. Steele was back at the Palladium again in 1983 and 1989, in the highly popular *Singin' In The Rain*, which he also directed. In the latter capacity he tried, too late as it transpired, to save impresario Harold Fielding's *Ziegfeld* (1988) from becoming a spectacular flop. Fielding had originally cast Steele in *Half A Sixpence* some 25 years earlier. Off-stage in the 80s, Steele published his first novel, a thriller, *The Final Run*; had one of his paintings exhibited at the Royal Academy; was commissioned by Liverpool City Council to fashion a bronze statue of 'Eleanor Rigby' as a tribute to the Beatles; and composed 'A Portrait Of Pablo' and 'Rock Suite - An Elderly Person's Guide To Rock'. The third, and least successful of Steele's movie-to-stage transfers was *Some Like It Hot* (1992). A hybrid of Billy Wilder's classic film, and the Broadway stage musical *Sugar* (1972), it received derisory reviews ('The show's hero is Mr Steele's dentist'), and staggered along for three months in the West End on the strength of its star's previous box-office appeal. In 1993 Steele was presented with the Hans Andersen Award at the Danish Embassy in London. A year later he was back on the road again with 'A Dazzling New Song & Dance Spectacular' entitled *What A Show!*.

Albums: *The Tommy Steele Stage Show* (1957), *The Tommy Steele Story* (1957), *Stars Of 6.05* (late 50s), *The Duke Wore Jeans* (1958, film soundtrack), *Tommy The Toreador* (1959, film soundtrack), *So This Is Broadway* (1964), *Light Up The Sky* (1959), *Cinderella* (1959, stage cast), *Get Happy With Tommy* (1960), *It's All Happening* (1962), *Half A Sixpence* (1963, stage recording), *Everything's Coming Up Broadway* (1967), *The Happiest Millionire* (1967), *My Life My Song* (1974), *Hans Andersen* (1978, London stage cast), with Sally Ann Howes *Henry Fielding's Hans Anderson* (1985). Compilations: *The Happy World Of Tommy Steele* (1969), *The World Of Tommy Steele, Volume 2* (1971), *Focus On Tommy Steele* (1977), *The Family Album* (1979), *20 Greatest Hits* (1983), *Tommy Steele And The Steelmen - The Rock 'N' Roll Years* (1988), *Handful Of Songs* (1993).

Further reading: *Quincy's Quest*, Tommy Steele, based on the children's television programme he scripted. *Tommy Steele*, John Kennedy.

Steiner, Max

b. Maximilian Raoul Steiner, 10 May 1888, Vienna, Austria, d. 28 December 1971, Hollywood, California, USA. A composer and conductor for some 300 films, from the late 20s through to the 60s, he was often called the leader in his field. Steiner studied at the Imperial Academy Of Music, and won the Gold Medal. In his teens he wrote and conducted his own operetta in Vienna, before travelling to London in 1904, and conducting in Music Halls in England and on the Continent. He returned to the USA in 1914 and conducted on Broadway, for concert tours, and spent some time as chief orchestrator for the Harms music publishing house. Steiner joined RKO in Hollywood in 1929, a couple of years after the movies began to talk, and worked, uncredited on *Rio Rita*, a 'lavish musical Western', starring Bebe Daniels and John Boles. From then, until 1934, his name appears on the titles of over 80 productions, mostly as the composer of the background music. They included *Check And Double Check* (film debut of Amos 'n' Andy), *Cimarron*, *Beau Ideal*, *A Bill Of Divorcement*, *The Half Naked Truth*, *The Lost Squadron*, *Little Women* and *Morning Glory*, both starring the young Katherine Hepburn, and *King Kong* 'the greatest monster movie of all'. In 1934, Steiner was nominated for an Academy Award for his score to *The Lost Patrol*, and, in the following year, won the Oscar for his work on John Ford's *The Informer*. His other scores in 30s included *Of Human Bondage*, *Alice Adams* (Hepburn again), *The Charge Of The Light Brigade*, (1936)

(Steiner's first, in a long series of films for Warner Brothers), *A Star Is Born* (1937), *The Garden Of Allah*, *The Life Of Emile Zola*, *Tovarich*, *Jezebel*, *The Adventures Of Tom Sawyer*, *Crime School*, *The Amazing Dr Clitterhouse*, *Four Daughters*, *The Sisters*, *Angels With Dirty Faces*, *The Dawn Patrol*, *The Oklahoma Kid*, *Dark Victory*, *We Are Not Alone*, and *Gone With The Wind*. Steiner's memorable score for the latter included the haunting 'Tara's Theme', which became a hit for Leroy Holmes and his Orchestra, and as 'My Own True Love' with a lyric by Mack David, for Johnny Desmond as well.

During the 30s, Steiner also served as musical director on several classic RKO Astaire-Rogers Musicals, such as *The Gay Divorcée*, *Follow The Fleet*, *Roberta*, and *Top Hat*. In the 40s, especially during the years of World War II, Steiner scored some of the most fondly remembered films in the history of the cinema, such as *Now Voyager* (1942) (Steiner's second Academy Award), which included the persuasive theme, 'It Can't Be Wrong' (lyric Kim Gannon), a smash hit for Dick Haymes, *Casablanca*, *The Corn Is Green*, *Johnny Belinda*, and *The Letter*. Other significant 40s films for which Steiner provided the music were *All This And Heaven Too*, *Sergeant York*, *They Died With Their Boots On*, *In This Our Life*, *Desperate Journey*, *Mission To Moscow*, *Watch On The Rhine*, *Passage To Marseilles* (including 'Someday I'll Meet You Again'), *The Adventures Of Mark Twain*, *Since You Went Away* (1944), starring Claudette Colbert and Joseph Cotton - Steiner's third Academy Award, *Arsenic And Old Lace*, *The Conspirators*, *Mildred Pearce*, *Saratoga Trunk* (including 'As Long As I Live'), *The Big Sleep*, *My Wild Irish Rose*, *Life With Father*, *The Treasure Of The Sierra Madre*, *Key Largo*, *The Adventures Of Don Juan*, and *White Heat* (1949). In 1950, Steiner received another of his 22 Academy Award nominations for his work on *The Flame And The Arrow*, starring Burt Lancaster, and, in the same year, he scored Tennessee Williams' *The Glass Menagerie*, starring UK Musical Comedy star, Gertrude Lawrence. His other 50s film music included *Operation Pacific*, *On Moonlight Bay*, *The Miracle Of Our Lady Fatima*, *The Jazz Singer*, *By The Light Of The Silvery Moon*, *The Caine Mutiny*, *Battle Cry* (including 'Honey-Babe'), *Marjorie Morningstar*, *The F.B.I. Story*, and *A Summer Place* (1959) (the theme was a US hit for Percy Faith And His Orchestra, and, with a lyric by Mack Discant, for the Lettermen (1965). Even though he was over 70, Steiner continued to work into the 60s on such movies as *The Dark At The Top Of The Stairs*, *Spencer's Mountain*, *Youngblood Hawk*, and *Two On A Guillotine*, although demand for his kind of romantic, powerful, yet tender, background music had declined. His work for television included the theme music for the popular *Perry Mason* series which starred Raymond Burr.

Selected albums: *King Kong* (1980), *Revisited* (1988).

Stept, Sam

b. Samuel H. Stept, 18 September 1897, Odessa, Russia, d. 1 December 1964, Los Angeles, California, USA. Stept was a popular composer during the 30s and 40s. He was taken to the USA in 1900, and grew up in Pittsburgh, Pennsylvania. After playing the piano for a local music publishing house, he served as an accompanist in Vaudeville for artists such as Mae West, Ann Chandler and Jack Norworth, and then led a dance band in Cleveland, Ohio in the early 20s. A few years later he started composing and in 1928, in collaboration with Bud Green, had a big hit with 'That's My Weakness Now', which Helen Kane made into one of her special numbers. It was featured in Reuben Mamoulian's critically acclaimed movie, *Applause* (1929), became a standard, and was included, over 45 years later, on Bobby Short's *The Mad Twenties*. During the late 20s and early 30s, Stept and Green combined on several songs for films, including 'Love Is A Dreamer', 'For The Likes O' You And Me', 'When They Sang "The Wearing Of The Green" In Syncopated Blues' (*Lucky In Love*); 'The World Is Yours and Mine' (*Mother's Boy*); 'There's A Tear For Every Smile In Hollywood' (*Showgirl*) and 'Tomorrow Is Another Day', 'Liza Lee' (*Big Boy*). With Green and Herman Ruby, Stept contributed 'Do Something' and 'I'll Always Be In Love With You' to the RKO backstage movie *Syncopation*. During the 30s his other compositions included 'Congratulations', 'Please Don't Talk About Me When I'm Gone' (Gene Austin/Johnnie Ray), 'I Beg Your Pardon', 'Mademoiselle', 'London On A Rainy Night', 'I'm Painting The Town Red', 'Tiny Little Fingerprints' and 'My First Impression Of You'. He also wrote songs for films with Sidney Mitchell, such as 'All My Life', 'Laughing Irish Eyes' (title track); 'Recollections Of Love' (*Dancing Feet*); and 'How Am I Doin' With You?' (*Sitting On The Moon*). Stept's other collaborators around this time included Ted Koehler, with whom he wrote 'We've Come A Long Way Together' (*Hullabaloo*); and 'Goodnight My Lucky Day', and 'We Happen To Be In The Army' (*23 And 1/2 Hours To Leave*). Stept also worked with Sidney Mitchell on 'All My Life' (*Johnny Doughboy*) and 'And Then' (*Twilight On The Prairie*); Ned Washington, 'Sweet Heartache' (*Hit Parade*); and 'The Answer Is Love' (*That's Right - You're Wrong*). For 30s stage shows Stept wrote 'Swing Little Thingy' (with Bud Green) for *Shady Lady*; 'So I Married The Girl' (with Herb Magidson) for *George White's Music Hall Varieties*; and most of the songs, with Lew Brown and Charles Tobias, for the 1939 hit, *Yokel Boy*. The score included 'I Can't Afford To Dream', 'Let's Make Memories Tonight', and 'Comes Love'. The show was filmed in 1942, starring Eddie Foy Jnr in the title role. In the same year Stept, again with Brown and Tobias, wrote 'Don't Sit Under The Apple Tree' for the Andrews Sisters to sing in *Private Buckaroo*. The

Stormy Weather

song became a big record hit for the Sisters, as well as Glenn Miller. Stept also contributed numbers to other early 40s movies such as *When Johnny Comes Marching Home* ('This Is Worth Fighting For', lyric by Eddie De Lange); and *Stars On Parade* ('When They Ask About You'). In the late 40s he was less active, but was still composing ballads such as 'I Was Here When You Left Me', and 'Next Time I Fall In Love'. He also contributed 'Yo Te Amo Mucho' to the movie *Holiday In Mexico* in 1946. In 1950, with Dan Shapiro, he wrote several numbers for the Broadway revue, *Michael Todd's Peep Show*, including 'We've Got What It Takes', and 'A Brand New Rainbow In The Sky'. After composing songs such as 'If You Should Leave Me', 'Star-Gazing' and 'Don't You Care A Little Bit About Me?' in the early 50s, Stept concentrated on his music publishing interests. In 1961, his 'Please Don't Talk About Me When I'm Gone' received a carefree rendering from Frank Sinatra on *Swing Along With Me*, the singer's second album for his own Reprise label.

Stormy Weather

Hollywood being what it was then, director Andrew Stone led an almost 'all-white' team behind the cameras for this otherwise 'all-black' musical. Never mind the routine and rather trite backstage storyline, the cast is superb. Led by Bill 'Bojangles' Robinson and Lena Horne, they romp through some magnificent musical numbers including spots by Cab Calloway And His Orchestra, including Shad Collins, Illinois Jacquet and J.C. Heard, Katharine Dunham And Her Dancers, and the fabulous Nicholas Brothers. For all this remarkable talent, however, the show is stolen by Fats Waller. In addition to acting in a couple of scenes he and an all-star band, including Slam Stewart, Benny Carter, the film's musical director (and the only black person in an off-camera role), and Zutty Singleton, the band's nominal leader, back Ada Brown for one number and are featured in two: 'Ain't Misbehavin'' and 'Moppin' And Boppin''. It was while returning east from Hollywood after appearing in this film that Waller died. Adding to this 1943 film's many marvels is the fact that at the time of its making Robinson, who was born around 1873, was long past his youthful prime.

Story Of Vernon And Irene Castle, The

All good things must come to an end, and this picure, which was released in 1939, was Fred Astaire and Ginger Rogers' last for RKO, although they reunited for MGM's *The Barkleys Of Broadway* some 10 years later. The 'Barkleys' were a product of writers Betty Comden and Adolph Green's fertile imagination, but Vernon and Irene Castle were a famous real-life dance team who became all the rage in America during

World War I. The screenplay, by Richard Sherman, Oscar Hammerstein II, and Dorothy Yost, traced the couple's tremendously successful career from their first meeting until Vernon's tragic death in an aircraft training accident in 1918. There was only one new song in the film's score, the charming 'Only When You're In My Arms', by Harry Ruby, Con Conrad and Bert Kalmar. The remainder consisted of carefully selected numbers from the dancing duo's heyday, and included several of their specialities such as 'Too Much Mustard (Castle Walk)', 'Rose Room (Castle Tango)', 'Little Brown Jug (Castle Polka)', 'Dengoza (Maxixe)', 'When They Were Dancing Around', 'Pretty Baby (Trés Jolie)', 'Millicent Waltz', 'Night Of Gladness', 'Missouri Waltz', and numerous other memories of bygone days. Astaire and Rogers excelled, especially in the ballroom dancing sequences, Edna May Oliver as the couple's agent, was also outstanding. However, the sight of Fred Astaire dying in a film was not most people's idea of fun, and the film reportedly lost some $50,000 dollars. It was the end of the RKO era for Astaire and Rogers. Ever-present dance director Hermes Pan was still there at the end, but producer Pandro S. Berman and director Mark Sandrich, who had contributed so much to the historic series, were replaced this time by George Haight and H.C. Potter. As one legendary dance team (Fred Astaire and Ginger Rogers) portrayed another (Vernon and Irene Castle), one half of a future highly talented duo was waiting to pick up the torch. Marge Belcher (later Marge Champion), who, together with her husband Gower, delighted cinema audiences in films such as *Show Boat* (1951), had a small part in *The Story Of Vernon And Irene Castle*.

Stowaway

Alice Faye had the two best songs, Mack Gordon and Harry Revel's 'Goodnight My Love' and 'One Never Knows, Does One?', but it was Shirley Temple's picture - clutching a pooch- that appeared on the sheet music for both numbers. Actually, she does flirt with the former number in the film - but not to any great effect. As usual, she plays her 'orphan of the storm' character, this time accidentally stowing away on a luxury yacht out of Shanghai. During the voyage, millionaire playboy Robert Young takes such a shine to her that he actually marries fellow passenger Alice Faye so that he can adopt the little darling - although the impression is given that the nuptials would probably have taken place anyway even if the curly-headed one had not been around. Naturally, she speaks Chinese fluently, although best wishes such as 'May the bird of prosperity continue to nest in your rooftop' are purveyed in English. When the ship reaches Hong Kong she becomes involved in a kind of Oriental talent contest, taking off Al Jolson and Ginger Rogers (complete with Fred Astaire dummy) while singing 'You've Gotta S-M-I-L-E If You Want

To Be H-A-Double P-Y'. It all ends in suitably sentimental style around the festive tree as Shirley gives forth with 'That's What I Want For Christmas' (Irving Caesar-Gerald Marks). Also involved in the shenanigans are Eugene Pallette, Helen Westley, Arthur Treacher, J. Edward Bromberg, Allan Lane, Astrid Allwyn, and Jayne Regan. William Conselman, Arthur Sheekman, and Nat Perrin wrote the screenplay from a story by Samuel G. Engel, and director William A Seiter kept it all moving along at good pace. Darryl F. Zanuck was in charge of production (executive producers Earl Carroll and Harold Wilson) and Arthur Miller photographed the film splendidly in black and white. It was released by 20th Century-Fox in 1936, and went on to become one of the year's biggest money-spinners.

Streisand, Barbra

b. 24 April 1942, New York City, New York, USA. From childhood Streisand was eager to make a career in show business, happily singing and 'playacting' for neighbours in Brooklyn, where she was born and raised. At the age of 15, she had a trial run with a theatrical company in upstate New York and by 1959, the year she graduated, was convinced that she could make a success of her chosen career. She still sang for fun, but was set on being a stage actress. The lack of opportunites in straight plays drove her to try singing instead and she entered and won a talent contest at The Lion, a gay bar in Greenwich Village. The prize was a booking at the club and this was followed by more club work, including an engagement at the Bon Soir which was later extended and established her as a fast-rising new singer. Appearances in off-Broadway revues followed, in which she acted and sang. Towards the end of 1961 she was cast in *I Can Get It For You Wholesale*, a musical play with songs by Harold Rome. The show was only moderately successful but Streisand's notices were excellent (as were those of another newcomer, Elliott Gould). She was invited to appear on an 'original cast' recording of the show, which was followed by another record date, to make an album of Rome's *Pins And Needles*, a show he had written 25 years earlier. The records and her Bon Soir appearances brought a television date and in 1962, on the strength of these, Columbia Records offered her a recording date of her own. With arrangements by Peter Matz, who was also responsible for the charts used by Noël Coward at his 1955 Las Vegas appearance, Streisand made her first album, which included such songs as 'Cry Me A River', 'Happy Days Are Here Again' and 'Who's Afraid Of The Big, Bad Wolf?'. Within two weeks of the album's release, in February 1963, Streisand was the top-selling female vocalist in the USA. Two Grammy Awards followed, for Best Album and for Streisand as Best Female Vocalist (for 'Happy Days Are Here Again'). Streisand's career was now unstoppable.

She had more successful club appearances in 1963 and released another strong album, which she followed by opening for Liberace at Las Vegas and appearing at Los Angeles's Coconut Grove and the Hollywood Bowl. That same remarkable year she married Elliott Gould and she was engaged to appear in a forthcoming Broadway show, *Funny Girl*. Based upon the life of Fanny Brice, *Funny Girl* had a troubled pre-production history, but once it opened it proved to have all the qualities its principal producer, Ray Stark, (who had nurtured the show for 10 years), believed it to have. With songs by Jule Styne and Ray Merrill, amongst which were 'People' and 'Don't Rain On My Parade', the show was a massive success, running for 1,348 performances and giving Streisand cover stories in *Time* and *Life* magazines. Early in 1966 Streisand opened *Funny Girl* in London but the show's run was curtailed when she became pregnant. During the mid-60s she starred in a succession of popular and award-winning television spectaculars. Albums of the music from these shows were big-sellers and one included her first composition, 'Ma Premiere Chanson'. In 1967, she went to Hollywood to make the film version of *Funny Girl*, the original Styne-Merrill score being extended by the addition of some of the songs Fanny Brice had performed during her own Broadway career. These included 'Second-Hand Rose' and 'My Man'. In addition to *Funny Girl*, Streisand's film career included roles in *Hello, Dolly!* and *On A Clear Day You Can See Forever*. The film of *Funny Girl* (1968) was a hit, with Streisand winning one of two Oscars awarded that year for Best Actress (the other winner was Katharine Hepburn).

By the time she came to the set to make her second Hollywood film, *Hello, Dolly!* (1969), Streisand had developed an unenviable reputation as a meddlesome perfectionist who wanted, and usually succeeded in obtaining, control over every aspect of the films in which she appeared. Although in her later films, especially those which she produced, her demands seemed increasingly like self-indulgence, her perfectionism worked for her on the many albums and stage appearances which followed throughout the 70s. This next decade saw changes in Streisand's public persona and also in the films she worked on. Developing her childhood ambitions to act, she turned more and more to straight acting roles, leaving the songs for her record albums and television shows. Among her films of the 70s were *The Owl And The Pussycat* (1970), *What's Up, Doc?* (1972), *The Way We Were* (1973), *Funny Lady* (1975), a sequel to *Funny Girl*, and *A Star Is Born* (1976). For the latter she co-wrote (with Paul Williams) a song, 'Evergreen', which won an Oscar as Best Song. Streisand continued to make well-conceived and perfectly executed albums, most of which sold in large numbers. She even recorded a set of the more popular songs written by classical composers such as Debussy and Schumann.

Although her albums continued to attract favourable reviews and sell well, her films became open season for critics and were markedly less popular with fans. The shift became most noticeable after *A Star Is Born* was released and its damaging self-indulgence was apparent to all. Nevertheless, the film won admirers and several Golden Globe Awards. She had an unexpected number 1 hit in 1978 with 'You Don't Bring Me Flowers', a duet with Neil Diamond, and she also shared the microphone with Donna Summer on 'Enough Is Enough', a disco number which reached Platinum, and with Barry Gibb on the album, *Guilty*. Her film career continued into the early 80s with *All Night Long* (1981) and *Yentl*, (1983) which she co-produced and directed. By the mid-80s Streisand's career appeared to be on cruise. However, she starred in and wrote the music for *Nuts* (1987), a film which received mixed reviews. Growing concern for ecological matters revealed themselves in public statements and on such occasions as the recording of her 1986 video/album, *One Voice*. In 1991 she was criticized for another directorial assignment on *Prince Of Tides*. As a performer, Streisand was one of the greatest showbiz phenomenons of the 60s. Her wide vocal range and a voice which unusually blends sweetness with strength, helps make Streisand one of the outstanding dramatic singers in popular music. Her insistence upon perfection has meant that her many records are exemplars for other singers. Her 1991 movie, *Prince Of Tides*, which she also directed, was nominated for seven Oscars. Two years later, she was being talked of as a close confidante and advisor to the newly elected US President Clinton, although she still found the time to return - on record at least - to where it all started, when she released *Back To Broadway*. In November 1993 it was reported that the singer had given away her £10 million Californian estate 'in an attempt to save the earth'. The 26 acres of landscaped gardens with six houses and three swimming pools would become the Barbra Streisand Centre For Conservancy Studies. She recouped the money early in January 1994, by giving two 90-minute concerts at MGM's new Grand Hotel and theme park in Las Vegas for a reported fee of £13 million. Later in the year she received mixed critical reviews for the four British concerts she gave at Wembley Arena in the course of a world tour. Her share of the box-office receipts - with tickets at an all-time high of £260 - and expensive merchandise is reported to have been in the region of £5 million.

Selected albums: *The Barbra Streisand Album* (1962), *The Second Barbra Streisand Album* (1963), *Barbra Streisand: The Third Album* (1964), *Funny Girl* (1964), *People* (1964), *My Name Is Barbra* (1965), *Color Me Barbra* (1966), *Je M'Appelle Barbra* (1967), *What About Today?* (1969), *Stoney End* (1970), *Greatest Hits* (1970), *Barbra Joan Streisand* (1971), *Classical Barbra* (1974), *Butterfly* (1975), *Lazy Afternoon* (1975), *Streisand*

Superman (1977), *Songbird* (1978), *Wet* (1979), *Guilty* (1980), *Memories* (1981), *Yentl* (1983, soundtrack), *Emotion* (1984), *The Broadway Album* (1985), *One Voice* (1986), *Nuts: Original Motion Picture Soundtrack* (1987), *Til I Loved You* (1988), *A Collection: Greatest Hits...And More* (1989), *Just For The Record...* (1991), *The Prince Of Tides* (1991, soundtrack), *Butterfly* (1992), *Back To Broadway* (1993).

Further reading: *Streisand: The Woman and the Legend*, James Spada. *Barbra Streisand, The Woman, The Myth, The Music*, Shawn Considine.

Strictly Ballroom

Made in Australia, and the hit of the 1992 Cannes Festival, this is probably the most enjoyable dance film to emerge since John Travolta strutted his extravagant stuff in *Saturday Night Fever* (1977). *Strictly Ballroom* is the brainchild of Baz Luhrmann who is better known 'down under' as the wunderkind of the Sydney Opera House. As director and screenwriter (with Craig Pearce), he presented the original 30 minute, and then 50 minute versions on stage before reshaping the concept for the screen. In this form it tells the story of Scott Hastings (Paul Mercurio) who has been preparing for the Australian Ballroom Dance Federation Championships since he was a young child. Having reached the semi-finals, he blows his chances by breaking the rules and improvising his own steps on the dance floor. This infuriates Scott's partner Liz Holt (Gia Carides), and she walks away. Also fuming are his domineering mother, Shirley, and coach, Les Kendall, (Pat Thompson and Peter Whitford) who together run the local dance school, and the powerful Federation President, Barry Fife (Bill Hunter). Out in the cold, Scott finds a new partner in Fran (Tara Morice), an unattractive beginner, and together, with the help of Fran's Spanish father and grandmother, they perfect a flamenco routine for the Pan-Pacific Grand Prix. As expected, it proves anathema to the judges but the audience love the sequence and go wild, joining the couple - who by now are preparing to dance off into the sunset together - on the floor for a spectacular celebration. It is not quite as simple as that - there are darker aspects involving Scott's father, Doug (Barry Otto), who, it turns out, was quite an innovative dancer himself in the old days, a fact which led to his wife Shirley turning to the cosy safety of Les Kendall. Also among the cast were John Hannan, Sonia Kruger, Kris McQuade, Pip Munshin, Leonie Page, Antonio Vargas (as Fran's father, Rico), Armonia Benedito, Jack Webster, and Lauren Hewett. John 'Cha Cha' O'Connell was the choreographer and the music score was composed by musical director David Hirschfelder. The songs used ranged from 'Perhaps, Perhaps, Perhaps (Quizas, Quizas, Quizas)' (Osvaldo Farres), 'La Cumparsita' (Rodriguez Ravern), 'Espana Carne' (Pascual Narro-Marquina), and 'Rhumba De Burros'

(Baz Lujrmann), to 'Time After Time' (Cyndi Lauper), 'Happy Feet' (Jack Yellen-Milton Ager), and 'Love Is In The Air' (Harry Vanda-George Young). It was beautifully photographed in Eastman Color by Steve Mason, and produced by Tristram Maill. This immensely likeable, charming and amusing film, with fine performances, especially from Scott Hastings, principal dancer and choreographer with the Sydney Dance Company, proved to be a box-office winner, not only in Australia, but worldwide.

Strike Up The Band (see *Babes In Arms*)

Strip, The

A would-be jazz drummer, Mickey Rooney, fresh out of the army, tangles with criminals. As directed by Leslie Kardos in this 1951 movie, all is very predictable but the pleasures in this film centre upon the band he joins, no less than Louis Armstrong And His All Stars. To meet some Hollywood executive's misconceived ideas on racial integration, apart from Rooney another white face appears on-screen in the band, behind the string bass. However, part of what you see and all of what you hear is the real All Stars back in the days when Armstrong's group truly merited the term: Jack Teagarden, Barney Bigard, Earl Hines, Arvell Shaw and William 'Cozy' Cole (the last two dubbing for their on-screen counterparts).

Armstrong recorded one of the film's songs, 'A Kiss To Build A Dream On', which became a minor hit for him. He also sings 'Shadrack' and the band plays a handful of other 'good old good ones' including 'Ole Miss'/'Bugle Call Rag' which is a feature for Rooney/Cole. In some scenes without the band Rooney may have played drums himself, something at which he was rather good although he was no Cozy Cole.

Student Prince, The

Mario Lanza walked out on MGM producer Joe Pasternak before filming had even started on Sigmund Romberg and Dorothy Donnelly's epic operetta which eventually reached the screen in 1954. Fortunately for all concerned, Lanza had recorded all the songs before he left, so it was simply a matter of matching his voice to the performing style of Edmund Purdom, the British actor chosen to co-star with Ann Blyth in this tale located in Old Heidelberg. Set in the late 1800s, Sonia Levien and William Ludwig's screenplay, which was based on Donnelly's Broadway libretto and Wilhelm Meyer-Forster's play, told the familiar story of the brief romance between the Student Prince Karl Franz (Purdom) and the waitress Kathy (Blyth) to the accompaniment of immortal songs from the 1924 hit stage production such as 'Serenade', 'Deep In My Heart, Dear', 'Drinking Song', 'Come Boys, Let's All Be Gay Boys', and 'Golden Days'. To these were added three new ones by Nicholas Brodszky and Paul Francis Webster, 'I Walk With God', Summertime In Heidelberg', and 'Beloved'. Louis Calhern, S.Z. Sakall, Edmund Gwenn, John Williams, Evelyn Vardon, Richard Anderson, and John Hoyt were among those taking part in this lavish production which was expertly photographed in Ansco Color and CinemaScope by Paul Vogel and directed by Richard Thorpe. An earlier, silent film of *The Student Prince*, directed by Ernst Lubitsch and starring Ramon Novarro and Norma Shearer, was released in 1927.

Styne, Jule

b. Julius K. Stein, 31 December 1905, London, England. Even before his family emigrated to the USA when he was aged seven, Styne had become an accomplished pianist. His studies continued in his new homeland and he was soon appearing as piano soloist with symphony orchestras. Deflected from a career as a concert pianist because his hands were thought to be too small, Styne tried composing popular songs. His first attempts included 'The Guy With The Polka-Dot Tie' and 'The Moth And The Flame'. After leaving school in 1922 he formed a band, which at one time included Benny Goodman in its ranks, but continued writing music. He had his first big success in 1926 with 'Sunday' (lyrics by Ned Miller) and continued working with Chicago-based jazz-orientated dance groups including the band led by Ben Pollack. In 1932 he adopted the spelling of his name by which he was thereafter known to avoid confusion with another musician named Jules Stein. Styne spent the mid-30s working in New York as a vocal coach and it was in this capacity that in 1937 he was hired to work in Hollywood. He continued to write songs and background music for films. Amongst his song successes from the 40s are 'Who Am I?' (lyrics by Walter Bulock), 'I've Heard That Song Before' (Sammy Cahn) and 'I Don't Want To Walk Without You' (Frank Loesser). Soon, Styne and Cahn formalized their partnership and theirs proved to be one of the most fruitful of such collaborations. Amongst their songs were 'I'll Walk Alone', 'There Goes That Song Again', 'And Then You Kissed Me', 'Five Minutes More', 'Time After Time', 'It's Magic', 'Three Coins In The Fountain', 'It's Been A Long, Long Time', 'Saturday Night (Is The Loneliest Night Of The Week)', 'Let It Snow! Let It Snow! Let It Snow!', 'The Things We Did Last Summer', 'I Fall In Love Too Easily', 'I Believe' and 'Give Me A Song With A Beautiful Melody'. In 1947, Styne and Cahn collaborated on a stage musical, *High Button Shoes*, which ran for 727 performances. The following year Styne formed a new partnership, this time with Leo Robin as his lyricist. This team wrote *Gentlemen Prefer Blondes* which ran for 740 performances thanks partly to the dynamism of Carol Channing in the lead and songs like 'Diamonds Are A Girl's Best Friend' and

'Bye Bye, Baby'. Styne's next few Broadway shows were undistinguished but he continued to write good songs for them, including 'Hold Me-Hold Me-Hold Me' (lyrics by Betty Comden and Adolph Green), 'How Do You Speak To An Angel?', 'Ev'ry Street's A Boulevard In Old New York' (both with Bob Hilliard) and 'Distant Melody' (Comden and Green). Styne hit again with *Bells Are Ringing* from which came 'Just In Time', 'Long Before I Knew You' and 'The Party's Over', all with lyrics by Comden and Green. In 1959 Styne had another Broadway success with *Gypsy*, from which came 'Everything's Coming Up Roses', 'Let Me Entertain You', and 'Together Wherever We Go', all with lyrics by Stephen Sondheim.

Although his next Broadway shows were less popular Styne still wrote some good songs, including 'Make Someone Happy' (Comden and Green) from *Do Re Mi* and 'Come Once In A Lifetime' (Comden and Green) from *Subways Are For Sleeping*. Next in Styne's musicals was *Funny Girl*, his greatest success, which made a star of Barbra Streisand. Styne's collaborator on this show was Bob Merrill and their songs included 'People' and 'Don't Rain On My Parade'. Later musicals for which Styne wrote suffered in comparison with *Funny Girl*'s huge success although *Sugar*, based upon Billy Wilder's 1959 film, *Some Like It Hot*, was better than several. He has continued to be active into the 90s, although his 1993 Broadway musical *Red Shoes* closed after only three days. Apart from writing for Broadway, Styne has also produced shows including the successful 1952 revival of *Pal Joey*. One of the most respected American songwriters, Styne has been the recipient of numerous awards and honours and even found time during the 80s to teach at New York University.

Subterraneans, The

This adaptation of a Jack Kerouac novel came too early for it to be successful. When this film was released in 1960, Hollywood was then still hidebound by its own peculiar code of sexual ethics. What could and could not be shown on the screen was a tangle which this film, directed by Ranald MacDougall, fails to unravel. Jazz fans have an excuse for watching it, however, as there are good moments from musicians such as André Previn, the film's musical director, Dave Bailey, Chico Hamilton, Art Farmer, Art Pepper, Bob Enevoldson, Russ Freeman, Red Mitchell, Shelly Manne, Bill Perkins and Gerry Mulligan, who also has an acting role.

Summer Holiday (1963)

The premis of *Summer Holiday* was deceptively simple. A group of teenagers, including the film's star Cliff Richard, take a London bus to Europe and the high jinx which follow are threaded together by a succession of innocent pop songs. The soundtrack

Summer Holiday (1963)

features several of the singer's best-known songs from the early 60s, including the double-sided chart topper 'The Next Time' and 'Bachelor Boy'. 'Summer Holiday' also reached the number 1 spot when issued as a single while Richard's backing group the Shadows, who appeared in various different guises throughout the film, reached the same position with the aptly-named 'Foot Tapper'. *Summer Holiday* captured an era about to be eclipsed. Released as the Beatles began their inexorable rise, it showed a perception of pop and, indeed, adolescence about to be changed forever.

Summer Holiday (1948)

Another wallow in turn-of-the-century small-town Americana of the kind that hardly ever failed at the box-office. This one was based on Eugene O'Neill's comedy *Ah, Wilderness!*, and was released by MGM in 1948. Frances Goodrich and Albert Hackett's screenplay retained much of the warmth and gentleness which had made the original so appealing, and Mickey Rooney, as a youngster making the often bewildering transition into manhood, was superb. Gloria De Haven was fine as his girlfriend, and so were parents Walter Huston and Selena Royle. The remainder of a strong cast included Frank Morgan, Agnes Moorehead, Jackie 'Butch' Jenkins', Marilyn Maxwell, and Anne Francis. Harry Warren and Ralph Blane's score was skilfully integrated into the story, and included 'Our Home Town', 'Independence Day', 'Afraid To Fall In Love', 'Weary Blues', 'I Think You're The Sweetest Kid I've Ever Known', 'All Hail Danville High', and the lively 'Stanley Steamer'. Charles Walters, who was renowned for his exuberant choreography, staged the dances, and Rouben Mamoulian, who set the standard for movie musicals with his *Love Me Tonight* (1933), directed with his usual flair and attention for detail and character. It was photographed brilliantly in Technicolor by Charles Schoenbaum, and produced by the famous Arthur Freed Unit. The modestly successful 1959 Broadway musical, *Take Me Along*, which had a score by Bob Merrill, was also based on O'Neill's *Ah, Wilderness!*.

Summer Stock

Of the three films in which Judy Garland and Gene Kelly starred together, their final project, *Summer Stock*, is the least impressive. Yet this 1950 MGM release still remains a favourite for many, and has some genuinely charming moments. It tells the tale of the two Falbury sisters - Jane (Garland) has remained at home in New England to run the farm, while Abigail (Gloria De Haven), has left the roost to pursue a showbiz career. To her sister's horror, Abigail brings the people, props and paraphernalia of a whole new show, written and organised by Joe D. Ross (Kelly), to rehearse on the farm. Jane insists that if the whole gang is going to live there and use the barn for rehearsals, they had better earn their keep. This results in some amusing shenanigans, with cows, chickens and an accident with a brand new tractor - disasters which Phil Silvers normally has something to do with. When Abigail suddenly leaves the production, Jane steps into her place, and does so with a hard working attitude and passion that her sister never showed. When Abigail arrives back to apologise half way through the opening night of the show, she not only finds that Jane's performance has been a triumph, but that Jane and Joe have fallen in love. Jane's fiancé, Orville (Eddie Bracken), is left out in the cold, but it looks like Abigail is going to help him recover from the blow. George Wells and Sy Gomberg's screenplay is a happy bundle of clichés - let's put a show on in a barn . . . you've only got a few days to learn the part etc. Not that anyone cares much, because *Summer Stock*, directed by Charles Walters and produced by Joe Pasternak, is good fun and indeed, several of the sequences are still quite memorable. Garland's singing and dancing in 'Get Happy' (Harold Arlen/Ted Koehler) combine to create one of her all-time best and sophisticated performances. During the rest of the film she was obviously overweight, but 'Get Happy' was shot two months after filming had officially ended, and by then she was back in fine condition. Whatever her physical problems, Garland's voice did not seem to be affected in renditions of the uplifting 'If You Feel Like Singing, Sing' and the poignant 'Friendly Star', both written by Harry Warren and Mack Gordon, who also contributed 'Happy Harvest', 'Blue Jean Polka', 'Dig-Dig-Dig For Your Dinner' and Mem'ry Island'. Garland and Kelly were perfect together, and Kelly and Silvers also had a great time with the more comic material, as they did in *Cover Girl* some six years earlier. Kelly's own personal mark of genius shows itself in the sequence when, while walking on the stage, he steps on a squeaky floorboard. Simply by using this, a sheet of newspaper and the accompaniment of 'You Wonderful You' (Warren-Jack Brooks-Saul Chaplin), he devises one of the film's most enchanting dances. Nick Castle handled the rest of the choreography, and the film was shot in Technicolor by Robert Planck. For UK audiences the title was changed to *If You Feel Like Singing*.

Sun Valley Serenade

Sun Valley Serenade

Such was the popularity of the Glenn Miller Band by 1941 that it just had to appear in a film, even if the story was as light as a feather and Miller himself was definitely no actor. Robert Ellis and Helen Logan's screenplay (from a story by Art Arthur and Robert Harari) was about a cute Norwegian refugee (Sonja Henie) whose arrival in America startles the band's pianist (John Payne) simply because he had agreed to sponsor a child. Inevitably, surprise turns to love on the snowy slopes of Sun Valley, Idaho. The musical sequences were tremendous, especially choreographer Hermes Pan's staging of 'Chattanooga Choo-Choo' (Harry Warren-Mack Gordon) which begins conventionally enough with Tex Beneke, Paula Kelly and the Modernaires singing with the band, and then segues into a spectacular song-and-dance routine featuring the amazing Nicholas Brothers and Dorothy Dandridge. Warren and Gordon contributed three other popular numbers, 'The Kiss Polka', 'I Know Why (And So Do You)', and 'It Happened In Sun Valley', while Joe Garland's 'In The Mood' also got an airing. Milton Berle supplied the wisecracks, and Lynn Bari and Joan Davis were in it too. Henie's big moment came in the impressive 'black ice' finalé when, accompanied by numerous white-clad couples, she gave a stunning display of ballet-style ice dancing. H. Bruce Humberstone directed, and *Sun Valley Serenade* was produced by Milton Sperling for 20th Century-Fox. Not much footage of the Miller Band exists, so this film and *Orchestra Wives* are continually re-viewed by lovers of the Swing Era.

Sven Klang's Kvintett

Based upon a stage play by Henric Holmberg and Ninne Olsson, this film made in 1976, directed by Stellan Olsson, tells the story of an amateur, and not-very-good, traditional jazz band in Sweden in the late 50s. The band is joined by an alto saxophonist who is not only a vastly superior musician but is also eagerly experimenting with bop. This character, portrayed by Christer Boustedt (who really does play alto), is loosely based upon alto and baritone saxophonist Lars Gullin who died in the year of the film's release. The film offers one of the best accounts of life on the road for jazz musicians, whatever their nationality.

Sweet And Low-Down

Only one good reason for staying up late to watch this 1944 film (if it is ever shown on television) and that is Benny Goodman. Fortunately, he and his orchestra and quartet are on-screen rather a lot in this tale of a swing band on tour. Although this was not Goodman's best band, there are still several good musicians on hand. Some are seen, others only heard while actors mime their instruments. Amongst the musicians are Bill Harris, Zoot Sims, Morey Feld, Jess Stacy, Sid Weiss, Allan Reuss, Heinie Beau and Al

Klink. (Alternative title: *Moment For Music*).

Sweet Charity

Director-choreographer Bob Fosse's 1969 screen adaptation of the hit Broadway musical was heavily criticized at the time of its release for its over-use of gimmicky cinematic trickery and the over-the-top central performance of Shirley MacLaine. However, in retrospect many observers feel that it wasn't so bad after all. Peter Stone's screenplay stayed closely to Neil Simon's stage libretto which told of dance hall hostess Charity Hope Valentine (MacLaine) who is all set achieve her ambition and marry strait-laced Oscar Lindquist (John McMartin) until he finds out where she works. At first he appears to be coming to terms with Charity's somewhat unconventional lifestyle, but after attending her rowdy farewell party at the Fan-Dango ballroom, he finds that he can't go through with the ceremony and jilts her at the very last minute. There were strong supporting performances from Ricardo Montalban as film star Vittorio Vidal, Sammy Davis Jnr. in the role of Big Daddy, an hilarious hippy evangelist, Stubby Kaye as the owner of the Fan-Dango, and Paula Kelly, Rita Moreno and the rest of the girls at the club who all want to get out themselves, but still hate to see Charity go. Also among the cast were Barbara Bouchet, Suzanne Charney, Alan Hewitt, Dante D'Paulo, Bud Vest, Ben Vereen, Lee Roy Reams, Al Lanti, John Wheeler, and Leon Bing. Most of Cy Coleman and Dorothy Fields's outstanding songs survived the journey from Broadway to Hollywood, and the team added some new ones to form a score which consisted of 'Big Spender', 'If My Friends Could See Me Now', 'My Personal Property', 'Rhythm Of Life', 'There's Gotta Be Something Better Than This', 'I'm a Brass Band', 'Rich Man's Frug', 'The Hustle', 'Where Am I Going?', 'I Love To Cry At Weddings', 'It's a Nice Face', and the title number. In spite of the carping of the critics, much of Bob Fosse's choreography and direction was superb, and stands repeated viewing. Robert Arthur was the producer for Universal, and the picture was photographed in Technicolor and Panavision by Robert Surtees.

Sweet Love, Bitter

Directed by Herbert Daniels in 1966, this is an uneven and slightly self-conscious attempt to examine racial problems in the USA through the life of a jazz musician. Based upon the novel, *Night Song*, by John Alfred Williams, the story is very loosely based upon Charlie Parker's final years Dick Gregory stars as the saxophone player, dubbed by Charles McPherson, and also heard are Chick Corea and Steve Swallow. The film's musical director is Mal Waldron. (Alternative title: *It Won't Rub Off, Baby*).

Sweethearts

Jeanette MacDonald and Nelson Eddy's fifth film together, which was released by MGM in 1938, eschewed the familiar costumes and wigs for a far more contemporary setting. Dorothy Parker and Alan Campbell's screenplay cast them as a successful musical comedy team in the long-running Broadway hit show, *Sweethearts*. Like so many stars in those days, the duo are attracted by the big money that Hollywood has to offer, but, in their case, it all goes sour, and they soon return to the theatre. Also among the strong cast were Ray Bolger, Frank Morgan, Herman Bing, Reginald Gardiner, Mischa Auer, and Florence Rice. The plot bore no relationship to the book of the real Broadway show called *Sweethearts*, which opened in 1913, although four of Victor Herbert's lovely songs were retained for the film version, albeit with new lyrics by Robert Wright and George Forrest. These were 'Pretty As A Picture', 'Wooden Shoes', 'Every Lover Must Meet His Fate', and the title number. The same team also contributed 'Summer Serenade', 'On Parade', and 'Game Of Love', and there were several other songs by various composers such as 'Little Grey Home In The West' (Herman Loehr-D. Eardly Wilmott) and 'Happy Day' (Herbert Stothart-Wright-Forrest). Albertina Rasch was the choreographer, and W.S. Van Dyke directed what was an effervescent and good natured affair in which MacDonald and Eddy were at their peak. It was the first MGM picture to be photographed in three-colour Technicolor, and Oliver T. Marsh and Allen Davey were awarded a special Oscar for their cinematography.

Swing Time

Released in August 1936, just a few months after *Follow the Fleet*, *Swing Time* gave Fred Astaire and Ginger Rogers fans another feast of sensational dance routines and marvellous songs. Screenwriters Howard Lindsay and Allan Scott's vivid imagination came up with a story in which dancer and gambler John 'Lucky' Garnett (Astaire) goes to New York to make his fortune after his future in-laws have rejected him as financially unsuitable for their daughter Margaret (Betty Furness). After meeting dance instructress Penny Carrol (Ginger Rogers), Margaret and money are forgotten, and the new team sing and dance their way to stardom. Jerome Kern and Dorothy Fields's score was full of outstanding numbers such as 'Pick Yourself Up', 'A Fine Romance', 'Never Gonna Dance', 'Waltz In Swing Time', and 'Bojangles Of Harlem' for which Astaire donned blackface for the only time in his long career. The lovely, tender ballad 'The Way You Look Tonight', which Fred sang to Ginger while she was shampooing her hair, won the Academy Award for best song. Most of the laughs were provided by the bumbling ex-vaudevillian

Swing Time

Victor Moore and two of the comical characters from previous Astaire-Rogers extravaganzas, Helen Broderick and Eric Blore. *Swing Time*, which was another big box-office hit for RKO, was directed by George Stevens. The dance director - almost inevitably - was Hermes Pan.

Swingmen In Europe
A succession of bandstand performances by visiting American jazzmen. Directed by Jean Mazeas, this 1977 film features Milt Buckner, Teddy Buckner, Gene 'Mighty Flea' Conner, Illinois Jacquet, Jo Jones, Sammy Price, J.C. Heard and Doc Cheatham.

Symphony In Black
A very short but musically fascinating film made in 1934 which offers an opportunity to see and hear Duke Ellington And His Orchestra and Billie Holiday. Ellington's musicians include Artie Whetsol, Cootie Williams, Joe Nanton, Lawrence Brown, Johnny Hodges, Harry Carney and Sonny Greer. Holiday, in the first of her few film appearances, sings 'Saddest Tale'.

Syncopation
Directed by William Dieterle, this 1942 film offers a Hollywood-eye view of the story of jazz. Predictably, accuracy goes out the window but there are some nice musical moments from a band of winners of a poll held by the *Saturday Evening Post*, whose readers seem to have heard of Benny Goodman and a few other swing era musicians but very little else. Apart from Goodman there are Harry James, Jack Jenney, Charlie Barnet, Joe Venuti, Bob Haggart and Gene Krupa. Stan Wrightsman dubbed the soundtrack for Bonia Granville, Bunny Berigan for Jackie Cooper, Rex Stewart for Todd Duncan.

T

Take Me Out To The Ball Game
A kind of a rehearsal for the historic *On The Town* which was released later in 1949, except that Frank Sinatra, Gene Kelly and Jules Munshin are dressed mostly in baseball gear in this one, instead of their more familiar sailor suits. Actually, at the beginning of the film, Dennis Ryan (Sinatra) and Eddie O'Brien (Kelly), are clad in natty striped suits and straw boaters while engaging in their off-season occupation as a song-and-dance team in vaudeville. When they rejoin Nat Goldberg (Munshin) and the rest of their Wolves team-mates at the Florida training camp, it is to find that the team has a new boss - Miss K.C. (Katharine) Higgins (Esther Williams). She takes the job so seriously that she is only spotted in the hotel swimming pool once. Under her strict supervision they are well on the way to winning the pennant when a bunch of racketeers try to knobble O'Brien, and his performance suffers. However, a little love and affection from Katharine soon raises his batting average again, and the Wolves go on to glory. Betty Garrett chases (and catches) Sinatra - as she does in *On The Town* - and their duet, 'It's Fate Baby, It's Fate' (Roger Edens), is one of the film's highspots. Sinatra is suitably romantic with 'The Right Girl for Me' (Betty Comden-Adolph Green-Edens), and Kelly has his moments - along with other members of the cast - in 'Yes Indeedy', 'O'Brien To Ryan To Goldberg', 'Strictly USA', (all Comden-Green-Edens), 'The Hat My Father Wore Upon St. Patrick's Day' (Jean Schwartz-William Jerome), and 'Take Me Out To The Ball Game' (Albert Von Tilzer-Jack Norworth). Also involved in Harry Tugend and George Wells's turn-of-the-century screenplay (adapted from a story by Kelly and Stanley Donen) were Edward Arnold, Richard Lane, Sally Forrest, Murray Alper, William Graff, and the Blackburn Twins. Kelly and Donen also staged some nifty dance routines, and the whole affair was presided over by another ace choreographer, director Busby Berkeley. George Folsey photographed the picture splendidly in Technicolor, and it was produced by Arthur Freed's MGM unit. It was re-titled *Everybody's Cheering* in the UK.

Take My Tip
Billed as a musical, but more of a farce, this immensely entertaining vehicle for the husband-and-wife team of Cicely Courtneidge and Jack Hulbert was produced by Gaumont-British Pictures in 1937. Lord and Lady Pilkington, otherwise known as George and Hattie (Hulbert and Courtneidge), have fallen on hard times due to George's extravagance and naiveté. The crunch finally comes when he purchases a non-existent oil well for £15,000 from a cove called Buchan (Harold Huth) after meeting him in a Turkish Bath. Happily, help is at hand in the person of George and Hattie's trusted servant, Paradine (Frank Cellier), who has recently bought an hotel in Dalmatia with the money he has made backing horses that his boss (George) *didn't* fancy. He offers his former employers jobs in the hotel as head waiter (George) and hostess (Hattie). While there they adopt various disguises (and somewhat devious means) to retrieve their money from Buchan - complete with a handsome £5,000 profit. All ends satisfactorily (and democratically) with Paradine, George and Hattie going into partnership together. Incidentally, Hattie is an ex-musical comedy

actress and George is a nifty hoofer, so there is plenty of excuse for the inclusion of songs such as, 'Birdie Out Of A Cage', 'Colonel Bogey' (Kenneth J. Alford), 'The Sleepwalker', 'Sentimental Agitation', 'I'm Turning The Town Upside Down', 'Everybody Dance', and the delightful duet, 'I Was Anything But Sentimental' (Sammy Lerner-Al Hoffman-Al Goodhart). Also taking part in the fun and games were Frank Pettingell, comedian Robb Wilton, Philip Buchel, H.F. Maltby, Elliot Makeham, and Paul Sheridan. In charge of the mayhem was director Herbert Mason.

Temple, Shirley

b. 23 April 1928, Santa Monica, California, USA. An actress, dancer and singer. By the time Shirley Temple was six years old she was a movie star of the first magnitude, and four years later became 20th Century-Fox - and Hollywood's top box-office attraction with reported annual earnings of $300,000. Her poise, acting and dancing, plus her incredible screen presence, even gave rise to scurrilous rumours to the effect that she was a dwarf. After taking dancing lessons from the age of three, she appeared in short films and played bit parts in several minor features before coming to prominence singing 'Baby Take A Bow' in the 1934 musical *Stand Up And Cheer*. Her nine pictures in 1934, including *Little Miss Marker* which made her a major film attraction, earned her a

special (miniature) Academy Award 'in grateful recognition of her outstanding contribution to screen entertainment during the year'. Throughout the rest of the 30s she sparkled in musicals such as *Bright Eyes, Curly Top, The Littlest Rebel, Captain January, Poor Little Rich Girl, Dimples, Stowaway, Rebecca Of Sunnybrook Farm, Little Miss Broadway, Just Around The Corner, The Blue Bird*, and *Young People* (1940). From out of these simple, yet mostly enormously popular films came songs such as 'On The Good Ship Lollipop', 'Animal Crackers In My Soup', 'When I Grow Up', 'Curly Top', 'At The Codfish Ball', 'Picture Me Without You', 'Oh, My Goodness', 'But Definitely', 'That's What I Want For Christmas', 'When I'm With You', 'We Should Be Together', 'Swing Me An Old-Fashioned Love Song' 'This Is a Happy Little Ditty', and 'I Want To Walk In The Rain'. By the end of the 30s Shirley Temple's career was in decline; the most successful child star of all-time could not sustain her appeal as a teenager. She left Fox and appeared throughout the 40s in a number of films for other studios - but only in straight roles - there were to be no more musicals. After marrying businessman Charles Black in 1950 she became known as Shirley Temple Black and retired from show business for a time, concentrating on her family and working extensively for charity. In the late 50s and into the early 60s, she appeared on US television in *The Shirley Temple Storybook* and *The Shirley Temple*

Shirley Temple

Show. Later in the 60s she was prominent in politics and ran unsuccessfully for Congress as a Republican candidate. She subsequently served as US Ambassador to the United Nations and Ghana, and US Chief of Protocol. In 1990 she was appointed US Ambassador to Czechoslovakia, and, two years later, received a career achievement award at the annual D.W. Griffith Awards in Manhattan. In 1982 she attended a lavish retrospective tribute to her films organized by the Academy of Motion Picture Arts and Sciences and was presented with a new, full-size Oscar to replace the miniature she received in 1934. In 1994 it was announced that some of her most popular films were being computer-coloured and released on video.

Further reading: *Shirley Temple*, L.C. Eby. *Temple*, J. Basinger. *Films Of Shirley Temple*, R. Windeler. *Shirley Temple: American Princess*, Anne Edwards. *Child Star* (her autobiography).

Thanks A Million

Taking a break from Warner Brothers, Ruby Keeler and the *Gold Diggers*, Dick Powell co-starred with the delightful Ann Dvorak in this bright and entertaining musical which was released by 20th Century-Fox in 1935. The distinguished writer, producer and director, Nunnally Johnson, came up with a pip of a satirical script in which Powell plays Eric Land, a crooner with a small troupe of travelling entertainers. They get stranded in a small town, and Powell reads the speech for the Commonwealth Party candidate for State Governor, A. Darius Culliman (Raymond Walburn), after the old boy is taken ill with indigestion (drunk). Powell is so impressive that leading members of the Party persuade him to run for the office himself. Naturally, they will expect cushy jobs for themselves after he wins, but he will have no part in their corruption, and, after exposing them, is triumphantly elected on a four-point ticket - one of which is that none of his political addresses will last for more than 30 seconds. Ann Dvorak played Powell's adoring girlfriend of course, and radio star Fred Allen was fine as his manager, a bit of a hustler who is intent on bringing some pizzazz into politics. Also among the cast were Paula Kelly, Benny Baker, Andrew Tomber, Alan Dinehart, Paul Harvey, Edwin Maxwell, and Margaret Irving. Paul Whitman and his Band with Zorina, and Rubinoff and the Yacht Club Boys made guest appearances. Gus Kahn and Arthur Johnston wrote the tuneful score which included 'Thanks A Million', 'Sittin' On A Hilltop', 'Pocketful Of Sunshine', 'New O'leans', 'Sugar Plum', 'Sing Brother', and 'The Square Deal Party'. Roy Del Ruth directed with verve and style, and it was nicely photographed in black and white by Peverell Marley. The producer was Darryl F. Zanuck. It was remade in 1946 as *If I'm Lucky*.

That Night In Rio

One of the most familiar (and entertaining) plots in movie musicals - it was the basis of *Folies Bergère De Paris* (1935) and *On The Riviera* (1951) - was utilised by screenwriters George Seaton, Bess Meredyth, and Hal Long, in this lively Technicolor 20th Century-Fox musical which burst on to the screen in 1941. Perhaps the theme, which was based on a play by Rudolph Lothar and Hans Adler, was so popular - especially among the ladies - because it entailed the (inevitably) good-looking leading man played two roles. It goes something like this: a nightclub entertainer (Don Ameche) resembles a philandering businessman (Don Ameche) so closely that he is hired to take the tycoon's place when he is out of town 'on business' with a 'client' (Carmen Miranda). The deception is so convincing that even the neglected wife (Alice Faye) does not know the difference. In only her second American film, Miranda had already got into the habit of stealing the honours from under the noses of the bigger stars. In this particular case she was aided and abetted by songwriters Harry Warren and Mack Gordon who presented her with two stunning numbers, 'I, Yi, Yi, Yi, Yi (I Like You Very Much)' and 'Chica Chica Boom Chic', and director Irving Cummings who (as he had done in *Down Argentine Way*) gave her the opening number. Choreographer Hermes Pan helped her too by designing some splendid settings in which to showcase her very individual talents. The rest of the score included 'They Met In Rio', 'Boa Noite', and 'The Baron Is In Conference' (Warren-Gordon), along with 'Cae Cae' (Roberto Martins-Pedro Berrios). The admirable supporting cast contained some very familiar names, including S.Z. Sakall, J. Carrol Naish, Curt Bois, Leonid Kinskey, along with the Banda Da Lua (Carmen Miranda's orchestra), and guest artists the Flores Brothers.

Theodorakis, Mikis

b. c.1926, Greece. Theodorakis was a poet, patriot, politician and composer of numerous film scores. He was seven years old when he learned to sing Byzantine hymns and Greek folk songs. His first film music of note was for *Barefoot Battalion* (1954), the true story of Greek orphans' struggle against the Germans during World War II; an apt theme in view of his own subsequent strife. His other movie scores, during the 50s and early 60s, included *Night Ambush*, *The Shadow Of The Cat*, *The Lovers Of Tereul*, *Phaedra*, *Electra* and *Five Miles To Midnight*. In 1964, the composer's memorable score for *Zorba The Greek* contributed to the film's enormous success. It was to be one of his last projects before his life changed dramatically in April 1967. Following the fascist colonels' military *coup d'etat* in Greece, Theodorakis, as a Communist, was forced underground, and eventually imprisoned and tortured. By Army Order, the people were banned from listening to and performing his works, although his music became a symbol of resistance for the his fellow islanders. In 1969, John Barry, a fellow composer for films, smuggled out tapes of Theodorakis singing new songs, reciting his own poems, and describing prison conditions, and sent them to U Thant, then Secretary General of the United Nations. Theodorakis' own version of his appalling experiences were detailed in his book, *Journals Of Resistance*, in 1973. After his escape from Greece, the composer was exiled for several years in Paris, and started writing for films again in the early 70s. These included *Biribi*, *Serpico*, *State Of Seige*, *Sutjeska*, *Partisans*, *Letters From Marusia*, *Iphighenia* and *Easy Road*. For 10 years, until 1986, Theodorakis was a Member of Parliament in Greece and, after his resignation began to give concerts in Europe and elsewhere, and resume composing including the music for the Turkish film, *Sis* (1989).

Selected albums: *Zorba The Greek* (1983), *The Bouzoukis Of Mikis Theodorakis* (1984), *Ballad Of Mauthausen* (1986), *Canto General* (1986), *All Time Greatest Hits* (1993).

There's No Business Like Show Business

Incongruous is perhaps an appropriate word to describe the casting of the 'Nabob of Sob', pop singer Johnnie Ray, in this, one of the last of the truly lavish screen musicals which was released by 20th Century-Fox in 1955. He plays one of the Donahues, a vaudeville act consisting of his brother and sister (Mitzi Gaynor and Donald O'Connor) and their parents (Dan Dailey and Ethel Merman). Ray even manages to induce a few of his trademark tears, although in this instance they swell up in the eyes of his proud old Mom and Dad after he has announced his decision to become a priest. That scene, and his strangulated version of 'If You Believe', one of the two new songs in Irving Berlin's otherwise entertaining score, should surely have won someone a bad-taste Oscar. Instead, the only whiff of an Academy Award was the nomination for Lamar Trotti's story (adapted for the screen by Henry and Phoebe Ephron). It deals with the triumphs and crises experienced by the family group, and O'Connor's initially ill-fated love affair with a cabaret singer played by Marilyn Monroe. After spending some time in the US Navy 'growing up', O'Connor joins the rest of the clan for the finalé and a rousing version of the title song. Before he went off to sea he had some of the best numbers, singing and dancing delightfully in 'A Man Chases A Girl (Until She Catches Him)' and (with Gaynor and Monroe) 'Lazy'. He also adopted a Scottish accent for his part in a spectacular setting of

There's No Business Like Show Business

'Alexander's Ragtime Band'. Gaynor gave the number a touch of the Parisian, Merman was gamely Germanic, and Johnnie Ray . . . well, his intended articulation was unclear. Other highlights were Monroe's sizzling versions of 'Heat Wave' and 'After You Get What You Want You Don't Want It', and Merman and Dailey's 'Play A Simple Melody', 'A Pretty Girl Is Like A Melody', 'Let's Have Another Cup Of Coffee', and 'You'd Be Surprised'. Jack Cole, who had worked with Monroe on *Gentlemen Prefer Blondes* two years earlier, staged her dances, and the remainder of the film's spirited routines were choreographed by Robert Alton. Sol C. Siegel was the producer, and it was directed by Walter Lang. The impressive DeLuxe Color and CinemaScope photography was by Leon Shamroy.

This Is The Army

Many of the same personnel, and most of Irving Berlin's original songs, made the journey from Broadway to Hollywood when this screen version of the 1942 all-soldier stage revue was released in the following year. Warner Brothers also linked the individual items with a story by Casey Robinson and Claude Binyon, which - guess what - was all about putting on a show that contained some of Berlin's most popular war-tinged and flag-waving numbers. The composer himself, dressed in his World War I uniform, sings 'Oh, How I Hate To Get Up In The Morning', and Kate Smith provides another of the highlights with her inspiring version of 'God Bless America'. The remaining songs are performed by the soldiers and a group of principals consisting of George Murphy, Joan Leslie, George Tobias, Charles Butterworth, Alan Hale, Frances Langford, Dolores Costello, and Gertude Nieson. These included 'I Left My Heart At The Stage Door Canteen', 'The Army's Made A Man Out Of Me', 'This Is The Army, Mr. Jones', 'We're On Our Way To France', 'I'm Getting Tired So I Can Sleep', 'How About A Cheer For The Navy?', 'American Eagles', 'With My Head In The Clouds', 'This Time', 'Poor Little Me, I'm On K.P.', 'Your Country And My Country', 'What The Well-Dressed Man In Harlem Will Wear', 'My Sweetie', and 'This Time Is The Last Time'. Future US President Ronald Reagan was in the cast, too. He plays Murphy's son who picks up the baton from his ageing producer father and puts on a US Forces revue in World War II - entitled *This Is The Army*. It was an unqualified success, as was this picture, which thrilled everyone who saw it. Much of the credit for that must go to director Michael Curtiz, choreographers LeRoy Prinz and Robert Sidney, musical director Ray Heindorf who won an Oscar for 'scoring of a musical picture', and producers Jack L. Warner and Hal B. Wallis. According to *Variety*, the five most commercially successful film musicals of the 40s were all Walt Disney features; *This Is The Army* was in sixth

place, but as a morale booster the picture was in a league of its own. All the profits from a US box-office gross of $8.5 million went to the Army Relief Fund.

This'll Make You Whistle

After co-starring with Hollywood actresses such as Fay Wray and Lili Damita, Jack Buchanan was reunited with his best-known partner, the very English Elsie Randolph, for this 1937 General Film Distributors screen adaptation of the hit West End musical. In Guy Bolton and Paul Thompson's screenplay, which was based on their original book, Bill Hopping (Buchanan) splits from his fiancé, Laura (Marjorie Brooks), because she is more passionate about horses than she is about him. Laura wants him back, and despatches her guardian uncle (Antony Holles) to look him over and give his approval. Having made alternative romantic arrangements with Joan (Jean Gillie), Bill and his pals Reggie and Archie (William Kendall and David Hutcheson), throw a 'Bohemian' party in order to put the uncle off. Unfortunately, he entirely approves of this kind of behaviour - even the presence of Bobbie Rivers (Elsie Randolph), an artist's model who is in the habit of removing her clothes even when she isn't working, does not put him off. However, after the action moves to Le Touquet, Reggie is the one who ends up with Laura. Maurice Sigler, Al Goodhart, and Al Hoffman were responsible for the lively and tuneful score which included 'I'm In Dancing Mood', 'There Isn't Any Limit To My Love', 'Without Rhythm', and 'This'll Make You Whistle'. The producer-director was Herbert Wilcox.

Thoroughly Modern Millie

This thoroughly entertaining pastiche of the 20s and the world of silent movies was released by Universal in 1967. Julie Andrews is Millie, the 'modern' of the title, and eager to marry one of New York's rich and eligible bachelors. She has a room at a boarding house which is reserved for single young women. Here she meets, and takes under her wing, a new resident, Miss Dorothy Brown (Mary Tyler Moore), who immediately attracts the attention of the landlady Mrs. Meers (Beatrice Lillie), a sinister (but hilarious) character with a serious interest in white slave trading. Millie sets out to capture her granite-jawed boss, Trevor Graydon (John Gavin), but he falls for Miss Dorothy and Millie is happy to end up with Jimmy Smith (James Fox), who (by heck) makes up dance-steps like 'The Tapioca' (Jimmy Van Heusen-Sammy Cahn) right there on the spot. Carol Channing as the wealthy Muzzy (step-mother of Miss Dorothy and Jimmy, as it turns out), makes one of her rare screen appearances, and renders delightful versions of 'Jazz Baby' (M.K. Jerome-Blanche Merrill) and 'Do It Again' (George Gershwin-Buddy De Sylva). Julie Andrews was splendid as Millie, especially when handling 'period' numbers such as 'Jimmy' (Kay

Thoroughly Modern Millie

Thompson), 'Baby Face' (Harry Askst-Benny Davis), 'Poor Butterfly' (Raymond Hubbell-John Golden), and the scene-setting title song by Cahn and Van Heusen. Her delicious all-round performance is some indication of how impressive she must have been on Broadway in 1954 when she starred in *The Boyfriend* - a pastiche in a similar vein. This upbeat, jolly movie had a screenplay by Richard Morris and was directed by George Roy Hill. The choreographer was Joe Layton, and it was photographed in Technicolor and Panavision by Russell Metty. Elmer Bernstein won an Oscar for his background music score.

Those Were The Happy Times (see *Star!*)

Thousands Cheer

Another effort by Hollywood in 1943 to lighten the war years by parading entertainers across the screen with only the most tenuous storyline to hold things together. Directed by George Sidney, amongst only a few bright moments are Bob Crosby And His Orchestra and Lena Horne, who is accompanied by a band led by Benny Carter.

Til The Butcher Cuts Him Down

An excellent documentary directed by Phillip Spalding in 1971, which shows many of the fine New Orleans veterans still around at the time of its making. Central to the film is Ernest 'Punch' Miller and also seen and heard are Kid Thomas Valentine, Kid Sheik Cola, Raymond Burke, Don Ewell, Emmanuel Sayles and Kid Ory. Amongst non-New Orleans musicians filmed are Bobby Hackett and Dizzy Gillespie. At the time of the film's making, Miller was terminally ill (he died in December 1971), but he plays to a festival audience with astonishing, and inevitably moving, verve and enthusiasm.

Till The Clouds Roll By

That was the title of a song from the 1917 hit musical *Oh, Boy!*, and its distinguished composer, Jerome Kern, is the subject of this film biography which was released by MGM in 1946. As usual, in these celebrity celebrations, the story owes more to the screenwriters not-so-vivid imagination than to reality, but the songs and their performers can always be relied upon to provide a feast of entertainment. Particularly in this case, when the tasty morsels on offer from the pen of 'the father of American popular music' are memorably performed by Lena Horne ('Can't Help Lovin' Dat Man' and 'Why Was I Born?'), Judy Garland ('Who?' and 'Look For The Silver Lining'), Dinah Shore ('They Didn't Believe Me' and 'The Last Time I Saw Paris'), June Allyson 'Leave It To Jane' and 'Cleopatterer'), Angela Lansbury ('How'd You Like To Spoon With Me?'), Kathryn Grayson and Tony Martin ('Make Believe'), and Virginia O'Brien ('Life Upon The Wicked Stage'). In spite of those and

others equally as wonderful, such as 'Long Ago And Far Away', 'A Fine Romance', 'All The Things You Are', and 'She Didn't Say Yes', the image most people seem to retain from this picture is the sight of a white-suited Frank Sinatra singing 'Ol' Man River' while standing on a lofty pedestal in the finalé. Robert Walker played Kern, with Dorothy Patrick as his wife, and also on hand were Lucille Bremer, Van Johnson, Van Heflin, Gower Champion, Cyd Charisse, Caleb Patterson, Ray McDonald, Sally Forrest, Wilde Twins, Mary Nash, Joan Wells, Paul Langton, and Harry Hayden. Myles Connolly and Jean Holloway were responsible for the storyline, and Robert Alton staged the dances. It was directed by Richard Whorf and Vincente Minnelli and produced by the Arthur Freed unit. Harry Stradling and George Folsey's Technicolor photography helped to make the whole thing look pretty good. *Till The Clouds Roll By* grossed nearly $5 million in the USA, and was highly placed in the Top 20 musicals of the 40s.

Tin Pan Alley

Pin-up girl Betty Grable followed up her splendid performance in *Down Argentine Way* (1940) with a more modest, but highly effective appearance later in the same year in this typical 20th Century-Fox musical. Set in the latter period of World War I, Robert Ellis and Helen Logan's screenplay concerns the singing Blane Sisters, Katie (Alice Faye) and Lily (Grable), who help a couple of songwriters, Harrigan and Calhoun, played by John Payne and Jack Oakie, to build up their own music publishing firm in New York's Tin Pan Alley. The boys and girls are parted for a time while the former 'do their bit' at the Front in France, but they are reunited following the Armistice, and march along together singing the latest Harrigan and Calhoun hit, 'K-K-K-Katie'. In fact, that song was actually written by Geoffrey O'Hara, and was one of the film's group of standards which included 'Honeysuckle Rose' (Andy Razaf-Fats Waller), 'Goodbye Broadway, Hello France' (Benny Davis-Francis Reisner-Billy Baskette), 'Moonlight Bay' (Percy Wenrich-Edward Madden), and 'America, I Love You' (Archie Gottler-Edgar Leslie). There was one new song, the appealing 'You Say The Sweetest Things, Baby' (Mack Gordon-Harry Warren), but the picture's musical highlight, which was staged by choreographer Semour Felix, was a sequence featuring another oldie, 'The Sheik Of Araby' (Ted Snyder-Harry B. Smith-Francis Wheeler). Billy Gilbert, as the Sheik, was serenaded by the hip-swaying Blane Sisters, and entertained in terpsichorean fashion by the scintillating be-turbanned and bare-torsoed Nicholas Brothers. Walter Land was the director who kept the whole thing moving at a smart rate, and the film, which was photographed in black and white by Leon Shamroy, was produced by Darryl F. Zanuck and Kenneth MacGowan. Alfred

Newman won an Oscar for his music score. *Tin Pan Alley* was remade as *I'll Get By* in 1950 starring June Haver and Gloria De Haven.

Tiomkin, Dimitri

b. 10 May 1894, St Petersburg, Russia, d. 11 November 1980. Taught music by his mother as a small child, Tiomkin later studied at the St. Petersburg Conservatory. He worked as a professional musician, playing on the concert platform and as a pianist in silent movie theatres, before moving to Berlin in 1921 to continue his studies. He gave numerous concert performances in Europe as both soloist and as a duettist with another pianist. In 1925 he made his first visit to the USA. In 1930 he returned to the USA when his wife, a ballet dancer and choreographer, was hired to work on some Hollywood films. Tiomkin was also engaged to write music for the films and was soon in great demand. His first major film score was for *Lost Horizon* (1937). Now an American citizen, Tiomkin quickly became one of the most successful and prolific film composers, writing scores and incidental music for films such as *The Westerner* (1940), *Duel In The Sun* (1946), *High Noon* (1952), for which he won Oscars for best score and best song (lyrics by Ned Washington), *The High And The Mighty* (1954), which won another Oscar, *Friendly Persuasion*, *Giant* (both 1956), *The Old Man And The Sea* (1958), which brought his fourth Oscar, *The Sundowners* (1960) and *55 Days At Peking* (1963). Among the songs which came from these and other films were 'Friendly Persuasion'/'Thee I Love' (lyrics by Paul Francis Webster), 'Wild Is The Wind' and 'Strange Are The Ways Of Love' (with Washington) and 'The Green Leaves Of Summer' (with Webster). In the late 50s Tiomkin wrote the theme music for the popular television series *Rawhide*. He also worked as executive producer on the Russian film, *Tchaikowsky* (1970), arranging the music of the film's subject. In the 70s Tiomkin moved to London, England, where he died in November 1980.

Tobias Brothers

This family group of songwriters comprised Charles Tobias (b. 15 August 1898, New York, USA, d. 7 July 1970), Harry Tobias (b. 11 September 1895, New York, USA) and Henry Tobias (b. 23 April 1905, Worcester, Massachusetts, USA). Charles Tobias was the most prolific of the trio, writing mainly lyrics, and occasionally music. After singing for publishing houses, on radio, and in Vaudeville, he formed his own New York publishing company in 1923, and started writing songs soon afterwards. In the late 20s these included 'On A Dew-Dew-Dewy Day' and 'Miss You' (with brothers Henry and Harry), which became hits for Dinah Shore, Bing Crosby and Eddie Howard. From 1928 through to the early 40s, Charles wrote sundry songs for Broadway shows, such as *Good Boy*, *Earl Carroll's Sketch Book* (1929 and 1935), *Earl Carroll's Vanities Of 1932*, *Hellzapoppin'*, *Yokel Boy* and *Banjo Eyes*. His contributions to films continued for another 10 years, until the early 50s. These included: *Life Begins In College* (1937), *Private Buckaroo* (1942), *Shine On, Harvest Moon* (1944), *Saratoga Trunk* (1945), *Tomorrow Is Forever* (1946), *Love And Learn* (1947), *The Daughter Of Rosie O'Grady* (1950), *On Moonlight Bay* (1951) and *About Face* (1952). From the shows, films and Tin Pan Alley, came popular songs such as 'When Your Hair Has Turned To Silver', 'Throw Another Log On The Fire', 'Don't Sweetheart Me', 'No Can Do', 'A Million Miles Away', 'Coax Me A Little Bit' and 'The Old Lamplighter'. His collaborators included Joe Burke, Murray Mencher, Sam Stept, Peter DeRose, Cliff Friend, Sammy Fain, Nat Simon, Jack Scholl, Lew Brown, Roy Turk and Charles Newman. In 1962, after a period of relative inactivity, Tobias wrote 'All Over The World' (with Al Frisch) and 'Those Lazy, Hazy, Crazy Days Of Summer' (with Hans Carste), both of which were successful for Nat 'King' Cole.

Charles' older brother Harry wrote lyrics for some songs in 1916, including 'That Girl Of Mine' and 'Take Me To Alabam' (both with Will Dillon). After military service in World War I, he spent several years in the real estate business before returning to songwriting in the late 20s. In 1931, with bandleader Gus Arnheim and Jules Lemare, he wrote 'Sweet And Lovely', which became Arnheim's theme song, and a big hit in the UK for Al Bowlly; and 'Goodnight My Love', which was featured in the film *Blondie Of The Follies* (1932). During the next 20 years, many of Tobias's lyrics were heard in films such as *Gift Of The Gab*, *Dizzy Dames*, *The Old Homestead*, *With Love And Kisses*, *Swing While You're Able*, *It's A Date*, *Stormy Weather*, *You're A Lucky Fellow, Mr. Smith*, *Sensations Of 1945*, *Brazil*, and *Night Club Girl*. His best-known songs included 'It's A Lonesome Old Town', 'Sail Along Sil'vry Moon', 'Wait For Me', 'No Regrets', 'Fascinating You', 'Go To Sleep, Little Baby', 'Oh Bella Maria' and 'Take Me Back To Those Wide Open Spaces'. His collaborators included Al Sherman, Roy Ingraham, Pinky Tomlin, Harry Barris, Neil Moret and Percy Wenrich. In the 50s he concentrated more on his music publishing interests.

The youngest of the three brothers, Henry Tobias, had a varied career. He wrote special material for artists such Sophie Tucker, Eddie Cantor and Jimmy Durante, was a producer and director for summer stock shows, and also worked for CBS Television as a producer and musical director. With his brother Charles he contributed to the Earl Carroll revues in the 30s, and also wrote many other popular numbers with Will Dillon, David Ormont, David Oppenheim, Don Reid, Milton Berle and Little Jack Little. These included 'Katinka', 'Cooking Breakfast For The One I

Love', 'We Did It Before And We Can Do It Again', 'The Bowling Song, 'You Walked Out Of The Picture', 'Easter Sunday With You' and 'I've Written A Letter To Daddy' (with Larry Vincent and Mo Jaffe), which was featured in the 1979 Janis Joplin biopic, *The Rose*, starring Bette Midler.

Tobias, Charles (see **Tobias Brothers**)

Too Late Blues

Director and star John Cassavetes, uncharacteristically turning out a Hollywood studio film in 1961, carefully evokes the personal and professional relationships between members of a jazz group. Cassavetes, who also appeared in the excellent *Johnny Staccato* television series about a jazzman-private eye, not only loves the music but clearly cares for the musicians who play it. Among the participating musicians, mostly off-screen, are Milt Bernhardt, Benny Carter, Slim Gaillard, Shelly Manne, Red Mitchell, Jimmy Rowles and Uan Rasey who dubs for Bobby Darin who has an acting role.

Top Hat

Probably the most fondly remembered of all the 10 movies Fred Astaire and Ginger Rogers made together, *Top Hat* was released by RKO in 1935. Dwight Taylor and Allan Scott's screenplay finds Jerry

Travers (Astaire) falling for swanky socialite Dale Tremont (Rogers) in London, and following her to Venice where she mistakes him for her best friend's husband. Jerry's problem is to divert Dale from the oily embraces of dress designer Alberto Beddini (Erik Rhodes), which he does in spite of being surrounded by the mayhem caused by other regular members of RKO's consistently droll 'repertory' company which included – besides Rhodes – Edward Everett Horton, Eric Blore and Helen Broderick. What made this musical so special and different to Astaire and Rogers' previous work, was the way in which the songs emerged so smoothly and naturally out of the story. And what songs! Irving Berlin came up with one of his best-ever film scores, and, in the process, gave Astaire his life-long identity number – 'Top Hat, White Tie And Tails'. There were four other marvellous dance sequences: 'Cheek To Cheek', during which, apparently, Fred became rather annoyed and frustrated because the feathers from Ginger's dress kept flying off and getting up his nose; 'No Strings', an Astaire solo which he reduced to a soft-shoe-shuffle after complaints from a sleepy Ginger in the apartment below; 'Isn't This A Lovely Day?', where the two are stranded in a bandstand during a thunder storm, a situation which leads to one of the most endearing all-time great movie moments; and 'The Piccolina', a lively dance finalé that gives Ginger

Top Hat

a rare solo vocal opportunity. Director Mark Sandrich and dance director Hermes Pan, along with an outstanding cast and Irving Berlin's wonderful music, all combined to make this a very special film.

Travolta, John

b. 18 February 1954, Englewood, New Jersey, USA, of Italian-Irish ancestry. Travolta left school at the age of 16 to become an actor. After working in off-Broadway productions and Hollywood bit-parts, he landed a lead in *Welcome Back Cotter*, a nationally-transmitted television series. Hating to see this exposure go to waste, Midsong Records engaged the handsome young thespian as a recording artist. Three singles, notably 1976's 'Let Her In', cracked the US Top 40 which, with his film roles in such as *Devil's Rain* (1975), *The Boy In The Plastic Bubble* (1976) and *Carrie* (1976), readied the public for his *pièce de résistance* as the star of *Saturday Night Fever* which turned disco into a multi-national industry. Travolta's pop and cinema interests combined in 1978's *Grease* for which he was singularly well-prepared, having once toured in a stage version of this musical. From the soundtrack, his duets with co-star Olivia Newton-John, 'You're The One That I Want' and 'Summer Nights', were world-wide number 1 hits with Travolta's solo highlights, 'Sandy' and 'Greased Lightning' also selling well. His chart career effectively ended after the fall of *Sandy* from album lists in 1979. *Staying Alive*, a 1983 sequel-of-sorts to *Saturday Night Fever*, was the most successful of Travolta's later movies, although he teamed up again with Newton-John in *Two Of A Kind* and they were heard on its tie-in album. He subsequently co-starred with Kirstie Allie in *Look Who's Talking*.

Albums: *Sandy* (1978), *Whenever I'm Away From You* (1978), *Two Of A Kind* (1983, film soundtrack). Compilation: *20 Golden Pieces* (1981).

Tucker, Sophie

b. Sophie (or Sonia) Kalish-Abuza, 13 January 1884, in transit between Russia and Poland, d. 9 February 1966. She was a singer of generous proportions, brassy and dynamic, who claimed to be 'The Last Of The Red-Hot Mamas'. The daughter of Russian parents, Tucker was taken to the USA when she was three years old. Sophie's father took the man's name and papers in an attempt to evade the Russian authorities. By the time she was 10-years-old Tucker was a singing waitress in her father's cafe in Hartford, Connecticut, and in 1906 she moved to New York to work at the Café Monopole, the German Village Cafe and then in burlesque, vaudeville and cabaret. Sometimes, because of her plain appearance she was persuaded to work in blackface, and made a reputation as a 'Coon-Shouter' in the ragtime era. After a teenage marriage failed (as did two later attempts), she added 'er' to her ex-husband's name of

'Tuck' to create her new stage name. In 1909 she played a small, but telling part in the Ziegfeld Follies. By 1911 she was a headliner, and was able to drop the dreaded blackface for good. In the same year she made her first recording of the song which was to become her life-long theme, forever associated with her. 'Some Of These Days' was written by composer-pianist Shelton Brooks (b. 4 May 1886, Amesburg, Ontario, Canada), who also wrote 'The Darktown Strutters Ball', and special material for Nora Bayes and Al Jolson. Other hits around this time were 'That Lovin' Rag', 'That Lovin' Two-Step Man', 'That Loving Soul Kiss' and 'Knock Wood'. When jazz music became the new craze during World War I, Tucker became known as 'The Queen Of Jazz', and toured with the band 'Sophie Tucker And Her Five Kings Of Syncopation'.

In 1919 she replaced 'shimmy dance' specialist, Gilda Gray in the Broadway show, *Schubert Gaieties*, and in 1921 hired pianist Ted Shapiro, who as well as writing some of her risque material, became her accompanist and musical director for the rest of her career. In the following year she made the first of many performances in London in the revue, *Round In 50*, based on the novel *Around The World In 80 Days*, by Jules Verne. She was back on Broadway in 1924 for the *Earl Carroll Vanities*, and was by now a major star. Her hits during the 20s included 'High Brown Blues', 'You've Gotta See Mama Ev'ry Night (Or You Won't See Mama At All)', 'Aggravatin' Papa', 'The One I Love Belongs To Somebody Else', 'Red-Hot Mama', 'Bugle Call Rag' (with Ted Lewis and his band), 'Fifty Million Frenchmen Can't Be Wrong', 'After You've Gone', 'I Ain't Got Nobody', 'Blue River', 'There'll Be Some Changes Made', 'The Man I Love', 'I'm The Last Of The Red-Hot Mamas', and two reputed million-sellers, a re-recording of her trademark song, 'Some Of These Days', and 'My Yiddishe Momme', written for her by Jack Yellen and Lew Pollack. She recorded the song in English on one side of the record, and in Yiddish on the other.

In 1929 Tucker made her movie debut in an early talkie, *Honky Tonk*, with songs by Yellen. She made several more films until 1944, including *Gay Love*, *Follow The Boys* and *Sensations Of 1945* - usually as a guest artist playing her larger-than-life self - although she gave critically acclaimed performances in *Thoroughbreds Don't Cry* and *Broadway Melody Of 1938*, co-starring with Judy Garland. In 1930 she returned to London's West End to star with Jack Hulbert in the musical comedy, *Follow A Star*. The London *Observer*'s theatre critic wrote: 'She hurls her songs like projectiles, in a very explosive manner'. Four years later she was back in London for the first of several Royal Command Performances, besides regular appearances at London's Kit Kat Club, music hall tours and cabaret. She made her final Broadway appearances in Cole Porter's *Leave It To Me* (1938), in which she sang 'Most Gentlemen Don't Like Love (They Just Like To Kick It Around') and *High Kickers* (1941). Her fame faded somewhat in the 50s and 60s, although she still worked in clubs and occasionally on television, including several appearances on the *Ed Sullivan Show*. She also played an effective cameo role in the bio-pic of comedian Joe E. Lewis, *The Joker Is Wild* (1957). In her later years, when her voice declined, she specialized in half-sung, half-spoken, philosophical songs and monologues, many written by Jack Yellen, sometimes in partnership with Ted Shapiro or Milton Ager. Her specialities included 'Life Begins At 40', 'I'm Having More Fun Now I'm 50', 'I'm Having More Fun Since I'm 60', 'I'm Starting All Over Again', 'The Older They Get', 'You've Got To Be Loved To Be Healthy', 'No One Man Is Ever Going To Worry Me' and 'He Hadn't Till Yesterday'. Her last appearances included New York's Latin Quarter, and The Talk Of The Town in London. She died in February 1966 in New York, USA. The 1963 Broadway musical *Sophie*, was based on her life.

Compilations: *Miff Mole's Molers 1927* (1971), *The Great Sophie Tucker* (1974), *Some Of These Days* (1976), *Harry Richman And Sophie Tucker* (1979), *Last Of The Red-Hot Mamas* (1983), *The Golden Age Of Sophie Tucker* (1985), *Follow A Star* (1987), *The Sophie Tucker Collection* (1987).

Further reading: *Some Of These Days*, Sophie Tucker.

U

Under Your Hat

This was one of the best – and the last – of the popular series of Cicely Courtneidge and Jack Hulbert musicals, although they did make the occasional comedy and dramatic picture together later in their careers. It was adapted from the successful couple's hit West End musical, and released in 1940 by Grand National (British Lion) Pictures. Courtneidge and Hulbert play film stars Kay and Jack Millett who get caught up in a web of espionage. A glamorous spy, Carole Markoff (Leonora Corbett), heads off to Europe with the intention of passing a top secret carburettor to Russian agent Boris Vladimir (Austin Trevor). Jack is despatched by the authorities to use his renowned charm on the lady in an effort to retrieve the stolen property, but Kay is not aware that his interest in Carole is purely platonic and in the national interest. However, she and her husband, with

the help of some hilarious disguises, eventually wrestle the booty from the Reds. Also involved in the fun and games were Cecil Parker, Charles Oliver, H.F. Maltby, Glynis Johns, Myrette Morvan, and Don Marino Barretto's Band. Most of the original stage score was dispensed with, and the songs in the film consisted of 'Keep It Under Your Hat' (Clive Erard-Claude Hulbert), 'I Won't Conga' (F. King-Hulbert), 'Tiger Rag' (Larocca), and 'Sur Le Pont D'Avignon' (Traditional). The well-known bandleader Lew Stone composed the atmospheric background music. Maurice Elvy was the director, and this amusing and typically English picture was produced by Jack Hulbert.

Up In Arms

Considering the impact Danny Kaye made in this, his first feature film, it could well have been re-titled *A Star Is Born*. Produced by Sam Goldwyn in Technicolor and released by RKO in 1944, *Up In Arms* is the story of a zany hypochondriac who leaves his job as an elevator boy and winds up in the US Army on an island in the South Pacific. With him is his buddy (Dana Andrews) and their girlfriends, played by Dinah Shore and Constance Dowling. The hectic storyline is interrupted occasionally by similarly hectic numbers such as 'Melody In 4-F' and 'The Lobby Song' ('Manic-Depressive Pictures presents . . .'), both written by Sylvia Fine and Max Liebman, and performed by Kaye in his own highly individual and brilliant style. If it was all getting a bit too frantic, audiences could relax for a few moments in the company of Dinah Shore and her lovely renderings of Harold Arlen and Ted Koeler's 'Now I Know' and 'Tess's Torch Song'. Not many were heard to complain, though, and this film launched the red-haired unique entertainer on his way to well-deserved world-wide acclaim. Joining in the fun were Louis Calhern, Lyle Talbot, Benny Baker, George Matthews, Walter Catlett, Margaret Dumont, Elisha Cook Jnr., and 24-year-old Virginia Mayo in only her second film. Danny Dare handled the choreography and the director was Elliot Nugent. *Up In Arms*, which had a screenplay by Don Hartman, Allan Boretz and Robert Pirosh, is sometimes considered to be a remake of *Whoopee!* (1930) which was based on Owen Davis's play *The Nervous Wreck*, and starred Eddie Cantor.

V

Vallee, Rudy

b. Hubert Prior Vallee, 28 July 1901, Island Pond, Vermont, USA, d. 3 July 1986, North Hollywood, California, USA. Vallee was an immensely popular singer during the 20s and 30s and is generally accepted as the first pop idol - someone able to generate mass hysteria among his audiences. He sang through a megaphone - the original 'crooner' - a precursor of Russ Columbo and Bing Crosby. He was brought up in Westbrook, Maine, and learnt to play the saxophone in his teens, taking the name 'Rudy' because of his admiration for saxophonist Rudy Weidoft. During 1924/5 he took a year off from university to play the saxophone in London with the Savoy Havana Band led by Reginald Batten. At this time his singing voice, which was rather slight and nasal, was not taken seriously. In 1928 he led his first band, at the exclusive Heigh-Ho Club on New York's 53rd Street. Billed as Rudy And His Connecticut Yankees, Vallee made an excellent front man complete with his famous greeting: 'Heigh-ho, everybody', and his smooth vocal delivery of his theme song at that time, Walter Donaldson's 'Heigh-Ho Everybody, Heigh-Ho'. When radio stations started to carry his shows in the club he became an instant success and admitted that he was 'a product of radio'. His next venue was the Versaille Club on 50th Street. After a few weeks, business was so good they renamed it the Villa Vallee. His success continued when he transferred his show to vaudeville. In 1929 he starred in his first feature film, the poorly-received Vagabond Lover, and in the same year began a weekly NBC network radio variety show sponsored by the Fleischmann's Yeast company (The Fleischmann Hour) which became a top attraction and ran for 10 years. His theme song for this production was 'My Time Is Your Time'. Artists he promoted on the show included radio ventriloquist Edgar Bergen, Frances Langford and Alice Faye. In 1931 and 1936 Vallee appeared on Broadway in George White's Scandals, and in 1934 starred in a film version of the show. From early in his career he had co-written several popular songs including 'I'm Still Caring', 'If You Haven't Got A Girl', 'Don't Play With Fire', 'Two Little Blue Little Eyes' and 'Oh, Ma-Ma'. He had big hits with some of his own numbers including 'I'm Just A Vagabond Lover', 'Deep Night', 'Vieni Vieni' and 'Betty Co-ed' (a song mentioning most of the US colleges).

Other record successes included 'Marie', 'Honey' (a number 1 hit), 'Weary River', 'Lonely Troubadour', 'A Little Kiss Each Morning (A Little Kiss Each Night)', 'Stein Song (University Of Maine)', 'If I Had A Girl Like You', 'You're Driving Me Crazy', 'Would You Like To Take A Walk?', 'When Yuba Plays The Rhumba On The Tuba', ' Let's Put Out The Lights', 'Brother Can You Spare A Dime?', 'Just An Echo In The Valley', 'Everything I Have Is Yours', 'Orchids In The Moonlight', 'You Oughta Be In Pictures', 'Nasty Man', 'As Time Goes By' and 'The Whiffenpoof Song'. During the 30s Vallee appeared in several popular musical films including Glorifying The American Girl, International House, Sweet Music, Gold Diggers Of Paris, and Second Fiddle. However, after Time Out For Rhythm, Too Many Blondes, and Happy-Go-Lucky (1943), he began a new movie career as a comedy actor. Discarding his romantic image, he began portraying a series of eccentric, strait-laced, pompous characters in films such as The Palm Beach Story, Man Alive!, and It's In The Bag. During World War II, Vallee led the California Coastguard orchestra which he augmented to 45 musicians. After the war he was back on the radio, in nightclubs, and making more movies including, The Bachelor And The Bobbysoxer, I Remember Mama, So This Is New York, Unfaithfully Yours, and The Beautiful Blonde From Bashful Bend. During the 50s he appeared regularly on television especially in talk shows, and featured in the films Gentlemen Marry Brunettes and The Helen Morgan Story. In 1961 he enjoyed a personal triumph in the role of J.B. Biggley, a caricature of a collegiate executive figure, in Frank Loesser's smash hit musical How To Succeed In Business Without Really Trying. Vallee re-created the part in the 1967 movie and in a San Francisco stage revival in 1975. In 1968 he contributed the narration to the William Friedkin film The Night They Raided Minsky's. He continued to make movies into the 70s (his last feature was the 1976 film Won Ton Ton, The Dog Who Saved Hollywood), and performed his one-man show up until his death from a heart attack.

Album: How To Succeed In Business Without Really Trying (1961, Original Broadway Cast). Compilations: Rudy Vallee And His Connecticut Yankees (1986), 'Heigh-Ho Everybody, This Is...' (1981), Sing For Your Supper (1989).

Further reading: Vagabond Dreams Come True, Rudy Vallee. My Time Is Your Time, Rudy Vallee. I Digress, Rudy Vallee.

Van Heusen, Jimmy

b. Edward Chester Babcock, 26 January 1913, Syracuse, New York, USA, d. 6 February 1990, Rancho Mirage, California, USA. Van Heusen was an extremely popular and prolific composer from the late 30s through to the 60s, particularly for movies. He was an affable, high-living, fun-loving character. His main collaborators were lyricists Johnny Burke and Sammy Cahn. While still at high school, Van Heusen worked at a local radio station, playing piano and singing. He changed his name to Van Heusen, after the famous shirt manufacturer. In the early 30s he studied piano and composition at Syracuse University, and met Jerry Arlen, son of composer Harold Arlen. Arlen Snr. gave Van Heusen the opportunity to write for Harlem's *Cotton Club Revues*.

His big break came in 1938 when bandleader Jimmy Dorsey wrote a lyric to Van Heusen's tune for 'It's The Dreamer In Me'. Ironically, the song was a big hit for rival bandleader Harry James. In the same year Van Heusen started working with lyricist Eddie DeLange. Their songs included 'Deep In A Dream', 'All This And Heaven Too', 'Heaven Can Wait' (a number 1 hit for Glen Gray), 'This Is Madness' and 'Shake Down The Stars' (a hit for Glenn Miller). In 1939 they wrote the score for the Broadway musical *Swingin' The Dream*, a jazzy treatment of Shakespeare's *A Midsummer Night's Dream*. Despite the presence in the cast of the all-star Benny Goodman Sextet, Louis Armstrong, Maxine Sullivan, and the Deep River Boys, plus the song, 'Darn That Dream', the show folded after only 13 performances. In 1940 Van Heusen was placed under contract to Paramount Pictures, and began his association with Johnny Burke. Their first songs together included 'Polka Dots And Moonbeams' and 'Imagination', both hits for the Tommy Dorsey Orchestra, with vocals by Frank Sinatra, who was to have an enormous effect on Van Heusen's later career. After contributing to the Fred Allen-Jack Benny comedy film, *Love Thy Neighbor* (1940), Van Heusen and Burke supplied songs for 16 Bing Crosby films through to 1953, including 'It's Always You' (*Road To Zanzibar*), 'Road To Morocco', 'Moonlight Becomes You' (*Road To Morocco*), 'Sunday, Monday Or Always' (*Dixie*), 'Swinging On A Star' (which won the 1944 Academy Award, from the film *Going My Way*), 'Aren't You Glad You're You?' (*The Bells Of St Mary's*), 'Personality' (*Road To Utopia*), 'But Beautiful', 'You Don't Have To Know The Language', 'Experience' (*Road To Rio*), 'If You Stub Your Toe On the Moon', 'Busy Doing Nothing' (*A Connecticut Yankee In King Arthur's Court*) and 'Sunshine Cake' (*Riding High*). Besides working on other films, Van Heusen and Burke also wrote the score for the 1953 Broadway musical *Carnival In Flanders*, which contained the songs, 'Here's That Rainy Day' and 'It's An Old Spanish Custom'. Other Van Heusen songs during this period include 'Oh, You Crazy Moon', 'Suddenly It's Spring' and 'Like Someone In Love' (all with Burke). The last song received a memorable delivery from Frank Sinatra on his first album, *Songs For Young Lovers* in 1953, as did 'I Thought About You', on Sinatra's *Songs For Swinging Lovers*. Van Heusen also wrote, along with comedian Phil Silvers, one of Sinatra's special songs, dedicated to his daughter, 'Nancy (With The Laughing Face)'.

When Burke became seriously ill in 1954 and was unable to work for two years, Van Heusen began a collaboration with Sammy Cahn. Cahn had recently ended his partnership with Jule Styne in style by winning an Oscar for their title song to the film *Three Coins In The Fountain* (1954). The new team had immediate success with another film title song, for the 1955 Sinatra comedy, *The Tender Trap*, and then won Academy Awards for their songs in two more Sinatra movies; 'All The Way' (from the Joe E. Lewis biopic, *The Joker Is Wild*) in 1957, and 'High Hopes' (from *A Hole In The Head*) in 1959. They also contributed songs to several other Sinatra movies, including 'Ain't That A Kick In The Head' (*Ocean's 11*), 'My Kind Of Town', 'Style' (*Robin And The Seven Hoods*), the title songs to *A Pocketful Of Miracles, Come Blow Your Horn* and several of Sinatra's best-selling albums, such as *Come Fly With Me, Only The Lonely, Come Dance With Me, No One Cares, Ring-A-Ding-Ding* and *September Of My Years*. Van Heusen and Cahn also produced his successful *Timex* television series (1959-60). They won their third Academy Award in 1963 for 'Call Me Irresponsible', from the film, *Papa's Delicate Condition*, and contributed songs to many other movies, including 'The Second Time Around' (*High Time*), and the title songs for *Say One For Me, Where Love Has Gone, Thoroughly Modern Millie* and *Star!*.

The duo also supplied the songs for a musical version of Thornton Wilder's classic play, *Our Town*, which included 'Love And Marriage' and 'The Impatient Years'. They wrote the scores for two Broadway musicals, *Skyscraper* in 1965 ('Everybody Has The Right To Be Wrong', 'I'll Only Miss Her When I Think Of Her') and *Walking Happy* in 1966, starring UK comedian Norman Wisdom. From then on, Van Heusen concentrated on his other interests such as music publishing (he had formed a company with Johnny Burke in 1944), photography, flying his own aeroplanes and helicopters, and collecting rare manuscripts by classical composers. He also continued to make television appearances, especially on tribute shows for composers. He died in 1990, after a long illness.

Vangelis

b Evangelos Odyssey Papathanassiou, 29 March 1943, Valos, Greece. A child prodigy, Vangelis gave his first public performance on the piano at the age of six. In the early 60s he joined the pop group Formynx, later forming Aphrodite's Child with vocalist Demis Roussos and Lucas Sideras (drums). The group moved to Paris in the late 60s, recording the international hit 'Rain And Tears'. After it disbanded in 1972, Vangelis concentrated on electronic music, composing classical works as well as film scores for wildlife documentaries by Frederic Rossif. He next built a studio in London where he further developed his fusion of electronic and acoustic sound. *Heaven And Hell* was a Top 40 hit in the UK while the concept album *Albedo 0.39* included the voices of astronauts landing on the moon, as well as the dramatic favourite 'Pulstar'. Returning to Greece in 1978, Vangelis collaborated with actress Irene Papas on settings of Byzantine and Greek traditional song, before joining forces with Yes vocalist Jon Anderson who had previously sung on *Heaven And Hell*. As Jon And Vangelis they had international success with 'I Hear You Now' (1980) and 'I'll Find My Way Home' (1982). The following year, Vangelis resumed his activities as a film music composer with the award-winning *Chariots Of Fire*. The title track was a world-wide hit and prompted scores of imitation 'themes'. This was followed by scores for Kuruhara's *Antarctica*, Ridley Scott's *Bladerunner* and Costas-Gavras' *Missing* and Donaldson's *The Bounty*. In 1988, he signed to Arista Records, releasing *Direct,* the first in a series of improvised albums which he composed, arranged and recorded simultaneously. His film credits in the early 90s included *Bitter Moon* and *1492: Conquest Of Paradise* (1993).

Albums: *Dragon* (1971), *L'Apocalypse Des Animaux* (1973), *Earth* (1974), *Heaven And Hell* (1975), *Albedo 0.39* (1976), *Spiral* (1977), *Beaubourg* (1978), *Hypothesis* (1978), *Odes* (1978), *China* (1979), *See You Later* (1980), *Chariots Of Fire* (1981, film soundtrack), *Opera Sauvage* (1981), *To The Unknown Man* (1981), *Soil Festivities* (1984), *Ignacio* (1985), *Invisible Connections* (1985), *Mask* (1985), *Direct* (1988), *Antarctica* (1988, film soundtrack), *The City* (1990), *1492 - The Conquest Of Paradise* (1992, film soundtrack), *Entends - Tu Les Chiens* (1993). Compilation: *The Best Of Vangelis* (1981), *Themes* (1989). As Jon And Vangelis: *Short Stories* (1980), *The Friends Of Mr Cairo* (1981), *Private Collection* (1983), *Page Of Life* (1991).

Vaughan, Frankie

b. Frank Abelson, 3 February 1928, Liverpool, England. While studying at Leeds College of Art, Vaughan's vocal performance at a college revue earned him a week's trial at the Kingston Empire music hall. Warmly received, he went on to play the UK variety circuit, developing a stylish act with trademarks which included a top hat and cane, a particularly athletic side kick, and his theme song 'Give Me The Moonlight' (Albert Von Tilzer-Lew Brown). His Russian-born maternal grandmother inspired his stage name by always referring to him as her 'Number Vorn' grandchild. After registering strongly in pre-chart days with 'That Old Piano Roll Blues', 'Daddy's Little Girl', 'Look At That Girl', and 'Hey, Joe' 1953), during the remainder of the 50s Vaughan was consistently in the UK Top 30 with songs such as 'Istanbul (Not Constantinople)', 'Happy Days And Lonely Nights', 'Tweedle Dee', Seventeen',

'My Boy Flat Top', 'Green Door', 'Garden Of Eden' (number 1), 'Man On Fire'/'Wanderin' Eyes', 'Gotta Have Something In the Bank Frank' (with the Kaye Sisters), 'Kisses Sweeter Than Wine', 'Can't Get Along Without You'/'We Are Not Alone', 'Kewpie Doll', 'Wonderful Things', 'Am I Wasting My Time On You', 'That's My Doll', 'Come Softly To Me' (with the Kaye Sisters), 'The Heart Of A Man', and 'Walkin' Tall'. In spite of the burgeoning beat boom he continued to flourish in the 60s with 'What More Do You Want', 'Kookie Little Paradise', 'Milord', 'Tower Of Strength' (number 1), 'Don't Stop Twist', Loop-De-Loop', 'Hey Mama', 'Hello Dolly', 'There Must Be A Way', 'So Tired', and 'Nevertheless' (1968). With his matinée idol looks he seemed a natural for films, and made his debut in 1956 in the Arthur Askey comedy *Ramsbottom Rides Again*. This was followed by a highly acclaimed straight role in *These Dangerous Years*, and a musical frolic with the normally staid Anna Neagle in *The Lady Is A Square*. Other screen appearances included *Wonderful Things! Heart Of A Man* with Anne Heywood, Tony Britton and Anthony Newley, and *It's All Over Town*, a pop extravaganza in which he was joined by current raves such as Acker Bilk, the Bachelors, the Springfields, and the Hollies. In the early 60s Vaughan began to experience real success in America, in nightclubs and on television, and he was playing his second season in Las Vegas when he was chosen to star with Marilyn Monroe and Yves Montand in the 20th Century-Fox picture *Let's Make Love*. Although he gave a creditable performance, especially when he duetted with Monroe on Sammy Cahn and Jimmy Van Heusen's 'Incurably Romantic', his disaffection for Hollywood ensured that a US film career was not pursued. At home, however, he had become an extremely well-established performer, headlining at the London Palladium and enjoying lucrative summer season work, appealing consistently to mainly family audiences. In 1985 he was an unexpected choice to replace James Laurenson as the belligerent Broadway producer Julian Marsh in the West End hit musical *42nd Street*. A one-year run in the show ended with ill-health and some acrimony. His career-long efforts for the benefit of young people, partly through the assignment of record royalties to bodies such as the National Association of Boys' Clubs, was recognized by an OBE in 1965. He was honoured further in 1993 when the Queen appointed him as the Deputy Lord Lieutenant of Buckinghamshire. In the preceding year he had undergone a life-saving operation to replace a ruptured main artery in his heart, but in 1994, when he was in cabaret at London's Café Royal, the legendary side-kick was still (gingerly) in evidence.

Selected albums: *Frankie Vaughan Showcase* (1958), *Frankie Vaughan At The London Palladium* (1959), *Frankie Vaughan Songbook* (1967), *There Must Be A*

Way (1967), *Double Exposure* (1971), *Frankie* (1973), *Frankie Vaughan's Sing Song* (1973), *Sincerely Yours, Frankie Vaughan* (1975), *Sings* (1975), *Seasons For Lovers* (1977), *Time After Time* (1986). Compilations: *Spotlight On Frankie Vaughan* (1975), *100 Golden Greats* (1977), *Golden Hour Presents Frankie Vaughan* (1978), *Greatest Hits* (1983), *Love Hits And High Kicks* (1985), *Music Maestro Please* (1986), *The Best Of* (1990), *The Essential Recordings 1955-65* (1993).

Vera-Ellen

b. Vera-Ellen Westmeyer Rohe, 16 February 1926, Cincinnati, Ohio, USA, d. 30 August 1981, Los Angeles, California, USA. A charming actress and one of the finest dancers in film musicals of the 40s and 50s. After taking dance lessons from the age of 10, as a teenager Vera-Ellen toured with the Major Bowes talent show before joining the Rockette line at the famous Radio City Musical Hall in New York. She made her Broadway debut in *Very Warm For May* (1939), and followed that with other roles in *Higher And Higher* (1940), *Panama Hattie* (1940), *By Jupiter* (1942) and *A Connecticut Yankee* (1943). Signed to 20th Century-Fox, she made two movies with Danny Kaye, *Wonder Man* and *The Kid From Brooklyn*, and then landed a seven year contract with MGM. She

was joined by Dick Haymes for her first film for the studio, *Carnival In Costa Rica* (1947). It proved to be fairly forgettable, but things improved with the Richard Rodgers and Lorenz Hart bio-pic *Words And Music* (1948) in which she and Gene Kelly provided the film's highspot with the classic ballet sequence, 'Slaughter On Tenth Avenue'. She was teamed with Kelly again a year later in the splendid *On The Town*, and then danced opposite that other great movie song-and-dance-man Fred Astaire in *Three Little Words* (1950) and *The Belle Of New York* (1952). Her last two pictures for MGM cast her opposite two completely contrasting personalities: in *The Big Leaguer* (1953) her co-star was Edward G. Robinson, and for *Call Me Madam*, which was released in the same year, she danced delightfully with the bright and breezy Donald O'Connor. During most of the 50s Vera-Ellen appeared in cabaret and made guest appearances on some of the top-rated US television variety shows, including the one hosted by Perry Como. In 1959, 10 years after she made her debut with him in *Wonder Man*, she was re-united with Danny Kaye in the immensely popular *White Christmas*, which also starred Bing Crosby and Rosemary Clooney. Her final film, *Let's Be Happy* (1957), was made in England, but even with Tony Martin, and songs by Nicholas Brodszky

Gwen Verdon and Bob Fosse (*Damn Yankees*)

and Paul Francis Webster, it was an unsatisfactory affair. At the end of the decade she retired from the screen, and, after she was divorced from her second husband the oil company executive Victor Rothschild in 1966, she lived in seclusion at her Hollywood home.

Verdon, Gwen

b. Gwyneth Evelyn Verdon, 13 January 1926, Culver City, California, USA. A vivacious, red-headed dancer, actress and singer, Verdon can be funny or tender, sassy or seductive, depending on the music and the mood. She studied dancing from an early age, and, after assisting the noted choreographer Jack Cole on *Magdalena* (1948), made her first appearance on Broadway two years later in *Alive And Kicking*. However, it was Cole Porter's *Can-Can* that made her a star in 1953. She played the (very) high-kicking Claudine, and won her first Tony Award. She won another for her portrayal of the bewitching Lola in *Damn Yankees* (1955), which was brilliantly choreographed by her future husband, Bob Fosse. He re-staged his innovative dance sequences for the 1958 film version, for which, instead of casting an already established film star, Verdon was invited to reprise her Broadway role. From then on, Fosse choreographed and/or directed all Verdon's shows. In 1957 she played Anna Christie in *New Girl In Town*, a musical adaptation of Eugene O'Neill's 1921 play, and on this occasion she shared the Tony with a fellow cast member, Thelma Ritter - the first time there had been a Tony-tie. In 1959, Verdon won outright - and for the last time - when she starred with Richard Kiley in *Redhead*. After that, Broadway audiences had to wait another seven years before they saw Verdon on the musical stage, but the wait was more than worthwhile. In *Sweet Charity* (1966) she played a dancehall hostess with a heart of gold who yearns for marriage and roses round the door. Cy Coleman and Dorothy Fields provided her with some lovely songs, including 'If My Friends Could See Me Now' and 'There's Gotta Be Something Better Than This'. Gwen Verdon's final Broadway musical (to date) was *Chicago* (1975), a razzle-dazzle affair set in the roaring 20s, full of hoods and Chita Rivera. In more recent times she has turned once more to films. She had appeared in several during the 50s, including *On The Riviera*, *Meet Me After The Show*, *David And Bathsheba*, *The Merry Widow*, *The I Don't Care Girl*, *The Farmer Takes A Wife*, as well as *Damn Yankees*. In 1983 she played a choreographer in the television movie *Legs*, and had several other good roles in big-screen features such as *The Cotton Club*, *Cocoon*, *Nadine*, *Cocoon-The Return*, and *Alice* (1990). In 1992 she donated a substantial amount of material documenting her own career and that of her late husband, Bob Fosse (he died in 1987), to the Library of Congress.

Victor/Victoria

In 1982, after finally breaking free from her 'goody goody' image by going topless in *S.O.B.* a year earlier, Julie Andrews went in for a touch of 'gender-bending' in this MGM release for which her husband, Blake Edwards, served as screenwriter, director and co-producer (with Tony Adams). Andrews plays singer Vicki Adams, down on her luck in Paris during the 60s. Desperate for work, and encouraged by a gay friend (Robert Preston), she takes a job as a female impersonator called Victor (ie as a woman, she impersonates a man who is masquerading as a woman). No wonder the businessman-hood (James Garner) who has just blown in from Chicago is confused. After seeing Vicki in cabaret, he falls for her/him before being entirely certain of the gender situation. Edwards invariably handles these kinds of situations well, and there are several marvellous moments in the film, such as when Garner sneaks into Vicki's room to try and discover once and for all if she is male or female, and another scene in which Garner's girlfriend, played by Lesley Ann Warren, having discovered Vicki's secret, thinks that he (Garner) may be homosexual. Henry Mancini and Leslie Bricusse won Academy Awards for their song score, which included 'The Shady Dame From Seville' 'Le Jazz Hot', 'Crazy World', 'You And Me', 'Gay Paree', and 'Chicago, Illinois'. Paddy Stone was the choreographer, and the film, which was either charming or crude depending on your point of view, was photographed in Metrocolor and Panavision. In 1994, following her successful comeback Off-Broadway in the Stephen Sondheim revue *Putting It Together*, there were persistent rumours that Julie Andrews would appear in a stage adaptation of *Victor/Victoria* in either London or New York.

Viva Las Vegas

Released by MGM in 1964, this was one of Elvis Presley's best film musicals, mainly due to the presence of Ann-Margret as his leading lady. They proved to be an irresistible combination in a screenplay which has Presley as an ambitious racing driving who takes a temporary job in an hotel after losing his bankroll when Ann-Margret pushes him into the swimming pool. At their first meeting she had mistaken him for a mechanic: She: 'I'd like you to check my motor - it whistles.' He: 'I don't blame it.' His persistent pursuit of her is aided by some pretty good songs, the best of which is their amusing love/hate duet 'The Lady Loves Me' (He: 'The lady's dying to be kissed.' She: 'The gentleman needs a psychiatrist.'). Sid Tepper and Roy C. Bennett wrote that one, and the rest of the score included 'I Need Somebody To Lean On' (Doc Pomus), 'Appreciation' and 'My Rival' (both Marvin Moore-Bernie Wayne), 'If You Think I Don't Need You' (Red West), 'Come On, Everybody' (Stanley Chianese), 'What'd I

Viva Las Vegas

Say?' (Ray Charles), and 'Today, Tomorrow And Forever' (Bill Giant-Bernie Baum-Florence Kaye). Naturally, Elvis wins the big race and the girl, and winds the whole thing up with the bustling 'Viva Las Vegas' (Pomus-Mort Shuman). Cesare Danova was his arch-rival for both prizes, and also among the cast were William Demarest, Nicky Blair, and Jack Carter. Sally Benson wrote the thin but diverting screenplay, David Winters was the choreographer, and director George Sidney kept up a lively pace. Sidney was also co-producer with Jack Cummings. According to *Variety*, this was the most commercially successful of all the Presley films, grossing well over $5 million. For the UK it was re-titled *Love In Las Vegas*. This was probably because the 1956 Dan Dailey-Cyd Charisse musical *Meet Me In Las Vegas* was called *Viva Las Vegas* when it was released in Britain.

W

Wabash Avenue (see *Coney Island*)

Walters, Charles

b. 17 November 1911, Pasadena, California, USA, d. 13 August 1982, Malibu, California, USA. A distinguished choreographer and director for some of the classic film musicals from the 40s through to 60s; his work is well-known, but his name is not so familiar. Walters studied at the University of Southern California before joining the famous Fanchon and Marco road shows as a dancer in 1934. In the late 30s he danced in several Broadway shows including *Between The Devil* and *Du Barry Was A Lady* (1939), and subsequently worked as a stage director before moving to Hollywood and making his debut as a choreographer for the Lucille Ball-Victor Mature RKO movie *Seven Days Leave* (1942). He then switched to MGM, and continued to direct the dance routines in top musicals such as *Presenting Lily Mars*, *Du Barry Was A Lady*, *Girl Crazy*, *Best Foot Forward*, *Broadway Rhythm*, *Meet Me In St. Louis*, *The Harvey Girls*, *Ziegfeld Follies*, and *Summer Holiday* (1947). At that stage producer Arthur Freed assigned Walters as director for the 1947 remake of *Good News* with June Allyson and Peter Lawford, and his deft handling of this fairly complicated project led to him directing a variety of mostly entertaining musicals starring some of the Studio's major stars such as Fred Astaire, Judy Garland, Esther Williams, Leslie Caron, and Frank

Sinatra. They included *Easter Parade*, *The Barkleys Of Broadway*, *Summer Stock*, *Texas Carnival*, *The Belle Of New York*, *Dangerous When Wet*, *Lili*, *Torch Song*, *Easy To Love*, *The Glass Slipper*, *The Tender Trap*, and *High Society* (1956). Actually, *The Tender Trap* was not really a musical - more a sophisticated comedy with music - and in the late 50s Walters directed other comedies such as *Don't Go Near The Water* and *Please Don't Eat The Daisies*. By then, of course, the sun had set on the big budget movie musical, and after directing *Billy Rose's Jumbo* (1962) and *The Unsinkable Molly Brown* (1964), Walters left MGM. He made just one more picture, *Walk, Don't Run*, for Columbia, which also happened to be Cary Grant's screen swansong. His best films - particularly *Lili*, *Easter Parade*, *High Society* and *Dangerous When Wet* - are notable for their charm and élan, and the way in which the director used the camera to create a wonderful feeling of movement. In later years Walters emerged from retirement intermittently to direct a few television sitcoms and Lucille Ball specials, and to give the occasional lecture. He died at the age of 70 of lung cancer.

Warren, Harry

b. Salvatore Guaragna, 24 December 1893, Brooklyn, New York, USA, d. 22 September 1981, Los Angeles, California, USA. Warren was one of the most important of all the popular movie composers, from the 20s up until the 50s. He is probably best remembered for the innovative 30s film musicals he scored in collaboration with lyricist Al Dubin. A son of Italian immigrants, from a family of 12, Warren taught himself to play accordion and piano, and joined a touring carnival show in his teens. Later, he worked in a variety of jobs at the Vitagraph film studios, and played piano in silent-movie houses. After serving in the US Navy in World War II, he started writing songs. The first, 'I Learned To Love You When I Learned My ABCs', gained him a job as a song-plugger for publishers Stark and Cowan, and in 1922 they published his 'Rose Of The Rio Grande', written with Edgar Leslie and Ross Gorman, which became a hit for popular vocalist, Marion Harris. During the remainder of the 20s his most successful songs were 'I Love My Baby, My Baby Loves Me' (with Bud Green), '(Home In) Pasadena' (with Edgar Leslie and Grant Clarke) and 'Nagasaki' (with Al Dubin). In the early 30s Warren contributed songs to several Broadway shows including Billy Rose's revue *Sweet And Low* ('Cheerful Little Earful' and 'Would You Like To Take A Walk?'), *Crazy Quilt* ('I Found A Million Dollar Baby'), and Ed Wynn's 1931 hit, *The Laugh Parade*, ('Ooh! That Kiss', 'The Torch Song' and 'You're My Everything'). Another of his 1931 songs, 'By The River Saint Marie', was a number 1 hit for Guy Lombardo and his Royal Canadians. Between 1929 and 1932, Warren wrote for a few minor movies, but, in 1933, made

Hollywood his permanent home when hired by Darryl F. Zanuck to work with Al Dubin on Warner Brothers' first movie-musical, *42nd Street*. Starring Dick Powell, Ruby Keeler and Bebe Daniels, and choreographed by Busby Berkeley, the film included songs such as 'Shuffle Off To Buffalo', 'You're Getting To Be A Habit With Me' and 'Young And Healthy'. During the 30s Warren and Dubin wrote songs for some 20 films, including several starring Dick Powell, such as *Gold Diggers Of 1933* (1933), 'We're In The Money', 'Pettin' In The Park', 'The Shadow Waltz', and the powerful plea on behalf of the ex-servicemen, victims of the depression, 'My Forgotten Man'; *Footlight Parade* (1933), co-starring James Cagney, and featuring 'By A Waterfall' and 'Shanghai Lil'; *Dames* (1934), 'I Only Have Eyes For You'; *Twenty Million Sweethearts* (1934), I'll String Along With You'; *Gold Diggers Of 1935* (1935), Warren's first Oscar-winner 'Lullaby Of Broadway', effectively sung by Winifred Shaw, 'The Words Are In My Heart'; *Broadway Gondolier* (1935), 'Lulu's Back In Town'; and *Gold Diggers Of 1937* (1936), 'All's Fair In Love And War', 'With Plenty Of Money And You'.

The team's other scores included the Eddie Cantor vehicle, *Roman Scandals* (1933), 'Keep Young And Beautiful'; *Go Into Your Dance* (1935), starring Al Jolson and his wife, Ruby Keeler, and featuring 'A Latin From Manhattan' and 'About A Quarter To Nine'; *Moulin Rouge* (1934), with Constance Bennett and Franchot Tone, and the song, 'The Boulevard Of Broken Dreams'. Warren and Dubin also contributed some numbers to *Melody For Two* (1937), including one of their evergreens, 'September In The Rain'. Shortly before taking his leave of Warners and Dubin in 1939, Warren joined with Johnny Mercer to write songs for two more Dick Powell films, *Going Places* (1938), featuring Louis Armstrong and Maxine Sullivan singing the Academy Award nominee, 'Jeepers Creepers', and *Hard To Get* (1938), with 'You Must Have Been A Beautiful Baby'. Warren's move to 20th Century-Fox led him to work with lyricist Mack Gordon, whose main composer collaborator was Harry Revel. During the 40s, with Gordon, Warren wrote some of World War II's most evocative songs. Together they composed for films such as *Down Argentine Way* (1940), starring Betty Grable and Don Ameche; *Tin Pan Alley* (1940), with 'You Say The Sweetest Things, Baby'; *That Night In Rio* (1941), featuring Carmen Miranda singing 'I, Yi, Yi, Yi, Yi, (I Like You Very Much)'; two films starring Glenn Miller And His Orchestra, *Sun Valley Serenade* (1941), 'Chattanooga Choo Choo', 'I Know Why', 'It Happened In Sun Valley, and *Orchestra Wives* (1942), 'Serenade In Blue', 'At Last', I've Got A Gal In Kalamazoo'; *Springtime In The Rockies* (1942), 'I Had The Craziest Dream'; *Iceland* (1942), 'There Will Never Be Another You'; *Sweet Rosie O'Grady* (1943),

'My Heart Tells Me', and *Hello, Frisco, Hello* (1943), starring Alice Faye singing Warren's second Oscar-winner, 'You'll Never Know'. While at Fox Warren also wrote the songs for another Alice Faye movie, in partnership with Leo Robin. In Busby Berkeley's *The Gang's All Here* (1943), Faye sang their ballad, 'No Love, No Nothin'', while Carmen Miranda was her usual flamboyant self as 'The Lady With The Tutti-Frutti Hat'. Warren wrote his last score at Fox, with Mack Gordon, for the lavish *Billy Rose's Diamond Horseshoe* (1945), starring Dick Haymes, Betty Grable, and Phil Silvers. Two songs from the film, 'I Wish I Knew' and 'The More I See You', are considered to be among their very best. From 1945-52 Warren worked for MGM Pictures, and won his third Oscar, in partnership with Johnny Mercer, for their song, 'On The Atchison, Topeka And The Santa Fe', from the Judy Garland and Ray Bolger film, *The Harvey Girls* (1946). Warren and Mercer also provided songs for the Fred Astaire/Vera-Ellen movie, *The Belle Of New York*, which included 'Baby Doll', 'Seeing's Believing', 'I Want To Be A Dancing Man' and 'Bachelor Dinner Song'. In 1949, after 10 years apart, MGM reunited Fred Astaire and Ginger Rogers, for their last musical together, *The Barkleys Of Broadway*. The musical score, by Warren and Ira Gershwin included the ballad, 'You'd Be Hard To Replace', the novelty, 'My One And Only Highland Fling' and the danceable, 'Shoes With Wings On'.

Other Warren collaborators while he was at MGM included Dorothy Fields, Arthur Freed and Mack Gordon, the latter for some songs to the Judy Garland/Gene Kelly film, *Summer Stock* (1950), including 'If You Feel Like Singing' and 'You, Wonderful You'. In 1952, Warren teamed with lyricist, Leo Robin, for Paramount's *Just For You*, starring Bing Crosby and Jane Wyman. The songs included 'A Flight Of Fancy', 'I'll Si Si Ya In Bahia' and 'Zing A Little Zong'. In the following year, together with Jack Brooks, he provided Dean Martin with one of his biggest hits, 'That's Amore', from the film *The Caddy* (1953), which sold over three million copies. Warren remained under contract to Paramount until 1961, writing mostly scores for dramatic films such as *The Rose Tattoo* (1955) and *An Affair To Remember* (1957). In the early 50s he went into semi-retirement. On his 80th birthday he was elected to the Songwriters Hall Of Fame. In the 80s, his 30s hits with Dubin were revived in the Broadway and London stage productions of *42nd Street*. One of most respected and energetic of the movie songwriters of the 30s and 40s, Warren died in 1981.

Compilations: *The Songs Of Harry Warren* (1979), featuring various artists *Who's Harry Warren?, Volume One: Jeepers Creepers* (1982), featuring various artists *Who's Harry Warren?, Volume Two: 42nd Street* (1982).

Washington, Ned

b. 15 August 1901, Scranton, Pennsylvania, USA, d. 20 December 1976, Beverly Hills, California, USA. A prolific lyricist, especially for films, from the 20s through to the 60s. As a child Washington had some of his poetry published, and, later, in the 20s worked in a variety of jobs in New York and Hollywood while writing songs in his spare time. His chief collaborators included composers Victor Young, Dimitri Tiomkin, Lester Lee, Allie Wrubel, Michael Cleary, George Duning, Max Steiner, Bronislaw Kaper, Jimmy McHugh, Waler Jurman, Sammy Stept, and Leigh Harline. In the late 20s and early 30s Washington contributed songs to Broadway shows such as *Earl Carroll's Vanities*, *Vanderbilt Revue*, *Murder At The Vanities*, *Blackbirds Of 1934*, and *Hello, Paris*. He had his first major hit with 'Can't We Talk It Over?' in 1932, and it was followed by 'I'm Getting Sentimental Over You' which Tommy Dorsey adopted as his signature tune. Washington's other notable songs in the 30s included 'Got The South In My Soul', 'A Hundred Years From Today' (immortalised by Jack Teagarden), 'Smoke Rings', (Glen Gray's theme tune), 'Love Is The Thing', 'My Love', and '(I Don't Stand A) Ghost Of A Chance'. From 1935 onwards he wrote prolifically for films. In the late 30s and 40s these included *Here Comes The Band*, *A Night At The Opera*, *The Hit Parade*, *Tropic Holiday*, *A Night At Earl Carroll's*, *I Wanted Wings*, *For Whom The Bell Tolls*, and *Passage To Marseilles*. His most successful songs of that period were 'You're My Thrill', 'The Nearness Of You', 'When I See An Elephant Fly' (from *Dumbo*), 'Stella By Starlight', and 'My Foolish Heart'. In 1940 he won an Academy Award for 'When You Wish Upon A Star' from the animated feature *Pinocchio*, and another Oscar for the original score. During his career he wrote the lyrics for some 40 movie titles songs. From 1950, through to the early 60s these included 'My Foolish Heart', 'High Noon (Do Not Forsake Me)' (for which he won his third Oscar in 1952), 'The Greatest Show On Earth', 'Take The High Ground', 'The High And The Mighty', 'The Man From Laramie', 'Land Of The Pharaohs', 'The Maverick Queen', 'Gunfight At The O.K Corral', 'Wild Is The Wind', 'Search For Paradise', 'The Roots Of Heaven', 'These Thousand Hills', 'The Unforgiven', 'Town Without Pity', 'Advise And Consent', 'Circus World' (1964 Golden Globe Award), and 'Ship Of Fools' (1965). He also wrote the lyrics for the *Rawhide* television theme, and two memorable numbers, 'The Heat Is On' and 'Sadie Thompson's Song' for the Rita Hayworth picture *Miss Sadie Thompson* (1953). Washington was a member of American Society of Composer and Publishers (ASCAP) from 1930, and served as its director from 1957-76.

Waters, Ethel

b. 31 October 1896, Chester, Pennsylvania, USA, d. 1 September 1977. One of the most influential of popular singers, Waters' early career found her working in vaudeville. As a consequence, her repertoire was more widely based and popularly angled than those of many of her contemporaries. It is reputed that she was the first singer to perform W.C. Handy's 'St Louis Blues' in public, and she later popularized blues and jazz-influenced songs such as 'Stormy Weather' and 'Travellin' All Alone', also scoring a major success with 'Dinah'. She first recorded in 1921 and on her early dates she was accompanied by artists such as Fletcher Henderson, Coleman Hawkins, James P. Johnson and Duke Ellington. Significantly, for her acceptance in white circles, she also recorded with Jack Teagarden, Benny Goodman and Tommy Dorsey.

From the late 20s, Waters appeared in several Broadway musicals, including *Africana*, *Blackbirds Of 1930*, *Rhapsody In Black*, *As Thousands Cheer*, *At Home Abroad*, and *Cabin In The Sky*, in which she introduced several diverting songs such as 'I'm Coming Virginia', 'Baby Mine', 'My Handy Man Ain't Handy No More', 'Till The Real Thing Comes Along', 'Suppertime', 'Harlem On My Mind', 'Heat Wave', 'Got A Bran' New Suit' (with Eleanor Powell), 'Hottentot Potentate', and 'Cabin In The Sky'. In the 30s she stopped the show regularly at the Cotton Club in Harlem with 'Stormy Weather', and appeared at Carnegie Hall in 1938. She played a few dramatic roles in the theatre, and appeared in several films, including *On With The Show*, *Check And Double Check*, *Gift Of The Gab*, *Tales Of Manhattan*, *Cairo*, *Cabin In The Sky*, *Stage Door Canteen*, *Pinky*, *Member Of The Wedding*, and *The Sound And The Fury* (1959). In the 50s she was also in the US television series *Beulah* for a while, and had her own Broadway show *An Evening With Ethel Waters* (1957).

Throughout the 60s and on into the mid-70s she sang as a member of the organization which accompanied evangelist Billy Graham. Although less highly regarded in blues and jazz circles than either Bessie Smith or Louis Armstrong, in the 30s Waters transcended the boundaries of these musical forms to far greater effect than either of these artists and spread her influence throughout popular music. Countless young hopefuls emulated her sophisticated, lilting vocal style and her legacy lived on in the work of outstanding and, ironically, frequently better-known successors, such as Connee Boswell, Ruth Etting, Adelaide Hall, Mildred Bailey, Lee Wiley, Lena Horne and Ella Fitzgerald. Even Billie Holiday (with whom Waters was less than impressed, commenting, 'She sings as though her shoes are too tight'), acknowledged her influence. A buoyant, high-spirited singer with a light, engaging voice that frequently sounds 'whiter' than most of her contemporaries,

Waters' career was an object lesson in determination and inner drive. Her appalling childhood problems and troubled early life, recounted in the first part of her autobiography, *His Eye Is On The Sparrow*, were overcome through grit and the application of her great talent.

Selected albums: *His Eye Is On The Sparrow* (c.1963), *Ethel Waters Reminisces* (c.1963). Compilations: *Ethel Waters* (1979), *The Complete Bluebird Sessions (1938-39)* (1986), *On The Air (1941-51)* (1986), *Ethel Waters On Stage And Screen (1925-40)* (1989), *Who Said Blackbirds Are Blue?* (1989), *Classics 1926-29* (1993).

Further reading: *His Eye Is On The Sparrow*, Ethel Waters. *To Me It's Wonderful*, Ethel Waters.

Waxman, Franz

b. Franz Wachsmann, 24 December 1906, Koenigshuette, Germany, d. 24 February 1967. An important composer; arranger and conductor of background film music from the middle 30s until the 60s. Waxman studied music in Berlin and Dresden, and earned his living as a nightclub pianist. After composing the music for Fritz Lang's film *Liliom* (1933), during the Austrian director's brief sojourn in France, on his way to the USA, Waxman, too, moved to Hollywood in 1934. Signed to Universal, his first music score, for the acclaimed *The Bride Of Frankenstein* (1935) ('a sophisticated masterpiece of black comedy'), was later reused in other movies. In a somewhat lighter vein, Waxman's next few projects included more conventional comedies such as *Diamond Jim* (co-composer Ferde Grofe); *Three Kids And A Queen*, and *Remember Last Night*. He also provided the music for the Robert Taylor-Irene Dunne sentimental film, *Magnificent Obsession*. In the late 30s, for MGM, Waxman's scores included *Captains Courageous*, *The Bride Wore Red*, *Test Pilot* (star combination: Clark Gable-Myrna Loy-Spencer Tracy), *The Young In Heart* (the first of Waxman's 11 Academy Award nominations), *A Christmas Carol* and *Huckleberry Finn*.

In 1941, Waxman composed the music for another highly- regarded horror film, the second re-make of *Dr Jekyll And Mr Hyde*, and for *On Borrowed Time*, a fantasy where death raised its ugly head. But yet again, he contrasted those scores with his music for two classic comedies starring Katherine Hepburn: *The Philadelphia Story* and *Woman Of The Year*, the film in which she met Spencer Tracy for the first time. Waxman's other 40s scores, sometimes as many as seven or eight a year, included: *On Borrowed Time*; *Rebecca*, *Suspicion*, *Strange Cargo*, *Boom Town*, *Tortilla Flat*, *Edge Of Darkness*, *Air Force*, *Old Acquaintance*, *Destination Tokyo*, *To Have And Have Not*, *Operation Burma!*, *The Horn Blows At Midnight*, *Mr Skeffington*, *Humoresque*, *Possessed*, *Dark Passage*, *Sorry, Wrong Number*; and *Johnny Holiday*. In 1947 Waxman founded the Los Angeles Music Festival, which introduced many new works by classical composers, and was its musical director until 1966. In the early 50s he won two Academy Awards for his scores to *Sunset Boulevard* (1950), and *A Place In The Sun* (1951). Also in 1950, he composed the music for *Dark City*, the film in which Charlton Heston made his Hollywood debut. Throughout the rest of the 50s, and into the 60s Waxman wrote some other memorable scores for movies such as: *The Blue Veil*, *Phone Call From A Stranger*, *My Cousin Rachel*, *Come Back, Little Sheba*, *Prince Valiant*, *Rear Window*, *The Silver Chalice*, *Untamed*, *Mister Roberts*, *The Virgin Queen*, *Crime In The Streets*, *The Spirit Of St. Louis*, *Peyton Place*, *Sayonara* ('Katsumi Love Theme' and 'Mountains Beyond The Moon', lyric by Carl Sigman), *Run Silent, Run Deep*, *Home Before Dark*, *The Nun's Story*, *The Story Of Ruth*, *My Geisha*; *Hemingway's Adventures Of Young Man*, *Taras Bulba*; *Lost Command*; and *The Longest Hundred Miles* (television movie) (1967). Waxman also composed several serious works, including 'Elegy For Strings'. A good deal of his soundtrack music was made available on records. He died in February 1967, in Los Angeles, California, USA.

We're Not Dressing

Just one of the movies to be based (in this case very loosely) on Scottish author J.M. Barrie's play, *The Admirable Crichton*. This 1934 Paramount release had a screenplay by Horace Jackson, Francis Martin, and George Marion Jnr. which retained the desert island theme while amending the characterization to suit the contracted stars. Carole Lombard plays the pampered rich girl whose yacht is shipwrecked on a Pacific island. Resourceful sailor Bing Crosby stops crooning long enough to build a shelter for the hardy cast which included Ethel Merman, Leon Errol, George Burns and Gracie Allen. He also has lots of comfort and affection for Lombard. Harry Revel and Mack Gordon came up with a great bunch of songs, such as 'Love Thy Neighbour', 'May I?', 'Once In A Blue Moon', 'She Reminds Me Of You', 'I Positively Refuse To Sing', 'Goodnight Lovely Little Lady', and 'Let's Play House'. Man-hungry Merman duetted with Errol on the splendid 'It's Just An Old Spanish Custom'. Norman Taurog directed this frothy confection which proved yet again, that at this stage of his career Crosby could do no wrong.

Webster, Paul Francis

b. 20 December 1907, New York City, New York, USA, d. 18 March 1984. Although highly educated, at Cornell and New York Universities, Webster was uninterested in pursuing his studies and dropped out, without graduating, to take a job teaching dance. He developed an interest in lyric writing and in 1932 had a hit with 'Masquerade' (music by John Jacob Loeb). Other songs of the 30s were 'Sweet Madonna' (music by Victor Young), 'Two Cigarettes In The Dark' (with Lew Pollack) and 'Got The Jitters' (Loeb). In 1934 Webster and Pollack were hired to write for films and it was while he was in Hollywood that Webster wrote lyrics for the show *Jump For Joy*, an all-black production with music by Duke Ellington, which opened in Los Angeles in 1941. Among the Ellington compositions to which Webster added lyrics was 'I Got It Bad And That Ain't Good'. He also had hits with 'Lily Of Laguna' (music by Ted Fio Rito) and a succession of songs composed by Hoagy Carmichael, among them 'Baltimore Oriole', 'The Lamplighter's Serenade' and 'Memphis In June'. Other popular songs were 'Black Coffee' (with Sonny Burke), 'The Loveliest Night Of The Year' (Irving Aaronson and Juventino Rosas) and 'Secret Love' (with Sammy Fain), for which he won an Oscar in 1953. Another Oscar winner in 1955 and again with Fain was 'Love Is A Many Splendoured Thing'. Other film successes for Webster and Fain, several of which were title songs, were 'April Love', 'A Certain Smile' and 'Tender Is The Night'. Webster also wrote with Dimitri Tiomkin, providing lyrics for 'Thee I Love', 'The Green Leaves Of Summer' and 'So Little Time'. Webster and Fain collaborated on some unsuccessful Broadway revues. Amongst Webster's other hit songs were 'Twelfth Of Never' (with Jerry Livingston), 'Like Young' (with André Previn) and 'The Shadow Of Your Smile' (with Johnny Mandel), for which he won his third Oscar. He also added lyrics to Maurice Jarre's 'Lara's Theme' from *Dr Zhivago* (1965), which later became known as 'Somewhere My Love'.

Wedding Bells (see *Royal Wedding*)

West Side Story

So many film musicals have been adapted from stage successes, but it can never be easy to follow up a ground-breaking and highly praised production with a film that keeps those same attractive qualities. *West Side Story*, released by United Artists in September 1961 (made for the Mirisch Company), did just that, and remains an historical musical movie. This contemporary interpretation of Shakespeare's *Romeo And Juliet* naturally benefited from the involvement of Jerome Robbins. He came up with the original idea, and is the film's choreographer and co-director with Robert Wise. The movie concentrates on the Sharks and Jets, two rival gangs who only mix when it is time to 'rumble' on the tough streets of New York. But life is never black and white, and complications are rife when the ex-leader of the Jets, Tony (Richard Beymer), falls in love with Maria (Natalie Wood), the sister of the Sharks' man-in-charge, Puerto Rican Bernardo (George Chakiris). The devoted couple do their best to isolate themselves from the action around them but it is almost impossible. Even when Bernardo's lover Anita (excellently played by Rita

West Side Story

Moreno) rushes to the drugstore in an attempt to warn the Jets of imminent trouble, she is almost raped by the gang who lose control. In the end everything goes tragically wrong. Tony tries to stop a fight between the gangs but ends up stabbing Bernardo, after the Sharks leader has himself killed the leader of the Jets (Russ Tamblyn). Desperate to see Maria, Tony almost goes on the run, knowing that the other Sharks will immediately be out for revenge. In a moving scene Tony is killed, and Maria weeps at his side. The final significant and poignant image is of both gangs joining together to carry Tony's body from the scene. *West Side Story*, with a screenplay by Ernest Lehman (Arthur Laurents wrote the original book for the 1957 show), is an extremely powerful piece. At some moments, its musical pace has an almost operatic feel about it. Individual performances are outstanding - Wood and Beymer make pleasant lovers, though they were not particularly known for their musical talent, and their voices had to be dubbed by Jim Bryant and Marni Nixon. Yet the love songs - 'Maria', 'Tonight', 'One Hand, One Heart', 'Somewhere' - and Wood's 'I Feel Pretty' - are all handled beautifully. However, it is really the ensemble work, particularly the sequences that involve dance and concentrate on the gang mentality, that make *West Side Story* stand out from the crowd. The combination of Leonard Bernstein's music, the young Stephen Sondheim's lyrics, and Robbins' staggering choreography puts the film in a league of its own. The opening, with its rapid focus in on the Jets, is hard hitting and sharp, as is the gang's attempts to calm their anger and frustration in 'Cool'. Moreno (dubbed by Betty Wand) also finely handles 'A Boy Like That' and the irresistible 'America', mocking the attractions of New York living. In a lighter moment, with a slightly serious underside, the Jets make fun of their upbringing and present social situation in 'Gee, Officer Krupke!' It's a joy to see performed and an early reminder of how witty Sondheim's lyrics could be ('My daddy beats my mummy/My mummy clobbers me/My grandpa is a Commie/my grandma pushes tea'). With all these factors in its favour it is not surprising that *West Side Story* collected 10 Oscars (including best picture) and was one of the 60s biggest successes at the box office, grossing more than any musical in 1962. Years later, although it appears a little dated in some respects, it retains a cult status, and more than that, is respected and loved by critics and audiences alike.

What Lola Wants (see Damn Yankees)

White Christmas

With a title like that, the score just had to be written by Irving Berlin, and a pretty good score it was too. The problem with this picture, which was released by Paramount in 1954, lay with the screenplay. It took three men, Norman Krasna, Norman Panama, and Melvin Frank, to come up with a story about Bob (Captain) Wallace (Bing Crosby) and Phil (Private First Class) Davis (Danny Kaye) who leave the US Army at the end of World War II and form a successful song-and-dance act, which eventually leads them to producing their own shows. After meeting with the Haynes Sisters singing duo (Rosemary Clooney and Vera-Ellen), the quartet end up at a Vermont holiday resort run by the ex-GI's' former (and much-respected) commanding officer (Dean Jagger). Business is bad owing to the lack of snow, but everything turns out fine when Wallace and Davis organize a benefit show which - surprise, surprise - ends with the much-needed flakes drifting down while everyone is singing 'White Christmas' and Crosby and Kaye are melting into the arms of Clooney and Vera-Ellen respectively. Irving Berlin 'borrowed' that song from the 1942 Crosby-Fred Astaire film *Holiday Inn* which was similar in many ways to *White Christmas*. The rest of the songs were a mixture of old and new. One of the most appealing was 'Sisters', with which Crosby and Kaye, waving feather boas and with their trousers rolled up to the knees, parody a typical Haynes Sisters routine. The remainder included 'The Best Things Happen While You're Dancing', 'The Old Man', 'Gee, I Wish I Was Back In The Army', 'Count Your Blessings Instead Of Sheep', 'Love, You Didn't Do Right By Me', 'Blue Skies', 'Choreography', 'Snow', 'What Can You Do With A General', 'I'd Rather See A Minstrel Show', and 'Mandy'. Also in the cast were Mary Wickes, John Brascia, Anne Whitfield, Grady Sutton, Sig Ruman, and the 21-year-old dancer George Chakiris. The dances and musical numbers were staged by Robert Alton and the film was nicely photographed in Technicolor and VistaVision by Loyal Griggs. The director was Michael Curtiz. *White Christmas* proved to be a tremendous box-office winner, becoming one of the Top 20 films of the 50s in the USA, and the fifth highest-grossing musical.

Whiting, Richard

b. 12 November 1891, Peoria, Illinois, USA, d. 19 February 1938, Beverly Hills, California, USA. A self-taught pianist with no formal tuition in composition, Whiting wrote his first songs in the years before World War I. Among them was 'It's Tulip Time In Holland', a very popular number which Whiting exchanged the rights to for a new piano. During the war years Whiting wrote several successful songs, some of which capitalized on the current vogue for minstrel-type music. These included 'Where The Black-Eyed Susans Grow' (lyric by David Darford), 'Mammy's Little Coal Black Rose' (Raymond Egan) and 'Where The Morning Glories Grow' (Gus Kahn). Whiting and Egan also collaborated on 'Till We Meet Again' which was an immensely popular hit, coming as it did in 1918, the final year of the war. In the post-war years, Whiting had further successes with 'The Japanese Sandman' (Egan), 'Ain't We Got Fun?' (Egan-Kahn), 'Sleepy Time Gal' (Egan-Joseph B. Alden), 'Ukelele Lady' (Kahn), 'Breezin' Along With The Breeze' and 'Honey' (both with Haven Gillespie-Seymour Simons). He also collaborated on both the music and lyric, with Neil Moret, for the beautiful (and successful) 'She's Funny that Way' (1928). Towards the end of the 20s Whiting went to Hollywood, and for the next decade wrote for films such as *Close Harmony*, *The Dance Of Life*, *Innocents Of Paris*, *Monte Carlo*, *Paramount On Parade*, *Safety In Numbers*, *My Weakness*, *Bottoms Up*, *Bright Eyes*, *Transatlantic Merry-Go-Round*, *Big Broadcast Of 1936*, *Rhythm On The Range*, *Sing, Baby, Sing*, *Ready, Willing And Able*, *Hollywood Hotel*, and *Cowboy From Brooklyn* (1938). From these came numerous songs such as 'Louise', 'My Ideal', 'I Can't Escape From You' (all with Leo Robin), 'Too Marvellous For Words' (with Johnny Mercer), 'Beyond The Blue Horizon' (Robin-additional music W. Frank Harling), 'On The Good Ship Lollipop' (Sidney Clare), 'Miss Brown To You' (Robin-additional music Ralph Rainger) and 'Hooray For Hollywood' and 'Have You Got Any Castles, Baby?' (both Mercer). Prior to 1920, Whiting had dabbled unsuccessfully on Broadway with shows such as *Robinson Crusoe Jr.*, *Toot Sweet*, *A Lonely Romeo*, and *George White's Scandals Of 1919*. In 1931 he tried again with *Free For All*, which was another failure, but in the following year he was moderately successful with *Take A Chance* in which Ethel Merman introduced his 'Eadie Was A Lady' (lyrics Buddy De Sylva, additional music Nacio Herb Brown). Merman and Jack Haley also duetted on one of the songwriters' future standards, 'You're An Old Smoothie'. Since Whiting died in February 1938 at the age of only 46, his daughter, the classy singer Margaret Whiting, has continued to include some of the best of his work on her records, and in her concert and cabaret performances - even into the 90s. Whiting's younger daughter, Barbara, is a lively, vivacious actress and singer who gave a particularly engaging performance in the Esther Williams film musical, *Dangerous When Wet*.

Whoopee!

Eddie Cantor recreated his original role in this screen version of the Broadway hit, *Whoopee!* ('A Musical Comedy Of The Great Wide West'), when it was released by United Artists in 1930. In William Conselman's screenplay, which was adapted from a story by Anthony McGuire and Owen Davis' play, *The Nervous Wreck*, Cantor played a manic hypochondriac who lands up on an Arizona ranch where he reveals his depression via lines such as 'Last week I bought a suit with two pair of pants - and burned a hole in the coat!' Nothing depressing about

the songs though, even if most of the Broadway originals were not retained. Among the survivors were Walter Donaldson and Gus Kahn's highly amusing title number and 'The Song Of The Setting Sun'. Donaldson and Kahn also wrote several songs especially for the film, including 'Stetson', the 'poignant' 'A Girl Friend Of A Boyfriend Of Mine' and the enduring 'My Baby Just Cares For Me'. Also in the cast were Eleanor Hunt, Ethel Shutta, Paul Gregory, John Rutherford, Spencer Charters, and Betty Grable in only her third film. The dances and ensembles were staged by Busby Berkeley who was making his screen debut. His innovative style was immediately established in the opening number in which an overhead camera displayed more than 60 cowboys and girls weaving a series of intricate patterns. *Whoopee!*, which made Eddie Cantor a box-office star and proved to be one of his biggest hits, was photographed in 'All Technicolor' (two colour Technicolor actually), produced by Samuel Goldwyn and Florenz Ziegfeld, and directed by Thorton Freeland.

Wilcox, Herbert

b. Herbert Sydney Wilcox, 19 April 1892, Cork, Eire, d. 15 May 1977, London, England. A distinguished producer and director, who was one of the leading figures in the British film industry from the 20s through to the 50s. The date and place of birth given here are those usually accepted, but other sources have suggested that Wilcox was born in Norwood, south London, in 1890. However, it is generally agreed that he went to school in Brighton and appeared as a chorus boy in one of the local theatres. Then he worked as a journalist for a time before serving as a pilot in the Royal Flying Corps during World War I. After being invalided out, he entered the film business in 1919, and produced his first picture, *The Wonderful Story*, in 1922. He had his first hit in the following year with a silent version of *Chu Chu Chow*, and from then on produced and/or directed (and occasionally wrote the screenplay) for a string of highly successful pictures. Among the comedies, dramas, and historical features, many of which starred his wife, Anna Neagle (they married in 1943), were several musicals. These included *Say It With Music* (1932), *Yes, Mr. Brown*, *Goodnight Vienna*, (USA: *Magic Night*), *Bitter Sweet*, *Limelight* (USA: *Backstage*), *This'll Make You Whistle*, and *London Melody* (USA: *Girls In The Street*) (1937). In 1939 Wilcox went to Hollywood to produce and direct several films. Included among them were the screen adaptations of three famous Broadway musicals: *Irene*, *No, No, Nanette*, and *Sunny*. Anna Neagle played the lead in each of the trio, and she was co-starred with the engaging British actor, Michael Wilding, when Wilcox returned to England and made his celebrated 'London' films, *Piccadilly Incident*, *The Courtneys Of Curzon Street* (USA: *The Courtney Affair*),

Herbert Wilcox (left), Anna Neagle and Frankie Vaughan

Spring In Park Lane, and *Maytime In Mayfair* (1950). These were enormously popular romantic comedies, containing just the occasional song. During the rest of the 50s, as well as making other acclaimed dramatic movies such as *Odette*, Wilcox worked on British musicals such as *Lilacs In The Spring* (USA: *Let's Make Up*), *King's Rhapsody*, *The Lady Is A Square*, and *The Heart Of A Man*. The latter was his final film. Changes in public taste, several box office flops, several unwise financial investments, and the advent of commercial television in Britain, are just some of the reasons given for Wilcox's subsequent financial decline which culminated in his much-publicized bankruptcy in 1964. He was discharged two years later, and, a year after that, his wife opened in the long-running musical comedy *Charlie Girl*, which ran for almost five and a half years. Wilcox is said to have suggested (uncredited) ideas for some of the songs, but otherwise he remained in retirement until his death in 1977. During his long career, he won numerous national and international awards, including the Gold Cup of All Nations at the Venice Film Festival in 1937. Although not considered an outstanding director, his flair and showmanship as a producer put him in the same league as the Hollywood greats.

Further reading: *Twenty-Five Thousand Sunsets* (his autobiography).

Wild Party, The

Football players, drop-outs, petty criminals and jazz musicians team up in an unlikely Hollywood farrago made in 1956 and directed by Harry Horner and starring Anthony Quinn and Nehemiah Persoff. Jazz, on-screen and off, is provided by a host of talented studio-cum-jazz musicians, who deserve better treatment. Amongst them are Georgie Auld, Teddy Buckner, Pete Candoli, Bob Cooper, Buddy De Franco, Maynard Ferguson, Frank Rosolino, Bud Shank and Alvin Stoller. Persoff's on-screen piano playing was dubbed by Pete Jolly.

Williams, Esther

b. 8 August 1921 or 1923, Inglewood, Los Angeles, California, USA. One of MGM's top film musicals stars in the 40s and 50s, Esther Williams's mother boasted that her daughter (one of five children) swam before she walked. By the time she was 15 she had won every national swimming competition and was set to represent the USA in the Olympic Games in Finland, but they were cancelled following the outbreak of World War II. She studied for a time at the University of Southern California before joining Billy Rose's Aquacade in San Francisco, in which her co-star was Johnny Weissmuller. While she was in the show she was spotted by MGM talent scouts, and made her film debut in 1942 as one of Mickey Rooney's girlfriends in *Andy Hardy's Double Life*. She

Esther Williams

had some swimming scenes in that one, and in *Bathing Beauty* (1944) and *Zeigfeld Follies* (1946), special water ballets were created for her. Her first starring role came in *Fiesta* (1947), with Richardo Montalban, and this was followed by a string of dazzling Technicolor movies in which her glamorous looks and pleasing personality were permanently on display. These included *This Time For Keeps*, *On An Island With You*, *Take Me Out To The Ball Game*, *Neptune's Daughter*, *The Duchess Of Idaho*, *Pagan Love Song*, *Texas Carnival*, *Skirts Ahoy!*, *Million Dollar Mermaid*, *Dangerous When Wet*, *Easy To Love*, and *Jupiter's Darling* (1955). With the demise of the big-budget Hollywood musicals she played several straight roles, but her appeal had diminished and her last picture, *The Magic Fountain*, was released in 1961. While MGM went to great lengths to show-case her superb swimming ability in some of the most lavish and spectacular aqua-sequences ever seen on the screen, and co-starred her with several attractive leading men (including cartoon characters Tom and Jerry), her acting ability was not allowed to develop, and her quite pleasant singing voice was rather neglected. However, she did sing a lovely version of 'The Sea Of The Moon' (Harry Warren-Arthur Freed) in *The Pagan Love Song*, and handled some of Arthur Schwartz and Johnny Mercer's numbers well in *Dangerous When Wet*. She also introduced Frank Loesser's Oscar-winning 'Baby, It's Cold Outside' with Ricardo Montalban in *Neptune's Daughter*. In 1967 she married her third husband, Fernando Lamas, and continued to concentrate on her commercial swimming pool interests.

Williams, John

b. John Towner Williams, 8 February 1932, Flushing, Long Island, New York, USA. A composer/arranger/conductor for film background music from the early 60s to the present. As a boy Williams learned to play several instruments, and studied composition and arranging in Los Angeles after moving there with his family in 1948. Later, he studied piano at the Juilliard School Of Music, before composing his first score for the film, *I Passed For White* in 1960. it was followed by others, such as *Because They're Young*, *The Secret Ways*, *Bachelor Flat*, *Diamond Head*, *Gidget Goes To Rome*, and *None But The Brave*, directed by, and starring Frank Sinatra. He scored Ronald Reagan's last film, *The Killers* in 1964 and continued with *Please Come Home*, *How To Steal A Million*, *The Rare Breed* and *A Guide For Married Men*. In 1967 Williams gained the first of more than 25 Oscar nominations for his adaptation of the score to *Valley Of The Dolls*, and after writing original scores for other movies such as *Sergeant Ryker*, *Daddy's Gone A-Hunting* and *The Reivers*. he won the Academy Award in 1971 for the best adaptation for *Fiddler On The Roof*. In the early 70s, Williams seemed to be

primarily concerned with 'disaster' movies, such as *The Poseidon Adventure*, *The Towering Inferno*, *Earthquake* and *Jaws*, for which he won his second Oscar in 1975. He then proceeded to score some of the most commercially successful films in the history of the cinema, including the epic *Star Wars*, *Close Encounters Of The Third Kind*, *Superman*, *The Empire Strikes Back*, *Raiders Of The Lost Ark*, *E.T. The Extra Terrestrial* - still the highest-grossing film of all time more than 10 years later - and another Academy Award winner for Williams. On and on Williams marched with: *The Return Of The Jedi*, *Indiana Jones And The Temple Of Doom*, *Indiana Jones And The Last Crusade*, *The River*, *The Accidental Tourist*, *Born On The Fourth Of July* and *Presumed Innocent* (1990). As for recordings, he had US singles hits with orchestral versions of several of his films' themes and main titles, and a number of his soundtracks entered the album charts. Real pop prestige came to Williams in 1977, when record producer Meco Monardo conceived a disco treatment of his themes for *Star Wars*, including music played in the film by the Cantina Band. 'Star Wars/Cantina Band' by Meco spent two weeks at number 1 in the USA. For his work in the early 90s Williams received Oscar nominations for the highly successful *Home Alone* (the score, and 'Somewhere In My Memory', lyric by Leslie Bricusse); the score for Oliver Stone's highly controversial *JFK*; and 'When You're Alone' (again with Bricusse), for Steven Spielberg's *Hook*. After contributing the music to *Far And Away* and *Home Alone 2: Lost In New York* (1992), Williams returned to Spielberg in 1993 to score the director's dinosaur drama, *Jurassic Park*, and another multi Oscar winner, *Schindler's List*. Williams himself won an Academy Award for his sensitive music for the latter picture. As well as his highly impressive feature film credits, Williams has written for television productions such as *Heidi*, *Jane Eyre* and *The Screaming Woman*. In 1985 he was commissioned by NBC Television to construct themes for news stories, which resulted in pieces such as 'The Sound Of The News', and featured a fanfare for the main bulletin and a scherzo for the breakfast show, and several others, including 'The Pulse Of Events' and 'Fugue For Changing Times'. Williams's quite sensational list of blockbuster movies is unlikely to ever be beaten.

Williams, Paul

b 19 September 1940, Omaha, Nebraska, USA. A pop composer, Williams wrote some of the 70s most enduring melodies and had further successes as a singer and soundtrack composer. Short in stature, Williams entered show business as a stunt man and film actor, appearing as a child in *The Loved One* (1964) and *The Chase* (1965). He turned to script and songwriting, collaborating with Roger Nichols on two of the Carpenters' biggest hits, 'We've Only Just Begun' and 'Rainy Days And Mondays'. The duo also provided material for Helen Reddy ('You And Me Against The World') and Three Dog Night ('Just An Old Fashioned Love Song'). Williams recorded his first solo album for Reprise in 1970 before moving to A&M Records the following year. None of these albums sold well but Williams developed a highly praised night-club act in the early 70s. His first film score was for *Phantom Of The Paradise*, Brian de Palma's update of the *Phantom Of The Opera* story, in which Williams starred. This was followed by songs for *A Star Is Born*, another modern version of an old movie which featured Kris Kristofferson and Barbra Streisand, but Williams' most impressive score was the 30s pastiche he provided for *Bugsy Malone*, the gangster spoof entirely acted by children. His later scores included *The End* (1977) and *The Muppet Movie* (1979). In 1998, Williams appeared at Michael's Pub in New York, and previewed some numbers intended for a future Broadway musical, as well as detailing his recovery from the ravages of drugs and alcohol. In 1992, he contributed music and lyrics for the songs in the feature film, *The Muppet Christmas Carol* which starred Michael Caine.

Albums: *Someday Man* (1970), *Just An Old Fashioned Love Song* (1971), *Life Goes On* (1972), *Here Comes Inspiration* (1974), *A Little Bit Of Love* (1974), *Phantom Of The Paradise* (1975, film soundtrack), *Ordinary Fool* (1975), *Bugsy Malone* (1975, film soundtrack). Compilation: *Classics* (1977).

With A Song In My Heart

Susan Hayward gave an outstanding performance in this 1952 20th Century-Fox film which was based on the life of the popular singer Jane Froman. There was hardly a dry eye in the house as producer Lamar Trotti's screenplay traced Froman's brave fightback to the top following a terrible air crash during World War II, which left her confined to a wheel chair. David Wayne was fine as her mentor and husband, and so was Thelma Ritter who played her hard-bitten nurse and companion. The 22-year-old Robert Wagner had a small but effective role as a shell-shocked young airman, and also in the fine supporting cast were Rory Calhoun, Richard Allan, Una Merkel, Helen Wescott, Leif Erikson, Max Showalter, and Lyle Talbot. It was Jane Froman's own voice that was heard on the soundtrack singing a marvellous selection of songs, many of which were associated with her. There were especially endearing versions of 'With A Song In My Heart' (Richard Rodgers-Lorenz Hart), 'I'll Walk Alone' (Jule Styne-Sammy Cahn), 'I'm Through With Love' (Gus Kahn-Matty Malneck-Fud Livingstone), and 'They're Either Too Young Or Too Old' (Frank Loesser), along with excellent readings of 'Embraceable You' (George and Ira Gershwin), 'It's A Good Day' (Peggy Lee-Dave Barbour), 'Indiana' (James Hanley-Ballard MacDonald), 'Blue Moon' (Rodgers-Hart), 'Deep In

The Heart Of Texas' (Don Swander-June Hershey), 'Tea For Two' (Vincent Youmans-Irving Caesar), 'That Old Feeling' (Lew Brown-Sammy Fain), and several more. Musical director Alfred Newman won an Oscar for his scoring. Billy Daniels staged the dance numbers and the impressive Technicolor photography was by Leon Shamroy. Walter Lang directed what was certainly one of the best films of its kind.

Wizard Of Oz, The

It is not an easy task to conjure up a fairy tale that genuinely wins over both children and adults alike, but *The Wizard Of Oz*, released by MGM in August 1939, succeeded in every respect and became the third-highest-grossing film in the US during the 30s. To this day, this adaptation of L. Frank Baum's tale *The Wonderful Wizard Of Oz* remains a constant family favourite for new generations. Considering the many production problems that besieged the film behind the scenes, it is ironic that the film appears to have few obvious flaws and is very complete in structure. Not only did the film have three writers - Florence Ryerson, Noel Langley and Edgar Allan Woolf - but producer Mervyn LeRoy (assisted by a budding Arthur Freed), had numerous problems engaging an appropriate director. Having considered at least three others, Victor Fleming was assigned the prestigious job. However, even then, Fleming was not able to stay with the project until its conclusion. A few weeks before shooting was completed he was re-assigned to *Gone With The Wind*. It fell to King Vidor, Fleming's replacement, to direct the famous 'Over the Rainbow' scene, which was nearly cut at one point in the filming. Even the actors who eventually played several of the leading parts were not the director's first choice. Indeed it is only because 11 years-old Shirley Temple was unavailable that Judy Garland, who was six years older (and many felt, too old) won the role of Dorothy. Life for Dorothy on a farm in Kansas is miserable, and she muses 'if happy little bluebirds fly beyond the rainbow, why oh why can't I?' Suddenly a tornado strikes, and before she knows what has happened, the strength of the winds have swept her up and taken her to another land far away. Up to this point in the film, Dorothy's world has been black and white, but the moment the door is opened to Oz, everything is more colourful (Technicolor photography by Harold Rasson and Allen Darby) than she and the audience could ever have imagined. Helped by Glinda the Good Witch (Billie Burke) and over a hundred midgets playing the Munchkins, Dorothy sets off down the yellow brick road to meet the Wizard in Emerald City, and eventually to find a way back home. During her journey, she meets the Scarecrow (Ray Bolger) who longs for a brain, the Tin Woodman (Jack Haley) anxious for a heart, and the Cowardly Lion (Bert Lahr) who strives to be

The Wizard Of Oz

brave. Together they defeat the Wicked Witch of the West (Margaret Hamilton), only to find the giant all-powerful Oz is simply Frank Morgan shouting into a loud microphone and pulling a few levers. However, Dorothy's friends are eventually convinced that they have gained the qualities they desire, and with the help of her magical ruby slippers, Dorothy is whisked back home, or rather, she wakes up, for it has all been a dream. Faced with all her family and friends, most of whom played leading roles in her dream of Oz, Dorothy famously declares that she will never run away again and 'there's no place like home'. This ending offended many fans of Baum's books because in his writings Oz is a real place, not just a figment of the imagination. Harold Arlen and E.Y. 'Yip' Harburg's charming score presented Garland with the immortal 'Over The Rainbow', which won an Oscar and proved to a be double-edged sword; in later years she would refuse to sing it for considerable periods of time. Other numbers included 'We're Off To See The Wizard', 'Follow The Yellow Brick Road', 'Ding-Dong! The Witch Is Dead', 'If I Were King Of The Forest', and 'The Merry Land Of Oz'. Ray Bolger gave a memorable comic performance in 'If I Only Had A Brain' (choreography was by Bobby Connolly). An extended dance sequence featuring Bolger in that number, which was removed from the final print, turned up in *That's Dancin'!*, a compilation

of MGM clips which was released in 1985. Even then, more than 45 years after it was first released, the magic of *The Wizard Of Oz* still lingered, and this was emphasised in 1994 when a highly acclaimed documentary, *In Search Of Oz*, was screened by BBC Television.

Further reading: *The Making Of 'The Wizard Of Oz'*, Al Jean Harmetz. *Who Put The Rainbow In The Wizard Of Oz? Yip Harburg, Lyricist*, Harold Meyerson and Ernie Harburg.

Wonder Man

The second of Danny Kaye's highly original and vastly entertaining films, and the first in which he played more than one role, was produced by Sam Goldwyn for RKO in 1945. Buzzy Bellew (Danny Kaye) is a loud and audacious nightclub performer who is set to marry his dance partner (Vera-Ellen) before he is killed by a bunch of hoodlums. His spirit enters the body of his twin brother, the meek and mild Edwin Dingle (Danny Kaye), and insists that he take revenge for the murder. This situation was tailor-made for Kaye to display the full range of his individual manic talents which were supplemented by the ingenious Oscar-winning special effects of John Fulton and A.W. Johns. The musical highlights included two hilarious spoofs, 'Opera Number' (Sylvia Fine) and the mangling of the Russian folk song 'Otchi

Tchorniya', along with 'Bali Boogie' (Fine) and 'So-o-o-o-o In Love' (Leo Robin-David Rose). Virginia Mayo plays Edwin's librarian girlfriend, and also in the strong supporting cast were Steve Cochran, Allen Jenkins, S.Z. Sakall, Donald Woods, Edward S. Brophy, Otto Kruger, Natalie Schafer, and, of course the stunning Goldwyn Girls. The screenplay was written by Don Hartman, Melville Shavelson and Philip Rapp, and was based on a story by Arthur Sheekam which was adapted by Jack Jevne and Eddie Moran. John Wray staged the dance numbers and this popular film, which confirmed Kaye as a star of world class, was beautifully photographed in Technicolor by Victor Milner. The director who made sense out of all the confusion was Bruce Humberstone.

Woods, Harry

b. Henry MacGregor Woods, 4 November 1896, North Chelmsford, Massachusetts, USA, d. 14 January 1970, Phoenix, Arizona, USA. This popular songwriter during the 20s and 30s, sometimes wrote both music and lyrics, but collaborated mostly with lyricist Mort Dixon. Woods was physically handicapped, lacking three - some say all - of the fingers of his left hand, but he still managed to play the piano with the other one. He was educated at Harvard, and then served in the US Army in World War I. He started writing songs in the early 20s, and 'I'm Going' South', was interpolated into the Broadway show *Bombo*, which starred Al Jolson. During the late 20s Woods provided Jolson with some of his biggest hits, such as 'When The Red Red Robin Comes Bob-Bob-Bobbin' Along' and 'I'm Looking Over A Four-Leaf Clover' (with Dixon). His other 20s songs included 'Paddlin' Madelin' Home', (a hit in 1925 for Cliff Edwards, and still remembered over 60 years later by 'revival bands' such as the Pasadena Roof Orchestra), 'Me Too', 'Is It Possible?', 'Just Like A Butterfly', 'Side By Side', 'Where The Wild Flowers Grow', 'Since I Found You', 'In The Sing Song Sycamore Tree', 'She's A Great Great Girl', 'Riding To Glory' and 'Lonely Little Bluebird'. In 1929, Woods wrote 'A Little Kiss Each Morning' and 'Heigh-Ho, Everybody, Heigh-Ho' for Rudy Vallee in his debut movie, *Vagabond Lover*. During the 30s he spent three years in England, writing songs for such movies as *Evergreen*, ('When You've Got A Little Springtime In Your Heart' and 'Over My Shoulder'), and *It's Love Again* ('I Nearly Let Love Go Slipping Through My Fingers', 'Gotta Dance My Way To Heaven'); *Jack Ahoy* ('My Hat's On The Wrong Side Of My Head'); *Aunt Sally* ('We'll All Go Riding On A Rainbow') and *Road House* ('What A Little Moonlight Can Do', a song which helped to launch Billie Holiday's career). Wood also collaborated with British songwriters and music publishers Jimmy Campbell and Reginald Connelly on 'Just An Echo In The Valley', and 'Try A Little Tenderness', one of his standards. Back in the USA, in 1936, Woods wrote big hits for Fats Waller ('When Somebody Thinks You're Wonderful') and Arthur Tracy ('The Whistling Waltz'). His other songs included 'Here Comes The Sun', 'It Looks Like Love', 'River Stay 'Way From My Door', 'All Of A Sudden', 'A Little Street Where Old Friends Meet', 'Loveable', 'Pink Elephants', 'We Just Couldn't Say Goodbye', 'Oh, How She Can Love', 'You Ought To See Sally On Sunday', 'Dancing With My Shadow', 'I'll Never Say "Never" Again' and 'So Many Memories'. His collaborators included Gus Kahn and Arthur Freed, Benny Davis, and Howard Johnson and Kate Smith, who worked with Woods on Smith's theme song, 'When The Moon Comes Over The Mountain'. Woods retired from songwriting in the early 40s, and eventually went to live in Arizona, where he died in January 1970, following a car crash.

Words And Music

Not the 1929 college musical of that name which starred the 22-year-old John (Duke) Wayne in his fifth film, but the lavish film biography of Richard Rodgers and Lorenz Hart, one of the most celebrated songwriting teams in the history of American popular music. It has been said many times that an authentic life story of Hart - a hard drinking, homosexual depressive - would make a fascinating movie, but in 1948 Hollywood obviously was not ready for that kind of reality, and so screenwriter Fred Finklehoffe turned in the usual fudged fairy tale which was typical of most bio-pics. Hart (Mickey Rooney) is portrayed as a cigar-smoking nice guy, whose first working meeting with Rodgers (Tom Drake) results in the assembly of the complicated lyric to 'Manhattan' which he has seemingly jotted down in various parts of a magazine on the way over. From then on, Rodgers, who in real life could be an extremely difficult man, is seen as having the patience of Job even when Hart goes off on his binges for weeks at a time - erratic behaviour which led to his death at the age of only 44. So much for the plot - it was irrelevant anyhow - given the marvellous songs and the talented performers who were on hand to sing them. In a film full of musical highlights, perhaps the most memorable were: Gene Kelly and Vera-Ellen's sizzling dance to 'Slaughter On Tenth Avenue'; Lena Horne's sparkling 'Where Or When' and 'The Lady Is A Tramp'; Mickey Rooney and Judy Garland reunited on film after a break of several years with 'I Wish I Were In Love Again', and Judy going to town by herself on 'Johnny One Note'; June Allyson and the Blackburn Twins with the delicious 'Thou Swell'; Mel Tormé ('Blue Moon'), Perry Como ('Blue Room' and 'Mountain Greenery' [with Allyn McLerie]), and not forgetting Rooney's charming version of 'Manhattan'. Also contributing were Betty Garrett, Ann Sothern, Cyd Charisse, Janet Leigh,

Words And Music

Marshall Thompson, Dee Turnell, Jeanette Nolan, Harry Antrim, and Clinton Sundberg. Robert Alton and Gene Kelly handled the choreography, and the director who put the whole complicated affair together was Norman Taurog. *Words And Music* was photographed in Technicolor and produced by Alan Freed's famous MGM unit. It grossed over $3.5 million in the USA and was one of the leading musicals of the decade.

Woodstock

The three-day music festival in Max Yasgur's Bethil farm has passed into legend, partly through the notion of survival in adversity, but largely because of the ensuing successful documentary film and album. *Woodstock* captures the spirit of those three-days in July 1969 - the haphazard organisation, the naive ideals, the storms - but most of all it showcases many of the era's finest acts. Several would later claim that their performance at *Woodstock* was poor, but there's no denying the excitement generated by Sly And The Family Stone and Santana, the sheer power of Joe Cocker and the Grease Band and the allegorical anguish pouring out of 'The Star-Spangled Banner' when in the hands of Jimi Hendrix. Although several performers on the *Woodstock* bill were not featured on the film or album, enough remains in both to give the full flavour of this extraordinary event. A recent director's cut adds previously-unseen footage and a related *Woodstock Diary* largely comprised of 'new' performances. The legend refuses to die.

Wrubel, Allie

b. 15 January 1905, Middletown, Connecticut, USA, d. 13 December 1973, Twentynine Palms, California, USA. This popular songwriter from the 30s through to the 50s, sometimes wrote both music and lyrics. He also played the saxophone and other reed instruments. After studying medicine at Columbia University, Wrubel played the saxophone with several dance bands, including a one-year stint with Paul Whiteman in the 20s, and toured England with his own band in 1924. He spent some time working as a theatre manager before having his first song published in 1931. 'Now You're In My Arms' (written with Morton Downey), was followed by 'As You Desire Me', 'I'll Be Faithful' (Jan Garber) and 'Farewell To Arms' (Paul Whiteman). In 1934, like many of his contemporaries, Wrubel began to write songs for films, often with lyricist Mort Dixon. Their 'Try To See It My Way' was interpolated into the Dubin-Warren score for *Dames*. During the 30s Wrubel also contributed to *Happiness Ahead* ('Pop! Goes Your Heart'); *Flirtation Walk* ('Mr And Mrs Is The Name');

I Live For Love ('Mine Alone'); *In Caliente* ('The Lady In Red'); *Sweet Music* ('Fare Thee Well, Annabelle' and 'I See Two Lovers'); *The Toast Of New York* ('The First Time I Saw You'); *Life Of The Party* ('Let's Have Another Cigarette'); and *Radio City Revels* ('Goodnight Angel' and 'There's A New Moon Over The Old Mill'). The films featured some of the biggest stars of the day, such as Dick Powell, Ruby Keeler and Rudy Vallee. Around that time Wrubel also wrote several numbers with Herb Magidson, such as 'Gone With The Wind', which went on to become a standard, recorded by Denny Dennis with the Roy Fox Orchestra, and Frank Sinatra; 'The Masquerade Is Over', sung by Dick Robertson, Sarah Vaughan and Patti Page; and 'Music Maestro Please', one of the most popular songs of the 30s, in versions by Tommy Dorsey and Lew Stone. During the 40s and 50s, Wrubel continued to write for movies, such as *Sing Your Way Home*, in which Anne Jeffreys sang Wrubel and Madgison's Oscar-nominated 'I'll Buy That Dream' ('A honeymoon in Cairo, in a brand-new autogiro/Then, home by rocket in a wink'); *Song Of The South* (an Oscar-winner, this time, with 'Zip-A-Dee-Doo-Dah', written with Ray Gilbert); *Duel In The Sun* ('Gotta Get Me Somebody To Love'); *The Fabulous Dorseys* ('To Me'); *I Walk Alone* ('Don't Call It Love'); two full-length Walt Disney cartoons, *Make Mine Music* in which the Andrews Sisters sang his 'Johnny Fedora And Alice Blue Bonnet'; and *Melody Time*, the Andrews again, with Wrubel's story about a tiny tugboat, 'Little Toot'.

During the 50s Wrubel's output declined, although he did contribute several songs to *Never Steal Anything Small* (1959), which featured an ageing James Cagney duetting with Cara Williams on 'I'm Sorry, I Want A Ferrari'. Wrubel also contributed 'What Does A Woman Do?' to the thriller, *Midnight Lace* (1960). During a career spanning nearly 30 years, his other songs included 'Gypsy Fiddler', 'The You And Me That Used To Be', 'I Can't Love You Anymore', 'I'm Home Again', 'I'm Stepping Out With A Memory Tonight' (a hit for Glenn Miller and Kate Smith), 'Where Do I Go From You?'), 'There Goes That Song Again' (revived by Gary Miller in the UK in 1961), 'The Lady From Twentynine Palms', '1400 Dream Street', 'Please, My Love' and 'Corabelle'. His collaborators included Walter Bullock, Nat Shilkret, Ned Washington, Abner Silver, and Charles Newman. Wrubel was a Charter member of the Composers Hall of Fame. He died, from a heart attack, in 1973, at the location of his one of his popular songs - Twentynine Palms - California, USA.

Yankee Doodle Dandy

James Cagney won best actor Oscar for his magnificent portrayal of Broadway showman George M. Cohan in one of the best film biographies ever to come out of Hollywood. Everything was right about this film, especially the screenplay by Robert Bruckner and Edmund Joseph. Beginning with Cohan being called to the White House to receive the Congressional Medal of Honour from President Roosevelt for his outstanding services to the American Musical Theatre, the veteran performer then relates his spectacular rise from young vaudevillian with the family act the Four Cohans, to his position as the legendary American theatrical actor, singer, songwriter, director and much else. Particularly fine, too, was the supporting cast, with Walter Huston as Cohan's father, Rosemary DeCamp as his mother, and Jeanne Cagney (the actor's own sister) in the role of sister Jeanne. Richard Whorf played Sam H. Harris, who co-produced many of Cohan's hits, and Joan Leslie was George's wife Mary. Also featured were Irene Manning, George Tobias, George Barbier, Frances Langford, S.Z. Sakall, Eddie Foy Jnr., Walter Catlett, and Odette Myril. But there was no doubt that it was Cagney's film. He also had started out as a song-and-dance man in vaudeville, and this early training served him well. The straight-legged strut and ebullient, cocky-style suited the character perfectly and was a joy to see, particularly the re-enactment of scenes from one of Cohan's most successful shows, *Little Johnny Jones* (1904) involving two immortal numbers, 'The Yankee Doodle Boy' and 'Give My Regards To Broadway'. Many of his other songs - several of them unashamed flag-wavers, were represented in the film as well, including 'Mary's A Grand Old Name', 'Harrigan', 'You're A Grand Old Flag', 'Over There', 'I Was Born In Virginia', 'The Man Who Owns Broadway', 'So Long, Mary', '45 Minutes From Broadway', 'Oh, You Wonderful Girl', and 'Off The Record'. Musical directors Ray Heindorf and Heinz Roemheld won Oscars for their 'scoring of a musical picture', and the superb dance sequences were staged by LeRoy Prinz, Seymour Felix, and John Boyle. The excellent black and white photography was by James Wong Howe, and the film was produced by Hal B. Wallis for Warner Brothers. The director of this classic all-time great musical was Michael Curtiz.

Yellen, Jack

b. 6 July 1892, Razcki, Poland, d. 17 April 1991, Springfield, New York, USA. Growing up in the

Yankee Doodle Dandy

USA after his family emigrated there in 1897, Yellen began writing both words and music for songs while still at school in Buffalo. Eventually he decided to concentrate on just lyrics, and, after working as a reporter on the local newspaper for a time, he moved to New York to pursue a professional songwriting career. During World War I he served in the US Army but still had some success with 'All Aboard For Dixie Land' (1913), 'Are You From Dixie?' (both with music by George L. Cobb) and 'How's Ev'ry Little Thing In Dixie?' and 'Peaches' (both with Albert Gumble). In 1920 he wrote 'Down By The O-H-I-O' with Abe Olman. Many of his songs of this period and in the 20s were used in Broadway revues and shows such as *What's In A Name?*, *Bombo*, *Rain Or Shine*, *John Murray Anderson's Almanac*, and *George White's Scandals*. After serving in the US Army during World War I, Yellen was introduced to composer Milton Ager and they began a fruitful association which initially resulted in 'A Young Man's Fancy', 'Who Cares?', 'Hard-Hearted Hannah, The Vamp Of Savannah', 'Crazy Words, Crazy Tune' and 'Ain't She Sweet?', one of the smash hit songs that typified the Roaring Twenties. In 1928, Yellen and Ager went to Hollywood where they collaborated on such songs as 'I'm The Last Of The Red Hot Mommas' (from the film *Honky Tonk*), 'Happy Feet', 'Glad Rag Doll' (with Dan Dougherty), 'A Bench In The Park' and 'Happy Days Are Here Again'. The latter became the theme song of the Democratic Party and President Franklin D. Roosevelt, and was synonymous with the promised emergence from the Depression and Roosevelt's New Deal. Much later, it was the enduring income from Barbra Streisand's highly individual, ironic and anti-political slow version of the song which she recorded on her first album in 1963, that helped to sustain Yellen in the last bed-ridden days of his life. In 1925 Yellen joined with Lew Pollock on both words and music for one song, written to record his emotions on the death of his mother. When it was sung by Sophie Tucker, 'My Yiddishe Momme', one of the all-time great 'sob' songs, became a huge success with audiences of all races and creeds. In the 30s Yellen also worked with Harold Arlen and Ray Henderson and wrote lyrics and/or screenplays for several musical films, including the early Technicolor *King Of Jazz*, *Chasing Rainbows*, *George White's Scandals*, *George White's Scandals Of 1935*, *Sing, Baby, Sing*, *King Of Burlesque*, *Happy Landing*, and two Shirley Temple vehicles, *Captain January* and *Rebecca Of Sunnybrook Farm*. From 1939 Yellen took another fling at Broadway, writing with

Sammy Fain, Henderson and others, for shows such as *George White's Scandals*, *Boys And Girls Together*, *Son O'Fun*, and *Ziegfeld Follies Of 1943*. Among the best songs from this period was 'Are You Havin' Any Fun?' and 'Something I Dreamed Last Night' (both Fain). Yellen was particularly associated with Sophie Tucker for whom he wrote several amusing songs over the years, including 'Stay At Home Papa' (with Dougherty), 'No One Man Is Ever Going To Worry Me' (Ted Shapiro), 'Life Begins At Forty' (Shapiro), and 'Is He My Boy Friend?' (Ager). Yellen retired in the late 40s to concentrate on his egg farm business, and was inducted into the US Songwriters Hall Of Fame in 1976. He was one of the first members of ASCAP in 1917, and served on its board from 1951-69.

Yellow Submarine

Named and inspired by one of the Beatles' most enduring pop songs, *Yellow Submarine* was a full-length animated feature which deftly combined comic-book imagery with psychedelia. Any lingering disappointment that the Beatles did not provide the voices for their characters vanished in a sea of colour and surrealism. Creations such as the anti-music Blue Meanies and their herald, Glove, were particularly memorable and if several songs were already-established Beatles favourites, the quartet did

contribute some excellent new compositions, including John Lennon's acerbic 'Hey Bulldog', George Harrison's anthemic 'It's All Too Much' and Paul McCartney's naggingly memorable 'All Together Now'. The group do briefly appear at the close singing the last-named song, but the film's strength lies in its brilliant combination of sound and visuals.

Yentl

With this 1984 release which was filmed in the UK and Czechoslovakia, Barbra Streisand became the first woman to write, produce, direct, sing and star in a movie. Her screenplay, written in collaboration with Jack Rosenthal, was adapted from Isaac Bashevis Singer's short story, *Yentl, The Yeshiva Boy*, and set in Eastern Europe at the turn of the century. Streisand plays Yentl, the Jewish girl who disguises herself as a young man so that she can study the Torah and make her way in a male-dominated community. Complications arise when Yentl marries Hadass (Amy Irving) who just happens to be the fiancée of Avigdor (Mandy Patinkin) the man Yentl actually loves. Most observers have commented that the scene in which Yentl, having walked away from the relationship, boards a ship bound for America, is very reminiscent of the famous 'Don't Rain On My Parade' sequence in her first picture, *Funny Girl*. The original song score, which won Academy Awards for composer

Yentl

Michel Legrand and lyricists Alan and Marilyn Bergman, was a Streisand *tour de force*, and consisted of mostly touching and emotional numbers such as 'Where Is It Written?', 'This Is One Of Those Moments', 'No Wonder', 'The Way He Makes Me Feel', 'Tomorrow Night', 'Will Someone Ever Look At Me That Way?', 'No Matter What Happens', and 'A Piece Of Sky'. An especially poignant song was 'Papa, Can You Hear Me' - the film is also a tribute from Streisand to the father she hardly knew. All in all, although far too long, *Yentl* is generally considered to be fine piece of work which certainly does not merit it's sometime nickname *Tootsie On The Roof*. Also among the cast were Steven Hill and Nehemiah Persoff, Bernard Spear, and David de Kyser. This MGM-United Artists release was beautifully photographed in Metrocolor and Panavision by David Watkin.

Yes Madam?

Bobby Howes, Bertha Belmore, and Vera Pearce, three of the stars of the original stage show which had a good run at the London Hippodrome in 1934/5, recreated their roles for this popular film version which was released by the Associated British Picture Corporation in 1938. Binnie Hale, who played the heroine on stage, was not present, but her part as Howes' cousin was played by the delightful Diana Churchill. In the somewhat frivolous plot, they are both obliged to work as servants for a month in order to qualify for an inheritance of more that £100,000. Obviously there will be many complications, especially when the supporting cast contains names such as Fred Emney, Wylie Watson, and Billy Milton. The score, with music by Jack Waller, Joseph Tunbridge, and Harry Weston, and lyrics by R.P. Weston, Bert Lee, and Clifford Grey, contained some jolly and engaging numbers, including 'Czechoslovakian Love Song', 'Dreaming A Dream', 'The Girl The Soldier Always Leaves Behind', 'Sitting Beside O' You', 'Too Many Outdoor Sports', 'What Are You Going To Do?', and 'Zip-Tee-Tootle-Tee-Too-Pom-Pom'. Stalwarts Clifford Grey, Bert Lee, and Freshman wrote the screenplay which was adapted from the musical play, which itself was based on a novel by K.R.G. Browne. Norman Lee produced this popular and harmless slice of fun, and the producer was Walter C. Mycroft. An earlier, non-musical film treatment of Browne's book starred Frank Pettingell and Kay Hammond.

Yes, Mr Brown

The celebrated stage duo of Jack Buchanan and Elsie Randolph came to the screen in this comedy-musical which was released by British & Dominion-Woolf & Freedom Films in 1933. Set in Vienna (as per usual) Douglas Furber's screenplay was adapted from the German play *Business With America* by Paul Frank and Ludwig Hershfield. It concerns Nicholas Baumann (Buchanan), the manager of a factory who is expecting a visit from his important American boss (Hartley Power). Just before he arrives, Nicholas's glamorous wife, Clary (Margot Grahame), walks out on him because he cannot stand the sight (or the smell) of her pet dog. Complications arise when he persuades his secretary, Ann Webber (Randolph), to stand in for her. Buchanan's deft comic touch supplemented his already established romantic image, and Randolph was her usual amusing self. Also in the cast were Vera Pearce and Clifford Heatherley. The songs included 'Leave A Little Love For Me' and 'Yes, Mr. Brown' (both Paul Abraham-Robert Gilbert-Armin Robinson-Douglas Furber). Herbert Wilcox was the producer, and he co-directed this diverting little film with Jack Buchanan.

You Were Never Lovelier

After their compatibility and box-office appeal was confirmed in *You'll Never Get Rich* in 1941, Fred Astaire and Rita Hayworth got together again a year later for this Columbia release which was set in Buenos Aires. The screenplay, by Michael Fessier, Ernest Pagano, and Delmar Daves, cast Astaire as an American nightclub dancer and gambler who goes to Argentina for the sport, but ends up working in Adolph Menjou's ritzy hotel when his money runs out. Fred's life becomes complicated when one of Menjou's daughters, played by Rita Hayworth, thinks he is wooing her with expensive flowers - when in fact they are being sent by her father in an attempt to 'get her off his hands'! Naturally, Fred gets the girl in the end with the assistance of some of Jerome Kern's most endearing music and Johnny Mercer's lyrics. Hayworth, whose singing was dubbed by Nan Wynn, 'danced her socks off' in 'Shorty George' and 'I'm Old Fashioned', and blended blissfully with Astaire for the delightfully romantic 'You Were Never Lovelier' and 'Dearly Beloved'. Xavier Cugat And His Orchestra provided a few genuine Latin-American rhythms in 'Chiu Chiu (Niconar Molinare)' and 'Wedding In The Spring' (both with Lina Romay), and 'Audition Dance' (with Astaire). Also in the cast was Larry Parks, just a few years before he hit the big time in *The Jolson Story*. The man who conceived the imaginative dance sequences was Val Raset, and *You Were Never Lovelier* was directed by William A. Seiter. Rita Hayworth's association with Fred Astaire had been a joy, and, two years later, she was marvellous all over again when she joined that other great screen dancer, Gene Kelly, in *Cover Girl*.

You'll Never Get Rich

Rita Hayworth confirmed her promise as a dancer, and her position as a major box-office attraction, when she partnered Fred Astaire in this 1941 Columbia release. With America on the brink of entry

You'll Never Get Rich

into World War II, Michael Fessier and Ernest Pagano's screenplay cast Astaire as a Broadway dance director who is smitten by chorus girl Rita Hayworth, but is drafted into the US Army before he can consolidate his position. He turns out to be a rather perverse soldier, and spends a good deal of time in the guardhouse. While there, he performs an incredibly fast solo tap dance accompanied by a moody version of 'Since I Kissed My Baby Goodbye', performed by the Delta Rhythm Boys. That number was part of the superb Cole Porter score which also included 'The Boogie Barcarolle', 'Dream Dancing' (a sadly underrated song), 'Shootin' The Works For Uncle Sam', and 'A-stairable Rag'. After Astaire has negotiated his release from detention in order to help produce a musical entertainment for the troops, he serenades Hayworth (naturally, she is one of stars of the show) on-stage with the lovely 'So Near And Yet So Far' ('I just start getting you keen on clinches galore with me/When fate steps in on the scene and mops up the floor with me/No wonder I'm a bit under par/For you're so near/And yet so far'), before the exuberant finale, 'Wedding Cake Walk'. Astaire and Hayworth were perfect together, and Robert Benchley, as the amorous producer who is responsible for their romantic involvement in the first place, was excellent too. Sidney Lanfield directed, and the choreographer was Robert Alton.

Youmans, Vincent

b. Vincent Miller (Millie) Youmans, 27 September 1898, New York, USA, d. 5 April 1946, Denver, Colorado, USA. Youmans was an important composer and producer for the stage during the 20s and 30s, whose career was cut short by a long illness. He worked for a Wall Street finance company before enlisting in the US Navy during World War I, and co-producing musicals at Great Lakes Naval Training Station. On leaving the navy he worked as a song-plugger for Harms Music, and as a rehearsal pianist for shows with music by influential composer, Victor Herbert. Youmans wrote his first Broadway score in 1921 for Two Little Girls In Blue, with lyrics by Ira Gershwin. One of the show's songs, 'Oh Me, Oh My, Oh You', was a hit for novelty singer Frank Crumit. Youmans' next show, Wildflower (1923), with book and lyrics by Otto Harbach and Oscar Hammerstein II, ran for a creditable 477 performances, and included 'April Blossoms', and 'Bambalina', recorded by Paul Whiteman and Ray Miller. Mary Jane McKane ('Toodle-oo', 'You're Never Too Old To Learn') and Lollipop ('Take A Little One-Step') both reached the Broadway stage in 1924, and in the following year Youmans, in collaboration with lyricist Irving Caesar, wrote a quintessential 20s score for No, No, Nanette, one of the decade's most successful musicals. The show contained several hits including 'Too Many Rings Around Rosie', 'You Can Dance With Any

Girl At All', and the much-recorded standards, 'I Want To Be Happy' and 'Tea For Two'. The show was filmed, with modifications to its score, in 1930, 1940, and in 1950 as Tea For Two, starring Doris Day and Gordon MacRae.

In contrast, Youman's 1926 show, Oh, Please, with songs such as 'I Know That You Know', and 'Like He Loves Me', with lyrics by Anne Caldwell, was a relative failure, despite the presence of Beatrice Lillie in the cast. For Hit The Deck (1927), Youmans assumed the role of producer in partnership with Lew Fields. The show was a substantial success, running for 352 performances, and featuring 'Sometimes I'm Happy' (lyric by Clifford Grey and Irving Caesar) and 'Halleluja' (lyric by Clifford Grey and Leo Robin). The show was filmed in 1930, and again in 1955 with an all-star cast including Tony Martin, Vic Damone, Debbie Reynolds, Jane Powell, and Ann Miller. The latter release contained a new Youmans song, 'Keepin' Myself For You', with a lyric by Sidney Clare. Despite containing some of his best songs, Youmans' next few shows were flops. Rainbow ran for only 29 performances; Great Day, with the title song, 'More Than You Know' and 'Without A Song' (lyrics by Billy Rose and Edward Eliscu), lasted for 36 performances; Smiles, starring Marilyn Miller, and Adele and Fred Astaire, and featuring 'Time On My Hands' (lyric by Mack Gordon and Harold Adamson), 63 performances; and Through The Years, with the title song, 'Kinda Like You'; and 'Drums In My Heart' (lyrics by Edward Heyman) 20 performances. Youmans' last Broadway show, Take A Chance, did much better. It starred Jack Haley and Ethel Merman and ran for 243 performances. Youmans contributed three songs with lyrics by Buddy De Sylva: 'Should I Be Sweet?', 'Oh, How I Long To Belong To You', and Miss Merman's show-stopper, 'Rise 'N' Shine', which was also a hit for Paul Whiteman. Apparently disenchanted with Broadway, Youmans moved to Hollywood and wrote his only major original film score for Flying Down To Rio (1933). Celebrated as the film that brought Fred Astaire and Ginger Rogers together as a dance team, the musical numbers, with lyrics by Gus Kahn and Edward Eliscu, consisted of 'The Carioca', 'Orchids In the Moonlight', 'Music Makes Me', and the peppy title number. Youmans' previous flirtations with the big screen, Song Of The West and What A Widow (both 1930), produced nothing particularly memorable, and the film adaptation of his stage show Take A Chance (with Lilian Roth replacing Ethel Merman) dispensed with most of the songs. However, the aforementioned Hit The Deck was a box-office favourite, and No, No, Nanette was filmed twice - as an early talkie with Bernice Claire in 1930, and 10 years later with Anna Neagle in the starring role.

In the early 30s Youmans contracted tuberculosis and spent much of the rest of his life in sanitoria. In 1934 his publishing company collapsed, and a year later he was declared bankrupt for over half a million dollars. In 1943 he seemed well enough to return to New York to plan his most ambitious project, an extravaganza entitled *The Vincent Youmans Ballet Revue* This was a combination of Latin-American music and classical music, including Ravel's 'Daphnis And Chloe', with choreography by Leonide Massine. It was a critical and commercial disaster, losing over four million dollars. Youmans retired to New York, then to Denver, Colorado, where he died in 1946. Despite his relatively small catalogue of songs and his penchant for rarely using the same collaborator, Youmans is rated among the elite composers of his generation. In 1971 an acclaimed revival of *No, No, Nanette* starring Ruby Keeler began its run of 861 performances on Broadway.

Compilations: *Through The Years With Vincent Youmans* (1972), *Wildflower/Gershwin's Tiptoes'* (1979).

Young At Heart

Adapted by Julius J. Epstein and Lenore Coffee from Fannie Hurst's novel, *Sister Act*, and the 1938 Claude Rains-John Garfield movie *The Four Sisters*, this 1954 Warner Brothers release provided a glimpse of American suburban family viewed through the proverbial rose-coloured glasses. It consisted of three sisters (one was dropped from the original), played by Doris Day, Dorothy Malone, and Elizabeth Fraser, who lived with their music teacher father (Robert Keith) and crusty aunt (Ethel Barrymore). Day is engaged to budding songwriter Gig Young until Frank Sinatra turns up on the doorstep and ruins the arrangement. Day jilts Young for Sinatra, but, after their marriage, his career prospects remain at zero (the people 'upstairs' never give him a break), and one dark snowy night he attempts to 'take the easy way out'. His will to live is re-kindled when his wife tells him they are about to become a threesome. Perhaps because of the film's sentimental character, the Sinatra-Day combination failed to work as well as might have been expected, although, individually, they had some satisfying moments. At the time, both were probably at the peak of their vocal powers, and a collection of engaging songs gave them ample chance to shine: Day with such as 'Hold Me In Your Arms' (Ray Heindorf-Charles Henderson-Don Pippin) and the more upbeat 'Ready, Willing And Able' (Floyd Huddleston-Al Rinker-Dick Gleason) and Sinatra on 'Someone To Watch Over Me' (George and Ira Gershwin), 'Just One Of Those Things' (Cole Porter), and 'One For My Baby' (Harold Arlen-Johnny Mercer). Sinatra sings a number of these while working in a local 'joint' for what he calls 'tips on a plate'. Other numbers included 'You, My Love' (Mack Gordon-Jimmy Van Heusen), 'There's A Rising Moon (For Every Falling Star)' (Paul Francis Webster-Sammy Fain), and 'Young At Heart' (Carolyn Leigh-Johnny Richards). Photographed in Warnercolor and directed by Gordon Douglas, this

The Young Ones

was the kind of film which - at the time - made audiences feel warm all over.

Young Man With A Horn

Directed by Michael Curtiz, this film made in 1950 follows broadly upon Dorothy Baker's novel which was in its turn very loosely based on the life of Bix Beiderbecke. Any chance of reality went out the window with the casting of Kirk Douglas and the choice of Harry James to dub the character's trumpet playing. Hoagy Carmichael appears as a pianist but despite the fact that he actually did play piano with Bix he was ghosted by Buddy Cole. Amongst other musicians involved, mostly off-screen, are Babe Russin, Nick Fatool, Jack Jenney, Willie Smith, Stan Wrightsman and Jimmy Zito. Doris Day plays Douglas's long-suffering girlfriend and has a chance to sing between the melodramatics. (Alternative title: *Young Man Of Music*).

Young Ones, The

Cliff Richard had already appeared in two films, *Expresso Bongo* and *Serious Charge*, prior to starring in this unashamedly teen-oriented vehicle. It combined many of the genre's sub-plots - unsympathetic adults, romance and an inevitable, jejune show which is finally performed despite adversity. Unashamedly light and frothy, *The Young Ones* also boasted a highly-popular soundtrack album. The memorable title track, a number 1 single in its own right, defines the innocence of Britain's pre-Beatles' 60s while 'When The Girl In Your Arms Is The Girl In Your Heart' remains one of the singer's most affecting ballads. *The Young Ones* confirmed Richard's status as one of the most popular entertainers of his era.

Young, Victor

b. 8 August 1900, Chicago, Illinois, USA, d. 11 November 1956, Palm Springs, California, USA. Young was a violinist, conductor, bandleader, arranger, and composer, responsible for over 300 film scores and themes. He studied at the Warsaw Conservatory in 1910 before joining the Warsaw Philharmonic as a violinist, and touring Europe. He returned to the USA at the outbreak of World War I, and later, in the early 20s, toured as a concert violinist, before becoming a concert master in theatre orchestras. On 'defecting' to popular music he served for a while as violinist-arranger with the popular pianist-bandleader Ted Fio Rito. During the 30s, Young worked a great deal on radio, conducting for many artists including Al Jolson, Don Ameche, and Smith Ballew. He also started recording with his own orchestra, and had a string of hits from 1931-54, including 'Gems From 'The Band Wagon', 'The Last Round-Up', 'Who's Afraid Of The Big Bad Wolf', 'The Old Spinning Wheel', 'This Little Piggie Went To Market' (featuring Jimmy Dorsey, Bunny Berigan

and Joe Venuti), 'Flirtation Walk', 'Ev'ry Day', 'Way Back Home', 'About A Quarter To Nine' and 'She's A Latin From Manhattan' (both from the Jolson movie, *Go Into Your Dance*), 'It's A Sin To Tell A Lie', 'Mona Lisa', 'The Third Man Theme', 'Ruby', 'Limelight Theme', and 'The High And The Mighty'. He also provided the orchestral accompaniments for other artists, including Dick Powell, Eddie Cantor, Deanna Durbin, Helen Forrest, Frances Langford, trumpet virtuoso Rafael Mendez, Cliff Edwards, the Boswell Sisters, and western movies singer Rex Allen. Most notably, it was Young's orchestra behind Judy Garland on her record of 'Over The Rainbow', the Oscar-winning song from the 1939 film, *The Wizard Of Oz*; and with Bing Crosby on two of his million-sellers, 'Too-Ra-Loo-Ra-Loo-Ral (That's An Irish Lullaby)', from *Going My Way*, the 'Best Picture' of 1944; and British doctor Arthur Colahan's somewhat unconventional song, 'Galway Bay' (1948). Young's extremely successful and prolific career as a film composer, musical director, conductor and arranger, initially for Paramount, started in the early 30s. Some of his best-known film works included *Wells Fargo* (1937), *Swing High, Swing Low* (1937), *Breaking The Ice* (1938), *Golden Boy* (1939), *Man Of Conquest* (1939), *Arizona* (1940), *I Wanted Wings* (1941), *Hold Back The Dawn* (1941), *Flying Tigers* (1942), *Silver Queen* (1942), *The Glass Key* (1942), *Take A Letter, Darling* (1942), *For Whom The Bell Tolls* (1943), *The Uninvited* (1944), *Samson And Delilah* (1949), *Rio Grande* (1950), *Scaramouche* (1952), *The Greatest Show On Earth* (1952), *Shane* (1953) and *Three Coins In The Fountain* (1954). Young was awarded a posthumous Academy Award for his score for the 1956 film, *Around The World In Eighty Days*, after his death in November 1956.

His record of the title song made the US charts in 1957, and had a vocal version by Bing Crosby on the b-side. He also wrote some television themes including 'Blue Star', for the US *Medic* series, and contributed music to two minor Broadway shows, *Pardon Our French* (1950) and *Seventh Heaven* (1955). Young's popular songs were written mostly with lyricist Ned Washington. These included 'Can't We Talk It Over?', 'A Hundred Years From Today' (from the show *Blackbirds Of 1933/34*), 'A Ghost Of A Chance' (with co-writer, Bing Crosby), 'Stella By Starlight' and 'My Foolish Heart' (film title song). Young's other lyricists included Will J. Harris ('Sweet Sue'), Wayne King, Haven Gillespie, and Egbert Van Alstyne ('Beautiful Love'), Sam M. Lewis ('Street Of Dreams'), Edward Heyman ('When I Fall In Love' and 'Love Letters') and Sammy Cahn (the film title song, 'Written On The Wind'). Young also wrote 'Golden Earrings' with the song writing team of Jay Livingston and Ray Evans.

Selected albums: *Around The World In 80 Days* (1957, film soundtrack), *Wizard Of Oz/Pinocchio* (1966),

Hollywood Rhapsodies (1974), *The Quiet Man/Samson And Delilah* (1979, film soundtrack).

Z

Ziegfeld Follies

William Powell, who had played the leading role in the 1936 screen biography, *The Great Ziegfeld*, portrayed the master showman again in this film which was released 10 years later. From his seat in that big theatre in the sky - heaven - Florenz Ziegfeld plans one final revue which will serve as his memorial. The resulting show, a collection of unconnected sketches and songs, was certainly spectacular, featuring as it did many of MGM's brightest stars of the day. Three of these, Fred Astaire, Cyd Charisse and Lucille Ball, accurately captured the Ziegfeld mood with 'Bring On The Beautiful Girls' (Earl Brent-Roger Edens) - followed closely by 'Bring On Those Beautiful Men' - and from then on the lavish production numbers, interspersed with the laughs, followed thick and fast. The lovely Lena Horne, eyes ablaze, raised the temperature with 'Love' (Ralph Blane-Hugh Martin), Judy Garland sent up the much-loved Greer ('Mrs. Miniver') Garson in 'Madame Crematon', and two refugees from the world of opera, James Melton and Marion Bell, rendered 'The Drinking Song' from Verdi's *La Traviata*. However, most of the honours went to Fred Astaire who, with Lucille Bremer, provided two of the films outstanding moments with the lovely ballad 'This Heart Of Mine' (Arthur Freed-Harry Warren) and the exquisitely staged 'Limehouse Blues' (Philip Braham-Douglas Furber). Astaire also revived a number called 'The Babbitt And The Bromide' (George Gershwin-Ira Gershwin), which he had introduced with his sister Adele in the Broadway musical *Funny Face* (1927). In this film Astaire performed it with his main 'rival', Gene Kelly - it was the first time they had danced on the screen together. Kathryn Grayson, surrounded by a substance that looked remarkably like foam, brought the curtain down on Ziegfeld's final performance with confirmation the impresario's lifelong creed: 'There's Beauty Everywhere' written by Earl Brent and Arthur Freed. Freed himself produced the whole stylish and extravagant affair which was directed by Vincente Minnelli and choreographed by Robert Alton.

Ziegfeld Girl

The trials and tribulations of a trio of showgirls in the most famous series of revues ever to grace Broadway - the *Ziegfeld Follies* - were discussed and dissected in this Pandro S. Berman MGM production which came to the screen in 1941. Judy Garland, Hedy Lamarr and Lana Turner were the three young hopefuls who were aiming for the top. Garland was the only one to make it in the end, with Lamarr and Turner swapping public acclaim for private happiness. The uneven, and sometimes maudlin screenplay was written by Marguerite Roberts and Sonia Levien. James Stewart, Tony Martin, Philip Dorn and Jackie Cooper were prominent in a splendid cast which also included Ian Hunter, Edward Everett Horton, Eve Arden, Dan Dailey, Paul Kelly, Fay Holden, and Felix Bressart. Charles Winninger played Ed Gallagher with Al Shean as himself in a recreation of the question and answer song 'Mr. Gallagher And Mr. Shean', which the famous vaudeville duo introduced in the Ziegfeld Follies of 1922. Garland was in fine form on a variety of numbers which included 'Minnie From Trinidad' (Roger Edens), 'You Never Looked So Beautiful' (Harold Adamson-Walter Donaldson), 'I'm Always Chasing Rainbows' (Joseph McCarthy-Harry Carroll), and 'Laugh? I Thought I'd Split My Sides' (Edens) (with Winninger), and Tony Martin gave a typically fine performance of 'You Stepped Out Of A Dream' (Nacio Herb Brown-Gus Kahn). Busby Berkeley's staging of the dance sequences was as brilliantly imaginative as always, and the lavish sets and costumes were created by Cedric Gibbons and Adrian respectively; the latter was coming to the end of his long and distinguished stint at MGM. The film contained several reminders of a previous celluloid tribute to the master showman, *The Great Ziegfeld*, including that enormous fluted spiral structure which amazed audiences again as it did the first time round. Robert Z. Leonard directed this opulent production which will be best remembered for its music and production numbers.

Zimmer, Hans

b. 1957, Frankfurt, Germany. From the age of six, Zimmer 'wanted to be a composer', although he had no formal musical education. At the age of 16 he went to school in England, and, during the 70s, toured with bands throughout the UK. After spending some time at Air-Edel, writing jingles for television commercials, he collaborated with the established movie composer, Stanley Myers, to write the score for Nicolas Roeg's *Eureka* (1981), and several other British films during the 80s, including *Moonlighting*; *Success Is The Best Revenge*; *Insignificance*; and *The Nature Of The Beast* (1988). His solo credits around that time included movies with such themes as apartheid (*A World Apart*); a psychological thriller (*Paperhouse*); a couple of eccentric comedies: (*Twister* and *Driving Miss Daisy*); a tough Michael Douglas detective yarn (*Black Rain*); and a 'stiflingly old-fashioned' version of a Stefan Zweig short story, *Burning Secret* (1988). In that year Zimmer is said to have provided the music for 14 films in the UK and abroad, including the blockbuster, *Rain Man*, starring Dustin Hoffman and Tom Cruise. *Rain Man* earned Zimmer a nomination for an Academy Award; ('When they found out that I was only 30, I didn't get it!'). He continued apace in the early 90s, with scores for such as *Bird On A Wire*; *Chicago Joe And The Showgirl* (written with Shirley Walker); *Days Of Thunder*; *Green Card*, starring Gerard Depardieu in his English-language debut); *Pacific Heights*; *Backdraft*; *K2* (a crashing, electro-Mahlerian score); *Regarding Henry*; *Thelma And Louise* ('a twanging, shimmering score'); *Radio Flyer*; *Toys* (with Trevor Horn); *The Power Of One*; *A League Of Their Own*; *Point Of No Return*, *Where Sleeping Dogs Lie* (with Mark Mancina) (1992), *The Assassin*, *Cool Runnings*, and *The House Of Spirits* (1993). In 1992, Zimmer composed the music for 'one of the most bizarre television re-creations to date', the 10-hour series, *Millennium*. His other work for the small screen includes the popular *First Born* (1988), and *Space Rangers* (1992). Zimmer is most certainly a major figure in music; his accomplishments in the film world for such a comparatively young man are already awesome.